A Mathematical Tour of Functions

Jorge Alberto Calvo

Department of Mathematics
Ave Maria University
Ave Maria, Florida, USA

Fourth Edition

ISBN 978-1-304-27932-3

Cover Photograph: *Bristlecone Under the Stars* by David G. Wilkins (2009).

The long exposure time used to produce this photograph reveals the circular motion of the stars in the night sky around Polaris, the north star. Ancient astronomers' observations of this motion contributed much to the birth of trigonometry and to the development of mathematics in general.

To Veronica, my beautiful wife and perfect complement.

To my Mom, who worked out all the solutions to the exercises.

And to Angelo DiDomenico and Ken Millett

for their lessons, advice, and friendship throughout the years.

We are told that it is faith which constructed the cathedrals of the Middle Ages. Without doubt, but faith would have constructed nothing at all if there had not also been arthitects; and if it is true that the façade of Notre Dame of Paris is a yearning of the soul toward God, that does not prevent its being also a geometrical work. It is necessary to know geometry in order to construct a façade which may be an act of love.... Everything is worth the trouble of being well done that is worth the trouble of being done for God.

E. H. Gilson
"Intelligence in the Service of Christ"
Christianity and Philosophy (1936)

Apology to the Student

Welcome to our mathematical tour! The theme of this book centers around the concept of **function**, a mathematical idea that has become increasingly important over the past two centuries. In these pages, you will read about many of the topics commonly covered in courses with impressive-sounding titles like *College Algebra*, *Trigonometry*, and *Precalculus*. A well-prepared student will already be familiar with the basic concepts of arithmetic, geometry, and algebra. In particular, it will be expected that you already know how, and how not, to manipulate fractions, multiply positive and negative numbers, and solve very simple equations. It is my hope that after reading this book you will be prepared – and perhaps even want – to move on to a course in Calculus. However, you should be warned that for a variety of reasons this book is probably different than any mathematics textbook that you may have used in the past, either in high school or even in college.

First of all, this book was originally written as a blueprint for a **university-level course**. If this is the case for you, there will no doubt be higher expectations placed on you, both in the amount of material that you need to learn and in the level at which you need to understand it. At times, you may feel overwhelmed by the fast pace of the course or the large number of homework exercises you will be asked to complete each night. To help you succeed, you will have access to tutors and to your instructor, both in class and in office hours. Make sure that you take advantage of these resources. In the end, the responsibility to keep up with the reading, to complete the homework, and to attend class on a regular basis falls squarely on *your* shoulders. Do not make the mistake of thinking that you can learn everything there is to know on the night before an exam.

Secondly, this book was designed as a part of the **core curriculum** emphasizing the liberal arts identity at Ave Maria University. This means that the material was written with an eye to highlight mathematics as an *art form*. Although it may come as a surprise to those students who were beaten down as youths with such mental tortures as multiplication tables and long division, mathematics is chock-full of beautiful ideas reflecting a perfect balance between creativity and logical consistency. This book will take you on a journey from the ancient problem of computing the square root of two to the complex affair of visualizing an imaginary number like the square root of negative one. Along the way, you will come across several historical figures, each of whom made his own contribution to the human endeavor that is the story of mathematics.

As you quickly skim through the first few pages of this text, you will notice that they are more than just a collection of examples, each working out a different type of problem, which you are to mimic in the homework exercises. The examples have been carefully chosen to give you an incrementally clearer picture of the concepts at hand, and of how you should be thinking about them. By the same token, some of the exercises in the problem sets will not look like any of the examples in the notes. Instead, some will ask you to perform a mathematical experiment; others will ask you to use your imagination and creativity to propose a reasonable conjecture. All of them will ask you to think. Be sure to give yourself plenty of time to work on these exercises.

You should read this book slowly, a few sentences at a time. Take your time. Make sure you understand what you read. If you don't, go back a few sentences and try again. Take an active role in the reading by working out the examples for yourself, and by asking yourself why one statement connects with the next. Remember that by approaching the reading as a mystery to be unraveled, rather than just as information and procedures to be memorized, you will bring out the best of your intellectual abilities until, ultimately, the mathematics itself will become clearer, more meaningful, and more beautiful.

If mathematics is a beautiful form of art, as I hope to convince you in the course of these pages, it is primarily an abstract art. This is a difficult concept with which to grapple, and it sometimes prompts the question of how any of this material applies to real life. The answer, presumably, depends on what you mean by "real life" in the first place. As a teenager, I delivered newspapers and cooked burgers in a fast-food restaurant; if that was my definition of real life then I would have to admit that, no, mathematics has no real bearing on everyday life. Of course, nowadays, mathematics is very much a part of my everyday life as a college professor. I suspect that the answer for you will lie somewhere in between these two extremes. Nevertheless, one could make the case that any educated person should be able to appreciate the beauty of an abstract painting by Pablo Picasso or Jackson Pollock, even if that is not one's particular preference in art. In the same way, any educated person ought to be able to appreciate the mathematical beauty driving today's science and technology; otherwise, their education would somehow be lacking.

Even if you have no plans to follow a career in mathematics, this book can help you become a better student, and perhaps even a better person. Wisdom, according to Solomon, "teaches temperance and prudence, justice and fortitude, and nothing in life is more useful than these" (Wisdom 8:7). A course in mathematics can do the same for you by challenging you to develop your intellectual habits of study and thereby grow in these cardinal virtues. Every problem set can be seen as an exercise in temperance, as you fight the temptations that distract you from the task at hand. Every difficult problem will test your fortitude as you resist your weaker impulses to avoid the strenuous work ahead. Justice is important when you study in groups; do not take credit for what others have done, and be sure to contribute your fair share of the group effort. Most concretely, prudence will point out the best course of action to be taken when confronted with a problem, mathematical or otherwise. Remember that the goal in this course is not simply to arrive at the correct answer, but to understand how the mathematical concepts fit together to lead you to that answer. It would be incorrect to say that

$$\frac{16}{64} = \frac{1}{4}$$

because the sixes cancel each other out, even though the final answer turns out to be the right one. The same logic is bound to fail, and lead you to the wrong answer, in nearly every other example. In order to successfully avoid the errors which at first seem obviously correct, you must develop a sense of what is right and what is wrong, and this mathematical sort of "conscience" can only be properly formed by training and experience, and by a firm understanding of the basic principles at work. The same lesson applies to all other areas of life.

As a final note, I would like to stress that this text is a work in progress. I have tried to stamp out all typographical errors, but one or two may have stubbornly survived all of my proofreading. If you find an error, please let me know! Furthermore, a lot of effort has been put into making these notes interesting and, yes, sometimes even entertaining reading. Whether I have succeeded or not is a matter of opinion. Nevertheless, I would consider it quite an insult if you did not at least giggle politely to yourself every once in a while. Now would be a good time to begin.

Good luck. And may all your problems be math problems!

jorge.calvo@avemaria.edu

Naples, Florida

July 2010

Table of Contents

CHAPTER 1

An Introduction To Functions

There are two types of functions – social functions and mathematical functions. Though completely different, they use much of the same terminology.

Social functions are also called mixers or gatherings. Usually they involve parties hosted by dormitory floors (or assistant deans) with kegs of beer (or little cucumber sandwiches). The location where the function takes place is known as the domain of the function. The place where the food is cooked is known as the range of the function. A function that lasts until morning is said to be continuous. One that is broken up by the police and resumed the next day is called discontinuous. The phone number of the dreamboat you met is called the value of the function. It often winds up in the range.

The same terminology is used by mathematicians to describe what they call a function. The main difference is that when a mathematician has a function, everyone gets exactly one value! No one leaves with two numbers at a mathematical function, and no one leaves with none.

C. Adams, J. Hass, and A. Thompson
How to Ace Calculus: the Streetwise Guide
page 218 (1998)

1.1. What Are Functions?

There is an old wives' tale that says that it is only safe to eat oysters in months that have an r in their spelling. Of course, most biologists will tell you that eating unpasteurized raw oysters is a bad idea any time of the year. Apparently, shellfish accumulate micro-organisms and toxins from the surrounding water during their filter-feeding process. Nevertheless, if you believe in old wives (and the tales they tell) then you can use Table 1.1 to make an assessment of the eating habits of thrill-seeking mollusk-eaters in each month of the year. This table gives us our very first example of what mathematicians call a function.

TABLE 1.1. An old wives' table.

In the month of...	eating oysters is...
January	safe
February	safe
March	safe
April	safe
May	risky
June	risky
July	risky
August	risky
September	safe
October	safe
November	safe
December	safe

A *function* is a rule that assigns to any given input a unique output value. The set of allowable inputs is called the *domain* of the function, and the set of possible outputs is called the *codomain* of the function. We can indicate that the function f has the set A as its domain and the set B as its codomain by using the following shorthand notation:

$$f : A \to B.$$

In this case, we say that the function f *maps* the domain A into the codomain B.

EXAMPLE 1.1. The table above describes a function f which assigns an output value of "safe" to months with an r in their spelling and an output value of "risky" to months with no r's. In this table, the input values (the names of the months of the year) are listed down the left hand column, while their corresponding output values (either "safe" or "risky") are listed down the right hand column. Evidently, the domain of this function is the set of

3

months in the year,

$$\text{Domain } f = \big\{\text{January, February, March}, \ldots, \text{December}\big\},$$

while its codomain is the two-element set

$$\text{Codomain } f = \big\{\text{safe, risky}\big\}.$$

We, therefore, write:

$$f : \big\{\text{January, February, March}, \ldots, \text{December}\big\} \to \big\{\text{safe, risky}\big\}.$$

We can describe this function by the **bubble diagram** in Figure 1.1. In this diagram, the bubble on the left represents the domain of the function while the bubble on the right represents the codomain. The lines connecting the two bubbles indicate how f assigns output values to points in the domain. The condition that this assignment is unique for each input in the domain translates in the diagram to having precisely one line leave each point of the domain. Notice, however, that it is perfectly legal for more than one line to come together at a point of the codomain.

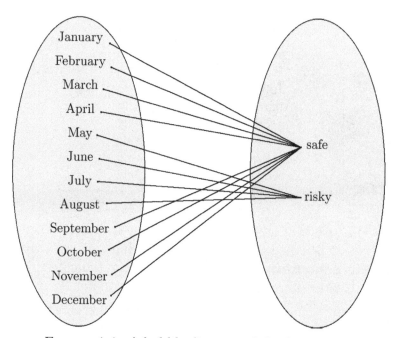

FIGURE 1.1. A bubble diagram of the function f.

Some mathematics textbooks use the word "range" as a synonym for codomain. In this case, the range of a function is the set of all *possible* output values. Other textbooks use the term "range" to describe the set of all output values *which are actually used*. We will call this second set the **image set** of the function. The difference between these two usages is subtle, but nevertheless important; we will illustrate it with a few examples. However, to avoid confusion, throughout the rest of this book we will refrain from using the word "range" altogether.

EXAMPLE 1.2. Consider what happens when the names of the letters of the English alphabet are written out. These are just words – strange words like "eff" and "aitch," but words nonetheless – so they can be alphabetized. We do this in Table 1.2. We can then define a function

$$g : \{a, b, c, \ldots, x, y, z\} \to \{1, 2, 3, \ldots\}$$

that takes as input a letter of the alphabet and returns as output the rank of this letter in the list. For instance, the letter h is assigned a value of 1, since h is the first letter in the list. Similarly, the letter a is assigned a value of 3 and the letter g is assigned a value of 16.

Since there are only 26 letters in the alphabet, there is no letter that is assigned the value of 27 (or any other number greater than 27, for that matter). Thus, 27 is an example of a potential value in the codomain of g that is not actually used by g. In particular, the image set of g is

$$\text{Image } g = \{1, 2, 3, \ldots, 24, 25, 26\},$$

which is significantly smaller than the codomain.

TABLE 1.2. The alphabet in alphabetical order.

1.	h	aitch	14.	x	ex
2.	r	are	15.	i	eye
3.	a	ay	16.	g	gee
4.	b	bee	17.	j	jay
5.	q	cue	18.	k	kay
6.	d	dee	19.	o	oh
7.	w	double you	20.	p	pea
8.	e	ee	21.	c	sea
9.	f	eff	22.	t	tea
10.	l	el	23.	v	vee
11.	m	em	24.	y	why
12.	n	en	25.	u	you
13.	s	ess	26.	z	zee

EXAMPLE 1.3. The domain and codomain are as much a part of a function as its rule of assignment. If we change either of these we obtain an entirely different function, even if the rule of assignment seems the same. For instance, as in the example above, we can define a *brand new* function

$$\tilde{g} : \{a, b, c, \ldots, x, y, z\} \to \{1, 2, 3, \ldots, 24, 25, 26\}$$

which assigns to each letter in the alphabet its rank in Table 1.2. At first sight, it might appear that g and $\tilde{g}$ are exactly the same function. However, since they have different codomains (one infinite and the other finite), they are, in fact, different functions.

If f is a function and a is an element of its domain, then the unique output value that f assigns to a is called the ***image*** of a under f. We shall use the notation $f(a)$ (pronounced "f of a") to refer to this output value. When we do this, we say that we are ***evaluating*** the function f at the input a. We may also say that f ***maps*** the input a to the output $f(a)$.

EXAMPLE 1.4. Let $h : \{1, 2, 3, \ldots\} \to \{1, 2, 3, \ldots\}$ be the function that maps each positive integer to the number of letters in its English name. Therefore h maps the number 1 to the value 3 (since "one" has three letters), the number 3 to the value 5 (since "three" has five letters), and the number 5 to the value 4 (since "five" has four letters). We can express all of these facts by writing:

$$h(1) = 3, \qquad h(3) = 5, \qquad \text{and} \qquad h(5) = 4.$$

Table 1.3 gives values of h for the first fifteen positive integers.

TABLE 1.3. The number of letters in a number's English name.

n	1	2	3	4	5	6	7	8	9	10	11	12	13	14	15
$h(n)$	3	3	5	4	4	3	5	5	4	3	6	6	8	8	7

EXAMPLE 1.5. Let $j : \{1, 2, 3, \ldots\} \to \{1, 2, 3, \ldots\}$ be the function that maps each positive integer to the number of letters in its Roman numeral representation. Actually, before we can call j a function, we should clarify *which* Roman numeral representation we mean. Certainly everyone agrees that the Roman numerals corresponding to the numbers one, two, three, and five are I, II, III, and V, respectively. However, four, which is usually written as IV, sometimes appears in older clocks as IIII. This is, for instance, the case with the Oltramontano clock in Saint Peter's Square in Vatican City. One possible explanation for this is that the IIII balances the VIII on the opposite side of the clock's face, thus providing a more pleasing symmetry. Another (somewhat dubious) explanation is that IV were the initials of the Roman god Jupiter (*Ivpiter*), and using the name of the head of the Roman pantheon in such a pedestrian object as a clock would have been considered blasphemous. Regardless of whether you find either of these explanations compelling, we will follow the lead of the clock in Saint Stephen's Tower in the Palace of Westminster in London (commonly known as Big Ben), which uses the traditional IV instead of IIII. With this issue cleared up, the values of j for the first fifteen positive integers are given by Table 1.4.

TABLE 1.4. The number of letters in a Roman numeral.

n	1	2	3	4	5	6	7	8	9	10	11	12	13	14	15
$j(n)$	1	2	3	2	1	2	3	4	2	1	2	3	4	3	2

It is important not to confuse the notation above for the evaluation of a function with the common practice in arithmetic of using parentheses to indicate multiplication. When we say that $h(10) = 3$, we do not mean that h times 10 equals 3. Rather, we mean that the function h takes the input value of 10 and returns the output value of 3. Said a different way, $h(10) = 3$ means that h maps the input 10 to the output 3. Keeping this in mind will become increasingly important when we begin to work with functions whose inputs and outputs are real numbers.[1]

EXAMPLE 1.6. Let $\mathbb{R}$ denote the set of all real numbers. The *identity function* on $\mathbb{R}$ is the function $I : \mathbb{R} \to \mathbb{R}$ that takes a real number as input and returns that exact same real number as output. For instance, I will map the number 5 to 5 and the number π to π. You can think of I as a childish function that is taking a game of "monkey see, monkey do" a little bit too far. We can describe this function's rule of assignment by the *formula*

$$I(x) = x.$$

The right hand side of this formula is a template or blueprint that we use to compute the value assigned by I to the input x. Since x represents any allowable input, it is called a *variable*. In order to compute $I\left(\frac{7}{4}\right)$, we replace every instance of the variable x in the formula above with $\frac{7}{4}$, obtaining

$$I\left(\tfrac{7}{4}\right) = \tfrac{7}{4}.$$

We can also replace x by another expression, including one involving the variable x itself, as long as each instance of x in the original formula is replaced by the new expression:

$$I(t) = t,$$
$$I(x + 1) = x + 1,$$
$$I(17 \cdot x^2) = 17 \cdot x^2.$$

Of course, we are not making use of any special property of the real numbers here. If A is any arbitrary set, we can always define the identity function $I : A \to A$ by the formula $I(a) = a$, where a is any element of the set A.

EXAMPLE 1.7. In his 1202 book *Liber Abaci*, Leonardo Fibonacci (c.1170 – 1250) introduced Europe to the Hindu-Arabic numerals that we use today. In the same book, he proposed a mathematical model describing the population of a hutch of rabbits as a function of time. According to the model, at the end of each month, every breeding pair of adult rabbits will produce a new pair of bunnies (one male and one female); after one month this new pair will, themselves, become adults and begin producing offspring of their own

---

[1] We will have a lot more to say about real numbers, as well as integers, rational, and irrational numbers, in Sections 1.2 and 1.3, so you should not despair if the details of the computations in the next few pages are not immediately clear. However, if this is the case, it would behoove you to come back and revisit these examples later on!

the month after that. The model begins on the first month with a single pair of newborn bunnies, who become adults by the second month and begin having bunnies in the third. Suppose that we let

$$\text{fib} : \{1, 2, 3, \dots\} \to \{1, 2, 3, \dots\}$$

be the function that gives the number of *pairs* of rabbits on a given month. Observe that, in this case, "fib" is simply the *name* of our function. The **bar graph** in Figure 1.2 depicts each value of this function using a two-toned bar, dark gray for the number of bunnies and light gray for the number of adults. Note in particular that since we start with a single pair of rabbits,

$$\text{fib}(1) = \text{fib}(2) = 1.$$

By the time the third month rolls along, we will have the original pair of rabbits, who are now adults, together with a brand new pair of bunnies:

$$\text{fib}(3) = \underbrace{1}_{\text{adults}} + \underbrace{1}_{\text{bunnies}} = 2.$$

On the fourth month, both of these pairs will be adults, and there will be another pair of bunnies – the second offspring of the original pair:

$$\text{fib}(4) = \underbrace{2}_{\text{adults}} + \underbrace{1}_{\text{bunnies}} = 3.$$

Since there are two pairs of adults at this point, we will see two new pairs of bunnies born on month five; these will join the previous three pairs of

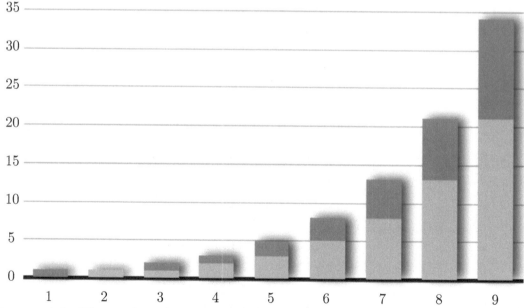

FIGURE 1.2. The number of pairs of rabbits in Fibonacci's hutch as a function of time. Bunnies are shown in dark gray and adults in light gray.

rabbits, all of whom are now adults:

$$\text{fib}(5) = \underbrace{3}_{\text{adults}} + \underbrace{2}_{\text{bunnies}} = 5.$$

From here onwards, the process skyrockets, so that by the ninth month there are more than thirty pairs of rabbits in the hutch.

If you take another look at Figure 1.2, you will notice that each light bar is the same height as the two-toned bar to its left. In other words, in any given month, the number of adult rabbits is equal to the total number of rabbits (adults plus bunnies) in the previous month. Thus, the number of pairs of adults in month number n is equal to $\text{fib}(n-1)$.

By the same token, each dark bar is the same height as the light bar to its left. This means that the number of bunnies in a particular month is equal to the total number of adults in the previous month, which, in turn, is equal to the total population of rabbits two months earlier. Thus, the number of pairs of bunnies in month number n is equal to $\text{fib}(n-2)$.

Since the total population of rabbits consists of these two quantities added together, our function is then described by the **recursive formula**

$$\underbrace{\text{fib}(n)}_{\text{total}} = \underbrace{\text{fib}(n-1)}_{\text{adults}} + \underbrace{\text{fib}(n-2)}_{\text{bunnies}}.$$

The word "recursive" refers to the fact that, in this formula, each output value of the function is defined on the basis of other output values of the *same* function. For instance, in order to determine the value of $\text{fib}(6)$, we first need to compute $\text{fib}(5)$ and $\text{fib}(4)$. Of course, thanks to our calculations above, we do know that $\text{fib}(5) = 5$ and $\text{fib}(4) = 3$. Thus, our recursive formula tells us that

$$\text{fib}(6) = \text{fib}(5) + \text{fib}(4) = 5 + 3 = 8,$$

so there will be a total of eight pairs of rabbits in our hutch during the sixth month.

Sometimes, it is convenient to define a function using more than a single formula, depending on the result of some test. For instance, we can describe the function from Example 1.1 by the expression

$$f(m) = \begin{cases} \text{safe} & \text{if } m \text{ is a month containing an } r, \\ \text{risky} & \text{otherwise.} \end{cases}$$

In this case, given a month m, we first test whether the statement "m is a month containing an r" is true or false. If it is true, then f maps m to the value "safe." If it is false, then f maps m to the value "risky." Functions defined in this way are typically called **piecewise functions**.

EXAMPLE 1.8. Let $q : \mathbb{R} \to \mathbb{R}$ be the function that maps each rational number to the value 1, and each irrational number to the value 0. Thus,

$$q(x) = \begin{cases} 1 & \text{if } x \text{ is a rational number,} \\ 0 & \text{if } x \text{ is an irrational number.} \end{cases}$$

Then $q(7) = q\left(\frac{2}{3}\right) = 1$ because 7 and $\frac{2}{3}$ are rational numbers, whereas $q(\pi) = q(\varphi) = 0$ since $\pi = 3.141\,592\ldots$ and $\varphi = 1.618\,033\ldots$ are irrational numbers.

EXAMPLE 1.9. The **absolute value function** has a domain and codomain of the real numbers and is defined as follows:

$$|x| = \begin{cases} x & \text{if } x \text{ is positive,} \\ 0 & \text{if } x \text{ is zero,} \\ -x & \text{if } x \text{ is negative.} \end{cases}$$

This function takes a real number as its input and, if that number is positive, returns the same number as output. If the input is negative, it returns the negative of the input (which then turns out to be positive). Finally, if the input is zero, the function returns an output of zero. Since any real number is bound to fall under one of these categories, this rule patently assigns a unique output value to each input, as required.

We need to be careful that our functions be **well-defined**. In other words, we need to check that the rule that assigns a unique output value to each input is clear and unambiguous. For the most part, this will be immediately transparent for the functions we will study. However, it is worth noting that difficulties can emerge from deceivingly simple-sounding rules, as the following intriguing example illustrates.

EXAMPLE 1.10. Suppose that we try to define a function H whose domain is the set of English adjectives by the expression

$$H(x) = \begin{cases} 1 & \text{if } x \text{ is an adjective that describes itself,} \\ 0 & \text{if } x \text{ is an adjective that does not describe itself.} \end{cases}$$

Note that the adjective "short," being a relatively short word, describes itself. Hence, $H(\text{short}) = 1$. On the other hand, the word "long" is not a long word at all, so it does not describe itself. Therefore $H(\text{long}) = 0$. Finally, the word "sesquipedalian," a rather lengthy synonym for "long," does describe itself, and so $H(\text{sesquipedalian}) = 1$.

One problem with H is that it is sometimes unclear what value it should assign to a word. For instance, is the word "good" a good word? Is the word "bad" a bad word? Whatever it is that makes a word good or bad seems to be a matter of personal opinion. What about the word "red"? Does it describe itself? Well, it does if it is written in red ink, but not if it is written in blue ink. It seems that for some words, the value of H depends on fleeting circumstances. This is certainly not proper behavior for a function!

An even more perplexing situation arises with the word "heterologous." A word is heterologous if it does not describe itself. What is H(heterologous)? If H(heterologous) $= 1$, that is, if "heterologous" describes itself, then it must be heterologous, which implies that it *does not* describe itself and so H(heterologous) $= 0$. On the other hand, if H(heterologous) $= 0$, that is, if "heterologous" does not describe itself, then it is heterologous, which implies that it *does* describe itself and so H(heterologous) $= 1$. In other words, H(heterologous) $= 0$ implies that H(heterologous) $= 1$, and vice versa. As soon as you decide on a value for H(heterologous), whatever that value might be, it immediately becomes the wrong one!

The source of all of these difficulties is that H is not well-defined over the entire domain of English adjectives. In fact, H is not even well-defined over the set of all adjectives that can be used to describe other words. The only way to turn H into a well-defined function is to restrict our domain to a small set of adjectives like $\{\text{short}, \text{long}, \text{sesquipedalian}\}$ in which we can always guarantee a unique output for each input.

The curious example above is loosely based on a famous paradox first set forth by Bertrand Russell (1872–1970). Russell was, himself, a curious character since he was not only a mathematician, but also a historian, logician, philosopher, and Nobel Laureate in literature. He was even imprisoned for a time during World War I for the many pacifist statements he made in public. True to form, he spent much of his time in prison writing about mathematics.

Reading Comprehension Questions for Section 1.1

A function is a ___(a)___ that assigns members of one set to members of a second set. When we see the notation $f : A \rightarrow B$, we say that the function f ___(b)___ the set ___(c)___ into the set ___(d)___. The set A is called the ___(e)___, and its members are the valid ___(f)___ of the function. The set B is called the ___(g)___, and its members are the possible ___(h)___ of the function. This set should not be confused with the image set of the function, which is the set of all ___(i)___ that are actually used by f. The notation $f(a)$ refers to the unique ___(j)___ that f assigns to the ___(k)___ a. It should not be confused with the product of ___(l)___ times ___(m)___.

A function can be described by a ___(n)___, a ___(o)___, or a ___(p)___. A formula is a sort of blueprint that we use to compute the output values assigned by a function; in this case, we use a ___(q)___ like the letter x to represent any allowable input to the function. A formula that defines each output value of a function based on other output values of the same function is called a ___(r)___. One example of this kind of formula is the model proposed by ___(s)___ to describe the population growth of ___(t)___. A ___(u)___ function is described by more than one formula; the choice of which formula applies for any given input depends on ___(v)___. For example, we can define the ___(w)___ function by mapping a real number x to ___(x)___, ___(y)___, or ___(z)___ depending on whether x is positive, zero, or negative, respectively.

Exercises for Section 1.1

1. There is a grain of truth behind every old wives' tale. Take another look at the data displayed in Table 1.1 on page 3. What do the four "risky" months have in common? Can you give a well-reasoned, scientific explanation for why consuming oysters on these months might be a risky business?

2. Which of the following descriptions produce a well-defined function and which do not? Explain. (You may assume that x refers to a person.)

   (a) $F(x)$ is x's mother.

   (b) $G(x)$ is x's grandmother.

   (c) $H(x)$ is x's older brother.

   (d) $J(x)$ is the number of x's siblings.

3. Which of the following descriptions produce a well-defined function and which do not? Explain. (You may assume that x refers to a person.)

   (a) $F(x)$ is the number of languages that x speaks fluently.

   (b) $G(x)$ is 1 if x speaks German and 2 if x speaks Russian.

   (c) $H(x)$ is 1 if x speaks Italian and 2 if x does not speak Italian.

   (d) $J(x)$ is 1 if x only speaks Spanish and 2 if x only speaks French.

4. Acute Alice left a mug of hot cocoa outside her door on a cold day and proceeded to record its temperature T in degrees Celsius as a function of the time (in minutes) since it was placed outside. Explain in a complete sentence the meaning of the statement $T(30) = 10$. Be sure to include units of measurement.

5. Obtuse Ollie wants to buy a used car. He finds that the cost C of a car (in thousands of dollars) is given as a function of its age (in years). Explain in a complete sentence the meaning of the statement $C(5) = 6$.

6. Scalene Sallie found a record of her hometown's population P (in thousands of people) as a function of the number of years that have elapsed since 1950. Explain in a complete sentence the meaning of the statement $P(35) = 12$.

7. Let h be the function in Example 1.4 on page 6, counting the letters in a given number's English name.

   (a) What is the smallest number in the image set of h?

   (b) How many numbers does h map to the value in part (a)?

   (c) What is the largest number n for which $h(n) = 5$?

8. Let j be the function in Example 1.5 on page 6, counting the letters in a given number's Roman numeral representation.

   (a) Find a number n for which $j(n) = 5$.

   (b) Is your answer to part (a) greater than, equal to, or less than $j(5)$?

   (c) Considering only values of n between 1 and 100, what is the largest that the value of $j(n)$ can be?

9. The bar graph shown below gives the number of moons (natural satellites) orbiting around each of the eight planets in our solar system, along with their relative position from the sun. Let

$$M : \{1, 2, 3, 4, 5, 6, 7, 8\} \to \{0, 1, 2, 3, \ldots\}$$

be the function mapping each integer n to the number of moons orbiting the planet in position n.

(a) Draw a bubble diagram for the function M.

(b) What is this function's domain?

(c) What is this function's codomain?

(d) What is this function's image set?

10. Let M be the function from Exercise 9 above.

(a) For which value(s) of n is $M(n)$ the largest?

(b) For which value(s) of n is $M(n)$ the smallest?

(c) For which value(s) of n does $M(n) = n + 5$?

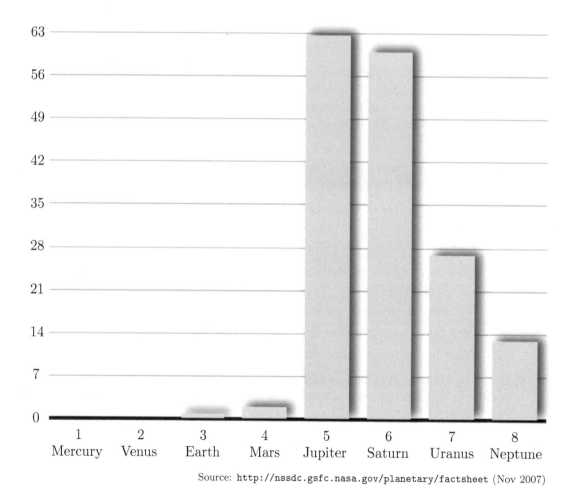

Source: http://nssdc.gsfc.nasa.gov/planetary/factsheet (Nov 2007)

In Exercises 11–20, determine whether each bubble diagram determines a function.

11.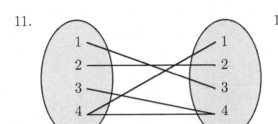

12.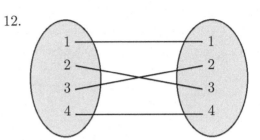

13.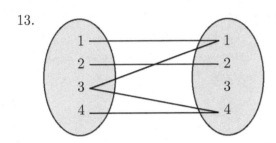

14.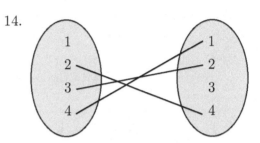

15.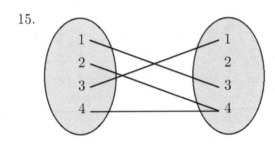

16.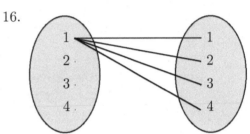

17.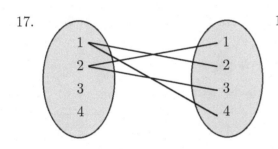

18.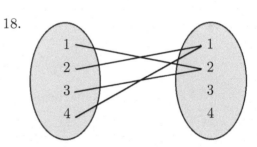

19.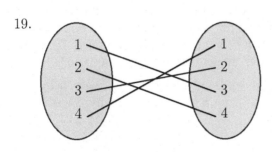

20.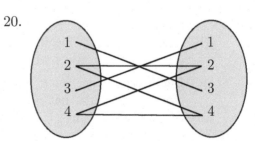

21. Let fib denote Fibonacci's function from Example 1.7 on page 7, which gives the population of rabbits in a hutch as a function of time.

    (a) Complete the table below with the values for this function.

n	1	2	3	4	5	6	7	8	9	10
fib(n)										

    (b) Find all of the integers n in this table for which the value fib(n) is even. What do all of these integers have in common? Do you detect a pattern?

    (c) Explain why the pattern you discovered in part (b) should continue indefinitely.

22. Consider the function $f : \{1, 2, 3, \ldots\} \to \{1, 2, 3, \ldots\}$ defined by the condition that $f(1) = 1$, together with the recursive formula

    $$f(n) = f(n-1) + 2.$$

    (a) Complete the table below with the values for this function.

n	1	2	3	4	5	6	7	8	9	10
$f(n)$										

    (b) What do all of the output values in this table have in common? Do you detect a pattern? Can you find a simpler, non-recursive formula for f?

    (c) Define a new function $F : \mathbb{R} \to \mathbb{R}$ whose output values are given by the non-recursive formula that you found in part (b). Explain why f and F are not the same function.

23. Consider the function $g : \{1, 2, 3, \ldots\} \to \{1, 2, 3, \ldots\}$ defined by the condition that $g(1) = 1$, together with the recursive formula

    $$g(n) = g(n-1) + (2n-1).$$

    (a) Complete the table below with the values for this function.

n	1	2	3	4	5	6	7	8	9	10
$g(n)$										

    (b) What do all of the output values in this table have in common? Do you detect a pattern? Can you find a simpler, non-recursive formula for g?

    (c) Define a new function $G : \mathbb{R} \to \mathbb{R}$ whose output values are given by the non-recursive formula that you found in part (b). Explain why g and G are not the same function.

24. After being shot out of a cannon, a dare-devil circus clown flies through the air at a height (in feet) of

$$H(t) = \begin{cases} -16\,t^2 + 95.5\,t + 3 & \text{if } 0 \le t \le 6 \\ 0 & \text{if } t > 6 \end{cases}$$

where t is the time (in seconds) after the cannon was fired.

(a) Complete the table below with the values for this function.

t	0	1	2	3	4	5	6	7	8	9
$H(t)$										

(b) According to your table, when does it seem that the dare-devil circus clown reaches the highest point of his journey?

(c) What happens to the dare-devil circus clown after 6 seconds?

25. A telecommunications company offers a monthly cellular phone plan which, for a flat rate, includes a limited number of peak-time minutes. Additional minutes beyond this limit may be purchased for a nominal fee. The monthly cost for a subscriber is given by the function

$$C(x) = \begin{cases} 24.99 & \text{if } 0 \le x \le 400 \\ 0.05\,x + 4.99 & \text{if } x > 400 \end{cases}$$

where x is the total number of peak-time minutes used that month.

(a) How much is the flat rate for this plan?

(b) What is the maximum number of peak-time minutes covered by this flat rate?

(c) How much does each additional peak-time minute cost after this limit has been reached?

26. Let $D : \{\text{January, February, March}, \dots, \text{November, December}\} \to \{1, 2, 3, \dots\}$ be the function that assigns to each month of the year the number of days in that month on a non-leap year. Express D as a piecewise function.

27. Describe the bubble diagram for the absolute value function from Example 1.9 on page 10. In particular, explain how many lines come out of each point of the domain and how many lines come in at each point of the codomain. Give as much detail as possible.

28. (a) How many different functions $f : \{1, 2, 3\} \to \{1, 2\}$ can you think of? For how many of these is the image set equal to the codomain?

(b) How many different functions $g : \{1, 2\} \to \{1, 2, 3\}$ can you think of? For how many of these is the image set equal to the codomain?

29. Suppose that the function h is defined by the formula

$$h(x) = 2x^3 - 7x^2 + 5x + A,$$

where A is a constant, that is, a number that does not depend on the variable x. Determine all of the possible values of A for which $h(2) = 3$.

30. Suppose that the function j is defined by the formula

$$j(x) = \frac{x - B}{x - C},$$

where B and C are constants. Determine all of the possible values of B and C for which $j(9) = 0$ and $j(3)$ is undefined.

1.2. Equations

Throughout most of this book, we will be looking at functions whose domains and codomains are sets of **real numbers**. The set of all real numbers, abbreviated using the fancy symbol $\mathbb{R}$, consists of nearly every kind of number you might run into in your everyday life. If a quantity can be expressed as a decimal, a fraction, or a mixed numeral, then it is a real number.

The simplest of all real numbers are the **positive integers**. These are the familiar "counting numbers" like 1, 2, 3, and so on, which we all learned about in honors kindergarten. We use a fancy $\mathbb{N}$ (which stands for "number") to designate this set:

$$\mathbb{N} = \{1, 2, 3, \dots\}.$$

If we add to these zero and the negative integers, we get the set of all **integers**, which we denote by a fancy $\mathbb{Z}$ (short for *Zahl*, the German word for "number"):

$$\mathbb{Z} = \{\dots, -3, -2, -1, 0, 1, 2, 3, \dots\}.$$

Next, we have the set of **rational numbers**. The word "rational" here says nothing about the particular temperament or mental state of these numbers; instead it refers to the fact that they are ratios (in other words, fractions) of integers. We represent this set by a fancy $\mathbb{Q}$, which stands for "quotient," yet another name for a fraction:

$$\mathbb{Q} = \left\{ \frac{p}{q} : p, q \in \mathbb{Z} \text{ and } q \neq 0 \right\}.$$

This is a good point to stop and briefly look at the **set-builder notation** we just used. The braces { and } in the definitions above indicate that we are looking at a set, while the symbol $\in$ is mathematical shorthand for the phrase "is an element of." The expression to the left of the colon is a template for the prototypical element of the set – in this case, a fraction of the form p/q – while the expression to the right of the colon gives the conditions that must be met when using this template. Here, the conditions are

$$\text{(i) } p, q \in \mathbb{Z} \qquad \text{and} \qquad \text{(ii) } q \neq 0.$$

The first of these says that p and q are elements of the set $\mathbb{Z}$, or in other words, that they are integers. The second says that q is not zero. This means that we can have any integer in the numerator of our fractions, but we may never have a zero in the denominator. Dividing by zero is about the worst thing you can do in mathematics. It is the equivalent of shouting "fire!" in a crowded theatre or joking with an airport security guard about carrying firearms in your luggage.

A fraction is in **lowest terms** when it is written as a ratio of integers with no common factors. If the denominator of a rational number in lowest terms is a product of 2's and 5's, then the rational number has a **decimal expansion** that terminates, as in

$$\frac{8}{5} = 1.6 \qquad \text{or} \qquad \frac{157}{50} = 3.14.$$

On the other hand, if the denominator has any other prime factor, the number's decimal expansion repeats indefinitely, as in

$$\frac{30}{11} = 2.727\,272\,727\,272\,727\,272\,727\,272\,727\,272\,\ldots.$$

Since a calculator will only show a few digits of any answer, you may jump to the incorrect conclusion that $30 \div 11 = 2.727\,272\,727$. (Try it and see!) However, you should remember that this is only an approximation and that the fraction's *true* decimal expansion is, in fact, infinitely long.

Every positive integer is an integer, and every integer is a rational number (with a denominator of 1 in lowest terms). Since there are infinitely many positive integers, there are also infinitely many rational numbers. However, this still leaves a great many real numbers that cannot be written as the ratio of two integers. For example, consider the famous number known as the **golden ratio**, which we express here as an infinite continued fraction:

$$\varphi = 1 + \cfrac{1}{1 + \cfrac{1}{1 + \cfrac{1}{1 + \cdots}}}.$$

The funny symbol φ is a Greek letter *phi*, which you can pronounce either as "fee" if you are a linguistic purist, or as "fie" if you are a member of a fraternity or sorority. Regardless of how you pronounce it, the decimal expansion for φ is

$$\varphi = 1.618\,033\,988\,749\,894\,848\,204\,586\,834\,365\,\ldots.$$

This decimal expansion neither terminates nor repeats. In fact, there is no discernible pattern to these digits. This means that, no matter how hard we try, we can never write φ as the ratio of two integers. In other words, whenever φ is written as a ratio (after all, it *is* called the golden ratio), either the numerator or the denominator (or both) will turn out to be a non-integer. Proving this, however, is not that easy!

A real number, like φ, that cannot be written as a fraction is said to be **irrational**. Without a doubt, the most famous irrational number of all is

$$\pi = 3.141\,592\,653\,589\,793\,238\,462\,643\,383\,279\,\ldots.$$

This number (called *pi*) describes, among other things, how many times the diameter of a circle may be wrapped around its circumference. Fairly soon, we shall encounter other important irrational numbers, all of which will have one thing in common: Their decimal expansions neither terminate nor repeat.

Irrational numbers are slippery little suckers! For instance, there are infinitely many irrational numbers whose decimal expansions start with precisely the same 32 digits as the expansion for π that we gave above, but only one of them is equal to π. Thus, to avoid problems, we usually refer to our special irrational numbers by their name (like π or φ) and not by their decimal expansion. On the rare occasion when we *do* use a decimal expansion, we must make sure that we also use an ellipsis (that is the fancy name for the "dot-dot-dot") as a reminder that the digits do go on and on. Otherwise, we might get confused and end up with a rational number that only approximates the irrational that we wanted to get our hands on in the first place.

EXAMPLE 1.11. Consider the number ζ (pronounced *zeta*), whose decimal expansion consists of increasingly longer runs of zeroes and ones:

$$\zeta = 0.101\,100\,111\,000\,111\,100\,001\,111\,100\,000\,111\ldots.$$

Since this pattern of digits continues indefinitely without ever repeating, the number ζ must be irrational. With a little bit of work, we can show that other numbers like $\zeta + \frac{1}{111}$ are also irrational.

Writing an expression like $\zeta + \frac{1}{111}$ leaves absolutely no question as to which number we are dealing with, even though we do not know its decimal expansion. Of course, given enough time we *could* determine at least the first few digits of this expansion:

$$\zeta + \frac{1}{111} = 0.110\,109\,120\,009\,120\,109\,010\,120\,109\,009\,120\ldots.$$

However, the point is that this is rarely necessary. For our purposes, it will usually be sufficient (and definitely more convenient) to refer to this number by its name (that is, as "$\zeta + \frac{1}{111}$") rather than by its decimal expansion.

In darker times, irrational numbers were a despised and persecuted lot. Legend has it that the Greek mathematician Hippasus of Metapontum (c. 520 BC) was taken out to sea and drowned by the secretive Order of Pythagoreans in punishment for revealing that the square root of two was irrational.[2] In our day and age, we should be more tolerant, remembering that, despite all of their apparent flaws, irrational numbers have feelings, too. We should not mistreat them in our mathematical wheeling and dealing. They are like eccentric relatives with bad fashion sense. We ought to be nice to them, the same as everyone else, even if they walk around wearing ruffled pirate shirts with poofy sleeves and a blue parrot on their shoulder.

---

[2] We shall have a chance to discuss the square root of two at length in Section 1.4.

Arithmetic involves combining real numbers by performing the familiar operations of addition, subtraction, multiplication, division, and exponentiation. When these operations are combined, they are performed in the following order:

> **The Order of Operations**
>
> ① exponentiation,
>
> ② multiplication and division,
>
> ③ addition and subtraction.

We use parentheses to modify this order of operations, computing the quantities inside the innermost parentheses first (following the order above), and then proceeding outward.

EXAMPLE 1.12. The expression $3 \cdot 5^2 - 7$ reduces to
$$3 \cdot 5^2 - 7 = 3 \cdot 25 - 7 = 75 - 7 = 68.$$

However, by adding parentheses we can change this result. Thus
$$3 \cdot (5^2 - 7) = 3 \cdot (25 - 7) = 3 \cdot 18 = 54$$
and
$$(3 \cdot 5)^2 - 7 = 15^2 - 7 = 225 - 7 = 218.$$

EXAMPLE 1.13. There are two symbols which we use to denote division: the **obelus** $\div$ and the **solidus** $/$. The latter is more common because it can be written horizontally, often eliminating the need for parentheses:
$$(2 + 9) \div (4^2 + 5) = (2 + 9)/(4^2 + 5) = \frac{2 + 9}{4^2 + 5} = \frac{11}{21}.$$

Since the use of the horizontal solidus is so much cleaner, the reign of the poor obelus has been reduced almost exclusively to the division button on your calculator.

EXAMPLE 1.14. Addition and multiplication obey the **associative** as and the **commutative properties**. This means that when we add together several numbers, it does not matter which we add first or in what order we do so; the same is true when we multiply several numbers together. Furthermore, subtracting simply means adding a negative number, and dividing means multiplying by a fraction, so the commutative and associative properties extend, from a certain point of view, to these operations as well. Thus,
$$3 - 4 + 5 = (3 - 4) + 5 = 3 + (-4 + 5) = (3 + 5) - 4 = (5 + 3) - 4 = 4$$
and
$$3 \cdot \frac{1}{4} \cdot 5 = \frac{3}{4} \cdot 5 = 3 \cdot \frac{5}{4} = \frac{3 \cdot 5}{4} = \frac{5 \cdot 3}{4} = \frac{15}{4}.$$

The term **algebra** is derived from the Arabic word *al-jabr* meaning "reduction." More precisely, the term refers to the famous book *Al-Jabr wa'l-Muqabala* by the eighth century Persian mathematician Abu Ja'far Muhammad ibn Musa Al-Khwarizmi (c. 780–850 AD). Nowadays, algebra refers to the use of letters (sometimes English, sometimes Greek) to take the place of unknown quantities in **equations**, and to the manipulation of these equations in order to discover the values of the unknowns that make these equations true. The values of the unknowns that turn an equation into a true statement are called the **solutions** of the equation. The process of reducing a complicated equation to its set of solutions is called **solving** the equation. There are three valid manipulations that can be used to solve for an unknown. All of algebra can be reduced to these three rules.

Algebra Rules

① Any real number may be added to (or subtracted from) each side of an equation:
$$A = B \qquad \Leftrightarrow \qquad A + C = B + C$$

② Each side of an equation may be multiplied times (or divided by) the same *non-zero* real number:
$$A = B \qquad \Leftrightarrow \qquad A \cdot C = B \cdot C \qquad \text{(if } C \neq 0)$$

③ If a product of numbers is equal to zero, then at least one of those numbers is also equal to zero:
$$A_1 \cdot A_2 \cdot A_3 \cdot \ldots \cdot A_n = 0 \quad \Leftrightarrow \quad A_1 = 0 \text{ or } A_2 = 0 \text{ or } \ldots \text{ or } A_n = 0$$

EXAMPLE 1.15. Suppose that we wish to solve the equation
$$7x - 3 = 4x + 9.$$

In order to solve a simple equation like this one, we first use Rule ① to move all of the terms involving the unknown x to one side of the equation and all of the constant terms (those not having an x) to the other side. This is known as "collecting like terms." Thus, we have:

$7x - 3 = 4x + 9$	original
$7x - 3 - 4x = 9$	subtracting $4x$ from both sides (Rule ①)
$7x - 4x = 9 + 3$	adding 3 to both sides (Rule ①)
$3x = 12$	simplifying

Next, we will use Rule ② to divide both sides of the equation by the number in front of the unknown x. This number is usually called the **coefficient** of x, and in our case, it happens to be 3. After dividing, we will have the unknown x by itself on the left hand side of our equation, as follows:

$$3x = 12 \qquad \text{result from above}$$

$$x = \tfrac{12}{3} \qquad \text{dividing both sides by 3 (Rule ②)}$$

$$x = 4 \qquad \text{simplifying}$$

We can check that we have arrived at a correct solution by replacing each instance of x in the original equation with the value 4; this is referred to as "substituting" $x = 4$:

$$x = 4 \quad \Rightarrow \quad \begin{cases} 7x - 3 = 7 \cdot 4 - 3 = 28 - 3 = 25, \\ 4x + 9 = 4 \cdot 4 + 9 = 16 + 9 = 25. \end{cases}$$

Since both sides of the equation end up equal to 25, we see that $x = 4$ is indeed a solution of the equation. The beauty of our Algebra Rules is that they guarantee that 4 is the *only* solution for this equation!

EXAMPLE 1.16. Solve the equation $x(x + 5)(2x - 3) = 0$.

Solution. We could multiply out the terms on the left hand side of the equation and get a new equation completely equivalent to the original one, namely

$$2x^3 + 7x^2 - 15x = 0.$$

However, this does little to help us find the values of x which satisfy the equation. In fact, it obfuscates the situation even further!

Instead, let us take a closer look at the original equation. It consists of three factors which multiply together to give zero. According to Rule ③ above, the only way to multiply a collection of numbers and get zero is if one of the numbers was equal to zero in the first place. Therefore, we can reduce our original problem to three simpler subproblems, each of which we solve independently from the others:

$$x = 0 \qquad \text{or} \qquad x + 5 = 0 \qquad \text{or} \qquad 2x - 3 = 0$$

$$x = -5 \qquad\qquad\qquad 2x = 3$$

$$x = \tfrac{3}{2}$$

The solution set is thus $\left\{0, -5, \tfrac{3}{2}\right\}$, as we can check by substituting back into our original equation as follows:

$$x = 0 \quad \Rightarrow \quad x\left(x + 5\right)\left(2x - 3\right) = (0) \cdot (5) \cdot (-3) = 0,$$

$$x = -5 \quad \Rightarrow \quad x\left(x + 5\right)\left(2x - 3\right) = (-5) \cdot (0) \cdot (-13) = 0,$$

$$x = \tfrac{3}{2} \quad \Rightarrow \quad x\left(x + 5\right)\left(2x - 3\right) = \left(\tfrac{3}{2}\right) \cdot \left(\tfrac{13}{2}\right) \cdot (0) = 0.$$

Before moving on, perhaps we should clarify a point which sometimes causes confusion. In the statement of Rule ③, the expressions A_1, A_2, A_3, and so on up to A_n simply represent the different factors which multiply together to give zero. Thus, in the example above, $A_1 = x$, $A_2 = x + 5$, and $A_3 = 2x - 3$. There is nothing particularly special about these expressions. The *indices* (that is what the little numbers on the bottom right of the A's are called) are there simply to allow us to refer to an unlimited number of distinct quantities all at once.

At its very core, the machinery of algebraic manipulation rests on the interaction between addition and multiplication. Without it, we would be unable to collect like terms, simplify, and in all but the simplest of situations solve equations. This interaction is succinctly expressed by the **distributive property**:

$$A \cdot (B + C) = A \cdot B + A \cdot C.$$

This property allows us to spread the effects of a multiplication among each of the terms in a sum, or conversely, to pull out a factor which is common to every term in a sum. We have already used the distributive property (albeit stealthily) in the solution in Example 1.15, when we pulled a common factor of x from the quantities $7x$ and $-4x$ in order to simplify $7x - 4x$ as

$$7x - 4x = (7 - 4)x = 3x.$$

The distributive property gives rise to several notable formulas, which we summarize in the following theorem. Committing these formulas to memory will be well worth your while!

Theorem 1.1. If a, b, and x are real numbers, then the following equations hold:

$$(1.1) \qquad\qquad (x + a)(x + b) = x^2 + (a + b)x + ab,$$

$$(1.2) \qquad\qquad (x + a)(x - a) = x^2 - a^2,$$

$$(1.3) \qquad\qquad (x + a)^2 = x^2 + 2ax + a^2,$$

$$(1.4) \qquad\qquad (x - a)^2 = x^2 - 2ax + a^2.$$

Proof. "The proof of the pudding is in the eating."[3] In our case, formula (1.1) is obtained by a direct computation using the distributive property four times:

$$(x + a)(x + b) = (x + a)x + (x + a)b = x^2 + ax + bx + ab = x^2 + (a + b)x + ab.$$

Formulas (1.2) and (1.3) follow from this one by setting $b = -a$ and $b = a$, respectively. Similarly, formula (1.4) is obtained by simultaneously replacing both a and b with $-a$. $\square$

----

[3] W. Camden, *Remains of a Greater Work Concerning Britain*, 266 (1605).

EXAMPLE 1.17. Find all of the solutions of the equation

$$x^2 + 6x + 9 = 0.$$

Solution. In order to apply Rule ③ to this equation, we will first need to factor the left hand side, and in order to do that, we need to look closely at our coefficients – in other words, the numbers in front of x^2 and x, as well as the number that has no x's at all. In the equation at hand, the coefficients are 1, 6, and 9. With a judicious eye, you might notice that $6 = 2 \cdot 3$ while $9 = 3^2$, so the expression on the left hand side of our equation is in the form of a **perfect square**, as in formula (1.3) above:

$$x^2 + 6x + 9 = x^2 + 2ax + a^2.$$

Here $a = 3$, so we can factor $x^2 + 6x + 9$ as $(x + 3)^2 = (x + 3)(x + 3)$. This gives us

$$(x + 3)(x + 3) = 0.$$

Now, observe that the two factors on the left are identical to each other, so we only need to worry about setting one of them equal to zero:

$$x + 3 = 0$$
$$x = -3.$$

Evidently, -3 is the only solution to our equation, as can be easily verified.

EXAMPLE 1.18. Suppose that we wish to solve the equation

$$x^2 - 12^2 = 5^2.$$

Now, Rule ③ only applies when one side of the equation is equal to zero. Therefore, before we attempt to factor the left hand side of the equation, we must first subtract 5^2 from both sides, thus setting the right hand side of the equation equal to zero:

$$x^2 - 12^2 - 5^2 = 0$$
$$x^2 - 169 = 0$$
$$x^2 - 13^2 = 0.$$

Notice that the expression on the left hand side of this equation consists of one perfect square, x^2, minus another, 13^2. For obvious reasons, this is called a **difference of two squares**. We can use formula (1.2) to factor this sort of expression. In this case, we get

$$(x + 13)(x - 13) = 0.$$

Thus, our original problem reduces to solving two simple equations:

$$x + 13 = 0 \qquad \text{or} \qquad x - 13 = 0$$
$$x = -13 \qquad\qquad\qquad x = 13.$$

Therefore, our solution set is $\{-13, 13\}$, as you can check for yourself.

Notice that in the last example we cannot just "cancel out the squares" as follows:

$$x^2 - 12^2 = 5^2 \quad \xrightarrow{\;\textcircled{!}\;} \quad x - 12 = 5.$$

Tempting as it might seem, there is no mathematical justification for this cancellation. In fact, following this approach would get us to the answer $x = 17$, which we know is not a solution. In the same way, a difference of two squares cannot be simplified as:

$$x^2 - 13^2 = 0 \quad \xrightarrow{\;\textcircled{!}\;} \quad x - 13 = 0.$$

Doing so would produce only one of the two solutions. Many an algebra student has fallen prey to this sort of wishful thinking. Do not follow in their steps. Beware of freshman dreams!

EXAMPLE 1.19. Solve the equation

$$x(x + 5) = 4x + 6.$$

Solution. We begin by multiplying out the product on the left hand side of the equation (using the distributive law) and then subtracting $4x + 6$ from both sides, thus setting the right hand side of the equation equal to zero:

$$x^2 + 5x = 4x + 6$$
$$x^2 + x - 6 = 0.$$

We would now like to factor $x^2 + x - 6$ as a product of the form $(x+a)(x+b)$. If we could do this, then, according to formula (1.1), we would have

$$x^2 + x - 6 = x^2 + (a + b)x + ab.$$

Comparing the coefficients on either side of this equation, we see that all we need to do is find two numbers (a and b) that add up to $a + b = 1$ and multiply to $ab = -6$. In order to find the required numbers, let us take a look at the integer factors of -6, and hope that we get lucky:

$$-6 = -6 \cdot 1 \quad \Rightarrow \quad -6 + 1 = -5,$$
$$-6 = -3 \cdot 2 \quad \Rightarrow \quad -3 + 2 = -1,$$
$$-6 = -2 \cdot 3 \quad \Rightarrow \quad -2 + 3 = 1,$$
$$-6 = -1 \cdot 6 \quad \Rightarrow \quad -1 + 6 = 5.$$

Note that $a = -2$ and $b = 3$ satisfy our requirements. Therefore,

$$x^2 + x - 6 = (x - 2)(x + 3) = 0.$$

Setting each factor equal to zero gives us

$$x - 2 = 0 \quad \text{or} \quad x + 3 = 0$$
$$x = 2 \qquad\qquad x = -3,$$

so our solution set is $\{2, -3\}$.

EXAMPLE 1.20. Solve the equation

$$4x^2 + 8x + 3 = 0.$$

Solution. Notice that the expression on the left hand side of this equation is a bit more complicated than the ones that appear in Theorem 1.1. In particular, the coefficient of x^2 in this equation is not equal to one. This means that we will need a slightly more refined strategy for factoring. Like a jeweler carefully cutting a fine gem with a chisel, we are going to figure out the perfect way to split the *middle* coefficient (which, in this case, is equal to 8) so the correct factorization shines through. However, coefficients are harder than diamonds, so we will need something with a little bit of bang. We call this the **sledgehammer method**.

What we will do is find two numbers (let us call them p and q) whose sum equals the coefficient of x (that is, $p + q = 8$) and whose product is equal to the product of the other two coefficients (in other words, $p \cdot q = 4 \cdot 3 = 12$). Since both 8 and 12 are positive, we can begin by looking at the positive integer factors of 12:

$$12 = 1 \cdot 12 \qquad \Rightarrow \qquad 1 + 12 = 13,$$
$$12 = 2 \cdot 6 \qquad \Rightarrow \qquad 2 + 6 = 8,$$
$$12 = 3 \cdot 4 \qquad \Rightarrow \qquad 3 + 4 = 7.$$

Evidently, choosing $p = 2$ and $q = 6$ will do the trick. Therefore, we will go back to our equation and split the coefficient of x as $8 = 2 + 6$:

$$4x^2 + (2 + 6)\,x + 3 = 0.$$

Then distributing, regrouping, and distributing twice more will give us the desired factorization:

$$4x^2 + (2 + 6)\,x + 3 = 0$$
$$4x^2 + (2x + 6x) + 3 = 0$$
$$(4x^2 + 2x) + (6x + 3) = 0$$
$$2x\,(2x + 1) + 3\,(2x + 1) = 0$$
$$(2x + 3)(2x + 1) = 0.$$

This means that we have either

$$2x + 3 = 0 \qquad \text{or} \qquad 2x + 1 = 0$$
$$2x = -3 \qquad\qquad\qquad 2x = -1$$
$$x = -\tfrac{3}{2} \qquad\qquad\qquad x = -\tfrac{1}{2},$$

so our solution set is $\left\{ -\tfrac{3}{2}, -\tfrac{1}{2} \right\}$, as you should verify.

Observe that there was nothing special about the order in which we split the middle coefficient above. We could have just as easily split it in the opposite order, as $8 = 6 + 2$. This alternate order produces the exact same factorization as before,

$$4x^2 + (6 + 2)\,x + 3 = 0$$

$$4x^2 + (6x + 2x) + 3 = 0$$

$$(4x^2 + 6x) + (2x + 3) = 0$$

$$2x\,(2x + 3) + 1\,(2x + 3) = 0$$

$$(2x + 1)(2x + 3) = 0,$$

and therefore results in exactly the same set of solutions.

EXAMPLE 1.21. Solve the equation

$$2x^3 - 6x = x^2.$$

Solution. As usual, we begin by clearing one side of the equation so it equals zero. We can do this by subtracting x^2 from both sides:

$$2x^3 - x^2 - 6x = 0.$$

Notice that every term on the left hand side of this equation has a factor of x, which we can factor out using the distributive property:

$$x\,(2x^2 - x - 6) = 0.$$

Next, we use our sledgehammer method to factor $2x^2 - x - 6$. Following the recipe outlined above, we need a pair of numbers, p and q, for which

$$p + q = -1 \qquad \text{and} \qquad p \cdot q = 2 \cdot (-6) = -12.$$

After examining all of the integer factors of -12, we find that choosing $p = 3$ and $q = -4$ will do the job. We can then split the middle coefficient as $-1 = 3 - 4$ and factor our expression as follows:

$$x\,(2x^2 + (3 - 4)\,x - 6) = 0$$

$$x\,(2x^2 + (3x - 4x) - 6) = 0$$

$$x\,((2x^2 + 3x) + (-4x - 6)) = 0$$

$$x\,(x\,(2x + 3) - 2\,(2x + 3)) = 0$$

$$x\,(x - 2)(2x + 3) = 0.$$

Then, according to Rule ③, we can split this equation into three simpler equations in which we set each factor independently equal to zero:

$$x = 0 \qquad \text{or} \qquad x - 2 = 0 \qquad \text{or} \qquad 2x + 3 = 0$$
$$x = 2 \qquad\qquad 2x = -3$$
$$x = -\tfrac{3}{2}.$$

Therefore, our solution set is $\left\{0, 2, -\tfrac{3}{2}\right\}$.

EXAMPLE 1.22. Solve the equation

$$\tfrac{3}{14}\, x^2 + \tfrac{1}{4}\, x - \tfrac{5}{7} = 0.$$

Solution. Since all three coefficients in this equation are fractions, we begin by multiplying everyone in sight by the lowest common denominator, which in this case happens to be 28. Much to the relief of any readers suffering from *quotientophobia* (an irrational fear of fractions), this will transform all of our coefficients into integers:

$$6x^2 + 7x - 20 = 0.$$

We are now ready to put our sledgehammer method to work. In particular, we seek two numbers, p and q, which add up to $p + q = 7$ and whose product is $p \cdot q = 6 \cdot (-20) = -120$. After searching amongst the factors of -120, of which there are many, we settle on $p = 15$ and $q = -8$. We can then complete the factorization as follows:

$$6x^2 + (15 - 8)\, x - 20 = 0$$

$$6x^2 + (15x - 8x) - 20 = 0$$

$$(6x^2 + 15x) + (-8x - 20) = 0$$

$$3x\, (2x + 5) - 4\, (2x + 5) = 0$$

$$(3x - 4)(2x + 5) = 0.$$

Then, using Rule ③, this reduces to

$$3x - 4 = 0 \qquad \text{or} \qquad 2x + 5 = 0$$
$$3x = 4 \qquad\qquad 2x = -5$$
$$x = \tfrac{4}{3} \qquad\qquad x = -\tfrac{5}{2}.$$

Therefore, our equation is solved by the set $\left\{\tfrac{4}{3}, -\tfrac{5}{2}\right\}$.

To understand exactly what the sledgehammer method is doing, we need to take a look at the general factorization formula

$$(ax + b)(cx + d) = acx^2 + (ad + bc)x + bd,$$

which we can derive, much like in Theorem 1.1, by repeated use of the distributive property. Notice that the coefficient of x is the sum of two numbers

$$p = ad \qquad \text{and} \qquad q = bc$$

whose product is equal to the product of the other two coefficients

$$p \cdot q = ad \cdot bc = ac \cdot bd.$$

This is precisely the recipe we follow in the sledgehammer method. In practice, when we look at expressions like

$$4x^2 + 8x + 3, \qquad 2x^2 - x - 6, \qquad \text{or} \qquad \tfrac{3}{14}x^2 + \tfrac{1}{4}x - \tfrac{5}{7},$$

the original numbers a, b, c, and d are all intermingled and scrambled about. The sledgehammer method helps us sift them out from the rubble. As long as a, b, c, and d are all integers, or even rational numbers, this is not too hard to do, and we are guaranteed to find the factorization. On the other hand, if a, b, c, or d are irrational numbers, factoring can be a very difficult affair, indeed!

EXAMPLE 1.23. Consider the equation

$$x^2 - x - 1 = 0.$$

In order to factor the expression on the left hand side of this equation with the sledgehammer method, we will need to find two numbers, p and q, that both add up and multiply to -1:

$$p + q = -1 \qquad \text{and} \qquad p \cdot q = -1.$$

A quick consideration of the factors of -1 shows that there are no *integers* that do this, so factoring $x^2 - x - 1$ may seem like a lost cause. As luck would have it, however, our old friend φ (a.k.a. the golden ratio) comes to the rescue just in the nick of time. If you look carefully at its definition back on page 20, you will observe that the denominator of the continued fraction on the right is exactly equal to φ itself:

$$\varphi = 1 + \cfrac{1}{1 + \cfrac{1}{1 + \cfrac{1}{1 + \cdots}}} = 1 + \frac{1}{\varphi}.$$

This means that the two numbers that we are looking for happen to be precisely $p = -\varphi$ and $q = \frac{1}{\varphi}$, since:

$$-\varphi + \tfrac{1}{\varphi} = -1 \qquad \text{and} \qquad -\varphi \cdot \tfrac{1}{\varphi} = -1.$$

The sledgehammer method then produces a truly mysterious factorization:

$$x^2 + \left(-\varphi + \tfrac{1}{\varphi}\right)x - 1 = 0$$

$$x^2 + \left(-\varphi\, x + \tfrac{1}{\varphi}\, x\right) - 1 = 0$$

$$\left(x^2 - \varphi\, x\right) + \left(\tfrac{1}{\varphi}\, x - 1\right) = 0$$

$$x\left(x - \varphi\right) + \tfrac{1}{\varphi}\left(x - \varphi\right) = 0$$

$$\left(x + \tfrac{1}{\varphi}\right)\left(x - \varphi\right) = 0.$$

We can now split our equation up as two simple equations:

$$x + \tfrac{1}{\varphi} = 0 \qquad \text{or} \qquad x - \varphi = 0$$

$$x = -\tfrac{1}{\varphi} \qquad\qquad\qquad x = \varphi.$$

Thus, we arrive at a solution set of $\left\{-\tfrac{1}{\varphi}, \varphi\right\}$.

EXAMPLE 1.24. Consider the equation

$$x^2 + 1 = 0.$$

First of all, we must avoid the temptation – strong as it might be – of factoring this expression as

$$x^2 + 1 = 0 \qquad \xrightarrow{\;\textcircled{!}\;} \qquad (x+1)^2 = 0.$$

Remember that formula (1.3) tells us that $(x + 1)^2 = x^2 + 2x + 1$, and this is *not* the same as $x^2 + 1$!

Instead, let us turn to the sledgehammer method. In this case, we need to find two numbers, p and q, with

$$p + q = 0 \qquad \text{and} \qquad p \cdot q = 1.$$

According to the first of these conditions, p and q must be opposites of each other, so one of these numbers is positive and the other is negative. On the other hand, the second condition requires that p and q be reciprocals of each other, so they are either both positive or both negative. Clearly, both conditions cannot be satisfied at the same time, so the sledgehammer method fails. This means that it is *impossible* to factor $x^2 + 1$, no matter how many sledgehammers we throw at it.

It turns out that our inability to factor x^2+1 is directly linked to the fact that there is no real number x that can turn our equation into a true statement. (We shall see why this is true in the next section.) Therefore, the solution set for this equation is the **empty set**: a set containing no values whatsoever, which we denote either by a lonely pair of braces {} with nothing to show for themselves, or by the symbol $\varnothing$.

As we see from the last two examples, factoring algebraic expressions can get pretty complicated. In Chapter 2, we will come back to the question of solving algebraic equations of the form

$$ax^2 + bx + c = 0.$$

There, we shall find a fool-proof method that can tell us exactly when and how a "quadratic" equation of this type may be solved. Later, in Chapter 5, we will consider equations of the form

$$ax^3 + bx^2 + cx + d = 0.$$

The solution for this "cubic" equation will lead us to the sixteenth century discovery of the complex numbers, an extension of the real numbers in which *every* algebraic equation, even those involving higher powers of x, has a solution.

Reading Comprehension Questions for Section 1.2

The set of ___(a)___, denoted by the symbol $\mathbb{R}$, contains nearly every kind of number you might run into in your everyday life. This set is divided into two large classes of numbers: the ___(b)___ numbers (those that can be written as fractions) and the ___(c)___ numbers (those that cannot). The set of ___(d)___ is denoted by the symbol $\mathbb{Q}$. Other important sets of numbers include $\mathbb{N}$ (the set of ___(e)___) and $\mathbb{Z}$ (the set of ___(f)___).

The purpose of algebra is to find all real numbers that make a given equation true. These numbers are called the ___(g)___ of the equation. To solve a simple equation like $5x + 2 = 3 - 4x$, we first move all of the x's to the left hand side by ___(h)___. Similarly, we move all the constant terms to the right hand side by ___(i)___. We can do both of these steps thanks to Algebra Rule Number ___(j)___. The result is now $9x = 1$, which we can solve for x by ___(k)___. We are allowed to do this thanks to Rule Number ___(l)___. Our final answer is then $x = $ ___(m)___.

To solve a more complicated equation like $6x^2 - 7x - 3 = 0$, we will use the ___(n)___ method. In this case, we will look at the product ___(o)___ and factor it as ___(p)___ $\times$ ___(q)___. Then we can split the middle coefficient and rewrite our equation as $($ ___(r)___ $) + ($ ___(s)___ $) = 0$. The first half factors as ___(t)___, while the second half factors as ___(u)___. This means that we can use the ___(v)___ property to pull out the common factor of ___(w)___ and rewrite our equation as $(2x - 3)(3x + 1) = 0$. Then by Rule Number ___(x)___, we can set each factor separately equal to zero. In particular, $2x - 3 = 0$ gives $x = $ ___(y)___, while $3x + 1 = 0$ gives $x = $ ___(z)___.

Exercises for Section 1.2

1. Express the value of the following product of 99 factors as a single fraction in lowest terms:

$$\left(1 - \tfrac{1}{2}\right) \cdot \left(1 - \tfrac{1}{3}\right) \cdot \left(1 - \tfrac{1}{4}\right) \cdots \cdots \left(1 - \tfrac{1}{98}\right) \cdot \left(1 - \tfrac{1}{99}\right) \cdot \left(1 - \tfrac{1}{100}\right).$$

2. Let ζ be the irrational number described in Example 1.11 on page 21.

  (a) What are the 45th, 46th, and 47th digits in the decimal expansion of ζ?

  (b) What are the 45th, 46th, and 47th digits in the decimal expansion of $\tfrac{1}{111}$?

  (c) What are the 45th, 46th, and 47th digits in the decimal expansion of $\zeta + \tfrac{1}{111}$?

3. Write each of the following numbers as a single fraction; then use a calculator or computer to determine its decimal expansion.

  (a) $1 + \cfrac{1}{1 + \cfrac{1}{1}}$

  (b) $1 + \cfrac{1}{1 + \cfrac{1}{1 + \cfrac{1}{1}}}$

  (c) $1 + \cfrac{1}{1 + \cfrac{1}{1 + \cfrac{1}{1 + \cfrac{1}{1}}}}$

  (d) $1 + \cfrac{1}{1 + \cfrac{1}{1 + \cfrac{1}{1 + \cfrac{1}{1}}}}$

  (e) The numbers in parts (a) through (d) are getting closer and closer to the golden ratio

$$\varphi = 1.618\,033\,988\ldots.$$

  How far must the pattern of fractions be continued before the decimal expansions agree with φ in their first four digits? In other words, how many fractions are required to produce a decimal expansion beginning with 1.618?

4. Add parentheses to the expression $3 + 2 \cdot 10 - 1$ so that it equals each of the following values:

  (a) 21   (b) 22   (c) 45   (d) 49

5. Add parentheses to the expression $3 \cdot 8 - 4 \div 2$ so that it equals each of the following values:

  (a) 6   (b) 10   (c) 18   (d) 22

6. You are given four numerals: 2, 3, 4, and 5. You also get one plus sign and one equals sign. Put all of these together to make a valid equation.

  (Hint: The 2 is smaller than the other three numbers.)

7. Obtuse Ollie claims that $x = 1$ is a solution to the following equation:

$$\frac{5x^2 + 3}{x + 3} = 4x + 1.$$

Acute Alice disagrees. What is wrong with Ollie's algebraic simplification?

Obtuse Ollie's Solution:

$$\frac{5x^2 + 3}{x + 3} = 4x + 1 \qquad \text{original}$$

$$\frac{5x^2}{x} = 4x + 1 \qquad \text{canceling the 3's}$$

$$5x = 4x + 1 \qquad \text{simplifying}$$

$$5x - 4x = 1 \qquad \text{subtracting } 4x$$

$$x = 1 \qquad \text{simplifying}$$

---

8. Scalene Sallie claims that $x = 0$ is the only solution to Obtuse Ollie's equation from Exercise 7 above. Once again, Acute Alice disagrees. What is wrong with Sallie's algebraic simplification?

Scalene Sallie's Solution:

$$\frac{5x^2 + 3}{x + 3} = 4x + 1 \qquad \text{original}$$

$$5x^2 + 3 = (4x + 1)(x + 3) \qquad \text{multiplying by } x + 3$$

$$5x^2 + 3 = 4x^2 + 3 \qquad \text{simplifying}$$

$$x^2 = 0 \qquad \text{subtracting } 4x^2 + 3$$

$$x = 0 \qquad \text{Rule ③}$$

---

9. Rewrite each of the following expressions in the form $A\,x^3 + B\,x^2 + C\,x + D$.

    (a) $x^3 - 2^3$ (b) $(x - 2)^3$

    (c) $x^3 + 2^3$ (d) $(x + 2)^3$

10. Rewrite each of the following expressions in the form $A\,x^3 + B\,x^2 + C\,x + D$.

    (a) $(2 - 5x)(3x^2 + 4x + 11)$ (b) $(2 - 5x)(3x^2 + 4x - 15)$

    (c) $(2 - 5x)(3x + 3)(x - 5)$ (d) $(2 - 5x)(3x + 5)(x - 3)$

In Exercises 11–28, solve each equation. Be sure to check your solutions.

11. $3x + 1 = 10$ 12. $6\,(x - 5) = 12$

13. $3 + 2x = 5x + 7$ 14. $\frac{7}{6}x - \frac{1}{5} = \frac{1}{2} + \frac{2}{3}x$

15. $\pi x - 1 = 3 + 2x$ 16. $x^2 - 9 = 16$

17. $x^2 + 8x + 16 = 0$ 18. $x^2 - 4x + 4 = 0$

19. $x^2 - 7x + 12 = 0$ 20. $x^2 + 7x + 10 = 0$

21. $x^2 - 1 = 5 - x$ 22. $5x^2 + 3x - 2 = 0$

23. $2x^2 + 5x - 3 = 0$ 24. $6x^2 + 5x + 1 = 0$

25. $\frac{2}{3}x^2 - \frac{19}{15}x + \frac{2}{5} = 0$ 26. $\frac{7}{8}x^2 - \frac{13}{4}x + \frac{1}{2} = \frac{3}{8}x$

27. $5x^3 = 9x^2 + 2x$ 28. $2x^4 + 7x^2 = 15x^3$

29. How many integers have the property that one half times the sum of the integer plus three is equal to the square of the integer?

30. Suppose that we define the function $f : \mathbb{R} \to \mathbb{R}$ by the expression

$$f(x) = \begin{cases} x^2 & \text{if } x \text{ is negative} \\ 4 & \text{if } x \text{ is zero} \\ 3x + 1 & \text{if } x \text{ is positive.} \end{cases}$$

Find all of the values of the input x for which $f(x) = 4$.

1.3. Inequalities

When ordered from lesser to greater, the set of all real numbers looks just like an infinite line, as shown in Figure 1.3 below. This assertion, sometimes called the **ruler postulate**, lies at the very heart of what it means to be a real number.

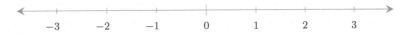

FIGURE 1.3. The real numbers arranged as points in a line.

An alert reader may have noticed that, back in Section 1.2, we did not actually define what the real numbers are, appealing instead to our intuition of what the real numbers *should be*, namely, numbers with possibly infinite decimal expansions. We could have just as easily used the ruler postulate to provide an alternate description of $\mathbb{R}$. In fact, mathematicians went for centuries without a rigorous definition of the real numbers until Georg Cantor (1845 – 1918) finally provided one in 1871. Cantor was somewhat of a troubled soul, suffering from chronic bouts of mental illness and depression that eventually led to his hospitalization. He was also a brilliant mathematician who developed the modern theory of sets. His crowning achievement was his proof that there are more irrational numbers than rational numbers; more precisely, he showed that, even though both sets are infinite, the set of irrational numbers has a larger "cardinality" or "degree of infinity" than the set of rational numbers.

To emphasize their geometric interpretation, we often refer to the set of real numbers as the **real line**. An **interval** is a convex subset of the real line, meaning that an interval has no holes: If an interval contains two real numbers, then it also contains every real number between those two numbers. In other words, intervals correspond to line segments and infinite rays in the real line.

EXAMPLE 1.25. Let J be the interval consisting of all real numbers strictly between -1 and 2. Let K be the interval consisting of all real numbers between -3 and 1, including -3 but not 1. Finally, let L be the set of all real numbers no smaller than -2. In set-builder notation, we would write each of these intervals as follows:

$$J = \{x : -1 < x < 2\}, \qquad K = \{x : -3 \leq x < 1\}, \qquad L = \{x : x \geq -2\}.$$

The shaded number lines in Figure 1.4 show graphically what these intervals look like. The "empty bubbles" at -1, 1, and 2 indicate that the shading goes all the way up to, but not including, these points, whereas the "filled-in bubbles" at -3 and -2 indicate that these points *do* form part of their respective intervals. Note that J and K form line segments in $\mathbb{R}$ but that L forms an infinite ray with no right hand endpoint.

We will often use the following shorthand to describe these intervals:

$$J = (-1, 2), \qquad K = [-3, 1), \qquad L = [-2, \infty).$$

39

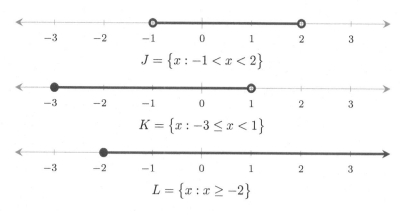

FIGURE 1.4. The intervals $J = (-1, 2)$, $K = [-3, 1)$, and $L = [-2, \infty)$.

In this ***interval notation***, the empty bubbles in our shaded number lines are replaced by round brackets, while the filled-in bubbles are replaced by square brackets.

The symbol ∞ is read "infinity" and embodies a quantity larger than any real number. Similarly, we will use the symbol $-\infty$ (read "negative infinity") to indicate a quantity smaller than any real number. We will sidestep any philosophical implications this might suggest and simply think of ∞ and $-\infty$ as useful pieces of notation. In particular, neither ∞ nor $-\infty$ represent real numbers, and so they can never belong to any interval; thus the brackets next to ∞ and $-\infty$ are necessarily always round.

An ***inequality*** is a statement about the relative sizes of two or more quantities. As in the example above, we formalize these statements by using the following symbols:

symbol	meaning
$<$	"is less than"
$>$	"is greater than"
$\leq$	"is less than or equal to"
$\geq$	"is greater than or equal to"

For example, the inequality

$$3x + 7 \geq 0$$

says that the quantity $3x + 7$ is greater than or equal to zero. Put a different way, this inequality says that $3x + 7$ is a non-negative number. The set of values of x which make this statement true is called the ***solution set*** of the inequality. The process by which we find this solution set is called ***solving*** the inequality. In order to solve an inequality, we are allowed to make algebraic manipulations similar to those we used for equations.

Algebra Rules for Inequalities

① Any real number may be added to (or subtracted from) each side of an inequality:

$$A < B \qquad \Leftrightarrow \qquad A + C < B + C$$

$$A > B \qquad \Leftrightarrow \qquad A + C > B + C$$

②a Each side of an inequality may be multiplied times (or divided by) the same *positive* real number:

$$A < B \qquad \Leftrightarrow \qquad A \cdot C < B \cdot C$$

$$A > B \qquad \Leftrightarrow \qquad A \cdot C > B \cdot C$$
$$(\text{if } C > 0)$$

②b Each side of an inequality may be multiplied times (or divided by) the same *negative* real number, as long as the inequality changes direction:

$$A < B \qquad \Leftrightarrow \qquad A \cdot C > B \cdot C$$

$$A > B \qquad \Leftrightarrow \qquad A \cdot C < B \cdot C$$
$$(\text{if } C < 0)$$

Note: The symbols $<$ and $>$ above may be replaced by $\leq$ and $\geq$.

EXAMPLE 1.26. Given the inequality $3x + 7 \geq 0$, we solve for x by collecting the unknowns on one side of the inequality and the constants on the other. Then we divide by the coefficient of x, just as if we were solving an equation:

$$3x + 7 \geq 0 \qquad \text{original}$$

$$3x \geq 0 - 7 \qquad \text{subtracting 7 from both sides (Rule ①)}$$

$$3x \geq -7 \qquad \text{simplifying}$$

$$x \geq -\tfrac{7}{3} \qquad \text{dividing both sides by 3 (Rule ②a)}$$

Evidently, our original inequality becomes a true statement when x is replaced by any real number greater than or equal $-\frac{7}{3}$. We can express this solution by using set-builder notation,

$$\left\{ x : x \geq -\tfrac{7}{3} \right\},$$

by using interval notation,

$$\left[-\tfrac{7}{3}, \infty \right),$$

or by shading a number line like so:

EXAMPLE 1.27. Solve the inequality

$$4 - 3x > 9.$$

Solution. We can use essentially the same strategy from our last example:

$4 - 3x > 9$	original
$-3x > 9 - 4$	subtracting 4 from both sides (Rule ①)
$-3x > 5$	simplifying
$x < -\frac{5}{3}$	dividing both sides by -3 (Rule ②b)

Note, however, that since we divided by a negative number, we had to change the direction of the last inequality, as prescribed by Rule ②b. The solution set is the interval $\left(-\infty, -\frac{5}{3}\right)$ illustrated below.

EXAMPLE 1.28. Solve the inequality

$$-5 < 2 - 3x < 8.$$

Solution. Actually, the expression above consists of two distinct inequalities:

$$-5 < 2 - 3x \quad \text{and} \quad 2 - 3x < 8.$$

We can solve both inequalities simultaneously by applying the appropriate Algebra Rules to all *three* sides at once, as follows:

$-5 < 2 - 3x < 8$	original
$-7 < -3x < 6$	subtracting 2 (Rule ①)
$\frac{6}{-3} < x < \frac{-7}{-3}$	dividing by -3 (Rule ②b)

Notice that instead of switching the direction of the inequalities (as per Rule ②b), we have swapped the $\frac{-7}{-3}$ with the $\frac{6}{-3}$. This is mostly for psychological reasons: It is more intuitive to write our quantities in increasing order from left to right, just like we place them on the number line and in our interval notation. After simplifying, our inequality becomes:

$$-2 < x < \frac{7}{3}$$

so the solution set is the interval $\left(-2, \frac{7}{3}\right)$ shown below.

Let us take a closer look at the Algebra Rules on pages 23 and 41. You will notice that Rule ① for equations matches up nicely with Rule ① for inequalities, just as Rule ② for equations matches up with Rules ②a and ②b for inequalities. However, Rule ③ for equations has no general counterpart for inequalities. Nevertheless, in some special circumstances we can get around this deficiency without too much difficulty.

EXAMPLE 1.29. Consider the inequality

$$(x + 7)(x + 1)(x - 5) < 0.$$

The solution to this inequality consists of all values of x which will turn the expression on the left hand side into a negative number. Instead, we shall first consider the values of x which make this expression *equal to zero*. In other words, we first look at the *equation*

$$(x + 7)(x + 1)(x - 5) = 0.$$

This equation has solutions at $x = -7$, $x = -1$, and $x = 5$. We plot these "critical points" on the number line below using empty bubbles to indicate that they are *not* solutions to our inequality (since zero is not a negative number):

The three critical points divide the real line into four intervals, namely,

$$(-\infty, -7), \qquad (-7, -1), \qquad (-1, 5), \qquad \text{and} \qquad (5, \infty).$$

Inside each one of these intervals, each of the factors from the left hand side of our inequality ($x + 7$, $x + 1$, and $x - 5$) is either exclusively positive or exclusively negative, regardless of the actual choice of x. We shall, therefore, examine each of these factors in each one of these intervals above. An easy way to do this is to pick a convenient value of x in each interval and substitute it into the formula for each of the factors. For instance, for the interval $(-\infty, -7)$, we might choose $x = -10$, in which case we find that all three factors are negative:

$$x = -10 \quad \Rightarrow \quad \begin{cases} x + 7 = -10 + 7 = -3 < 0, \\ x + 1 = -10 + 1 = -9 < 0, \\ x - 5 = -10 - 5 = -15 < 0. \end{cases}$$

On the other hand, for the interval $(-1, 5)$, we might choose $x = 0$, revealing that, here, two factors are positive and one is negative:

$$x = 0 \quad \Rightarrow \quad \begin{cases} x + 7 = 0 + 7 = 7 > 0, \\ x + 1 = 0 + 1 = 1 > 0, \\ x - 5 = 0 - 5 = -5 < 0. \end{cases}$$

Of course, since the values of each factor remain exclusively positive or exclusively negative within each interval, it does not matter which value of x we pick for each interval. In the chart below, we mark those intervals in which a particular factor takes on positive values by a plus sign; similarly, we mark those intervals in which a factor takes on negative values by a minus sign. These signs then help us to determine whether the product $(x + 7)(x + 1)(x - 5)$ is, itself, positive or negative inside each interval.

	$(-\infty, -7)$	$(-7, -1)$	$(-1, 5)$	$(5, \infty)$
$x + 7$	$-$	$+$	$+$	$+$
$x + 1$	$-$	$-$	$+$	$+$
$x - 5$	$-$	$-$	$-$	$+$
$(x + 7)(x + 1)(x - 5)$	$-$	$+$	$-$	$+$

Since we are looking for the values of x for which $(x + 7)(x + 1)(x - 5)$ is negative, our solution set consists of the **union** of the two intervals marked by minus signs (shown in bold font) on the bottommost row of our chart:

$$(-\infty, -7) \cup (-1, 5).$$

Remember that a union of sets (denoted by the symbol $\cup$) is the mathematical equivalent of the word "or". The shorthand expression above stands for the set of real numbers which are less than -7 *or* are strictly between -1 and 5. We illustrate this solution set graphically on the number line below:

EXAMPLE 1.30. Solve the inequality $2x^4 + 8x^2 \leq 17x^3$.

Solution. We first subtract $17x^3$ from both sides of the inequality, thereby setting the right hand side equal to zero. Next, we use the distributive property to pull out the common factor of x^2 from all three terms on the left, and finish the factorization by using the sledgehammer method:

$$2x^4 - 17x^3 + 8x^2 \leq 0$$
$$x^2(2x^2 - 17x + 8) \leq 0$$
$$x^2(2x^2 - x - 16x + 8) \leq 0$$
$$x^2\big(x(2x - 1) - 8(2x - 1)\big) \leq 0$$
$$x^2(x - 8)(2x - 1) \leq 0.$$

The product on the left hand side of this inequality equals zero when $x = 0$, $x = 8$, or $x = \frac{1}{2}$. Since this is a "less than or equal" type of inequality, these three critical points are automatically solutions of our inequality, so we plot them on a number line using filled-in bubbles:

These points are the endpoints of four intervals: $(-\infty, 0)$, $\left(0, \frac{1}{2}\right)$, $\left(\frac{1}{2}, 8\right)$, and $(8, \infty)$. We now look at whether the values of the factors x^2, $x-8$, and $2x-1$ are positive or negative in each of these intervals, recording our findings in the chart below.

	$(-\infty, 0)$	$\left(0, \frac{1}{2}\right)$	$\left(\frac{1}{2}, 8\right)$	$(8, \infty)$
x^2	$+$	$+$	$+$	$+$
$x-8$	$-$	$-$	$-$	$+$
$2x-1$	$-$	$-$	$+$	$+$
$x^2(x-8)(2x-1)$	$+$	$+$	$-$	$+$

Now, we are looking for values of x for which $x^2(x-8)(2x-1)$ is negative. According to the chart above, this only happens in the interval marked by a minus sign, that is, in $\left(\frac{1}{2}, 8\right)$. If we add this single interval to the three points that we plotted earlier, where $x^2(x-8)(2x-1)$ was equal to zero, we obtain a graphical representation of our solution:

Evidently, our solution set is the union of the single-point set $\{0\}$ together with the interval $\left[\frac{1}{2}, 8\right]$:

$$\{0\} \cup \left[\tfrac{1}{2}, 8\right].$$

EXAMPLE 1.31. Solve the inequality $\dfrac{x-3}{x-7} \geq -1$.

Solution. Since neither side of the inequality is zero, we will begin by clearing the right hand side (the simpler side) by adding 1 to both sides. This gives us a new inequality:

$$\frac{x-3}{x-7} + 1 \geq 0.$$

We can then combine the two terms on the left by finding a lowest common denominator and adding the resulting fractions together. In this case, the lowest common denominator happens to be $x - 7$, so we can simplify our inequality as follows:

$$\frac{x-3}{x-7} + \frac{x-7}{x-7} \geq 0$$

$$\frac{(x-3)+(x-7)}{x-7} \geq 0$$

$$\frac{2x-10}{x-7} \geq 0.$$

Observe that the fraction on the left hand side of this last inequality will be equal to zero precisely when its numerator is zero. On the other hand, the fraction will be undefined whenever its denominator is zero, since dividing by zero is forbidden. In particular, our expression will be zero when $2x - 10 = 0$ and undefined when $x - 7 = 0$. By solving each of these equations, we arrive at two critical points:

$$2x - 10 = 0 \qquad\qquad x - 7 = 0$$
$$x - 5 = 0 \qquad\qquad x = 7.$$
$$x = 5$$

Since this is a "greater than or equal" type of inequality, the first of these critical points is automatically a solution of our inequality, while the second is definitely not a solution. Hence, when we plot these points on a number line, we will have a filled-in bubble for $x = 5$ and an empty bubble for $x = 7$:

These two points divide the real line into three intervals: $(-\infty, 5)$, $(5, 7)$, and $(7, \infty)$. Within each of these intervals, the values of the expressions $x - 5$ and $x - 7$ are either exclusively positive or exclusively negative. We, therefore, examine each of these expressions, noting in the following chart whether they are positive or negative within each interval. We can then determine where the fraction on the left hand side of our inequality is positive and where it is negative.

	$(-\infty, 5)$	$(5, 7)$	$(7, \infty)$
$x - 5$	$-$	$+$	$+$
$x - 7$	$-$	$-$	$+$
$\dfrac{x-5}{x-7}$	$+$	$-$	$+$

Since we are looking for values of x which make the fraction on the left hand side of our inequality greater than or equal to zero, our solution set will consist of the two intervals marked by plus signs, $(-\infty, 5)$ and $(7, \infty)$, along with the critical point $x = 5$:

In interval notation, this is equal to the union $(-\infty, 5] \cup (7, \infty)$.

EXAMPLE 1.32. Solve the inequality $x + \dfrac{12}{x} \geq 7$.

Solution. As in the previous example, we begin by subtracting 7 from both sides of the inequality in order to set the right hand side equal to zero:

$$x + \frac{12}{x} - 7 \geq 0.$$

Next, we combine the three terms on the left hand side into a single fraction with a common denominator of x:

$$\frac{x^2}{x} + \frac{12}{x} - \frac{7x}{x} \geq 0$$

$$\frac{x^2 - 7x + 12}{x} \geq 0.$$

We can then factor the numerator of our new fraction using a sledgehammer:

$$\frac{x^2 + (-4 - 3)x + 12}{x} \geq 0$$

$$\frac{x^2 - 4x - 3x + 12}{x} \geq 0$$

$$\frac{x(x - 4) - 3(x - 4)}{x} \geq 0$$

$$\frac{(x - 3)(x - 4)}{x} \geq 0.$$

Now that the left hand side of this inequality is completely factored, we recognize that this fraction is zero when $x = 3$ or $x = 4$, and undefined when $x = 0$. This means that the first two of these points are solutions of the inequality, while the third point is not. We plot all three critical points on the number line below, using filled-in bubbles for $x = 3$ and $x = 4$ and an empty bubble for $x = 0$:

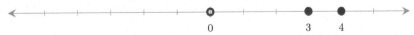

These points divide the line into the intervals $(-\infty, 0)$, $(0, 3)$, $(3, 4)$, and $(4, \infty)$. We look at the values of $x - 3$, $x - 4$, and x in each of these intervals to determine where they are positive and where they are negative, recording our findings in the following chart:

	$(-\infty, 0)$	$(0, 3)$	$(3, 4)$	$(4, \infty)$
$x - 3$	$-$	$-$	$+$	$+$
$x - 4$	$-$	$-$	$-$	$+$
x	$-$	$+$	$+$	$+$
$\dfrac{(x-3)(x-4)}{x}$	$-$	$+$	$-$	$+$

According to this chart, our solution consists of the two intervals marked with plus signs, namely $(0, 3)$ and $(4, \infty)$, together with the two critical points $x = 3$ and $x = 4$:

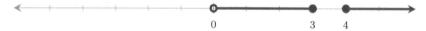

In other words, our solution set is the union $(0, 3] \cup [4, \infty)$.

Observe that our method for solving the inequalities in the last few examples depended on us having a bunch of simple terms multiplied or divided together on one side of the inequality, and on having a *zero* on the other side. In any other situation, we will first need to clear one side of the inequality and then factor whatever remains on the other side. However, as we saw in Section 1.2, we will occasionally encounter expressions which cannot be factored completely. In such cases, we will be forced to rely on perspicacity, chicanery, and a little bit of luck.

EXAMPLE 1.33. Solve the inequality $(x - 4)(x + 4) \leq -17$.

Solution. We begin by clearing the right hand side of the inequality and simplifying:

$$(x - 4)(x + 4) + 17 \leq 0$$

$$x^2 - 16 + 17 \leq 0$$

$$x^2 + 1 \leq 0.$$

Before moving on, we should once again point out a common mistake: The expression on the left hand side of the inequality is a sum of squares which will not factor. In fact, a quick look back at Example 1.24 on page 32 should convince you that not even the sledgehammer method can help us here.

Since we cannot factor $x^2 + 1$, we are going to have to consider this quantity more closely. First of all, notice that

$$x^2 \geq 0,$$

regardless of whether x is positive, negative, or zero. Adding 1 to both sides of this inequality proves that

$$x^2 + 1 \geq 1,$$

which, in turn, tells us that $x^2 + 1$ is *never* zero or less. This confirms our earlier assertion from Example 1.24 that the equation

$$x^2 + 1 = 0$$

has no solutions. More generally, it says that there are *no* values of x which will turn the inequality

$$x^2 + 1 \leq 0$$

into a true statement. Therefore, our solution set is once again the empty set, which we can denote either by an pair of lonesome braces {}, by the symbol $\varnothing$, or by a completely unshaded number line:

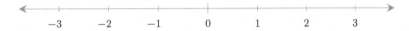

Having completed our quick review of algebra, we next return to the discussion of functions that we started back in Section 1.1. If you found our preliminary statements about real numbers in that section (especially those in Examples 1.6 through 1.9 on pages 7–10) somewhat mystifying, now would be an excellent time to go back and revisit those examples.

Reading Comprehension Questions for Section 1.3

An inequality is a mathematical statement comparing the __(a)__ of two or more quantities. It uses symbols like $<$ and $\geq$ to express the notions of " __(b)__ " and " __(c)__ ." The solution to an inequality is usually the union of one or more __(d)__, which in turn correspond to __(e)__ and __(f)__ in the real line. We solve inequalities by using three Algebra Rules that are very similar to those used for solving equations; the main differences are (i) that there are two different versions of Rule Number __(g)__ (depending on whether we multiply times a __(h)__ or a __(i)__ number), and (ii) that there is no equivalent of Rule Number __(j)__.

To solve an inequality like $5 - 4x \leq -3$, we begin by moving all of the constant terms to the right hand side. We will do this by __(k)__ using Rule Number __(l)__. This reduces our inequality to $-4x \leq -8$, which we can solve by __(m)__. Since we are using Rule Number __(n)__, we need to remember to __(o)__. The final solution can then be written in interval notation as __(p)__.

To solve a more complicated inequality like

$$\frac{2x^2 - 9x - 5}{x - 3} \geq 0$$

we first need to __(q)__ the expression on the left hand side. For example, we can do this using the sledgehammer method. The result is an inequality of the form

$$\frac{(x - 5)(2x + 1)}{x - 3} \geq 0.$$

We note that the fraction on the left hand side is equal to zero when $x =$ __(r)__ and $x =$ __(s)__, and that it is undefined when $x =$ __(t)__. Thus, we set up a chart with rows labeled $x-5$, $2x+1$, and $x-3$, and columns labeled __(u)__, __(v)__, __(w)__, and __(x)__. By looking at the bottom row of our completed chart, we select all of the intervals marked with a __(y)__ sign and arrive at the solution __(z)__.

Exercises for Section 1.3

In Exercises 1–24, solve each inequality. In each case, express your answer using both set-builder notation and interval notation, and illustrate it by shading an appropriately labeled number line.

1. $-2(x+3) < 8$

2. $2x - 2 \le 3 + x$

3. $8 - 4(2 - x) \ge -2x$

4. $(x-1)(x+1) > (x-3)(x+5)$

5. $(x-4)(x+4) > (x+2)(x-3)$

6. $x(4x+3) \ge (2x+1)^2$

7. $4 \le 2x - 2 \le 10$

8. $-5 \le 4 - 3x < 2$

9. $x(x-7) > 8$

10. $(x-1)(x-2)(x-3) \le 0$

11. $(x+2)(x^2 - 2x + 1) > 0$

12. $x^3 - 2x^2 - 3x < 0$

13. $6x^2 \le 6 + 5x$

14. $x^4 \ge 4x^2$

15. $0 < \dfrac{3-x}{3} \le 1$

16. $-3 < \dfrac{2x-1}{4} < 4$

17. $\dfrac{x-3}{x+1} > 0$

18. $\dfrac{(x-3)^2}{x^2 - 1} \le 0$

19. $\dfrac{(x-1)(x+1)}{x} \le 0$

20. $\dfrac{x^2 - 3x + 2}{x^2} \ge 0$

21. $\dfrac{x^2 - 2x + 1}{x^2 + 3x - 10} \le 0$

22. $x - \dfrac{6}{x} > 1$

23. $\dfrac{7x-3}{x+6} \le 2$

24. $\dfrac{4}{x-6} \ge \dfrac{3}{x+2}$

25. Write each of the following sets as a single interval.

   (a) $(0,3] \cup (-3,0]$

   (b) $(-1,2] \cup [-2,4)$

   (c) $(3,5) \cup \{5\} \cup (5,6)$

   (d) $\{4\} \cup \{7\} \cup (3,7) \cup (1,4)$

26. Find a single inequality whose solution set is $[-2,-1) \cup [1,2)$.

27. Find a single inequality whose solution set is $\{-5\} \cup [5, \infty)$.

28. Suppose that we define the function $f : \mathbb{R} \to \mathbb{R}$ by the expression

$$f(x) = \begin{cases} x^2 & \text{if } x < 0 \\ 5 & \text{if } x = 0 \\ 3x + 2 & \text{if } x > 0. \end{cases}$$

Find all of the values of the input x for which $f(x) \geq 4$.

29. Let $q : \mathbb{R} \to \mathbb{R}$ be the piecewise function described in Example 1.8 on page 10. Identify each of the following sets, first giving a short description and then using an appropriate mathematical notation.

    (a) $\{x : q(x) > 0\}$ (b) $\{x : q(x) \geq 0\}$ (c) $\{x : q(x) < 0\}$

30. Suppose that p and q are two positive numbers with $p < q$.

    (a) Acute Alice claims that $\dfrac{p}{q} < 1$. Is she correct? Explain.

    (b) Scalene Sallie also claims that $\dfrac{1}{q} < \dfrac{1}{p}$. Is she correct? Explain.

    (c) Obtuse Ollie thinks that the two statements above would still be true even if p and q were negative. Is he correct? Explain.

1.4. Functions and Formulas

Recall that a function $f : A \to B$ is a *rule* for mapping each input value in the domain A to a unique output value from the codomain B. When A and B are sets of numbers, one convenient way to describe such a rule is by means of a formula. In this section we shall look at four types of functions defined by formulas.

First, suppose that n is a non-negative integer and that a is a fixed real number. We can define a function f by the formula

$$f(x) = a \cdot x^n.$$

We call f a **power function of degree n**. The formula informs a user how to evaluate the function: we start with any real number x, raise it to the nth power, and then multiply the result by the coefficient a.

EXAMPLE 1.34. Imagine that as part of a physics experiment we release a compact object, say a cat, from the top of a tall building and observe its free fall. Now, it is important to note that we would be simply holding the cat over the edge of the building and then releasing it to the force of gravity; to actually toss the cat would be considered cruel and probably make us liable to legal action on the part of the cat's estate. This experiment would produce data similar to that shown in Table 1.5. In this table, $d(t)$ measures the distance (in feet) that the cat has fallen after t seconds from the moment it entered free fall. Now physicists, who have plenty of experience in tossing objects such as cats from the tops of tall buildings, know that the distance travelled by a free-falling cat is described by the power function with formula

$$d(t) = 16\,t^2.$$

If we evaluate d at several values of t, then we can quickly verify that the data presented in Table 1.5 is indeed predicted by this function.

EXAMPLE 1.35. Suppose that g is the zero-degree power function defined by the formula

$$g(x) = a \cdot x^0.$$

Before we can evaluate g, we need to discuss exactly what it means to raise a number to the zeroth power. For a positive integer n, x^n simply means

TABLE 1.5. The distance, in feet, that a free-falling cat travels in t seconds.

t	0.0	0.5	1.0	1.5	2.0	2.5	3.0	3.5	4.0	4.5	5.0	5.5
$d(t)$	0	4	16	36	64	100	144	196	256	324	400	484

the result of multiplying x by itself n times, so that

$$x^1 = x, \qquad x^2 = x \cdot x, \qquad x^3 = x \cdot x \cdot x, \qquad x^4 = x \cdot x \cdot x \cdot x,$$

and so on. Notice that in these expressions we can go from one power of x to the next by multiplying by x:

$$x^2 = x^1 \cdot x, \qquad x^3 = x^2 \cdot x, \qquad x^4 = x^3 \cdot x, \qquad x^5 = x^4 \cdot x.$$

It seems reasonable to expect that the same behavior holds for x^1 and for x^0:

$$x^1 = x^0 \cdot x.$$

We, therefore, assert that $x^0 = 1$ for all real numbers x. In this case,

$$g(x) = a \cdot x^0 = a \cdot 1 = a.$$

This means that g is a function which always returns the same output a regardless of what input it is given. We say g is a **constant function**, since its output never changes. If in addition $a = 0$, so that g maps every single input to the output 0, then we will call g the **zero function**.

A **polynomial function** consists of the sum of several power functions of various degrees:

$$\boxed{h(x) = a_n \, x^n + a_{n-1} \, x^{n-1} + a_{n-2} \, x^{n-2} + \cdots + a_2 \, x^2 + a_1 \, x + a_0.}$$

In this formula, n is a non-negative integer and the coefficients a_0, a_1, a_2, ..., a_{n-2}, a_{n-1}, and a_n are fixed real numbers. The use of indices (the little subscript numbers to the right of each "a") in this definition provides us with a convenient way to denote the coefficients of a polynomial, even when the polynomial is a sum of hundreds or even thousands of different power functions. The **degree** of h is equal to the degree of the highest power function in h having a non-zero coefficient.

EXAMPLE 1.36. Suppose that we take a piece of cardboard measuring 24 inches by 36 inches and that, from each of the four corners, we cut a square measuring x inches by x inches. This produces four flaps, which are then folded up to form an open box – ideal for carrying a cat from one physics experiment to the next – as indicated by Figure 1.5. Depending on the value of x, the bottom of the box (the rectangle formed in the middle of the cardboard when the flaps are folded up) will measure $24 - 2x$ inches by $36 - 2x$ inches, while each of the sides of the box (the four flaps) will be x inches tall. Therefore, the volume of the box (in cubic inches) is given by the polynomial function

$$V(x) = x(24 - 2x)(36 - 2x) = 4x^3 - 120x^2 + 864x.$$

According to the notation above, this is a polynomial of degree three with coefficients $a_3 = 4$, $a_2 = -120$, $a_1 = 864$, and $a_0 = 0$.

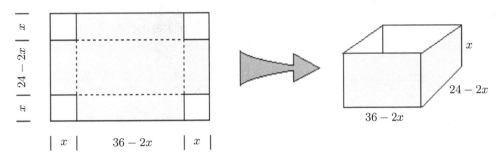

FIGURE 1.5. Forming an open box from a rectangular piece of cardboard.

A **rational function** is the ratio of two polynomials p and q, where q is not the zero function:

$$F(x) = \frac{p(x)}{q(x)}.$$

Observe that this function is well-defined for all values of x which make $q(x)$ non-zero.

EXAMPLE 1.37. A 5 kilogram cat weighs approximately 11 pounds on the surface of the earth but only 1.9 pounds on the surface of the moon. If the moon is in its apogee – the point on its orbit farthest from the earth, about 406 million meters away – and the cat is placed directly between the centers of the earth and the moon at a distance of x million meters from the center of the earth, then the weight of the cat (in pounds) will be given by the rational function

$$W(x) = \frac{450}{x^2} - \frac{11}{2(406 - x)^2} = \frac{148\,352\,400 - 730\,800\,x + 889\,x^2}{2\,x^2\,(406 - x)^2}.$$

Table 1.6 gives the value of W for several choices of x between 6.4 million meters (at the surface of the earth) and 404.3 million meters (at the surface of the moon). The last two entries are negative, indicating that at those distances the force of gravity pulls the cat towards the moon rather than the earth. Indeed, as we shall soon see, somewhere around 365.5 million meters above the center of the earth, the gravitational pull from the moon will exactly counteract the gravitational pull from the earth, rendering our cat completely weightless!

TABLE 1.6. The weight, in pounds, of a 5 kg cat x million meters from the center of the earth.

x	6.4	10	50	100	150	200	250	300	350	400	404.3
$W(x)$	11.0	4.5	0.18	0.045	0.020	0.011	0.007	0.005	0.002	−0.15	−1.9

Notice that the power function $d(t) = 16t^2$ from Example 1.34 is also a polynomial function, since it is a sum of *one* power function. Furthermore, the polynomial $V(x)$ from Example 1.36 is also a rational function:

$$V(x) = 4x^3 - 120x^2 + 864x = \frac{4x^3 - 120x^2 + 864x}{1} = \frac{4x^3 - 120x^2 + 864x}{x^0}.$$

There is nothing mysterious going on here: *Every* power function is a polynomial and *every* polynomial is a rational function!

Our fourth type of function is called a **radical function**. These functions are defined by formulas that look very much like polynomials or rational functions, but which also contain square roots, cube roots, and so on. This is not to say that a radical function like

$$f(x) = \sqrt{2x - 3}$$

is exceedingly liberal, and supports strict gun control laws and a large government welfare program; nor does it mean that a radical function like

$$g(x) = \sqrt[3]{3x + 5}$$

spends all of its free time at the beach trying to catch the perfect wave on its surfboard. Instead, the use of the adjective "radical" here goes back to the original sense of the Latin root word *radix*, meaning "root." Before exploring radical functions further, perhaps we ought to talk a little bit about what exactly we mean when we say, "square roots, cube roots, and so on."

One number is said to be a **square root** of another number if its square is equal to that second number. For example, 5 and -5 are both square roots of 25 because the square of each of these numbers is equal to 25:

$$5^2 = 25 \qquad \text{and} \qquad (-5)^2 = 25.$$

Square roots typically come in pairs like this: one positive and one negative. To avoid confusion, whenever x is positive, we will use the symbol $\sqrt{x}$ to denote its positive square root. Therefore, despite the fact that -5 is *a* square root of 25, we will say that 5 is *the* square root of 25:

$$\sqrt{25} = 5.$$

This is never an issue for zero since, in that case, we have a unique square root, namely zero itself:

$$\sqrt{0} = 0.$$

Finally, since squares are never negative, we would do well to avoid taking the square root of any negative number. These are always undefined in the set of real numbers.[4]

---

[4] In Chapter 5, we will discuss the "imaginary" square roots of negative numbers. Of course, these will *not* be real numbers.

As an example, suppose that we wish to compute the square root of two. In other words, suppose that we wish to find a positive real number y for which

$$y^2 = 2.$$

Initially, it may seem difficult to pin-point the exact value of this mysterious number. Certainly, y is not an integer, and after some experimentation you might begin to suspect that it is not even a fraction. (You might want to keep these suspicions to yourself, lest you suffer the same fate as poor, old Hippasus!)

Instead of worrying about the *exact* value of y, we shall construct a sequence of *approximations* y_1, y_2, y_3, y_4, and so on, each of whose square is *almost* equal to two. Furthermore, we will make sure that y_n, the nth number in this sequence, is a better approximation than any of the numbers that came before. We can then think of y as the **limit** of this sequence of approximations.

To begin, let us assume that we have somehow, through good fortune or guile, found a number y_n whose square is approximately equal to two:

$$y_n{}^2 \approx 2.$$

Notice that this is equivalent (by dividing both sides by y_n) to having

$$y_n \approx \frac{2}{y_n}.$$

The point of this second expression is that it allows us to gauge how closely our approximation y_n comes to the as-of-yet unknown value of the square root of two by measuring the distance between two numbers that we *do* know, namely y_n and $\frac{2}{y_n}$. The closer these two numbers are to one another, the closer our approximation is to the exact value of y. Now, it turns out that we can always improve the accuracy of our approximations simply by setting the next number in our sequence equal to the average of y_n and $\frac{2}{y_n}$:

$$y_{n+1} = \frac{1}{2}\left(y_n + \frac{2}{y_n}\right).$$

With just a dash of algebra, we can show that the distance between y_{n+1} and $\frac{2}{y_{n+1}}$ is smaller than the distance between y_n and $\frac{2}{y_n}$, meaning that our new approximation really is closer to the elusive square root of two.

Let us, then, start by setting $y_1 = 1$. Admittedly, this is not a particularly good approximation for the square root of two. However, we are guaranteed a better approximation if we follow the recipe outlined above. In particular, we shall let y_2 be the average of $y_1 = 1$ and $\frac{2}{y_1} = 2$:

$$y_2 = \tfrac{1}{2}\big(1 + 2\big) = \tfrac{3}{2} = 1.5.$$

Next, we let y_3 be the average of $y_2 = \frac{3}{2}$ and $\frac{2}{y_2} = \frac{4}{3}$:

$$y_3 = \tfrac{1}{2}\big(\tfrac{3}{2} + \tfrac{4}{3}\big) = \tfrac{17}{12} = 1.416\,666\,666\,666\ldots.$$

Finally, we let y_4 be the average of $y_3 = \frac{17}{12}$ and $\frac{2}{y_3} = \frac{24}{17}$:

$$y_4 = \tfrac{1}{2}\big(\tfrac{17}{12} + \tfrac{24}{17}\big) = \tfrac{577}{408} = 1.414\,215\,686\,274\ldots.$$

By this point, our approximation is greatly improved. Of course, this process can be repeated over and over again, and each time we obtain a better approximation to the square root of two. We record our sequence of approximations in Table 1.7.

Observe that, as our approximations become more accurate, their corresponding decimal expansions will have more digits in common. For example, the first three digits of $y_3 \approx 1.41$ also appear in all subsequent approximations. The same is true for the first six digits of $y_4 \approx 1.414\,21$ and for the first twelve digits of $y_5 \approx 1.414\,213\,562\,37$. In other words, the digits in these approximations are slowly **stabilizing**, and once they are stable, they will not change in any subsequent approximation. In $y_6 \approx 1.414\,213\,562\,373$, all thirteen digits shown have stabilized. This means that every approximation after y_6 begins with the same thirteen digits. Therefore, we can say our mystery number is

$$\sqrt{2} = 1.414\,213\,562\,373\ldots,$$

meaning that the decimal expansion of the real number whose square is equal to 2 begins precisely in this way. We still have no idea of what any of the digits past the twelfth decimal place are, but we could always repeat the process above to compute more digits, if we ever felt that we needed to.

We can adapt the method described above to find the square root of any positive real number. What we obtain is an ancient example of what mathematicians call an **algorithm**, a word derived from the Latinized version of the name of Abu Al-Khwarizmi, whom we met back on page 23. At one point in history, algorithms referred exclusively to the use of the Hindu-Arabic numerals that Fibonacci brought to Europe at the start of the thirteenth century. The familiar method of long division that we all learned about in grammar school is just one example of an algorithm in the classical sense of the word. Nowadays, the term is used more broadly to describe any

TABLE 1.7. Computing the square root of two using the Babylonian algorithm.

n	y_n	$\frac{2}{y_n}$	$\frac{1}{2}\big(y_n + \frac{2}{y_n}\big)$
1	1.0	2.0	1.5
2	1.5	$1.333\,333\,333\,333\ldots$	$1.416\,666\,666\,666\ldots$
3	$1.416\,666\,666\,666\ldots$	$1.411\,764\,705\,882\ldots$	$1.414\,215\,686\,274\ldots$
4	$1.414\,215\,686\,274\ldots$	$1.414\,211\,438\,474\ldots$	$1.414\,213\,562\,374\ldots$
5	$1.414\,213\,562\,374\ldots$	$1.414\,213\,562\,371\ldots$	$1.414\,213\,562\,373\ldots$
6	$1.414\,213\,562\,373\ldots$	$1.414\,213\,562\,373\ldots$	$1.414\,213\,562\,373\ldots$

computational recipe leading to some mathematical result, regardless of the writing system used. The square root algorithm that we described above dates back to the Greek mathematician Heron of Alexandria (c. 10–75 AD). However, there is good evidence (in the form of cuneiform writing on clay tablets) that it was actually used by the Babylonians as far back as 1700 BC!

The Babylonian Algorithm

To find the square root of a positive real number x:

① Begin with an approximation $y_1 > 0$.

② Obtain a better approximation by using the rule

$$y_{n+1} = \frac{1}{2}\left(y_n + \frac{x}{y_n}\right).$$

③ Repeat Step ② as needed.

EXAMPLE 1.38. Use the Babylonian algorithm to determine the decimal expansion for the square root of three.

Solution. Starting with $y_1 = 1$, we compute a sequence of approximations by following the rule

$$y_{n+1} = \frac{1}{2}\left(y_n + \frac{3}{y_n}\right);$$

our results are shown in Table 1.8. (A computer spreadsheet like *Microsoft Excel* can help us to quickly produce such a table.) After six iterations of the algorithm, all thirteen digits of our approximation have stabilized, giving us

$$\sqrt{3} = 1.732\,050\,807\,568\ldots.$$

TABLE 1.8. Computing the square root of three using the Babylonian algorithm.

n	y_n	$\frac{3}{y_n}$	$\frac{1}{2}\left(y_n + \frac{3}{y_n}\right)$
1	1.0	3.0	2.0
2	2.0	1.5	1.75
3	1.75	$1.714\,285\,714\,285\ldots$	$1.732\,142\,857\,142\ldots$
4	$1.732\,142\,857\,142\ldots$	$1.731\,958\,762\,886\ldots$	$1.732\,050\,810\,014\ldots$
5	$1.732\,050\,810\,014\ldots$	$1.732\,050\,805\,123\ldots$	$1.732\,050\,807\,568\ldots$
6	$1.732\,050\,807\,568\ldots$	$1.732\,050\,807\,568\ldots$	$1.732\,050\,807\,568\ldots$

EXAMPLE 1.39. The square root of an integer is typically an irrational number. For instance, as we just saw, both $\sqrt{2}$ and $\sqrt{3}$ are irrational. The only exceptions to this rule are the square roots of perfect squares like 25, which, naturally, are always integers. Fortunately, the square root of a product can always be factored as the product of the individual square roots:

$$\sqrt{a \cdot b} = \sqrt{a} \cdot \sqrt{b}.$$

This property becomes particularly useful for simplifying the square root of a large number like 252, which is divisible by more than one perfect square:

$$252 = 4 \cdot 9 \cdot 7 = 2^2 \cdot 3^2 \cdot 7.$$

Applying the property above, we obtain

$$\sqrt{252} = \sqrt{4} \cdot \sqrt{9} \cdot \sqrt{7} = 2 \cdot 3 \cdot \sqrt{7} = 6\sqrt{7}.$$

We recognize that this expression is as simple as possible since 7 is not a perfect square.

EXAMPLE 1.40. The square root of a quotient can always be factored as the quotient of the individual square roots. This means that the square root of a fraction like $\frac{7}{4}$, whose denominator is a perfect square, can be expressed as a fraction with an integer denominator:

$$\sqrt{\frac{7}{4}} = \frac{\sqrt{7}}{\sqrt{4}} = \frac{\sqrt{7}}{2}.$$

It turns out that we can do this, even when the original denominator is not a perfect square. We simply need to coax the denominator into becoming a perfect square by multiplying both the numerator and the denominator by some carefully chosen number. This process is known as ***rationalizing the denominator***. For instance, consider the square root of $\frac{4}{7}$. In this case, the denominator can be turned into a perfect square by multiplying top and bottom by 7. Thus, we have

$$\sqrt{\frac{4}{7}} = \sqrt{\frac{4}{7} \cdot \frac{7}{7}} = \frac{\sqrt{28}}{\sqrt{49}} = \frac{2\sqrt{7}}{7}.$$

The trick here was to find the right number by which to multiply. In the case of a more complicated radical expression like

$$\frac{5 - \sqrt{2}}{3 + \sqrt{2}}$$

we will need to multiply both the numerator and the denominator by $3 - \sqrt{2}$. Note that this is almost the same as the original denominator, except for the fact that it has a minus sign where the denominator had a plus sign. The opposite signs make the new denominator easy to compute as the difference of the squares of 3 and $\sqrt{2}$, the two terms in the original denominator:

$$\frac{5 - \sqrt{2}}{3 + \sqrt{2}} = \frac{5 - \sqrt{2}}{3 + \sqrt{2}} \cdot \frac{3 - \sqrt{2}}{3 - \sqrt{2}} = \frac{15 - 5\sqrt{2} - 3\sqrt{2} + 2}{9 - 2} = \frac{17 - 8\sqrt{2}}{7}.$$

Becoming comfortable with this sort of arithmetic manipulation will undoubtedly prove a useful skill later on.

One number is said to be a **cube root** of another number if its cube is equal to the second number. For instance, 3 is a cube root of 27 and -3 is a cube root of -27 because

$$3^3 = 27 \qquad \text{and} \qquad (-3)^3 = -27.$$

Every real number, be it positive, negative, or zero, has a unique cube root. In particular, the cube root of a positive number is positive, the cube root of a negative number is negative, and the cube root of zero is zero.

More generally, one number is a $\boldsymbol{p^{\text{th}}}$ **root** of another number, where p is some positive integer, if the first number raised to the pth power is equal to the second number. Thus, 3 is a fifth root of 243 and -2 is a tenth root of 1024, since

$$3^5 = 243 \qquad \text{and} \qquad (-2)^{10} = 1024.$$

When p is odd, every real number x has a unique p^{th} root. In this case, we use the symbol $\sqrt[p]{x}$ to denote the unique root. However, when p is even, only non-negative numbers will have p^{th} roots. Furthermore, when p is even, positive numbers will have two p^{th} roots, one positive and one negative. In this case, we shall let $\sqrt[p]{x}$ denote the positive root. In either case, p^{th} roots can be found by approximation by using a modified version of the Babylonian algorithm. (For example, see Exercise 5.)

There is an important psychological difference between radical functions and the power, polynomial, and rational functions that we discussed earlier. For instance, take the power function from Example 1.34. The formula

$$d(t) = 16\, t^2$$

tells us exactly how to evaluate this function: We can find out that $d(5) = 400$ by first squaring 5 and then multiplying by 16. On the other hand, the output values of the radical function

$$f(x) = \sqrt{2x - 3}$$

are given only through approximation by the Babylonian algorithm. Even though this formula tells us that $f(4) = \sqrt{2 \cdot 4 - 3} = \sqrt{5}$, we might have no clear notion of what number this is (or rather, of what the decimal expansion for this number is) until we run through several iterations of the algorithm and arrive at the answer

$$\sqrt{5} = 2.236\,067\,977\,499\ldots.$$

Even then, we will still only know the first thirteen digits of the answer. In this case, our formula seems to tell us precious little about the numerical values of f.

Nevertheless, the remarkable thing about radical functions is that we can deal with them algebraically, just as with any other function given by an "honest-to-goodness" formula. In particular, when you think about $f(4) = \sqrt{5}$, you should be less concerned with its decimal expansion (which you can always figure out either by using the Babylonian algorithm or by punching some buttons in a calculator), and more with its definition as the unique positive real number whose square is equal to five.

EXAMPLE 1.41. Solve the equation $\sqrt{2x - 3} = 9$.

Solution. We will square both sides of the equation (which we are allowed to do since this amounts to multiplying both sides by the same number) and then solve for x using our usual algebraic techniques:

$$2x - 3 = 9^2 = 81$$

$$2x = 81 + 3 = 84$$

$$x = \frac{84}{2} = 42.$$

Notice that this is a valid solution since substitution back into our original equation yields:

$$x = 42 \quad \Rightarrow \quad \sqrt{2x - 3} = \sqrt{2 \cdot 42 - 3} = \sqrt{81} = 9.$$

EXAMPLE 1.42. Solve the equation $\sqrt{2x - 3} = -5$.

Solution. Remember that the output values produced by the square root function are always non-negative. This means that there is no value of x which will ever make the left hand side of this equation negative. Hence, our equation has no solution. Let us suppose, however, that we did not immediately notice the insolubility of our equation. In this case, we would have proceeded as in the example above, squaring both sides of the equation and solving for x as follows:

$$2x - 3 = (-5)^2 = 25$$

$$2x = 25 + 3 = 28$$

$$x = \frac{28}{2} = 14.$$

At this point, substitution back into our original equation will reveal that all is not right with this alleged solution:

$$x = 14 \quad \Rightarrow \quad \sqrt{2x - 3} = \sqrt{2 \cdot 14 - 3} = \sqrt{25} = 5 \neq -5.$$

This is called a *spurious solution* since it was not the legitimate solution that it was purported to be. Indeed, $x = 14$ is the only solution to the equation we obtained *after squaring*, but not to our original equation. Once again, we come to the conclusion that our original equation has no solution.

EXAMPLE 1.43. Solve the following equation:

$$\sqrt{2x-3} = 3 - x.$$

Solution. Observe that the right hand side of this equation depends on the unknown value of x. This means that some values of x will make this side positive and some will make it negative. Since the left hand side is always non-negative, we will need to be extra vigilant to verify the validity of our solutions. Putting such alliterative worries aside for the moment, we begin by squaring both sides of our equation:

$$2x - 3 = (3 - x)^2 = 9 - 6x + x^2.$$

We can then clear the left hand side of the equation, simplify, and factor:

$$0 = (9 - 6x + x^2) - (2x - 3)$$

$$0 = x^2 - 8x + 12$$

$$0 = (x - 6)(x - 2).$$

Thus, we find two potential solutions:

$$x = 6 \qquad \text{or} \qquad x = 2.$$

However, upon further investigation, we observe that only one of these is a legitimate solution to our equation. In particular, note that $x = 6$ is a spurious solution which makes the left hand side positive and the right hand side negative:

$$x = 6 \qquad \Rightarrow \qquad \begin{cases} \sqrt{2x-3} = \sqrt{2 \cdot 6 - 3} = \sqrt{9} = 3, \\ \\ 3 - x = 3 - 6 = -3. \end{cases}$$

On the other hand, substitution confirms that $x = 2$ is our only solution:

$$x = 2 \qquad \Rightarrow \qquad \begin{cases} \sqrt{2x-3} = \sqrt{2 \cdot 2 - 3} = \sqrt{1} = 1, \\ \\ 3 - x = 3 - 2 = 1. \end{cases}$$

EXAMPLE 1.44. Solve the following equation:

$$\sqrt[3]{3x + 5} = -4.$$

Solution. In this case, we are dealing with cube roots, so there is no problem with the right hand side of the equation being negative. In order to solve, we first eliminate the root by cubing both sides of the equation, producing

$$3x + 5 = (-4)^3 = -64.$$

We can now solve for x by subtracting 5 from both sides of the equation and then dividing by 3, as follows:

$$3x = -64 - 5 = -69$$

$$x = -\frac{69}{3} = -23.$$

It is then a relatively easy task to verify that this is a valid solution:

$$x = -23 \quad \Rightarrow \quad \sqrt[3]{3x+5} = \sqrt[3]{3 \cdot (-23) + 5} = \sqrt[3]{-64} = -4.$$

EXAMPLE 1.45. Suppose that we wish to solve the equation

$$x^2 - 6x + 9 = \pi.$$

Instead of clearing one side of the equation and factoring, we will develop a new technique called the ***square root method***. We begin by noticing that the left hand side of the equation can be rewritten as a perfect square:

$$(x - 3)^2 = \pi.$$

According to this equation, the expression $x - 3$ represents a number which, after squaring, produces an answer of π. There are two numbers that do this, namely $\sqrt{\pi}$ and $-\sqrt{\pi}$. We can refer to these two numbers simultaneously by using the shorthand notation $\pm\sqrt{\pi}$, which we can read as "plus or minus the square root of *pi*." Our equation can now be simplified as follows:

$$(x - 3)^2 = \pi$$

$$x - 3 = \pm\sqrt{\pi}$$

$$x = 3 \pm \sqrt{\pi}.$$

All that remains for us to do is substitute our two solutions, $x = 3 + \sqrt{\pi}$ and $x = 3 - \sqrt{\pi}$, back into our original equation to check that they are valid, as indeed they are.

EXAMPLE 1.46. Solve the equation $x^2 + 4x + 4 = 49$.

Solution. We could solve this equation by subtracting 49 from both sides and using the sledgehammer method to factor. Instead, since we recognize that the left hand side of this equation can be factored as a perfect square, we shall use the square root method described above. In particular, after factoring the left hand side, we take the square root of each side of our equation and finish by solving for x as follows:

$$(x + 2)^2 = 49$$

$$x + 2 = \pm\sqrt{49} = \pm 7$$

$$x = -2 \pm 7.$$

Therefore, our solutions consist of $x = -2 + 7 = 5$ and $x = -2 - 7 = -9$, as you should verify.

The success of the square root method depends largely on the fact that there is an ***inverse relationship*** between squaring and taking square roots. In other words, we can use a square root to undo the work of a square, just like we can use a square to undo the effects of a square root:

$$y = x^2 \qquad \Leftrightarrow \qquad x = \pm\sqrt{y}.$$

Of course, this inverse relationship is not perfect, since there are two square roots for each positive number. In particular, a square root cannot undo the job of squaring a negative number, since the square root function always returns non-negative numbers. This is precisely why we need to include the "plus or minus" symbol whenever we use the square root method.

EXAMPLE 1.47. Consider the function $h : \mathbb{R} \to \mathbb{R}$ defined by the formula

$$h(x) = \sqrt{x^2}.$$

This function maps a real number x to the non-negative real number whose square equals x^2. If x happens to be positive or zero, then x itself is this number; however, if x is negative, then $-x$ is the non-negative real number whose square equals x^2. Therefore, we can describe what h does in an entirely different way: It takes a real number as input and, if that number is positive or zero, it returns the same number as output; if the input is negative, it returns the opposite of the input. We have already seen a function that does precisely this, namely the absolute value function from Example 1.9. In particular, we have the following curious identity:

$$\sqrt{x^2} = |x|.$$

Although a formula describes the rule of assignment for a function, it says almost nothing about its domain and codomain. A formula is kind of like the photograph on your passport or driver's licence: It describes you well enough to get you into the country or to allow you to purchase a refreshing alcoholic beverage (assuming that you are old enough, of course) but it says little about the type of person you are or the sort of values that you hold near and dear to your heart. In the same way, a formula tells you how to evaluate a function, but it does not say much about the sort of input or output values allowed. When only supplied with a formula for a function, we will assume that the domain of the function is the largest set for which that formula makes sense. We will also assume that the codomain of the function is all of $\mathbb{R}$. Note, however, that the actual domain or codomain of the function may, in fact, be smaller. For instance, suppose that the building in Example 1.34 is 484 feet tall. Then the cat's free fall will end in a soft "thud" as she lands gracefully on her feet after 5.5 seconds. (Cats always land on their feet!) This means that the domain of the function d is the interval $[0, 5.5]$, even though the formula $d(t) = 16t^2$ makes computational sense for all real numbers, including negative values of t.

EXAMPLE 1.48. Find the largest possible domain for the function

$$f(x) = 3x^2 + 10x + 3.$$

Solution. Since f is a polynomial function, we have nothing to fear when it comes to evaluating f. In particular, the only operations at work here are addition and multiplication, so there is nothing preventing us from evaluating the function f at any real number. Hence, the largest possible domain for this function is the entire real line:

$$\text{Domain } f = \mathbb{R}.$$

EXAMPLE 1.49. Find the largest possible domain for the function

$$g(x) = \frac{3x^2 + 10x + 3}{x^2 - 5x + 4}.$$

Solution. As a rational function, the formula for g involves division. This means that we need to avoid dividing by zero at all costs.. Thus, the largest possible domain for g consists of all values of x for which the denominator is non-zero:

$$\text{Domain } g = \left\{ x : x^2 - 5x + 4 \neq 0 \right\}.$$

We determine the contents of this domain by factoring the denominator (perhaps using the sledgehammer method) as follows:

$$x^2 - 5x + 4 = (x - 1)(x - 4).$$

Evidently, we should not attempt to evaluate g at either $x = 1$ or $x = 4$, since those input values will cause us to divide by zero. All other values of x will yield valid output values for $g(x)$, so

$$\text{Domain } g = \left\{ x : x \neq 1 \text{ and } x \neq 4 \right\} = (-\infty, 1) \cup (1, 4) \cup (4, \infty).$$

We represent this domain graphically on the number line below.

EXAMPLE 1.50. Find the largest possible domain for the function

$$h(x) = \frac{7x^3 + 4x}{2x^2 + 4x}.$$

Solution. Again, h is a rational function, so we need only avoid the values of x for which the denominator equals zero:

$$\text{Domain } h = \left\{ x : 2x^2 + 4x \neq 0 \right\}.$$

As before, we can analyze this domain by first factoring the denominator as

$$2x^2 + 4x = 2x\,(x+2).$$

It is now clear that $x = 0$ and $x = -2$ are the only values of x which would force us to divide by zero, making $h(x)$ undefined. Therefore,

$$\text{Domain } h = \{x : x \neq -2 \text{ and } x \neq 0\} = (-\infty, -2) \cup (-2, 0) \cup (0, \infty).$$

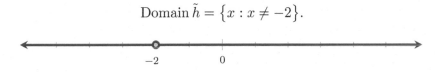

EXAMPLE 1.51. The formula defining h in the example above is not in lowest terms, as the numerator and the denominator have a common factor of x. If we were to cancel this common factor, we would get a new rational function

$$\tilde{h}(x) = \frac{7x^2 + 4}{2x + 4}.$$

Note that h and $\tilde{h}$ really *are* different functions, even though their output values are equal wherever their domains overlap. In particular, observe that $\tilde{h}(0) = 1$ whereas $h(0)$ is not defined. The difference, of course, is that the domain of $\tilde{h}$ contains one more point than the domain of h:

$$\text{Domain } \tilde{h} = \{x : x \neq -2\}.$$

This phenomenon is true in general: A rational function which is not in lowest terms might have smaller domain than the corresponding lowest term function. In such a case, the *values* of the functions will agree whenever they are both defined, but the *functions* themselves will be different.

EXAMPLE 1.52. Find the largest possible domain for the function

$$F(x) = 1 - \sqrt{3x + 5}\,.$$

Solution. In this case, F is a radical function involving a square root, so we need to be careful not to take the square root of a negative number. Thus, the largest possible domain for F consists of all x which will make the expression inside the square root greater than or equal to zero:

$$\text{Domain } F = \{x : 3x + 5 \geq 0\}.$$

This domain is characterized by an inequality, which we can solve as follows:

$$3x + 5 \geq 0$$

$$3x \geq -5$$

$$x \geq -\tfrac{5}{3}.$$

Therefore, we have

$$\text{Domain } F = \left\{ x : x \geq -\tfrac{5}{3} \right\} = \left[-\tfrac{5}{3}, \infty \right).$$

EXAMPLE 1.53. Determine the largest possible domain for the function

$$G(x) = \frac{\sqrt{x^2 + 8x + 15}}{x - 1}.$$

Solution. Note that G is a radical function combining both square roots and division. Hence, we need to eliminate all values of x which might lead us to take the square root of a negative number or to divide by zero. In particular, the domain of G consists of all values of x which make the expression under the square root non-negative and the denominator non-zero:

$$\text{Domain } G = \left\{ x : x^2 + 8x + 15 \geq 0 \text{ and } x - 1 \neq 0 \right\}.$$

The first of these conditions is simply an inequality, which we can factor (perhaps using the sledgehammer method) as:

$$x^2 + 8x + 15 = (x + 5)(x + 3) \geq 0.$$

This factorization gives us two critical points to consider, namely $x = -5$ and $x = -3$. These points separate the real line into three intervals in which each of the expressions $x + 5$ and $x + 3$ is either exclusively positive or exclusively negative. As before, we consider the sign of each of these expressions in each one of the three intervals, and record our findings in the following chart:

	$(-\infty, -5)$	$(-5, -3)$	$(-3, \infty)$
$x + 5$	$-$	$+$	$+$
$x + 3$	$-$	$-$	$+$
$(x + 5)(x + 3)$	$+$	$-$	$+$

By selecting the intervals marked with a plus sign, we find that the square root in our formula for G is well-defined in the subset

$$(-\infty, -5] \cup [-3, \infty).$$

Next, we turn to the second condition in our domain, the non-equality

$$x - 1 \neq 0.$$

This is clearly satisfied as long as $x \neq 1$. Therefore, by removing this single point from the subset above, we find that the largest possible domain for our function is

$$\text{Domain } G = (-\infty, -5] \cup [-3, 1) \cup (1, \infty).$$

EXAMPLE 1.54. Determine the largest possible domains for the function

$$H(x) = \frac{\sqrt[3]{x^2 + 8x + 15}}{x - 1}.$$

Solution. Note that H is a radical function whose formula involves a cube root. Like all odd roots, the cube root in this formula does not cause any problems during evaluation: As long as the expression inside the root is well-defined, so is the value of cube root. In this function, the expression inside the cube root is simply a polynomial, which is always well-defined. Therefore, we only need to be careful not to divide by zero. Hence

$$\text{Domain } H = \big\{ x : x - 1 \neq 0 \big\} = (-\infty, 1) \cup (1, \infty).$$

The last few examples illustrate how square roots tend to wipe out large portions of the domain a function, while division by zero eliminates only a handful of points. To use a military analogy, a square root is like a cannon ball blasting its way through the hull of a ship. The devastation is usually massive as it wreaks all kinds of havoc, mayhem, and bedlam. In contrast, division by zero is more like a high-precision rifle in the hands of a well-trained sniper. Although the outcome is catastrophic for the few points in question, the nearby points escape unscathed and unharmed.

Reading Comprehension Questions for Section 1.4

A function defined by a formula such as $f(x) = a \cdot x^n$ is known as a ___(a)___. In this formula, the number ___(b)___ is called the degree of the function. The largest valid domain for this type of function consists of ___(c)___. A sum of several power functions of various degrees is known as a ___(d)___. For this type of function, the degree is equal to the degree of the ___(e)___ with a nonzero coefficient, and the largest valid domain consists of ___(f)___. A ___(g)___ function is the ratio $p(x)/q(x)$ of two polynomials where q is not the ___(h)___. The largest valid domain for such a function consists of the set of all real numbers x for which ___(i)___. Every ___(j)___ is a polynomial and every polynomial is a ___(k)___. A function defined by a formula that contains square roots, cube roots, and so on, is called a ___(l)___. The output values of the square root function can be computed using a technique known as the ___(m)___; unlike other functions, these values are not produced directly, but by a sequence of ___(n)___. The largest valid domain for the square root function is ___(o)___, while that for the cube root function is ___(p)___.

To find the largest valid domain for the function

$$f(x) = \frac{3 + \sqrt{x^2 + 4x - 5}}{x - 3},$$

we must first solve the inequality ___(q)___. After factoring, this becomes

$$(x + \underline{\quad(r)\quad})(x - \underline{\quad(s)\quad}) \geq 0.$$

The critical points $x = $ ___(t)___ and $x = $ ___(u)___ make the left hand side of this inequality equal to zero. Completing a chart reveals that points in the interval ___(v)___ will make this quantity negative, and must therefore be thrown out of the domain for f; otherwise, we will end up taking the square root of a ___(w)___ number, which is never allowed. We must also remove the point $x = $ ___(x)___, where we would be dividing by ___(y)___. Therefore, the largest valid domain for f is the set ___(z)___.

Exercises for Section 1.4

1. Consider the volume function V from Example 1.36 on page 54.

   (a) Determine the values of x that make $V(x) < 0$.

   (b) Given that V describes the volume of a box, what is the domain of V?

   (Hint: Consider the signs of each of the three dimensions of the box, instead of just its volume.)

2. Consider the weight function W from Example 1.37 on page 55.

   (a) For what values of x is the formula for W undefined? What do those values mean in terms of the cat's position?

   (b) Given that W gives the weight of a cat placed somewhere between the surface of the earth and the surface of the moon, what is the domain of W?

3. (a) Scalene Sallie is making an open box from a square piece of cardboard 24 inches on each side by cutting out a square from each corner and folding the sides up. Express the volume of Sallie's box as a function of the length x of the side of the square cut from each corner.

   (Hint: Compare with Example 1.36.)

   (b) Obtuse Ollie is convinced that Sallie's box will have the largest volume if she cuts out 6-inch squares from each corner. Acute Alice thinks that Sallie can make a bigger box if she cuts out 3-inch squares instead. Whose suggestion will produce the bigger box?

   (c) Can you propose an even better suggestion for Sallie?

4. Use the Babylonian algorithm to determine the decimal expansion of $\sqrt{7}$ accurate to seven decimal places. Starting with $y_1 = 1$, how many steps does this take?

5. The Babylonian algorithm can be modified to compute the cube root of x by using the following rule for improving our approximations:

$$y_{n+1} = \frac{1}{3}\left(2\,y_n + \frac{x}{y_n{}^2}\right).$$

   Use this modification to determine the decimal expansion of $\sqrt[3]{5}$ accurate to seven decimal places. Starting with $y_1 = 1$, how many steps does this take?

6. Use a calculator or a computer to determine the decimal expansion for each of the following four numbers:

   (a) $\sqrt{1+\sqrt{1}}$

   (b) $\sqrt{1+\sqrt{1+\sqrt{1}}}$

   (c) $\sqrt{1+\sqrt{1+\sqrt{1+\sqrt{1}}}}$

   (d) $\sqrt{1+\sqrt{1+\sqrt{1+\sqrt{1+\sqrt{1}}}}}$

(e) The decimal expansions in parts (a) through (d) are getting closer to the irrational number given by the infinitely-nested radical

$$\sqrt{1+\sqrt{1+\sqrt{1+\sqrt{1+\cdots}}}}.$$

Can you guess which irrational number this is? Explain.

7. Use a calculator or a computer to determine the decimal expansion for each of the following four numbers:

(a) $2 \cdot \dfrac{2}{\sqrt{2}}$

(b) $2 \cdot \dfrac{2}{\sqrt{2}} \cdot \dfrac{2}{\sqrt{2+\sqrt{2}}}$

(c) $2 \cdot \dfrac{2}{\sqrt{2}} \cdot \dfrac{2}{\sqrt{2+\sqrt{2}}} \cdot \dfrac{2}{\sqrt{2+\sqrt{2+\sqrt{2}}}}$

(d) $2 \cdot \dfrac{2}{\sqrt{2}} \cdot \dfrac{2}{\sqrt{2+\sqrt{2}}} \cdot \dfrac{2}{\sqrt{2+\sqrt{2+\sqrt{2}}}} \cdot \dfrac{2}{\sqrt{2+\sqrt{2+\sqrt{2+\sqrt{2}}}}}$

(e) The decimal expansions in parts (a) through (d) are getting closer to the irrational number given by the infinite product

$$2 \cdot \dfrac{2}{\sqrt{2}} \cdot \dfrac{2}{\sqrt{2+\sqrt{2}}} \cdot \dfrac{2}{\sqrt{2+\sqrt{2+\sqrt{2}}}} \cdot \dfrac{2}{\sqrt{2+\sqrt{2+\sqrt{2+\sqrt{2}}}}} \cdots.$$

Can you guess which irrational number this is? Explain.

8. Each number in the first row below is equal to some number in the second row. Without using a calculator, find each matching pair of numbers.

(a) $\sqrt{4+2\sqrt{3}}$ (b) $\sqrt{9-4\sqrt{5}}$ (c) $\sqrt{5-2\sqrt{6}}$ (d) $\sqrt[3]{5\sqrt{2}+7}$

I. $1+\sqrt{2}$ II. $\sqrt{3}-\sqrt{2}$ III. $\sqrt{3}+1$ IV. $\sqrt{5}-2$

In Exercises 9–12, solve each equation. Be sure to check for spurious solutions.

9. $\sqrt{2x + 3} = 5$

10. $\sqrt{x^2 - 2x + 9} = x + 1$

11. $\sqrt{4x - 3} = x - 2$

12. $\sqrt{6 - x} = 4 - x$

In Exercises 13–16, solve each equation using the square root method.

13. $(2x + 3)^2 = 9$

14. $x^2 - 4x + 4 = 144$

15. $9x^2 - 12x + 4 = 9$

16. $x^2 + 2x + 1 = 5$

In Exercises 17–26, determine the largest possible domain for each function. In each case, express your answer using both set-builder notation and interval notation, and illustrate it by shading an appropriately labeled number line.

17. $f(x) = \dfrac{7x - 3}{x + 4}$

18. $f(x) = -\dfrac{5x^2}{(x - 3)(2x + 3)}$

19. $f(x) = \dfrac{x - x^2}{3x^2 + 5x + 2}$

20. $f(x) = \dfrac{2x^2 - 3x}{2x^2 - 5x + 3}$

21. $f(x) = \sqrt{5x - 10}$

22. $f(x) = \sqrt{-x - 6}$

23. $f(x) = \sqrt{x^2 - 7x + 12}$

24. $f(x) = \sqrt{\dfrac{4}{x - 8}}$

25. $f(x) = \sqrt{\dfrac{3 + x}{3 - x}}$

26. $f(x) = \dfrac{\sqrt{x^2 - 4}}{x + 7}$

In Exercises 27–30, determine the formula for a function which is only defined on the given set.

27. $(-\infty, 1) \cup (1, \infty)$

28. $(-\infty, 7]$

29. $(-\infty, -1] \cup [5, \infty)$

30. $(-\infty, -2) \cup (4, \infty)$

1.5. Cartesian Coordinates

Since its beginnings in the ancient world, mathematics was divided in two by a fine line: On the one side was geometry; on the other, algebra. And even though the notion of number permeated throughout both of these arenas, most mathematicians of the sixteenth century would have considered the two to be altogether different fields of study. Then along came the famous French philosopher and mathematician René Descartes (1596 – 1650) and, in one fell swoop, the whole universe changed.

Descartes, at the time a soldier in the army of Prince Maurice of Orange, was encamped for the winter on the banks of the Danube River when one night, in a dream, the idea came to him of taking two copies of the real line and setting them down at right angles to each other, one horizontally and one vertically, so that they met at their common zero, as in Figure 1.6. The horizontal line became known as the **x-axis**, the vertical line as the **y-axis**, and the point where they meet (labeled zero in each of their scales) as the **origin**. The plane determined by these axes is called the **xy-plane** or, more formally, the **Cartesian plane**. The term "Cartesian" refers to Descartes himself, or rather to his Latinized *nom de plume*, Renatus Cartesius.

The x- and y-axes serve as a frame of reference for identifying points on the Cartesian plane. If P is any point on the plane, we define its **x-coordinate** as the horizontal distance from P to the y-axis, chosen to be a positive number in the case that P lies to the right of the axis and a negative number in the case that P lies to the left of the axis. Similarly, its **y-coordinate** is defined as the vertical distance

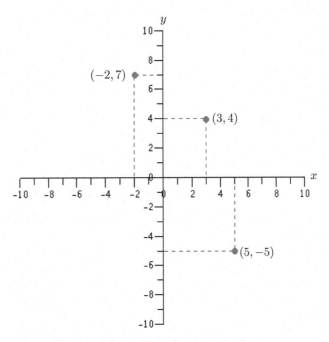

FIGURE 1.6. The Cartesian plane.

from P to the x-axis, again, chosen to be positive if P is located above the axis and negative if P is located below the axis. These two quantities, which by convention are arranged as an **ordered pair** with x-coordinate first and y-coordinate second, completely distinguish P from any other point on the xy-plane.

EXAMPLE 1.55. We consider the three points marked in Figure 1.6 from left to right. The first of these is located 2 units to the left of the y-axis and 7 units above the x-axis; hence, this point has an x-coordinate of -2 and a y-coordinate of 7. The next point lies 3 units to the right of the y-axis and 4 units above the x-axis, so its x-coordinate is 3 and its y-coordinate is 4. Finally, the third point, 5 units to the right of the y-axis and 5 units below the x-axis, has an x-coordinate of 5 and a y-coordinate of -5. Thus, these points are denoted by the ordered pairs $(-2, 7)$, $(3, 4)$, and $(5, -5)$.

EXAMPLE 1.56. The x- and y-axes separate the xy-plane into four regions, called **quadrants**, depending on the sign of their x- and y- coordinates, as follows:

quadrant	x	y	location
I	$+$	$+$	upper right quarter of the plane
II	$-$	$+$	upper left quarter of the plane
III	$-$	$-$	lower left quarter of the plane
IV	$+$	$-$	lower right quarter of the plane

Observe that the point $(3, 4)$ is quadrant I, that $(-2, 7)$ is in quadrant II, and that $(5, -5)$ is in quadrant IV. (Take another look at Figure 1.6.)

Descartes's genius came in realizing that we can visualize *algebraic* relationships as *geometric* sets in the xy-plane, and conversely, that we can describe *geometric* objects by *algebraic* expressions. In particular, we define the **graph of an equation** with two variables, x and y, as the set of all points in the xy-plane whose x- and y-coordinates make the equation true. With this definition in mind, we can apply our geometric intuition whenever we are trying to solve algebraic problems, and our algebraic tools whenever we are trying to solve geometric problems. In other words, thanks to Descartes, that fine line separating the algebraic from the geometric worlds has been blurred away!

EXAMPLE 1.57. The graph of the equation $x = 5$ consists of all points whose x-coordinates are equal to 5. These points are precisely those which lie 5 units to the right of the y-axis, so they form a vertical line. On the other hand, the graph of $y = -2$ consists of all points which have y-coordinates of -2. Since these points lie 2 units below the x-axis, they form a horizontal line. Figure 1.7 shows both of these lines plotted on the same plane.

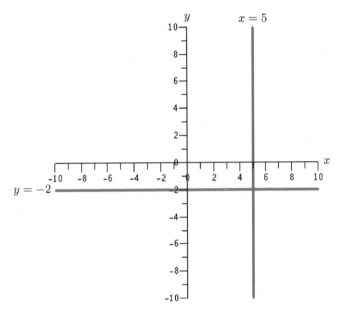

FIGURE 1.7. The graphs of $x = 5$ and $y = -2$.

Notice that we can generalize these observations to arbitrary horizontal and vertical lines. If a is any fixed real number, then the graph of the equation $x = a$ is a vertical line, and the graph of the equation $y = a$ is a horizontal line. In particular, the equation of the x-axis is $y = 0$ and the equation of the y-axis is $x = 0$. (Yes, this *does* seem counterintuitive at first!)

EXAMPLE 1.58. Consider the graph of the equation $y = x^2 - 7$.

If we let $x = 5$ and $y = 18$, then the left and right hand sides of the equation will equal each other,

$$(x, y) = (5, 18) \quad \Rightarrow \quad \begin{cases} y = 18, \\ x^2 - 7 = 5^2 - 7 = 18, \end{cases}$$

and the equation becomes a true statement. On the other hand, if we let $x = 4$ and $y = 11$, the two sides of the equation yield different results,

$$(x, y) = (4, 11) \quad \Rightarrow \quad \begin{cases} y = 11, \\ x^2 - 7 = 4^2 - 7 = 9, \end{cases}$$

This means that the point $(5, 18)$ is a point on this graph, but $(4, 11)$ is not. If we wish to sketch the graph of $y = x^2 - 7$, we can pick a bunch of values for x, substitute them into the equation, and obtain the corresponding values of y which will make the equation true. For instance, when $x = 0$ we will have

$$x = 0 \quad \Rightarrow \quad y = x^2 - 7 = 0^2 - 7 = -7.$$

Similarly, if $x = 3$ then we find that

$$x = 3 \quad \Rightarrow \quad y = x^2 - 7 = 3^2 - 7 = 2.$$

Thus, the points $(0, -7)$ and $(3, 2)$ belong to the graph. We record our findings in Table 1.9. Even though these are only eleven points, when plotted together, as in Figure 1.8, they give us an idea of the general contour of the graph of our equation, in this case a shapely curve known as a **parabola**. Plotting more points, of course, will give us a better picture of the graph. In fact, the thin curve connecting the heavy points in Figure 1.8 consists of several thousand points plotted so closely together that we hardly notice any gaps between them. Our eyes trick us into thinking that we are actually looking at a smooth curve!

TABLE 1.9. Points in the graph of $y = x^2 - 7$.

x	-5	-4	-3	-2	-1	0	1	2	3	4	5
y	18	9	2	-3	-6	-7	-6	-3	2	9	18

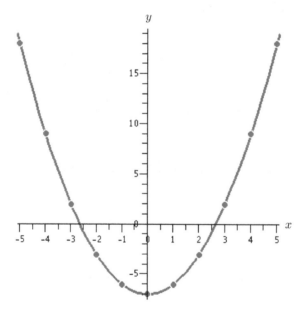

FIGURE 1.8. The graph of $y = x^2 - 7$.

Each "tick mark" on the y-axis in the graph in Figure 1.8 represents one unit. Hence, the fifth tick above the origin is labeled 5, the tenth is labeled 10, and so on. On the other hand, the second tick mark to the right of the origin is labeled 1; this means that each tick mark on the x-axis represents only a half of a unit. We will often use different scales for the x- and y-axes in order to see a greater portion of the graph all at once. Had we used equal scales on the axes, the parabola would have appeared to be two and a half times taller than it does in Figure 1.8, and would have taken up almost an entire page.

EXAMPLE 1.59. Sketch the graph of the equation $x^2 - y^2 = 1$.

Solution. As before, we shall pick a few values of x and substitute them into the equation to obtain their corresponding values of y. This time, however, there is a catch: Depending on the value of x with which we begin, we might end up with zero, one, or two values of y. For instance, if we take $x = 2$ then we obtain the equation

$$4 - y^2 = 1,$$

which is solved as $y = \pm\sqrt{3}$. If, instead, we look at $x = 1$, we get

$$1 - y^2 = 1;$$

this has the unique solution $y = 0$. Finally, if we set $x = 0$, we have

$$0 - y^2 = 1,$$

which has *no* solutions at all. Table 1.10 gives a list some of the points we obtain by substituting in various values of x. These points are then plotted in Figure 1.9, which also shows a sketch of the graph – a cute little "two-piece" curve called a **hyperbola**.

TABLE 1.10. Points in the graph of $x^2 - y^2 = 1$.

x	-3	-2	-1	0	1	2	3
y	$\pm\sqrt{8}$	$\pm\sqrt{3}$	0	—	0	$\pm\sqrt{3}$	$\pm\sqrt{8}$

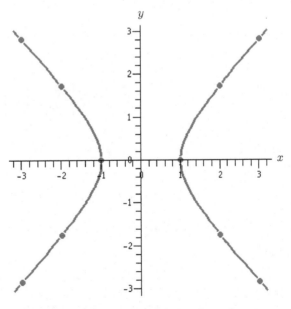

FIGURE 1.9. The graph of $x^2 - y^2 = 1$.

A point where a graph crosses the x-axis is called an **x-intercept** of the graph, and a point where it crosses the y-axis is called a **y-intercept**. Since every point on the x-axis has a y-coordinate equal to zero, we can find the x-intercepts of the graph of any equation algebraically by simply substituting $y = 0$ into the equation and solving for x. Similarly, we can find the y-intercepts of the graph by substituting in $x = 0$ and solving for y. For instance, in the case of the parabola $y = x^2 - 7$ shown in Figure 1.8, we have:

x-intercepts:	**y-intercepts:**
$0 = x^2 - 7$	$y = 0^2 - 7$
$x^2 = 7$	$y = -7$
$x = \pm\sqrt{7}$	

This means that this parabola has two x-intercepts at $\left(\sqrt{7}, 0\right)$ and $\left(-\sqrt{7}, 0\right)$, and a single y-intercept at $(0, -7)$. On the other hand, for the hyperbola $x^2 - y^2 = 1$ in Figure 1.9, we have:

x-intercepts:	**y-intercepts:**
$x^2 - 0^2 = 1$	$0^2 - y^2 = 1$
$x^2 = 1$	$y^2 = -1$
$x = \pm 1$	$\varnothing$

Therefore, this hyperbola has two x-intercepts at $(1, 0)$ and $(-1, 0)$, but no y-intercepts.

EXAMPLE 1.60. Find the x and y-intercepts of the graph of the equation
$$x^2 + y^2 = 6x - 8y.$$

Solution. As in the discussion above, we shall find the required intercepts by setting x and y, in turn, equal to zero and solving the resulting equation for the other unknown:

x-intercepts:	**y-intercepts:**
$x^2 + 0^2 = 6x - 8 \cdot 0$	$0^2 + y^2 = 6 \cdot 0 - 8y$
$x^2 = 6x$	$y^2 = -8y$
$x^2 - 6x = 0$	$y^2 + 8y = 0$
$(x - 6)x = 0$	$(y + 8)y = 0$
$x = 6$ or $x = 0$	$y = -8$ or $y = 0$

This means that the graph in question has two x-intercepts at $(6, 0)$ and $(0, 0)$, and two y-intercepts at $(0, -8)$ and $(0, 0)$.

In order to measure the distance between two points on the xy-plane, we will need the following classical theorem about right triangles. This result dates back, in one form or another, some four thousand years to the ancient Egyptians, Babylonians, Indians, and Chinese, but is primarily linked to the Greeks – specifically to Pythagoras of Samos (c. 569 – 475 BC). Pythagoras was the leader of a strange and secretive cult whose philosophy was an odd mix of mathematics and mysticism. Those belonging to the Order of Pythagoreans held that *number* was the center of reality, not simply as a means to describing reality, but rather as the building blocks of reality itself. Turning back to the theorem in question, recall that the longest of the three sides of a right triangle – the one located opposite the right angle – is called the **hypotenuse** of the triangle. The other two sides are called the **legs**.

Theorem 1.2. (Pythagoras's Theorem) The square of the length of the hypotenuse of a right triangle equals the sum of the squares of the lengths of the other two sides. In other words, if a right triangle has legs measuring a and b, respectively, and a hypotenuse measuring c, then

$$a^2 + b^2 = c^2.$$

Proof. Consider a square measuring $a + b$ by $a + b$ with four transversals splitting each of its sides into a segment of length a and a segment of length b, as in Figure 1.10(a). Each transversal is the hypotenuse of a right triangle with legs measuring a and b. Since each of these is congruent to our right triangle, each transversal measures c. Thus, the transversals divide the large square into four copies of our right triangle and a square of area c^2. The four triangles can also be rearranged as in Figure 1.10(b). Our large square now consists of our four triangles as well as two smaller squares with area a^2 and b^2, respectively. Since the area of the two white squares in Figure 1.10(b) adds up to the area of the white square in Figure 1.10(a), we have $a^2 + b^2 = c^2$ as desired. $\square$

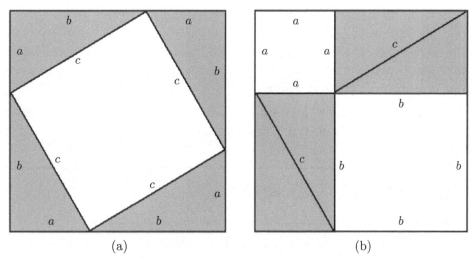

FIGURE 1.10. Proving Pythagoras's Theorem.

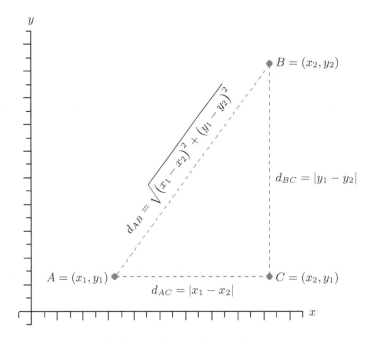

FIGURE 1.11. The points (x_1, y_1), (x_2, y_2), and (x_2, y_1) determine a right triangle.

Let us consider two arbitrary points A and B on the xy-plane corresponding to the coordinates (x_1, y_1) and (x_2, y_2), respectively. These two points, together with a third point at $C = (x_2, y_1)$, form a right triangle with one horizontal leg and one vertical leg, as shown in Figure 1.11.

Since the points A and C live on a horizontal line, the distance between them is given by the difference in their x-coordinates, that is, by either $x_1 - x_2$ or $x_2 - x_1$, whichever of these two numbers happens to be positive. Similarly, points B and C live on a vertical line, so the distance between them is given by the difference in their y-coordinates, either $y_1 - y_2$ or $y_2 - y_1$, depending on which of these is positive. For convenience, we can use absolute values to ensure that we get positive answers regardless of the order in which we subtract. Thus, in Figure 1.11, we express these distances as $d_{AC} = |x_1 - x_2|$ and $d_{BC} = |y_1 - y_2|$, respectively.

According to Pythagoras's theorem, we can find the length of the hypotenuse connecting A and B by first adding together the squares of each of these distances, and then taking the square root:

$$\boxed{\text{The distance from } A \text{ to } B \text{ is } d_{AB} = \sqrt{\left(x_1 - x_2\right)^2 + \left(y_1 - y_2\right)^2}.}$$

This result is known as the ***distance formula***. Observe that the absolute values are no longer necessary in this formula because the two squares will eliminate any annoying negative signs that might arise from subtracting the x- or y-coordinates in the "wrong order."

EXAMPLE 1.61. Let us once again consider the three points $(-2, 7)$, $(3, 4)$, and $(5, -5)$ illustrated in Figure 1.12. A quick glance at this figure should convince you that these points are the vertices of a scalene triangle with three sides of different lengths. In particular, the side joining $(-2, 7)$ and $(3, 4)$ is shorter than the side joining $(3, 4)$ and $(5, -5)$, which in turn is shorter than the side joining $(5, -5)$ and $(-2, 7)$. The distance formula confirms these observations:

The distance from $(3, 4)$ to $(-2, 7)$ is $\sqrt{\left(3 - (-2)\right)^2 + \left(4 - 7\right)^2} = \sqrt{34}$.

The distance from $(3, 4)$ to $(5, -5)$ is $\sqrt{\left(3 - 5\right)^2 + \left(4 - (-5)\right)^2} = \sqrt{83}$.

The distance from $(5, -5)$ to $(-2, 7)$ is $\sqrt{\left(5 - (-2)\right)^2 + \left((-5) - 7\right)^2} = \sqrt{193}$.

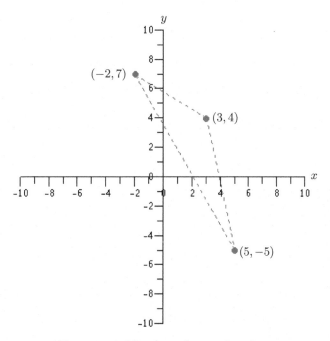

FIGURE 1.12. A scalene triangle.

Suppose that $r > 0$ is a positive real number. Then, by definition, the circle of radius r with center at (h, k) consists of the set of all points (x, y) a distance of r from the center. Therefore this circle is described by the equation

$$\boxed{\left(x - h\right)^2 + \left(y - k\right)^2 = r^2,}$$

which is simply the square of the appropriate distance formula. (You can verify this for yourself by taking the square root of each side.) This expression is called the **general equation of a circle**.

EXAMPLE 1.62. Consider the equation

$$x^2 + y^2 = 81.$$

Observe that this equation can easily be put in the form of the general equation of a circle by setting $h = 0$, $k = 0$ and $r = 9$:

$$(x - 0)^2 + (y - 0)^2 = 9^2.$$

Therefore, our equation describes a circle with center at the origin $(0, 0)$ and with radius 9. As with our previous graphs, we can find the x- and y-intercepts for this circle algebraically by setting y or x, respectively, equal to zero and solving for the other variable:

x-intercepts:	y-intercepts:
$x^2 + 0^2 = 81$	$0^2 + y^2 = 81$
$x^2 = 81$	$y^2 = 81$
$x = \pm\sqrt{81} = \pm 9$	$y = \pm\sqrt{81} = \pm 9$

Of course, for an equation this simple, all this work is hardly necessary. In particular, the locations of the intercepts, nine units above, below, and to either side of the origin, become self-evident as soon as we take a close look at the graph in Figure 1.13.

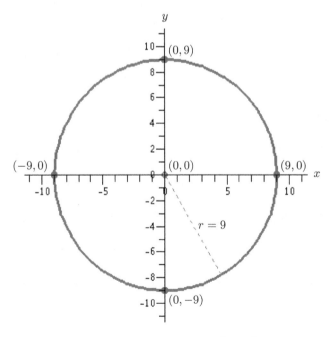

FIGURE 1.13. The graph of $x^2 + y^2 = 81$.

EXAMPLE 1.63. The equation

$$(x - 2)^2 + (y + 3)^2 = 64$$

is precisely in the form of the general equation of a circle. In this case, $h = 2$, $k = -3$, and $r = \sqrt{64} = 8$. Hence, its graph is a circle with radius 8 whose center is $(2, -3)$. See Figure 1.14.

In order to find the x- and y-intercepts for this circle, all we need to do is set one variable equal to zero and solve for the other one. In either case, we get an equation that is ripe for using the square root method:

<table>
<tr><td align="center">x-intercepts:</td><td align="center">y-intercepts:</td></tr>
<tr><td align="center">$(x - 2)^2 + (0 + 3)^2 = 64$</td><td align="center">$(0 - 2)^2 + (y + 3)^2 = 64$</td></tr>
<tr><td align="center">$(x - 2)^2 + 9 = 64$</td><td align="center">$4 + (y + 3)^2 = 64$</td></tr>
<tr><td align="center">$(x - 2)^2 = 64 - 9 = 55$</td><td align="center">$(y + 3)^2 = 64 - 4 = 60$</td></tr>
<tr><td align="center">$x - 2 = \pm\sqrt{55}$</td><td align="center">$y + 3 = \pm\sqrt{60}$</td></tr>
<tr><td align="center">$x = 2 \pm \sqrt{55}$</td><td align="center">$y = -3 \pm \sqrt{60}$</td></tr>
</table>

These computations show that the circle crosses the x-axis at

$$(2 + \sqrt{55}, 0) \approx (9.416, 0) \qquad \text{and} \qquad (2 - \sqrt{55}, 0) \approx (-5.416, 0),$$

and that it crosses the y-axis at

$$(0, -3 + \sqrt{60}) \approx (0, 4.746) \qquad \text{and} \qquad (0, -3 - \sqrt{60}) \approx (0, -10.746).$$

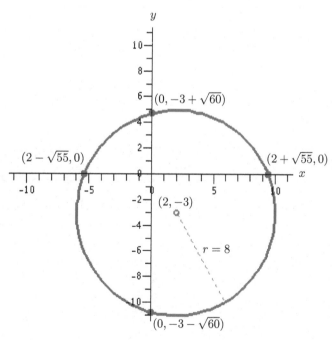

FIGURE 1.14. The graph of $(x - 2)^2 + (y + 3)^2 = 64$.

EXAMPLE 1.64. Although the equation

$$x^2 + 2x + y^2 = 48$$

does not look like the general equation of a circle, we can put it in the proper form by observing that the first two terms in this equation agree with the first two terms in the perfect square $(x + 1)^2 = x^2 + 2x + 1$. Therefore, adding 1 to both sides of the equation will **complete the square**, giving:

$$x^2 + 2x + 1 + y^2 = 48 + 1 = 49$$
$$(x + 1)^2 + (y - 0)^2 = 7^2.$$

Hence the graph of this equation is the circle of radius 7 centered at $(-1, 0)$ shown in Figure 1.15 below. As in the examples above, we can locate the x- and y-intercepts for this circle by setting each variable equal to zero and solving for the other one using the square root method:

x-intercepts:	**y-intercepts:**
$(x + 1)^2 + 0^2 = 7^2$	$(0 + 1)^2 + y^2 = 7^2$
$(x + 1)^2 = 7^2$	$1 + y^2 = 7^2 = 49$
$x + 1 = \pm 7$	$y^2 = 49 - 1 = 48$
$x = -1 \pm 7$	$y = \pm\sqrt{48}$
$x = -8 \quad \text{or} \quad x = 6$	

In this case, the circle has x-intercepts at $(-8, 0)$ and $(6, 0)$, and y-intercepts at $(0, \pm\sqrt{48}) \approx (0, \pm 6.928)$.

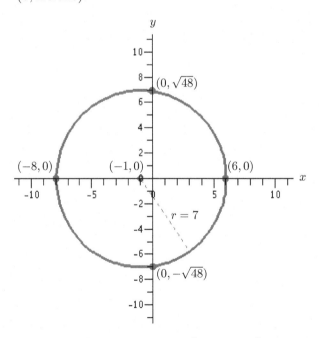

FIGURE 1.15. The graph of $x^2 + 2x + y^2 = 48$.

EXAMPLE 1.65. Consider the equation

$$x^2 + y^2 = 6x - 8y$$

from Example 1.60. As in the example above, we shall put this equation in the proper form of a circle by completing the squares twice. We start by moving the terms involving x and y over to the left, as follows:

$$x^2 - 6x + y^2 + 8y = 0.$$

First of all, we look at the part of the equation involving x, namely $x^2 - 6x$. Because the coefficient of x is negative, we will write this as a perfect square of the form $(x - h)^2$, in which case we must have

$$x^2 - 6x + \boxed{???} = (x - h)^2 = x^2 - 2hx + h^2.$$

To determine the unknown constant that we need to add, we will first take the coefficient of x and divide it by two. In this case, the coefficient in question is $2h = 6$, so dividing by two gives $h = 3$. This means that we will be able to complete the square by adding $h^2 = 9$ to this part of our equation. This would produce the factorization

$$x^2 - 6x + 9 = (x - 3)^2.$$

Next, we turn to the part of our equation involving y, that is, $y^2 + 8y$. Since the coefficient of y is positive, we will complete this part of the equation as a perfect square of the form $(y + k)^2$:

$$y^2 + 8y + \boxed{???} = (y + k)^2 = y^2 + 2ky + k^2.$$

Again, we shall look at the coefficient of y, which in this case is $2k = 8$. Dividing this coefficient by two gives us $k = 4$. Then squaring this gives us $k^2 = 16$, the constant needed to complete this part of the equation as a perfect square:

$$y^2 + 8y + 16 = (y + 4)^2.$$

After adding $9 + 16 = 25$ to both sides, our equation then becomes

$$(x^2 - 6x + 9) + (y^2 + 8y + 16) = 25$$

$$(x - 3)^2 + (y + 4)^2 = 5^2.$$

It is now clear that our original equation describes a circle of radius 5 with center at $(3, -4)$, as shown in Figure 1.16. As you can readily see in this figure, our circle intersects the x-axis twice, at the origin and at the point $(0, 6)$. It also intersects the y-axis twice, at the origin and at $(-8, 0)$. This confirms our results from Example 1.60 on page 80.

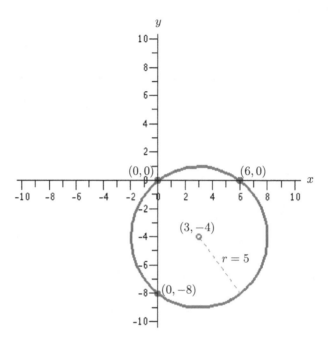

FIGURE 1.16. The graph of $x^2 + y^2 = 6x - 8y$.

EXAMPLE 1.66. Determine the radius, center, and intercepts of the circle

$$9x^2 + 42x + 9y^2 - 120y = 176.$$

Solution. Observe that the coefficients of x^2 and y^2 in the general equation of a circle are both one. In this equation, they are both 9. Therefore we will begin by dividing both sides of our equation by 9, which after simplifying becomes:

$$x^2 + \tfrac{14}{3}x + y^2 - \tfrac{40}{3}y = \tfrac{176}{9}.$$

Note that the coefficient of x is positive while the coefficient of y is negative. Thus, we shall complete the first part of this equation as a perfect square of the form

$$x^2 + \tfrac{14}{3}x + \boxed{???} = (x + h)^2 = x^2 + 2hx + h^2,$$

and the second part as a perfect square of the form

$$y^2 - \tfrac{40}{3}y + \boxed{???} = (y - k)^2 = y^2 - 2ky + k^2.$$

With this in mind, we take the coefficients of x and y, divide them by two, and square them, obtaining

$$h^2 = \left(\tfrac{7}{3}\right)^2 = \tfrac{49}{9} \qquad \text{and} \qquad k^2 = \left(-\tfrac{20}{3}\right)^2 = \tfrac{400}{9}.$$

Adding both of these constants to each side of our equation gives us

$$\left(x^2 + \tfrac{14}{3}x + \tfrac{49}{9}\right) + \left(y^2 - \tfrac{40}{3}y + \tfrac{400}{9}\right) = \tfrac{176}{9} + \tfrac{49}{9} + \tfrac{400}{9} = \tfrac{625}{9}.$$

Therefore, after factoring each of the perfect squares, our equation becomes

$$\left(x + \tfrac{7}{3}\right)^2 + \left(y - \tfrac{20}{3}\right)^2 = \left(\tfrac{25}{3}\right)^2.$$

This means that our equation describes a circle centered at $\left(-\tfrac{7}{3}, \tfrac{20}{3}\right)$ with a radius of $\tfrac{25}{3}$. We can determine its intercepts algebraically as follows:

x-intercepts:

$$\left(x + \tfrac{7}{3}\right)^2 + \left(0 - \tfrac{20}{3}\right)^2 = \tfrac{625}{9}$$

$$\left(x + \tfrac{7}{3}\right)^2 + \tfrac{400}{9} = \tfrac{625}{9}$$

$$\left(x + \tfrac{7}{3}\right)^2 = \tfrac{625}{9} - \tfrac{400}{9} = \tfrac{225}{9}$$

$$x + \tfrac{7}{3} = \pm\sqrt{\tfrac{225}{9}} = \pm\tfrac{15}{3}$$

$$x = -\tfrac{7}{3} \pm \tfrac{15}{3}$$

$$x = \tfrac{8}{3} \quad \text{or} \quad x = -\tfrac{22}{3}$$

y-intercepts:

$$\left(0 + \tfrac{7}{3}\right)^2 + \left(y - \tfrac{20}{3}\right)^2 = \tfrac{625}{9}$$

$$\tfrac{49}{9} + \left(y - \tfrac{20}{3}\right)^2 = \tfrac{625}{9}$$

$$\left(y - \tfrac{20}{3}\right)^2 = \tfrac{625}{9} - \tfrac{49}{9} = \tfrac{576}{9}$$

$$y - \tfrac{20}{3} = \pm\sqrt{\tfrac{576}{9}} = \pm\tfrac{24}{3}$$

$$y = \tfrac{20}{3} \pm \tfrac{24}{3}$$

$$y = \tfrac{44}{3} \quad \text{or} \quad y = -\tfrac{4}{3}$$

Thus, this circle has two x-intercepts at $\left(\tfrac{8}{3}, 0\right)$ and $\left(-\tfrac{22}{3}, 0\right)$, and two y-intercepts at $\left(0, \tfrac{44}{3}\right)$ and $\left(0, -\tfrac{4}{3}\right)$, as indicated in Figure 1.17.

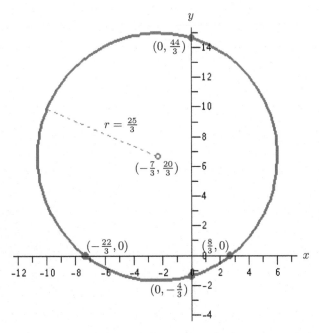

FIGURE 1.17. The graph of $9x^2 + 42x + 9y^2 - 120y = 176$.

In the next section, we shall use graphs in the Cartesian plane in order to visualize the behavior of functions. Before we move on, however, we should point out that René Descartes had a tremendous influence in many areas of Western thought, not just mathematics. He gained notoriety as a philosopher for his famous proclamation *"Cogito ergo sum"* (I think therefore I am), a statement which inaugurated the turn in modern philosophy toward human subjectivity. He was also the first to systematize the scientific method, and even made important discoveries in the physics of light and the theory of optics.

Despite all of his positive attributes and celebrity, however, Descartes was not particularly known for his social skills. He would often receive invitations to different social functions, but he always turned them down. However, it turns out that in 1649, having just arrived in Sweden to tutor Queen Christina, Descartes was invited to a formal ball to be held at the Royal Palace in his honor. Now, formal balls were the sorts of events which no one, not even Descartes, could turn down without a really good excuse. Anyone who was anyone in seventeenth century Stockholm would be there. And to Descartes's credit, he knew that it would be a monumental *faux pas* to turn down an invitation to a party thrown in his honor. Not wishing to insult his new employer, René Descartes reluctantly accepted.

Queen Christina was tickled pink to escort Descartes around the ball and introduce him to everyone on the Swedish A-list. When they walked past the hors d'oeuvres table, she turned to her tutor and asked, "Monsieur Descartes, would you care for some lutefisk?"

"Lutefisk," exclaimed Descartes in a tone of disdain that only a French accent properly refined by the best Jesuit education could convey. "Lutefisk? I think not!"

And just like that – *poof* – he disappeared!

Reading Comprehension Questions for Section 1.5

The Cartesian plane was first developed by __(a)__. Points in this plane are distinguished from one other by an __(b)__ of numbers. The first number in the pair is called the __(c)__; it gives the horizontal distance between the point and a vertical line called the __(d)__. The second number in the pair is called the __(e)__; it gives the vertical distance between the point and a horizontal line called the __(f)__. For example, the point $P = (12, -5)$ lives 12 units to the __(g)__ (right or left) of the y-axis and 5 units __(h)__ (above or below) the x-axis.

Geometric shapes in the Cartesian plane are described by equations involving the variables __(i)__ and __(j)__. For instance, the horizontal and vertical lines passing through the point P above are described, respectively, by the equations __(k)__ and __(l)__. On the other hand, the equation for the circle of radius 13 centered at the point P is described by __(m)__. We can check that this circle goes through the origin by substituting $x =$ __(n)__ and $y =$ __(o)__ into the equation. This gives us __(p)__, which is a true statement. Alternatively, we can use the __(q)__ formula to show that the point P is 13 units away from the origin.

We might guess that the equation $x^2 - 4x + y^2 = 12$ describes a __(r)__ because it contains terms with both x^2 and y^2. To determine the exact shape of the graph, we first need to complete the __(s)__, thereby putting the equation in the proper form. We first look at the coefficient of __(t)__, which in this case is __(u)__. If we divide this by two and square, we get __(v)__. After adding this to both sides of the equation and factoring, we get

$$(x - \underline{\quad (w) \quad})^2 + y^2 = \underline{\quad (x) \quad}.$$

This shows that the equation describes a circle with a radius of __(y)__ and center at __(z)__.

Exercises for Section 1.5

1. Determine the quadrant that contains each of the following points. Then plot all six points together in the xy-plane.

   (a) $(-3, 2)$ (b) $(-6, -1)$ (c) $(-2, -2)$

   (d) $(6, 5)$ (e) $(4, -3)$ (f) $(-6, 3)$

2. Find the coordinates for each of the six points plotted below. You may assume that all of these points have integer coordinates.

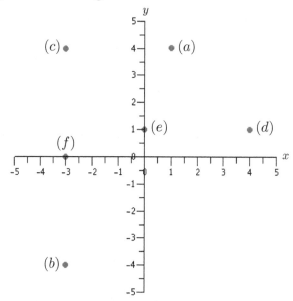

3. Determine whether each of the following points belongs to the graph of $y^2 = x^4 - x^2$.

   (a) $(1, 0)$ (b) $(-2, 12)$ (c) $(0, 2)$

   (d) $(2, \sqrt{12})$ (e) $(3, -3)$ (f) $(\sqrt{5}, 2\sqrt{5})$

4. Determine whether each of the following points belongs to the graph of $y^2 = x^2 + 9$.

   (a) $(-3, 0)$ (b) $(1, 10)$ (c) $(4, -5)$

   (d) $(0, -3)$ (e) $(\sqrt{7}, 4)$ (f) $(\sqrt{2}, 2\sqrt{3})$

5. Carefully plot the points $(2, 3)$ and $(6, 6)$ on the xy-plane. Then use your plot to determine the x- and y-intercepts of the line containing these points.

6. Scalene Sallie has drawn a triangle with vertices at $(1, 2)$, $(5, 6)$, and $(-2, 5)$.

   (a) Find the perimeter of Sallie's triangle.

   (b) Is Sallie's triangle equilateral, isosceles, or scalene?

   (c) Is Sallie's triangle acute, right, or obtuse?

7. Acute Alice and Obtuse Ollie want to draw an equilateral triangle. They begin by placing two vertices at $(1, 0)$ and $(-1, 0)$. They plan to put the third vertex somewhere on the y-axis.

   (a) Ollie suggests placing the third vertex at the point $(0, 1)$, but Alice thinks this would be a mistake. Explain why Alice is correct.

   (b) Alice reminds Ollie that every point on the y-axis is of the form $(0, y)$. What algebraic condition(s) must the number y satisfy at the third vertex of the equilateral triangle?

   (c) Where should Acute Alice and Obtuse Ollie place the third vertex of their equilateral triangle?

In Exercises 8–11, find the coordinates for the endpoints of each line segment, and use these coordinates to determine the length of each line segment. You may assume that all of these endpoints have integer coordinates.

8.

9.

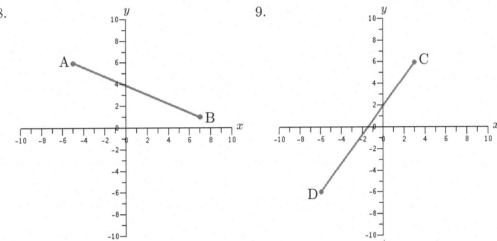

10.

11.

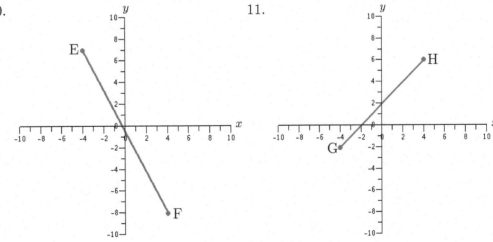

In Exercises 12–15, determine the x- and y-intercepts of the graph of each equation.

12. $5x + 2y = 10$ 13. $y + 3 = 7 - x^2$

14. $x^2 - 7y^2 + 8x + 8 = 1$ 15. $y^2 + 7y + 10 = 2x^2 - 8x$

In Exercises 16–20, make a sketch of each graph described and determine its equation.

16. The line passing through the points $(7, -2)$ and $(7, 5)$.

17. The line passing through the points $(-1, 3)$ and $(4, 3)$.

18. The circle with center $(4, -2)$ and radius $r = 5$.

19. The circle with center $(5, 12)$ which passes through the origin.

20. The circle with intercepts at $(8, 0)$, $(0, 15)$, and $(0, 0)$.

In Exercises 21–30, determine whether the graph of each equation is a horizontal line, a vertical line, or a circle. Then graph each equation by hand, labeling its intercepts. In the case of a circle, also label its center and its radius.

21. $x^2 + y^2 = 49$ 22. $2x - 7 = 3$

23. $15 - y = 2y$ 24. $(x + 3)^2 + y^2 = 25$

25. $x^2 + y^2 + 10x + 9 = 0$ 26. $x^2 + y^2 + 6y = 16$

27. $2x + y^2 = 14 + y^2$ 28. $2x^2 + 2y^2 - 8x = 0$

29. $3y - 5 = 4 - 3y$ 30. $3x^2 - 6x = 12y - 3y^2 + 12$

1.6. Functions and Graphs

The great breakthrough of Descartes's coordinate system lies in that it allows us to put our geometric intuition to work when we are trying to answer questions of an algebraic nature. Suppose, then, that $f : A \to B$ is a function whose domain and codomain are subsets of $\mathbb{R}$. We shall define the **graph of the function** f as the set of points (x, y) on the Cartesian plane satisfying the equation

$$y = f(x).$$

As we shall see, the graph of a function will prove an invaluable tool when we try to understand the function's overall behavior.

EXAMPLE 1.67. Consider the open box described in Example 1.36 on page 54, which was obtained by cutting a square measuring x inches on a side from each of the four corners of a 24 by 36 inch piece of cardboard and then folding the sides up. The volume of this box, in cubic inches, is given by the polynomial function

$$V(x) = x(24 - 2x)(36 - 2x) = 4x^3 - 120x^2 + 864x.$$

Figure 1.18 shows the graph of this polynomial when considered as a function over the entire domain of real numbers.

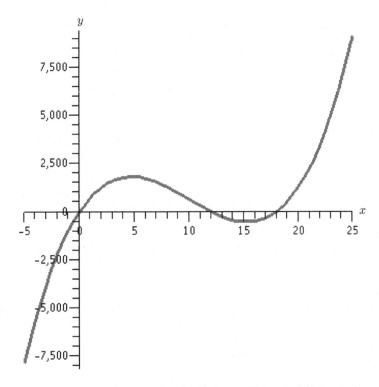

FIGURE 1.18. The graph of $V(x) = x(24 - 2x)(36 - 2x)$.

As this graph reminds us, the formula for $V(x)$ makes computational sense for all real values of x. Nevertheless, if we consider V in the context of building a box, we realize that x can never be negative. Nor can x ever be larger than half of the shorter side of our rectangular piece of cardboard. Therefore, the actual domain of V is only the interval $[0, 12]$. In fact, you will notice that $V(x)$ is negative when $x < 0$ and when $12 < x < 18$, and, of course, negative volumes are a physical impossibility. Evidently, the actual graph of $V : [0, 12] \to \mathbb{R}$ consists only of those points between the x-intercepts at $(0, 0)$ and $(12, 0)$ in Figure 1.18.

Before making any cuts into our cardboard, it would be desirable to find the value of x which will make $V(x)$ the largest. A quick glance at the graph in Figure 1.18 should convince you that this happens somewhere near $x = 5$. In fact, if we were to trace the graph from left to right, starting when $x = 0$, we would see the values of V get larger and larger until we reach the optimal volume of about $2\,000$ cubic inches just slightly to the left of $x = 5$. We say that the graph of V is *increasing* on this interval. The values of V would then start to get smaller and end back at 0 cubic inches when $x = 12$. We say that the graph of V is *decreasing* on this second interval. The optimal point is called a *local maximum* because its y-coordinate is larger than that of any of the nearby points in the graph.

Unfortunately, the resolution of the graph in Figure 1.18 is far too coarse to make a better estimation of the local maximum. In contrast, Figure 1.19 shows a zoomed-in version of the graph with much finer detail. From this close-up of the graph, we can tell that the optimal value occurs when $x \approx 4.7$. Zooming in further will allow us make even sharper approximations.

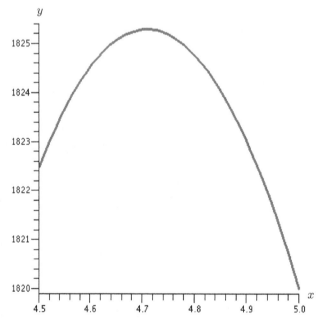

FIGURE 1.19. A close-up of the local maximum in the graph of $V(x)$.

Finding the exact location of the graph's local maximum directly from the formula for V involves the techniques of calculus, which we will not discuss here. It turns out, however, that the local maximum occurs precisely at

$$x = 10 - 2\sqrt{7} = 4.708\,497\,377\,870\ldots.$$

There is also a **local minimum** (a point with a smaller y-coordinate than any of its neighboring points) at

$$x = 10 + 2\sqrt{7} = 15.291\,502\,622\,129\ldots.$$

If you find these assertions intriguing, you should consider taking a calculus course sometime in the near future!

EXAMPLE 1.68. Recall the rational function

$$W(x) = \frac{450}{x^2} - \frac{11}{2(406-x)^2} = \frac{148\,352\,400 - 730\,800\,x + 889\,x^2}{2\,x^2\,(406-x)^2}$$

from Example 1.37 on page 55. This function gives the weight in pounds of a 5 kg "astrocat" placed in orbit between the earth and the moon, at a distance of x million meters above the center of the earth. Since we cannot divide by zero, the formula for $W(x)$ is only defined on the set $\{x : x \neq 0 \text{ and } x \neq 406\}$. With this domain, the formula above determines a rational function, which we graph in Figure 1.20. By picking values of x close enough to 0 or 406, we can find values of W which are arbitrarily large or arbitrarily small, so W has no maximum or minimum. However, it only makes sense for our cat to find herself somewhere between the *surface* of the earth and the *surface* of the moon. This corresponds to the domain $[6.4, 404.3]$, on which W has a maximum when $x = 6.4$ and a minimum when $x = 404.3$.

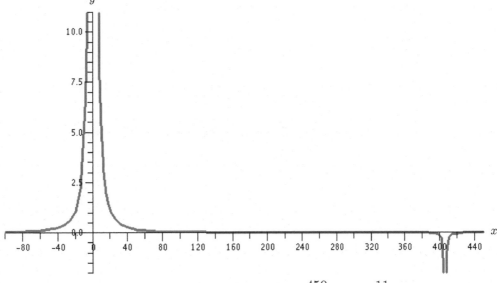

FIGURE 1.20. The graph of $W(x) = \dfrac{450}{x^2} - \dfrac{11}{2(406-x)^2}$.

Figure 1.21 (a) shows a more detailed version of the graph of W. From this graph, we can tell that W has an x-intercept somewhere near $x = 360$. This intercept corresponds to the point at which the gravitational pull from the earth and the moon cancel each other out, making our cat weightless. Of course, we can determine the exact value of the intercept by setting $W(x) = 0$ and solving for x:

$$\frac{148\,352\,400 - 730\,800\,x + 889\,x^2}{2\,x^2\,(406 - x)^2} = 0.$$

Since the fraction on the left hand side of the equation will be zero precisely when its numerator is, we are faced with the formidable task of solving the equation

$$148\,352\,400 - 730\,800\,x + 889\,x^2 = 0.$$

The problem, of course, is that the polynomial on the left does not factor easily. Nevertheless, we can obtain a reasonable approximation to the intercept by zooming in closer on the graph, as in Figure 1.21 (b). In this case, we can see that $x \approx 365.5$ at the x-intercept.

We will not develop the tools necessary to solve an equation like the one above until Chapter 2. When we do, however, we will be able to show that the exact location of the x-intercept for G occurs precisely when

$$x = \frac{52\,200 - 1740\sqrt{11}}{127} = 365.583\,250\,903\,792\ldots.$$

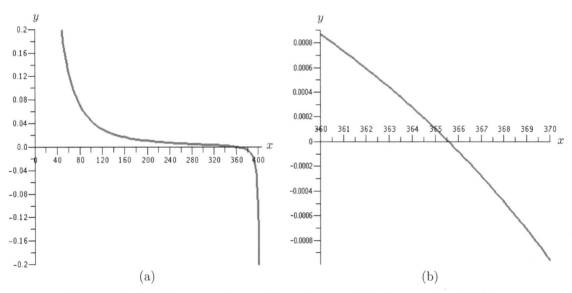

(a)   (b)

FIGURE 1.21. Close up views of the x-intercept in the graph of $W(x)$.

EXAMPLE 1.69. Let us examine the graphs of each of the following six "model" functions:

$$f_1(x) = x \qquad\qquad f_2(x) = x^2$$

$$f_3(x) = x^3 \qquad\qquad f_4(x) = \frac{1}{x}$$

$$f_5(x) = |x| \qquad\qquad f_6(x) = \sqrt{x}.$$

Figure 1.22 shows these graphs, which may be obtained by evaluating each function on a representative collection of input values and plotting the corresponding output values. The following chart can serve as a field guide when you encounter these functions in your mathematical outings.

function	description
$f_1(x) = x$	A straight line that passes diagonally through the origin, making a 45° angle with both the x- and y-axes.
$f_2(x) = x^2$	A parabola opening upward with increasing steepness on either side of its local minimum at the origin; similar to the graph in Example 1.58.
$f_3(x) = x^3$	An increasing graph with varying steepness: shallowest when it crosses the origin and very steep to either side.
$f_4(x) = \frac{1}{x}$	A hyperbola with points arbitrarily close to the x- and y-axes; similar to the graph in Example 1.59, but rotated counterclockwise by 45°.
$f_5(x) = |x|$	A V-shaped graph formed by two diagonal rays that meet at the origin and make a 45° angle with both the x- and y-axes.
$f_6(x) = \sqrt{x}$	The top half of a sideways parabola which starts at the origin and opens up to the right of the xy-plane.

You should take some time to memorize the basic shape of these graphs, what naturalists might call their "jizz," so that you can quickly draw a relatively accurate rendition of each one by only looking at the formula and without plotting lots of points. You should also be able to produce the correct formula when presented with one of these graphs.

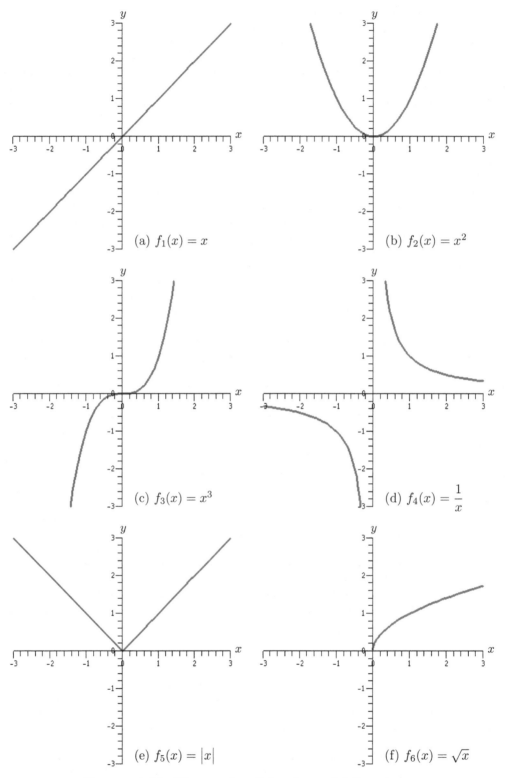

FIGURE 1.22. The graphs of the six model functions.

Familiarity with the six model functions is not only useful in and of itself, but can also assist us in graphing other functions. For instance, in Chapter 2, we will investigate a whole family of functions which are derived in very simple ways from these functions. The graphs of those "linear transformations" will have the same over-all shape as the graphs of our model functions, differing only in the minor details.

Our model functions can also serve as "local guides" as we try to sketch the graph of other polynomial and rational functions, especially when those functions can be factored into a collection of simple terms of degree one. In the case of polynomials, each of these factors produces an x-intercept. Depending on the number of times that a given factor appears in the formula for the polynomial, the graph can behave in one of three different ways near the corresponding intercept:

① If the factor in question appears only once, then the graph will cross the x-axis transversally, that is to say along a diagonal, like the graph of $f_1(x) = x$. In this case, we will say that the function exhibits a **transversal intercept**.

② If the factor appears an even number of times, then the graph will only touch the x-axis momentarily before turning around and continuing in the direction from which it came, as in the graph of $f_2(x) = x^2$. Thus, the graph exhibits what we might call a **turning intercept**.

③ Finally, if the factor appears an odd number of times (but more than once), then the graph will cross the x-axis tangentially, bending into a horizontal before proceeding on its way to the other side of the axis, like the graph of $f_3(x) = x^3$. We shall refer to this as a **tangential intercept**.

Like the graphs of these three model functions, the graph of any polynomial consists of a single smooth curve that stretches its way to the left and to the right as far as the eye can see. As it does so, the output values of our polynomial will also head up to positive infinity or down to negative infinity.

EXAMPLE 1.70. Suppose that we wish to sketch the graph of the function

$$f(x) = (x + 5)(x - 2)(x - 7).$$

Since this polynomial is already factored, it equals zero precisely when:

$$x + 5 = 0 \qquad \text{or} \qquad x - 2 = 0 \qquad \text{or} \qquad x - 7 = 0$$

$$x = -5 \qquad\qquad\qquad x = 2 \qquad\qquad\qquad x = 7.$$

Therefore, our graph has three x-intercepts at $(-5, 0)$, $(2, 0)$, and $(7, 0)$. Furthermore, since each factor appears only once in the formula for f, our graph must cross the x-axis transversally at each intercept.

Next, let us determine the regions where our function takes on positive or negative values. As in Section 1.3, we do this by examining the values of each of the three factors in each of the four intervals separated by the critical points $x = -5$, $x = 2$, and $x = 7$, as in the following chart:

	$(-\infty, -5)$	$(-5, 2)$	$(2, 7)$	$(7, \infty)$
$x + 5$	$-$	$+$	$+$	$+$
$x - 2$	$-$	$-$	$+$	$+$
$x - 7$	$-$	$-$	$-$	$+$
$(x+5)(x-2)(x-7)$	$-$	$+$	$-$	$+$

The alternating pattern of signs in the last row of our chart tells us that the graph of f starts below the x-axis, and winds its way up, then down, and then up again. This means that, on the far left, our curve heads towards negative infinity, while on the far right, it heads towards positive infinity. Figure 1.23 shows a sketch of this graph.

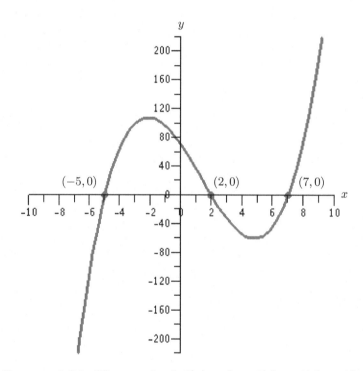

FIGURE 1.23. The graph of $f(x) = (x + 5)(x - 2)(x - 7)$.

Observe that, as we move from one intercept to the next, the graph in Figure 1.23 inevitably encounters some local maxima or minima. As we noted earlier, finding these maxima and minima requires computational tools beyond the scope of this book, so you do not need to be particularly concerned with their exact location in your sketches. At this stage of the game, all that we are concerned with is finding the general shape of each graph.

EXAMPLE 1.71. The graph of the polynomial function

$$g(x) = (15 - 2x)(x + 4)^2,$$

has two x-intercepts corresponding to where each factor equals zero:

$$15 - 2x = 0 \qquad \text{or} \qquad x + 4 = 0$$
$$x = \tfrac{15}{2} \qquad\qquad\qquad x = -4.$$

Since the factor $(15 - 2x)$ appears only once in our factorization for $g(x)$, the graph will cross the x-axis transversally at the intercept $\left(\tfrac{15}{2}, 0\right)$. On the other hand, the factor $(x + 4)$ appears twice in the factorization (notice the exponent of 2 in the formula) so the graph has a turning intercept at $(-4, 0)$. This becomes even clearer when we investigate where our function takes on positive or negative values. We do this in the following chart:

	$\left(-\infty, -4\right)$	$\left(-4, \tfrac{15}{2}\right)$	$\left(\tfrac{15}{2}, \infty\right)$
$15 - 2x$	$+$	$+$	$-$
$(x + 4)^2$	$+$	$+$	$+$
$(15 - 2x)(x + 4)^2$	$+$	$+$	$-$

Notice that $(x + 4)^2$ is never negative; hence the sign of $g(x)$ always agrees with that of $15 - 2x$. In particular, this means that the values of $g(x)$ are positive whenever x is chosen from either the first or second interval, and only become negative when x is taken from the third interval. Thus, the graph of g starts off above the x-axis and decreases until it touches the axis at $(-4, 0)$. At this point, the graph will begin to increase until it reaches a local maximum (whose location will remain undisclosed to protect the innocent). The graph will then decrease once again so that it can cross the x-axis at $\left(\tfrac{15}{2}, 0\right)$. To the left, our graph heads towards positive infinity, while to the right, it heads towards negative infinity, as can be seen in Figure 1.24.

EXAMPLE 1.72. Consider the polynomial function

$$h(x) = (3x + 17)(x - 3)^3,$$

which returns an output value of zero when

$$3x + 17 = 0 \qquad \text{or} \qquad x - 3 = 0$$
$$x = -\tfrac{17}{3} \qquad\qquad\qquad x = 3.$$

Since the factor $(3x + 17)$ appears only once in the factorization for $h(x)$, the graph crosses the x-axis transversally at $\left(-\tfrac{17}{3}, 0\right)$. In contrast, the factor

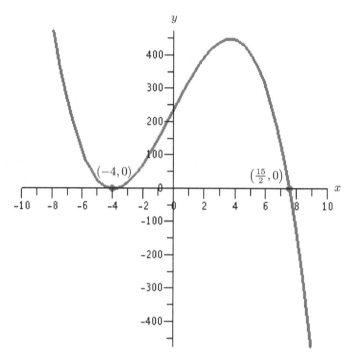

FIGURE 1.24. The graph of $g(x) = (15 - 2x)(x + 4)^2$.

$(x-3)$ appears three times in the factorization (again, note the exponent), so the graph crosses the x-axis tangentially at $(3,0)$. We can determine where our function takes on positive or negative values by noting the behavior of each factor inside each of the intervals surrounding the critical points $x = -\frac{17}{3}$ and $x = 3$ corresponding to the x-intercepts. As before, we do this in the following chart:

	$\left(-\infty, -\frac{17}{3}\right)$	$\left(-\frac{17}{3}, 3\right)$	$(3, \infty)$
$3x + 17$	$-$	$+$	$+$
$(x - 3)^3$	$-$	$-$	$+$
$(3x + 17)(x - 3)^3$	$+$	$-$	$+$

Evidently, our graph starts above the x-axis, dips down below the axis, and then comes back up. At either end, the graph heads towards positive infinity. Figure 1.25 shows a sketch of the graph. You should take particular note of how the curve bends in order to intersect the x-axis tangentially at $(3,0)$.

Sketching the graph of a rational function in lowest terms (at least one that has been factored into simple terms of degree one) is similar to sketching the graph of a polynomial, with two minor complications.

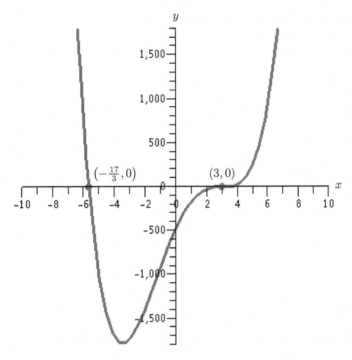

FIGURE 1.25. The graph of $h(x) = (3x + 17)(x - 3)^3$.

First of all, while each factor in the numerator determines the location of an x-intercept, each factor in the denominator determines the location of a **pole** where the function is not defined. For instance, the model function $f_4(x) = \frac{1}{x}$ has a pole at $x = 0$. If we get close to any pole, the function explodes with output values approaching either positive or negative infinity. The explosively large values are a direct result of dividing by a denominator that is almost – although not quite – zero. In the graph of the function, this explosion is characterized by a **vertical asymptote**, that is, by a vertical line that splits the graph at the pole into two pieces, much like the y-axis separates the graph of $f_4(x) = \frac{1}{x}$ into two pieces. Although the asymptote, itself, is not a part of the graph, it is nevertheless useful to draw it (perhaps as a dashed line) along with the graph.

The second difficulty that arises when we sketch the graph of a rational function is determining what happens at the far left and right of the graph. Again, there are three possible scenarios:

① If the degree of the numerator is greater than the degree of the denominator, then the left and right ends of the graph will head up to positive infinity or down to negative infinity, as in the graph of a polynomial.

② If the degree of the denominator is greater than the degree of the numerator, then the left and right ends of the graph will get closer and closer to the x-axis, as in the graph of $f_4(x) = \frac{1}{x}$. In this case, we call the x-axis a **horizontal asymptote**.

③ If the degrees of the numerator and the denominator are equal, then the left and right ends of the graph will get arbitrarily close to a different horizontal asymptote determined by the ratio of the highest degree coefficients in the numerator and the denominator.

We shall now take a look at each of these possibilities in turn.

EXAMPLE 1.73. Suppose that we wish to sketch the graph of the function
$$F(x) = \frac{(x-1)(x-7)}{3x+6}.$$

Setting each factor in this formula equal to zero and solving for x we arrive at three critical points:

$$x - 1 = 0 \qquad\qquad x - 7 = 0 \qquad\qquad 3x + 6 = 0$$
$$x = 1 \qquad\qquad x = 7 \qquad\qquad x = -2.$$

Since the first two of these points make the numerator zero, they correspond to two transversal x-intercepts at $(1,0)$ and $(7,0)$. In contrast, the third point makes the denominator zero, so it corresponds to a pole at $x = -2$. As before, we can determine where the function is positive and where it is negative by looking at the values of each of the factors inside each of the four intervals determined by these critical points:

	$(-\infty, -2)$	$(-2, 1)$	$(1, 7)$	$(7, \infty)$
$x - 1$	$-$	$-$	$+$	$+$
$x - 7$	$-$	$-$	$-$	$+$
$3x + 6$	$-$	$+$	$+$	$+$
$\dfrac{(x-1)(x-7)}{3x+6}$	$-$	$+$	$-$	$+$

The bottom row in our chart now makes our graph's behavior near the vertical asymptote at $x = -2$ clear. In particular, observe that our function is negative on the interval $(-\infty, -2)$ and positive on the interval $(-2, 1)$. This means that our graph must approach negative infinity on the left side of the asymptote and positive infinity on its right.

Finally, note that the numerator has degree two (since it is the product of two factors of degree one) while the denominator only has degree one. This means that the graph heads towards negative infinity on the far left of the plane and to positive infinity on the far right of the plane. Consequently, the graph has a local maximum on the left of the pole in addition to the local minimum between the two x-intercepts, as shown in Figure 1.26.

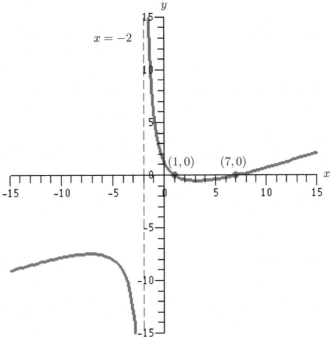

FIGURE 1.26. The graph of $F(x) = \dfrac{(x-1)(x-7)}{3x+6}$.

EXAMPLE 1.74. The rational function

$$G(x) = \frac{3x-6}{(x+3)(x-6)^2}$$

has an x-intercept and two poles; as before, these can be found by setting each factor in the formula for G equal to zero and solving for x:

$$3x - 6 = 0 \qquad\qquad x + 3 = 0 \qquad\qquad x - 6 = 0$$

$$x = 2 \qquad\qquad x = -3 \qquad\qquad x = 6.$$

In the following chart, we examine the sign of each one of our three factors, and by extension that of G, in the four intervals between these points:

	$(-\infty, -3)$	$(-3, 2)$	$(2, 6)$	$(6, \infty)$
$3x - 6$	$-$	$-$	$+$	$+$
$x + 3$	$-$	$+$	$+$	$+$
$(x - 6)^2$	$+$	$+$	$+$	$+$
$\dfrac{3x-6}{(x+3)(x-6)^2}$	$+$	$-$	$+$	$+$

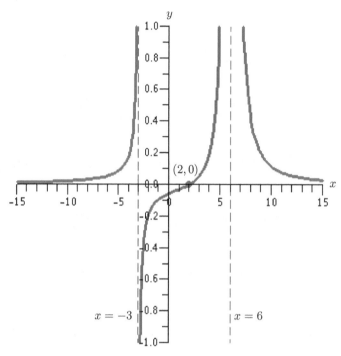

FIGURE 1.27. The graph of $G(x) = \dfrac{3x - 6}{(x + 3)(x - 6)^2}$.

Our chart indicates that the graph of G starts off above the x-axis and approaches positive infinity to the left of the first pole at $x = -3$. On the right of this pole, the graph increases from negative infinity, intersects the x-axis at $(2, 0)$, and once again approaches positive infinity on the left side of the second pole at $x = 6$. Finally, on the right of this pole, the graph remains above the x-axis, making its way down from positive infinity. Since the numerator has degree one while the denominator has degree three, the far right and left ends of our graph get arbitrarily close to a horizontal asymptote at the x-axis, as shown in Figure 1.27.

EXAMPLE 1.75. Consider the rational function

$$H(x) = \frac{2x + 7}{x - 6}.$$

By setting its numerator and denominator equal to zero and solving for x,

$$2x + 7 = 0 \qquad\qquad x - 6 = 0$$
$$x = -\tfrac{7}{2} \qquad\qquad x = 6,$$

we will discover that H has an x-intercept at $\left(-\tfrac{7}{2}, 0\right)$ and a pole at $x = 6$. Furthermore, in the intervals determined by these two critical points, the function alternates between positive and negative values, as illustrated by the following chart:

	$\left(-\infty, -\frac{7}{2}\right)$	$\left(-\frac{7}{2}, 6\right)$	$(6, \infty)$
$2x + 7$	$-$	$+$	$+$
$x - 6$	$-$	$-$	$+$
$\dfrac{2x + 7}{x - 6}$	$+$	$-$	$+$

According to this chart, the graph of H starts above the x-axis, crosses the axis at the intercept at $\left(-\frac{7}{2}, 0\right)$, and then heads towards negative infinity on the left hand side of the vertical asymptote at $x = 6$. On the right hand side of the asymptote, the graph descends from positive infinity and remains above the x-axis the rest of the way.

Finally, observe that the numerator and denominator have equal degree. This means that the right and left ends of the graph will get arbitrarily close to a horizontal asymptote determined by the ratio of the largest degree coefficients in the numerator and denominator. In our particular case, the largest degree coefficient in $2x + 7$ is 2, while the largest degree coefficient in $x - 6$ is 1. Therefore, the ends of our graph approach the horizontal line $y = \frac{2}{1} = 2$, as illustrated in Figure 1.28.

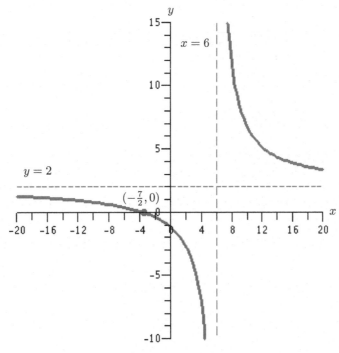

FIGURE 1.28. The graph of $H(x) = \dfrac{2x + 7}{x - 6}$.

There are some functions which arise naturally from their graphs. For example, Figure 1.29 shows the results of a medical examination called an electrocardiogram, also known as an EKG. An electrocardiogram measures a heart's electrical impulse as a function of time; however, this function is rarely expressed by a formula. Instead, a doctor looks at the pattern of heartbeats, and from this pattern makes a diagnosis. Since there is no explicit formula associated with this function, we say that the function is **defined implicitly** by its graph.

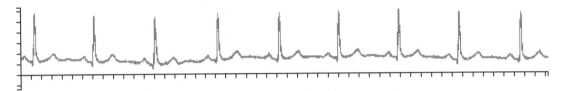

FIGURE 1.29. Normal adult electrocardiogram.

Most graphs do not define functions. For instance, suppose that we try to define a function f implicitly from the hyperbola $x^2 - y^2 = 1$ shown in Figure 1.30. For a given choice of x, we will find that this graph may produce zero, one, or two values of y. Now, it is not a big problem if a choice like $x = 0$ does not correspond to any y; this simply means that our specific choice of x is not in the domain of f. Such values of x can simply be disregarded. On the other hand, a choice like $x = 2$, which produces multiple values of y, does cause a problem. In order for f to be a well-defined function, we need to be clear about which output value is assigned to each input. Since the hyperbola contains two points with $x = 2$, there is not enough information to determine whether $f(2)$ should be equal to $\sqrt{3}$ or to $-\sqrt{3}$. Thus, f is not a function after all. As the following theorem intimates, our main difficulty here lies in the fact that this hyperbola intersects some vertical lines, like $x = 2$, more than once.

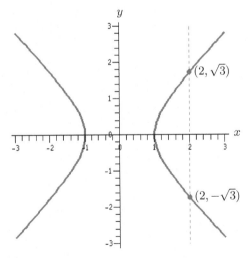

FIGURE 1.30. The hyperbola $x^2 - y^2 = 1$ does not define a function.

Theorem 1.3. (Vertical Line Test) A graph implicitly defines a function precisely when every vertical line intersects the graph in at most one point. In this case, the domain of the function is the set of the x-coordinates of the points of the graph.

Proof. Let G be a graph and A be the set of real numbers a for which the vertical line $x = a$ intersects G at least once. If every vertical line intersects G in at most one point, then we can define $f : A \to \mathbb{R}$ by letting $f(a)$ be the y-coordinate of the *unique* point of intersection between G and the line $x = a$. Since this rule assigns a unique value to each real number in A, f is a well-defined function whose graph is equal to G.

On the other hand, suppose that the vertical line $x = a$ intersects G more than once. This means that G has more than one point with an x-coordinate of a. However, the only point with an x-coordinate of a on the graph of a function f is $(a, f(a))$. Hence the graph of f cannot contain every point of G, and therefore G does not define a function. $\square$

EXAMPLE 1.76. Consider the graph of the equation

$$x^2 + y^2 = 25$$

shown in Figure 1.31 (a). Since this circle intersects the vertical line $x = 3$ at the points $(3, 4)$ and $(3, -4)$, it *does not* define a function. In contrast, the set

$$\{(x, y) : x^2 + y^2 = 25 \text{ and } y \geq 0\}$$

contains only those points on our circle which live on or above the x-axis, as seen in Figure 1.31 (b). This semicircle intersects each vertical line at most once, so it *does* define a function implicitly. As a matter of fact, we can find an explicit formula for this function by solving for y as follows:

$$x^2 + y^2 = 25$$

$$y^2 = 25 - x^2$$

$$y = \sqrt{25 - x^2}.$$

Note that, when we take square roots in the third step above, we do not need a $\pm$ symbol because we know ahead of time that all of the points in this graph have non-negative values of y. Since the formula on the right hand side gives a unique output value for each input x, it explicitly defines y as a function of x, and thus we can write:

$$y(x) = \sqrt{25 - x^2}.$$

Next, take the set

$$\{(x, y) : x^2 + y^2 = 25 \text{ and } x \geq 0\},$$

which consists of the semicircle to the right of the y-axis, as illustrated in Figure 1.31 (c). This set intersects the vertical line $x = 3$ at two points.

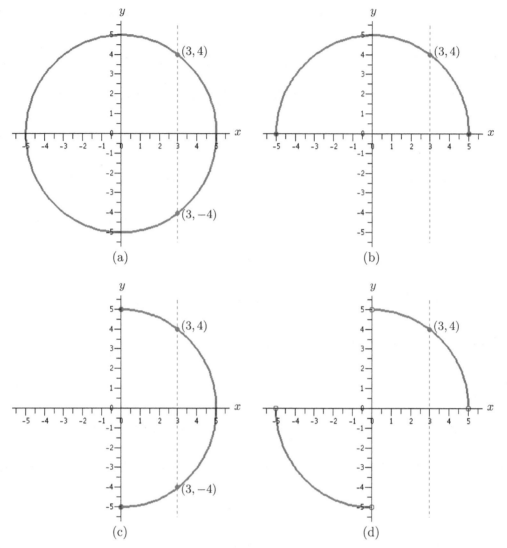

FIGURE 1.31. Some graphs implicitly define functions; others do not.

Hence it *does not* implicitly define a function. Finally, consider the set

$$\big\{(x, y) : x^2 + y^2 = 25 \text{ and } xy > 0\big\}.$$

This last graph consists of the two quarter circles shown in Figure 1.31 (d). Since it intersects each vertical line at most once, this graph *does* implicitly define a function. In fact, you can verify for yourself that this is the graph of the piecewise function

$$y(x) = \begin{cases} \sqrt{25 - x^2} & \text{if } x > 0, \\ -\sqrt{25 - x^2} & \text{if } x < 0. \end{cases}$$

EXAMPLE 1.77. The graph of a function may have several x-intercepts. For instance, the graph of the polynomial function

$$V(x) = x(24 - 2x)(36 - 2x)$$

has three x-intercepts (see Figure 1.18 on page 95), while the graph of the rational function

$$W(x) = \frac{450}{x^2} - \frac{11}{2(406 - x)^2}$$

has two. (The second x-intercept for W lies just outside the field of vision of Figure 1.20 on page 97, at $x \approx 456.5$.) On the other hand, the y-axis is, itself, a vertical line. Thus, according to the vertical line test, it can intersect the graph of a function at most once. This means that the graph of any function will have at most one y-intercept. As a case in point, the graph of V has its unique y-intercept at the origin, while the graph of W does not have any y-intercepts at all.

EXAMPLE 1.78. Let us take another look at the piecewise function from Example 1.8 on page 10:

$$q(x) = \begin{cases} 1 & \text{if } x \text{ is rational,} \\ 0 & \text{if } x \text{ is irrational.} \end{cases}$$

The German mathematician Peter Gustav Lejeune Dirichlet (1805–1859) first put forward q as an example of a function whose graph, illustrated in Figure 1.32, has some rather unexpected properties.

Observe that the graph of q consists of two types of points: those of the form $(x, 1)$ where x is a rational number, and those of the form $(x, 0)$ where x is an irrational number. These points belong to two distinct horizontal lines, namely, $y = 1$ and $y = 0$. Of course, our graph does not contain *every* point in these two lines: The point $(\varphi, 1)$ is missing from the top line because the golden ratio φ is an irrational number. Similarly, the point $\left(-\frac{1}{2}, 0\right)$ is missing from the bottom line since $-\frac{1}{2}$ is rational. We indicate that these two points are missing from the graph of q by using a pair of empty bubbles in Figure 1.32, recognizing that the indicated vertical lines intersect the graph only at the filled-in bubbles at $\left(-\frac{1}{2}, 1\right)$ and $(\varphi, 0)$. Since each real number is either rational or irrational, every vertical line will intersect the graph at exactly one point, thus satisfying the vertical line test.

Now, it turns out that the rational and irrational numbers are inextricably mixed together in the real line. Between any two irrational numbers, there are infinitely many rational numbers to be found. By the same token, between any two rational numbers, there are infinitely many irrationals lurking about. This means that it is simply impossible to see all of the holes in this graph, regardless of how much we zoom in. To the eye of a naked observer, the graph looks just like two solid lines with no gaps whatsoever!

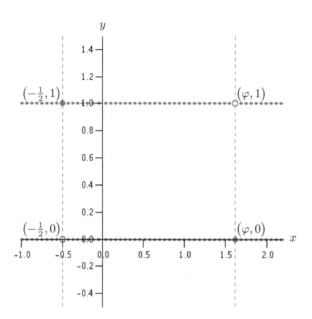

FIGURE 1.32. The graph of Dirichlet's function satisfies the vertical line test.

It was Dirichlet who, in 1837, first proposed our modern definition of a function (the one that appears at the beginning of this chapter) as a rule for mapping input values from a domain to output values in a codomain. Before then, the term *function* was essentially a synonym for *formula*. Since Dirichlet's time, mathematicians have discovered the value of defining functions by tables, graphs, and algorithms in addition to just formulas.

Reading Comprehension Questions for Section 1.6

The graph of a function f is the set of points (x, y) satisfying the equation ___(a)___. The graph of the function $f_1(x) = x$ is a ___(b)___, while that of the function $f_2(x) = x^2$ is a ___(c)___. The graph of $f_3(x) = x^3$ is said to be ___(d)___ because its points move up on the Cartesian plane as we trace them from left to right. The graph of $f_4(x) = \frac{1}{x}$ is a ___(e)___ with points arbitrarily close to the x- and y-axis. The graph of $f_5(x) = |x|$ is shaped like the letter ___(f)___. The graph of $f_6(x) = \sqrt{x}$ is the top half of a ___(g)___ opening to the right. All of these graphs satisfy the ___(h)___, which says that a graph implicitly defines a function if every ___(i)___ intersects the graph in at most one point.

The graph of a polynomial consists of a single ___(j)___ stretching all the way from the left to the right of the Cartesian plane. The x-intercepts for such a graph are found by ___(k)___ the polynomial into simple terms of degree one. For example, a factor of the form $(ax + b)$ indicates an intercept at $x =$ ___(l)___. When a factor appears only once, the graph crosses the x-axis in a ___(m)___ intercept. When it appears an even number of times, the graph has a ___(n)___ intercept and does not cross the x-axis. When it appears an odd number of times (but more than once), the graph crosses the x-axis in a ___(o)___ intercept. For instance, the function

$$g(x) = (2x - 3)(x + 5)^2(x + 1)^3$$

has a tangential intercept at $x =$ ___(p)___, a transversal intercept at $x =$ ___(q)___, and a turning intercept at $x =$ ___(r)___.

The graph of a rational function behaves much like that of a polynomial, except that it can also include ___(s)___ at the poles, where the denominator becomes ___(t)___. For example, the function

$$h(x) = \frac{(2x - 5)(x + 2)^2}{(x - 7)^3}$$

has x-intercepts at $x =$ ___(u)___ and $x =$ ___(v)___ and a pole at $x =$ ___(w)___. Since the degree of the denominator is ___(x)___ (greater than or less than or equal to) the degree of the numerator, the left and right hand sides of the graph also exhibit a ___(y)___; its location is determined by the ratio of the highest-degree coefficients, which in this case happens to be $y =$ ___(z)___.

Exercises for Section 1.6

1. Suppose that the astrocat from Examples 1.37 and 1.68 is standing on the far side of the moon with the Earth directly below her feet. Will she feel the force of gravity pulling towards or away from the Earth? Does your answer agree with the graph in Figure 1.20 on page 97? Explain.

2. Acute Alice leaves a mug of hot cocoa outside her door on a cold $-30°C$ day. Sketch a graph of its temperature in degrees Celsius as a function of the time since it was put outside. Will the temperature of the cocoa continue to decrease indefinitely? What is the significance of the x- and y-intercepts of your graph in terms of the temperature of the cocoa?

3. Obtuse Ollie wants to buy a used car. He finds that the cost C of a car (in thousands of dollars) is given as a function of its age (in years). Sketch a possible graph of C. Is C an increasing or decreasing function? What is the significance of the x- and y-intercepts of the graph in terms of the cost of the car?

4. According to the historical record, the population in Scalene Sallie's hometown boomed during the 1950's and 60's, and fell during the 70's. Since then, the town has grown again, reaching an all-time high of $12\,000$ people in 1995. In recent years, it has not changed dramatically. Sketch a graph of the town's population as a function time. Identify the local minima and maxima in your graph.

5. After being shot out of a cannon, a dare-devil circus clown flies through the air at a height (in feet) of

$$H(t) = \begin{cases} -16\,t^2 + 95.5\,t + 3 & \text{if } 0 \le t \le 6 \\ 0 & \text{if } t > 6 \end{cases}$$

where t is the time (in seconds) after the cannon was fired. Make a table of values for this function (or consult your answer to Exercise 24(a) in Section 1.1). Then use your table to sketch the graph of this function on the domain $\{t : 0 \le t \le 9\}$.

6. The monthly cost for a subscriber to a telecommunications company's cellular phone plan is given by the function

$$C(x) = \begin{cases} 24.99 & \text{if } 0 \le x \le 400 \\ 0.05\,x + 4.99 & \text{if } x > 400 \end{cases}$$

where x is the total number of peak-time minutes used that month. Complete the table below with the values for this function. Then use your table to sketch the graph of this function on the domain $\{x : 0 \le x \le 900\}$.

x	0	100	200	300	400	500	600	700	800	900
$C(x)$										

7. Complete the following table with the values for the function f graphed below.

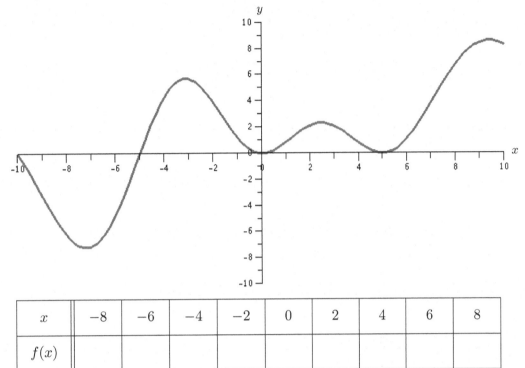

x	-8	-6	-4	-2	0	2	4	6	8
$f(x)$									

8. Complete the following table with the values for the function g graphed below.

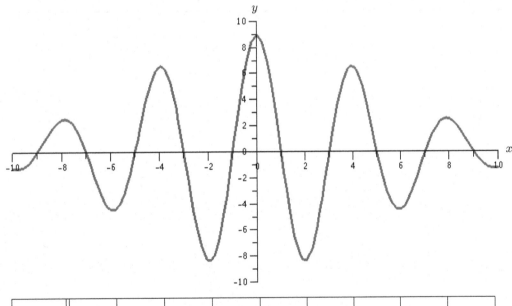

x	-8	-6	-4	-2	0	2	4	6	8
$g(x)$									

9. Consider the function $f : [-10, 10] \to [-10, 10]$ from Exercise 7.

    (a) What is the image set of this function?

    (b) Find the x- and y-intercepts of the graph of f.

    (c) For what values of x is $f(x)$ positive?

    (d) For what values of x is $f(x)$ negative?

    (e) For how many values of x does $f(x) = 5$?

10. Consider the function $g : [-10, 10] \to [-10, 10]$ from Exercise 8.

    (a) What is the image set of this function?

    (b) For what values of x does g reach a local maximum?

    (c) For what values of x is g increasing?

    (d) For what values of x is g decreasing?

    (e) For how many values of x does $g(x) = x$?

In Exercises 11–24, sketch the graph of each polynomial or rational function by hand. Be sure to label all intercepts and asymptotes. Note that in some cases, you will first need to factor.

11. $f(x) = (x + 3)(2x - 7)$

12. $f(x) = (x + 9)(x - 2)(3x - 8)$

13. $f(x) = (1 - 2x)(x - 5)^2$

14. $f(x) = (x + 4)(x + 3)(x + 2)(x + 1)$

15. $f(x) = (6x - 1)(x + 4)^3$

16. $f(x) = (x + 6)(4x - 7)^4$

17. $f(x) = 2x^2 + 7x + 3$

18. $f(x) = x^2 - 8x + 16$

19. $f(x) = \dfrac{x - 5}{(x + 8)(3x - 2)}$

20. $f(x) = \dfrac{(x + 4)(x + 6)}{x - 4}$

21. $f(x) = \dfrac{2x - 5}{(x - 6)^2}$

22. $f(x) = \dfrac{4x + 1}{x + 7}$

23. $f(x) = \dfrac{(x + 4)^2}{(2x - 9)(x - 4)}$

24. $f(x) = \dfrac{7x + 3}{x^2 - 8x - 9}$

In Exercises 25–30, determine whether each graph satisfies the vertical line test.

25.

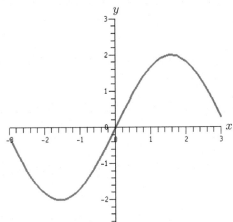

26.

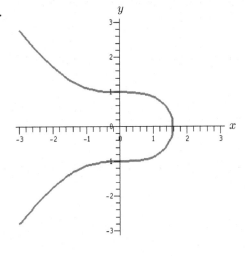

27.

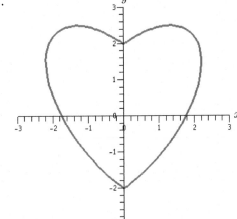

28.

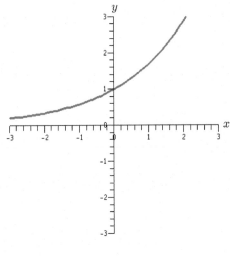

29.

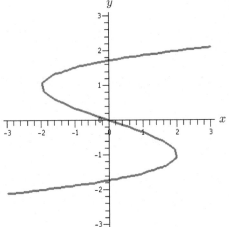

30.

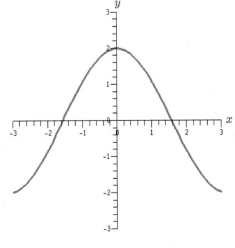

Review of Chapter 1

Vocabulary with which you should now be familiar:

- absolute value function
- Cartesian plane
- codomain
- coefficient
- constant function
- decreasing graph
- domain
- formula
- equation
- function
- graph of equation
- graph of function
- horizontal asymptote
- identity function
- image set
- increasing graph
- inequality
- integer
- intercept
- interval
- irrational number
- local maximum
- local minimum
- piecewise function
- polynomial function
- power function
- quadrant
- radical function
- rational function
- rational number
- real number
- solution of equation
- solution of inequality
- tangential intercept
- transversal intercept
- turning intercept
- variable
- vertical asymptote
- well-defined
- zero function

Tasks you should now be prepared to perform:

- evaluate functions described by words, tables, formulas, or graphs.
- solve simple equations involving polynomial, radical, or rational functions.
- solve simple inequalities involving polynomials or rational functions.
- determine the domain of a polynomial, radical, or rational function.
- determine the equation of an arbitrary vertical line, horizontal line, or circle.
- determine the center and radius of a circle from its equation.
- locate the x- and y-intercepts of the graph of an equation or a function.
- sketch the graph of the six model functions.
- sketch the graph of a factored polynomial or rational function.

CHAPTER 2

Polynomials

I am the very model of a modern Major General,
I've information vegetable, animal, and mineral,
I know the kings of England, and I quote the fights historical
From Marathon to Waterloo, in order categorical.

I'm very well acquainted, too, with matters mathematical,
I understand equations, both the simple and quadratical,
About binomial theorem I'm teeming with a lot of news,
With many cheerful facts about the square of the hypotenuse.

I'm very good at integral and differential calculus;
I know the scientific names of beings animalculous.
In short, in matters vegetable, animal, and mineral
I am the very model of a modern Major General!

W. S. Gilbert and A. Sullivan
"I Am the Very Model of a Modern Major General"
The Pirates of Penzance (1879)

2.1. Linear Functions

It is difficult for us to consider exactly what kind of cat thoughts might be passing through the feline brain of a cat that finds herself plummeting towards earth from the top of a tall building, as in Example 1.34 on page 53. However, it is fairly safe to assume that our cat is probably less concerned with how *far* she has fallen, and more with how *fast* she is falling. In particular, our cat will probably find the *rate* at which the values of the function d (summarized in the second row of Table 2.1 below) are changing more important than the values themselves. This rate is what we normally call **velocity** or **speed**.

For instance, consider what happens over the first half-second of the cat's free fall. In this half-second, the cat falls a distance of 4 feet. If the cat were to continue falling at exactly the same rate for an entire second, then she would travel a total distance of 8 feet. Therefore, we say that the velocity of the cat over the first half-second interval is, on average, 8 feet per second (abbreviated 8 feet/sec). Observe the importance of the phrase "on average." The cat is actually speeding up, so the longer she has been falling, the greater her velocity. In particular, the cat is moving faster at the end of this half-second, when $t = 0.5$ seconds, than when she first started to fall at $t = 0$ seconds. The average velocity of 8 feet/sec describes what happened throughout the entire half-second interval and not necessarily at any specific moment in time.

We can compute an average velocity by looking at a **difference quotient**, that is, a quotient (division) of differences (subtractions), that gives us the change in distance divided by the corresponding change in time. For example, between $t = 1.5$ and $t = 2$ seconds, the distance that the cat has fallen changes from 36 feet to 64 feet. This is a change of 28 feet which takes place over a half a second. We often use the Greek letter Δ (read *delta*) to indicate "change," so that our change in distance is denoted by Δd while our change in time is denoted by Δt. This makes our difference quotient

$$\frac{\Delta d}{\Delta t} = \frac{d(2.0) - d(1.5)}{2.0 - 1.5} = \frac{64 - 36}{2.0 - 1.5} = \frac{28}{0.5} = 56 \text{ feet/sec.}$$

The third row of Table 2.1 gives the average velocity of our free-falling cat over each half-second interval of free fall. According to this table, by the time the cat has been falling for 5 seconds, she has built up quite a formidable velocity. In fact,

TABLE 2.1. The average velocity, in feet/sec, of a free-falling cat.

t	0.0	0.5	1.0	1.5	2.0	2.5	3.0	3.5	4.0	4.5	5.0	5.5
$d(t)$	0	4	16	36	64	100	144	196	256	324	400	484
average velocity		8	24	40	56	72	88	104	120	136	152	168

between $t = 5.0$ and $t = 5.5$ seconds, her average velocity is a whopping

$$\frac{\Delta d}{\Delta t} = \frac{d(5.5) - d(5.0)}{5.5 - 5.0} = \frac{484 - 400}{5.5 - 5.0} = \frac{84}{0.5} = 168 \text{ feet/sec.}$$

Since the velocity of the cat measures how quickly the output of the distance function d changes as its input changes, we say that the velocity gives the rate of change of distance. As we shall see, all sorts of other functions have interesting rates of change. In particular, suppose that f is a function and that $[a, b]$ is an interval in its domain. Then we shall define the ***average rate of change*** of the function f between $x = a$ and $x = b$ by the following difference quotient:

$$\boxed{\text{The average rate of change of } f \text{ is } \frac{\Delta f}{\Delta x} = \frac{f(b) - f(a)}{b - a}.}$$

EXAMPLE 2.1. Let v be the function which gives the average velocity of our free-falling cat from our discussion above over the half-second interval starting at time t. In other words, $v(t)$ gives the average rate of change of the distance function d over the interval $[t, t + 0.5]$. According to our computations up above, we have $v(0.0) = 8$ feet/sec, $v(1.5) = 56$ feet/sec, and $v(5.0) = 168$ feet/sec. We can use Table 2.2 to read the values of v for several other inputs. We can also use these values to determine the average rate of change of v over various time intervals. For instance, the average rate of change of v between $t = 0$ and $t = 5$ is given by the difference quotient

$$\frac{\Delta v}{\Delta t} = \frac{v(5.0) - v(0.0)}{5.0 - 0.0} = \frac{168 - 8}{5.0 - 0.0} = \frac{160}{5.0} = 32.$$

This quantity – the average rate of change of the average rate of change of distance – represents the number of feet per second by which the average velocity increases each second. Hence, the units of measure for this average rate of change are "feet per second per second," or simply "feet per second squared." We shall write this as feet/sec^2 for short. The bottom row of Table 2.2 gives the values of the average rate of change of v over several half-second intervals. Note that every single one of the rates of change computed turns out to be equal to 32 feet/sec^2!

TABLE 2.2. The average rate of change, in feet/sec^2, of the velocity function v.

t	0.0	0.5	1.0	1.5	2.0	2.5	3.0	3.5	4.0	4.5	5.0
$v(t)$	8	24	40	56	72	88	104	120	136	152	168
rate of change		32	32	32	32	32	32	32	32	32	32

EXAMPLE 2.2. Kittens at *Felines-R-Us* sell for $15 each. This means that two kittens will cost $30, three kittens $45, four kittens $60, and so on. In each case, the total cost is computed by multiplying the price of a single kitten times the number of kittens purchased. In other words, the total cost is **proportional** to the number of kittens purchased. If K is the function that gives the cost (in dollars) of buying x kittens, then it will be described by the formula

$$K(x) = 15 \cdot x.$$

Table 2.3 gives the values of this cost function for several choices of the input x; it also gives the average rates of change of K for several intervals. You will notice that each of these average rates of change is equal to 15 dollars per kitten, regardless of which interval we look at. For instance, the average rate of change of K between $x = 2$ and $x = 3$ is equal to

$$\frac{\Delta K}{\Delta x} = \frac{K(3) - K(2)}{3 - 2} = \frac{45 - 30}{3 - 2} = \frac{15}{1} = 15;$$

the average rate of change of K between $x = 4$ and $x = 8$ equals

$$\frac{\Delta K}{\Delta x} = \frac{K(8) - K(4)}{8 - 4} = \frac{120 - 60}{8 - 4} = \frac{60}{4} = 15;$$

and the average rate of change of K between $x = 24$ and $x = 32$ is

$$\frac{\Delta K}{\Delta x} = \frac{K(32) - K(24)}{32 - 24} = \frac{480 - 360}{32 - 24} = \frac{120}{8} = 15.$$

The same is true for any other interval as well. This makes sense because the rate of change of cost – sometimes called the **marginal cost** – indicates how much it would cost to add one more kitten to our purchase. Since the price of each additional kitten does not depend on the number of kittens that we are already buying, this rate is constant no matter which interval we consider.

TABLE 2.3. The cost of buying x kittens at *Felines-R-Us*.

x	0	1	2	3	4	8	12	16	20	24	32
$K(x)$	0	15	30	45	60	120	180	240	300	360	480
rate of change		15	15	15	15	15	15	15	15	15	15

EXAMPLE 2.3. Suppose that we want to start a business making identification tags for cats. This involves buying the appropriate machinery to stamp out little kitty-face-shaped tags from large sheets of metal, to polish the tags, and to engrave the tags with each cat's name, phone number, and email address. The amount of money required to purchase all of this machinery is called our company's **start-up costs**. Suppose that these costs add up to

$100. This represents the amount of money we need to invest regardless of the number of id tags that we plan to produce.

Suppose further that the materials required to make a single id tag cost approximately $0.25. If we only produce one id tag, then we will have invested $100.25 for that single tag. On the other hand, if we make one hundred tags, we will have spent a total of $125, so that each tag ends up costing us an average of $1.25. Producing a thousand tags costs $350, so the average production cost for each tag is then only $0.35 a piece.

Let c be the function that gives the total cost of producing x id tags, so that

$$c(x) = 100 + 0.25\,x.$$

Note that the 100 in this formula represents the start-up costs, while the 0.25 represents the cost of materials for a single tag. As in the example above, the average rate of change of c (the marginal cost) is the same over any interval. This is easy to see by computing the difference quotient for the interval between two arbitrary inputs, say $x = a$ and $x = b$:

$$\frac{\Delta c}{\Delta x} = \frac{c(b) - c(a)}{b - a}$$

$$= \frac{(100 + 0.25\,b) - (100 + 0.25\,a)}{b - a}$$

$$= \frac{100 + 0.25\,b - 100 - 0.25\,a}{b - a}$$

$$= \frac{0.25\,b - 0.25\,a}{b - a}$$

$$= \frac{0.25\,(b - a)}{b - a}$$

$$= 0.25.$$

Evidently, the marginal cost is equal to the cost of materials for producing a single id tag. It does not change with the number of tags that we produce. In particular, the marginal cost is *not* equal to the average cost per tag, which, as we saw above, does depend on the total number of tags produced.

The functions in the last three examples all have one special property in common: Their average rate of change was the same regardless of which interval we looked at. We shall say that a function f is **linear** if its average rate of change remains constant over every interval in its domain. This rather strange use of the word "linear" comes from the curious fact that, if the average rate of change of f is constant, then all of the points in the graph of f will lie along a single straight line. In fact, the average rate of change of f completely determines the pitch at which this line slants. For this reason, the average rate of change is often called the **slope** of the linear function. As we shall see, the larger the slope of a function, the steeper its graph.

EXAMPLE 2.4. Suppose that f is a linear function with $f(0) = b$. Remember that this means that the graph of f has its y-intercept at $(0, b)$. Let m be the slope of f, and choose x to be an arbitrary non-zero point in the domain of f. Then the average rate of change corresponding to the interval between 0 and x is given by the difference quotient

$$m = \frac{f(x) - f(0)}{x - 0} = \frac{f(x) - b}{x}.$$

We can solve this equation for $f(x)$ by multiplying by x (this is allowed since x is not zero) and adding b:

$$\boxed{f(x) = m\,x + b.}$$

Notice that this final formula holds for all values of x (zero and non-zero alike). Because the two coefficients in this expression consist of the function's slope (m) and y-intercept (b), it is commonly called the ***slope-intercept formula*** for f.

Take another look at the slope-intercept formula above. Since every linear function has a formula of this type, we could have also defined a linear function as a polynomial whose degree equals one. In that case, we would interpret the coefficient of x (whom we called a_1 back on page 54) as the slope of our function, and the constant coefficient (formerly known as a_0) as the y-intercept.

EXAMPLE 2.5. Consider the function v from Example 2.1. As we can see in Table 2.2, this function has a slope of 32 and a y-intercept of 8. Therefore the slope-intercept formula for this function is

$$v(t) = 32\,t + 8.$$

By simply looking at this formula, we can immediately see that the graph of v must go through the point $(0, 8)$. Furthermore, since the slope of v is

$$m = \frac{\Delta v}{\Delta t} = 32,$$

a change in the input of $\Delta t = 1$ will cause the value of v to increase by

$$\Delta v = m \cdot \Delta t = 32 \cdot 1 = 32.$$

Therefore, if we move 1 unit to the right and 32 units up from the y-intercept, we will arrive at a second point in the graph of v, namely $(1, 40)$. Since two points determine a line, the graph of v must be the line passing through $(0, 8)$ and $(1, 40)$, as shown in Figure 2.1.

This last example illustrates an important interpretation of slope. Suppose that we are looking at an arbitrary linear function $f(x) = m\,x + b$. If we choose a specific value of Δx and multiply by m, we get the corresponding value of Δf. Geometrically, Δx represents a horizontal distance in the graph of f, while Δf represents the

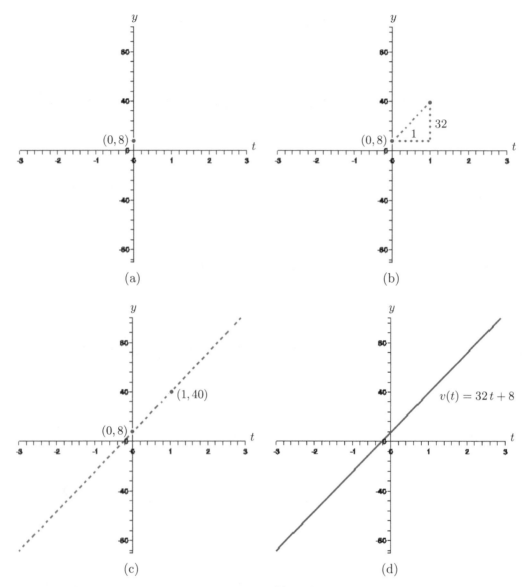

FIGURE 2.1. In order to draw the graph of $v(t) = 32\,t + 8$, we begin by (a) identifying the y-intercept, (b) using the slope of the function to find a second point on the graph, and (c) connecting the two points with a line. The final graph appears in (d).

corresponding vertical distance. It is sometimes customary to call Δf a "rise" and Δx a "run." You may have run into fellow students at recess repeating to themselves, "Slope equals rise over run," *ad nauseam*. This is what they were talking about.

We can think of the slope m as a conversion multiplier, allowing us to transform a given run in the graph of our function into the corresponding rise. In fact, this is precisely what we are doing in Figure 2.1 (b), where a run of $\Delta t = 1$ was converted into a rise of $\Delta v = 32$. When thought of in this way, a slope behaves a lot like a conversion rate at the bank. You go in with several pounds of Canadian coins – all of which were returned as defective by the soda machine at your moment of greatest need for caffeine – and the nice bank teller gives you the equivalent amount in *real money*. (Just kidding, eh?) The amount of money you get back is determined by multiplying the amount of Canadian change you turned in times a conversion rate.[1]

The following two remarks are slightly off-topic (but at least we can admit it):

① Some people are often confused by the fact that the word "slope" does not start with the letter m. Interestingly enough, these people never seem to worry about the fact that the phrase "y-intercept" does not start with (or even contain) the letter b, but that is neither here nor there.

Every so often, someone on the internet will try to resurrect the theory that the m comes from the French word *monter*, which means "to go up" or "to climb." Unfortunately, the evidence for this is pretty weak since most French mathematics textbooks do not even use the letter m for slope; they use a letter k, as in $f(x) = k\,x + b$. It turns out that French roosters do not say "cock-a-doodle-doo," either; instead, they say "co-co-rico." So much for universal constants! At any rate, if you are the type of person who cannot handle mystery in your life, try this on for size: The letter m stands for "multiplier." Not too shabby, huh?[2]

② Here is a useful suggestion for what to do with your Canadian change:

Drop it in the collection basket at church on Sunday. That way, you fulfill your duty to tithe and it gives your priest a reason to visit with the nice bank teller on Monday morning!

The slope of a linear function slope says a lot about that function's personality. For example, if f has a positive slope then it is an optimistic sort of function. Every positive run will produce a positive rise so that, as we move from left to right, the graph of f goes up, higher and higher. Remember that this means that the graph of f is increasing. This was precisely the case in Example 2.5 above. On the other hand, a function f with a negative slope will have a rather pessimistic outlook on life. Every positive run will turn into a negative rise so, as we move to the right, the graph of the function goes down, sinking ever deeper into a state of existential angst. In this case, the graph of f is decreasing. Finally, suppose that f has zero slope. Then $f(x) = 0 \cdot x + b = b$ is a constant function whose graph extends indefinitely to the left and to the right, never going up or down. In other words, the graph of f is a horizontal line. In this case, f is the sort of function which sees the glass as neither half-full nor half-empty; rather the glass is simply twice as large as necessary. People with this personality trait usually grow up to be accountants and engineers.

---

[1] The conversion rate in question is constantly changing. Over the past few years, the value of one Canadian dollar has varied anywhere from \$0.62 in January 2002 to \$1.10 in November 2007.

[2] Again, this is a total fabrication, but if it helps you to remember that slopes are multipliers, who are we to argue?

Slope and the Personality of a Linear Function

Consider the linear function $f(x) = m\,x + b$ with slope m.

○ If $m > 0$, then the graph of f is an increasing line.

○ If $m < 0$, then the graph of f is a decreasing line.

○ If $m = 0$, then the graph of f is a horizontal line.

EXAMPLE 2.6. Suppose that f is a linear function with a slope of $m = -0.3$ and a y-intercept of $b = 5$. Then the slope-intercept formula for f is

$$f(x) = -0.3\,x + 5.$$

Observe that the graph of f must pass through the point $(0, 5)$. In order to find a second point on this graph, we shall pick an run Δx and compute its corresponding rise Δf. Now, if we wanted to, we could certainly pick $\Delta x = 1$; however, we are free to choose any value of Δx that we like. In particular, since we can write the slope of f as a fraction, namely

$$m = -0.3 = -\tfrac{3}{10},$$

it will be more convenient for us to select $\Delta x = 10$, in which case

$$\Delta f = m \cdot \Delta x = -\tfrac{3}{10} \cdot 10 = -3.$$

This corresponds to moving ten units to the right and three units down from the y-intercept, which places us at the point $(10, 2)$. The graph of f is the line determined by these two points, as shown in Figure 2.2.

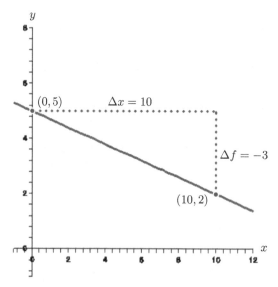

FIGURE 2.2. The graph of the linear function $f(x) = -0.3x + 5$.

EXAMPLE 2.7. Find a formula for the linear function f with slope 5 such that $f(-2) = 3$.

Solution. Since f has a slope of 5, the slope-intercept formula for f is

$$f(x) = 5x + b$$

for an appropriate value of b. Evaluating this at $x = -2$, we obtain

$$3 = 5(-2) + b = -10 + b,$$

At this point, we certainly could solve for the unknown y-intercept b in the second equation and substitute it into the original formula for f. Instead, we will do something slightly fancier. We will cancel out b by subtracting the second equation from the first as follows:

$$f(x) - 3 = (5x + b) - (-10 + b) = 5x + b + 10 - b = 5x + 10.$$

Then simplifying gives us the equation we seek:

$$f(x) = 5x + 13.$$

EXAMPLE 2.8. Consider a linear function f with slope m such that $f(p) = q$. We can generalize the method that we used in the last example to find a formula for $f(x)$. In particular, we have

$$f(x) = mx + b \quad \text{and} \quad q = mp + b.$$

In these equations, we should think of m, p, and q as numbers that we already know, in contrast to x (which is a variable) and b (which is the unknown value of the y-intercept). Subtracting the second equation from the first gives

$$f(x) - q = (mx + b) - (mp + b) = mx - mp = m(x - p),$$

or, equivalently,

$$\boxed{f(x) = m(x - p) + q.}$$

Although this is not our usual slope-intercept formula, it is a perfectly good formula for our function. Since it describes f in terms of its slope and a random point in its graph, it is known as the ***point-slope formula*** for f.

EXAMPLE 2.9. Find the point-slope and slope-intercept formulas for the linear function f with slope $m = 7$ such that $f(1) = 2$.

Solution. The point-slope formula is immediate:

$$f(x) = 7(x - 1) + 2.$$

The slope-intercept formula then follows from the distributive property:

$$f(x) = 7x - 7 + 2 = 7x - 5.$$

EXAMPLE 2.10. Find a formula for the linear function g with $g(3) = 5$ and $g(6) = 7$.

Solution. We know that the graph of g is the unique line which goes through the points $(3, 5)$ and $(6, 7)$, so we begin by determining its slope as the difference quotient corresponding to these two points:

$$m = \frac{\Delta g}{\Delta x} = \frac{5 - 7}{3 - 6} = \frac{-2}{-3} = \frac{2}{3}.$$

Then we can use either of the points to compute a point-slope formula for the g. For instance, using the fact that $g(3) = 5$, we obtain the formula

$$g(x) = \tfrac{2}{3}(x - 3) + 5.$$

On the other hand, if we use the fact that $g(6) = 7$, we find an alternate formula,

$$g(x) = \tfrac{2}{3}(x - 6) + 7.$$

Both of these are in point-slope form; they only look different because they arose from different points. Nevertheless, they *do* describe the same function, since they both simplify to exactly the same slope-intercept formula:

$$g(x) = \tfrac{2}{3}x + 3.$$

This shows that any given linear function can have many different point-slope formulas, but only one slope-intercept formula. Of course, all of these formulas will turn out to be equivalent in the end.

EXAMPLE 2.11. Find the slope-intercept formula for the function h whose graph is the line passing through the points $(2, -3)$ and $(-2, 5)$.

Solution. Just like in the example above, we begin by computing the slope of function based on the two points that we know:

$$m = \frac{\Delta h}{\Delta x} = \frac{(-3) - (5)}{(2) - (-2)} = \frac{-8}{4} = -2.$$

Since the graph of h passes through the point $(2, -3)$, we have $h(2) = -3$. Thus

$$h(x) = -2(x - 2) - 3 = -2x + 4 - 3 = -2x + 1.$$

Of course, we could just as well look at the point $(-2, 5)$. Since the graph of h also goes through this point, we have $h(-2) = 5$, so

$$h(x) = -2(x - (-2)) + 5 = -2(x + 2) + 5 = -2x - 4 + 5 = -2x + 1.$$

Either way, we find that

$$h(x) = -2x + 1.$$

EXAMPLE 2.12. Consider the functions $g(x) = \frac{2}{3}x + 3$ and $h(x) = -2x + 1$ from the previous two examples. Since they have different slopes, their graphs slant with different pitches, and so they must intersect each other. The typical point in the graph of g is of the form $(x, g(x))$ and the typical point in the graph of h is of the form $(x, h(x))$. Wherever the lines meet, these points must agree in both their x- and y-coordinates. Thus, we can find the point of intersection by setting the y-coordinates of these points equal to each other and solving for x:

$$g(x) = h(x)$$

$$\tfrac{2}{3}x + 3 = -2x + 1$$

$$\tfrac{2}{3}x + 2x = 1 - 3$$

$$\tfrac{8}{3}x = -2$$

$$x = -2 \cdot \tfrac{3}{8} = -\tfrac{3}{4}.$$

We can check our work by evaluating

$$g\left(-\tfrac{3}{4}\right) = \tfrac{2}{3}\left(-\tfrac{3}{4}\right) + 3 = -\tfrac{1}{2} + 3 = \tfrac{5}{2}$$

and

$$h\left(-\tfrac{3}{4}\right) = -2\left(-\tfrac{3}{4}\right) + 1 = \tfrac{3}{2} + 1 = \tfrac{5}{2}.$$

Since the output values of the functions agree at the same input, the two graphs must intersect at the point $\left(-\tfrac{3}{4}, \tfrac{5}{2}\right)$, as in Figure 2.3.

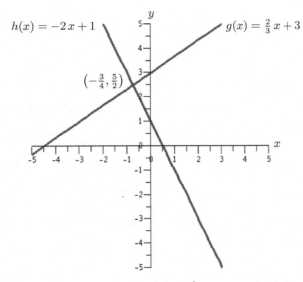

FIGURE 2.3. The graphs of the functions $g(x) = \frac{2}{3}x + 3$ and $h(x) = -2x + 1$ intersect at the point $\left(-\tfrac{3}{4}, \tfrac{5}{2}\right)$.

Even though the questions in Examples 2.10, 2.11, and 2.12 were written in the language of functions, they really dealt with lines. We could have just as easily asked them in the following way:

Question. What is the equation of the line passing through $(3, 5)$ and $(6, 7)$?

Answer. $y = \frac{2}{3} x + 3$.

Question. What is the equation of the line passing through $(2, -3)$ and $(-2, 5)$?

Answer. $y = -2 x + 1$.

Question. Where do these two lines intersect?

Answer. At the point $\left(-\frac{3}{4}, \frac{5}{2}\right)$.

Our answers involve y rather than $g(x)$ or $h(x)$ because we are no longer talking about those functions, but about their graphs. However, the difference simply lies in the semantics and not in the mechanics. All of our mathematical tools will still work in exactly the same way. For instance, up until now, we have talked about the slope of a *linear function*. We can also talk about the slope of a *line*. Since the line $y = \frac{2}{3} x + 3$ is the graph of a function with a slope of $\frac{2}{3}$, we shall say that the line *itself* has a slope of $\frac{2}{3}$. Similarly, we say that the line $y = -2 x + 1$ has a slope of -2. A horizontal line like $y = -2$ has a slope of zero since it is the graph of a constant function with zero slope.

This leaves only one difficulty: A vertical line like $x = 5$ is not the graph of *any* function, linear or otherwise. Observe, in particular, that it fails the vertical line test (Theorem 1.3) and quite badly at that! Therefore, we shall say that a vertical line has *no slope* whatsoever. This does not mean that a vertical line has a slope of $m = 0$, like a horizontal line. The slope of a vertical line does not exist. If slopes were bank accounts, horizontal lines would be perpetually broke, having a zero balance in the bank day-in and day-out, but at least they would have an account. Vertical lines do not even get to have an account. They do not get a line of credit. They do not get an ATM card or checks with pictures of cute little kittens on them. Why, they are not even allowed within fifty feet of the premises. Life is rough when you are a vertical line!

Let us now turn our attention back to our falling cat from Example 1.34. In that example, the function d provides us with a rather simplified model of the cat's fall. The actual distance travelled by the cat as she plummets towards earth depends on many factors. Mathematical modeling – the art of finding an appropriate mathematical function to describe a real-life event – depends heavily on having a good feel for which factors are important and which can be ignored. For instance, our simplified model d accounts for the force of gravity (clearly the major factor determining our cat's fall) but it completely neglects air resistance.

TABLE 2.4. A revised model for the distance (in feet) travelled by falling cat.

t	0.0	0.5	1.0	1.5	2.0	2.5	3.0	3.5	4.0	4.5	5.0	5.5
$d(t)$	0	4	16	34	57	84	114	151	189	227	265	303
average velocity		8	24	36	46	54	60	74	76	76	76	76

A more complicated model for our cat's journey – one which incorporates the effects of air resistance – might reveal data similar to that in Table 2.4. According to this data, as the cat builds up speed, its fur collides with more and more air molecules, producing an upward force (called "drag") which counteracts the pull of gravity. Eventually, the drag will become large enough to balance the force of gravity and the cat will stop accelerating. Make no mistake about it: The cat is still falling, but her velocity has stabilized. The cat is then said to have reached **terminal velocity**.

Now, it turns out that cats instinctively abhor acceleration. An otherwise perfectly happy cat will completely freak out when she feels herself accelerating against her will. This explains why cats make absolutely horrible companions on road trips, and why you hardly ever see a cat riding on a roller coaster. When a cat begins to fall towards earth, she will first become very grumpy and nearly immediately tense all of her muscles. If, as bad luck would have it, the cat were to collide with a 5.97×10^{24} kilogram planet while in this tense state, she would run a serious risk of shattering on impact into a thousand tiny little cat-shaped pieces. On the other hand, if the cat is allowed to reach terminal velocity, she will realize that she is no longer accelerating and, despite the annoying whistling of air rushing past her whiskers, she will relax her muscles. When she finally hits the ground (feet first, of course!) she stands a good chance of being able to just shake off the impact. This is why a cat is more likely to survive a long fall than a short one.

Reading Comprehension Questions for Section 2.1

The average __(a)__ of a function is a measure of how quickly that function is changing. We can determine it by computing an expression called a __(b)__. In the case of an interval $[a, b]$ in the domain of the function f, this involves looking at the difference __(c)__ divided by the difference __(d)__. The first of these differences represents a change in the __(e)__ of the function, while the second represents a corresponding change in the __(f)__.

A function is said to be __(g)__ if its average rate of change remains __(h)__ over all intervals in its domain. The graph of such a function is always part of a __(i)__, in which case the average rate of change is also called the __(j)__ of the graph.

In the formula $g(x) = m\,x + b$, the coefficient m represents the __(k)__ while the coefficient b represents the __(l)__. For this reason, this is known as the __(m)__ formula. For instance, the graph of the function $g(x) = 5\,x - 3$ is a line that crosses the y-axis at the point $(0, \underline{\quad(n)\quad})$ and __(o)__ (rises or falls) with a slope of __(p)__. This means that the graph of f passes through the points $(1, \underline{\quad(q)\quad})$, $(2, \underline{\quad(r)\quad})$, and $(3, \underline{\quad(s)\quad})$.

To find the linear function whose graph passes through the points $(2, 6)$ and $(4, -2)$, we first compute the slope as $m = \underline{\quad(t)\quad}$. Then we can use the __(u)__ formula and write either $h(x) = -4(x - 2) + \underline{\quad(v)\quad}$ or $h(x) = -4(x - 4) + \underline{\quad(w)\quad}$. Both of these formulas can be simplified to $h(x) = -4x + \underline{\quad(x)\quad}$, indicating that our function has a slope of __(y)__ and a y-intercept of __(z)__.

Exercises for Section 2.1

1. Recall the function $V(x) = x(24-2x)(36-2x)$ defined in Example 1.36 on page 54. Compute the average rate of change of V over each of the following intervals:

   (a) $[0,3]$ (b) $[3,6]$ (c) $[6,9]$ (d) $[9,12]$

2. Compute the average of the four average rates of change in Exercise 1. Compare this value with the average rate of change of V over the interval $[0,12]$.

3. Compute the average rate of change of the function W from Example 1.37 on page 55 over the interval $[6.4, 404.3]$. Does this function appear to be linear? (Hint: Look both at the data in Table 1.6 and at the graph in Figure 1.20.)

4. Carefully plot the data for the function K given in Table 2.3 on page 127, and verify that K is, indeed, a linear function.

5. Let $a(x)$ be the average production cost when manufacturing x id tags under the business plan discussed in Example 2.3 on page 127. According to our earlier computations, $a(1) = 100.25$, $a(100) = 1.25$, and $a(1000) = 0.35$. Does a appear to be a linear function? Explain.

6. Find a formula for the linear function f with a slope of $m = 3$ and $f(5) = 2$.

7. Find a formula for the linear function g with $g(1) = 5$ and $g(7) = -1$.

8. Find a formula for the linear function h with $h(1) = h(3) = 3$.

9. Find a formula for the linear function j with an x-intercept of 6 and a y-intercept of 2.

In Exercises 10–15, each equation defines a linear function of x. Find the slope and y-intercept of each function and use these to sketch its graph.

10. $f(x) = 2x + 3$

11. $x + 2g(x) = 6$

12. $5h(x) - 2x = 10$

13. $8f(x) + 2x = 13 + f(x)$

14. $x = -5g(x) + 3$

15. $h(x) = 5(x+1) + 4(x-1)$

In Exercises 16–21, find the x- and y-intercepts of the line containing the two given points.

16. $(3,5)$ and $(6,8)$

17. $(1,9)$ and $(7,3)$

18. $(0,8)$ and $(4,3)$

19. $(2,1)$ and $(-1,7)$

20. $(4,6)$ and $(3,2)$

21. $(5,0)$ and $(1,1)$

In Exercises 22–25, find a formula for the linear function f implicitly defined by each graph. You may assume that every intercept shown has integer coordinates.

22.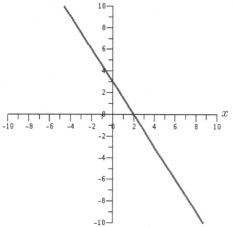

23.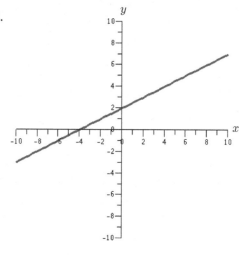

24.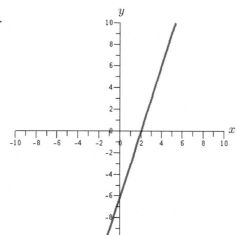

25.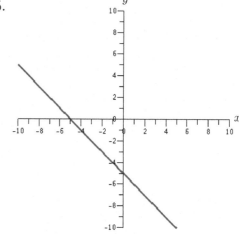

26. A telecommunications company offers a monthly cellular phone plan which, for a flat rate, includes a limited number of peak-time minutes. Additional minutes beyond this limit may be purchased for a nominal fee. The monthly cost for a subscriber is given by the function

$$C(x) = \begin{cases} 24.99 & \text{if } 0 \le x \le 400 \\ 0.05\,x + 4.99 & \text{if } x > 400 \end{cases}$$

where x is the total number of peak-time minutes used that month. Since the formula for C consists of two linear pieces, we say that C is a **piecewise-linear function**.

(a) What is the slope of the first linear piece in the formula for C? What is its y-intercept? Sketch a graph of this function over the domain $[0, 400]$.

(b) What is the slope of the second linear piece in the formula for C? What is its y-intercept? Sketch a graph of this function over the domain $[400, \infty)$.

(c) Sketch a graph of C by merging the graphs from parts (a) and (b). Do the two pieces of the graph form a single, connected graph?

27. Obtuse Ollie wants to buy a used car. He finds that the cost C of the car (in thousands of dollars) is given as a function of its age (in years). The car originally cost \$19 000 when it was brand new, and it has been depreciating in value by \$1 500 every year.

(a) Find a formula for the linear function which gives the cost of the car when it is x years old.

(b) When will the car be worth \$2 000?

28. When Acute Alice got up at sunrise to work on a term paper, she noticed that the outside temperature was 64°F. Suppose that the temperature increased by 0.4°F every 15 minutes, so that a few hours later, when Alice finished her paper and left her dorm, it was 70°F.

(a) Find a formula for the linear function which gives the temperature x hours after sunrise.

(b) How long did it take Alice to finish her paper? Express your answer in hours and minutes.

29. (a) Pet owners are more likely to purchase cat food in greater quantities when they can do so at a lower price. In economics terms, this is known as **demand**. Suppose that, on a given day, customers at *Felines-R-Us* will buy 1 200 cans of cat food if the price of one can is \$1.00, but only 700 cans if the price of one can is \$3.00. Write a formula for the demand function, measured in numbers of cans, assuming it is a linear function of the price.

(b) Pet stores are willing to stock more cans of cat food on their shelves when they can charge a higher price for it. In economics terms, this is known as **supply**. Suppose that the store manager at *Felines-R-Us* will stock 1 500 cans if the price of one can is \$2.75, but only 700 cans if the price of one can is \$1.25. Write a formula for the supply function, measured in numbers of cans, assuming it is a linear function of the price.

30. The price for which the value of the demand function for a product is equal to the value of the supply function for the same product is known as the **equilibrium price**.

(a) What will happen at *Felines-R-Us* if the supply of cat food is greater than the demand?

(b) What will happen if the demand is greater than the supply?

(c) What is the equilibrium price for cat food given the supply and demand functions in Exercise 29?

2.2. Least Squares Regression

Ultimately, the "real world" is data-driven. This means that, most of the time, our experience of a function comes from the output data it produces, rather than from the rule – the formula, the algorithm, *etc.* – which produced that data. For example, we can tune in to the nightly business report each evening and find out the price of our favorite stocks, but we should be wary of anyone trying to sell us a sure-fire method to predict what these prices are going to be tomorrow, next week, or next month. Nevertheless, it would be nice to be able to look at some data and say something meaningful about the function that produced it. In particular, we might wish to determine whether the function responsible for producing the data is linear.

As an example, let us take another look at the data from Tables 2.1 and 2.2 back on pages 125 and 126. Observe that the input values in both of these tables are evenly spaced in increments of 0.5 seconds:

$$t: \ 0.0 \xrightarrow{+0.5} 0.5 \xrightarrow{+0.5} 1.0 \xrightarrow{+0.5} 1.5 \xrightarrow{+0.5} 2.0 \xrightarrow{+0.5} 2.5 \xrightarrow{+0.5} 3.0 \xrightarrow{+0.5} \cdots$$

Whenever we see a progression of numbers which are evenly spaced like this, we will say that they form an **arithmetic sequence**. The output values in Table 2.2 also form an arithmetic sequence, this time with equal increments of 16 feet per second:

$$v: \ 8 \xrightarrow{+16} 24 \xrightarrow{+16} 40 \xrightarrow{+16} 56 \xrightarrow{+16} 72 \xrightarrow{+16} 88 \xrightarrow{+16} 104 \xrightarrow{+16} 120 \xrightarrow{+16} \cdots$$

This behavior is typical of linear functions, since equal increments in the input are converted into equal increments in the output. (Remember that this conversion is accomplished by multiplying by the slope.) On the other hand, the output values in Table 2.1 do *not* form an arithmetic sequence:

$$d: \ 0 \xrightarrow{+4} 4 \xrightarrow{+12} 16 \xrightarrow{+20} 36 \xrightarrow{+28} 64 \xrightarrow{+36} 100 \xrightarrow{+44} 144 \xrightarrow{+52} 196 \xrightarrow{+60} \cdots$$

Since equal increments in the input produce different increments in the output, the distance function d cannot possibly be linear.

EXAMPLE 2.13. The data illustrated in Table 2.5 describes the consumer demand for avocados at a roadside vegetable stand as a function of their price in dollars. In this case, h gives the number of crates of avocados sold in one week if the grocer charges x dollars per pound. Thus, according to the table, the grocer can expect to sell 33 crates a week if the price is $0.75 a pound, but only 3 crates when the price is $2.75 a pound.

TABLE 2.5. A linear demand function h.

x	0.75	0.95	1.15	1.35	1.55	1.75	1.95	2.15	2.35	2.55	2.75
$h(x)$	33	30	27	24	21	18	15	12	9	6	3

Observe that both the input and the output values in this table form arithmetic sequences. The first one increases in steps of $\Delta x = 0.2$,

$$x: \; 0.75 \xrightarrow{+0.2} 0.95 \xrightarrow{+0.2} 1.15 \xrightarrow{+0.2} 1.35 \xrightarrow{+0.2} 1.55 \xrightarrow{+0.2} \cdots,$$

while the other decreases in steps of $\Delta h = -3$,

$$h: \; 33 \xrightarrow{-3} 30 \xrightarrow{-3} 27 \xrightarrow{-3} 24 \xrightarrow{-3} 21 \xrightarrow{-3} 18 \xrightarrow{-3} \cdots.$$

Therefore, without ever computing a single difference quotient, we can be assured that the function h is linear. Of course, should we wish to find a formula for h, we could always use the point-slope formula. In this case, we would find that h has a slope of

$$m = \frac{\Delta h}{\Delta x} = \frac{-3}{0.2} = -15,$$

so that h is given by the formula

$$h(x) = -15(x - 0.75) + 33 = 44.25 - 15\,x.$$

We should touch on a technical point: If we only know *some* of the output values of a function, as we did in the previous example, then we can only make conclusions about the function in a limited domain. For instance, we should be careful when we say that the demand function above is linear. This is certainly true *in the domain given by the table*. If the function were defined on a larger domain, it is entirely possible that h might not really be linear, a fact that would become apparent when we looked at more data points. There is no telling what strange behavior we may discover at those new input values. For the sake of sanity, however, in this book we will usually assume that the data that we look at is representative of the overall behavior of the function. In other words, if all of the evidence available suggests that a function is linear, then you can assume that it really is. Nevertheless, you should be warned that, when dealing with "real world" data, this is likely *not* to be the case!

EXAMPLE 2.14. The absolute value function $|x|$ is not linear, as can be deduced from the data in Table 2.6. In particular, since the input values in this table are evenly spaced in increments of $\Delta x = 1$, they form an arithmetic sequence:

$$x: \; -4 \xrightarrow{+1} -3 \xrightarrow{+1} -2 \xrightarrow{+1} -1 \xrightarrow{+1} 0 \xrightarrow{+1} 1 \xrightarrow{+1} 2 \xrightarrow{+1} 3 \xrightarrow{+1} 4.$$

TABLE 2.6. The absolute value function is not linear.

x	-4	-3	-2	-1	0	1	2	3	4
$|x|$	4	3	2	1	0	1	2	3	4

However, the output values are decreasing on the left half of the table, but then they are increasing on the right half of the table:

$$|x| : \ 4 \xrightarrow{-1} 3 \xrightarrow{-1} 2 \xrightarrow{-1} 1 \xrightarrow{-1} 0 \xrightarrow{+1} 1 \xrightarrow{+1} 2 \xrightarrow{+1} 3 \xrightarrow{+1} 4.$$

Since the output values do not form an arithmetic sequence, $|x|$ is not a linear function. Of course, this should hardly come as a surprise. After all, the graph of the absolute value function is V-shaped, and hence not a straight line. (See Figure 1.22 (b) on page 100.)

Imagine that we somehow obtain a set of data from a "real world" experiment. For example, consider the data in Table 2.7, which describes the volume (in milliliters) of a liquid – say, real Florida orange juice – which drips from a pipet into a beaker. (Beakers and pipets are real pieces of laboratory equipment which may be found in "real world" chemistry laboratories.) More specifically, suppose that f is the function giving the volume of orange juice accumulated after x seconds.

TABLE 2.7. Data from a "real world" pipet experiment.

x	0	60	120	180	240	300
$f(x)$	12.0	13.0	14.2	15.4	16.3	17.1

A quick look at the data shows that f is not linear. In particular, the input data forms an arithmetic sequence (it is evenly spaced in increments of $\Delta x = 60$ seconds) while the output data does not. If we were to compute difference quotients for f, we would observe that the average rates of change depend on the intervals we look at. For instance, the average rate of change between $x = 0$ and $x = 60$ is

$$\frac{\Delta f}{\Delta x} = \frac{13.0 - 12.0}{60 - 0} = \frac{1.0}{60} \approx 0.016\,666\,666 \ \text{ml/sec},$$

while that between $x = 60$ and $x = 120$ is

$$\frac{\Delta f}{\Delta x} = \frac{14.2 - 13.0}{120 - 60} = \frac{1.2}{60} = 0.02 \ \text{ml/sec},$$

and that between $x = 240$ and $x = 300$ is

$$\frac{\Delta f}{\Delta x} = \frac{16.3 - 17.1}{300 - 240} = \frac{0.8}{60} \approx 0.013\,333\,333 \ \text{ml/sec}.$$

Since there is not a unique choice for the slope, this data does not come from a linear function.

But what if f was *supposed* to be linear? What if the various rates of change turned out to be different not because of the function that produced them, but rather due to faulty second-hand laboratory equipment or an over-worked, under-paid, and sleep-deprived lab technician in charge of measuring the data? How can we find the true linear function hidden behind this layer of experimental "noise"?

Well, the bad news is that we can never be entirely certain of the exact function responsible for our data since we can never be entirely certain of which points are tainted by the dark hand of experimental error. The good news is that we can come to a reasonable compromise. Take a look at Figure 2.4 (a), which shows a plot of the six data points in Table 2.7. We call this a **scatter plot** of the data. It is clear from this graph that the data is very close to lying on a single line. In fact, we have supplied one such line in Figure 2.4 (b).

Of course, this is just a guess of what the graph of the mystery linear function that produced the data really looks like. Note that there are three points ($x = 120$, $x = 180$, and $x = 240$) which live above the line and three points ($x = 0$, $x = 60$, and $x = 300$) which live below. We can take heart that the overestimates of the first three points are balanced by the underestimates of the other three. Depending on the situation, it is sometimes enough to visually find a line which strikes a good balance between the overestimates and the underestimates. In our case, this "eyeball estimate" is good enough to tell us that there were approximately 14.6 milliliters of orange juice in the beaker after 150 seconds.

Suppose that we let f_* be the hypothetical *linear* function originally responsible for producing the data in Table 2.7 before it was disturbed by experimental error. A mathematician would call this function "f star". This is not the same function as f, which is riddled with errors, but instead it is a shiny, brand-new, sparklingly clean and error-free linear version of f. Furthermore, suppose that the slope-intercept formula for f_* is

$$f_*(x) = m_* x + b_*.$$

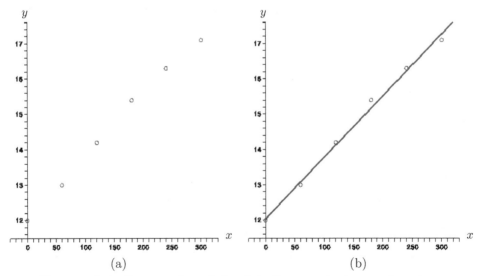

(a)   (b)

FIGURE 2.4. Scatter plot of the data from a pipet experiment.

Then the errors between the real and the observed data at each value of x are given by the following expressions:

$$\text{error}_1 = f_*(0) - f(0) = \big(m_* \cdot 0 + b_*\big) - 12.0,$$

$$\text{error}_2 = f_*(60) - f(60) = \big(m_* \cdot 60 + b_*\big) - 13.0,$$

$$\text{error}_3 = f_*(120) - f(120) = \big(m_* \cdot 120 + b_*\big) - 14.2,$$

$$\text{error}_4 = f_*(180) - f(180) = \big(m_* \cdot 180 + b_*\big) - 15.4,$$

$$\text{error}_5 = f_*(240) - f(240) = \big(m_* \cdot 240 + b_*\big) - 16.3,$$

$$\text{error}_6 = f_*(300) - f(300) = \big(m_* \cdot 300 + b_*\big) - 17.1.$$

You will note that depending on the specific choice of m_* and b_*, these individual errors can be positive, negative, or zero. A positive error simply means that the lab assistant must have recorded a slightly lower value than f_* produced, while a negative error means that the lab assistant recorded a slightly higher value. If the error is zero, then the measurement was completely accurate.

Amongst all of the possible choices for m_* and b_* that we could have used when defining f_*, we wish to find the one that minimizes the effects of all of these errors. This means that we would like to see each error as close to zero as possible. However, we should not try to eliminate one error at the expense of making another error large; instead we need to find a line which strikes a good balance between the positive and the negative errors. An equitable strategy – one that does not sacrifice one error for the sake of the others – is to choose the values of m_* and b_* which minimize the sum of the squares of the individual errors:

$$E = \big(\text{error}_1\big)^2 + \big(\text{error}_2\big)^2 + \big(\text{error}_3\big)^2 + \big(\text{error}_4\big)^2 + \big(\text{error}_5\big)^2 + \big(\text{error}_6\big)^2.$$

The idea here is that squaring the individual errors eliminates their differences in sign, so the positive errors do not cancel out the negative ones when we add them together. When this aggregate error is small (close to zero), each individual error must also be small, and so we have a good candidate for the function f_*. We call the minimum value of this sum the **least squares error**. The graph of the linear function f_* with the optimal choice of m_* and b_* is the line that fits the given data the best, so it is called the **line of best fit**. Since finding this line involves "going backwards" from the data to the function, it is also called a **line of regression**. The following theorem makes it possible for us to get our hands on the line of regression that achieves this least squares error. Both Adrien-Marie Legendre (1752–1833) and Carl Friedrich Gauss (1777–1855) fought bitterly over the credit for this result, each accusing the other of stealing his ideas; alas, this was just one more point of contention in a lifelong feud between these two brilliant mathematicians.

Theorem 2.1. (Least Squares Regression) Suppose that we are given a total of n data points:

$$(x_1, y_1),\ (x_2, y_2),\ (x_3, y_3),\ \ldots,\ (x_n, y_n).$$

Let X be the sum of their x-values, Y be the sum of their y-values, S be the sum of the squares of their x-values, and P be the sum of the products of their x- and y-values, as follows:

$$X = x_1 + x_2 + x_3 + \ldots + x_n,$$

$$Y = y_1 + y_2 + y_3 + \ldots + y_n,$$

$$S = x_1{}^2 + x_2{}^2 + x_3{}^2 + \ldots + x_n{}^2,$$

$$P = x_1 y_1 + x_2 y_2 + x_3 y_3 + \ldots + x_n y_n.$$

Then the linear function best fitting this data is given by the formula

$$\boxed{\,f_*(x) = \frac{P\,n - X\,Y}{S\,n - X^2}\,x + \frac{S\,Y - P\,X}{S\,n - X^2}.\,}$$

Proof. Let j be an arbitrary integer between 1 and n. Then the square of the jth error term is given by

$$\begin{aligned}
\left(\text{error}_j\right)^2 &= \left(f_*(x_j) - y_j\right)^2 \\
&= \left(m_* x_j + b_* - y_j\right)^2 \\
&= m_*^2 x_j{}^2 + b_*^2 + y_j{}^2 + 2\,m_* b_* x_j - 2\,m_* x_j y_j - 2\,b_* y_j.
\end{aligned}$$

This means that the squares of all n errors add up to a total error of

$$\begin{aligned}
E &= \left(\text{error}_1\right)^2 + \ldots + \left(\text{error}_n\right)^2 \\
&= \left(f_*(x_1) - y_1\right)^2 + \ldots + \left(f_*(x_n) - y_n\right)^2 \\
&= \left(m_*^2 x_1{}^2 + \ldots + m_*^2 x_n{}^2\right) + \left(b_*^2 + \ldots + b_*^2\right) \\
&\quad + \left(y_1{}^2 + \ldots + y_n{}^2\right) + \left(2\,m_* b_* x_1 + \ldots + 2\,m_* b_* x_n\right) \\
&\quad\quad - \left(2\,m_* x_1 y_1 + \ldots + 2\,m_* x_n y_n\right) - \left(2\,b_* y_1 + \ldots + 2\,b_* y_n\right) \\
&= \left(m_*^2 S\right) + \left(b_*^2 n\right) + \left(y_1{}^2 + \ldots + y_n{}^2\right) + \left(2\,m_* b_* X\right) - \left(2\,m_* P\right) - \left(2\,b_* Y\right).
\end{aligned}$$

We can obtain the line of best fit to our data by making this total error as small as possible.

Now, we can interpret the total error E as a function of either m_* or b_*. In each case, we will have

$$E(m_*) = S\,m_*^2 + 2\left(b_*\,X - P\right)m_* + \left(b_*^2\,n + y_1{}^2 + \ldots + y_n{}^2 - 2\,b_*\,Y\right)$$

or

$$E(b_*) = n\,b_*^2 + 2\left(m_*\,X - Y\right)b_* + \left(m_*^2\,S + y_1{}^2 + \ldots + y_n{}^2 - 2\,m_*\,P\right).$$

As it turns out (see Exercise 30 at the end of section 2.4), the choices of m_* and b_* which minimize this error must satisfy the equations

$$S\,m_* + X\,b_* = P \qquad \text{and} \qquad X\,m_* + n\,b_* = Y.$$

Then it is a relatively easy matter (see Exercise 30 at the end of this section) to verify that the best choice of slope and intercept are given by the formulas

$$m_* = \frac{P\,n - X\,Y}{S\,n - X^2} \qquad \text{and} \qquad b_* = \frac{S\,Y - P\,X}{S\,n - X^2}. \qquad \square$$

The least squares regression formula above is a generalization of the point-slope formula from Section 2.1 (see page 133). Whereas the point-slope formula gives us the unique linear function determined by two data points, the regression formula gives us the best linear function fitting n data points. In particular, it should not be too difficult for you to believe that the line that best fits a data set consisting of exactly two data points happens to be precisely the line determined by the two points.

EXAMPLE 2.15. Let us return to our pipet experiment data in Table 2.7, which consists of six data points. In order to find the linear function f_* that best fits this data, we will first compute the values of n, X, Y, S, and P using the following organizational chart:

j	x_j	y_j	$x_j{}^2$	$x_j\,y_j$
1	0	12.0	0	0
2	60	13.0	3 600	780
3	120	14.2	14 400	1 704
4	180	15.4	32 400	2 772
5	240	16.3	57 600	3 912
6	300	17.1	90 000	5 130
$n = 6$	$X = 900$	$Y = 88$	$S = 198\,000$	$P = 14\,298$

With these values in hand, we can apply the formula from Theorem 2.1. First, we compute the three quantities

$$P\,n - X\,Y = 14\,298 \cdot 6 - 900 \cdot 88 = 6\,588,$$

$$S\,Y - P\,X = 198\,000 \cdot 88 - 14\,298 \cdot 900 = 4\,555\,800,$$

$$S\,n - X^2 = 198\,000 \cdot 6 - (900)^2 = 378\,000.$$

Then, we combine these quantities and discover that the line of regression is given by the function

$$f_*(x) = \frac{6\,588}{378\,000}\,x + \frac{4\,555\,800}{378\,000} \approx 0.017\,428\,571\,x + 12.052\,380\,952.$$

Table 2.8 compares the observed values of f with the values produced by the regression function f_*. As before, the individual errors listed down the fourth column of this table are determined by subtracting each value of f from the corresponding value of f_*. As you can see for yourself, these errors vary in size between approximately -0.210 and 0.181 milliliters.

One useful way to gauge the significance of these errors involves dividing each individual error by the corresponding value of f_*. This produces what is commonly known as the ***relative error***. For instance, in the case when $x = 0$, we have a relative error of

$$\frac{f_*(0) - f(0)}{f_*(0)} \approx \frac{0.052}{12.052} \approx 0.004\,346,$$

or approximately 0.435%. Similarly, when $x = 240$, the relative error is

$$\frac{f_*(240) - f(240)}{f_*(240)} \approx \frac{-0.065}{16.235} \approx -0.003\,989,$$

or approximately -0.399%. The relative errors for our pipet experiment, listed down the fifth column of Table 2.8, range between -1.386% and 1.047%. Whether this is an acceptable level of accuracy depends on the specific situation we are trying to model.

TABLE 2.8. Gauging the accuracy of our linear fit.

x	$f(x)$	$f_*(x)$	error	relative error
0	12.0	12.052	0.052	0.435%
60	13.0	13.098	0.098	0.749%
120	14.2	14.144	−0.056	−0.397%
180	15.4	15.190	−0.210	−1.386%
240	16.3	16.235	−0.065	−0.399%
300	17.1	17.281	0.181	1.047%

TABLE 2.9. Nutritional content in one serving of breakfast cereal.

brand	A	B	C	D	E	F	G	H	I	J
carbs (g)	25	23	22	26	38	45	43	48	46	44
sugar (g)	0	6	9	3	5	20	13	4	17	12
protein (g)	2	4	3	2	5	3	4	6	7	5
fat (g)	1	1	1.5	0.5	1	1	3	1	3	6
fiber (g)	14	10	2	1	5	4	3	7	5	4
calories	60	80	110	120	160	190	200	200	230	240

Source: http://www.acaloriecounter.com/breakfast-cereal.php (2010)

EXAMPLE 2.16. Consider the data in Table 2.9, which lists the nutritional content, per recommended serving size, for ten different national brands of breakfast cereal. According to this data, the number of calories in a serving of cereal is not a function of the amount of dietary fiber. In particular, there are two types of cereal containing 4 grams of fiber per serving (Brand F with 190 calories and Brand J with 240 calories) and two different types of cereal containing 5 grams of fiber per serving (Brand E with 160 calories and Brand I with 230 calories). Nevertheless, we can use the regression formula from Theorem 2.1 to find the linear function f_* that best predicts the number of calories in a serving of cereal containing x grams of fiber. To do this, we begin by putting together an organizational chart as follows:

j	x_j	y_j	$x_j{}^2$	$x_j y_j$
1	14	60	196	840
2	10	80	100	800
3	2	110	4	220
4	1	120	1	120
5	5	160	25	800
6	4	190	16	760
7	3	200	9	600
8	7	200	49	1 400
9	5	230	25	1 150
10	4	240	16	960
$n = 10$	$X = 55$	$Y = 1\,590$	$S = 441$	$P = 7\,650$

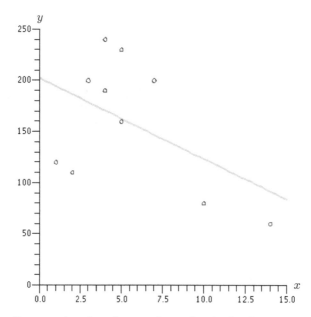

FIGURE 2.5. Line of regression for the number of calories in a serving of cereal with x grams of fiber.

Following the indications of Theorem 2.1, we have

$$P\,n - X\,Y = 7\,650 \cdot 10 - 55 \cdot 1\,590 = -10\,950,$$

$$S\,Y - P\,X = 441 \cdot 1\,590 - 7\,650 \cdot 55 = 280\,440,$$

$$S\,n - X^2 = 441 \cdot 10 - (55)^2 = 1\,385,$$

so our line of best fit is given by the function

$$f_*(x) = -\frac{10\,950}{1\,385}\,x + \frac{280\,440}{1\,385} \approx -7.906\,137\,184\,x + 202.483\,754\,513.$$

Figure 2.5 shows a scatter plot of the data as well as the line of regression. Observe that the line's negative slope indicates that high fiber cereals are generally lower in calories than low fiber cereals. Note also how the points of this scatter plot are not packed as closely to the line of regression as in the previous example. Indeed, as we can see in Table 2.10, the relative errors for this data range between -41.1% and 41.1%.

Statisticians use the term ***correlation*** to describe the quality of the fit between a given data set and its line of regression. For instance, in light of the results of Example 2.16, we could say that the amount of dietary fiber in a serving of cereal is ***weakly correlated*** to the number of calories in that cereal. This means that the errors involved in this fit are fairly significant. In contrast, the volume of orange juice accumulated in the beaker of Example 2.15 is ***strongly correlated*** to the duration of the experiment since the regression function there produced fairly small errors.

TABLE 2.10. Gauging the accuracy of our linear fit.

x	$f(x)$	$f_*(x)$	error	relative error
14	60	91.798	31.798	34.7%
10	80	123.422	43.422	35.2%
2	110	186.671	76.671	41.1%
1	120	194.578	74.578	38.3%
5	160	162.953	2.953	1.8%
4	190	170.859	−19.141	−11.2%
3	200	178.765	−21.235	−11.9%
7	200	147.141	−52.859	−35.9%
5	230	162.953	−67.047	−41.1%
4	240	170.859	−69.141	−40.5%

We can also say that Example 2.16 shows that the amount of fiber is **negatively correlated** to number of calories, meaning that the line of regression which (almost) relates these two quantities to one another has a negative slope. Similarly, the volume of orange juice in the pipet experiment of Example 2.15 is **positively correlated** to the duration of the experiment since the line of regression there has a positive slope.

It is very important to remember that correlation does not necessarily imply **causation**. In other words, just because two phenomena are related to one another, it does not mean that one is the cause of the other, or vice versa. Certainly, in the case of our pipet experiment, the causation is clear: The amount of orange juice in the beaker is a direct result of the length of time that we run the experiment. However, simply because high fiber cereals tend to be lower in calories does not mean that the lack of calories is caused by the fiber. Indeed, like any other carbohydrate, dietary fiber provides about four calories per gram. Of course, since fiber is not easily digested, it turns out that these calories are typically not absorbed by the body. At any rate, it is entirely possible that producers of breakfast cereal, knowing from experience that their health-minded consumers will be interested in cereals which are both high in fiber *and* low in calories, design their products to satisfy both of these concerns. Then again, it may just be that our sample of data is just too small to be representative of the entire breakfast cereal industry, and that the correlation we observed was purely coincidental or statistically insignificant.

As you might suspect, performing least square regressions on large data sets can become a rather tedious process. Computers and calculators can be very useful in this regard. For instance, our organizational charts for computing the values of n, X, Y, S, and P in the examples above can be readily constructed on any electronic spreadsheet like *Microsoft Excel*. Furthermore, with a computer algebra system like *Maxima*,[3] we can conjure up a line of regression in just a few keystrokes. For instance, to determine the line of best fit from Example 2.15, we would simply give *Maxima* the following instructions:

```
load(stats);
data : [[0, 12.0], [60, 13.0], [120, 14.2], [180, 15.4],
    [240, 16.3], [300, 17.1]];
simple_linear_regression(data);
```

Here, the first command loads a special library of statistical functions that we will need for our least squares regression. The next command stores the input and output data values in the computer's memory; notice that the data sets are entered as lists of ordered pairs separated by commas and surrounded by square brackets. The final command computes the line of regression based on the stored data. In reply to these instructions, *Maxima* will return the formula for our line of best fit (along with several other statistics) in a fraction of a second:

SIMPLE LINEAR REGRESSION

$\text{model} = .01742857142857143\,x + 12.05238095238095$

$\text{correlation} = .9974813540841126$

$\text{v\_estimation} = .02419047619047623$

$\text{b\_conf\_int} = [.01570812551246419, .01914901734467866]$

$\text{hypotheses} = H0 : b = 0, H1 : b\#0$

$\text{statistic} = 28.12612202486292$

$\text{distribution} = [student\_t, 4]$

$\text{p\_value} = 1.0638746601454585\,10^{-6}$

Similarly, we can perform the least squares regression in Example 2.16 by entering the following commands:

```
load(stats);
data : [[14, 60], [10, 80], [2, 110], [1, 120], [5, 160],
    [4, 190], [3, 200], [7, 200], [5, 230], [4, 240]];
simple_linear_regression(data);
```

---

[3] *Maxima* is an open-source computer algebra system originally developed in the late 1960's by the Project for Mathematics and Computation at the Massachusetts Institute of Technology with funding from the U.S. Department of Energy. *Maxima* contains a number of symbolic routines for manipulating and solving equations algebraically, numerical algorithms for providing estimates where exact solutions do not exist, and graphics commands for visualizing complicated mathematical information. At present, *Maxima* is maintained as a collaborative effort by a group of volunteers from around the world, and is available as a free download at **http://maxima.sourceforge.net**.

These will produce the response:

SIMPLE LINEAR REGRESSION

$$\text{model} = 202.4837545126354 - 7.906137184115523\,x$$

$$\text{correlation} = -.4911368305921179$$

$$\text{v\_estimation} = 3404.097472924187$$

$$\text{b\_conf\_int} = [-19.33850499967173, 3.526230631440684]$$

$$\text{hypotheses} = H0 : b = 0, H1 : b\#0$$

$$\text{statistic} = 1.594733946124518$$

$$\text{distribution} = [student\_t, 8]$$

$$\text{p\_value} = .1452360531850145$$

Whether you choose to use *Maxima* or some other computer program, the process for performing a least squares regression will be essentially the same, varying only in the **syntax**, that is, in the collection of "grammar rules" that the computer understands. The colons, semicolons, parentheses, and square brackets in the commands above form part of *Maxima*'s syntax. Without these symbols in their proper place, *Maxima* would not understand what it is that we are asking her to do. Other programs will require slightly different syntax, but the overall procedure will be very similar to the one described here.

Note that you *do not* need to memorize the least squares regression formula from Theorem 2.1. Indeed, the truth of the matter is that it is extremely unlikely that you will ever explicitly use this formula again, choosing instead to use a computer to do the work for you. This is a perfectly reasonable choice. Instead of wasting your time with hours of mindless arithmetic, it is much more important that you understand what the result of a least squares regression is telling you – the formula of the linear function which comes closest to producing the given data set – and to make good use that result. After all, *that* is what mathematics is really all about! However, because you have now seen the least squares regression formula in action, you should be immune from the altogether too common impression that regression is some sort of mathematical *hocus pocus*, the understanding of which is reserved to a select few.

Reading Comprehension Questions for Section 2.2

A linear function maps equal increments in the input to __(a)__ in the output. In other words, if the input values form an __(b)__, then the corresponding output values form one as well. For example, suppose that f is a linear function that maps the inputs 0, 1, 2, and 3 respectively to -5, 2, 9, and 16. Here, the inputs are all separated by increments of $\Delta x = $ __(c)__ while the outputs are separated by increments of $\Delta f = $ __(d)__. Then we can conclude that $f(4) = $ __(e)__ because this is __(f)__ more than $f(3) = $ __(g)__. On the other hand, if g maps the inputs 0, 1, 2, and 3 to the outputs 4, 2, 1, and -2, then we can tell that g __(h)__ (is or is not) linear because the outputs did not form an __(i)__.

We can find the linear function that best fits a set of data by using a process known as least-squares __(j)__. For instance, consider the data for the function g given above; it consists of a total of $n = $ __(k)__ data points. We first compute four numbers:

- the sum of the x-values, $X = $ __(l)__,
- the sum of the y-values, $Y = $ __(m)__,
- the sum of the squares of the x-values, $S = $ __(n)__,
- the sum of the products of the x- and y-values, $P = $ __(o)__.

Then, we use these numbers to determine the values of three expressions:

- $Pn - XY = $ __(p)__,
- $SY - PX = $ __(q)__,
- $Sn - X^2 = $ __(r)__.

According to these values, the data above is best described by the linear function

$$g_\star(x) = \underline{\quad(s)\quad} x + \underline{\quad(t)\quad}.$$

This function maps the inputs 0, 1, 2, and 3 to the outputs __(u)__, __(v)__, __(w)__, and __(x)__. The sum of the squares of the errors between g and $g_\star$ is then

$$E = \big(g_\star(0) - g(0)\big)^2 + \big(g_\star(1) - g(1)\big)^2 + \big(g_\star(2) - g(2)\big)^2 + \big(g_\star(3) - g(3)\big)^2 = \underline{\quad(y)\quad}.$$

Since this is the smaller error among all possible linear functions $g_\star$ approximating the data, it is known as the __(z)__ error.

Exercises for Section 2.2

In Exercises 1–10, determine whether or not each table describes a linear function. If it does, find a formula for the function. If it does not, draw a scatter plot of the data and make a good visual guess for the line that best fits the data.

1.

x	1	2	3	4	5
$f(x)$	1	4	7	10	13

2.

x	1	2	3	4	5
$f(x)$	15	14	11	9	7

3.

x	1	2	3	4	5
$f(x)$	2	4	8	6	10

4.

x	1	2	3	4	5
$f(x)$	3	5	7	9	11

5.

x	1	2	3	4	5
$f(x)$	7	5	3	0	-3

6.

x	1	2	3	4	5
$f(x)$	-7	-3	1	5	9

7.

x	1	2	3	4	5
$f(x)$	8	6	4	2	0

8.

x	1	2	3	4	5
$f(x)$	1	3	6	10	15

9.

x	1	2	3	4	5
$f(x)$	8	5	3	2	1

10.

x	1	2	3	4	5
$f(x)$	25	21	17	13	9

11. (a) Draw a scatter plot of the data in Table 1.3 on page 6. In your scatter plot, can you detect a positive or a negative correlation between a number and the length of its English name?

   (b) What is the slope of the line connecting the first and last points on your scatter plot? How many points in your scatter plot live above this line? How many points live below this line?

   (c) What is slope of the line of best fit for this data? How many points in your scatter plot live above this line? How many points live below this line?

12. (a) Draw a scatter plot of the data in Table 1.4 on page 6. In your scatter plot, can you detect a positive or a negative correlation between a number and the length of its Roman numeral?

   (b) What is the slope of the line connecting the first and last points on your scatter plot? How many points in your scatter plot live above this line? How many points live below this line?

(c) What is slope of the line of best fit for this data? How many points in your scatter plot live above this line? How many points live below this line?

13. (a) Draw a scatter plot of the data in Figure 1.2 on page 8.

(b) What is the slope of the line connecting the first and last points on your scatter plot? How many points in your scatter plot live above this line? How many points live below this line?

(c) What is slope of the line of best fit for this data? How many points in your scatter plot live above this line? How many points live below this line?

14. (a) Draw a scatter plot of the data in Table 1.5 on page 53.

(b) What is the slope of the line connecting the first and last points on your scatter plot? How many points in your scatter plot live above this line? How many points live below this line?

(c) What is slope of the line of best fit for this data? How many points in your scatter plot live above this line? How many points live below this line?

In Exercises 15–18, refer to the data in Table 2.9 on page 151, which depicts the nutritional content for eight different national brands of breakfast cereal.

15. Find a formula predicting the number of calories in a 100 gram serving of cereal as a linear function of the amount of carbohydrates. Does your formula reveal a positive or a negative correlation?

16. Find a formula predicting the number of calories in a 100 gram serving of cereal as a linear function of the amount of sugar. Does your formula reveal a positive or a negative correlation?

17. Find a formula predicting the number of calories in a 100 gram serving of cereal as a linear function of the amount of protein. Does your formula reveal a positive or a negative correlation?

18. Find a formula predicting the number of calories in a 100 gram serving of cereal as a linear function of the amount of fat. Does your formula reveal a positive or a negative correlation?

In Exercises 19–22, refer to the data in Table 2.11, which provides the average distance to the sun and the duration of a year (a revolution around the sun) for each planet in our solar system.

19. In his 1619 *Harmonices Mundi*, German astronomer Johannes Kepler (1571 – 1630) published his third law of planetary motion, asserting that the duration of a year on any planet in our solar system is proportional to the square root of the cube of its distance to the sun.

(a) Compute the square root of the cube of the distance to the sun for each of the eight planets in our solar system.

(b) Find a formula predicting the duration of a year as a linear function of the values in part (a).

TABLE 2.11. The average distance to the sun (in millions of kilometers) and the duration of a year (in earth days) for each of the eight planets in our solar system.

planet	distance to sun	duration of year
Mercury	57.9	88.0
Venus	108.2	224.7
Earth	149.6	365.2
Mars	227.9	687.0
Jupiter	778.6	4 331
Saturn	1 433.5	10 747
Uranus	2 872.5	30 589
Neptune	4 495.1	59 800

Source: http://nssdc.gsfc.nasa.gov/planetary/factsheet (Nov 2007)

20. How well does your formula from Exercise 19 predict the actual data shown in Table 2.11? Express your answers as a percentage of the actual values. Does your answer seem to confirm Kepler's third law?

21. In 2006, the International Astronomical Union declared that Pluto is no longer considered a planet. Instead, Pluto is now classified as a dwarf planet. What does your formula from Exercise 19 predict as the duration of a year on Pluto, which is 5 870 million kilometers away from the sun?

22. How does the value from Exercise 21 compare to the actual value of 90 588 days? Express your answer as a percentage of this actual value. Do you think your answer warrants Pluto's dismissal from the roster of planets? Or do you think that the IAU must have had other reasons for its decision?

In Exercises 23–26, refer to the data in Table 2.12, which provides the birth rate, gross domestic product, average life expectancy, and rate of internet usage in several European nations.

23. (a) Find a formula predicting the average life expectancy as a linear function of the birth rate of a typical European nation.

(b) Does your formula reveal a positive or a negative correlation?

(c) Do you believe that there are underlying causes behind this correlation? In other words, do you believe that a nation's birth rate directly affects its life expectancy? Explain.

24. (a) Find a formula predicting the rate of internet usage as a linear function of the gross domestic product of a typical European nation.

(b) Does your formula reveal a positive or a negative correlation?

TABLE 2.12. The birth rate (in births per hundred people), gross domestic product (in thousands of dollars per person), average life expectancy (in years), and rate of internet usage (as a percentage of the population) for fifteen European nations.

nation	birth rate	g.d.p.	life expectancy	internet usage
Albania	1.516	5.7	77.6	13.293
Andorra	0.845	38.8	83.5	33.207
Belgium	1.029	33.0	78.9	46.554
Germany	0.820	31.9	79.0	46.831
Ireland	1.440	44.5	77.9	36.201
Italy	0.854	30.2	79.9	49.701
Luxembourg	1.184	71.4	79.0	73.267
Moldova	1.088	2.0	70.2	16.366
Norway	1.127	46.3	79.7	89.058
Portugal	1.059	19.8	77.9	30.478
Russia	1.092	12.2	65.9	17.867
San Marino	0.989	34.1	81.8	54.029
Spain	0.998	27.4	79.9	46.121
Ukraine	0.945	7.8	67.9	11.617
United Kingdom	1.067	31.8	78.7	55.639

Source: https://www.cia.gov/library/publications/the-world-factbook (2006)

    (c) Do you believe that there are underlying causes behind this correlation? In other words, do you believe a nation's gross domestic product directly affects its internet usage? Explain.

25. The United States has a birth rate of 1.416% and a life expectancy of 78 years. How closely does your formula from Exercise 23 predict this average life expectancy? Express your answers as a percentage of the actual values.

26. The United States has a gross domestic product of $44 000 per person and an internet usage of 70.983%. How closely does your formula from Exercise 24 predict this rate of internet usage? Express your answers as a percentage of the actual values.

27. Carbon dioxide (CO_2) is called a "greenhouse gas" because it traps heat in the atmosphere and helps to increase the average surface temperature of the earth. Climatologists believe that, without greenhouse gases, the earth would be as much as 33°C colder. According to some proponents of global warming, CO_2 should be considered a pollutant since higher levels of this gas in the atmosphere are purportedly the main cause of higher surface temperatures on earth. Which of the

statements below support the conclusion that higher CO_2 levels *are correlated* to higher temperatures? Which statements support the conclusion that higher CO_2 levels *actually cause* the higher temperatures? Which statements support neither conclusion?

(a) Ice core records from the Vostok Research Station in Antarctica show that, over the past million years, colder glacial periods have been marked by lower atmospheric CO_2 levels, while warmer interglacial periods have been marked by higher CO_2 levels.

(b) The same ice core records show that the rise in temperature at the start of each interglacial period precedes the corresponding rise in CO_2 levels by about 800 years.

(c) Scientists have found no evidence that the level of CO_2 in the atmosphere changed during Medieval Warm Period (c. 950 – 1250 AD) or during the Little Ice Age (c. 1550 – 1850 AD).

(d) Over the last 150 years, the level of CO_2 in the atmosphere has increased from 270 ppm to 390 ppm. Over the same time span, the surface of the earth has warmed by $0.8°C$.

28. Suppose that we are given two data points (x_1, y_1) and (x_2, y_2) with different x-coordinates. Verify that the slope of the linear function given by Theorem 2.1 is equal to

$$m_* = \frac{y_1 - y_2}{x_1 - x_2}.$$

What is the geometric significance of this result?

29. Suppose that we are given three different data points (x_1, y_1), (x_1, y_2), and (x_1, y_3), all with precisely the same x-coordinate. Explain why the slope m_* and the y-intercept b_* of the linear function given by Theorem 2.1 are both undefined. What is the geometric significance of this result?

30. Verify that the slope m_* and the y-intercept b_* of the linear function given by Theorem 2.1 satisfy each of the following equations.

(a) $S\, m_* + X\, b_* = P$ 　　　　　　　　　(b) $X\, m_* + n\, b_* = Y$

2.3. Linear Transformations

As you brush your teeth in front of the bathroom mirror every morning, you may have noticed that the person that you see on the other side of the mirror holds his toothbrush with the opposite hand than you do. This happens because mirrors swap points on the left with points on the right, and vice versa. In contrast, mirrors do not swap points vertically, interchanging up with down. This is certainly unremarkable, until we ask ourselves how the mirror knows the difference. How *does* a mirror distinguish between left and right and up and down? And how can it continue to do so even after it is rotated, hung on its side, or taken up to the International Space Station where the effects of gravity are otherwise negligible? These questions might lead us to seriously ponder the inner-workings of mirrors.

As it turns out, the answer to our conundrum rests on the fact that the person looking into the mirror is (presumably) a human being from planet Earth, and not a giant hyperintelligent amoeboid from the Betelgeuse solar system, if you believe in that sort of thing. The human body has **bilateral symmetry**, which is just a fancy way of saying that a human body with left and right swapped still looks human. The human mind, which is instinctively aware of this fact, will subconsciously interpret the image on the mirror as a person with left and right swapped simply because this is the most reasonable interpretation available. It makes perfect sense to imagine ourselves walking around to the back of the mirror and standing side-by-side next to our reflection. In fact, this is precisely the sort of mental comparison which we are making when we say that the mirror swaps left with right but not up with down. On the other hand, it seems entirely improbable to imagine ourselves jumping up, doing a half-somersault over the top of the mirror, and landing head-first next to our rather impressed, if somewhat surprised, reflection. However, if we were to do so, we would find that our left and right sides would match those of our reflection, but that up and down have now been swapped. The point is that we can only make a statement about which directions (left and right or up and down) have been swapped by a mirror if we can place the original image side-by-side with its reflection. In the case of our own reflection, this side-by-side comparison can only happen in our imagination.

This sort of difficulty does not hamper us when we look at the reflection of a graph in the Cartesian plane because, in this case, the original graph and its mirror image *can* be placed side-by-side. In particular, a reflection in the xy-plane can swap points horizontally, vertically, or both. For example, consider the graph of the square root function

$$f(x) = \sqrt{x}$$

which looks like the top half of a parabola starting at the origin and opening to the right, as illustrated in Figure 2.6 (a). We can reflect this graph across the y-axis by moving every point on the right hand side of the graph to the left hand side, and vice versa. More precisely, imagine lifting the graph up, out of the Cartesian plane, flipping it by 180° around the y-axis, and placing it back on the plane. This flip

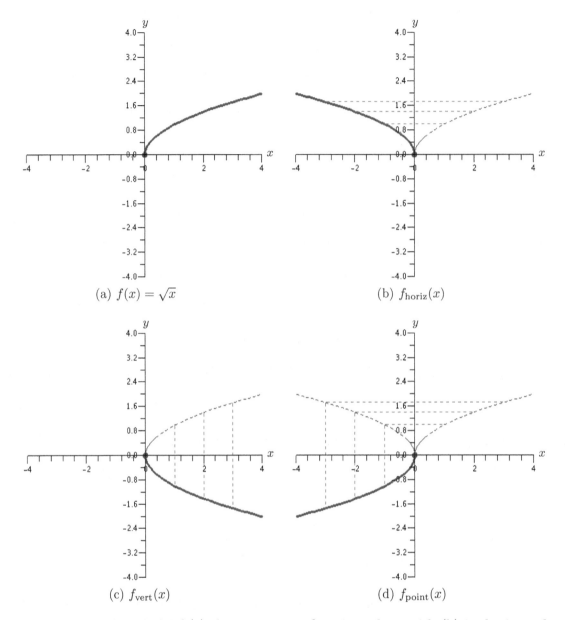

(a) $f(x) = \sqrt{x}$ (b) $f_{\mathrm{horiz}}(x)$

(c) $f_{\mathrm{vert}}(x)$ (d) $f_{\mathrm{point}}(x)$

FIGURE 2.6. The graph of (a) the square root function, along with (b) its horizontal reflection, (c) its vertical reflection, and (d) its point reflection about the origin. Note that the modifiers "vertical" and "horizontal" do not refer to the axis of reflection, but rather to the *motion* (dashed lines) of the reflection.

moves every point on the graph horizontally to a spot the same distance away from, but on the opposite side of, the y-axis. In particular, points on the right are swapped with points on the left and vice versa, as in Figure 2.6 (b). Notice that the result is the top half of a parabola that opens to the left instead of the right. This new graph defines a function f_{horiz} that we shall call the ***horizontal reflection*** of f about the y-axis.

We can also reflect our graph vertically, swapping the points above the x-axis with those below. As before, we can think of this reflection as lifting the graph out of the plane, flipping it by 180° around the x-axis, and placing it back in the plane. Such a reflection will move each point on the graph vertically, to the opposite side of the x-axis. In our case, the result will be the bottom half of a parabola opening to the right, as shown in Figure 2.6 (c). We refer to the function f_{vert} described by this graph as the **vertical reflection** of f about the x-axis.

A third possibility consists of reflecting our graph both horizontally *and* vertically. Observe that the result does not depend on whether we reflect first horizontally and then vertically, as we have done in Figure 2.6 (d), or the other way around. Either way, we obtain a copy of the original graph rotated, just like a pinwheel, 180° around origin. In particular, this type of reflection will move each point in our graph to a spot the same distance away from, but on the opposite side of, the origin. The function f_{point} defined by this new graph is called the **point reflection** of f about the origin. This is the sort of reflection that you might see when you look into a concave spherical mirror such as the inside of a well-polished silver spoon.

Let us consider an arbitrary point (x, y) in the graph of an arbitrary function f. A horizontal reflection will swap this point with one an equal distance away from, but on the opposite side of, the y-axis. In other words, a horizontal reflection will change the sign in the x-coordinate of our point:

$$(x, y) \quad \xleftarrow{\text{horizontal reflection}} \quad (-x, y).$$

In terms of the function f, this change of sign corresponds to multiplying the input to the function (corresponding to the x-coordinates in its graph) times negative one before evaluating the function, so

$$\boxed{f_{\text{horiz}}(x) = f(-x).}$$

On the other hand, a vertical reflection will interchange an arbitrary point in the graph of f with one an equal distance away from, but on the other side of, the x-axis. Again, we can think of this reflection as a simple change of sign, this time in the y-coordinate of our point:

$$(x, y) \quad \xleftarrow{\text{vertical reflection}} \quad (x, -y).$$

Hence, the vertical reflection of f about the x-axis is obtained by multiplying the output values of the function (corresponding to the y-coordinates in its graph) times negative one after the function is evaluated,

$$\boxed{f_{\text{vert}}(x) = -f(x).}$$

Finally, a point reflection about the origin will perform both of these sign changes simultaneously:

$$\big(x, y\big) \quad \xleftrightarrow{\text{point reflection}} \quad \big(-x, -y\big).$$

Therefore, the point reflection of f about the origin is obtained by multiplying both the input and the output values of f times negative one,

$$\boxed{f_{\text{point}}(x) = -f(-x).}$$

Although all of these formulas look deceivingly similar, you should keep in mind that, for most functions, these three reflections produce entirely different results.

EXAMPLE 2.17. Let us take another look at the square root function

$$f(x) = \sqrt{x},$$

whose horizontal, vertical, and point reflections are given by the formulas

$$f_{\text{horiz}}(x) = f(-x) = \sqrt{-x},$$

$$f_{\text{vert}}(x) = -f(x) = -\sqrt{x},$$

$$f_{\text{point}}(x) = -f(-x) = -\sqrt{-x}.$$

In each case, the reflection is well-defined whenever the number inside the square root in the formula is non-negative; furthermore, the square root in each formula will only produce non-negative values. Therefore, we have

$$\text{Domain } f_{\text{horiz}} = \big(-\infty, 0\big], \qquad \text{Image } f_{\text{horiz}} = \big[0, \infty\big),$$

$$\text{Domain } f_{\text{vert}} = \big[0, \infty\big), \qquad \text{Image } f_{\text{vert}} = \big(-\infty, 0\big],$$

$$\text{Domain } f_{\text{point}} = \big(-\infty, 0\big], \qquad \text{Image } f_{\text{point}} = \big(-\infty, 0\big].$$

These differences in domain and image become self-evident when we re-examine the graphs pictured in Figure 2.6. They point to the fact that f and its three reflections really are distinct functions.

EXAMPLE 2.18. Consider the linear function

$$f(x) = 3x + 6.$$

As noted above, we obtain formulas for this function's horizontal and vertical reflections by multiplying its input or output values times minus one:

$$f_{\text{horiz}}(x) = f(-x) = 3(-x) + 6 = -3x + 6,$$

$$f_{\text{vert}}(x) = -f(x) = -(3x + 6) = -3x - 6.$$

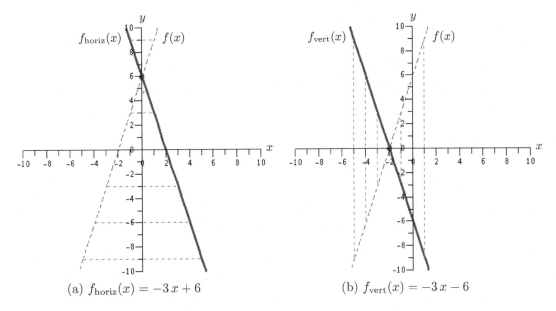

(a) $f_{\mathrm{horiz}}(x) = -3\,x + 6$ (b) $f_{\mathrm{vert}}(x) = -3\,x - 6$

FIGURE 2.7. The graphs of the (a) horizontal and (b) vertical reflections of the linear function $f(x) = 3\,x + 6$.

Figure 2.7 shows how the graph of each one of these reflections is a line. This, of course, is to be expected since a reflection should not change the general shape of a graph. After all, reflecting a line always will always produce another line. You should observe how the slopes have changed from 3 in the original function to -3 in each reflection. Although the reflections are decreasing instead of increasing, they are just as steep as the original graph. Furthermore, you should note how the original function f shares its y-intercept at $(0, 6)$ with f_{horiz} and its x-intercept at $(-2, 0)$ with f_{vert}. Once again, this will be true in general: A horizontal reflection will keep all of the points of the y-axis (including any y-intercepts) fixed in place, just as a vertical reflection will keep all of the points of the x-axis (including any x-intercepts) fixed in place.

A function and its reflections are cousins of sorts. Although they each have their own distinguishing features, they are members of the same family of functions, all bearing a strong resemblance to one another both in their formulas and in the overall shape of their graphs. The slight differences arise as the input and output values of our original function are modified in some relatively simple way. In the case of our horizontal, vertical, and point reflections, the modification involved multiplication times negative one, but this is only one of many possibilities, each presenting us with a new branch in our function's family tree. For instance, we might choose to multiply by a different constant, or perhaps to add a constant, or maybe to perform some other combination of adding and multiplying. Each one of these possibilities is called a **_linear transformation_** of our original function, and has a slightly different effect on the graph of our function. We shall consider each possibility in turn.

First, let us suppose that the *output* of a function f is multiplied by a positive constant a (with $a \neq 1$), thereby producing a new function g defined as follows:

$$g(x) = a \cdot f(x).$$

When a is a large number, the graph of g will look like a stretched version of the graph of f, in which all points have moved vertically away from the x-axis. For instance, the vertical distance from each point to the x-axis will be doubled if $a = 2$, tripled if $a = 3$, quintupled if $a = 5$, and so on. On the other hand, if a is a small number, the graph of g will look like a compressed version of the graph of f in which all points have moved vertically towards the x-axis. For example, the vertical distance to the x-axis will be cut in half when $a = \frac{1}{2}$, by a third when $a = \frac{1}{3}$, and by two fifths when $a = \frac{2}{5}$. The distinction between "large" and "small" depends on whether $a > 1$ (in which case the graph is stretched) or $0 < a < 1$ (in which case the graph is compressed). In either case, the new graph will be a replica of the old graph of f, except that it will be a times as tall as the original. Thus, we shall refer to our new function g as the **vertical dilation** of f by a factor of a.

EXAMPLE 2.19. Consider the vertical dilations of the square root function

$$f(x) = \sqrt{x}$$

by a factor of two and by a factor of one half. As we discussed above, these two functions are given by the formulas

$$g(x) = 2\sqrt{x} \qquad \text{and} \qquad h(x) = \tfrac{1}{2}\sqrt{x}.$$

Note that the graphs of these dilations, which are displayed in Figure 2.8, have the general shape of a half-parabola that opens to the right, just like the graph of the model function f, which appears as a dashed curve in each figure. However, the graph of g is a stretched version of the graph of f. It is as if each point in the original graph had been pushed vertically away from the x-axis, following the dashed lines in Figure 2.8 (a), to a location twice its original distance from the axis. Only the x-intercept at the origin remains unmoved throughout this dilation. The end result is that the graph of g appears to be twice as tall as the original graph of f.

In contrast, the graph of h is a compressed version of the graph of f. In this case, the dilation has pulled each point in the original graph closer toward the x-axis, along the dashed lines in Figure 2.8 (b), until it lies at half its original distance from the axis. Again, only the x-intercept at the origin escapes the compressing effects of the dilation. In the end, the graph of h appears to be only half as tall as the original graph.

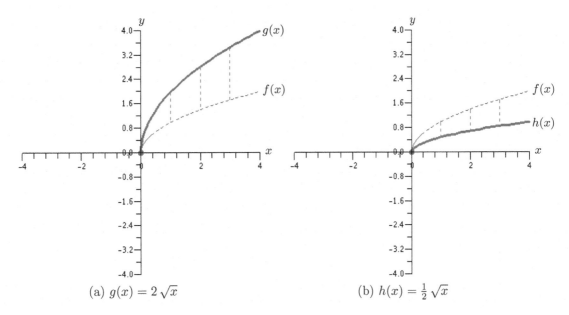

(a) $g(x) = 2\sqrt{x}$ (b) $h(x) = \frac{1}{2}\sqrt{x}$

FIGURE 2.8. The graphs of two vertical dilations of the function $f(x) = \sqrt{x}$.

Next, suppose that the *input* values to the function f are multiplied by a positive constant b (with $b \neq 1$) before the function is evaluated, as in the formula below:

$$g(x) = f(b \cdot x).$$

As in our discussion above, depending on the value of the constant b, the graph of the function g will be either a stretched or a compressed version of the original graph. However, in this case the situation is somewhat more delicate. In particular, the points of the new graph will be closer to the y-axis when b is a large number, and farther away from the y-axis when b is a small number. As before, the distinction between "large" and "small" depends on whether $b > 1$ or $0 < b < 1$, except that this time around, it is the large values of b that will compress the graph horizontally towards the y-axis, and it is the small values of b that will stretch it away from the y-axis. For example, the horizontal distance from any given point to the y-axis will be cut in half when $b = 2$, to one third when $b = 3$, and to one seventh when $b = 7$. In contrast, the same distance will be doubled when $b = \frac{1}{2}$, tripled when $b = \frac{1}{3}$, and multiplied by seven when $b = \frac{1}{7}$. You might find this situation a bit counterintuitive at first, especially since it is precisely the opposite of what happened earlier, when we were looking at vertical dilations. At any rate, the new graph will appear to be $\frac{1}{b}$ times as wide as the original, so we refer to our new function as the ***horizontal dilation*** of f by a factor of $\frac{1}{b}$.

EXAMPLE 2.20. We can recognize the functions defined by the formulas

$$g(x) = \sqrt{4\,x} \qquad \text{and} \qquad h(x) = \sqrt{\tfrac{1}{4}\,x}$$

as horizontal dilations of the square root function $f(x) = \sqrt{x}$ because their inputs are multiplied by 4 and by $\tfrac{1}{4}$, respectively, before the square roots are evaluated. Both of their graphs, shown in Figure 2.9, have the same overall shape as that of the graph of f (shown as a dashed curve). However, the graph of g is compressed by a dilation factor of $\tfrac{1}{4}$ as its points are pulled horizontally from the original graph, along the dashed lines in Figure 2.9 (a), until they lie at one fourth of their original distance to the y-axis. Thus, the new graph appears to be one fourth as wide as the original. In the meanwhile, the graph of h is stretched out horizontally by a dilation factor of 4, as all of the points in the graph of f are pushed away from the y-axis, following the dashed lines in Figure 2.9 (b). This makes the graph of h appear to be four times as wide as the original graph of f. As is to be expected, in each case, the y-intercept at the origin remains fixed by the horizontal dilation.

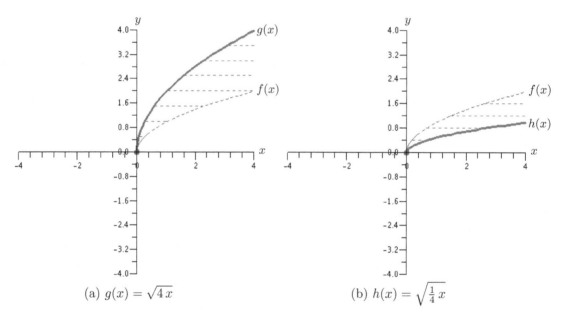

(a) $g(x) = \sqrt{4\,x}$ \qquad\qquad (b) $h(x) = \sqrt{\tfrac{1}{4}\,x}$

FIGURE 2.9. The graphs of two horizontal dilations of the function $f(x) = \sqrt{x}$.

Perhaps you noticed that the graphs in Figures 2.8 and 2.9 look suspiciously similar. Indeed, both figures show the graphs of exactly the same pair of functions:

$$g(x) = 2\,\sqrt{x} = \sqrt{4\,x} \qquad \text{and} \qquad h(x) = \tfrac{1}{2}\,\sqrt{x} = \sqrt{\tfrac{1}{4}\,x}.$$

In each case, the only distinction between a vertical and a horizontal dilation is a positive constant that can be moved in or out of the square root. Of course, there is a cost to moving the constant; for instance, a 2 outside the root becomes a 4 inside, and a $\tfrac{1}{4}$ inside the root becomes a $\tfrac{1}{2}$ outside. Nevertheless, it is not too difficult to show that any vertical dilation of the square root function is automatically a horizontal dilation, and vice versa, although in general the dilation factors will be different. This is a special property that the square root function shares with the other five model functions. Evidently, for these model functions, interpreting a dilation as either horizontal or vertical is purely a matter of taste. However, as the next example points out, for the vast majority of functions there is a real distinction between horizontal and vertical dilations.

EXAMPLE 2.21. If you will recall from Example 1.76 (see page 111), the graph of the function

$$f(x) = \sqrt{25 - x^2}$$

is a semicircle of radius 5 living above the x-axis, as shown in Figure 2.10 (a). If we multiply this function's output values by $\frac{3}{5}$, we obtain a vertical dilation of the original function, namely

$$g(x) = \frac{3}{5} \sqrt{25 - x^2}.$$

As we can see in Figure 2.10 (b), the graph of this new function is a sort of half-oval (technically, the top half of an **ellipse**) which is just as wide as the original semicircle, but measures only three units from top to bottom. In particular, it has two x-intercepts at $(5, 0)$ and $(-5, 0)$ and a y-intercept at the point $(0, 3)$.

Alternatively, multiplying the input of f by $\frac{5}{2}$ produces a horizontal dilation by a factor of $\frac{2}{5}$:

$$h(x) = \sqrt{25 - \left(\frac{5}{2} x\right)^2}.$$

Note that, in this formula, the multiplication occurs before the input x is even squared. Again, the resulting graph is half of an ellipse, this time just as tall at the original semicircle, but measuring only four units from side to side. See Figure 2.10 (c). Its graph has its x-intercepts at $(2, 0)$ and at $(-2, 0)$, and its y-intercept at $(0, 5)$.

Finally, consider what happens when we multiply the output of f by $\frac{3}{5}$, and at the same time we multiply its input by $\frac{5}{2}$:

$$j(x) = \frac{3}{5} \sqrt{25 - \left(\frac{5}{2} x\right)^2}.$$

In this case, j will be a **composition** (in other words, a combination) of the two dilations above. For instance, we might imagine starting with the graph of f, dilating vertically by a factor of $\frac{3}{5}$, and then dilating a second time, horizontally, by a factor of $\frac{2}{5}$. Of course, we could also perform the two dilations in the opposite order – first horizontally and then vertically. In either case, the end result would be the half-ellipse measuring four units from side to side, and three units from top to bottom, as shown in Figure 2.10 (d).

Observe that f and g share the same x-intercepts, so that their graphs are equally wide. Similarly, f and h share the same y-intercept, making their graphs equally tall. This means that, in the case of this specific function, there is no confusing a vertical with a horizontal dilation. In particular, the graph of j, which is distinctly thinner and shorter than the graph of f, cannot be the result of a single dilation.

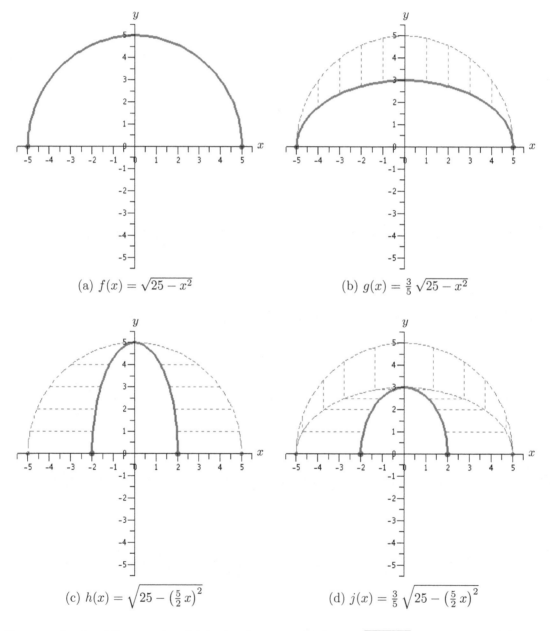

(a) $f(x) = \sqrt{25 - x^2}$

(b) $g(x) = \frac{3}{5}\sqrt{25 - x^2}$

(c) $h(x) = \sqrt{25 - \left(\frac{5}{2}x\right)^2}$

(d) $j(x) = \frac{3}{5}\sqrt{25 - \left(\frac{5}{2}x\right)^2}$

FIGURE 2.10. The graph of (a) the function $f(x) = \sqrt{25 - x^2}$, along with (b) its vertical dilation by a factor of $\frac{3}{5}$, (c) its horizontal dilation by a factor of $\frac{2}{5}$, and (d) the composition of both of these dilations together.

EXAMPLE 2.22. If we multiply either the input or the output of a function by a *negative* constant, then we can consider the result as the composition of a reflection together with a dilation. For instance, suppose that we multiply the output values of the square root function

$$f(x) = \sqrt{x}$$

times negative two, producing the new function

$$g(x) = -2\sqrt{x}.$$

In essence, this amounts to multiplying f twice: first by -1, thereby causing a vertical reflection, and then by 2, producing a vertical dilation:

$$\boxed{f(x) = \sqrt{x}} \xrightarrow{\text{reflection}} \boxed{f_{\text{vert}}(x) = -\sqrt{x}} \xrightarrow{\text{dilation}} \boxed{g(x) = -2\sqrt{x}}$$

Figure 2.11 shows each of the steps in this composition. Of course, we would have been perfectly justified in doing things in the opposite order, first dilating and then reflecting, just as we we would have been perfectly justified in multiplying first by 2 and then by -1. In either case, the final effect would still be the same: a mathematical sort of "fun-house mirror" in which our graph is not only reflected but also stretched out. Thus, the graph of g consists of the bottom half of a parabola which dips twice as far below the x-axis as the original graph of f went above the axis.

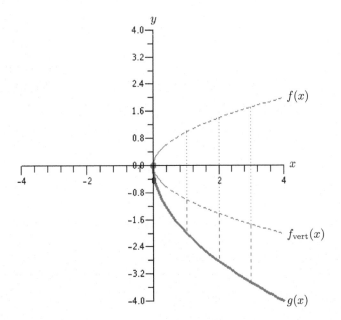

FIGURE 2.11. The composition of a vertical reflection (dotted lines) and a vertical dilation (dashed lines) of the square root function $f(x) = \sqrt{x}$.

The last type of transformation that we will consider occurs when a constant (which may be either a positive or a negative number) is added either to the input or to the output values of the function f, as in the functions

$$g(x) = f(x + c) \qquad \text{and} \qquad h(x) = f(x) + d.$$

The graph of each of these functions is an identical copy of the original graph of f that has been moved either to the left or to the right (in the case of g) or up or down (in the case of h), depending on whether the constant in question is positive or negative. For example, the graph of g will slide to the left when c is positive, and to the right when c is negative. We refer to g as a **horizontal translation** of the function f. On the other hand, the graph of the function h slides up when d is positive, and down when d is negative. We shall refer to h as a **vertical translation** of the original function f. In either case, the distance that the translated graph moves is given by the absolute value of the constant added, which of course is always positive.

EXAMPLE 2.23. Consider the following four translations of the square root function $f(x) = \sqrt{x}$:

$$g_1(x) = \sqrt{x + \tfrac{3}{2}}, \qquad\qquad g_2(x) = \sqrt{x - \tfrac{3}{2}},$$

$$h_1(x) = \sqrt{x} + \tfrac{3}{2}, \qquad\qquad h_2(x) = \sqrt{x} - \tfrac{3}{2}.$$

Their graphs are shown in Figure 2.12. Since the functions g_1 and g_2 are the result of adding $\pm\tfrac{3}{2}$ to the input of the square root, they are both horizontal translations of f. In contrast, the functions h_1 and h_2 are obtained by adding $\pm\tfrac{3}{2}$ to the output of the square root, and so they are both vertical translations of f. Note that the four graphs are identical to the original graph of f (shown in dashed lines in Figure 2.12), except for the fact that they start at points $\tfrac{3}{2}$ units to the left of, or to the right of, or above, or below the origin, respectively.

Observe that horizontal dilations and horizontal translations behave somewhat counterintuitively. In each of these transformations, you modify the input to a function before that function is evaluated, and in each case, that modification has the opposite effect of what you might otherwise expect. Thus, multiplying by a large number causes the graph to shrink, while multiplying by a small number causes the graph to expand. Similarly, adding a positive number causes the graph to slide to the left (in other words, in the direction of negative x's), while adding a negative number causes it to slide to the right (in the direction of positive x's). This experience might remind you of working with a microscope in one of your biology classes. If you want the paramecium that you are looking at to go in one direction, then you have to move the slide it is sitting on in the opposite direction. For these horizontal transformations, as well as for microscopes, the rule of thumb is to always do the opposite of what your instincts first tell you to do.

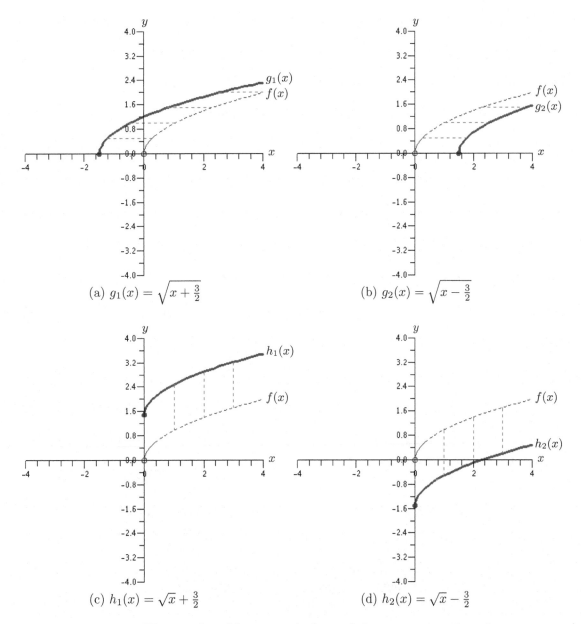

FIGURE 2.12. The graphs of four translations of the square root function.

Now that we understand the individual effects of modifying either the input or the output of a function by adding or multiplying by a constant, we can consider a **general linear transformation** in which all of these modifications might occur at once. In particular, suppose that f is a function and that a, b, c, and d are all constants, and let us define a new function g by the formula

$$g(x) = a \cdot f\big(b\left(x + c\right)\big) + d.$$

Depending on the values of the constants, our new function will be some composition of reflections, dilations, and translations of the original function f. In particular, this linear transformation will consist of:

① a vertical reflection about the x-axis if a is negative,

② a horizontal reflection about the y-axis if b is negative,

③ a vertical dilation by a factor of $|a|$ (expanding if $|a| > 1$ and contracting if $0 < |a| < 1$),

④ a horizontal dilation by a factor of $\left|\frac{1}{b}\right|$ (contracting if $|b| > 1$ and expanding if $0 < |b| < 1$),

⑤ a horizontal translation by $|c|$ units (sliding to the left if c is positive and to the right if c is negative),

⑥ a vertical translation by $|d|$ units (sliding up if d is positive and down if d is negative).

Together with a good field guide of model functions (such as the one provided in Example 1.69 on pages 99 and 100), this decomposition into linear transformations enables us to graph an entire menagerie of functions, all without the hassles of plotting lots of points. As we do so, we need to keep in mind that the order in which we perform these steps is important. In particular, we must complete all of our reflections and dilations before we even consider any translations. Following a different order is likely to affect the end result and leave us with the wrong answer.

EXAMPLE 2.24. Consider the function

$$g(x) = 1 - \sqrt{3x + 5},$$

which we first rewrite in the form of a general linear transformation as:

$$g(x) = -1 \cdot \sqrt{3\left(x + \tfrac{5}{3}\right)} + 1.$$

Note that this requires that we factor the quantity inside the square root. In terms of the formula for a general linear transformation, we have $a = -1$, $b = 3$, $c = \frac{5}{3}$, and $d = 1$. Thus, our transformation is the composition of:

① a vertical reflection (since a is negative),

② a horizontal dilation contracting by a factor of $\frac{1}{3}$ (since $b = 3$),

③ a horizontal translation sliding to the left by $\frac{5}{3}$ units (since $c = \frac{5}{3}$),

④ a vertical translation sliding up by 1 unit (since $d = 1$).

In particular, observe that our transformation does not include any vertical dilations (since $|a| = 1$) or any horizontal reflections (since b is positive). We can interpret this composition as a sequence of steps, as illustrated in Figure 2.13. As expected, the graphs of four intermediate steps have the same general shape, but each one has its own distinguishing peculiarities.

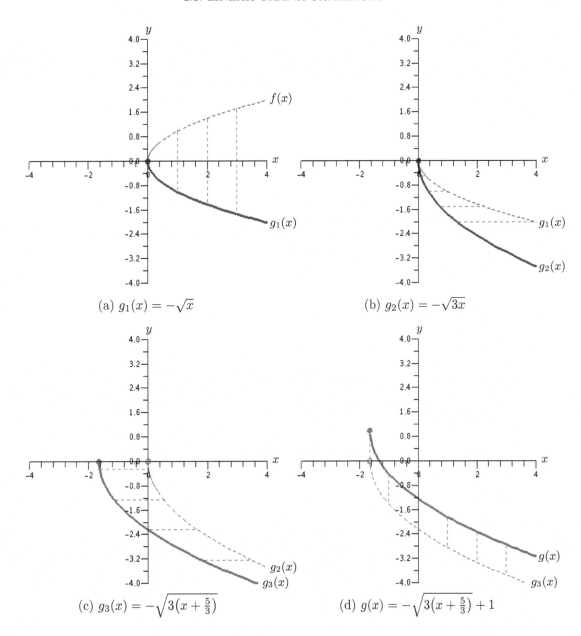

(a) $g_1(x) = -\sqrt{x}$

(b) $g_2(x) = -\sqrt{3x}$

(c) $g_3(x) = -\sqrt{3\left(x + \frac{5}{3}\right)}$

(d) $g(x) = -\sqrt{3\left(x + \frac{5}{3}\right)} + 1$

FIGURE 2.13. The function $g(x) = 1 - \sqrt{3x + 5}$ as a composition of linear transformations of the square root function $f(x) = \sqrt{x}$. The composition consists of (a) a vertical reflection, (b) a horizontal dilation contracting by a factor of $\frac{1}{3}$, (c) a horizontal translation moving $\frac{5}{3}$ units to the left, and (d) a vertical translation moving 1 unit up:

$$\boxed{f(x)} \xrightarrow[\text{reflection}]{\text{vertical}} \boxed{g_1(x)} \xrightarrow[\text{dilation}]{\text{horizontal}} \boxed{g_2(x)} \xrightarrow[\text{translation}]{\text{horizontal}} \boxed{g_3(x)} \xrightarrow[\text{translation}]{\text{vertical}} \boxed{g(x)}$$

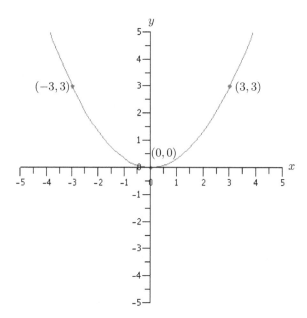

FIGURE 2.14. The graph of a mystery function g.

EXAMPLE 2.25. Consider the function g whose graph is shown Figure 2.14. Since we recognize this graph as a parabola, we will presume that g is a linear transformation of the model function

$$f(x) = x^2.$$

We begin our analysis by noting that our parabola opens upward, just like the model function. Therefore, our linear transformation will not involve any reflections.

Next, we take note of the local minimum at the origin. This minimum is a uniquely recognizable point in the graph of g, and must therefore correspond to the local minimum in the graph of the model function. Since both local minima occur at the origin, we can conclude that our linear transformation does not exhibit any translations either.

To determine whether our mystery function is a dilation of f, we shall measure a horizontal run and a vertical rise between two points in our mystery graph, and compare them to the corresponding rise and run in the graph of the model function. For the two points in the graph of g, we might consider our local minimum at $(0,0)$ and the point $(3,3)$. This gives us a run of $\Delta x = 3$ and a rise of $\Delta y = 3$.

Let us suppose, then, that our mystery function g is a vertical dilation of f, stretching vertical distances but leaving horizontal distances intact. In the graph of the model function, a horizontal run of $\Delta x = 3$ would take us from the local minimum at $(0,0)$ to a point with $x = 3$. Since $f(3) = 9$, the point in question is $(3,9)$, which then marks a rise of $\Delta y = 9$. This means that the rise of $\Delta y = 9$ in the graph of f is contracted to a rise of $\Delta y = 3$ in the graph of g, as shown below:

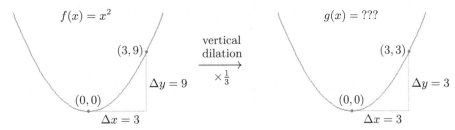

Evidently, our mystery function must be the result of a vertical dilation contracting the the graph of f by a factor of $\frac{1}{3}$, and can therefore be described by the formula

$$g(x) = \tfrac{1}{3}\, x^2.$$

Alternatively, we could assume that g is a horizontal dilation of the model function f. In that case, we would find that horizontal distances would be stretched and vertical distance would remain the same. In particular, we note that a rise of $\Delta y = 3$ in the graph of f would take us from the local minimum at $(0,0)$ to a point with $y = 3$, which we can locate by solving the equation

$$x^2 = 3.$$

The point in question is $(\sqrt{3}, 3)$, indicating a run of $\Delta x = \sqrt{3}$. This means that the run of $\Delta x = \sqrt{3}$ in the graph of f has been expanded to a run of $\Delta x = 3$ in the graph of g, as illustrated below:

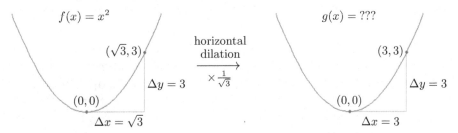

Consequently, our mystery function is a horizontal dilation of f by a factor of $\sqrt{3}$. Remembering to multiply the input of our model function by the reciprocal of this dilation factor, we arrive at the formula

$$g(x) = \left(\tfrac{1}{\sqrt{3}}\, x\right)^2.$$

Of course, either approach results in an equivalent formula for g, since

$$g(x) = \left(\tfrac{1}{\sqrt{3}}\, x\right)^2 = \tfrac{1}{3}\, x^2.$$

As we noted earlier, for our six model functions from Example 1.69, which point of view we take is purely a matter of personal preference.

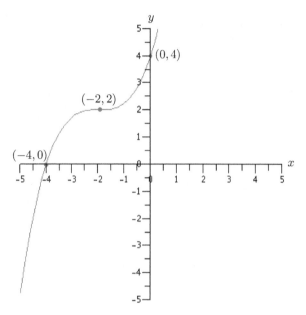

FIGURE 2.15. The graph of a mystery function h.

EXAMPLE 2.26. Consider the function h whose graph appears in Figure 2.15. This graph has the same over-all shape as the graph of the model cubic function shown in Figure 1.22 (d) on page 100, so we can think of our function as a general linear transformation of $f(x) = x^3$:

$$h(x) = a \cdot \big(b(x + c)\big)^3 + d.$$

Since our graph is increasing throughout the entire domain, the linear transformation in question must not involve any reflections. On the other hand, note the flat spot at the point $(-2, 2)$. This point corresponds to the flat spot at the origin in the graph of the model function f, indicating that h has been translated two units to the left and two units up. Finally, observe that between the flat spot at $(-2, 2)$ and the y-intercept at $(0, 4)$ there is a run of $\Delta x = 2$ and a corresponding rise of $\Delta y = 2$. Now, in the graph of the model cubic function, the same run of $\Delta x = 2$ would take us from the origin to the point $(2, 8)$, and thus corresponds to a rise of $\Delta y = 8$:

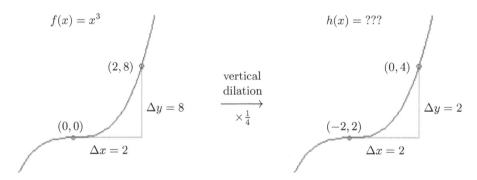

This indicates a vertical dilation by a factor of $\frac{1}{4}$. Collecting all of these facts together, we arrive at the conclusion that our linear transformation must be a composition of:

① a vertical dilation contracting by a factor of $\frac{1}{4}$,

② a horizontal translation sliding to the left by 2 units,

③ a vertical translation sliding up by 2 units.

Consequently, the general linear transformation above must have $a = \frac{1}{4}$ (to produce the vertical dilation), $c = 2$ (to produce the horizontal translation), and $d = 2$ (to produce the vertical translation). Furthermore, since we do not need any horizontal reflections or dilations, we must have $b = 1$. Hence our mystery function is described by the formula

$$h(x) = \tfrac{1}{4}(x+2)^3 + 2.$$

EXAMPLE 2.27. The graph of the function j displayed in Figure 2.16 is shaped like an upside-down letter V. Thus, j is a linear transformation of the absolute value function:

$$j(x) = a \cdot \big| b(x+c) \big| + d.$$

Since the graph of the absolute value function is shaped like a right-side-up V, our linear transformation must involve a vertical reflection. Furthermore, our graph's maximum at the point $(2, 3)$ corresponds to the absolute value's minimum at the origin. This means that our graph has also been translated two units to the right and three units up. Finally, in order to determine

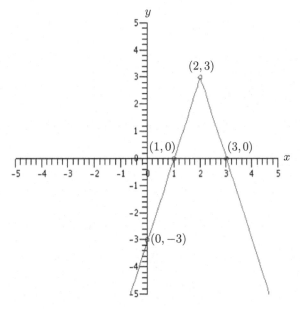

FIGURE 2.16. The graph of a mystery function j.

whether any dilations form part of our transformation, we note that, between the local maximum at $(2,3)$ and the x-intercept at $(3,0)$, our graph has a horizontal run of $\Delta x = 1$ and a corresponding vertical rise of $\Delta y = 3$. On the graph of the absolute value function, however, a horizontal run of $\Delta x = 1$ corresponds to a vertical rise of $\Delta y = 1$. This indicates a vertical dilation by a factor of 3, as shown below:

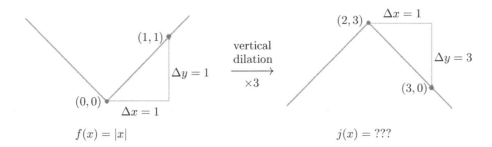

In summary, then, our linear transformation must be a composition of:

① a vertical reflection,

② a vertical dilation expanding by a factor of 3,

③ a horizontal translation sliding to the right by 2 units,

④ a vertical translation sliding up by 3 units.

To produce the vertical reflection and dilation, we must set $a = -3$; similarly, to produce the translations, we must set $c = -2$ and $d = 3$. Furthermore, since we have no horizontal reflections or dilations, we must once again set $b = 1$. Therefore, our mystery function is given by the formula

$$j(x) = -3\left|x - 2\right| + 3.$$

As we have seen in the examples above, having a clear understanding of linear transformations can enhance our ability to graph a variety of functions. In some cases, it also provides us with an effective method for moving from the graph of a function to its formula. In the next section, we will explore these ideas further as we set our sights specifically on the model function $f(x) = x^2$ and all of its linear transformations.

Reading Comprehension Questions for Section 2.3

A linear transformation of f is a function defined by a combination of ___(a)___ (through which points on one side of the graph are moved to the other side, and vice versa), ___(b)___ (through which the graph is expanded or contracted), and ___(c)___ (through which the graph is moved rigidly on the xy-plane). All of these effects can be created by ___(d)___ or ___(e)___ the input or output of f with a constant.

Modifying the ___(f)___ of f results in a vertical transformation. If a positive number is added to it, then the graph moves ___(g)___; if a negative number is added to it, the graph moves ___(h)___. Similarly, multiplying times a large positive number (greater than ___(i)___) makes the graph appear to be ___(j)___ (shorter or taller). On the other hand, multiplying times a small number (between ___(k)___ and ___(l)___) makes the graph appear ___(m)___ (shorter or taller). Finally, multiplying times a ___(n)___ number swaps the points on the top of the graph with those on the bottom of the graph.

In contrast, modifying the ___(o)___ of f results in a horizontal transformation. If a positive number is added to it, then the graph moves to the ___(p)___; if a negative number is added to it, the graph moves to the ___(q)___. Multiplying times a large positive number makes the graph appear ___(r)___ (thinner or wider), while multiplying times a small number makes the graph appear to be ___(s)___ (thinner or wider). Finally, multiplying times a ___(t)___ number swaps the points on the left of the graph with those on the right of the graph.

For example, consider the function

$$g(x) = 5 - \sqrt{3(x - 2)},$$

which is a linear transformation of the model function $f(x) = $ ___(u)___. Its graph will look similar to that of the model function, except that it will be reflected ___(v)___ (horizontally or vertically), ___(w)___ (contracted or expanded) horizontally, and translated both vertically and horizontally. When all of these transformations are taken into account, we will observe the graph will look like a sideways half-parabola that starts at the point ___(x)___ and extends ___(y)___ (up or down) and to the ___(z)___ (right or left).

Exercises for Section 2.3

In Exercises 1–6, each graph illustrates a linear transformation that was applied to one of the six model functions from Example 1.69. Determine the model function, the linear transformation, and the formula for the resulting function.

1.

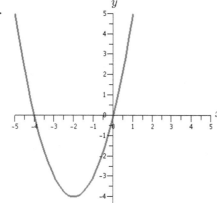

2.

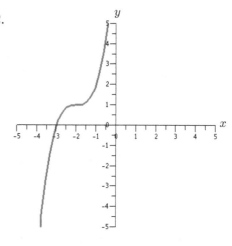

3.

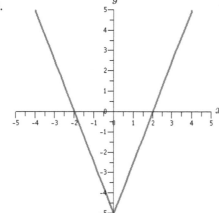

4.

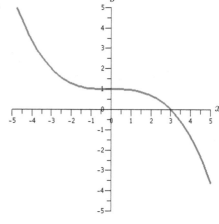

5.

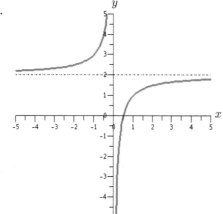

6.

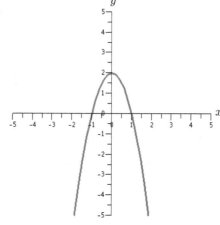

In Exercises 7–18, interpret each function as a linear transformation of one of the six model functions from Example 1.69. Use this information to sketch its graph.

7. $g(x) = (x - 2)^2$

8. $g(x) = |x| - 7$

9. $g(x) = -2 \cdot \dfrac{1}{x}$

10. $g(x) = \sqrt{3x}$

11. $g(x) = |x + 5|$

12. $g(x) = -\dfrac{1}{x - 4}$

13. $g(x) = 3(x + 1)^2$

14. $g(x) = 1 + |2x|$

15. $g(x) = 5\sqrt{x} - 2$

16. $g(x) = \dfrac{1}{3x} + 1$

17. $g(x) = (6 - 2x)^3$

18. $g(x) = \dfrac{1}{3x - 3} + 1$

In Exercises 19–24, each function is given by two equivalent formulas. First, verify that both formulas really are equivalent. Then, sketch the graph of the function by applying the techniques described in Section 1.6 to the first formula. Finally, sketch the graph a second time by interpreting the second formula as a linear transformation of one of the six model functions from Example 1.69. Do the two graphs agree with one another?

19. $g(x) = (x + 5)(x - 1) = (x + 2)^2 - 9$

20. $g(x) = \dfrac{x - 3}{x - 4} = \dfrac{1}{x - 4} + 1$

21. $g(x) = (1 - x)(x - 9) = -1 \cdot (x - 5)^2 + 16$

22. $g(x) = \dfrac{3x - 7}{x - 2} = -1 \cdot \left(\dfrac{1}{x - 2}\right) + 3$

23. $g(x) = (2x + 4)(x + 4) = 2 \cdot (x + 3)^2 - 2$

24. $g(x) = \dfrac{2x - 6}{x - 4} = 2 \cdot \left(\dfrac{1}{x - 4}\right) + 2$

25. A function f is said to be **even** if it equals its own horizontal reflection about the y-axis. In other words, f is even if and only if

$$f(-x) = f(x).$$

Determine which of the six model functions from Example 1.69 are even.

26. A function f is said to be **odd** if it equals its own point reflection about the origin. In other words, f is odd if and only if

$$f(-x) = -f(x).$$

Determine which of the six model functions from Example 1.69 are odd.

27. Which of the following power functions are even? Which are odd? For power functions, how does the characterization of "even" and "odd" depend on the formula for the function?

(a) $f(x) = 3\,x^2$ (b) $f(x) = 2\,x$

(c) $f(x) = \sqrt{5}\,x^{10}$ (d) $f(x) = \frac{2}{43}\,x^{42}$

(e) $f(x) = \pi\,x^{13}$ (f) $f(x) = \frac{5}{7}\,x^{57}$

28. Which of the following polynomial functions are even? Which are odd? For polynomials, how does the characterization of "even" and "odd" depend on the formula for the function?

(a) $f(x) = 2\,x + \pi\,x^{13} + \frac{5}{7}\,x^{57}$ (b) $f(x) = \sqrt{5}\,x^{10} + \frac{2}{43}\,x^{42} + \frac{5}{7}\,x^{57}$

(c) $f(x) = 3\,x^2 + 2\,x + \pi\,x^{13}$ (d) $f(x) = 3\,x^2 + \sqrt{5}\,x^{10} + \frac{2}{43}\,x^{42}$

29. Suppose that the function g is defined by the formula

$$g(x) = (A - 1)\,x^6 + A\,x^5 + 2\,B\,x + C,$$

where A, B, and C are constants. Suppose further that g is an odd function whose graph has an x-intercept at $x = -1$. Determine the values of the constants A, B, and C.

30. Although we use the words "even" and "odd" to describe both integers and functions, the way these adjectives interact in each setting is quite different. Complete the following table comparing the two distinct behaviors.

	integers	functions
even + even		
odd + odd		
even + odd		
even × even		
odd × odd		
even × odd		

2.4. Quadratic Functions

To be fair, J. G. Büttner was probably not so terrible as to deserve the label of "a virile brute ... whose idea of teaching the hundred or so boys in his charge was to thrash them into such a state of terrified stupidity that they forgot their own names."[4] Nevertheless, Master Büttner's fate was sealed on that morning in the winter of 1787, when he walked into his cold, one-room German schoolhouse in Brunswick only to find the pile of ungraded arithmetic quizzes that he had forgotten to take home with him the night before. With a sigh of disgruntlement, he turned to his pupils and announced the day's assignment: "Find the sum of all the numbers from one to a hundred." That should keep the little scoundrels out of trouble while he graded those papers, he thought to himself.

Immediately, the entire class went straight to work: One plus two is three. Three plus three is six. Six plus four is ten... They could not have gotten much farther than that when Carl, a shy little ten-year-old, went up to the teacher and turned in 'his slate. Instead of adding each number one at a time, like all of his classmates were doing, Carl had imagined the whole sum, which we might call S, all at once:

$$S = 1 + 2 + 3 + \cdots + 98 + 99 + 100.$$

Carl figured that he would get the same answer by adding the numbers in the opposite order:

$$S = 100 + 99 + 98 + \cdots + 3 + 2 + 1.$$

What is more, adding these two expressions together gave him a sum consisting of one hundred terms, all equal to 101:

$$2S = \underbrace{101 + 101 + 101 + \cdots + 101 + 101 + 101}_{\text{100 copies of 101}}.$$

This he could easily compute by multiplying,

$$2S = 100 \times 101 = 10100,$$

and thus, after dividing by 2, he arrived at his final answer of

$$S = 5050.$$

To Master Büttner's surprise, the young Carl Friedrich Gauss (whom we already met in passing on page 147) had found the correct answer after just a moment of thought. So much for his quiet morning of grading papers!

There are plenty of lessons to learn from this quaint little story, not the least of which is to never underestimate the insight of a perspicacious grammar school genius. More importantly for us, however, is to note that by taking a clue from young Gauss's

---

[4] E. T. Bell, "Gauss, the Prince of Mathematicians," *Men of Mathematics* (1937).

method, we can add up the terms of any arithmetic sequence such as, for instance, the first n positive odd numbers.

EXAMPLE 2.28. Let $s(n)$ denote the sum of the first n positive odd numbers. Now, the odd numbers form an arithmetic sequence which is evenly spaced by increments of 2:

$$1 \xrightarrow{+2} 3 \xrightarrow{+2} 5 \xrightarrow{+2} 7 \xrightarrow{+2} 9 \xrightarrow{+2} 11 \xrightarrow{+2} 13 \xrightarrow{+2} \cdots .$$

Therefore, the nth odd number, which we shall call $t(n)$, is given by a linear function with slope 2. In particular, since $t(1) = 1$, the point-slope formula gives

$$t(n) = 2(n-1) + 1 = 2n - 1.$$

This means that we can write $s(n)$ as the sum

$$s(n) = 1 + 3 + 5 + \cdots + (2n-5) + (2n-3) + (2n-1).$$

Of course, we can also rewrite this sum in the opposite order, obtaining

$$s(n) = (2n-1) + (2n-3) + (2n-5) + \cdots + 5 + 3 + 1.$$

Adding these two expressions together gives us a sum of n terms, each one of which is equal to $2n$:

$$2\,s(n) = \underbrace{2n + 2n + \cdots + 2n + 2n}_{n \text{ copies of } 2n} = n \cdot 2n = 2n^2.$$

Now, dividing by two, we obtain a more manageable formula for s, namely,

$$s(n) = n^2.$$

This formula tells us that $s(n)$, originally defined as a large and unwieldy sum, is actually a simple polynomial of degree two.

A function f is said to be **quadratic** if it is a polynomial of degree two. This means that f is defined by a formula of the form

$$\boxed{f(x) = a\,x^2 + b\,x + c,}$$

where the coefficients a, b, c are fixed real numbers and a is not zero. These same coefficients were called a_2, a_1, and a_0 back on page 54, but after all, "what's in a name? That which we call a rose by any other name would smell as sweet."[5] The word "quadratic" comes from the Latin word for square. This is a good way to remember that the most complicated thing in the formula for a quadratic function is supposed to be the square of the input. Anything more or anything less and you

---

[5] W. Shakespeare, *Romeo and Juliet*, act II, scene ii (1597).

TABLE 2.13. The values of the function $s(n) = n^2$.

n	1	2	3	4	5	6	7	8	9	10	11
$s(n)$	1	4	9	16	25	36	49	64	81	100	121
Δs		3	5	7	9	11	13	15	17	19	21

will not be dealing with a quadratic function. "Quadratic" is also a good word to remember because Q's are worth 10 points in *Scrabble*.

We can generalize our computations in Example 2.28 to show that the sum of the terms in any arithmetic sequence determines a quadratic function. In fact, we can say something even stronger. Consider the values of the function $s(n) = n^2$, as given in Table 2.13. Notice that the input values in this table form an arithmetic sequence:

$$1 \xrightarrow{+1} 2 \xrightarrow{+1} 3 \xrightarrow{+1} 4 \xrightarrow{+1} 5 \xrightarrow{+1} 6 \xrightarrow{+1} 7 \xrightarrow{+1} 8 \xrightarrow{+1} 9 \xrightarrow{+1} \cdots .$$

The same holds true for the successive *increments* Δs in the output values:

$$3 \xrightarrow{+2} 5 \xrightarrow{+2} 7 \xrightarrow{+2} 9 \xrightarrow{+2} 11 \xrightarrow{+2} 13 \xrightarrow{+2} 15 \xrightarrow{+2} 17 \xrightarrow{+2} \cdots .$$

It turns out that every quadratic function can be characterized by this property: Given an arithmetic sequence of inputs, a quadratic function produces a sequence of output values whose successive increments form an arithmetic sequence. We shall refer to this type of sequence as a **quadratic sequence**.

EXAMPLE 2.29. Consider the function g defined by the values in Table 2.14. Observe that the input values in this table form an arithmetic sequence:

$$1 \xrightarrow{+2} 3 \xrightarrow{+2} 5 \xrightarrow{+2} 7 \xrightarrow{+2} 9 \xrightarrow{+2} 11 \xrightarrow{+2} 13 \xrightarrow{+2} \cdots .$$

Furthermore, the corresponding output values in this table define a quadratic sequence, that is, the increments Δg form an arithmetic sequence:

$$18 \xrightarrow{-7} 11 \xrightarrow{-7} 4 \xrightarrow{-7} -3 \xrightarrow{-7} -10 \xrightarrow{-7} -17 \xrightarrow{-7} \cdots .$$

Therefore g is a quadratic function.

TABLE 2.14. A function defined by a quadratic sequence.

x	1	3	5	7	9	11	13
$g(x)$	-3	15	26	30	27	17	0
Δg		18	11	4	-3	-10	-17

One rather slick way to find a formula for $g(x)$ is to first express our function in the form
$$g(x) = A + B\,(x-1) + C\,(x-1)(x-3).$$
Here, the first term is a constant, the second term is a linear function that disappears at the first input in our table, and the third term is a quadratic function that disappears at the first two inputs in our table. We can determine the values of the constants A, B, and C by evaluating g at each of our first three inputs, as follows:
$$g(1) = A = -3,$$
$$g(3) = A + B \cdot 2 = 15,$$
$$g(5) = A + B \cdot 4 + C \cdot 4 \cdot 2 = 26.$$
Now, the first of these equations tells us that $A = -3$. Then, solving the second equation for B gives
$$B = \frac{15 - A}{2} = \frac{15 + 3}{2} = \frac{18}{2} = 9.$$
Finally, solving the third equation for C yields
$$C = \frac{26 - A - 4B}{8} = \frac{26 + 3 - 36}{8} = -\tfrac{7}{8}.$$
Therefore, our quadratic function is given by the formula
$$g(x) = -3 + 9\,(x-1) - \tfrac{7}{8}\,(x-1)(x-3) = -\tfrac{7}{8}x^2 + \tfrac{25}{2}x - \tfrac{107}{8}.$$

As noted in Example 1.69, the graph of the quadratic function $f(x) = x^2$ is a $\cup$-shaped graph called a **parabola**. To be sure, this fact requires some further explanation since it is not the case that every $\cup$-shaped graph is a parabola. Parabolas have a long-standing history dating back to the time of the great geometer Apollonius of Perga (c. 262 – 190 BC). It was Apollonius who first gave parabolas (as well as their cousins, the hyperbolas and the ellipses) their name. Apollonius's greatest contribution to mathematics was his eight-volume study of **conic sections**, in which he investigated the various ways in which a flat plane can cut through a cone. From this point of view, a parabola is defined as the intersection of a cone (a right circular cone, to be precise) and a plane that is tilted at the same pitch as the slant of the cone. To better appreciate what this means, perhaps a mental experiment is in order.[6]

Suppose that you shine a flashlight directly in front of a wall. The tiny reflectors behind the lightbulb will redirect the light coming from the bulb so that when it leaves the flashlight it forms a thick beam in the shape of a cone. If you hold the flashlight so that the center of the beam hits the wall at a right angle, you will see a bright

---

[6] Since this is only a *mental* experiment, we will not need a cat. However, performing this experiment for real could be kind of fun, especially if you were caught in an electrical blackout with a flashlight and nothing else to do. In that case, the cat would be optional.

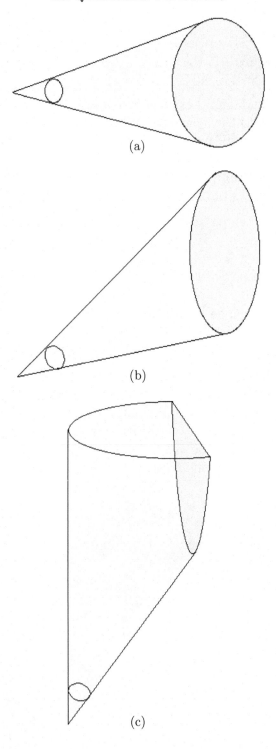

FIGURE 2.17. Three different kinds of conic sections: (a) a circle, (b) an ellipse, and (c) a parabola. The fourth type of conic section (a hyperbola) is not shown here.

circle of light on the wall in front of you, as illustrated in Figure 2.17 (a). If you tilt the flashlight ever so slightly upwards, the circle of light will appear to stretch and form an ellipse, as in Figure 2.17 (b). More tilting will result in even more stretching, until eventually the top of the ellipse will hit the edge of the ceiling.

Now suppose that you did not have a ceiling above you, and that the wall in front of you stretches up as far as the eye can see. You can then continue tilting the flashlight upward until the top of the beam of light becomes vertical. See Figure 2.17 (c). At that instant, the ellipse on the wall would have been stretched as far as it could go, its top-most point having been relegated to the infinite confines of outer space. At that very moment, you would be looking at a parabola!

As described in our mental experiment, a parabola is a smiling ∪-shaped curve with a single local minimum. In this case, we say that the parabola is **concave up**. Of course, this is just a matter of perspective. If we had tilted the flashlight downwards instead of upwards, we would have ended up with a frowning ∩-shaped curve with a single local maximum. This, too, would be a parabola, but this time it would be **concave down**. The local minimum or maximum is called the **vertex** of the parabola. It marks the center of symmetry for the parabola. On either side of the vertex, the parabola evolves in precisely the same way, increasing (if concave up) or decreasing (if concave down) without bounds as it goes off to infinity.

Let us take another look at the graph of the function $f(x) = x^2$. The graph in Figure 2.18 shows a close-up view of this parabola near its vertex. It also shows the point $F = \left(0, \frac{1}{4}\right)$ as well as the horizontal line $\mathcal{D}$ with equation $y = -\frac{1}{4}$. Observe that every point on the parabola is the same distance away from F as it is from $\mathcal{D}$. For instance, the distance from the point $(-1, 1)$ to F is given by the distance formula

$$\sqrt{\left(-1-0\right)^2 + \left(1 - \left(\frac{1}{4}\right)\right)^2} = \sqrt{\left(-1\right)^2 + \left(\frac{3}{4}\right)^2} = \sqrt{1 + \frac{9}{16}} = \sqrt{\frac{25}{16}} = \frac{5}{4},$$

while the shortest distance between $(-1, 1)$ and the line $\mathcal{D}$ is simply given by the difference in their y-coordinates:

$$\left|1 - \left(-\frac{1}{4}\right)\right| = \frac{5}{4}.$$

Similarly, the distance between $\left(\frac{\sqrt{2}}{2}, \frac{1}{2}\right)$ and F is

$$\sqrt{\left(\frac{\sqrt{2}}{2} - 0\right)^2 + \left(\frac{1}{2} - \left(\frac{1}{4}\right)\right)^2} = \sqrt{\left(\frac{\sqrt{2}}{2}\right)^2 + \left(\frac{1}{4}\right)^2} = \sqrt{\frac{1}{2} + \frac{1}{16}} = \sqrt{\frac{9}{16}} = \frac{3}{4},$$

while that between $\left(\frac{\sqrt{2}}{2}, -\frac{5}{2}\right)$ and $\mathcal{D}$ is

$$\left|\frac{1}{2} - \left(-\frac{1}{4}\right)\right| = \frac{3}{4}.$$

Apollonius proved that *every* parabola has this property, so that we can think about a parabola as the set of points which are the same distance away from a fixed point

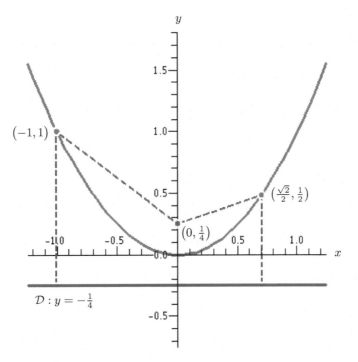

FIGURE 2.18. Each point of the parabola $y = x^2$ is the same distance away from the focus $F = \left(0, \frac{1}{4}\right)$ as from the directrix $\mathcal{D}$ determined by the equation $y = -\frac{1}{4}$.

(called the **focus**) and a fixed line (called the **directrix**). With this alternate definition in hand, we can show that the graph of every quadratic function is in the shape of a parabola. (For the details, see Exercise 29 at the end of this section.)

EXAMPLE 2.30. Consider the quadratic function defined by the formula

$$g(x) = x^2 - x - 1.$$

Finding the y-intercept of the graph of this function is as easy as evaluating at $x = 0$:

$$g(0) = 0^2 - 0 - 1 = -1.$$

On the other hand, we can find its x-intercepts by factoring the formula for g as we did back in Example 1.23 on page 31:

$$g(x) = \left(x - \varphi\right)\left(x + \tfrac{1}{\varphi}\right).$$

Remember that, in this formula, φ is our favorite irrational number, the golden ratio. Thus the graph of g is a parabola with a y-intercept at $y = -1$ and x-intercepts at $x = -\frac{1}{\varphi}$ and $x = \varphi$.

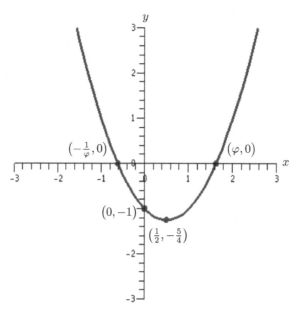

FIGURE 2.19. The graph of the quadratic function $g(x) = x^2 - x - 1$.

We can determine the exact shape of this parabola by first finding the constant which completes $x^2 - x$ as a square:

$$x^2 - x + \boxed{\text{ ??? }} = \left(x - h\right)^2 = x^2 - 2hx + h^2.$$

We do this by taking the coefficient of x (namely, -1), dividing by 2, and squaring. Thus, the square is completed by adding $\frac{1}{4}$:

$$x^2 - x + \tfrac{1}{4} = \left(x - \tfrac{1}{2}\right)^2.$$

With this information in hand, we can rewrite our formula for g as

$$\begin{aligned}
g(x) &= x^2 - x - 1 \\
&= x^2 - x + \tfrac{1}{4} - \tfrac{1}{4} - 1 \\
&= \left(x^2 - x + \tfrac{1}{4}\right) - \left(\tfrac{1}{4} + 1\right) \\
&= \left(x - \tfrac{1}{2}\right)^2 - \tfrac{5}{4}.
\end{aligned}$$

Note that in the second line above, we simply added zero, cleverly disguised as $\frac{1}{4} - \frac{1}{4}$, to our formula; this, of course, did not change the value of g at all. When the dust settles, we see that the graph of g consists of an identical copy of our model parabola $f(x) = x^2$ which has been translated half a unit to the right and five fourths of a unit down. In particular, it is a concave up parabola that has its vertex at the point $\left(\frac{1}{2}, -\frac{5}{4}\right)$, as shown in Figure 2.19.

EXAMPLE 2.31. Sketch the graph of the quadratic function defined by the formula

$$g(x) = -4x^2 - 8x - 3.$$

Solution. First of all, notice that the coefficient of x^2 is equal to -4. We can factor this coefficient from all three terms in the formula for f, obtaining

$$g(x) = -4\left(x^2 + 2x + \tfrac{3}{4}\right).$$

We can then complete $x^2 + 2x$ as a square:

$$x^2 + 2x + \boxed{\ ???\ } = \left(x + h\right)^2 = x^2 + 2hx + h^2.$$

Evidently, in this case, we need to add (and subtract) 1 inside the parentheses of our factored expression for g:

$$\begin{aligned}
g(x) &= -4\left(x^2 + 2x + \tfrac{3}{4}\right) \\
&= -4\left(x^2 + 2x + 1 - 1 + \tfrac{3}{4}\right) \\
&= -4\left((x + 1)^2 - \tfrac{1}{4}\right) \\
&= -4\left(x + 1\right)^2 + 1.
\end{aligned}$$

This means that the graph of g is a copy of our model parabola reflected across the x-axis, dilated vertically by a factor of 4, and translated to the left by one unit and up by one unit. This places the vertex of our new parabola at the point $\left(-1, 1\right)$.

As before, we can find the y-intercept of this parabola by evaluating

$$g(0) = -4 \cdot 0^2 - 8 \cdot 0 - 3 = -3.$$

On the other hand, finding the x-intercepts is a little bit more involved. In particular, we are looking for all the values of x at which $g(x) = 0$. As it turns out, our new expression for g is perfectly suited for using the square root method from Section 1.4:

$$\begin{aligned}
-4\left(x + 1\right)^2 + 1 &= 0 \\
-4\left(x + 1\right)^2 &= -1 \\
\left(x + 1\right)^2 &= \tfrac{1}{4} \\
x + 1 &= \pm\sqrt{\tfrac{1}{4}} = \pm\tfrac{1}{2} \\
x &= -1 \pm \tfrac{1}{2}.
\end{aligned}$$

Therefore our graph has a y-intercept at $y = -3$ and x-intercepts at $x = -\tfrac{1}{2}$ and $x = -\tfrac{3}{2}$. See Figure 2.20.

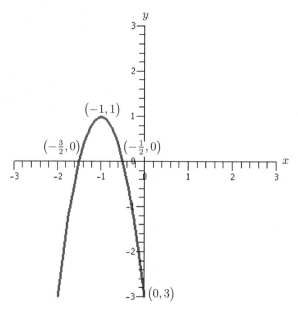

FIGURE 2.20. The graph of the function $g(x) = -4x^2 - 8x - 3$.

We can take the same approach as in the two previous examples to determine the exact shape of the graph of the general quadratic function

$$g(x) = a\,x^2 + b\,x + c.$$

In particular, we shall first factor the coefficient of x^2 from all three terms in the formula for g:

$$g(x) = a\left(x^2 + \frac{b}{a}\,x + \frac{c}{a}\right).$$

Of course, we can only do this if $a \neq 0$, but this is hardly a concern; if a were zero, then g would actually be a linear function and we would not be having this conversation. Next, we look at the expression inside the parentheses and complete the square:

$$x^2 + \frac{b}{a}\,x + \boxed{\ \ ???\ \ } = \left(x + h\right)^2 = x^2 + 2hx + h^2.$$

As before, we take the coefficient of x, divide by 2, and square. In this case, we find that we can complete the square by adding and subtracting

$$\left(\frac{b}{2a}\right)^2 = \frac{b^2}{4a^2}.$$

Doing so gives us

$$g(x) = a\left(x^2 + \frac{b}{a}\,x + \frac{b^2}{4a^2} - \frac{b^2}{4a^2} + \frac{c}{a}\right)$$

$$g(x) = a\left(\left(x + \frac{b}{2a}\right)^2 - \frac{b^2 - 4ac}{4a^2}\right)$$

$$= a\left(x + \frac{b}{2a}\right)^2 - \frac{b^2 - 4ac}{4a}.$$

What this last expression lacks in physical appearance, it certainly makes up in personality. For one thing, this formula is teeming with gossip as it shows us that the graph of g is simply a linear transformation of our model parabola $f(x) = x^2$. Specifically, it consists of a copy of the model parabola which has been:

① reflected across the x-axis if a is negative,

② dilated vertically by a factor of a,

③ translated to the left by $\dfrac{b}{2a}$,

④ translated down by $\dfrac{b^2 - 4ac}{4a}$.

The resulting parabola will be concave up when a is positive, and concave down when a is negative. Furthermore, its vertex will be located at the point

$$\text{vertex} = \left(-\frac{b}{2a}, -\frac{b^2 - 4ac}{4a}\right).$$

Finally, in order to find the x-intercepts, all we need to do is consider the equation

$$g(x) = a\left(x + \frac{b}{2a}\right)^2 - \frac{b^2 - 4ac}{4a} = 0,$$

which we can solve by using the square root method:

$$a\left(x + \frac{b}{2a}\right)^2 = \frac{b^2 - 4ac}{4a}$$

$$\left(x + \frac{b}{2a}\right)^2 = \frac{b^2 - 4ac}{4a^2}$$

$$x + \frac{b}{2a} = \pm\frac{\sqrt{b^2 - 4ac}}{2a}$$

$$x = \frac{-b \pm \sqrt{b^2 - 4\,a\,c}}{2a}.$$

This last expression was first given by the Indian mathematician and astronomer Brahmagupta (598–668 AD) as part of his magnificent work *Brahmasphutasiddhanta.* Roughly translated as "The Opening of the Universe," this book is impressive not only because of its sophisticated level of mathematics, including the early use of zero and negative numbers, but also because it was written completely in verse. Many of our grandparents might have referred to formula above as the "Indian formula." Nowadays, it is universally known as the **quadratic formula** and even though we do not learn it in verse, we can still sing it to the tune of "Pop Goes the Weasel!"

EXAMPLE 2.32. As we observed in Example 1.37 on page 55, the weight (in pounds) of a 5 kg cat placed in orbit directly between the earth and the moon is given by the rational function

$$W(x) = \frac{889\,x^2 - 730\,800\,x + 148\,352\,400}{2\,x^2\,(406 - x)^2},$$

where x is the cat's distance (measured in millions of meters) from the center of the earth. The graph of W, shown in Figure 1.21 (see page 98), has an x-intercept somewhere around $x \approx 365.6$ million meters. This intercept corresponds to the spot where the pull of gravity from the earth is precisely cancelled by that from the moon, so that our cat becomes weightless. In terms of the function W, this corresponds to a value of x which will make $W(x) = 0$. We can determine this value by setting the numerator in the formula for W equal to zero and solving for x:

$$889\,x^2 - 730\,800\,x + 148\,352\,400 = 0.$$

Our main problem in solving this equation comes from the fact that the coefficients involved are rather unmanageable. (Would you like to try the sledge-hammer method and find all the possible ways to factor $889 \cdot 148\,352\,400 = 131\,885\,283\,600$?) With the quadratic formula in hand, however, these difficulties are a thing of the past! All we have to do is substitute the values of our coefficients ($a = 889$, $b = -730\,800$, and $c = 148\,352\,400$) into the quadratic formula:

$$x = \frac{730\,800 \pm \sqrt{(-730\,800)^2 - 4 \cdot 889 \cdot 148\,352\,400}}{2 \cdot 889}.$$

After some number-crunching, this becomes

$$x = \frac{52\,200 \pm 1\,740\,\sqrt{11}}{127}.$$

Of these two values, the solution with the plus sign is

$$x = \frac{52200 + 1740\sqrt{11}}{127} = 456.463\,993\,190\ldots,$$

and hence falls outside the physical domain of our function. (If you recall, the function W is supposed to give the weight of a cat *between* the earth and the moon, so that $6.4 \le x \le 404.3$.) Therefore, the only x-intercept for W that matters to us is

$$x = \frac{52200 - 1740\sqrt{11}}{127} = 365.583\,250\,861\ldots.$$

This gives us the precise location (in millions of meters above the center of the earth) where our "astrocat" becomes completely weightless.

The example above illustrates how the quadratic formula can be used to solve an equation of the form

$$a\,x^2 + b\,x + c = 0.$$

Observe that the right-hand side of this equation defines a quadratic function while the left-hand side is zero. For obvious reasons, an equation of this form is called a **quadratic equation**. Notice that this gives us three phrases that sound very similar, but refer to three very different kinds of mathematical objects. In particular, we have the *quadratic formula* which can be used to find either the x-intercepts of a *quadratic function* or the solutions to a *quadratic equation*. It might seem pedantic at first, but you should strive to use the right word in the right situation.

EXAMPLE 2.33. Back in Section 1.2, we solved several quadratic equations by factoring or by using the sledgehammer method. We can now solve these much more efficiently with the quadratic formula. In particular, consider the following equations:

① $x^2 + 6x + 9 = 0$ has $a = 1$, $b = 6$, and $c = 9$, so

$$x = \frac{-6 \pm \sqrt{6^2 - 4 \cdot 1 \cdot 9}}{2 \cdot 1} = \frac{6 \pm 0}{2} = 3.$$

② $x^2 - 169 = 0$ has $a = 1$, $b = 0$, and $c = -169$, so

$$x = \frac{0 \pm \sqrt{0^2 - 4 \cdot 1 \cdot (-169)}}{2 \cdot 1} = \frac{0 \pm 26}{2} = \pm 13.$$

③ $x^2 + x - 6 = 0$ has $a = 1$, $b = 1$, and $c = -6$, so

$$x = \frac{-1 \pm \sqrt{1^2 - 4 \cdot 1 \cdot (-6)}}{2 \cdot 1} = \frac{-1 \pm 5}{2} = 2 \text{ or} - 3.$$

④ $4x^2 + 8x + 3 = 0$ has $a = 4$, $b = 8$, and $c = 3$, so

$$x = \frac{-8 \pm \sqrt{8^2 - 4 \cdot 4 \cdot 3}}{2 \cdot 4} = \frac{-8 \pm 4}{8} = -\tfrac{1}{2} \text{ or} - \tfrac{3}{2}.$$

⑤ $2x^2 - x - 6 = 0$ has $a = 2$, $b = -1$, and $c = -6$, so

$$x = \frac{1 \pm \sqrt{(-1)^2 - 4 \cdot 2 \cdot (-6)}}{2 \cdot 2} = \frac{1 \pm 7}{4} = 2 \text{ or} - \tfrac{3}{2}.$$

You should take a moment to compare these answers to our results from Examples 1.17 through 1.21 (see pages 26 through 29). In particular, note all of the hard work that the Quadratic Formula saves us from!

Depending on the situation in question, the quadratic formula will generate zero, one, or two values. Which of these three possibilities prevails is determined by the number

$$b^2 - 4ac$$

inside the square root in the quadratic formula; this value is called the ***discriminant*** of the equation. When this number is positive (as in equations ② through ⑤ above), the quadratic formula will churn out two values: one corresponding to the plus sign and the other corresponding to the minus sign. Thus, the graph of a quadratic function with a positive discriminant will be a parabola that intersects the x-axis twice, once on either side of the vertex, as in Figures 2.19 and 2.20. On the other hand, if the discriminant is zero (as in equation ①), adding or subtracting zero gives the same answer, so the quadratic formula will produce precisely one solution. This means that the graph of a quadratic function with a zero discriminant will be a parabola which barely touches the x-axis once, at its vertex, as in Figure 2.18. Finally, the third possibility arises when the discriminant is negative. In this case, the quadratic formula calls for an impossible square root of a negative number. Therefore the graph of a quadratic function with a negative determinant will not have any x-intercepts at all.

The Discriminating Discriminant

Consider the quadratic function $g(x) = a\,x^2 + b\,x + c$.

- If $b^2 - 4ac > 0$, then the graph of f has two x-intercepts.
- If $b^2 - 4ac = 0$, then the graph of f has one x-intercept.
- If $b^2 - 4ac < 0$, then the graph of f has zero x-intercepts.

EXAMPLE 2.34. The quadratic function

$$f(x) = x^2 + 1$$

has a negative discriminant of

$$b^2 - 4ac = 0^2 - 4 \cdot 1 \cdot 1 = -4.$$

Since this discriminant is negative, the graph of f does not have any x-intercepts. Indeed, the graph of f is a copy of our model parabola that has been translated up by one unit. Since the vertex of this concave up parabola is located above the x-axis at the point $(0, 1)$, the graph of f cannot possibly intersect the x-axis.

Let us turn our attention back to the quadratic function

$$f(x) = x^2 - x - 1$$

from Example 2.30. As we saw in that example, the graph of this function is a concave up parabola with x-intercepts at $x = \varphi$ and $x = -\frac{1}{\varphi}$. These intercepts were obtained from our curious factorization of f back in Example 1.23. What does the quadratic formula say about these intercepts? If we substitute the values of our coefficients ($a = 1$, $b = -1$, and $c = -1$) into the quadratic formula, we discover that the x-intercepts of f occur at

$$x = \frac{1 \pm \sqrt{1^2 - 4 \cdot 1 \cdot (-1)}}{2 \cdot 1} = \frac{1 \pm \sqrt{5}}{2}.$$

Notice that $\sqrt{5} > 1$, so the intercept with the plus sign is positive, while the intercept with the minus sign is negative. Therefore, we must have

$$\varphi = \frac{1 + \sqrt{5}}{2}. \tag{2.1}$$

This equations gives us a new way of thinking about the golden ratio. You should take a minute to verify that this new formula gives us precisely the same decimal expansion as the one we saw back on page 20.

Reading Comprehension Questions for Section 2.4

A quadratic function is a polynomial of degree ___(a)___. This means that every quadratic function can be described by a formula of the form $g(x) = $ ___(b)___. We can also think of a quadratic function as a linear transformation of the model function $f(x) = $ ___(c)___. Thus, the graph of every quadratic function is a ___(d)___. If the coefficient of x^2 is ___(e)___ (positive or negative), then the graph is shaped like a $\cup$ and we say that it is ___(f)___; in contrast, if the coefficient of x^2 is ___(g)___ (positive or negative), then the graph is shaped like a $\cap$ and we say it is ___(h)___.

If we can factor a quadratic function, then we can read off the x-intercepts directly from the factorization. Alternatively, we can use the ___(i)___ to find the x-intercepts from the unfactored function. For instance, applying this formula to the quadratic function $g(x) = 3x^2 - 5x + 2$ produces

$$ x = \frac{\text{(j)} \pm \sqrt{\text{(k)}}}{\text{(l)}}. $$

This simplifies to $x = $ ___(m)___ and $x = $ ___(n)___. The quantity under the square root in this formula is known as the ___(o)___. If this quantity is ___(p)___ then the graph has no x-intercepts; if it is ___(q)___ then it has only one x-intercept; and if it is ___(r)___, as in our example above, the graph has two x-intercepts.

A quadratic function will map any arithmetic sequence of input values to a ___(s)___ sequence of output values. For example, the function g above maps the input values 0, 1, 2, and 3, respectively, to the output values ___(t)___, ___(u)___, ___(v)___, and ___(w)___. Although these values are not separated by equal increments, the increments in question, namely ___(x)___, ___(y)___, and ___(z)___, do form an arithmetic sequence.

Exercises for Section 2.4

In Exercises 1–6, determine whether or not each table describes a quadratic function. If it does, find a formula for the function. If it does not, what is the least number of output values that must be changed in order to make f quadratic?

1.

x	1	2	3	4	5
$f(x)$	10	8	7	8	10

2.

x	1	2	3	4	5
$f(x)$	8	11	12	11	8

3.

x	1	2	3	4	5
$f(x)$	10	8	6	4	2

4.

x	1	2	3	4	5
$f(x)$	-7	-2	5	14	25

5.

x	1	2	3	4	5
$f(x)$	10	8	5	1	-4

6.

x	1	2	3	4	5
$f(x)$	-10	-3	1	8	16

In Problems 7–16, solve each equation using the quadratic formula.

7. $x^2 - 7x + 10 = 0$

8. $x^2 - 4x + 1 = 0$

9. $x^2 - x + 6 = 0$

10. $x^2 + 8x + 9 = 0$

11. $2x^2 + 5x + 2 = 0$

12. $4x^2 - x + 2 = 0$

13. $x^2 + 2x = 1 - x^2$

14. $x^2 + 4 = 4x + 2$

15. $5x^2 + 2x = 5x + 1$

16. $5x + 2 = 4x^2 + 7$

In Problems 17–24, sketch a graph of each function. Be sure to label the x- and y-intercepts, as well as the vertex of each parabola.

17. $f(x) = 25 - x^2$

18. $f(x) = 16x^2 - 8x + 1$

19. $f(x) = 2x^2 + 12x + 10$

20. $f(x) = -3x^2 - 2x - 1$

21. $f(x) = 2x^2 + 3x - 2$

22. $f(x) = -3x^2 + 4x + 2$

23. $f(x) = x^2 + \sqrt{2}x + 1$

24. $f(x) = x^2 - \sqrt{2}x - 1$

25. After being shot out of a cannon, a circus clown flies through the air at a height (in feet) of

$$H(t) = \begin{cases} -16\,t^2 + 95.5\,t + 3 & \text{if } 0 \leq t \leq 6 \\ 0 & \text{otherwise} \end{cases}$$

where t is the time (in seconds) after the cannon was fired. When does the clown reaches the highest point of his journey? Does this value agree with your answer to Exercise 24 in Section 1.1?

26. Consider the graph of the quadratic function $f : \mathbb{R} \to \mathbb{R}$ shown below.

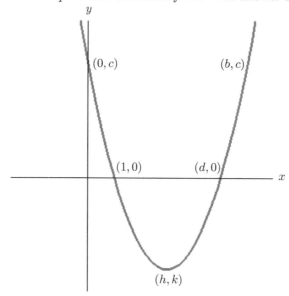

(a) Which of the following formulas best describes f? Explain.

    (i) $f(x) = a\,(x+3)^2 - 8$ (ii) $f(x) = a\,(x-3)^2 - 8$

    (iii) $f(x) = a\,(x-3)^2 + 8$ (iv) $f(x) = a\,(x+3)^2 + 8$

(b) According to the formula you chose in part (a), what are the coordinates of the vertex (h, k)?

(c) The graph of f has x-intercepts at the points $(1, 0)$ and $(d, 0)$. Appealing to the symmetry of the parabola, determine the value of the constant d.

(d) The graph of f has a y-intercept at the point $(0, c)$. If the horizontal line passing through this y-intercept crosses the graph a second time at the point (b, c), what is the value of the constant b?

(e) The constant a in the formula from part (a) determines a dilation of the model parabola. What is the value of the dilation factor a?

(f) Determine the value of the y-intercept c of the graph.

27. Find all of the values of the constant A for which the quadratic function

$$g(x) = Ax^2 + 2x + A$$

has exactly one x-intercept.

28. Find all of the values of the constant B for which the quadratic function

$$g(x) = 2x^2 - Bx + 4$$

has more than one x-intercept.

29. Let $f(x) = ax^2 + bx + c$ be a quadratic function and set

$$h = -\frac{b}{2a}, \qquad k = \frac{4ac - b^2 + 1}{4a}, \qquad d = \frac{4ac - b^2 - 1}{4a}.$$

(a) Verify the following equation by factoring the left hand side as the difference of two squares:

$$(y - d)^2 - (y - k)^2 = (k - d)(2y - (k + d)).$$

(b) Observe that $k - d = \dfrac{1}{2a}$ and that $k + d = 2c - \dfrac{b^2}{2a}$. Conclude that

$$(y - d)^2 - (y - k)^2 = \frac{y - c}{a} + h^2.$$

(c) Substitute $f(x)$ for y in the expression above and show that

$$(f(x) - d)^2 - (f(x) - k)^2 = x^2 - 2hx + h^2 = (x - h)^2.$$

(d) The equation in part (c) implies that

$$(x - h)^2 + (f(x) - k)^2 = (f(x) - d)^2.$$

Explain why this means that any point $(x, f(x))$ on the graph of f is equidistant from the focus (h, k) as from the directrix $y = d$.

30. In the proof of Theorem 2.1 on page 148, we considered the total error E obtained from approximating a data set by a line of regression as a quadratic function of either the regression line's slope or its y-intercept. Since the graph of each of these functions is a parabola, we can make E as small as possible by choosing the values of m_* and b_* corresponding to the vertices of these parabolas.

(a) Find the value of m_* that corresponds to the vertex of the quadratic function

$$E(m_*) = S\, m_*^2 + 2\left(b_* X - P\right) m_* + \left(b_*^2\, n + y_1{}^2 + \ldots + y_n{}^2 - 2\, b_* Y\right).$$

(b) Find the value of b_* that corresponds to the vertex of the quadratic function

$$E(b_*) = n\,b_*^2 + 2\left(m_*\,X - Y\right)b_* + \left(m_*^2\,S + y_1{}^2 + \ldots + y_n{}^2 - 2\,m_*\,P\right).$$

(c) Conclude that the total error E is at its minimum value whenever

$$S\,m_* + X\,b_* = P \qquad \text{and} \qquad X\,m_* + n\,b_* = Y.$$

2.5. Systems of Equations

It stands to reason that savvy consumers at a roadside vegetable stand are more likely to purchase greater quantities of fresh produce when they could do so at a lower price. In contrast, a grocer hoping to make a profit will be willing to stock more crates of produce at his vegetable stand if he can charge a higher price. For instance, in Example 2.13, we saw that the number of crates of avocados that a grocer can expect to sell each week at a price of x dollars per pound was given by the **demand function**

$$h(x) = 44.25 - 15\,x.$$

Let us also suppose that the number of crates of avocados that our grocer can afford to stock each week is given by the **supply function**

$$g(x) = 14\,x + 1.04,$$

where x is the price per pound that he plans to charge. Figure 2.21 shows the graphs of these supply and demand functions, drawn on the same set of axes.

The price at which the value of the demand function is equal to the value of the supply function is known as the **equilibrium price**. In Figure 2.21, this equilibrium price corresponds to the point at which the supply and demand lines intersect. If our grocer charges less than the equilibrium price, then he will find himself to the left of this intersection point, where the demand for avocados will be greater than he can supply, and he will run out of avocados before the week is up. Eventually, he will realize that he can raise prices to improve his bottom line. If, on the other hand, our grocer charges more than the equilibrium price, then he will find himself to the

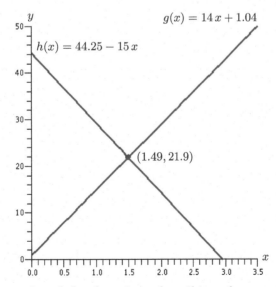

FIGURE 2.21. The graphs of the functions describing the supply and demand at a vegetable stand.

right of the intersection point, where his supply of avocados will be greater than his customers demand, and by the end of the week he will have leftover avocados. In order to sell the leftovers, our grocer will feel compelled to lower his prices. In either case, the grocer experiences a sort of "social pressure" to match the equilibrium price. In economics terms, this is known as the ***law of supply and demand***.

In the situation above, we can find the equilibrium price by setting our supply and demand functions equal to each other, and solving for x:

$$14\,x + 1.04 = 44.25 - 15\,x$$
$$14\,x + 15\,x = 44.25 - 1.04$$
$$29\,x = 43.21$$
$$x = 1.49.$$

Thus, the equilibrium price for avocados at our vegetable stand is \$1.49 per pound. At this price, we will have

$$g(1.49) = 14 \cdot 1.49 + 1.04 = 21.9,$$
$$h(1.49) = 44.25 - 15 \cdot 1.49 = 21.9,$$

so both the supply and the demand will consist of 21.9 crates of avocados per week; therefore, by week's end, the grocer will have sold all of his avocados and never had to turn away a willing customer empty-handed.

The intersection point between the supply and demand lines in Figure 2.21 corresponds to a single pair of x- and y-values that turn the equation for each of these lines into a true statement. In other words, the pair $x = 1.49$ and $y = 21.9$ simultaneously satisfies the equations

$$\begin{cases} y = 44.25 - 15\,x, \\ y = 14\,x + 1.04. \end{cases}$$

A collection of two or more equations grouped together in this way is usually called a ***system of equations***. It is customary to use a large brace, as we have done above, to hold the equations in the system together so that they do not go wandering off on their own and get lost. The values of the unknowns which simultaneously satisfy these equations are called the ***solutions*** of the system. The process through which these solutions are found is called ***solving*** the system of equations; it involves precisely the same Algebra Rules as solving a single equation (see page 23).

EXAMPLE 2.35. Consider the following system of equations:

$$\begin{cases} 2\,x + 3\,y = 7, \\ x - y = 1. \end{cases}$$

We can find the solutions of this system of equations by using a strategy known as the ***substitution method***. We begin by solving the first equation for one of the two unknowns (let us say y), and substituting the resulting expression wherever that unknown appears in the second equation. The second equation can then be solved for the other unknown (in this case x) using our usual algebraic techniques. The final solution is then obtained by substituting the resulting value of x back into our expression for y.

In our case, we begin by solving the first equation for y as follows:

$$2\,x + 3\,y = 7$$

$$3\,y = 7 - 2\,x$$

$$y = \tfrac{7}{3} - \tfrac{2}{3}\,x.$$

Notice that this gives us an expression for y in terms of the unknown x. We substitute this expression anywhere that y appears in the second equation of our system and solve as follows:

$$x - y = 1$$

$$x - \left(\tfrac{7}{3} - \tfrac{2}{3}\,x\right) = 1.$$

$$x - \tfrac{7}{3} + \tfrac{2}{3}\,x = 1$$

$$x + \tfrac{2}{3}\,x = 1 + \tfrac{7}{3}$$

$$\tfrac{5}{3}\,x = \tfrac{10}{3}$$

$$x = \tfrac{10}{3} \cdot \tfrac{3}{5} = 2.$$

Finally, we substitute this value of x back into our earlier expression for y:

$$y = \tfrac{7}{3} - \tfrac{2}{3}\,x$$

$$= \tfrac{7}{3} - \tfrac{2}{3} \cdot 2$$

$$= \tfrac{7}{3} - \tfrac{4}{3} = 1.$$

Therefore, the solution to our system is the pair of values $x = 2$ and $y = 1$, as indicated in Figure 2.22.

Looking back at the previous example, a curious reader may wonder what ever happened to all of our functions. The answer is that they are still there, lurking in the background and hiding behind the equations of our system. For example, take the first equation

$$2\,x + 3\,y = 7.$$

This equation implicitly defines y as a linear function of x. This becomes clear once we solve the equation for y and find that

$$y(x) = \tfrac{7}{3} - \tfrac{2}{3}\,x.$$

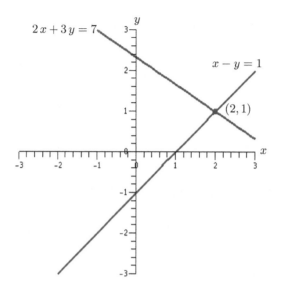

FIGURE 2.22. The solutions to a system of equations correspond to the points of intersection between two or more graphs.

Here, we have written "$y(x)$" instead of just "y" to emphasize the fact that y is, indeed, a function of x. In the same way, the second equation

$$x - y = 1$$

implicitly defines y as a *different* linear function of x, namely

$$y(x) = x - 1.$$

Technically, we are abusing our notation by giving the two functions in question the same name. However, we are only interested in finding the input values for which both of these functions produce the same output value, so our abuse of notation should cause little to no confusion. In any case, the solution

$$x = 2 \qquad \text{and} \qquad y = 1$$

to our system of equations corresponds to the point $(2, 1)$ where the graphs of these functions intersect. (See Figure 2.22.)

EXAMPLE 2.36. Solve the following system of equations:

$$\begin{cases} x - y = 1, \\ y = 2x - x^2 + 1. \end{cases}$$

Solution. As in our previous example, we shall employ the substitution method. In this case, however, we shall first take the second equation, which

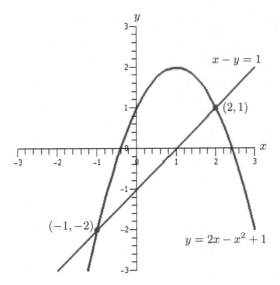

FIGURE 2.23.   The solutions to a system of equations correspond to the points of intersection between two or more graphs.

is already solved for y, and substitute it into the first:

$$x - (2x - x^2 + 1) = 1.$$

After simplifying, we obtain the quadratic equation

$$x^2 - x - 2 = 0,$$

which we can then solve using the quadratic formula as follows:

$$x = \frac{1 \pm \sqrt{(-1)^2 - 4 \cdot 1 \cdot (-2)}}{2} = \frac{1 \pm 3}{2}.$$

Evidently, we have two possible values of x, namely $x = \frac{1+3}{2} = 2$ and $x = \frac{1-3}{2} = -1$. When each of these values is substituted back into our formula for y, we obtain:

$$x = 2 \quad \Rightarrow \quad y = 2x - x^2 + 1 = 2 \cdot 2 - 2^2 + 1 = 1,$$

$$x = -1 \quad \Rightarrow \quad y = 2x - x^2 + 1 = 2 \cdot (-1) - (-1)^2 + 1 = -2.$$

Therefore, our system of equations has two solutions,

$$x = 2 \text{ and } y = 1 \quad \text{or} \quad x = -1 \text{ and } y = -2,$$

corresponding to the two intersection points between the line $x - y = 1$ and the parabola $y = 2x - x^2 + 1$. (See Figure 2.23.)

EXAMPLE 2.37. Typically, we measure temperature in one of two scales: Fahrenheit and Celsius. For instance, the temperature at which water freezes can be measured as either 32°F or 0°C; similarly, the temperature at which water boils is either 212°F or 100°C. Now, it turns out that there is a *linear correspondence* between the temperature in degrees Fahrenheit and the equivalent temperature in degrees Celsius. In other words, the temperature in one scale is a linear function of the temperature in the other.

Determine the temperature at which both a Fahrenheit thermometer and a Celsius thermometer will read the same value.

Solution. ① There are two types of quantities in this problem: temperatures in degrees Celsius and temperatures in degrees Fahrenheit. Let

$$x = \text{the temperature in degrees Celsius},$$

$$y = \text{the temperature in degrees Fahrenheit}.$$

Then, we can think of y as a linear function of x with

$$y(0) = 32 \qquad \text{and} \qquad y(100) = 212.$$

② The slope of this function is

$$m = \frac{\Delta y}{\Delta x} = \frac{212 - 32}{100 - 0} = \frac{180}{100} = \frac{9}{5},$$

so by the slope-intercept formula,

$$y = \tfrac{9}{5}x + 32.$$

③ We are looking for the temperature at which both scales agree, that is, where

$$y = x.$$

In other words, we are looking for a solution to the system of equations

$$\begin{cases} y = \tfrac{9}{5}x + 32 \\ y = x. \end{cases}$$

④ Since each equation already shows the value of y in terms of x, we can solve the system of equations by setting the right hand sides of the equations equal to one another and then solving for the unknown value of x:

$$\tfrac{9}{5}x + 32 = x$$

$$\tfrac{4}{5}x = -32$$

$$x = -32 \cdot \tfrac{5}{4} = -40.$$

Evidently, the two scales will measure equal temperatures when

$$x = y = -40.$$

In other words, we have just found that $-40°\text{C} = -40°\text{F}$.

⑤ Substituting the value $x = -40$ back into either of the equations in our original system gives us the same value of y:

$$x = -40 \qquad \Rightarrow \qquad \begin{cases} y = \frac{9}{5}x + 32 = \frac{9}{5} \cdot (-40) + 32 = -40, \\ y = x = -40. \end{cases}$$

Thus, the pair $x = -40$ and $y = -40$ is a solution to our system of equations. Furthermore, note that going from $-40°\text{F}$ to $32°\text{F}$ is a change of $72°$, while going from $-40°\text{C}$ to $0°\text{C}$ is a change of $40°$. This corresponds to an average rate of change of

$$\frac{\Delta y}{\Delta x} = \frac{72}{40} = \frac{9}{5}.$$

Similarly, going from $-40°\text{F}$ to $212°\text{F}$ is a change of $252°$, while going from $-40°\text{C}$ to $100°\text{C}$ is a change of $140°$. This also corresponds to an average rate of change of

$$\frac{\Delta y}{\Delta x} = \frac{252}{140} = \frac{9}{5}.$$

Both of these rates of change are consistent with the slope we computed earlier. Therefore, the point $(-40, -40)$ lies on the same straight line as $(0, 32)$ and $(100, 212)$, so our answer must be correct.

This last example heralds our transition from abstract systems of equations to "story problems." Before we proceed, we should point out that solving problems is a creative endeavor, more of an art than a science. A particular problem might be solved in a variety of ways, including entirely arithmetic or guess-and-check methods which do not use any algebra at all. In practice, these are perfectly acceptable methods which often show great cunning and imagination; however, these methods also tend to be rather specialized to the type of problem at hand. Sometimes, a more general algebraic approach will be required.

Below, we outline one such method which is typically efficacious for solving story problems. That being said, you should be aware that there is no universal method that will solve every single problem. At some point, you might encounter a problem which does not fit the usual pattern, a problem that seems intractable, a problem which will challenge you to rise above all adversities and use your ingenuity to invent a solution. Some people (mostly mathematicians) spend entire years working on the same math problem; some emerge victorious, while others fail and fade into oblivion. It falls squarely on your shoulders to determine which of the two fates will be yours.

Zen and the Art of Mathematical Problem-Solving

① **Read the problem.** You should try to "read for understanding," paying close attention to the details. Read slowly. If necessary, read the problem two or three times. Make a list of all of the relevant unknown quantities, and identify any relationships between them. Sometimes you might want to draw a diagram, a table, or a chart. In particular, look for key phrases which define one quantity as a function of another.

② **Write equations for all of the facts.** If you are dealing with a linear function, you might use either the slope-intercept or point-slope formulas, based on the information given. This may involve calculating a slope first. If you are dealing with a quadratic function you might be given information about its graph's x-intercepts or vertex, from which you can reconstruct the formula for the function. And remember that you can sometimes construct a quadratic function by multiplying two linear functions together.

③ **Determine what your goal is.** What is the problem asking for? What are you looking for? This usually involves looking at the last sentence in the problem (the one with the question mark), but it might also involve looking at the extra information from the other sentences in the problem. Once you know what it is you are looking for, write a mathematical equation for it.

④ **Solve your system of equations and find an answer.** This is the time to impress your instructor (as well as your potential love interests) with your algebraic prowess. We will cheer you on: Al-ge-bra! Al-ge-bra! Al-ge-bra!

⑤ **Check your answer.** You should make sure that your answer makes sense, both mathematically and in the context of the problem. Look for arithmetic or algebraic mistakes. Make sure that you are answering the right question. This is also a good time to check your units.

Each step in this process above is important. After reading a problem, many students will try to jump straight to writing the system of equations, without first clearly explaining what quantity each variable stands for (see Step ①). Inevitably, chaos ensues. Other students might miss an important fact or two (see Step ③) and are then confused when their system does not seem to have enough equations. A good rule of thumb is that a system should have the same number of equations as unknowns. Finally, there are some students who do not go back and check that their answers make sense (see Step ⑤), proposing solutions that should have been ruled out after a just moment's thought. You should do your best to avoid each of these traps by training yourself to proceed slowly and methodically.

This is not to say that every step in the process is necessarily easy. Translating written phrases into mathematical equations (see Step ②) can be difficult, and, of course, there will probably be a fair bit of algebra to contend with (see Step ④). However, all of this does get easier with practice, so practice you must. The following examples, and the exercises at the end of this section, will give you ample opportunity to put your problem-solving skills to the test.

> EXAMPLE 2.38. Acute Alice has a total of $2 700 to invest, some in stocks and some in mutual funds. Her financial advisor recommends to her that the amount she invests in stocks be no more than 35% of the amount invested in mutual funds. How much should she invest in each?
>
> *Solution.* ① In this problem, we have two types of investment vehicles: stocks and mutual funds. Thus, we shall let
>
> $$x = \text{the amount invested in mutual funds,}$$
>
> $$y = \text{the amount invested in stocks.}$$
>
> ② The amount invested in mutual funds will determine the largest amount to be invested in stocks. Suppose that as much money is invested in stocks as is advisable. Then the amount invested in stocks will equal 35% of the amount invested in mutual funds; we translate this statement into an algebraic equation as follows:
>
> $$y = 0.35\,x.$$
>
> ③ We want to determine how much of Alice's $2 700 should be invested in stocks and how much should be invested in mutual funds. Since the total amount to be invested is $2 700, we seek values of x and y for which
>
> $$x + y = 2\,700.$$
>
> In other words, we must solve the following system of equations:
>
> $$\begin{cases} y = 0.35\,x \\ x + y = 2\,700. \end{cases}$$
>
> ④ We solve the system by taking the expression on the right hand side of the first equation (which is already solved for y), substituting it for y in the second equation, and then solving for x:
>
> $$x + \big(0.35\,x\big) = 2\,700$$
>
> $$1.35\,x = 2\,700$$
>
> $$x = \tfrac{2\,700}{1.35} = 2\,000.$$

Then, substituting this value for x in the first equation gives

$$y = 0.35 \cdot 2\,000 = 700.$$

Hence Acute Alice should invest at least $2\,000$ in mutual funds and at most $700 in stocks.

⑤ By direct computation, $700 is 35% of $2\,000$. Since these add up to $2\,700$, we can see that our answer must be correct.

The example above is a typical ***mixture problem***, in which two or more types of objects (in this case, two different types of investments) are combined in order to produce some desired result. Other types of mixture problems may involve coins, regular and overtime pay, people's ages, or even different flavors of milk, but the overall idea pretty much remains the same.

EXAMPLE 2.39. The dairy cooperative in Scalene Sallie's hometown wishes to produce a brand-new flavor of milk by blending its popular chocolate milk with its less successful banana-flavored milk. Normally, a gallon of chocolate milk sells for $2.49 while a gallon of banana-flavored milk sells for $4.49. Each gallon of the new milk will sell for $2.99. The cooperative is expecting to make an additional profit of $0.10 from the sale of each gallon of the new milk. How much chocolate milk and how much banana-flavored milk is needed to make one gallon of the new milk?

Solution. ① In this problem, we have two types of flavored milk (chocolate and banana) and their respective costs. Thus, we let

$x =$ a quantity of banana-flavored milk (in gallons),

$y =$ a quantity of chocolate milk (in gallons),

$b =$ the cost of mixing x gallons of banana-flavored milk,

$c =$ the cost of mixing y gallons of chocolate milk.

② In each case, the cost is proportional to the amount of milk that is mixed. In fact, the slope of each cost function is equal to the price of one gallon of the respective type of milk. Thus,

$$b = 4.49\,x,$$
$$c = 2.49\,y.$$

③ We are looking for the amount of chocolate milk and banana-flavored milk needed to make one gallon of the new milk, so that

$$x + y = 1.$$

Furthermore, each gallon of the new milk is supposed to be sold for $2.99 and produce $0.10 in profits (after the cost of the milk used is taken into account), so that

$$b + c + 0.10 = 2.99.$$

Therefore, we must solve the following system of equations:

$$\begin{cases} b = 4.49\,x \\ c = 2.49\,y \\ x + y = 1 \\ b + c + 0.10 = 2.99. \end{cases}$$

④ We will solve this system by repeated substitution, noting that the first two equations are already solved for b and c, respectively. We shall substitute the right hand sides of these two equations into the fourth, which then becomes

$$\big(4.49\,x\big) + \big(2.49\,y\big) + 0.10 = 2.99.$$

We can also solve the third equation for y, giving us

$$y = 1 - x.$$

Substituting this expression into our modified fourth equation and solving for x yields

$$4.49\,x + 2.49\big(1 - x\big) + 0.10 = 2.99$$

$$4.49\,x + 2.49 - 2.49\,x + 0.10 = 2.99$$

$$4.49\,x - 2.49\,x = 2.99 - 2.49 - 0.10$$

$$2.00\,x = 0.40$$

$$x = \tfrac{0.40}{2.00} = 0.2\;.$$

Substituting back in our expression for y gives

$$y = 1 - \big(0.2\big) = 0.8.$$

Therefore, each gallon of the new milk should consist of 0.2 gallons of banana-flavored milk and 0.8 gallons of chocolate milk.

⑤ The price of $x = 0.2$ gallons of banana-flavored milk is

$$b = 0.2 \cdot 4.49 = \$0.898,$$

while the price of $y = 0.8$ gallons of the chocolate milk is

$$c = 0.8 \cdot 2.49 = \$1.992.$$

Together, this comes to $2.89, so selling each gallon of the new milk for $2.99 will produce the desired $0.10 in additional profits.

The following is an example of a ***rate problem***, in which some task must be accomplished in a given amount of time or at a given speed. Sometimes, the task at hand involves traveling some distance. Other times, the task corresponds to some work that needs to be completed, like emptying a tank, painting a room, or filling a swimming pool.

EXAMPLE 2.40. Obtuse Ollie is filling a swimming pool using a large fire hose. Under normal circumstances, it would take Ollie 5 hours to fill the pool. However, unbeknownst to Ollie, the bottom of the pool has a leak which can completely empty the pool in 23 hours. How long will it take Obtuse Ollie to fill the pool?

Solution. ① The task at hand is to fill a swimming pool. In a given amount of time, the hose will add some water to the pool while the leak will take away some water from the pool. In each case, the amount of water put into or taken out of the pool is proportional to the amount of time elapsed. We shall let

t = the amount of time elapsed (in hours),

x = the amount of water added in t hours by the hose,

y = the amount of water removed in t hours by the leak.

Since the size of the pool is not given, we can measure both x and y as a fraction of the whole pool. For instance, $x = 0.5$ corresponds to half a pool's worth of water, $x = 0.25$ corresponds to a quarter pool's worth of water, and so forth.

② We know it should take Obtuse Ollie 5 hours to completely fill the pool in the absence of a leak, so the hose is adding water at a rate of $\frac{1}{5}$ of a pool per hour. Similarly, since the leak can drain the pool in 23 hours, it is removing water from the pool at a rate of $\frac{1}{23}$ of a pool per hour. Therefore, we can write rate equations for both x and y in terms of t:

$$x = \tfrac{1}{5}\, t,$$

$$y = \tfrac{1}{23}\, t.$$

③ We are looking for the time at which the water added by the hose minus the water removed by the leak equals an entire pool's worth of water:

$$x - y = 1.$$

In other words, we are looking for for the value of t in the solution to the system of equations

$$\begin{cases} x = \tfrac{1}{5}\, t \\ y = \tfrac{1}{23}\, t \\ x - y = 1. \end{cases}$$

④ We solve the system of equations by substituting the right hand sides of the first and second equations (which are already solved for x and for y, respectively) into the third:

$$\tfrac{1}{5}\, t - \tfrac{1}{23}\, t = 1.$$

We can then solve for t as follows:

$$\left(\tfrac{1}{5} - \tfrac{1}{23}\right)t = 1$$

$$\tfrac{18}{115}\,t = 1$$

$$t = \tfrac{115}{18}.$$

Therefore it will take Obtuse Ollie $\frac{115}{18}$ hours (that is, 6 hours, 23 minutes, and 20 seconds) to fill the pool.

⑤ In $t = \frac{115}{18}$ hours, the hose will pump $x = \frac{1}{5} \cdot \frac{115}{18} = \frac{23}{18}$ pools' worth of water. In the same amount of time, $y = \frac{1}{23} \cdot \frac{115}{18} = \frac{5}{18}$ pools' worth of water will leak out of the bottom. Therefore the net amount of water left in the pool will be

$$x - y = \tfrac{23}{18} - \tfrac{5}{18} = \tfrac{18}{18} = 1.$$

In other words, the pool will be completely full. Of course, the pool will continue to leak after Ollie is finished filling it, but that is another matter.

The following rate problem deals with the relationship between distance, speed, and time:

$$\boxed{\text{distance} = \text{speed} \times \text{time.}}$$

This relationship holds as long as the speed is constant. Notice that, in addition, the solution to this problem depends on Pythagoras's Theorem (see page 81).

EXAMPLE 2.41. Scalene Sallie and her best friend are going sailing in the Gulf of Mexico. Sallie sets out on her sailboat at noon and heads directly west at 8 kilometers per hour. An hour later, Sallie's friend takes her boat out from the same port and sails at 9 kilometers per hour due south. If they each travel in a straight line, at what time will the two boats be 30 kilometers apart?

Solution. ① There are three distances that will be changing with time: the distance that each of the two boats has travelled, and the distance between the boats. Thus we let

$t =$ the amount of time elapsed since noon,

$x =$ the distance travelled by Scalene Sallie's boat,

$y =$ the distance travelled by Sallie's friend's boat,

$z =$ the distance between the two boats.

Each distance is measured in kilometers and t is measured in hours.

② Because Sallie left port at noon, she has been sailing at a speed of 8 kilometers per hour for a period of t hours, so

$$x = 8t.$$

In contrast, Sallie's friend left port an hour later, so she has been sailing at a speed of 9 kilometers per hour for only $t - 1$ hours. Thus

$$y = 9\,(t - 1) = 9\,t - 9.$$

Finally, the two boats' trajectories were perpendicular to each other, so the distance between the boats is given by Pythagoras's Theorem:

$$x^2 + y^2 = z^2.$$

③ We are searching for the time when the two boats are 30 kilometers apart:

$$z = 30.$$

Thus, we are looking for the value of t in the solution to the system of equations

$$\begin{cases} x = 8\,t \\ y = 9\,t - 9 \\ x^2 + y^2 = z^2 \\ z = 30. \end{cases}$$

④ We solve the system of equations by substituting the formulas for x, y, and z in the first, second, and fourth equations into the third equation of our system. In particular, this gives us a quadratic equation in t to solve:

$$\left(8\,t\right)^2 + \left(9\,t - 9\right)^2 = 30^2$$

$$\left(64\,t^2\right) + \left(81\,t^2 - 162\,t + 81\right) = 900$$

$$145\,t^2 - 162\,t - 819 = 0.$$

The quadratic formula then gives us two possible answers,

$$t = \frac{162 \pm \sqrt{162^2 + 4 \cdot 145 \cdot 819}}{2 \cdot 145} = \frac{162 \pm \sqrt{501\,264}}{290} = \frac{162 \pm 708}{290}.$$

Therefore, either

$$t = \tfrac{162 + 708}{290} = \tfrac{870}{290} = 3 \qquad \text{or} \qquad t = \tfrac{162 - 708}{290} = -\tfrac{546}{290} \approx -1.883.$$

Of course, only the first of these answers makes sense, so the distance between the boats will be 30 kilometers at three in the afternoon.

⑤ When $t = 3$ hours, Scalene Sallie will have travelled a distance of

$$x = 8 \cdot 3 = 24 \text{ kilometers}$$

due west, while her friend will have only travelled

$$y = 9 \cdot 2 = 18 \text{ kilometers}$$

due south. Therefore, at that time, the distance between the two boats is

$$z = \sqrt{24^2 + 18^2} = 30 \text{ kilometers},$$

as desired.

The next example, which pertains to the total amount of money generated by the sale of some commodity, is known as a **revenue problem**. In this type of problem, the price of the item for sale determines the number of items that can be sold by means of a demand function, and that number will control the total revenue produced from the sale. Thus, the connection between price and revenue is given by an equation of the form

$$\boxed{\text{revenue} = \text{price} \times \text{demand}.}$$

Note in particular that if demand is a linear function of price, then revenue will be a quadratic function of price.

EXAMPLE 2.42. Obtuse Ollie is working as a part-time handyman in an apartment complex. The complex manager knows from experience that all 120 apartments will be occupied if rent is set to $300 per month. In addition, experience shows that for every $5 increase in the rent, on average one more unit remains unoccupied. What should the manager charge for rent in order to guarantee a revenue of exactly $40,000?

Solution. ① The problem describes how the number of apartments that are rented out depends on the monthly rent (in other words, the price) charged for each apartment. Let

x = the amount of monthly rent (in dollars),

y = the number of apartments rented at that price (the demand),

z = the total rent brought in at that price (the revenue).

② Since revenue is the product of price times demand, we begin with the equation

$$z = x \cdot y.$$

Now, we are only given two values for the demand function, so we will have to assume that y is a linear function of x. In particular, if the rent is set at $300 then all 120 apartments are rented, but if the rent is increased to $305 then only 119 apartments will be rented. This means that

$$y(300) = 120 \qquad \text{and} \qquad y(305) = 119.$$

Thus the slope of the demand function is

$$m = \frac{\Delta y}{\Delta x} = \frac{119 - 120}{305 - 300} = -\frac{1}{5}.$$

The point-slope formula then gives

$$y = -\tfrac{1}{5} \cdot \left(x - 300\right) + 120 = -\tfrac{1}{5}x + 60 + 120 = 180 - \tfrac{1}{5}x.$$

③ We are looking for the monthly rent that will guarantee a revenue of precisely $40,000:

$$z = 40\,000.$$

Therefore, we will consider the values of x which solve the system of equations

$$\begin{cases} z = x \cdot y \\ y = 180 - \frac{1}{5}x \\ z = 40\,000. \end{cases}$$

④ We will take the value of y from the second equation and the value of z from the third equation, and substitute them into the first equation, obtaining:

$$40\,000 = x \cdot \left(180 - \tfrac{1}{5}x\right)$$
$$40\,000 = 180\,x - \tfrac{1}{5}x^2$$
$$\tfrac{1}{5}x^2 - 180\,x + 40\,000 = 0$$
$$x^2 - 900\,x + 200\,000 = 0.$$

Note that we simplified the last equation by multiplying all terms by 5. The quadratic formula then gives us two values of x,

$$x = \frac{900 \pm \sqrt{900^2 - 4 \cdot 1 \cdot 200\,000}}{2} = \frac{900 \pm \sqrt{810\,000 - 800\,000}}{2} = \frac{900 \pm 100}{2}$$

so x is either $\frac{900-100}{2} = 400$ or $\frac{900+100}{2} = 500$. Therefore, if Ollie's apartment manager charges either \$400 or \$500 in rent, then he can expect to collect exactly \$40,000 of revenue.

⑤ If rent is set at $x = \$400$, then $y = 180 - \frac{1}{5} \cdot 400 = 100$ apartments will be rented, bringing in a total revenue of $z = 400 \cdot 100 = \$40\,000$. On the other hand, if rent is set at $x = \$500$, then only $y = 180 - \frac{1}{5}500 = 80$ apartments will be rented, but this will also bring in a total revenue of $z = 500 \cdot 80 = \$40\,000$, as desired.

Although the following example appears at first to be a simple revenue problem like the one above, its solution does not require us to solve a system of equations at all. Instead, this is an ***optimization problem***, in which we search for the local maximum or minimum of some function. In the case of a quadratic function, this optimum value will always occur at the vertex of the corresponding parabola. This type of problem is included in this section (and in the exercises) to keep you on your toes!

EXAMPLE 2.43. During the tourist season, Acute Alice makes shell necklaces which she then sells at the beach by the Naples pier. Last winter, Alice sold necklaces for \$10 each and she averaged 18 sales per day. When she increased the price to \$11, she lost about three sales per day. If it costs her \$2 to make one necklace, for what price should Acute Alice sell each necklace to maximize her profit?

① The problem describes how the number of necklaces that Alice sells (in other words, the demand) depends on the price she charges for each necklace.

Let

$$x = \text{the price of one necklace (in dollars)},$$
$$y = \text{the number of necklaces sold at that price},$$
$$z = \text{the total profit brought in at that price}.$$

② As in the previous example, we shall assume that the demand function y is linear. Since Alice can sell 18 necklaces when she charges \$10 apiece, but only 15 when she increased the price to \$11, the demand function satisfies the conditions

$$y(10) = 18 \qquad \text{and} \qquad y(11) = 15.$$

This indicates a slope of

$$m = \frac{\Delta y}{\Delta x} = \frac{15 - 18}{11 - 10} = -3.$$

Then the point-slope formula give us a demand of

$$y = -3 \cdot (x - 10) + 18 = -3\,x + 30 + 18 = 48 - 3\,x.$$

Now the total profit is the amount of money that Alice makes over and above what it costs her to make the necklaces she sells. Since the sale of each necklace brings in $x - 2$ dollars of profit over the manufacturing cost, the total profit from y sales each day is given by

$$z = (x - 2) \cdot y.$$

③ We are looking for the price that will produce the largest profit. Therefore, we want to consider profit as a function of the price,

$$z(x) = (x - 2) \cdot (48 - 3\,x) = -3\,x^2 + 54\,x - 96,$$

and determine the value of x which will produce the maximum value for this function.

④ The graph of $z(x)$ is a concave-down parabola because its coefficient of x^2 is negative. Therefore z has a local maximum at

$$x = -\frac{b}{2a} = -\frac{54}{-6} = 9.$$

Therefore the price that generates the greatest profits is \$9 per necklace.

⑤ If Alice charges $x = \$9$ for each necklace, she will be selling

$$y(9) = 48 - 3 \cdot 9 = 21 \text{ necklaces}$$

and making a daily profit of

$$z(9) = (9 - 2) \cdot (48 - 3 \cdot 9) = 7 \cdot 21 = \$147.$$

If, on the other hand, she charged either \$8 or \$10, then she would only make an average daily profit of \$144:

$$z(8) = (8 - 2) \cdot (48 - 3 \cdot 8) = 6 \cdot 24 = 144,$$
$$z(10) = (10 - 2) \cdot (48 - 3 \cdot 10) = 8 \cdot 18 = 144.$$

Admittedly, our final problem has a ridiculous number of quantities for us to keep track of. However, it serves as a reminder to us that our substitution method works just the same, even on this "over-the-top" monkey problem.

EXAMPLE 2.44. Over the top of a fence hangs a rope, with the same amount hanging on each side. The rope weighs a third of a pound per foot. On one end of the rope hangs a monkey holding a banana; on the other end is an anvil weighing the same amount as the monkey and the banana put together. The banana weighs two ounces per inch. The length of the rope (in feet) is equal to the age of the monkey, and the weight of the monkey (in ounces) is as much as the age of the monkey's mother. The ages of the monkey and his mother add up to thirty years. The weight of the banana plus one half the weight of the monkey is one quarter as much as the sum of the weights of the anvil and the rope, where all weights are in the same units. The monkey's mother is one half as old as the monkey will be when he is three times as old as his mother was when she was one half as old as the monkey will be when he is twice as old as he is now.

How old is the monkey? And how long is the banana?

Solution. In this problem, we have two different lengths (the banana's and the rope's), four weights (the anvil's, the banana's, the monkey's, and the rope's) and two ages (the monkey's and his mother's). These quantities, and the relationships between them, are illustrated in Figure 2.24. You should take a moment to identify each of the arrows in this diagram as a sentence in the our story problem above.

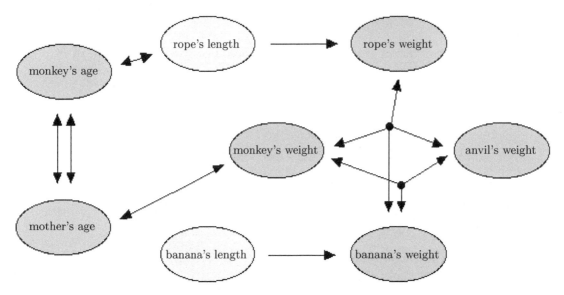

FIGURE 2.24. Quantities in the "monkey-with-a-banana-hanging-from-a-rope" problem. Can you determine which arrow corresponds to each statement from the problem?

We shall first find the monkey's age, and not worry about the length of his banana until later.

① Consider the ages of the monkey and his mother. In particular, let

$$x = \text{the age of the monkey},$$

$$y = \text{the age of the monkey's mother}.$$

② The last statement (the sentence before the two questions) describes a linear relationship between the mother's age and the monkey's age. We shall go over that last statement with fine tooth comb:

> "The monkey's mother is one half as old as the monkey will be when he is three times as old as his mother was when she was one half as old as the monkey will be when he is twice as old as he is now."

The monkey's age is now x. It will be $2x$ when the monkey is twice as old as he is now. When the monkey's mother was half as old as that, her age was $\frac{1}{2} \cdot 2x = x$. When the monkey is three times as old as that, his age will be $3x$. So the monkey's mother is now half as old as that:

$$y = \tfrac{1}{2} \cdot 3x = \tfrac{3}{2} x.$$

In addition, there is one more statement describing the relationship between x and y:

> "The ages of the monkey and his mother add up to thirty years."

In other words, we also have

$$x + y = 30.$$

③ We are looking for the age of the monkey, that is, for the value of x in the solution of the system of equations

$$\begin{cases} y = \tfrac{3}{2} x \\ x + y = 30. \end{cases}$$

④ We solve the system by substituting the right hand side of the first equation for y in the second equation, and then solving for x:

$$x + \left(\tfrac{3}{2} x \right) = 30$$

$$\tfrac{5}{2} x = 30$$

$$x = \tfrac{2}{5} \cdot 30 = 12.$$

Therefore the monkey is 12 years old.

⑤ Since the monkey is $x = 12$ years old, his mother is $y = \frac{3}{2} \cdot 12 = 18$ years old. Thus, their ages add up to $x + y = 12 + 18 = 30$, as required.

Now, let us deal with the banana:

① Suppose that we let

$$x = \text{the length (in inches) of the banana,}$$
$$y = \text{the length (in feet) of the rope,}$$
$$z = \text{the weight (in ounces) of the anvil,}$$
$$u = \text{the weight (in ounces) of the banana,}$$
$$v = \text{the weight (in ounces) of the monkey,}$$
$$w = \text{the weight (in ounces) of the rope.}$$

② Since the rope weighs $\frac{1}{3}$ pound (or $\frac{1}{3} \cdot 16 = \frac{16}{3}$ ounces) per foot, we have

$$w = \tfrac{16}{3}\, y.$$

Notice the change of units! Similarly, the anvil weighs the same as the monkey and the banana put together,

$$z = u + v,$$

while the banana weighs 2 ounces per inch,

$$u = 2\, x.$$

Furthermore, the rope is 12 feet long (since the monkey is 12 years old),

$$y = 12,$$

and the monkey weights 18 ounces (since the monkey's mother is 18 years old),

$$v = 18.$$

Finally, the weight of the banana plus one half the weight of the monkey is one quarter as much as the sum of the weights of the anvil and the rope:

$$u + \tfrac{1}{2} v = \tfrac{1}{4}(z + w).$$

③ Since we are looking for the length of the banana, we need to find the value of x in the solution to the system

$$\begin{cases} w = \tfrac{16}{3}\, y \\ z = u + v \\ u = 2\, x \\ y = 12 \\ v = 18 \\ u + \tfrac{1}{2} v = \tfrac{1}{4}(z + w). \end{cases}$$

④ We solve this system of equations by substituting, in turn, each of the expressions from the first five equations into the last equation. First, we substitute $w = \frac{16}{3}\,y$:

$$u + \tfrac{1}{2}\,v = \tfrac{1}{4}\big(z + \tfrac{16}{3}\,y\big),$$

then $z = u + v$:

$$u + \tfrac{1}{2}\,v = \tfrac{1}{4}\big(u + v + \tfrac{16}{3}\,y\big),$$

then $u = 2\,x$:

$$2\,x + \tfrac{1}{2}\,v = \tfrac{1}{4}\big(2\,x + v + \tfrac{16}{3}\,y\big),$$

then $y = 12$:

$$2\,x + \tfrac{1}{2}\,v = \tfrac{1}{4}\big(2\,x + v + \tfrac{16}{3}\cdot 12\big),$$

and finally $v = 18$:

$$2\,x + \tfrac{1}{2}\cdot 18 = \tfrac{1}{4}\big(2\,x + 18 + \tfrac{16}{3}\cdot 12\big).$$

We can then simplify this equation by collecting like terms, multiplying both sides by 4, and solving for x as follows:

$$2\,x + 9 = \tfrac{1}{4}\big(2\,x + 82\big)$$

$$8\,x + 36 = 2\,x + 82$$

$$6\,x = 46$$

$$x = \tfrac{46}{6} = \tfrac{23}{3}.$$

Therefore the banana is $\frac{23}{3}$ (that is, seven and two thirds) inches long.

⑤ Since the banana is $x = \frac{23}{3}$ inches long, it weighs $u = 2 \cdot \frac{23}{3} = \frac{46}{3}$ ounces. On the other hand, the rope is $y = 12$ feet long and weighs $w = \frac{16}{3} \cdot 12 = 64$ ounces, that is, 4 pounds. The anvil weighs $z = 18 + 2 \cdot \frac{23}{3} = \frac{100}{3}$ ounces. Thus, the weight of the banana plus one half the weight of the monkey is

$$u + \tfrac{1}{2}\,v = \tfrac{46}{3} + \tfrac{1}{2}\cdot 18 = \tfrac{73}{3},$$

while one quarter as much as the sum of the weights of the anvil and the rope is equal to

$$\tfrac{1}{4}\big(z + w\big) = \tfrac{1}{4}\big(\tfrac{100}{3} + 64\big) = \tfrac{1}{4}\cdot\tfrac{292}{3} = \tfrac{73}{3}.$$

Observe that these two quantities are, indeed, equal so we have solved the problem.

Reading Comprehension Questions for Section 2.5

The ___(a)___ of a system of equations is the set of all values that make all of the equations in the system simultaneously ___(b)___. An effective strategy for finding these values involves solving for one unknown in the first equation and then ___(c)___ the result into the other equations, thus eliminating that unknown from the system. The same process is then ___(d)___ over and over again, until all but one of the unknowns are eliminated. Eventually, we find the value of the last unknown, which can then be ___(e)___ back to find the values of the unknowns that were eliminated earlier. This approach is known as the ___(f)___ method. As an example, consider the system

$$\begin{cases} 5\,x - 3\,y = 10, \\ -4\,x + 7\,y = 2. \end{cases}$$

Graphically, each equation in this system describes a ___(g)___, and the solution represents the unique point where these graphs ___(h)___. If we solve the first equation for x, we arrive at the equivalent equation $x = $ ___(i)___ $y + $ ___(j)___. This expression is substituted into the second equation, which then simplifies to $y = $ ___(k)___. Substituting this value back into our expression above gives $x = $ ___(l)___. Thus, the two graphs intersect at the unique point (___(m)___, ___(n)___).

You can solve "story problems" by translating them into systems of equations. To do this, your first step is to ___(o)___, paying special attention to the ___(p)___. This is a good time to make a list of all the ___(q)___ you will need and explain carefully what each of them means. Next, you should write an ___(r)___ for each fact of the story. Before proceeding, you should decide what your ___(s)___ is, perhaps writing it as an ___(t)___ as well. With all these preparations in place, you can ___(u)___ your system of equations and find your answer. Finally, you should ___(v)___, making sure that it makes sense and that it answers the question you were asked.

Some types of problems that can be solved as a system of equations include ___(w)___ problems (in which several types of objects are combined to produce some desired result), ___(x)___ problems (in which some task must be accomplished in a given amount of time or at a given speed), and ___(y)___ problems (which deal with the total amount of money generated by the sale of some commodity). Problems of the last type should not be confused with ___(z)___ problems, in which we search for the local maximum or minimum of some function.

Exercises for Section 2.5

In Exercises 1–4, solve each system of equations in two ways. First, graph the two equations on the same set of axes and find their point of intersection. Then, use the rules of algebra to arrive at the same solution.

1. $\begin{cases} 3x + 4y = 11 \\ 6x - 2y = 2 \end{cases}$

2. $\begin{cases} 7x + 4y = 3x + 4 \\ 2x - 2y = 2y + 8 \end{cases}$

3. $\begin{cases} 6y - 2x = x + y \\ 5x + y = 4x + 8 \end{cases}$

4. $\begin{cases} 2y - x = 3x - 2 \\ x^2 + 9 = 5y - 7 \end{cases}$

In Exercises 5–30, answer each story problem by solving a system of equations or by finding the vertex of a quadratic function, as appropriate.

5. While studying for a philosophy exam, Acute Alice and Scalene Sallie decided to order some food. They paid a total of $16, including tip, for a pizza pie that was cut into eight slices. Alice ate two slices; Sallie ate three slices. They decided to save the leftovers for Obtuse Ollie, who would be joining them later.

    (a) Assuming that Acute Alice and Scalene Sallie decide to split the cost of the pizza based on the number of slices they each ate, how much should each one pay?

    (b) Suppose that, when Obtuse Ollie arrives, he wants to pay Acute Alice and Scalene Sallie for his share of the pizza. How much should he give each one?

6. The boiling point of water depends on the elevation. For instance, in a city like Boston, which is located at sea level, water boils at 100°C. On the other hand, in Denver, at an altitude of 1 655 meters above sea level, water boils at only 94.25°C. Assuming that the relationship between boiling point and altitude is linear, at what temperature should water boil at the top of Alaska's Mount McKinley, at an altitude of 6 196 meters above sea level? At the top of Mount Everest, at an altitude of 8 848 meters above sea level?

7. Acute Alice bought a telescope tripod at her local photography shop. Because she is a frequent customer, the shop owner gave her a 20% discount. After paying the 6% sales tax, Alice saved $19 over the original price of the tripod. How much did Acute Alice pay for her tripod?

8. Scalene Sallie is organizing a one-day trip to the Florida Everglades for a local retirement home. If 20 senior citizens go on the trip, Sallie can charter a bus for $15 a person. If more seniors go, then the charter company agrees to reduce the price of every ticket by $0.10 for each additional passenger in excess of 20, up to a maximum of 44, the capacity of the bus. If the final bill from the charter company comes to $482.40, how many seniors are going on Scalene Sallie's trip, and how much is each of them paying?

231

9. Obtuse Ollie has a part-time job at a landscaping supply store. The manager tells Ollie that the store can sell 900 heavy duty lawn mowers at the price of $2 000, but only 775 lawn mowers at the price of $2 250. What price should be charged to maximize the revenue at Obtuse Ollie's store?

10. According to an old matchmaker's rule of thumb, it is considered socially unacceptable for a man to court a woman that is younger than half his age plus seven years. According to this rule, at what age does it become socially acceptable for a man to court a woman that is eleven years younger than he is?

11. After her physics class, Acute Alice called her roommate for a ride and then started her six mile trek home, walking at 5 miles per hour. Alice's roommate quickly got ready, hopped in her car, and drove at 35 miles per hour to pick Alice up.

    (a) If Alice's roommate started driving as soon as she got the call, for how long will Acute Alice have to walk? Express your answer in minutes.

    (b) If Alice's roommate took 12 minutes to get ready before leaving, for how long will Acute Alice have to walk? Express your answer in minutes.

12. Scalene Sallie is volunteering for an ecological foundation which has just acquired a tract of land in a mangrove forest on the coast of Florida. According to the stipulations of the agreement, the parcel of land must be in the shape of a rectangle enclosed by 10 miles of fence on three sides; the fourth side will be along the Gulf of Mexico and will not require a fence. What is the area of the largest tract of land that the foundation can obtain?

13. After working 52 hours last week at the local ice cream shop, Obtuse Ollie received a paycheck for $435. Any work over and beyond 40 hours in a week counts as overtime, and earns Ollie time and a half. What is Obtuse Ollie's hourly wage?

14. At noon, a train leaves New York for Toronto while another leaves Toronto for New York. It takes one train 8 hours and the other 22 hours to complete the trip. Both maintain constant speeds, traveling in opposite directions along the same route. At what time will the trains pass each other?

15. Acute Alice invested $1000 of her savings in stocks from two start-up companies. After a year, the stocks for one company had gained 25% in value, but the stocks for the other company had lost 5% in value. At that point in time, Alice sold both stocks for a total of $1160. How much did Acute Alice originally invest in each company?

16. Scalene Sallie's friend owns a jet-ski that can travel at a constant speed of 14 miles per hour relative to the water. Sallie took the jet-ski on a river and traveled upstream for 20 minutes; she then turned around and made the return trip in 15 minutes. Suppose that the river's constant current decreased Sallie's speed on her trip upstream by the same amount that it increased her speed on the way downstream. How far did Scalene Sallie travel in total?

17. Obtuse Ollie is working as a courier making evening deliveries for a local attorney. Whenever he makes a delivery run, Ollie is paid $18. Some nights, however, no

deliveries are necessary, and Ollie is paid \$5 just for being on call. At the end of 40 nights, he is paid \$538. How many nights was Obtuse Ollie running deliveries and how many nights was he on call?

18. An architect is planning to put a Norman style window on the front of the new church he is designing. The window, which consists of a rectangle crowned by a semicircular arch, is supposed to have a perimeter of 15 feet. Describe the window which will let in the most light. In other words, find the dimensions of the window with the largest area.

19. Acute Alice and her roommate are painting their dormitory room. If they worked together, they could complete the job in six hours. If Alice can paint twice as fast as her roommate, how much time would it take her to paint the room by herself? How about her roommate?

20. Scalene Sallie took some classmates to visit a retirement home, where groups of students and seniors citizens sat together and played card games. At each table, there were either three seniors and one student, or four seniors and two students. If there were 23 students and 61 seniors citizens in all, how many tables were there?

21. Obtuse Ollie is working during the summer at an orange grove. The owner of the grove has determined that if 120 orange trees are planted per acre, each tree will yield approximately 60 boxes of oranges over the growing season. The state agricultural service advices that because of crowding, each additional tree will reduce the average yield per tree by about 2 boxes. How many trees per acre should be planted to maximize the total yield of oranges, and what is the maximum yield of the crop?

22. A freight train leaves Albuquerque at nine in the morning, traveling at 30 miles an hour. An hour and a half later, a passenger train takes the same route but travels at 50 miles an hour. If both trains maintain constant speeds, at what time will the passenger train pass the freight train?

23. Acute Alice has determined that the 15 kilograms of 4% salt solution which she prepared for a chemistry experiment is too weak. She decides to make a more concentrated 10% salt solution by either letting some of the water evaporate away, or adding more salt.

    (a) How much water must Acute Alice allow to evaporate away?

    (b) How much salt must Acute Alice add to the mixture?

24. Scalene Sallie's friend owns a jet-ski, which Sallie is going to take up the coast to examine some buoys. On her way out, Sallie will be sailing with the wind at her back, so she can travel at 30 kilometers per hour. However, on her way back, she will be traveling against the wind, so she can only go at 10 kilometers per hour. If she has enough fuel for a two hour round trip, how far out can Scalene Sallie travel and still make it back home?

25. Obtuse Ollie has a part-time job at a metalworking shop. He has been assigned to construct a box from a square piece of sheet metal by removing a 10 cm by 10

cm square from each corner and folding the remaining flaps up. What should the dimensions of the piece of sheet metal be if the box is to hold 160 cubic centimeters?

26. A 1 000 cubic foot oil tanker semi-trailer can be emptied in three hours through a large valve on the back of the tank. It can also be emptied in seven hours through a smaller valve on the side of the tank. How long will it take to empty the tank using both valves at the same time? Express your answer in hours and minutes.

27. Acute Alice has a piece of rope which is 30 feet long. Alice intends to splice the ends of the rope together and hold this loop taut to mark off a right triangle with a 13 foot hypotenuse. What will be area of Acute Alice's triangle?

28. Obtuse Ollie was looking for his television remote control between the cushions on his couch. Instead, Ollie found $3.92 in loose change. When he examined all of the coins that he had found, he noticed that half of all the coins were pennies. In addition, there were twice as many quarters as nickels, and two more nickels than dimes. How many coins of each type did Obtuse Ollie find?

29. Last weekend, Scalene Sallie went on a 9 mile canoe trip which took 6 hours. For the first 4.5 miles of the trip, Sallie rowed with the current of the river, which was flowing at 1 mile per hour. For the second 4.5 miles of the trip, she rowed against the current. Assuming that she went at a constant speed relative to the water, how fast was Scalene Sallie rowing?

30. Scalene Sallie and Obtuse Ollie are running around a circular track. Sallie makes it all the way around the track in 6 minutes, while Ollie does it in 10 minutes.

    (a) How often will they run past each other if they go around the track in opposite directions? Express your answer in minutes.

    (b) How often will they run past each other if they go around the track in the same direction? Express your answer in minutes.

Review of Chapter 2

Vocabulary with which you should now be familiar:

- arithmetic sequence
- average rate of change
- causation
- concave down
- concave up
- correlation
- difference quotient
- discriminant
- equation of a line
- horizontal dilation
- horizontal reflection
- horizontal translation
- least squares regression
- linear function
- linear transformation
- parabola
- point reflection
- point-slope formula
- quadratic equation
- quadratic formula
- quadratic function
- quadratic sequence
- scatter plot
- slope
- slope-intercept formula
- system of equations
- vertex of parabola
- vertical dilation
- vertical reflection
- vertical translation

Tasks you should now be prepared to perform:

- compute the average rate of change of a function over a given interval.
- recognize a linear or quadratic function from a table of data points.
- determine the formula for the linear function determined by two data points.
- determine the formula for the linear function that best fits n data points.
- locate the x- and y-intercepts of any linear or quadratic function.
- locate the local maximum or minimum of any quadratic function.
- sketch the graph of a linear or quadratic function.
- sketch the graph of a transformation of one of the six model functions.
- solve systems of linear and quadratic equations.

CHAPTER 3

Exponentials and Logarithms

In mathematics the base of all bases is the transcendental number $e = 2.71828\ldots$. It is a number of strange, Sicilian dignity. The most natural definition of the logarithmic function, the definition that is the most mathematical, leads us to the most natural definition of the exponential function, which in turn leads to the number e. The intellectual movement is one of a soapy wave washing forward to define the logarithmic function, washing backward to reveal the exponential function, and exposing in the back and forth motion the number e, the black jewel of the calculus.

D. Berlinski
A Tour of the Calculus
pages 82–83 (1997)

3.1. Exponential Functions

A long time ago, in a far away land, there lived a King by the name of Shirhâm who was very depressed. Sure, King Shirhâm had all the comforts that any monarch in a minor principality might come to expect. He lived in an enormous castle with high ceilings, white alabaster walls, and pink and blue onion-shaped domes on top of three tall minarets. He had a huge, soft, down bed on which to sleep, a large bathtub full of warm sudsy water in which to bathe, indoor plumbing, and a legion of attendants at his beck and call, ready to cater to his every whim. To many, it would have seemed an idyllic existence. And yet the king yearned for excitement and adventure.

It was a time of prosperity in the kingdom. There were no wars to fight, no famines to overcome, no pestilences to ward off. What is worse, the king had managed to master all of the usual games that would normally engage the attention of the royal court in the short periods between war, famine, and pestilence. Tic-tac-toe, rock-paper-scissors, tiddlywinks... none of these seemed like a challenge anymore. One lazy afternoon, while sipping on his tall glass of iced chai, King Shirhâm realized that he was terribly bored, and this realization made the King feel even more depressed.

And so it happened that the Grand Vizier Sissa Ben Dahir, one of Shirhâm's cleverest subjects, was commissioned to put together a game worthy of, well, a king. After many sleepless nights, Sissa took a square board, divided it into sixty-four smaller squares, eight on each side, and filled it with moveable pieces representing kings and queens, knights and bishops, castles, and of course lots of pawns to do the king's bidding. (He thought that King Shirhâm would like that sort of thing.) He also came up with a complex set of rules for moving each piece, all leading to the ultimate goal of putting the opponent's king under a direct attack from which escape was impossible. Thus, the game of chess was born.

When King Shirhâm saw his new game, he was thrilled to pieces and offered the Grand Vizier any reward in the kingdom that he felt daring enough to claim. At first, Sissa hesitated, declaring that he was a humble man who was only concerned with feeding his family and pleasing his king, and that no reward was necessary. However, at the king's insistence, Sissa eventually relented, asking for a single grain of wheat for the first square on his chessboard, two grains for the second square, four for the third square, and so on, doubling the number of grains of wheat for each square of the chessboard.

King Shirhâm, well pleased by Sissa's modesty, happily accepted until he realized that he had been duped. For although the reward began meekly enough with one, two, four, and eight grains of wheat, it quickly became alarmingly exorbitant, as can be seen in Table 3.1. In fact, had it all been gathered together, Sissa's reward would have consisted of a grand total of over 18 quintillion grains of wheat weighing about six hundred trillion tons. To put this number in perspective, on a good year, the

TABLE 3.1. The Grand Vizier's reward.

square	grains of wheat	square	grains of wheat
1	1	33	4 294 967 296
2	2	34	8 589 934 592
3	4	35	17 179 869 184
4	8	36	34 359 738 368
5	16	37	68 719 476 736
6	32	38	137 438 953 472
7	64	39	274 877 906 944
8	128	40	549 755 813 888
9	256	41	1 099 511 627 776
10	512	42	2 199 023 255 552
11	1 024	43	4 398 046 511 104
12	2 048	44	8 796 093 022 208
13	4 096	45	17 592 186 044 416
14	8 192	46	35 184 372 088 832
15	16 384	47	70 368 744 177 664
16	32 768	48	140 737 488 355 328
17	65 536	49	281 474 976 710 656
18	131 072	50	562 949 953 421 312
19	262 144	51	1 125 899 906 842 624
20	524 288	52	2 251 799 813 685 248
21	1 048 576	53	4 503 599 627 370 496
22	2 097 152	54	9 007 199 254 740 992
23	4 194 304	55	18 014 398 509 481 984
24	8 388 608	56	36 028 797 018 963 968
25	16 777 216	57	72 057 594 037 927 936
26	33 554 432	58	144 115 188 075 855 872
27	67 108 864	59	288 230 376 151 711 744
28	134 217 728	60	576 460 752 303 423 488
29	268 435 456	61	1 152 921 504 606 846 976
30	536 870 912	62	2 305 843 009 213 693 952
31	1 073 741 824	63	4 611 686 018 427 387 904
32	2 147 483 648	64	9 223 372 036 854 770 808
		total	18 446 744 073 709 551 615

United States only produces about sixty million tons of wheat. This means that it would take the U.S. about 10 million years to produce enough wheat to pay Sissa's price. Presumably, the only thing in the kingdom greater than the Grand Vizier's reward would have been the King's wrath when dealing with his humble servant.

Take a closer look at the sequence of numbers displayed under the two columns labeled "grains of wheat" in Table 3.1; you will notice that each number is obtained by multiplying the previous number times two:

$$1 \xrightarrow{\times 2} 2 \xrightarrow{\times 2} 4 \xrightarrow{\times 2} 8 \xrightarrow{\times 2} 16 \xrightarrow{\times 2} 32 \xrightarrow{\times 2} 64 \xrightarrow{\times 2} 128 \xrightarrow{\times 2} \cdots.$$

A progression of this type, in which new values are generated by multiplying old values by a fixed number, is known as a **geometric sequence**. The fixed number by which we multiply over and over again (two, in the case of the values in the table) is called the **base** of the geometric sequence. We can always forecast a value in a geometric sequence by multiplying its **initial value** (the first number in the sequence) by an appropriate power of the base. Thus, if a geometric sequence has an initial value of a and a base of b, then its values will form the progression

$$a \xrightarrow{\times b} a \cdot b \xrightarrow{\times b} a \cdot b^2 \xrightarrow{\times b} a \cdot b^3 \xrightarrow{\times b} a \cdot b^4 \xrightarrow{\times b} a \cdot b^5 \xrightarrow{\times b} \cdots.$$

Suppose that a and b are two fixed real numbers; suppose further that b is positive. Then we can define a function $f : \mathbb{R} \to \mathbb{R}$ by the expression

$$\boxed{f(x) = a \cdot b^x.}$$

We say that f is an **exponential function**. The number b is called the **base** of the exponential and the number a is called its **initial value**. As we shall see, exponential functions turn an arithmetic sequence of inputs into a geometric sequence of outputs.

EXAMPLE 3.1. Table 3.2 gives the population p (in thousands of inhabitants) of a small city, as recorded by the clerk in City Hall on January 1st of each year throughout the early 1980's. By measuring time t in years and letting $t = 0$ represent the year 1980, we can define p as a function of t. Note in particular that p is *not* a linear function, as the output values in the table do not form an arithmetic sequence:

$$67.38 \xrightarrow{+1.75} 69.13 \xrightarrow{+1.80} 70.93 \xrightarrow{+1.84} 72.77 \xrightarrow{+1.89} 74.66 \xrightarrow{+1.94} 76.60 \xrightarrow{+1.99} 78.59.$$

TABLE 3.2. The population of a small city, measured in thousands of inhabitants.

year	1980	1981	1982	1983	1984	1985	1986
t	0	1	2	3	4	5	6
$p(t)$	67.38	69.13	70.93	72.77	74.66	76.60	78.59

However the values of p in the table *do* come very close to forming a geometric sequence. This is easy to see if we divide each value by its predecessor:

$$\frac{69.13}{67.38} \approx 1.025972, \qquad \frac{70.93}{69.13} \approx 1.026038, \qquad \frac{72.77}{70.93} \approx 1.025941,$$

$$\frac{74.66}{72.77} \approx 1.025972, \qquad \frac{76.60}{74.66} \approx 1.025985, \qquad \frac{78.59}{76.60} \approx 1.025979.$$

Evidently, we go from one value of p to the next by multiplying by a common base, in this case approximately 1.026:

$$67.38 \xrightarrow{\times 1.026} 69.13 \xrightarrow{\times 1.026} 70.93 \xrightarrow{\times 1.026} 72.77 \xrightarrow{\times 1.026} 74.66 \xrightarrow{\times 1.026} 76.60 \xrightarrow{\times 1.026} 78.59.$$

This means that we can arrive at the value of $p(t)$ by starting with our initial value of $p(0) = 67.38$ and multiplying by the base 1.026 a total of t times. Therefore p is an exponential function described by the formula

$$p(t) = 67.38 \cdot 1.026^{t}.$$

We can use this formula to make predictions about the future population of our city. For instance, according to our formula, the population at the start of the year 2005 should have been:

$$p(25) = 67.38 \cdot 1.026^{25} \approx 128.001.$$

Whether there really were 128 001 people living in our city in 2005 is a matter for the record books; if there were, then we would say that our exponential function p did a good job of modeling the real behavior of this population. If this were the case, then we could also say that the population is exhibiting ***exponential growth***.

EXAMPLE 3.2. Carbon-14 (also known as C-14) is a radioactive isotope of carbon which "decays" over time with a ***half-life*** of about 5 730 years. This means that if we start with, say, 10 grams of C-14, then after about 5 730 years we will only have 5 grams left; the rest will have turned into more stable nitrogen. After a second half-life, there will only be 2.5 grams of C-14 left in our sample, and after yet another half-life, there will only be 1.25 grams. No matter how much C-14 we start off with, after any period of 5 730 years, there will only be half as much as there was in the beginning. Therefore, we can describe how much C-14 (in grams) we have in our sample after t years by the exponential function

$$g(t) = 10 \cdot 0.5^{t/5\,730}.$$

This function takes the initial amount of 10 grams and multiplies it by 0.5 a total of $\frac{t}{5\,730}$ times, once for every half-life that has elapsed in the t years.

Thus, after 57 300 years (or after 10 half-lives), our sample will contain only a minuscule amount of C-14:

$$g(57\,300) = 10 \cdot 0.5^{\,57\,300/5\,730} = 10 \cdot 0.5^{\,10} = 0.009\,765\,625 \text{ grams.}$$

This sort of behavior is called **exponential decay**.

EXAMPLE 3.3. Suppose that a sum of \$3 000.00 is deposited in a savings account that pays an annual interest of 4.5%. At the end of each year, the amount of interest earned is computed by multiplying the principal (the amount of money in the account – in this case \$3 000.00) times 0.045:

$$\text{interest} = 3\,000 \times 0.045 = 135.00;$$

Thus, after one year, we will have \$3 135.00 in our savings account. Assuming there are no withdrawals, the principal plus interest will accrue more interest the following year, more the year after that, and so on. Thus, the bank account will grow in value from the initial \$3 000.00 to \$3 135.00 to \$3 276.08 to \$3 423.50, and so forth. In general, a principal of P dollars will accrue $P \cdot 0.045$ dollars in interest, so after one year the new principal will be

$$
\begin{aligned}
\text{new principal} &= \text{old principal} + \text{interest} \\
&= P + P \cdot 0.045 \\
&= P \cdot (1 + 0.045) \\
&= P \cdot 1.045.
\end{aligned}
$$

In other words, each time interest is **compounded**, the new principal is equal to the old principal times 1.045. In this case, the fractional part of 0.045 corresponds to the 4.5% interest, while the whole number part of 1 refers to the original deposit. (There is not much of a market for savings accounts that pay interest *in exchange for*, rather than *in addition to*, the original deposit.) Therefore, after t years, the principal $P(t)$ in our account is found by taking the initial principal balance of \$3 000 and multiplying by 1.045 a total of t times:

$$P(t) = 3\,000 \cdot 1.045^t.$$

Thus, after seven years, our savings account will have a balance of

$$P(7) = 3\,000 \cdot 1.045^{\,7} \approx 4\,082.59.$$

In the last three examples we were careful to make sure that the power to which we were raising each base was always a positive integer. In particular, we only considered the population of a city on January 1st of each year, the amount of carbon-14 after a whole number of half-lifes, and the principal balance in our savings account immediately after the yearly interest had been accrued. In reality, however, these quantities vary continuously over time. We might be interested in the population of our city on, say, March 14th, 2007 (when t = 27.2), or the amount of carbon-14 after

1000 years (approximately 0.175 of the half-life). The bank might even need to calculate the interest earned in the first three months of the year (when $t = 0.25$) if we decided to close our account as an April Fools' prank. In each of these scenarios, our formulas would require us to compute an exponential with a fractional, or perhaps even an irrational, power.

Before we contemplate what exponentials mean in the real numbers, we must first consider exponentials in the realm of positive integers. There, exponentiation is simply a shorthand for repeated multiplication. Thus, we have

$$1.026^{25} = \underbrace{1.026 \cdot 1.026 \cdot 1.026 \cdots 1.026 \cdot 1.026 \cdot 1.026}_{25 \text{ copies of } 1.026} = 1.899\,696\ldots,$$

$$0.5^{10} = \underbrace{0.5 \cdot 0.5 \cdot 0.5 \cdot 0.5 \cdot 0.5 \cdot 0.5 \cdot 0.5 \cdot 0.5 \cdot 0.5 \cdot 0.5}_{10 \text{ copies of } 0.5} = 0.000\,977\ldots,$$

$$1.045^{7} = \underbrace{1.045 \cdot 1.045 \cdot 1.045 \cdot 1.045 \cdot 1.045 \cdot 1.045 \cdot 1.045}_{7 \text{ copies of } 1.045} = 1.360\,862\ldots.$$

Observe that each one of our exponentials above obeys the following key property:

$$(3.1) \qquad b^p \cdot b^q = \underbrace{b \cdot b \cdots b \cdot b}_{p \text{ copies of } b} \cdot \underbrace{b \cdot b \cdots b \cdot b}_{q \text{ copies of } b} = \underbrace{b \cdot b \cdots b \cdot b}_{p+q \text{ copies of } b} = b^{p+q}.$$

We call this formula the ***defining property*** for exponentials with base b because it succinctly captures the notion of repeated multiplication. For example, we have

$$b \cdot b = b^1 \cdot b^1 = b^{1+1} = b^2,$$

$$b \cdot b \cdot b = b^2 \cdot b^1 = b^{2+1} = b^3,$$

$$b \cdot b \cdot b \cdot b = b^3 \cdot b^1 = b^{3+1} = b^4,$$

$$b \cdot b \cdot b \cdot b \cdot b = b^4 \cdot b^1 = b^{4+1} = b^5,$$

and so on. Of course, this property only holds when p and q are positive integers; otherwise, the expressions b^p and b^q are meaningless. That is, they are meaningless until *we define what they should mean*. In particular, when our intuition fails us, we shall rely on mathematical consistency to guide us. For instance, back in Example 1.35 on page 53, we asserted that

$$\boxed{b^0 = 1.}$$

This is the only choice that preserves the integrity of the defining property. Indeed, with this definition in place, we have

$$b^p \cdot b^0 = b^p \cdot 1 = b^p = b^{p+0},$$

which is perfectly consistent with our computation above. We can take things one step further by defining b^{-p} as the reciprocal of b^p:

$$b^{-p} = \frac{1}{b^p}.$$

Again, this definition is the only choice that would be consistent with our defining property, since it gives us

$$b^p \cdot b^{-p} = b^p \cdot \frac{1}{b^p} = 1 = b^0 = b^{p-p}.$$

Finally, note that if p is a positive integer, then the defining property implies that

$$\underbrace{b^q \cdot b^q \cdot b^q \cdot \ldots \cdot b^q \cdot b^q \cdot b^q}_{p \text{ copies of } b^q} = b^{\overbrace{q+q+q+\cdots+q+q+q}^{p \text{ copies of } q}}.$$

This gives us the following property for raising an exponential b^q to an integer power p:

$$\left(b^q\right)^p = b^{p \cdot q}.$$

In the special case that $q = \frac{1}{p}$, this property becomes

$$\left(b^{\frac{1}{p}}\right)^p = \underbrace{b^{\frac{1}{p}} \cdot b^{\frac{1}{p}} \cdot b^{\frac{1}{p}} \cdot \ldots \cdot b^{\frac{1}{p}} \cdot b^{\frac{1}{p}} \cdot b^{\frac{1}{p}}}_{p \text{ copies of } b^{\frac{1}{p}}} = b^{\overbrace{\frac{1}{p}+\frac{1}{p}+\frac{1}{p}+\cdots+\frac{1}{p}+\frac{1}{p}+\frac{1}{p}}^{p \text{ copies of } \frac{1}{p}}} = b^{p \cdot \frac{1}{p}} = b^1 = b,$$

which in turn tells us that we ought to define $b^{\frac{1}{p}}$ as the pth root of b:

$$b^{\frac{1}{p}} = \sqrt[p]{b}.$$

As before, this definition is the only possible choice that would be consistent with our defining property. In particular, it gives us

$$\left(b^{\frac{1}{p}}\right)^p = \left(\sqrt[p]{b}\right)^p = b,$$

which, again, agrees with the desired result above.

EXAMPLE 3.4. With all of the above stipulations in place, the exponential b^x is now well-defined for any positive base b and any rational number $x \in \mathbb{Q}$. For instance, we have:

$$4^{-5} = \frac{1}{4^5} = \frac{1}{1024},$$

$$25^{3/2} = \left(25^{1/2}\right)^3 = \left(\sqrt{25}\right)^3 = 5^3 = 125,$$

$$27^{-4/3} = \left(27^{1/3}\right)^{-4} = \left(\sqrt[3]{27}\right)^{-4} = 3^{-4} = \frac{1}{3^4} = \frac{1}{81}.$$

EXAMPLE 3.5. Earlier, in Example 3.2, we considered a chemical sample containing 10 grams of carbon-14, noting that the amount of radioactive material in the sample after t years is given (in grams) by the exponential function

$$g(t) = 10 \cdot 0.5^{t/5\,730}.$$

Going back in time 11 460 years, or two half-lives ago, our sample would have consisted of 40 grams of carbon-14:

$$
\begin{aligned}
g(-11\,460) &= 10 \cdot 0.5^{-11\,460/5\,730} \\
&= 10 \cdot 0.5^{-2} \\
&= 10 \cdot \left(\tfrac{1}{0.5}\right)^2 \\
&= 10 \cdot 2^2 \\
&= 40.
\end{aligned}
$$

Of course, this is perfectly reasonable since there should have been twice as much carbon-14 (in other words, 20 grams) in the sample one half-life ago, and twice that amount (40 grams) two half-lives ago.

On the other hand, we can expect that 1 146 years (one fifth of a half-life) from now, our sample will only contain approximately 8.706 grams of carbon-14:

$$
\begin{aligned}
g(1146) &= 10 \cdot 0.5^{1146/5730} \\
&= 10 \cdot 0.5^{1/5} \\
&= 10 \cdot \sqrt[5]{0.5} \\
&= 8.705\,505\,633\ldots.
\end{aligned}
$$

Observe that, according to this computation, about 13% of the carbon-14 has decayed away in one fifth of a half-life. Perhaps you might have expected that only 10% (that is, one fifth of one half) would have been lost in this time, and that the sample would still contain 90% (compared to 87%) of the original carbon-14. However, that would be reasoning linearly, and not exponentially.

Having tackled exponentials in the rational numbers, we are now prepared to face one of the strangest and most esoteric creatures in all of mathematics: an exponential with an irrational power. For example, let us consider the value of 2^π. As before, we shall proceed by sheer force of will, asserting that if q is a rational number near π, then the value of 2^q should also be near the mysterious value of 2^π:

$$q \approx \pi \qquad \Leftrightarrow \qquad 2^q \approx 2^\pi.$$

In particular, since we know that

$$\pi = 3.141\,592\,653\,589\,793\,238\,462\,643\,383\,279\ldots,$$

we can take a look at the following sequence of numbers:

$$2^3 = 8,$$

$$2^{3.1} = 2^{31/10} = \left(\sqrt[10]{2}\right)^{31} = 8.574\,187\,700\ldots,$$

$$2^{3.14} = 2^{314/100} = \left(\sqrt[100]{2}\right)^{314} = 8.815\,240\,927\ldots,$$

$$2^{3.141} = 2^{3\,141/1\,000} = \left(\sqrt[1\,000]{2}\right)^{3\,141} = 8.821\,353\,304\ldots,$$

$$2^{3.141\,5} = 2^{31\,415/10\,000} = \left(\sqrt[10\,000]{2}\right)^{31\,415} = 8.824\,411\,082\ldots,$$

$$2^{3.141\,59} = 2^{314\,159/100\,000} = \left(\sqrt[100\,000]{2}\right)^{314\,159} = 8.824\,961\,595\ldots,$$

$$2^{3.141\,592} = 2^{3\,141\,592/1\,000\,000} = \left(\sqrt[1\,000\,000]{2}\right)^{3\,141\,592} = 8.824\,973\,829\ldots.$$

In each case, we are raising 2 to a rational power, and so we can compute the value of the exponential by taking an appropriate power of a root of 2. After a few computations, you should notice that our answers are getting closer and closer to one another, and that we see more and more digits stabilizing.[1] In fact, by our seventh computation, we might already suspect that the first five digits of our answer are stable. This is indeed the case. Our answers are getting closer and closer to some elusive number which we shall define as 2^π – a real number always a millimeter or two beyond our grasp and yet revealing itself to us a few digits at a time as:

$$2^\pi = 8.824\,977\,827\,076\,287\,623\,856\,429\,604\,208\ldots.$$

---

[1] If you don't remember what it means for the digits to stabilize, take another look at the description of the Babylonian Algorithm in pages 58 – 59.

We shall take the approach described above to define b^x whenever x is irrational: Namely, we shall consider a sequence of rational approximations getting closer and closer to x, raise b to each of these rational approximations, and then look at the real number that these rational powers of b get closer and closer to. In other words, the value of b^x is defined to be the limit of this sequence of approximations. That the sequence of approximations we choose does not affect the outcome of the limiting process, and, indeed, that there is always a result to get closer and closer to, is a truly deep and remarkable result of mathematical analysis. Equally remarkable is the fact that our defining property survives this limiting process. Consequently, we also have the following set of properties, each of which can be deduced from the defining property as we did in pages 244 and 245.

Exponential Rules

For any positive base $b \neq 1$ and any pair of real exponents x and y:

① $b^{x+y} = b^x \cdot b^y$,

② $b^{x-y} = b^x / b^y$,

③ $b^{x \cdot y} = \left(b^x\right)^y = \left(b^y\right)^x$,

④ $b^{x/y} = \sqrt[y]{b^x} = \left(\sqrt[y]{b}\right)^x$,

⑤ $b^x = b^y$ if and only if $x = y$.

The first four of these properties allow us to move arithmetic operations from inside the exponent to outside the exponential, and vice versa. Thus, addition inside the exponent becomes multiplication outside the exponential, subtraction inside the exponent becomes division outside the exponential, and so on. In contrast, the fifth property tells us that two exponentials of the same base can only be equal to one another if the exponents in question are also equal to each other.

EXAMPLE 3.6. Solve the equation $3^{x+1} = 27$.

Solution. Observe that $27 = 3^3$, so we can rewrite our equation as:
$$3^{x+1} = 3^3.$$

We now have two exponentials, both with a base of 3, that are equal to each other. According to Exponential Rule ⑤, the only way this can happen is if the two exponents are equal. This means that we must have:
$$x + 1 = 3.$$

Therefore $x = 2$ is the only solution to our equation.

EXAMPLE 3.7. Solve the equation $2^{-x^2} = \dfrac{4^x}{8}$.

Solution. Again, our goal will be to express each side of the equation as a single exponential. We can do this since $4 = 2^2$ and $8 = 2^3$ are both powers of 2. Thus, we can use Exponential Rules ③ and ② (in that order) to simplify the expression on the right hand side of our equation as follows:

$$\frac{4^x}{8} = \frac{\left(2^2\right)^x}{2^3} = \frac{2^{2x}}{2^3} = 2^{2x-3}.$$

Our equation has now been transformed into a pair of exponentials of the same base that are set equal to one another:

$$2^{-x^2} = 2^{2x-3}.$$

Therefore, using Exponential Rule ⑤, we can set the exponents equal to each other and solve for x as follows:

$$-x^2 = 2x - 3$$

$$0 = x^2 + 2x - 3$$

$$0 = (x+3)(x-1).$$

Evidently, our solution set is $\{-3, 1\}$.

EXAMPLE 3.8. Solve the equation $\left(7^x\right)^{x-1} - 7 = 0$.

Solution. We use Exponential Rule ③ to simplify our equation as follows:

$$\left(7^x\right)^{x-1} - 7 = 0$$

$$\left(7^x\right)^{x-1} = 7$$

$$7^{x(x-1)} = 7^1.$$

This gives us two exponentials of the same base that are equal to each other, so we can use Exponential Rule ⑤ to set the two exponents equal:

$$x(x-1) = 1$$

$$x^2 - x - 1 = 0.$$

Then by applying the quadratic formula (or by factoring as in Example 1.23 on page 31), we find that our equation has two solutions:

$$x = \frac{1 + \sqrt{5}}{2} = \varphi \qquad \text{and} \qquad x = \frac{1 - \sqrt{5}}{2} = -\frac{1}{\varphi}.$$

EXAMPLE 3.9. Solve the equation $4^x - 2^x = 12$.

Solution. This equation involves exponentials in two different bases. However, since $4 = 2^2$ is a power of 2, we can rewrite our equation in terms of two exponentials with base 2. We do this by noting that, according to Exponential Rule ③, we have

$$4^x = \left(2^2\right)^x = 2^{2x}.$$

Thus, our equation becomes

$$2^{2x} - 2^x = 12.$$

The main difficulty we now confront is that it is not entirely clear how to simplify the left side of this equation. You will note that the Exponential Rules allow us to combine products, fractions, powers, and even roots of exponentials, but there is no rule that helps us simplify exponentials that are added together or subtracted from one another. In particular, observe that Exponential Rule ② does not apply here because the minus sign is *outside* the exponentials, not *inside* the exponent.

As it turns out, there is an ingenious trick for solving this kind of problem. They key is to observe that we can invoke Exponential Rule ③ in order to express the more complicated exponential 2^{2x} in terms of the simpler 2^x:

$$2^{2x} = \left(2^x\right)^2.$$

Thus, by replacing 2^x with the "dummy variable" z, we can transform our original equation into the more manageable

$$z^2 - z = 12.$$

The point is that we are now trying to solve a quadratic equation, which is relatively simple for us now that we have the quadratic formula. In this case, however, we can even factor our equation as follows:

$$z^2 - z = 12$$

$$z^2 - z - 12 = 0$$

$$\left(z + 3\right)\left(z - 4\right) = 0.$$

This tells us that either $z = -3$ or $z = 4$. Putting things back in terms of x, we arrive at two possibilities:

$$2^x = -3 \qquad \text{or} \qquad 2^x = 4.$$

Now, for the first of these, we note that an exponential of the form 2^x is always positive. This is certainly true when x is a positive integer, in which case 2^x is some number of copies of the number 2 multiplied together. It remains true even if we let x be a negative integer, a fraction, or an irrational number. This will become clear very soon, when we sketch the graph of the exponential function $f(x) = 2^x$. For now, let us simply accept the fact that 2^x can never equal -3, which leaves us with only one possibility:

$$2^x = 4.$$

Rewriting $4 = 2^2$ as a power of 2 and applying Exponential Rule ⑤,

$$2^x = 2^2$$

$$x = 2,$$

allows us to conclude that our only solution is $x = 2$, as you can promptly verify by substituting back into our original equation.

We can sketch the graph of any exponential function by plotting points. As in our earlier expeditions with graphing functions, the more points we plot, the better a picture of the graph we get. For example, in the case of the function

$$f(x) = 2^x,$$

plotting just a few hundred points (a task not as enjoyable as you might otherwise expect) reveals the curve shown in Figure 3.1.

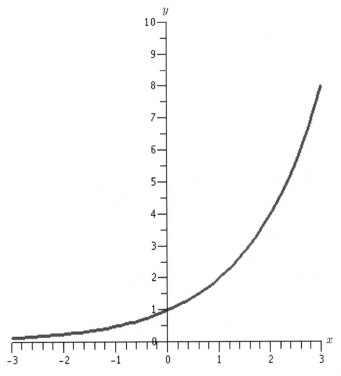

FIGURE 3.1. The graph of the exponential function $f(x) = 2^x$.

This curve has several features worth mentioning. First of all, note that

$$f(0) = 2^0 = 1,$$

so the graph of f has its y-intercept at the point $(0,1)$. To one side of this intercept, as the values of x get large and positive, the output values of f will grow faster and faster without bound, as we already saw in Table 3.1. Thus, the right hand side of the graph heads off to infinity. In contrast, as we move to the left of the intercept and the values of x get large but negative, the corresponding output values of f will get smaller and smaller. Indeed, these output values will be the reciprocals of the values we saw on the right hand side of the graph. They will get arbitrarily small, but never quite reach zero, and certainly never become negative. This means that the left hand side of the graph of f will exhibit a horizontal asymptote along the negative x-axis, getting closer and closer to it, but without ever touching it.

Once you have seen the graph of one exponential function, you have pretty well seen them all. For instance, consider the function $g(x) = 4^x$. Since the base $4 = 2^2$ is a power of two, we can rewrite the formula for g as

$$g(x) = 4^x = \left(2^2\right)^x = 2^{2x} = f(2x).$$

This means that the graph of $g(x) = 4^x$ is simply a copy of the graph of $f(x) = 2^x$ that has been compressed horizontally by a dilation factor of $\frac{1}{2}$. The dilation will make the ascent to infinity on the right of the graph steeper and the asymptotic behavior towards zero on the left faster, but other than that the graphs will look pretty much the same, as you can see in Figure 3.2 (a). As before, we say this graph exhibits exponential growth.

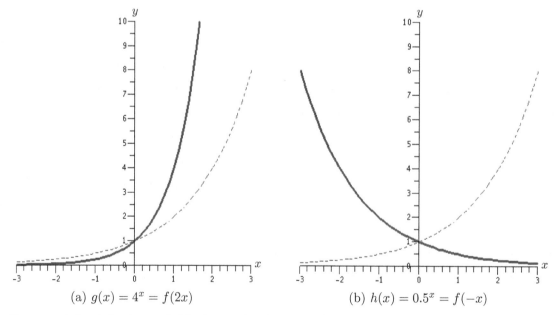

(a) $g(x) = 4^x = f(2x)$ (b) $h(x) = 0.5^x = f(-x)$

FIGURE 3.2. A horizontal dilation and reflection of the exponential function $f(x) = 2^x$.

In contrast, consider the graph of the function $h(x) = 0.5^x$. Again, we can express the base $0.5 = 2^{-1}$ as a power of two, this time with a negative exponent. Thus,

$$h(x) = 0.5^x = \left(2^{-1}\right)^x = 2^{-x} = f(-x),$$

so that $h(x) = 0.5^x$ is the horizontal reflection of $f(x) = 2^x$ across the y-axis. The graph still has a y-intercept at $(0, 1)$, but it now heads towards infinity on the left and asymptotes towards the x-axis on the right, as shown in Figure 3.2 (b). In other words, this graph exhibits exponential decay.

It turns out that the graph of any exponential function whatsoever may be found through some linear transformation of this type. The only exception is the exponential with base 1, whose graph is just the horizontal line $y = 1^x = 1$. In all other cases, the key will be to express the base b of the exponential in question as a power of two. Since the graph in Figure 3.1 forms a continuous curve with no gaps, every positive number b may, indeed, be written as some power of two:

$$b = 2^p.$$

If the base b happens to be greater than one, then the corresponding power p will be a positive number and the desired graph will be a dilated version of the graph of f. In particular, the function will exhibit exponential growth. On the other hand, if b is less than one, then the exponent p will be a negative number. Consequently, our graph will also be reflected horizontally, and thus, will exhibit exponential decay. In either case, the long-term behavior of our exponential function, whether it is growth or decay, is entirely determined by the base b.

The Basic Behavior of Exponentials

Let $f(x) = b^x$ be an exponential function with base $b > 0$.

- If $b = 1$, then the graph of f is a horizontal line.
- If $b > 1$, then the graph of f exhibits exponential growth.
- If $0 < b < 1$, then the graph of f exhibits exponential decay.

It should be noted that, except in the simplest of cases, determining the precise value of the power that corresponds to any given positive number can be a rather tedious and uninspiring affair. For example, we can see in Figure 3.3 that the number $b = 3$ can be written as a power of two by taking $p \approx 1.585$:

$$3 \approx 2^{1.585}.$$

Finding the exact value of the power p, however, will require significantly more work. Nevertheless, towards the end of the sixteenth century, the Scottish mathematician

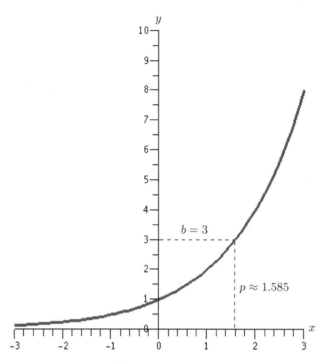

FIGURE 3.3. The number 3 can be written as a power of 2.

John Napier (1550–1617) invested the considerable peace and quiet afforded him by his position of nobility as Laird of Merchiston Castle, near Edinburgh, to address this very question. In 1614, Napier published a large table of "ratio numbers," or "logarithms," in which one could look up a number b and find the corresponding power p. (Actually, Napier used the base $0.999\,999\,9$ instead of 2, but the idea is essentially the same.) It took him twenty years to complete this table, but his work had deep repercussions in the way people computed for the next three hundred and fifty years. Indeed, it was not until the advent of the electronic hand-held calculator in the 1960's and 1970's that Napier's logarithms finally went out of vogue. We shall return to the topic of logarithms in Section 3.3, after we take a closer, more in-depth look at the graphs of these exponential functions.

Reading Comprehension Questions for Section 3.1

An exponential function maps ___(a)___ sequences of inputs to ___(b)___ sequences of outputs. This means that we can find each output value by ___(c)___ the previous value times a fixed number b. This number b is sometimes called the ___(d)___ of the exponential function. We can describe the exponential function by the formula $f(x) = a \cdot b^x$. Here, the number a is called the ___(e)___ and represents the ___(f)___ in the graph of the function.

If b is a positive number greater than ___(g)___, the values of the function grow faster and faster without bound. This phenomenon is known as ___(h)___, and can be used to model the way that the ___(i)___ of a city grows in times of prosperity. It also describes the way that ___(j)___ is added to the principal balance in a savings account. For example, suppose that we invest $100 and earn 5% annually. Then, every year, we can compute our new principal by multiplying the old one times ___(k)___. Thus, after one year we will have $___(l)___, after two years we will have $___(m)___, and after three years we will have $___(n)___.

On the other hand, if b is a positive number between ___(o)___ and ___(p)___, the values of the function decrease, and become closer and closer to ___(q)___. This phenomenon is known as ___(r)___. It is used to model the way that ___(s)___ decay over time into other more stable elements. Regardless of the amount of material we start off with, it takes the same amount of time T for half of the original material to decay away. In this case, T is known as the ___(t)___ of the material. For example, suppose that we start with 100 grams of carbon-14. Then, after $T = 5\,730$ years, we will only have ___(u)___ grams; after $2 \times 5\,730 =$ ___(v)___ years, we will have ___(w)___ grams; and after $3 \times 5\,730 =$ ___(x)___ years, we will have ___(y)___ grams of carbon-14. According to this model, the amount of carbon-14 will never completely decay away since the graph of an exponential function has a ___(z)___ and never touches the x-axis or becomes negative.

Exercises for Section 3.1

In Exercises 1–6, determine whether each table describes an exponential function. If it does, find a formula for the function. If it does not, determine whether the table describes a linear or a quadratic function.

1.
x	0	1	2	3	4
$f(x)$	3	6	12	21	33

2.
x	0	1	2	3	4
$f(x)$	$\frac{1}{4}$	1	4	16	64

3.
x	0	1	2	3	4
$f(x)$	$\frac{2}{3}$	1	$\frac{3}{2}$	$\frac{9}{4}$	$\frac{27}{8}$

4.
x	0	1	2	3	4
$f(x)$	1	3	5	7	9

5.
x	0	1	2	3	4
$f(x)$	100	10	1	0.1	0.01

6.
x	0	1	2	3	4
$f(x)$	0.25	0.5	1	1.75	2.75

7. Determine the exact value of each expression below without using a calculator or computer.

   (a) $8^{5/3}$ (b) $32^{2/5}$ (c) $49^{3/2}$ (d) $81^{3/4}$

8. Suppose that we set $b = \frac{1}{4}$. Using a calculator or a computer, determine the decimal expansions for the following numbers, remembering that, according to the order of operations, the value of the exponents must be computed first.

   (a) b^b (b) b^{b^b} (c) $b^{b^{b^b}}$ (d) $b^{b^{b^{b^b}}}$

   (e) The numbers in the sequence above are getting closer and closer to the number

$$b^* = b^{b^{b^{b^{\cdot^{\cdot^{\cdot}}}}}}$$

   where the powers repeat indefinitely. Find the exact value of b^*.

9. Let φ denote the golden ratio (see page 20), and consider the exponential function

$$f(x) = \frac{1}{\sqrt{5}} \cdot \varphi^x.$$

   (a) Complete the table below with the values for this function.

   (b) Round each of your answers from part (a) to the nearest integer. Do these values seem familiar? What kind of population might $f(x)$ be used to model?

n	1	2	3	4	5	6	7	8	9	10
$f(n)$										

In Exercises 10–15, interpret each function as a linear transformation of a model function of the form $f(x) = b^x$, for an appropriate choice of b. Use this information to sketch its graph. Be sure to label at least three points in the graph and find the equation of the horizontal asymptote.

10. $g(x) = 3 \cdot 4^x$

11. $g(x) = 5 + 2^x$

12. $g(x) = 7^{-x/2}$

13. $g(x) = 2^{x-4} + 1$

14. $g(x) = 7 - 2^{-x}$

15. $g(x) = 5^{2-x} - 3$

In Exercises 16–21, solve each equation. Be sure to check your solutions.

16. $2^{2x-1/2} = 32\sqrt{2}$

17. $5^{x+2} = 25^{x-1}$

18. $6^{x^2} \cdot 6^{7x} \cdot 6^{12} = 1$

19. $3^{1-2x} = 27^{x^2}$

20. $4^x + 9 \cdot 2^x + 8 = 0$

21. $x^{2/3} + 6x^{1/3} - 7 = 0$

22. Find a formula for the exponential function $f(x) = a\,b^x$ whose graph passes through the points $(1, 3)$ and $(3, 15)$.

23. Suppose that the function $g : \mathbb{R} \to \mathbb{R}$ is defined by the formula

$$g(x) = A + B^x,$$

where A and B are constants. Suppose further that the graph of g goes through the points $(1, 4)$ and $(2, 10)$. Determine the values of A and B. (Remember that $g(x)$ should be defined for all real numbers x.)

24. As part of a photography project, Acute Alice is experimenting with different types of tinted glass. If a single pane of tinted glass obliterates 3% of the light passing through it, then the percent of light that passes through x successive panes is given by the function

$$p(x) = 100 \cdot 0.97^x.$$

What percent of light will pass through 10 panes? Through 25 panes?

25. Obtuse Ollie wants to buy a used car. He finds that the cost C of a car that is x years old is given by the function

$$C(x) = 16\,630 \cdot 0.9^x.$$

How much does a car cost when it is 3 years old? When it is 9 years old?

26. Scalene Sallie is volunteering at a retirement community that houses 700 residents. Suppose that a rumor is spreading throughout the community, and that the function

$$R(t) = 700\left(1 - 2^{-0.2t}\right)$$

describes the number of residents who have heard the rumor after t days. How long will it be before half of the retirees have heard the rumor? How long before 75% of them have heard it?

27. It is typical for a bank to pay interest periodically, say twice, four times, or twelve times a year. In that case, each installment of interest is computed as a fraction of the annual interest, depending on the total number of installments, according to the formula

$$P(t) = P_0 \cdot \left(1 + \frac{r}{n}\right)^{nt},$$

where P_0 is the initial principal in the account, r is the annual interest rate (written as a decimal), and n is the number of times interest is paid out every year.

   (a) Suppose that $100 is deposited in a savings account that pays an annual interest rate of 4%, compounded twice a year. How much interest is generated in one year?

   (b) Suppose that $100 is deposited in a savings account that pays an annual interest rate of 4%, compounded quarterly. How much interest is generated in one year?

   (c) Suppose that $100 is deposited in a savings account that pays an annual interest rate of 4%, compounded monthly. How much interest is generated in one year?

   (d) Why is receiving interest in small installments throughout the year better for a short-term investor than receiving a single lump sum payment at the end of the year? Why is it better for a long-term investor? How does paying interest in small installments benefit the bank?

28. According to Figure 3.3 on page 254, we can express 3 as a power of 2,

$$3 = 2^p,$$

by taking $p \approx 1.585$. One way to see this is by observing that $2^{1.584} \approx 2.998$ is slightly less than 3, while $2^{1.586} \approx 3.002$ is slightly greater than 3. Use a calculator or computer to find the decimal expansion for the power p accurate to six places after the decimal point.

29. Obtuse Ollie noticed the definition for an exponential function required that the base b be a positive number. He is trying to understand why $b = 0$ should not be considered a viable base. To help him out, Alice suggests that he try to evaluate

the expression

$$y = 0^x$$

under a variety of conditions. For which of the following is y well-defined? What is the value of y in each of those cases?

(a) When x is a positive integer.

(b) When x is a negative integer.

(c) When x is a rational number.

(d) When x is an irrational number.

30. Scalene Sallie also noticed that the definition for an exponential function required that the base b be a positive number. She is trying to understand why $b = -1$ should not be considered a viable base. Again, Alice suggests that she try to evaluate the expression

$$y = (-1)^x$$

under a variety of conditions. For which of the following is y well-defined? What is the value of y in each of those cases?

(a) When x is an even integer.

(b) When x is an odd integer.

(c) When x is a rational number.

(d) When x is an irrational number.

3.2. Rates of Change Revisited

With one notable exception, the graph of every exponential function comes in one of two flavors: exponential growth or exponential decay. Certainly, the graph of each function is distinguished by its y-intercept (determined by the function's initial value) and by the particular speed at which it grows or decays (determined by its base). However, except for these minor details, the graph of every exponential function looks pretty much the same. For instance, the graph of the function

$$f(x) = 2^x$$

consists of a continuous curve that crosses the y-axis at the point $(0, 1)$. To the left of this point, the graph slowly approaches the x-axis, coming ever closer to its asymptote. To the right, the graph curves upward, climbing faster and faster towards infinity. Now this curvature is best appreciated from relatively far away, as in Figure 3.4 (a). If we were to zoom in close enough to some portion of the graph, then we would no longer be able to recognize the curvature at all. Instead, we might even confuse the graph with a perfectly straight line. We can observe this phenomenon in Figure 3.4 (b), which shows a zoomed-in version of the graph of f, together with a carefully chosen line passing through the same y-intercept at the point $(0, 1)$. Notice that in this close-up view, the graph of our exponential function is essentially indistinguishable from the straight line. For this reason, we say that the graph of an exponential function is ***locally linear***.

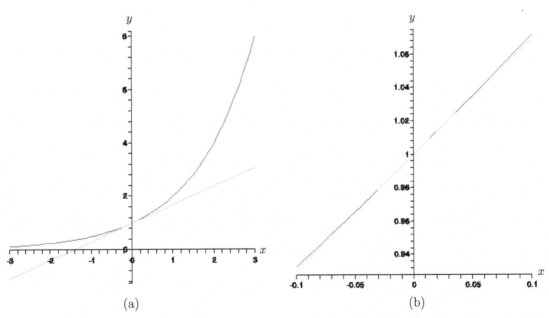

(a)   (b)

FIGURE 3.4. The graph of $f(x) = 2^x$ and a carefully-chosen line passing through the point $(0, 1)$.

261

EXAMPLE 3.10. Nearly every graph that we have looked at so far – every circle, every parabola, and every hyperbola, for instance – has been locally linear. The only exception has been the graph of Dirichlet's function

$$q(x) = \begin{cases} 1 & \text{if } x \text{ is rational} \\ 0 & \text{if } x \text{ is irrational} \end{cases}$$

from Example 1.78, which is *not* locally linear. To see why not, remember that this graph, shown in Figure 1.32 on page 114, consists of points distributed between two horizontal lines. Even though these points are densely packed in each line, so that there are no large appreciable gaps, we can always detect some nearby "holes" no matter how close we zoom in to the graph. In fact, the more we zoom in, the more holes we can detect. Therefore, we will never be able to think of any portion of this graph as a single line!

The slope of the line in Figure 3.4 represents the rate at which the exponential function f is changing at the very instant that its graph crosses the y-axis. Therefore, we shall refer to this slope as the ***instantaneous rate of change*** of f when $x = 0$. We can obtain an approximate value for this slope by calculating the *average* rate of change of f on a small interval containing the point $x = 0$. For instance, the average rate of change of f on the interval $[-1, 1]$ is given by the difference quotient

$$\frac{\Delta f}{\Delta x} = \frac{f(1) - f(-1)}{1 - (-1)} = \frac{2^1 - 2^{-1}}{2} = \frac{2 - 0.5}{2} = \frac{1.5}{2} = 0.75.$$

Of course, this is only a rough approximation to the instantaneous rate of change when $x = 0$. We can get a better approximation by choosing a smaller interval. For example, if we instead look at the interval $[-0.1, 0.1]$, we shall find an average rate of change of

$$\frac{\Delta f}{\Delta x} = \frac{f(0.1) - f(-0.1)}{0.1 - (-0.1)} = \frac{2^{0.1} - 2^{-0.1}}{0.2} = 0.693\,702\,354\ldots.$$

Better still, if we consider the interval $[-0.01, 0.01]$, then we find an average rate of change of

$$\frac{\Delta f}{\Delta x} = \frac{f(0.01) - f(-0.01)}{0.01 - (-0.01)} = \frac{2^{0.01} - 2^{-0.01}}{0.02} = 0.693\,152\,730\ldots.$$

Table 3.3 shows the average rates of change of f over these, and even smaller intervals, all containing the point $x = 0$. In each case, the smaller the interval, the closer the average rate of change comes to the instantaneous rate of change that we are looking for. Notice that the digits in these approximations are stabilizing! If we were to compute more difference quotients over even smaller intervals, we would eventually

TABLE 3.3. The average rate of change of the exponential function $f(x) = 2^x$ over a sequence of smaller and smaller intervals about $x = 0$.

interval	average rate of change
$[-1, 1]$	$\dfrac{\Delta f}{\Delta x} = \dfrac{2^1 - 2^{-1}}{2} = 0.75$
$[-0.1, 0.1]$	$\dfrac{\Delta f}{\Delta x} = \dfrac{2^{0.1} - 2^{-0.1}}{0.2} = 0.693\,702\,354\ldots$
$[-0.01, 0.01]$	$\dfrac{\Delta f}{\Delta x} = \dfrac{2^{0.01} - 2^{-0.01}}{0.02} = 0.693\,152\,730\ldots$
$[-0.001, 0.001]$	$\dfrac{\Delta f}{\Delta x} = \dfrac{2^{0.001} - 2^{-0.001}}{0.002} = 0.693\,147\,236\ldots$
$[-0.000\,1, 0.000\,1]$	$\dfrac{\Delta f}{\Delta x} = \dfrac{2^{0.000\,1} - 2^{-0.000\,1}}{0.000\,2} = 0.693\,147\,181\ldots$
$[-0.000\,01, 0.000\,01]$	$\dfrac{\Delta f}{\Delta x} = \dfrac{2^{0.000\,01} - 2^{-0.000\,01}}{0.000\,02} = 0.693\,147\,180\ldots$
$[-0.000\,001, 0.000\,001]$	$\dfrac{\Delta f}{\Delta x} = \dfrac{2^{0.000\,001} - 2^{-0.000\,001}}{0.000\,002} = 0.693\,147\,180\ldots$

see our average rates of change get closer and closer to the irrational number

$$0.693\,147\,180\,559\,945\,309\,417\,232\,121\,458\ldots.$$

This value is the precise rate of change of f at the very instant that $x = 0$. In other words, this number gives the exact slope of the line that best resembles the graph of f as it crosses the y-axis.

We can perform a series of computations like the one above using any other exponential function with any other base. For instance, consider the function

$$g(x) = 3^x.$$

The graph of this function is also locally linear so, as before, we can approximate the rate of change at the very instant that it crosses the y-axis by calculating its average rates of change over a sequence of smaller and smaller intervals around the point $x = 0$. The results of these computations appear in Table 3.4. As before, you should observe the stabilizing digits in these approximations.

TABLE 3.4. The average rate of change of the exponential function $g(x) = 3^x$ over a variety of intervals.

interval	average rate of change
$[-1, 1]$	$\dfrac{\Delta g}{\Delta x} = \dfrac{3^1 - 3^{-1}}{2} = 1.333\,333\,333\ldots$
$[-0.1, 0.1]$	$\dfrac{\Delta g}{\Delta x} = \dfrac{3^{0.1} - 3^{-0.1}}{0.2} = 1.100\,823\,570\ldots$
$[-0.01, 0.01]$	$\dfrac{\Delta g}{\Delta x} = \dfrac{3^{0.01} - 3^{-0.01}}{0.02} = 1.098\,634\,388\ldots$
$[-0.001, 0.001]$	$\dfrac{\Delta g}{\Delta x} = \dfrac{3^{0.001} - 3^{-0.001}}{0.002} = 1.098\,612\,509\ldots$
$[-0.000\,1, 0.000\,1]$	$\dfrac{\Delta g}{\Delta x} = \dfrac{3^{0.000\,1} - 3^{-0.000\,1}}{0.000\,2} = 1.098\,612\,290\ldots$
$[-0.000\,01, 0.000\,01]$	$\dfrac{\Delta g}{\Delta x} = \dfrac{3^{0.000\,01} - 3^{-0.000\,01}}{0.000\,02} = 1.098\,612\,288\ldots$
$[-0.000\,001, 0.000\,001]$	$\dfrac{\Delta g}{\Delta x} = \dfrac{3^{0.000\,001} - 3^{-0.000\,001}}{0.000\,002} = 1.098\,612\,288\ldots$

Evidently, the average rates of change for this function are getting closer and closer to the irrational number

$$1.098\,612\,288\,668\,109\,691\,395\,245\,236\,922\ldots.$$

This computation proves that, when it crosses the y-axis, an exponential with base 3 is growing about 1.585 times faster than an exponential with base 2. (Does this value seem familiar?)

Suppose that b is an arbitrary positive number, which we shall think of as the base of an exponential function. We define the ***natural logarithm*** of b as the instantaneous rate of change of the exponential function

$$f(x) = b^x$$

when $x = 0$. In other words, the natural logarithm of b is the slope of the line that best resembles the graph of f as it crosses the y-axis. For purely historical reasons, it is customary to denote the natural logarithm of b by the symbol

$$\boxed{\ln(b),}$$

which is supposed to remind you of its original Latin name, *logarithmus naturalis*. When you read this symbol aloud, you should pronounce it either as "log bee" or as "ellen bee." Occasionally, you will hear someone say "lynn bee" or "lawn bee," but these are the same sort of people who are likely to tell you all about their new "idears" for safe and renewable "new-cue-lar" energy obtained from cold fusion. We leave it up to you to decide whether you want to be associated with *that* crowd. At any rate, as in our examples above, we can determine the natural logarithm of any positive number as the limit of a sequence of average rates of change of an exponential function over smaller and smaller intervals containing the point $x = 0$. Table 3.5 gives the values of the natural logarithm of every integer between one and ten.

TABLE 3.5. A short table of natural logarithms.

b	$\ln(b)$
1	0
2	$0.693\,147\,180\ldots$
3	$1.098\,612\,288\ldots$
4	$1.386\,294\,361\ldots$
5	$1.609\,437\,912\ldots$
6	$1.791\,759\,469\ldots$
7	$1.945\,910\,149\ldots$
8	$2.079\,441\,541\ldots$
9	$2.197\,224\,577\ldots$
10	$2.302\,585\,092\ldots$

EXAMPLE 3.11. Remember that the graph of the exponential function

$$f(x) = 1^x = 1$$

is a horizontal line which exhibits neither exponential growth nor decay. Since the slope of this horizontal line is zero, we define the natural logarithm of one to be equal to zero, as indicated in Table 3.5.

EXAMPLE 3.12. The natural logarithm describes how quickly an exponential function is growing, not just at the moment that its graph crosses the y-axis, but throughout its entire domain. For instance, suppose that we once again consider the function

$$f(x) = 2^x.$$

As we know, the graph of this function crosses the y-axis with a slope of $\ln(2)$, or about $0.693\,147\,180$. Let us examine the instantaneous rate of change of f at a different spot on the graph, say, at the point $(3, 8)$. We shall do this by defining a new exponential function with the same base but with a different initial value:

$$g(x) = 8 \cdot 2^x = 8 \cdot f(x).$$

Evidently, g is a vertical dilation of f. This dilation causes the slope of graph of g as it crosses the y-axis to be 8 times that of the graph of f. In other words, the instantaneous rate of change of g at the point $(0, 8)$ must be equal to $8 \cdot \ln(2)$, as indicated in Figure 3.5.

On the other hand, according to the rules of exponentials, we also have

$$g(x) = 8 \cdot 2^x = 2^3 \cdot 2^x = 2^{x+3} = f(x + 3),$$

so g is also a horizontal translation of f by 3 units to the left. Since translating a graph does not change its slope at any point, the instantaneous rate of change of f at the point $(3, 8)$ is equal to the instantaneous rate of change of g at the point $(0, 8)$. In other words, this rate of change is also equal to $8 \cdot \ln(2)$. See Figure 3.5.

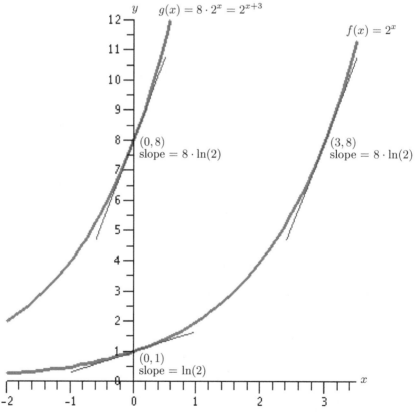

FIGURE 3.5. The slopes of the graphs of $f(x) = 2^x$ and $g(x) = 8 \cdot 2^x = 2^{x+3}$.

Of course, our choices of $b = 2$ and $x = 3$ above were entirely arbitrary. Without much work, we can easily show that the instantaneous rate of change of any exponential function f with base b at the point $\big(x, f(x)\big)$ is equal to

$$\text{rate of change of } f \text{ at the point } \big(x, f(x)\big) = f(x) \cdot \ln(b).$$

Said another way, the instantaneous rate of change of f at any given point in its domain is proportional to the the value of f at that point, and the constant of proportionality happens to be the natural logarithm of b. This means that the value of $\ln(b)$ describes how quickly f is changing (relative to its size) throughout its domain. For this reason, we sometimes refer to $\ln(b)$ as the **growth rate** of the exponential function.

A quick look at the values in Table 3.5 might make us wonder whether there is some base which has a natural logarithm equal to one. If there were such a base, it seems reasonable that it would live somewhere between 2 and 3, so that is where we begin our search. After a few computations, we would discover that the desired base is found somewhere between 2.718 and 2.719:

b	$\ln(b)$
2	$0.693\,147\,180\ldots$
2.7	$0.993\,251\,773\ldots$
2.71	$0.996\,948\,634\ldots$
2.718	$0.999\,896\,315\ldots$
2.719	$1.000\,264\,165\ldots$
2.72	$1.000\,631\,880\ldots$
2.8	$1.029\,619\,417\ldots$
3	$1.098\,612\,288\ldots$

Continuing in this way, we would eventually zero in on the number

$$e = 2.718\,281\,828\,459\,045\,235\,360\,287\,471\,352\ldots.$$

This strange little number has the distinction of being the unique positive number with a natural logarithm of one:

$$\ln(e) = 1.$$

It also has many other curious properties, as we will soon discover. For instance, in 1737, the celebrated Swiss mathematician Leonhard Euler (1707–1783) proved that e is an irrational number, so it cannot be written as a fraction and its decimal expansion never repeats. However, e is unlike many of the other irrational numbers, like φ and $\sqrt{2}$, that we have come across so far. Such irrationals are said to be **algebraic numbers** because they can each be written as a combination of sums, products, fractions, and radicals of integers. For example, as we saw on page 203, the golden ratio φ can be written as

$$\varphi = \frac{1 + \sqrt{5}}{2}.$$

More generally, a number is said to be algebraic if it is the solution of a polynomial equation with integer coefficients. For instance, $\sqrt{2}$ and φ solve the equations

$$x^2 - 2 = 0 \quad \text{and} \quad x^2 - x - 1 = 0,$$

respectively. Even an intimidating number like

$$\sqrt[3]{\sqrt[7]{5} + 13}$$

is algebraic since it is a solution of the polynomial equation

$$(x^3 - 13)^7 - 5 = 0.$$

In contrast, e is never the solution of a polynomial equation with integer coefficients, as was shown in 1873 by the French mathematician Charles Hermite (1822–1901). This means that unlike the golden ratio, it is impossible to write e as a combination of sums, products, fractions, or radicals. This property of "transcending" the usual operations of algebra earns e the mystical title of **transcendental number**. Hermite's proof was the first result of its kind, but it was quickly followed by others like it. For instance, in 1882, the German mathematician Ferdinand von Lindemann (1852–1939) showed that π is also a transcendental number.

EXAMPLE 3.13. Solve the equation $e^{-x^2} = \frac{1}{e} \cdot \left(e^x\right)^2$.

Solution. We begin by using Exponential Rules ②, ③, and ① to simplify our equation as follows:

$$e^{-x^2} = e^{-1} \cdot \left(e^x\right)^2$$

$$e^{-x^2} = e^{-1} \cdot e^{2x}$$

$$e^{-x^2} = e^{2x-1}.$$

Then, using Exponential Rule ⑤, we set the exponents equal to each other, obtaining

$$-x^2 = 2x - 1$$

or, after clearing the left hand side,

$$0 = x^2 + 2x - 1.$$

Finally, the quadratic formula renders our two solutions as

$$x = \frac{-2 \pm \sqrt{8}}{2} = \frac{-2 \pm 2\sqrt{2}}{2} = -1 \pm \sqrt{2}.$$

We refer to the exponential function with base e as the **natural exponential function**, sometimes denoted as

$$\exp(x) = e^x.$$

Thus, with this notation in hand, the equation in Example 3.13 becomes:

$$\exp(-x^2) = \frac{1}{e} \cdot \big(\exp(x)\big)^2.$$

The natural exponential function is *the* exponential function *par excellence*. One of its most important properties – in fact, the one that makes it more "natural" than any other exponential function – is that its instantaneous rate of change at any point is not only *proportional*, but in fact *equal*, to its value. Thus, as the graph of $\exp(x)$ crosses the y-axis at the point $(0, 1)$, it does so with a slope of 1. At the point $(1, e)$, the graph of $\exp(x)$ has a slope of e. And at the point $(-2, e^{-2})$, the slope of the graph of $\exp(x)$ is e^{-2}. See Figure 3.6.

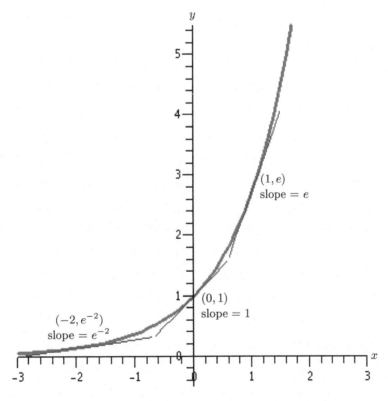

FIGURE 3.6. The graph of the natural exponential function $\exp(x) = e^x$.

The true power of the natural exponential function, however, can be seen in the graph of the function

$$g(x) = e^{kx} = \exp(kx)$$

where we let k be some nonzero constant. Notice that g is a horizontal dilation of the natural exponential function. This dilation either compresses or stretches the graph of $\exp(x)$, producing a graph that crosses the y-axis with a slope of k, as shown in Figure 3.7. On the other hand, since we can also rewrite the formula for g as

$$g(x) = e^{kx} = \left(e^k\right)^x,$$

we recognize that g is simply an exponential with base $b = e^k$. This means that the natural logarithm of e^k (that is, the slope with which the graph of g crosses the y-axis) is simply k:

(3.2) $$\ln\left(e^k\right) = k.$$

We will have a lot more to say about how to interpret this result in the next section, but for the time being, we shall simply observe that it gives us two distinct ways of describing the growth or decay of an exponential function. On the one hand,

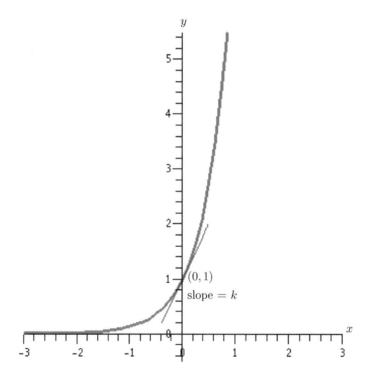

FIGURE 3.7. The exponential function $g(x) = e^{kx}$ has a growth rate of k.

we have the function's base b, which is a long-term measure of the function's behavior:

$$f(x) = a\,b^x.$$

In this case, the base describes how the output values of the function increase as we vary the input over large steps of a fixed size. For instance, if we take steps of size $\Delta x = 1$, the output values of this exponential function will form the geometric sequence

$$a \longrightarrow a\,b \longrightarrow a\,b^2 \longrightarrow a\,b^3 \longrightarrow \dots.$$

On the other hand, we have the function's growth rate k, which describes the behavior of the function in the short term:

$$f(x) = a\,e^{kx}.$$

In particular, the growth rate gives the instantaneous rate of change at which the function grows relative to its present value. (See Example 3.12.)

Equation (3.2) informs us of how these two descriptions of the same exponential function are related to one other. In particular, if we know the function's growth rate k, then we can determine its base by computing the natural exponential of k; if we know the function's base b, then we can determine its growth rate by computing the natural logarithm of b:

$$\boxed{b = \exp(k) \qquad \Leftrightarrow \qquad k = \ln(b).}$$

As we shall see in Section 3.5, which of these two approaches (base or growth rate) we use to describe an exponential function is simply a matter of personal taste and convenience, predicated only by the information we have at hand.

EXAMPLE 3.14. Suppose that a laboratory technician is analyzing two different strains of bacteria, each of which is exhibiting exponential growth.

The first bacteria culture was inoculated into a test tube of liquid medium several days ago, and in that time has consistently doubled in size every 14 hours. Since this culture started with an initial population of 200 cells, the size of the culture is described as a function of time (in hours) by the formula

$$p_1(t) = 200 \cdot 2^{t/14} = 200 \cdot \left(2^{1/14}\right)^t.$$

In other words, the function describing the exponential growth of the first strain of bacteria has an initial value of 200 and a base of

$$b_1 = 2^{1/14} = 1.050\,756\dots.$$

This means that the growth rate for this culture is given by

$$k_1 = \ln(b_1) = \ln\!\left(2^{1/14}\right) = 0.049\,510\dots,$$

or about 4.95% per hour, as you can verify for yourself by using a calculator.

On the other hand, the second bacteria culture is only a few minutes old. After some early observations, the laboratory technician determines that, with an initial population of 800 cells, a new cell created approximately every 100 seconds. The technician, thus, concludes that the colony is exhibiting a growth rate of $\frac{1}{100} = 0.01$ cells per second, or equivalently,

$$k_2 = \frac{0.01 \text{ cells/sec}}{800 \text{ cells}} \times 60 \, \frac{\text{sec}}{\text{min}} \times 60 \, \frac{\text{min}}{\text{hour}} = 0.045,$$

or 4.5% per hour. Therefore, the size of the second culture is described by an exponential function with a base of

$$b_2 = \exp(k_2) = e^{0.045} = 1.046\,027\ldots,$$

namely

$$p_2(t) = 800 \cdot \left(e^{0.045}\right)^t = 800 \, e^{0.045t}.$$

With all of this information in hand, the laboratory technician can now compare the two strains of bacteria. In particular, since the first strain has a larger base and a larger growth rate than the second strain, the technician can tell that it will also grow faster than the second strain.

The example above demonstrates one way in which the natural exponential and the natural logarithm go hand in hand as we solve problems involving exponential growth and decay. As it turns out, this relationship between exponential and logarithm goes deeper than we might at first suspect.

Reading Comprehension Questions for Section 3.2

The graph of the exponential function $f(x) = b^x$ has a y-intercept at the point ___(a)___, regardless of the value of b. The more we zoom in closer to this point, the more the graph looks like a ___(b)___. Its slope, which describes how quickly the exponential function is changing at the instant that it crosses the ___(c)___, is known as the ___(d)___ rate of change when $x = 0$, or more simply as the ___(e)___. Its value depends on b. For example, if b is larger than ___(f)___, then f exhibits exponential ___(g)___, and the slope is ___(h)___ (positive or negative); on the other hand, if b is between ___(i)___ and ___(j)___, then f exhibits exponential ___(k)___, and the slope is ___(l)___ (positive or negative).

We can determine the instantaneous rate of change of $f(x) = b^x$ when $x = 0$ by computing a sequence of ___(m)___ taken over smaller and smaller intervals of the form $[-z, z]$. Each one of these will look like

$$\frac{\Delta f}{\Delta x} = \frac{f(z) - f(-z)}{z - (-z)} = \underline{\quad(n)\quad}.$$

The values in this sequence will get closer and closer to a number (denoted by $\ln(b)$) that is known as the ___(o)___ of b. For example, for $f(x) = 2^x$, the instantaneous rate of change is $\ln(2) = $ ___(p)___; for $f(x) = 3^x$, it is $\ln(3) = $ ___(q)___; and for $f(x) = 4^x$, it is $\ln(4) = $ ___(r)___.

There is precisely one real number x that has $\ln(x) = 1$. This number, which is denoted by the letter ___(s)___, happens to be an ___(t)___ number whose decimal expansion begins as ___(u)___. We use this number to define the natural exponential function, $\exp(x) = $ ___(v)___. The graph of this function crosses the y-axis with a slope of ___(w)___.

By considering $g(x) = (e^k)^x = e^{kx} = \exp(kx)$ as a horizontal dilation of the natural exponential function, we see that $\ln(e^k) = $ ___(x)___. In other words, if we know the base b of an exponential function then we can compute its growth rate as $k = $ ___(y)___, and if we know the growth rate k of an exponential function then we can compute its base as $b = $ ___(z)___.

Exercises for Section 3.2

1. (a) Compute a decimal expansion for the quantity $\ln(2) + \ln(5)$.

    (b) How does the quantity in part (a) compare to the value of $\ln(2+5) = \ln(7)$?

    (c) Do you recognize the quantity in part (a) as the natural logarithm of some other number?

2. (a) Compute a decimal expansion for the quantity $2\ln(3)$.

    (b) How does the quantity in part (a) compare to the value of $\ln(2 \cdot 3) = \ln(6)$?

    (c) Do you recognize the quantity in part (a) as the natural logarithm of some other number?

3. (a) Compute a decimal expansion for the quantity $\ln(8) - \ln(4)$.

    (b) How does the quantity in part (a) compare to the value of $\ln(8-4) = \ln(4)$?

    (c) Do you recognize the quantity in part (a) as the natural logarithm of some other number?

4. If n is a positive integer, then the quantity $n!$ (read "n factorial") is defined as the product of all positive integers between 1 and n:
$$n! = 1 \cdot 2 \cdot 3 \cdots \cdots (n-2) \cdot (n-1) \cdot n.$$

    Make a table containing the values of $n!$ for every integer n between 1 and 10.

5. (a) Order the following numbers from smallest to largest:

    (i) 2^{10} (ii) 10^2 (iii) $10!$ (iv) 10^{10}

    (b) How many digits make up each of the numbers above?

    (c) How many zeroes are there at the end of each of these numbers?

6. Determine the decimal expansions for each of the following sums:

    (a) $1 + \dfrac{1}{1!} + \dfrac{1}{2!}$

    (b) $1 + \dfrac{1}{1!} + \dfrac{1}{2!} + \dfrac{1}{3!}$

    (c) $1 + \dfrac{1}{1!} + \dfrac{1}{2!} + \dfrac{1}{3!} + \dfrac{1}{4!}$

    (d) $1 + \dfrac{1}{1!} + \dfrac{1}{2!} + \dfrac{1}{3!} + \dfrac{1}{4!} + \dfrac{1}{5!}$

    (e) The decimal expansions in parts (a) through (d) are getting closer to e. In other words, we can think of e as the result of the infinite sum
$$e = 1 + \frac{1}{1!} + \frac{1}{2!} + \frac{1}{3!} + \frac{1}{4!} + \frac{1}{5!} + \frac{1}{6!} + \cdots.$$

    How far must this pattern of sums be continued before the decimal expansions agree with e in their first six digits?

7. Determine the decimal expansions for each of the following numbers:

(a) $2 + \cfrac{1}{1 + \cfrac{1}{2+2}}$

(b) $2 + \cfrac{1}{1 + \cfrac{1}{2 + \cfrac{2}{3+3}}}$

(c) $2 + \cfrac{1}{1 + \cfrac{1}{2 + \cfrac{2}{3 + \cfrac{3}{4+4}}}}$

(d) $2 + \cfrac{1}{1 + \cfrac{1}{2 + \cfrac{2}{3 + \cfrac{3}{4 + \cfrac{4}{5+5}}}}}$

(e) The decimal expansions in parts (a) through (d) are getting closer to e. In other words, we can think of e as the infinite continued fraction

$$e = 2 + \cfrac{1}{1 + \cfrac{1}{2 + \cfrac{2}{3 + \cfrac{3}{4 + \cfrac{4}{5 + \cfrac{5}{6 + \cdots}}}}}}.$$

How far must this pattern of fractions be continued before the decimal expansions agree with e in their first six digits?

8. Determine the decimal expansions for each of the following numbers:

(a) $\left(1 + \dfrac{1}{10}\right)^{10}$

(b) $\left(1 + \dfrac{1}{50}\right)^{50}$

(c) $\left(1 + \dfrac{1}{100}\right)^{100}$

(d) $\left(1 + \dfrac{1}{500}\right)^{500}$

(e) The decimal expansions in parts (a) through (d) are getting closer to e. In other words, we can think of e as the "limit as n approaches infinity" of the expression

$$\left(1 + \frac{1}{n}\right)^{n}.$$

How large must n become before the decimal expansion of this expression agrees with e in its first four digits?

In Exercises 9–14, interpret each function as a linear transformation of the natural exponential function $f(x) = e^x$. Use this information to sketch its graph. Be sure to label at least three points in the graph together with their slopes, and find the equation of the horizontal asymptote.

9. $g(x) = e^{-x}$ 10. $g(x) = -e^x$

11. $g(x) = e^{x+1}$ 12. $g(x) = e^x - 1$

13. $g(x) = 5 + e^{-x}$ 14. $g(x) = 9 + 3e^x$

In Exercises 15–28, solve each equation for x.

15. $e^{x-5} = e^{2x}$ 16. $\exp(3x) = \exp(9)$

17. $e^{x^2} = e^{25}$ 18. $\exp(x^3) - \exp(27) = 0$

19. $e^{x^2} \cdot e^{9x} \cdot e^8 = 1$ 20. $\exp(x^2) = \exp(3x) \cdot \exp(-2)$

21. $\left(e^4\right)^x \cdot e^{x^2} = e^{12}$ 22. $\exp(x^{2/3}) = \dfrac{(\exp(x^{1/3}))^6}{e^8}$

23. $e^2 \cdot \left(e^{x^2}\right)^3 = e^{6x}$ 24. $\exp(2x) = \sqrt{e} \cdot \exp(x)$

25. $e^6 \cdot e^{x^2} = e^{5x}$ 26. $\exp(2x) + 2\exp(x) = 3$

27. $\dfrac{3 - 7\ln(x)}{1 - 5\ln(x)} = 1$ 28. $\bigl(3 - \ln(x)\bigr)\bigl(3 + \ln(x)\bigr) = 9 - \ln(x)$

29. Scalene Sallie is confused about how a horizontal dilation can affect the graph of an exponential function. Acute Alice suggests answering the following questions:

   (a) Consider a line that crosses the y-axis with the same slope as the graph of the exponential function $f(x) = b^x$. On this line, what is the value of the rise Δy that corresponds to a run of $\Delta x = 1$?

   (b) What would a horizontal dilation $g(x) = b^{kx}$ do to the rise and run in part (a)? With what slope does the graph of g cross the y-axis?

   (c) Confirm your answer to part (b) by examining the specific case of $f(x) = 2^x$ and $g(x) = 2^{1.585\,x} \approx 3^x$.

30. Obtuse Ollie is also confused about how a vertical dilation can affect the graph of an exponential function. Acute Alice suggests answering the following questions:

   (a) Consider a line that crosses the y-axis with the same slope as the graph of the exponential function $f(x) = b^x$. On this line, what is the value of the rise Δy that corresponds to a run of $\Delta x = 1$?

   (b) What would a vertical dilation $h(x) = k\,b^x$ do to the rise and run in part (a)? With what slope does the graph of h cross the y-axis?

   (c) On a graphing calculator or computer, examine the graphs of $g(x) = 2^{1.585\,x}$ and $h(x) = 1.585 \cdot 2^x$. What similarities and differences do you notice between these graphs? Do the graphs ever cross each other? Which graph heads faster to infinity? Which asymptotes faster to zero?

3.3. Logarithmic Functions

When we took our first look at natural logarithms, we defined them as *numbers*. In particular, the number $\ln(b)$ was defined as the growth rate of the exponential function $f(x) = b^x$, that is to say, as the slope of its graph as it crosses the y-axis. We shall now make a paradigm shift and, instead, think of the natural logarithm as a *function*. In fact, we shall think of the natural logarithm as one member of a large family of functions, each identified by its own positive base.

Suppose that b is a positive real number which is not equal to 1. We define the **logarithm with base b** as the function $\log_b : (0, \infty) \to \mathbb{R}$ given by the ratio

$$\log_b(x) = \frac{\ln(x)}{\ln(b)}.$$

This ratio depends on the values of both $\ln(b)$ and $\ln(x)$, which are well-defined only when b and x are viable bases of an exponential; hence, b and x can be neither zero nor negative. In the case of the base b, the extra condition that $b \neq 1$ comes from the observation that dividing by $\ln(1) = 0$ is forbidden. On the other hand, the condition that the input x be strictly positive implies that the domain of any logarithmic function is always restricted to the set $(0, \infty)$.

EXAMPLE 3.15. Recall that the irrational number e was defined as the unique real number with a natural logarithm of one,

$$\ln(e) = 1.$$

Therefore, the natural logarithm is simply the logarithm with base e:

$$\log_e(x) = \frac{\ln(x)}{\ln(e)} = \frac{\ln(x)}{1} = \ln(x).$$

EXAMPLE 3.16. Suppose that we start with any positive number x and compute its natural logarithm. Let us call the result y, so that we have

$$\ln(x) = y.$$

According to equation (3.2), this value is precisely the same as the natural logarithm of e^y:

$$\ln(e^y) = y.$$

We can think of x and e^y as two exponential bases, each of which exhibits the same growth rate of y. However, as our numerical experiments in Section 3.2 showed, different exponential bases will produce different growth rates. For instance, consider the results in Table 3.5. Therefore, the two bases in question must, in fact, be the same base. In other words, we have the following inverse relationship between the natural logarithm and the natural exponential function:

$$y = \ln(x) \qquad \Leftrightarrow \qquad x = e^y.$$

EXAMPLE 3.17. Let b be any positive base, and consider the logarithm with base b of a positive number x. As in the example above, we shall call this result y:

$$\log_b(x) = y.$$

Solving for $\ln(x)$ in the definition of $\log_b(x)$ produces the following logarithmic equation:

$$\ln(x) = \ln(b) \cdot y.$$

We can then exploit the inverse relationship between the natural logarithm and the natural exponential in Example 3.16 to rewrite this equation in exponential form and simplify it as follows:

$$x = e^{\ln(b) \cdot y} = \left(e^{\ln(b)}\right)^y = b^y.$$

This produces another inverse relationship – this time between the logarithm and the exponential function with base b:

$$y = \log_b(x) \qquad \Leftrightarrow \qquad x = b^y.$$

The inverse relationships in Examples 3.16 and 3.17 give us a new way of interpreting logarithms, natural or otherwise: $\log_b(x)$ is the *exponent* to which the base b must be raised in order to produce a value of x. This observation makes computing $\log_b(x)$ relatively simple whenever x can be easily expressed as a power of the base b.

EXAMPLE 3.18. According to the values in Table 3.5, we have:

$$\ln(2) \approx 0.693\,147\,180, \qquad \ln(4) \approx 1.386\,294\,361, \qquad \ln(8) \approx 2.079\,441\,541.$$

Therefore, by a direct computation, we can approximate

$$\log_2(4) = \frac{\ln(4)}{\ln(2)} \approx \frac{1.386\,294\,361}{0.693\,147\,180} \approx 2.000\,000\,001,$$

$$\log_2(8) = \frac{\ln(8)}{\ln(2)} \approx \frac{2.079\,441\,541}{0.693\,147\,180} \approx 3.000\,000\,001,$$

$$\log_4(8) = \frac{\ln(8)}{\ln(4)} \approx \frac{2.079\,441\,541}{1.386\,294\,361} \approx 1.499\,999\,999.$$

However, since we can write 4 and 8 as powers of 2 and 4, we can employ the inverse relationship between exponentials and logarithms to determine the exact values of $\log_2(4)$, $\log_2(8)$, and $\log_4(8)$. In particular, we have

$$4 = 2^2 \quad \Rightarrow \quad \log_2(4) = 2,$$

$$8 = 2^3 \quad \Rightarrow \quad \log_2(8) = 3,$$

$$8 = 4^{3/2} \quad \Rightarrow \quad \log_4(8) = \tfrac{3}{2}.$$

EXAMPLE 3.19. A typical scientific calculator can compute logarithms via one of two buttons, labeled `ln` and `log`. Obviously, the first of these computes the natural logarithm. The other computes the logarithm with base 10, also known as the **common logarithm**. This function gives the exponent needed to express a given number as a power of 10. Thus, for a perfect power of 10, the common logarithm gives the number of zeroes following the initial one:

$$100 = 10^2 \quad \Rightarrow \quad \log_{10}(100) = 2,$$

$$10\,000 = 10^4 \quad \Rightarrow \quad \log_{10}(10\,000) = 4,$$

$$1\,000\,000 = 10^6 \quad \Rightarrow \quad \log_{10}(1\,000\,000) = 6.$$

For other positive numbers, the common logarithm, when rounded up to the next integer, gives the total number of digits to the left of the decimal point. Thus:

$$\log_{10}(98) = 1.991\,226\ldots \quad \Rightarrow \quad 2 \text{ digits},$$

$$\log_{10}(34\,576) = 4.538\,774\ldots \quad \Rightarrow \quad 5 \text{ digits},$$

$$\log_{10}(123\,456.789) = 5.091\,514\ldots \quad \Rightarrow \quad 6 \text{ digits}.$$

You can use either the `ln` or `log` button to compute logarithms of any base, but you should do so with a modicum of care. For instance, to compute $\log_2(3)$, you might evaluate either:

$$\log_2(3) = \frac{\ln(3)}{\ln(2)} \approx \frac{1.098\,612\,288}{0.693\,147\,180} \quad \text{or} \quad \log_2(3) = \frac{\log_{10}(3)}{\log_{10}(2)} \approx \frac{0.477\,121\,255}{0.301\,029\,996}.$$

The last computation gives the correct answer since

$$\frac{\log_{10}(3)}{\log_{10}(2)} = \frac{\dfrac{\ln(3)}{\ln(10)}}{\dfrac{\ln(2)}{\ln(10)}} = \frac{\ln(3)}{\ln(2)} = \log_2(3).$$

Evidently, regardless of which approach we take, we will reach the same approximation of $\log_2(3) \approx 1.584\,962\,501$.

EXAMPLE 3.20. Towards the end of Section 3.1 (see page 254), we noted that the number 3 may be expressed as a power of 2,

$$3 = 2^x,$$

if we let the exponent x take on a value very close to 1.585. To find the exact value needed, we can use the inverse relationship to convert this exponential equation into an equivalent equation involving logarithms:

$$3 = 2^x \quad \Rightarrow \quad x = \log_2(3).$$

We note that this is a reasonable answer since, according to our computation in Example 3.19,

$$x = \log_2(3) \approx 1.584\,962\,501.$$

EXAMPLE 3.21. Solve the following equation:

$$3x + 2 = \log_5\left(\tfrac{1}{125}\right).$$

Solution. We first evaluate the logarithm on the right side of the equation by writing $\frac{1}{125}$ as a power of the base 5 and applying the inverse relationship between exponentials and logarithms:

$$\tfrac{1}{125} = 5^{-3} \quad \Rightarrow \quad \log_5\left(\tfrac{1}{125}\right) = -3.$$

With this simplification, we arrive at a linear equation that we may solve using our algebraic techniques from Chapter 1:

$$3x + 2 = -3$$

$$3x = -5$$

$$x = -\tfrac{5}{3}.$$

EXAMPLE 3.22. Solve the following equation:

$$\log_3(x) = 4.$$

Solution. In order to solve this equation, we must somehow get rid of the logarithm base 3 on the left hand side. For this purpose, we will use the inverse relationship, rewriting our logarithmic equation above in exponential form as follows:

$$\log_3(x) = 4 \quad \Rightarrow \quad x = 3^4.$$

Note that this operation replaced the logarithm on the left of the equation with an exponential (of the same base) on the right. However, this is precisely what we needed, since our unknown x is now by itself on the left hand side of the equation. Then our solution of $x = 3^4 = 81$ becomes self-evident.

EXAMPLE 3.23. Solve the following equation:

$$\log_4(2x - 1) = \tfrac{1}{2}.$$

Solution. Again, our inverse relationship helps us rewrite our equation in exponential form and thus eliminate the logarithm on the left hand side:

$$\log_4(2x - 1) = \tfrac{1}{2} \quad \Rightarrow \quad 2x - 1 = 4^{1/2}.$$

As before, this operation replaced the logarithm on the left of the equation with an exponential on the right. Happily, this exponential is easily evaluated as $4^{1/2} = 2$. Thus, we are now looking at a simple linear equation, which we can solve in the usual manner:

$$2x - 1 = 2$$
$$2x = 3$$
$$x = \tfrac{3}{2}.$$

EXAMPLE 3.24. Solve the following equation:

$$5 + 8\ln(3x) = 1.$$

Solution. Since the inverse relationship only becomes useful when one side of an equation contains a single logarithm by itself, we begin by solving for $\ln(3x)$ as follows:

$$5 + 8\ln(3x) = 1$$
$$8\ln(3x) = -4$$
$$\ln(3x) = -\tfrac{4}{8} = -\tfrac{1}{2}.$$

Next, we use our inverse relationship to convert this logarithmic equation into exponential form:

$$\ln(3x) = -\tfrac{1}{2} \quad \Rightarrow \quad 3x = e^{-1/2}.$$

Therefore, after dividing by 3, we arrive at the solution of

$$x = \frac{1}{3}e^{-1/2} = \frac{1}{3\sqrt{e}}.$$

EXAMPLE 3.25. Solve the following equation:

$$\log_2\!\left(2x^2 - 5x + 1\right) = 3.$$

Solution. Once again, we undo the work of the logarithm on the left side of the equation by transforming it into an exponential on the right:

$$\log_2\!\left(2x^2 - 5x + 1\right) = 3 \quad \Rightarrow \quad 2x^2 - 5x + 1 = 2^3.$$

The result is then a quadratic equation, which we can solve by factoring:

$$2x^2 - 5x + 1 = 8$$

$$2x^2 - 5x - 7 = 0$$

$$(2x - 7)(x + 1) = 0.$$

Separating the two linear factors and solving produces two solutions:

$$2x - 7 = 0 \qquad \text{or} \qquad x + 1 = 0$$

$$x = \tfrac{7}{2} \qquad\qquad\qquad x = -1.$$

We leave it up to you to verify that substituting either of these into our original equation yields $\log_2(8) = 3$, which is, of course, a true statement.

EXAMPLE 3.26. Solve the following equation:

$$\log_3\left(x^2 + 5x - 3\right) = 2.$$

Solution. As in the previous examples, we eliminate the logarithm on the left of the equation and replace it with an exponential with the same base on the right hand side of the equation:

$$\log_3\left(x^2 + 5x - 3\right) = 2 \qquad \Rightarrow \qquad x^2 + 5x - 3 = 3^2.$$

This gives a quadratic equation, but one that does not appear to factor:

$$x^2 + 5x - 3 = 9$$

$$x^2 + 5x - 12 - 0.$$

Thus, we turn to the quadratic formula, which in due course yields two solutions:

$$x = \frac{-5 \pm \sqrt{25 - 4(-12)}}{2} = \frac{-5 \pm \sqrt{25 + 48}}{2} = \frac{-5 \pm \sqrt{73}}{2}.$$

The results, admittedly, are not as pretty as those in the previous examples; however, it is not hard (and only a little tedious) to check that substituting either $x = \frac{-5+\sqrt{73}}{2} \approx 1.772\,001\,873$ or $x = \frac{-5-\sqrt{73}}{2} \approx -6.772\,001\,873$ into our original equation yields the true statement $\log_3(9) = 2$.

EXAMPLE 3.27. Solve the following equation:

$$5^{3-x} = 7.$$

Solution. In this case, we need to eliminate an exponential to get our hands on the unknown x. Therefore, we use the inverse relationship to find the logarithmic form of this exponential equation:

$$5^{3-x} = 7 \qquad \Rightarrow \qquad 3 - x = \log_5(7).$$

Observe that this operation removed the exponential on the left hand side of the equation, replacing it with a logarithm on the right. You should not be overly concerned by the sudden appearance of the number $\log_5(7)$. What is important here is that this is just a number – an irrational number approximately equal to $1.209\,061\,955$ – but a number nonetheless. This means that we are now looking at a simple linear equation, which we can solve as follows:

$$3 - x = \log_5(7)$$

$$-x = \log_5(7) - 3$$

$$x = 3 - \log_5(7).$$

Therefore, our solution is $x = 3 - \log_5(7) \approx 1.790\,938\,045$.

EXAMPLE 3.28. Solve the following equation:

$$\exp(x^2 + 2) = 7 \cdot \exp(-2x).$$

Solution. We begin by writing each instance of the natural exponential as a power of e. In particular, since $\exp(x^2 + 2) = e^{x^2+2}$ and $\exp(-2x) = e^{-2x}$, we should consider the equation

$$e^{x^2+2} = 7 \cdot e^{-2x}.$$

The various powers of e can then be combined into a single exponential on the left hand side of the equation as follows:

$$\frac{e^{x^2+2}}{e^{-2x}} = 7$$

$$e^{x^2+2x+2} = 7.$$

Next, to get rid of the exponential, we invoke the inverse relationship and rewrite our equation in logarithmic form as follows:

$$e^{x^2+2x+2} = 7 \qquad \Rightarrow \qquad x^2 + 2x + 2 = \ln(7).$$

This gives us a quadratic equation,

$$x^2 + 2x + \big(2 - \ln(7)\big) = 0,$$

which we can solve using the quadratic formula:

$$x = \frac{-2 \pm \sqrt{4 - 4\big(2 - \ln(7)\big)}}{2} = -1 \pm \sqrt{\ln(7) - 1}\,.$$

Both of these solutions are valid because $\ln(7) - 1 \approx 0.946$ is positive and hence causes no problems when we try to take its square root. In particular, we end up with the solutions $x = -1 + \sqrt{\ln(7) - 1} \approx -0.027\,420\,878$ and $x = -1 - \sqrt{\ln(7) - 1} \approx -1.972\,579\,122$.

EXAMPLE 3.29. It is probably a good idea to consider two things that could have gone wrong as we were solving the equation in Example 3.28 above.

The first of these traps would arise if our equation instead looked like:

$$\exp(x^2 + 2) = -7 \cdot \exp(-2x).$$

As before, we would combine the natural exponentials as a single power of e, obtaining

$$e^{x^2+2x+2} = -7.$$

The problem occurs when we try to put this equation in logarithmic form:

$$e^{x^2+2x+2} = -7 \qquad \Rightarrow \qquad x^2 + 2x + 2 = \ln(-7).$$

Since -7 is negative, it falls outside of the domain of the natural logarithm function. Therefore, the expression $\ln(-7)$ is undefined and our equation has no solutions.

The second trap – trickier to catch than the first – occurs when our equation looks like:

$$\exp(x^2 + 2) = \tfrac{7}{3} \cdot \exp(-2x).$$

In this case, we would also combine the exponentials as

$$e^{x^2+2x+2} = \tfrac{7}{3}$$

and rewrite the equation in logarithmic form:

$$e^{x^2+2x+2} = \tfrac{7}{3} \qquad \Rightarrow \qquad x^2 + 2x + 2 = \ln\!\left(\tfrac{7}{3}\right).$$

We would then solve this equation using the quadratic formula, obtaining

$$x = 1 \pm \sqrt{\ln\!\left(\tfrac{7}{3}\right) - 1}\,.$$

The problem now is that $\ln\!\left(\tfrac{7}{3}\right) - 1 \approx -0.152$ is negative and, therefore, falls outside the domain of the square root function. Again, there are no solutions for this equation.

The inverse relationship tells us that, for any given base b, the input values for the logarithm become output values for the exponential, and vice versa. In terms of graphs, this corresponds to interchanging the x- and y-coordinates of each point:

$$\big(x, y\big) = \big(x, \log_b(x)\big) \qquad \longleftrightarrow \qquad \big(y, x\big) = \big(y, b^y\big).$$

Swapping coordinates in this fashion has the effect of reflecting our graphs across the diagonal line $y = x$. Thus, the graph of the logarithmic function $\log_b(x)$ is simply a copy of the graph of the exponential b^x, but reflected across this diagonal line. For example, Figure 3.8 shows the graph of the natural logarithm function, which is, of course, just a reflected copy of the graph of the natural exponential function that we saw in Figure 3.6 back on page 269.

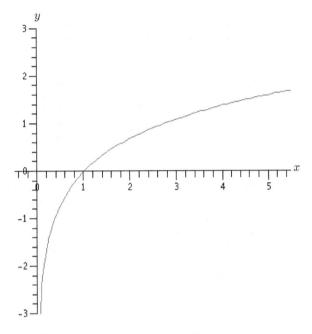

FIGURE 3.8. The graph of the natural logarithm function $\ln(x)$.

You should take a moment to observe some of the peculiarities of this graph. First of all, you will notice that it has a single x-intercept at the point $(1,0)$ and no y-intercepts at all. Instead, as the input x gets closer to 0, the value of $\ln(x)$ gets large and negative. This means the graph gets arbitrarily close to a vertical asymptote along the negative y-axis without ever touching it. On the other hand, as x gets large and positive on the right hand side of the graph, the value of $\ln(x)$ grows larger and larger without bound, but it does so extremely slowly. The natural logarithm's slow crawl to infinity might remind you of the behavior exhibited by the square root function, but it is actually much slower than that. Indeed, by using the techniques of calculus, we can prove that the natural logarithm goes off to infinity slower than any radical function. "Slow but steady wins the race," the tortoise-like logarithm reminds us with a sigh of subdued indolence.

EXAMPLE 3.30. To appreciate just how slowly a logarithm actually grows, let us consider the mind-bogglingly large number nicknamed **googol**:

$$\text{googol} = 10^{100}.$$

This number, whose decimal representation consists of a one followed by a hundred zeroes, was invented (or perhaps "discovered" is a better word) in 1938 by the American mathematician Edward Kasner (1878 – 1955) and his nine-year-old nephew Milton, as they took a walk through the New Jersey Palisades. A googol is unimaginably large – larger than the number of atoms in the observable universe[3] – and yet its common logarithm is puny:

$$\log_{10}(\text{googol}) = \log_{10}(10^{100}) = 100.$$

Given this rather disappointing showing, it seems entirely unlikely that the values of the common logarithm are heading towards infinity.

However, there are numbers much larger than even the mighty googol. For instance, consider the **googolplex**, originally defined by young Milton as a one "followed by writing zeros until you get tired," and later refined by his uncle as a one followed by a googol zeroes:

$$\text{googolplex} = 10^{\text{googol}} = 10^{10^{100}}.$$

As Kasner later explained in his book *Mathematics and the Imagination*,

> A googolplex is much bigger than a googol. You will get some idea of the size of this very large but finite number from the fact that there would not be enough room to write it, if you went to the farthest star, touring all the nebulae and putting down zeros every inch of the way.[4]

Actually, matters are much worse than this. Since the decimal representation for a googolplex has more zeroes than there are atoms in the universe, we would surely run out of ink well before we were done writing it down! Not surprisingly, the googolplex has an equally impressive common logarithm,

$$\log_{10}(\text{googolplex}) = \log_{10}(10^{\text{googol}}) = \text{googol},$$

restoring our faith that logarithms do, in fact, go off to infinity ... just really, really, *really* slowly!

---

[3] A typical "back-of-the-envelope" calculation estimates that there are only about 10^{78} atoms in the observable universe. For more details, we direct the interested reader to the following website: http://www.madsci.org/posts/archives/oct98/905633072.As.q.html.

[4] E. Kasner and J. R. Newman, *Mathematics and the Imagination*, p. 23 (1940).

Reading Comprehension Questions for Section 3.3

The logarithm with base $b > 0$ is defined as the function given by the formula $\log_b(x) = \underline{\quad(a)\quad}$. Since $\ln(e) = \underline{\quad(b)\quad}$, this means that we can think of the natural logarithm as the logarithm with base $\underline{\quad(c)\quad}$. From our definition follows the following inverse relationship:

$$y = \log_b(x) \qquad \Leftrightarrow \qquad \underline{\quad(d)\quad}.$$

This says that the $\underline{\quad(e)\quad}$ and $\underline{\quad(f)\quad}$ functions of the same base will "undo" each other's work. In other words, we can think of $y = \log_b(x)$ as the $\underline{\quad(g)\quad}$ to which we need to raise the base $\underline{\quad(h)\quad}$ to arrive at the answer $\underline{\quad(i)\quad}$. For example, we know that $\log_2(32) = 5$ because $\underline{\quad(j)\quad}$ raised to the power $\underline{\quad(k)\quad}$ is equal to $\underline{\quad(l)\quad}$.

We can use logarithms to solve exponential equations like $3^{x-5} = 4$. In this case, we undo the exponential with base $\underline{\quad(m)\quad}$ on the left hand side by writing it as a $\underline{\quad(n)\quad}$ of the same base on the right. This yields $x - 5 = \underline{\quad(o)\quad}$. We can then solve for x by $\underline{\quad(p)\quad}$, giving us $x = \underline{\quad(q)\quad}$.

Conversely, we can use exponential functions to solve logarithmic equations like $\log_5(3x + 1) = 2$. Here, we undo the logarithm with base $\underline{\quad(r)\quad}$ on the left hand side by writing it as an $\underline{\quad(s)\quad}$ of the same base on the right: $3x + 1 = \underline{\quad(t)\quad}$. Then we can solve for x by first $\underline{\quad(u)\quad}$ and then $\underline{\quad(v)\quad}$, thus producing $x = \underline{\quad(w)\quad}$.

The graph of a logarithmic function looks a little like that of an exponential function, except that the roles of the x- and y-coordinates have been $\underline{\quad(x)\quad}$. It has a $\underline{\quad(y)\quad}$ asymptote along the y-axis and, on the right, heads towards infinity very $\underline{\quad(z)\quad}$ (slowly or fast).

Exercises for Section 3.3

1. Change each of the following exponential expressions into an equivalent expression involving logarithms.

   (a) $a^3 = 5$ (b) $b^4 = \pi$ (c) $e^{15} = x$ (d) $10^{\sqrt{2}} = 4y$

2. Change each of the following logarithmic expressions into an equivalent expression involving exponentials.

   (a) $\log_a(3) = 6$ (b) $\log_b(4) = 2$ (c) $\log_3(2) = x$ (d) $\log_{10}(y) = 4$

In Problems 3–12, find the exact value of each expression without using a calculator or computer.

3. $\log_2(8)$ 4. $\log_3\left(\frac{1}{9}\right)$

5. $\log_{10}\left(\sqrt{1000}\right)$ 6. $\log_5\left(\sqrt[3]{25}\right)$

7. $\log_{\sqrt{2}}(16)$ 8. $\ln\left(e^{-4}\right)$

9. $3^{\log_3(71)}$ 10. $2^{\log_2(7)}$

11. $e^{\ln(5)}$ 12. $\left(\log_3(8)\right) \cdot \left(\log_2(81)\right)$

In Problems 13–24, first find the exact solution for each equation. Then, using a calculator or computer if necessary, determine an approximate value.

13. $\log_3(x) = 2$ 14. $\log_x(17) = 2$

15. $\log_3(3x - 2) = 2$ 16. $\log_2(2x + 1) = 3$

17. $\log_2\left(2x^2 - x + 6\right) = 4$ 18. $\log_3\left(x^2 + 5x + 3\right) = 3$

19. $\ln\left(x^2 + 2x\right) = 1$ 20. $\exp(3x + 4) = 5$

21. $2^{5x-2} = 7$ 22. $\exp\left(x^2 - 7x + 12\right) = 1$

23. $2^{x^2 + 5x - 6} = -4$ 24. $3^{x^2 - 2x + 3} = 7$

In Problems 25–30, find the largest possible domain of each function.

25. $f(x) = \ln(x - 3)$

26. $f(x) = 3 + \log_2(x^2 - 1)$

27. $f(x) = \ln(x^2 - 2x + 1)$

28. $f(x) = \log_5(x^3 - 3x^2 + 2x)$

29. $f(x) = \log_{10}\left(\dfrac{x+1}{x}\right)$

30. $f(x) = \log_2(\sqrt{7 - 2x})$

3.4. Logarithms Up Close and Personal

There is a famous scene in an old-fashioned Cold War era film in which a Soviet submarine breaches the ocean surface at an improbable angle before crashing back under water and setting off its countermeasure flares. The Soviet sailors, who had evacuated the submarine under their captain's orders, cheer on from a flotilla of yellow emergency rafts, believing that he is giving battle to the American submarine that has been hunting them down for several days. Their shouts of joy slowly die down as they see the remnants of the flares and begin to fear the demise of the two submarines.

This unlikely nautical analogy can help us remember the inverse relationship that we discovered in Section 3.3. We can think about our logarithmic and exponential functions as submarines from different camps, which, if they get too close to one another, can annihilate each other:

$$b^{\log_b(x)} = x \qquad \text{and} \qquad \log_b(b^x) = x.$$

We shall refer to these two equations as the **_cancellation principle_**. In either case, whether we look at an exponential of a logarithm or the other way around, all that is left is the input x, much like all that remains from our two submarines are the sailors floating in the yellow rafts.

EXAMPLE 3.31. Suppose that we wish to solve the following equation:

$$e^{3+4\ln(x)} = 1.$$

Instead of making direct use of the inverse relationship between logarithms and exponentials, as we did in Section 3.3, we shall begin by taking the natural logarithm of both sides of the equation, which in this case gives us

$$\ln(e^{3+4\ln(x)}) = \ln(1) = 0.$$

Then, we can apply the cancellation principle to obtain

$$3 + 4\ln(x) = 0.$$

This, of course, agrees completely with what the inverse relationship would have given us, but the point is that we got here by following a "method of cancellation." In particular, taking the natural logarithm of both sides cancels the natural exponential that featured prominently in the original equation. We can continue the cancellation, first by subtracting 3 (to undo an addition), and then by dividing by 4 (to undo a multiplication) as follows:

$$3 + 4\ln(x) = 0$$
$$4\ln(x) = -3$$
$$\ln(x) = -\tfrac{3}{4}.$$

We can now eliminate the natural logarithm on the left by taking the natural exponential of both sides:

$$e^{\ln(x)} = e^{-3/4}$$

$$x = e^{-3/4}.$$

Hence, our only solution is $x = e^{-3/4}$.

The cancellation principle transforms the Exponential Rules in Section 3.1 (see page 248) into a corresponding list of rules for logarithms. For instance, suppose that we wish to add two logarithms $\log_b(x) + \log_b(y)$. Placing this sum within an exponential and simplifying using Exponential Rule ① gives us

$$b^{\log_b(x)+\log_b(y)} = b^{\log_b(x)} \cdot b^{\log_b(y)} = x \cdot y.$$

Observe how the sum has been turned into a product. In the same way, consider a difference of logarithms $\log_b(x) - \log_b(y)$ and place it within an exponential. Then, applying Exponential Rule ② produces:

$$b^{\log_b(x)-\log_b(y)} = \frac{b^{\log_b(x)}}{b^{\log_b(y)}} = \frac{x}{y}.$$

Note that the difference has been turned into a quotient. Next, consider multiplying a logarithm $\log_b(x)$ times y. Placing this product in an exponential and invoking Exponential Rule ③ transforms it into a power:

$$b^{y\log_b(x)} = \left(b^{\log_b(x)}\right)^y = x^y$$

Similarly, thanks to Exponential Rule ④, dividing $\log_b(x)$ by y becomes a radical:

$$b^{\frac{1}{y}\log_b(x)} = \sqrt[y]{b^{\log_b(x)}} = \sqrt[y]{x}$$

Now, we can recover our original sum, difference, product, or quotient by moving to the logarithmic version of each of the equations above, in each case replacing the exponential on the left with a logarithm (of the same base) on the right. For example, our first equation becomes the logarithmic rule

$$\log_b(x) + \log_b(y) = \log_b(x \cdot y).$$

We will obtain similar rules for the other three equations.

Finally, for an analog of Exponential Rule ⑤, all we need to do is observe that if we start with two numbers whose logarithms are the same, then putting both logarithms inside exponentials give the same result, which according to the cancellation principle are the two numbers themselves:

$$\log_b(x) = \log_b(y) \quad \Leftrightarrow \quad b^{\log_b(x)} = b^{\log_b(y)} \quad \Leftrightarrow \quad x = y.$$

We summarize all five logarithmic rules below.

Logarithm Rules

For any positive base $b \neq 1$ and any pair of positive real numbers x and y:

① $\log_b(x) + \log_b(y) = \log_b(x \cdot y)$,

② $\log_b(x) - \log_b(y) = \log_b\left(\frac{x}{y}\right)$,

③ $y \log_b(x) = \log_b\left(x^y\right)$,

④ $\frac{1}{y} \log_b(x) = \log_b\left(\sqrt[y]{x}\right)$,

⑤ $\log_b(x) = \log_b(y)$ if and only if $x = y$.

As was the case with the Exponential Rules, the first four of these properties allow us to move arithmetic operations in and out of a logarithm. However, in the case of logarithms, addition outside the logarithm becomes multiplication inside, subtraction outside the logarithm becomes division inside, and so on. Observe that this is precisely the opposite of the situation with exponential functions.

EXAMPLE 3.32. Expand the following expression as a sum or difference of simple logarithms:
$$y = \log_2\left(x\sqrt{x^2 - 1}\right).$$

Solution. Our expression is the logarithm of a product of two factors, so we first use Logarithmic Rule ① to split it into a sum of logarithms:
$$y = \log_2\left(x\sqrt{x^2 - 1}\right) = \log_2(x) + \log_2\left(\sqrt{x^2 - 1}\right).$$

Next, we remove the square root inside the second logarithm by pulling out a factor of $\frac{1}{2}$ according to Logarithmic Rule ④:
$$y = \log_2(x) + \tfrac{1}{2}\log_2\left(x^2 - 1\right).$$

Now, we can factor the expression inside the second logarithm as a difference of two squares, so we apply Logarithmic Rule ① once again to split that single logarithm into a sum:
$$y = \log_2(x) + \tfrac{1}{2}\log_2\left((x-1)(x+1)\right)$$
$$= \log_2(x) + \tfrac{1}{2}\left(\log_2(x-1) + \log_2(x+1)\right).$$

Finally, we observe that we have no Logarithmic Rule for simplifying a sum or a difference appearing inside a logarithm. Thus, the terms $\log_2(x-1)$

and $\log_2(x+1)$ in the expression above cannot be simplified any further. The only thing left for us to do, then, is to distribute the coefficient of $\frac{1}{2}$ to each of the appropriate terms, bringing us to our final answer of

$$y = \log_2(x) + \tfrac{1}{2}\log_2(x-1) + \tfrac{1}{2}\log_2(x+1).$$

EXAMPLE 3.33. Expand the following expression as a sum or difference of simple logarithms:

$$y = \ln\left(\frac{x^2}{(x-1)^3}\right).$$

Solution. This time, our expression is the logarithm of a quotient of two powers, so we use Logarithmic Rule ② to write our logarithm as a difference of two logarithms:

$$y = \ln\left(x^2\right) - \ln\left((x-1)^3\right).$$

Next, we invoke Logarithmic Rule ③ to pull out the powers from inside each of the logarithms:

$$y = 2\ln(x) - 3\ln(x-1).$$

Again, this is as simple an expression as we can find.

EXAMPLE 3.34. Expand the following expression as a sum or difference of simple logarithms:

$$y = \log_{10}\left(\frac{x^5\sqrt[3]{x^2+1}}{(x+1)^4}\right).$$

Solution. The given expression is a fraction with the product of a power and a cube root in the numerator, and a power in the denominator. Thus, we apply Logarithmic Rules ②, ①, ③, and ④ (in that order) as follows:

$$y = \log_{10}\left(\frac{x^5\sqrt[3]{x^2+1}}{(x+1)^4}\right) = \log_{10}\left(x^5\sqrt[3]{x^2+1}\right) - \log_{10}\left((x+1)^4\right)$$

$$= \log_{10}\left(x^5\right) + \log_{10}\left(\sqrt[3]{x^2+1}\right) - \log_{10}\left((x+1)^4\right)$$

$$= 5\log_{10}(x) + \log_{10}\left(\sqrt[3]{x^2+1}\right) - 4\log_{10}(x+1)$$

$$= 5\log_{10}(x) + \tfrac{1}{3}\log_{10}\left(x^2+1\right) - 4\log_{10}(x+1).$$

Note that there is nothing further to do because $x^2 + 1$ does not factor.

EXAMPLE 3.35. Combine the following expression into a single logarithm:

$$y = 2 + 2\log_3(x) + \log_3\left(x^2+1\right) - \log_3(6).$$

Solution. In order to apply our Logarithmic Rules, we must first make sure that every term in our expression is written as a logarithm of the same base. In our case, this involves writing the 2 on the left as a logarithm with base 3:

$$2 = \log_3(3^2) = \log_3(9).$$

Then, we can combine the various terms in our expression using Logarithmic Rules ③, ①, and ② as follows:

$$y = \log_3(9) + 2\log_3(x) + \log_3(x^2 + 1) - \log_3(6)$$

$$= \log_3(9) + \log_3(x^2) + \log_3(x^2 + 1) - \log_3(6)$$

$$= \log_3(9 \cdot x^2 \cdot (x^2 + 1)) - \log_3(6)$$

$$= \log_3\left(\frac{9x^4 + 9x^2}{6}\right).$$

After putting this fraction in lowest terms, we arrive at our final answer of

$$y = \log_3\left(\frac{3x^4 + 3x^2}{2}\right).$$

EXAMPLE 3.36. Solve the following equation:

$$\log_4(x^2) = 1 + \log_4(9).$$

Solution. We shall first rewrite the expression on the right hand side of this equation as a single logarithm:

$$1 + \log_4(9) = \log_4(4) + \log_4(9) = \log_4(4 \cdot 9) = \log_4(36).$$

This transforms our equation into

$$\log_4(x^2) = \log_4(36).$$

Then using Logarithmic Rule ⑤, we can set the inputs to these logarithms equal to each other, obtaining

$$x^2 = 36.$$

Finally, we use the square root method and find that we have two solutions:

$$x = \pm 6.$$

You should check that each of these values constitutes a valid solution by substituting them back into our original equation.

EXAMPLE 3.37. Solve the following equation:

$$\log_6(x+3) + \log_6(x-2) = 1.$$

Solution. As above, we begin by combining each side of the equation as a single logarithm. For the left hand side, we use Logarithmic Rule ① to write

$$\log_6(x+3) + \log_6(x-2) = \log_6\big((x+3)(x-2)\big).$$

In contrast, for the right hand side, we have

$$1 = \log_6(6),$$

so that our equation becomes

$$\log_6\big((x+3)(x-2)\big) = \log_6(6).$$

We can then use Logarithmic Rule ⑤ to eliminate the two logarithms:

$$(x+3)(x-2) = 6.$$

Distributing on the left hand side, clearing the right hand side, and factoring yields:

$$x^2 + x - 6 = 6$$
$$x^2 + x - 12 = 0$$
$$(x-3)(x+4) = 0.$$

Evidently, we have $x = 3$ or $x = -4$. However, only one of these turns out to be a valid solution. In particular, substituting in $x = -4$ causes problems, since

$$\log_6(-4+3) = \log_6(-1) \qquad \text{and} \qquad \log_6(-4-2) = \log_6(-6)$$

are both undefined. Therefore, $x = -4$ is a spurious solution. On the other hand, $x = 3$ does satisfy our equation, as you can verify for yourself. In particular, $x = 3$ is the only solution to our equation.

EXAMPLE 3.38. Solve the equation $5^{x-2} = 3^{3x+4}$.

Solution. This equation involves exponentials in two different bases, neither of which and we cannot easily express one base as a power of the other. Therefore, it is difficult to say which of the two exponentials we should try to eliminate with the inverse property. Fortunately, thanks to Logarithmic Rule ③, there is nothing to worry about. Indeed, we can eliminate both exponentials simultaneously by taking the natural logarithm of both sides of the equation, as follows:

$$5^{x-2} = 3^{3x+4}$$

$$\ln\left(5^{x-2}\right) = \ln\left(3^{3x+4}\right)$$

$$(x-2)\ln(5) = (3x+4)\ln(3).$$

Although the coefficients in this equation might seem intimidating, we are only looking at a linear equation that we can solve without much fanfare:

$$x\ln(5) - 2\ln(5) = 3x\ln(3) + 4\ln(3)$$

$$x\ln(5) - 3x\ln(3) = 2\ln(5) + 4\ln(3)$$

$$x\left(\ln(5) - 3\ln(3)\right) = 2\ln(5) + 4\ln(3)$$

$$x = \frac{2\ln(5) + 4\ln(3)}{\ln(5) - 3\ln(3)}$$

We can then use our Logarithmic Rules to combine this expression into a single logarithm as follows:

$$x = \frac{\ln\left(5^2 \cdot 3^4\right)}{\ln\left(\frac{5}{3^3}\right)} = \frac{\ln(2025)}{\ln\left(\frac{5}{27}\right)} = \log_{5/27}(2025) = -4.514\,545\,602\ldots.$$

Reading Comprehension Questions for Section 3.4

Logarithmic and exponential functions exhibit an __(a)__ relationship. This means that we can use a logarithm to __(b)__ an exponential, and vice versa. Because of this relationship, each of the __(c)__ has a corresponding version for logarithms.

For example, the product of two exponentials with the same base can be written as a single exponential; the exponent in the product is the __(d)__ of the original exponents. The analogous rule for logarithms says that the logarithm of a __(e)__ can be written as the __(f)__ of two logarithms of the same base, that is, $\log_b(x \cdot y) =$ __(g)__. Similarly, the quotient of two exponentials with the same base can be written as a single exponential; in this case the exponent in the quotient is the __(h)__ of the original exponents. In the language of logarithms, this means that the logarithm of a __(i)__ can be written as the __(j)__ of two logarithms of the same base, that is, $\log_b\left(\frac{x}{y}\right) =$ __(k)__.

Again, when we raise an exponential to the yth power, we multiply the old exponent times __(l)__, and when we take the yth root of an exponential, we multiply the old exponent times __(m)__. Therefore, in the logarithm of a yth power, we can "pull out" a factor of __(n)__ from inside the logarithm, while in the logarithm of a yth root, we can pull out a factor of __(o)__. Hence, $\log_b(x^y) =$ __(p)__ and $\log_b\left(\sqrt[y]{x}\right) =$ __(q)__. Finally, we know that two exponentials of the same base are equal if and only if their powers are equal. Consequently, two logarithms of the same base are equal if and only if their __(r)__ are equal.

The logarithm rules allow us to solve logarithmic equations when all the bases are the same. For instance, to solve the equation

$$\log_3(x+1) + \log_3(x-2) - \log_3(2) = 2,$$

we would first combine the expression on the left hand side as a single logarithm:

$$\log_3\left(\underline{\quad(s)\quad}\right) = 2.$$

We can then turn to the exponential form of this equation, replacing the logarithm on the left with the exponential __(t)__ on the right. This yields a quadratic equation that simplifies to

$$x^2 - x - \underline{\quad(u)\quad} = 0.$$

We can solve it either by factoring or by using the quadratic formula; in either case, we obtain $x =$ ___(v)___ or $x =$ ___(w)___. However, only one of these values turns out to be a solution to the original equation; the other one is a ___(x)___ solution that would force us to take the logarithm of a ___(y)___ number, which is undefined. Therefore, our equation has only one solution, namely, $x =$ ___(z)___.

Exercises for Section 3.4

In Problems 1–10, find the exact value of each logarithmic expression without using a calculator or computer.

1. $\log_8(2) + \log_8(4)$

2. $\log_6(9) + \log_6(4)$

3. $\log_6(18) - \log_6(3)$

4. $\log_8(16) - \log_8(2)$

5. $\log_2(6) \cdot \log_6(4)$

6. $2\log_{10}(5) + \frac{1}{2}\log_{10}(16)$

7. $3^{\log_3(5)-\log_3(4)}$

8. $5^{\log_5(6)-\log_5(7)}$

9. $e^{\log_{e^2}(16)}$

10. $e^{\ln(5)+\ln(3)}$

11. Write each of the following expressions as a single logarithm.

   (a) $3\log_5(u) + 4\log_5(v)$

   (b) $2\log_3(u) - \log_3(v)$

   (c) $\log_4(x^2 - 1) - 2\log_4(x + 1)$

   (d) $2\ln(x + 1) - \ln(x^2 + 3x + 2)$

12. Write each of the following logarithms as a combination of $\ln(2)$ and $\ln(3)$.

   (a) $\ln(6)$

   (b) $\ln(1.5)$

   (c) $\ln(54)$

   (d) $\ln\left(\sqrt[5]{6}\right)$

13. Write each of the following logarithms as a combination of $\ln(2)$ and $\ln(3)$.

   (a) $\log_3(24)$

   (b) $\log_2(18)$

   (c) $\log_6\left(\frac{4}{9}\right)$

   (d) $\log_{2/3}(48)$

14. Find the value of the product of logarithms

$$\log_2(3) \cdot \log_3(4) \cdot \log_4(5) \cdots \log_{125}(126) \cdot \log_{126}(127) \cdot \log_{127}(128)$$

without using a calculator or computer.

In Problems 15–30, first find the exact solution for each equation. Then, using a calculator or computer if necessary, determine an approximate value.

15. $e^{3x} = 10$

16. $e^{2x+5} = 13$

17. $\log_4(x + 2) = \log_4(8)$

18. $\frac{1}{2} \log_3(x) = 2 \log_3(2)$

19. $2 \log_5(x) = 3 \log_5(4)$

20. $3 \log_2(x - 1) - \log_3(81) = \log_5(25)$

21. $\log_6(x) + \log_6(x + 9) = 2$

22. $\log_4(x) + \log_4(x - 3) = 1$

23. $\ln(x) + \ln(x + 2) = 4$

24. $\ln(x + 1) - \ln(x) = 2$

25. $e^{2x} + 9e^x + 8 = 0$

26. $2^{2x} - 4 \cdot 2^x - 5 = 0$

27. $3^{2x} - 3^{x+1} + 2 = 0$

28. $12e^x + 12e^{-x} = 25$

29. $2^{5x-4} = 7^{x+3}$

30. $3^{12x-7} = 4^{5-3x}$

3.5. Exponential Growth and Decay

Recall that a physical quantity will exhibit **exponential growth** if it can grow at a rate proportional to the quantity itself. A typical example of this sort of behavior is a population of plants, animals, or bacteria that has plenty of room to grow, plenty of food to consume, and no natural predators to fear. In mathematical biology, this is usually called the **law of uninhibited growth**. The exponential growth of such a population can be described either by a base $b > 1$ or by a growth rate $k > 0$. In particular, the population will be given by a function of the form

$$f(t) = P_0 \, b^t \qquad \text{or} \qquad f(t) = P_0 \, e^{kt},$$

where P_0 gives the initial population at time $t = 0$. The decision of whether to use a base or a growth rate to describe the growth is usually made based on the data at hand.

EXAMPLE 3.39. A colony of bacteria grows according to the law of uninhibited growth with a growth rate of 4.5% per day. Initially, there are 100 cells in the colony. How many cells will there be after five days?

Solution. According to the given information, our initial population consists of $P_0 = 100$ cells and the colony grows exponentially with a growth rate of $k = 0.045$. Therefore, the population is described by the exponential function

$$f(t) = 100 \, e^{0.045t}.$$

After five days, this population will consist of

$$f(5) = 100 \, e^{0.045 \cdot 5} \approx 125 \text{ cells}.$$

EXAMPLE 3.40. A colony of bacteria doubles in number every three hours. Scientists refer to this as the **doubling time** of the colony. How long will it take for the number of cells to triple?

Solution. Since we are not given a growth rate, we shall model our population by the function

$$f(t) = P_0 \, b^t,$$

where P_0 is the initial number of cells, b is the base of the exponential growth, and t is given in hours. Now, we do know that after three hours, the size of our colony will be double its initial value, so

$$f(3) = P_0 \, b^3 = 2 \, P_0.$$

If we solve this equation for b, we will know how quickly our colony is growing. In particular, we have

$$P_0 \, b^3 = 2 \, P_0$$
$$b^3 = 2$$
$$b = 2^{1/3}.$$

305

This means that

$$f(t) = P_0 \, (2^{1/3})^t = P_0 \, 2^{t/3}.$$

Then, to determine how long it will take our colony to triple in size, we simply set $f(t)$ equal to $3\,P_0$ and solve for t:

$$P_0 \, 2^{t/3} = 3\,P_0$$
$$2^{t/3} = 3$$
$$\tfrac{t}{3} = \log_2(3)$$
$$t = 3\log_2(3) \approx 4.755.$$

Therefore, the colony will triple in size in approximately 4 hours and 45 minutes.

Although the examples above deal specifically with bacteria, the law of uninhibited growth also applies to larger plants and animals that are guided only by instinct. However, one should take care not to apply the same law to human populations. This is because the biological drive to reproduce can be tempered in human beings by many social and economic factors. For instance, we might consider the case of the English vicar Thomas Robert Malthus (1766–1834). In an essay in 1798, Malthus observed that food production grows arithmetically, like a linear function of time, while people grow geometrically, like an exponential function. Since exponential functions grow faster than linear functions, Malthus predicted that the world would run out of food by 1890, and advocated the repeal of the Poor Laws, which he thought contributed to the problem of human overpopulation. A similar call to arms was made almost two centuries later by American biologist Paul Ehrlich. In his 1968 best-selling book *The Population Bomb*, Ehrlich predicted rampant famines in the 1970's and 1980's due to the world's exponential population growth. Needless to say, neither Malthus's nor Ehrlich's predictions materialized in the end. Thanks in part to human ingenuity, and in particular the technological innovations that became known as the "green revolution," there is still enough food to sustain everyone around the world; localized famines are only a result of corruption and poor means of distribution rather than overpopulation.[5]

Let us now turn to a second example of exponential growth, namely that of investing for the future. Some quantity of money is deposited in a savings account (or some other guaranteed investment vehicle) and generates interest over time. The speed with which the principal balance in the account grows depends both on the interest rate that the bank offers as well as on the frequency of the interest payments. In this setting, the formula to use – described by a base or a growth rate – depends on the frequency that interest is accrued.

---

[5] For an excellent treatment of the question of over population, the reader is invited to visit the Population Research Institute's POP 101 video series at `overpopulationisamyth.com`.

EXAMPLE 3.41. The Bank of Brandenburg offers its customers several choices in savings accounts. For its most patient of investors, the *Adagio* account provides a single payment of 7% at the end of every year. The principal balance for an account with an initial investment of $125 would be given as a function of time (in years) by the formula

$$A(t) = 125 \cdot 1.07^t.$$

For those investors wishing for more liquidity in their funds, the *Allegro* account, pays compound interest in four quarterly installments. Although the bank advertises an annual interest rate of 6.4% for this type of account, only one fourth of this percentage is paid at a time, making each installment only 1.6% of the principal. Since payments occur four times as often as in the *Adagio* account, the principal balance for this type of account, assuming an initial investment of $125, is given by the formula

$$B(t) = 125 \cdot 1.016^{4t}.$$

Finally, for those investors requiring instant gratification, the bank offers the *Presto* account, paying **continuous interest** in infinitesimally small increments, allowing the principal to grow at an instantaneous rate of change of 6%. Assuming, as above, an initial deposit of $125, the principal in this account would grow according to the formula

$$C(t) = 125 \cdot e^{0.06t}.$$

Which of these accounts is best depends, at least in part, on the investor. If one is only interested in short-term gains, then perhaps the *Presto* account is preferable. For instance, after only five months (when $t = \frac{5}{12}$ years), the principal in this account has grown to

$$C\left(\tfrac{5}{12}\right) = 125 \cdot e^{0.06 \cdot \frac{5}{12}} \approx \$128.16.$$

In this time, the *Allegro* account has paid only one installment of interest (after one quarter, when $t = \frac{1}{4}$), while the *Adagio* has not paid any interest at all. Thus, after five months, the principal balances in these accounts would be

$$A(0) = 125 \cdot 1.07^0 = \$125.00,$$

$$B\left(\tfrac{1}{4}\right) = 125 \cdot 1.016^{4 \cdot \frac{1}{4}} = \$127.00.$$

The point, of course, is that the bank only promises to pay an impatient investor the interest he is due if he can afford to wait until the end of the quarter or of the year. A premature withdrawal can result in forfeiting the interest, and perhaps other penalties as well.

On the other hand, for the long-term investor, the *Adagio* provides the most lucrative results. Indeed, after one year (when $t = 1$), the balance in each account would be

$$A(1) = 125 \cdot 1.07 = \$133.75,$$

$$B(1) = 125 \cdot 1.016^4 \approx \$133.19,$$

$$C(1) = 125 \cdot e^{0.06} \approx \$132.73.$$

Certainly, a difference of a few cents is not much to speak of now, but in time, it will grow into a significant amount – almost \$500 in forty years:

$$A(40) = 125 \cdot 1.07^{40} = \$1871.81,$$

$$B(40) = 125 \cdot 1.016^{4 \cdot 40} \approx \$1584.54,$$

$$C(40) = 125 \cdot e^{0.06 \cdot 40} \approx \$1377.90.$$

Behold the power of compound interest at work!

In contrast to populations following the law of uninhibited growth or savings accruing interest, other quantities exhibit **exponential decay** when they continually decrease at a rate proportional to the quantity itself. This behavior is pre-eminently illustrated by substances that experience **radioactive decay**. In this case, the decay is described either by a base $b < 1$ or by a **decay rate** $k > 0$. Again, if P_0 is the initial amount of radioactive substance present, then the substance is described by a function of the form

$$f(t) = P_0 \, b^t = P_0 \, e^{-kt}.$$

Notice that the decay rate is defined to be a *positive* number, so a negative sign is added to the second formula above.

EXAMPLE 3.42. Traces of burned wood along with ancient stone tools in an archaeological dig in Uruguay were found to contain approximately 1.7% of the amount of C-14 present in living organisms. This difference is due to the fact that the C-14 in the wood has been decaying ever since the tree from which it came was chopped down. If the half-life of C-14 is approximately 5 730 years, when was the tree cut and burned?

Solution. Suppose that the amount of C-14 in the wood, as a function of the time since the tree was cut down, is given by

$$f(t) = P_0 \, b^t$$

where P_0 is the original amount and t is measured in years. Then, since C-14 has a half-life of 5 730 years,

$$f(5\,730) = P_0 \, b^{5\,730} = \tfrac{1}{2} \, P_0.$$

Solving this equation for b gives

$$P_0\, b^{5\,730} = \tfrac{1}{2}\, P_0$$
$$b^{5\,730} = \tfrac{1}{2} = 2^{-1}$$
$$b = 2^{-1/5\,730},$$

so that

$$f(t) = P_0\left(2^{-1/5\,730}\right)^t = P_0\, 2^{-t/5\,730}.$$

Now, the wood presently contains only 1.7% of the original amount of C-14, so we can determine the time since the tree was chopped down by setting $f(t)$ equal to $0.017\, P_0$ and solving for t:

$$P_0\, 2^{-t/5\,730} = 0.017\, P_0$$
$$2^{-t/5\,730} = 0.017$$
$$-t/5\,730 = \log_2(0.017)$$
$$t = -5\,730\log_2(0.017) = 33\,682.781\,870\,749\ldots.$$

In other words, the tree was cut approximately $33\,700$ years ago.

Our second example of exponential decay comes by way of Sir Isaac Newton (1643–1727). Newton, of course, is best known for his 1687 groundbreaking treatise *Philosophiæ Naturalis Principia Mathematica* (known also as the *Principia*), in which he set forth his laws of motion and universal gravitation, thus giving modern physics the solid mathematical footing that it lacked at the time. Of particular interest to us here is **Newton's Law of Heating and Cooling**. According to this law, the difference in temperature between a small object and its surroundings will decay exponentially as time passes. If the object is hotter than its surroundings then it will cool down until its temperature is essentially the same as that of its surroundings. Similarly, if it is cooler than its surroundings then it will warm up. In either situation, we shall assume that the surrounding space is large enough not to be affected by the smaller object.

> EXAMPLE 3.43. A mug of water is heated in a microwave oven to a temperature of $100°C$ until it starts to boil. A tea bag is placed in the water and allowed to brew on the counter in a $20°C$ room. After five minutes, the tea is $85°C$. How long will it be before the tea is cool enough to drink, at a temperature of $50°C$?

Solution. Let $f(t)$ give the temperature difference between the tea and its surroundings after t minutes of brewing. Initially, this difference is

$$f(0) = 100 - 20 = 80°C.$$

Since this difference in temperature decays exponentially with time, we can assume that f is given by the formula

$$f(t) = 80\, b^t$$

for an appropriate choice of base b. After five minutes, the tea has cooled down to 85°C, so the difference in temperatures is

$$f(5) = 85 - 20 = 65°\text{C}.$$

Setting $f(5) = 80\,b^5$ and solving for b gives

$$80\,b^5 = 65$$

$$b^5 = \tfrac{65}{80} = \tfrac{13}{16}$$

$$b = \left(\tfrac{13}{16}\right)^{1/5},$$

so that

$$f(t) = 80\left(\left(\tfrac{13}{16}\right)^{1/5}\right)^t = 80\left(\tfrac{13}{16}\right)^{t/5}.$$

When the tea is cool enough to drink, the difference in temperatures will only be $50 - 20 = 30°\text{C}$, so we can determine how long that will take by setting $f(t)$ equal to 30 and solving for t:

$$80\left(\tfrac{13}{16}\right)^{t/5} = 30$$

$$\left(\tfrac{13}{16}\right)^{t/5} = \tfrac{30}{80} = \tfrac{3}{8}$$

$$\ln\left(\tfrac{13}{16}\right)^{t/5} = \ln\left(\tfrac{3}{8}\right)$$

$$\tfrac{t}{5}\ln\left(\tfrac{13}{16}\right) = \ln\left(\tfrac{3}{8}\right)$$

$$t = 5\frac{\ln\left(\tfrac{3}{8}\right)}{\ln\left(\tfrac{13}{16}\right)} = 5\frac{\ln(3) - \ln(8)}{\ln(13) - \ln(16)} = 23.618\,576\,710\ldots.$$

Therefore, the tea will be cool enough to drink in about 24 minutes.

Reading Comprehension Questions for Section 3.5

An exponential function can be described by either a base b, as in the formula $f(t) = $ _____(a)_____, or by a growth rate k, as in the formula $f(t) = $ _____(b)_____. If we know the growth rate k, we can compute the base as $b = $ _____(c)_____, whereas if we know the base b, we can compute the growth rate as $k = $ _____(d)_____. Thus, a function exhibits exponential growth when its base is greater than _____(e)_____, and when its growth rate is _____(f)_____ (positive or negative). In contrast, a function exhibits exponential decay when its base is between _____(g)_____ and _____(h)_____, and when its growth rate is _____(i)_____ (positive or negative). However, for ease of computation, some scientists prefer the formula $f(t) = P_0\, e^{-kt}$, where k now represents the _____(j)_____ rate, which by definition is always _____(k)_____ (positive or negative).

In theory, we can move back and forth between these two formulations of base and growth rate, but in practice, we usually pick whichever of the two is simplest for the given information. For example, consider a colony of 250 bacteria cells that has plenty of room and nutrients; such a colony is subject to the law of _____(l)_____, which says that its population will exhibit exponential _____(m)_____. If we are told that the colony doubles in size every seven hours, then we can model its population by an exponential function using the _____(n)_____ (base or growth rate) formulation as follows: $f(t) = $ _____(o)_____. On the other hand, if we are told that the colony grows at a rate of 9.9% per hour, then we can model its population using the _____(p)_____ (base or growth rate) formulation as follows: $f(t) = $ _____(q)_____. To find how many bacterial cells we will have after one hour, we need to determine the value of _____(r)_____. Conversely, to find how long it will take for the colony to triple in size, we need to solve the equation _____(s)_____. The first formulation gives _____(t)_____ cells and _____(u)_____ hours, while the second formulation gives _____(v)_____ cells and _____(w)_____ hours. Both formulations give essentially the same answers because they describe essentially the same exponential function. Indeed, the growth rate for the first is $k = $ _____(x)_____, while the base for the second is $b = $ _____(y)_____ $\approx 2^{1/7} = $ _____(z)_____.

311

Exercises for Section 3.5

1. The size of a certain insect population at time t (measured in days) is described by the function

$$P(t) = 500\, e^{0.02\, t}.$$

(a) What is the initial population of insects at time $t = 0$?

(b) By what percentage does the insect population grow in one day?

(c) What is the growth rate of this population?

(d) How long does it take before the number of insects has doubled?

2. The number of cells in a bacterial culture at time t (measured in hours) is described by the function

$$P(t) = 250 \cdot 1.4^t.$$

(a) What is the initial population of cells at time $t = 0$?

(b) By what percentage does the culture grow in one hour?

(c) What is the growth rate of this population?

(d) How long does it take before the number of cells has doubled?

3. After t years of earning interest compounded annually, the principal balance of a savings account is described by the function

$$P(t) = 700 \cdot 1.05^t.$$

(a) How large was the initial deposit when the account was originally opened?

(b) At what annual percentage rate is interest accrued in this account?

(c) At what interest rate would a savings account that pays compound interest every month produce the same return as this account?

(d) At what interest rate would a savings account that pays continuous interest produce the same return as this account?

4. After t years of earning interest compounded monthly, the principal balance of a savings account is described by the function

$$P(t) = 625 \cdot 1.005^{12\, t}.$$

(a) How large was the initial deposit when the account was originally opened?

(b) What is the annual percentage rate at which interest is accrued?

(c) At what interest rate would a savings account that pays compound interest every year produce the same return as this account?

(d) At what interest rate would a savings account that pays continuous interest produce the same return as this account?

312

5. After t years of earning continuous interest, the principal balance of a savings account is described by the function

$$P(t) = 435 \cdot e^{0.03\,t}.$$

(a) How large was the initial deposit when the account was originally opened?

(b) What is the annual percentage rate at which interest is accrued?

(c) At what interest rate would a savings account that pays compound interest every year produce the same return as this account?

(d) At what interest rate would a savings account that pays compound interest every month produce the same return as this account?

6. The amount of radioactive cobalt-60 (in grams) contained in a mineral sample at time t (in years) is given by the function

$$A(t) = 37.5 \cdot e^{-0.131\,527\,t}.$$

(a) What is the initial amount of cobalt-60 present in the sample?

(b) What is the decay rate of cobalt-60 in the sample?

(c) By what percentage does the amount of cobalt-60 decay in one year?

(d) How long does it take before half of the cobalt-60 has decayed away?

7. The amount of radioactive radium-226 (in grams) contained in a mineral sample at time t (in years) is given by the function

$$A(t) = 3.5 \cdot 2^{-t/1\,601}.$$

(a) What is the initial amount of radium-226 present in the sample?

(b) What is the decay rate of radium-226 in the sample?

(c) By what percentage does the amount of radium-226 decay in one year?

(d) How long does it take before half of the radium-226 has decayed away?

8. The concentration of the narcotic drug oxycodone (measured in micrograms per milliliter of blood) in the bloodstream of a hospital patient t hours after the drug was administered is given by the function

$$C(t) = 74 \cdot e^{-0.175\,t}.$$

(a) What is the concentration at time the drug was administered?

(b) What is the decay rate of oxycodone in the patient's bloodstream?

(c) How long does it take before half of the oxycodone has been eliminated by the patient's kidneys?

(d) How long does it take before the drug concentration falls below 0.1 micrograms per milliliter, thus becoming effectively undetectable?

9. The temperature (measured in degrees Celsius) of a spear of broccoli steamed over boiling water at time t (in minutes) is given by the function

$$T(t) = 100 - 93 \cdot e^{-0.19\,t}.$$

   (a) What is the broccoli's temperature when it was first put in the steamer at time $t = 0$?

   (b) How long does it take for the broccoli to reach a temperature of 85°C?

   (c) Assuming that the steamer can operate indefinitely without running out of water, what will the temperature of the broccoli be after one hour in the steamer? What about after two hours? After ten hours?

10. In her biology laboratory, Acute Alice is studying a bacteria culture that triples in size every 4 hours. If initially she counts 127 bacteria cells in the culture, how many cells will there be after 5 hours?

11. Scalene Sallie's financial advisor has found two investment vehicles for her to consider. The first pays 40% interest compounded yearly. The second pays 34% continuous interest. Which will give Sallie the better return?

12. Obtuse Ollie is working in a pizza restaurant to make some extra cash. He notes that when he takes a pizza out of the oven, its temperature is 450°F. After three minutes of sitting in a 70°F room, the temperature of the pizza is 300°F. When will the pizza be cool enough to eat at 150°F?

13. While working at an archaeological dig, Acute Alice found the fossilized shell of an ancient mollusk. Laboratory results confirm that the fossil contains 63% of the usual amount of carbon-14 found in living tissue. Assuming that the carbon-14 in the fossil has been decaying with a half-life of 5 730 years since the mollusk died, what can Alice conclude about the age of the fossil?

14. Scalene Sallie has a summer job at the mosquito control office in her hometown. On the first rainy day of the season, she surveys a local park and determines that there are approximately 1 000 mosquitoes living in the vicinity of a pond. Three days later, a similar survey of the pond shows that there are 1 800 mosquitoes. Assuming that the population of mosquitoes in the pond grows exponentially, how long will it be before there are 10 000 mosquitoes living in the pond?

15. Obtuse Ollie wants to buy a car. He finds that the cost of a brand new car is $23 000, but that after two years the same model costs only $17 500. Assuming that the cost of a car decreases over time like an exponential function, how long would Ollie need to wait before the same car costs less than $5 000?

16. Acute Alice left a mug of hot cocoa outside her door on a cold 5°C day and proceeded to record its temperature in degrees Celsius as a function of time (in minutes) since it was placed outside. Alice noted that after 10 minutes the cocoa's temperature was 49°C, and that after 30 minutes it was 16°C. What was the temperature of the cocoa when Alice first set it outside?

17. Scalene Sallie received an inheritance of \$5 000 from a long lost aunt, and she decided to invest all of it in a municipal bond that guarantees 9% continuous interest. How long will it take before Sallie's investment doubles in value?

18. As part of his business baking and selling artisan breads, Obtuse Ollie is making a sourdough culture consisting of wild yeast and lactobacillus bacteria. According to the recipe he is following, the number of cells in his culture grows exponentially, doubling every twelve hours. How long does it take before the number of yeast cells triples in size?

19. As part of a biology experiment, Acute Alice injects a laboratory rat with one milliliter of the radioactive tracer technetium-99m before scanning the rat's heart. If the half-life of technetium-99m is 6.006 hours, how long will it be before the rat has less than 0.001 milliliters of the tracer?

20. Scalene Sallie is checking her financial records and finds that the \$3 500 she invested in stocks last year depreciated in value at a continuous rate of 16% during the first quarter of the year, but then rebounded in value at a continuous rate of 11% for the rest of the year. By how much did her investment grow? Give your answer both as a dollar amount and as a percentage of the original investment.

21. Obtuse Ollie is going to grill a steak for dinner, so he decides to let it thaw in a 70°F room during the afternoon. If the steak was 30°F an hour after coming out of the freezer and 50°F an hour after that, what was the temperature of the freezer?

22. Acute Alice takes a thermometer reading 72°F and places it in a refrigerator where the temperature is a constant 38°F. After 2 minutes, the thermometer reads 60°F. What will it read after 5 additional minutes?

23. Scalene Sallie found a record of her hometown's population during the first half of the nineteenth century. According to this record, there were 2 200 people living in her hometown in 1800, but by 1850 this number had grown to 5 800 people. Assuming that the population grew exponentially over the last two hundred years, how many people were living in Sallie's hometown in the year 2000?

24. Obtuse Ollie has invested \$2 500 in a certificate of deposit (CD) that pays 8% annual interest. However, he does not know whether interest is compounded yearly, monthly, daily, or continuously. When he checked his financial statements, he found that one year after his initial deposit the principal balance was \$2 708.19. How often is interest compounded in Ollie's CD?

25. On April 26, 1986, an accident in a nuclear power plant in Chernobyl, Ukraine, released radioactive material into the atmosphere over much of Europe. As a result, the hay in Austria was contaminated with Iodine-131, a radioactive isotope with a half-life of 8 days. If the hay was safe enough for cows to consume when 10% of the original contamination remained, how long did Austrian farmers need to wait before using this hay?

26. The Shroud of Turin is a mysterious 14-foot long linen cloth that bears the faint image of a crucified man. Although the Catholic Church has not given a definitive opinion on the matter, many faithful Christians believe it to be the burial shroud of Jesus Christ. In an attempt to validate this claim, a group of scientists in 1988 conducted a radiocarbon dating of a small sample of the shroud and determined that it contained 92% of the usual amount of carbon-14 found in living tissue. Unfortunately, the small sample was taken from an outside corner of the shroud, where it had been handled hundreds of times over the centuries. It is even likely that the sample came from a part of the shroud that was repaired after it was nearly destroyed in a fire in 1532. Because of these reasons, the radiocarbon dating has largely been discredited as scientifically unreliable.[6]

    (a) Assuming that carbon-14 has a half-life of 5 730 years, how old does the 1988 radiocarbon dating test indicate the shroud to be? Round your answer to the nearest year.

    (b) Assuming that the shroud is an authentic 2 000-year-old relic, how much carbon-14 should it contain? Round your answer to the nearest percent.

27. According to the U.S. Census Bureau, the population of the state of Florida increased from 528 500 people in 1900 to 2 771 300 people in 1950.

    (a) Assuming that the population grew exponentially, what was its growth rate between 1900 and 1950?

    (b) If the population continued increasing exponentially at the same rate, what would the population of Florida be in the year 2000?

    (c) The latest census revealed a population of 15 983 000 people in the year 2000. Is this greater than or less than the value predicted by the exponential model?

    (d) What historical phenomena might explain your answer to (c)?

28. Table 3.6 gives the total world population over the last sixty years.

    (a) Assuming that the population grew exponentially between 1960 and 1970, find a formula describing the world's population as a function of time.

    (b) If the population continued increasing exponentially at the same rate during the next fifty years, what would the world population be in the years 1980, 1990, 2000, and 2010?

    (c) Is the data given in the table less than or greater than the values predicted by the exponential model?

TABLE 3.6. World population (in millions of persons) between 1960 and 2010.

year	1960	1970	1980	1990	2000	2010
population	3 043	3 712	4 451	5 287	6 090	6 864

Source: http://www.census.gov/population/international/data/worldpop (Mar 2013)

---

[6] For example, see G. Fanti and S. Gaeta, *Il Mistero della Sindone* (2013).

29. Carbon dioxide (CO_2) is called a "greenhouse gas" because it traps heat in the atmosphere and increases the average surface temperature of the earth. As a result of the industrial revolution and the burning of coal, oil, and natural gas that went with it, the level of CO_2 in the atmosphere has increased from 270 ppm (parts per million) 150 years ago to the present level of 390 ppm. This increase has resulted in a global increase in temperature of about 0.8°C. Scientists believe that, all other factors being equal, a doubling of CO_2 from the present levels to 780 ppm will cause a global warming of about 1°C.[7] Assuming that CO_2 levels have been growing exponentially for the past 150 years, and continue to do so in the future, how long will it take before CO_2 levels double to 780 ppm?

30. According to Samuel Arbesman, many so-called scientific facts have a expiration dates, meaning that in time they are eventually proven to be wrong. He cites the number of chemical elements in the periodic table or whether eating red meat is good for you as examples of such "meso-facts" that have changed drastically over the last fifty years. Arbesman argues that knowledge in most scientific fields evolves in a predictable way, so that statements taken as fact at some point in time eventually decay exponentially.[8]

    (a) Suppose that the meso-facts a given scientific field decay with a half-life of 30 years. What percentage of the meso-facts in this field are still believed to be true after one century?

    (b) What would be the half-life of a scientific field in which 90% of the meso-facts are still believed to be true after one century?

---

[7] W. Happer, The Truth About Greenhouse Gases, *First Things* No. 214 (June/July 2011).

[8] S. Arbesman, *The Half-Life of Facts: Why Everything We Know Has an Expiration Date* (2012).

Review of Chapter 3

Vocabulary with which you should now be familiar:

- base of exponential
- base of logarithm
- compound interest
- continuous interest
- decay rate
- doubling time
- exponential decay
- exponential function
- exponential growth
- geometric sequence
- growth rate

- half-life
- initial value
- instantaneous rate of change
- inverse relationship
- law of cooling and heating
- law of uninhibited growth
- locally linear
- logarithmic function
- natural logarithm
- natural exponential
- the number e

Tasks you should now be prepared to perform:

- evaluate an exponential function at any real number.
- evaluate the natural logarithm of any positive number.
- recognize an exponential function from a table of data points.
- determine the formula for the exponential function determined by two data points.
- determine the domain of an exponential or logarithmic function.
- locate the x- and y-intercepts of the graph of an exponential or logarithmic function.
- locate the asymptote of the graph of an exponential or logarithmic function.
- sketch the graph of an exponential or logarithmic function.
- translate between the exponential and logarithmic forms of an equation.
- solve equations involving exponentials and logarithms.
- solve "story problems" involving exponential growth or decay.

CHAPTER 4

Trigonometry

In the story of π we find both the mythical and the mystical, the profound and the profoundly silly. π teaches us about the limits of our own comprehension, clearly marking the boundary between the finite and the infinite. We know π best from the circle ratio, and yet it appears throughout mathematics, physics, statistics, engineering, architecture, biology, astronomy, and even the arts. π lies hidden in the rhythms of both sound waves and ocean waves, ubiquitous in nature as well as in geometry.

There is little doubt that if we understood this number better – if we could find a pattern in its digits or a deeper awareness of why it appears in so many seemingly unrelated equations – we'd have a deeper understanding of mathematics and the physics of our universe. But the number has always held its cards tight to its chest, ceding little ground in the battle for human comprehension.

D. Blatner
The Joy of π
page 3 (1999)

4.1. Angles, Circles, and Triangles

An *angle* consists of the region between two infinite rays meeting at a common point. This common point is called the *vertex* of the angle, and the rays are called its *initial side* and its *terminal side*, respectively. It is typical to place an angle on the Cartesian plane so that its vertex is at the origin with its initial side lying horizontally along the positive x-axis. In this case, the angle is said to be in *standard position*. For example, consider the two angles depicted in Figure 4.1. They have the same initial and terminal sides meeting at the same vertex at the origin, so we refer to them as *coterminal angles*. However, they are, in fact, different angles since they consist of different regions of the plane.

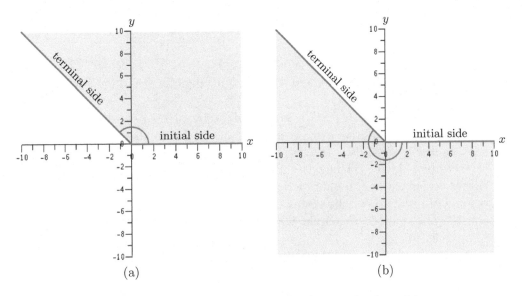

FIGURE 4.1. Two coterminal angles in standard position.

We can think of the angle in Figure 4.1(a) as the region swept out by an infinite ray which travels counterclockwise around the origin from the initial side to the terminal side. On the other hand, the angle in Figure 4.1(b) consists of the region swept out as our ray moves clockwise from the initial side to the terminal side. When an angle corresponds to the counterclockwise motion about the origin, as in Figure 4.1(a), we say it is a *positive angle*; when it corresponds to the clockwise motion, as in Figure 4.1(b), we say it is a *negative angle*.

The size or *measure* of an angle is determined as a fraction of a circle drawn around the angle's vertex. For instance, if we drew a small circle around the origin, then about $\frac{3}{8}$ of this circle would be covered by the angle in Figure 4.1(a). In contrast, the angle in Figure 4.1(b) would cover about $\frac{5}{8}$ of the same circle. There are several ways in which we can express angle measure, but in all of them, the number that we obtain is simply a measure of the portion of a circle covered by the angle.

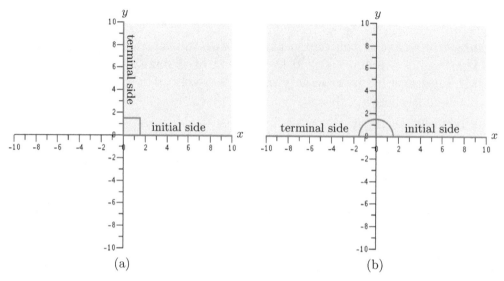

(a)   (b)

FIGURE 4.2. A right angle and a straight angle in standard position.

EXAMPLE 4.1. We can form a *right angle* by placing the initial side, as usual, along the positive x-axis, and the terminal side along the positive y-axis, as in Figure 4.2(a). In contrast, we form a *straight angle* by moving the terminal side to the negative x-axis, as shown in Figure 4.2(b). Observe that it is conventional to mark a right angle by drawing a little square corner, instead of an arc, near the vertex of the angle. The measure of a right angle consists of a quarter of a circle, while that of a straight angle consists of half of a circle.

EXAMPLE 4.2. An angle is said to be *acute* if it measures less than a right angle. It is said to be *obtuse* if it measures more than a right angle, but less than a straight angle. Finally, it is said to be *reflex* if it measures more than a straight angle. Accordingly, the angle shown in Figure 4.1(a) is a positive obtuse angle, while that in Figure 4.1(b) is a negative reflex angle.

EXAMPLE 4.3. Two acute angles are *complementary* if they add up to a right angle. Two angles are *supplementary* if they add up to a straight angle.

The use of *degrees* to measure angles dates back to Babylon, some four thousand years ago, where ancient astronomers observed the stars in the night sky slowly circling around Polaris, the north star. Of course, the apparent movement of the stars is really just the effect of the earth's own motion around the solar system. Nevertheless, from the vantage point of the Babylonian astronomers, the stars completed slightly more than one rotation every twenty-four hours, so that their position would appear to advance gradually from one night to the next, coming full circle after one year. Since one year was reckoned as 360 days in the Babylonian calendar,[1] the circle was divided into 360 equal pieces, called degrees, each measuring the nightly advance of the stars. As is common practice, we use a little superscript circle to denote degrees. Thus, we can assert that a full circle is equivalent to 360°.

Dividing the circle into 360 degrees turned out to have some nice consequences. For one thing, 360 is sufficiently large so that, for many purposes, the measure of any angle can be reasonably approximated to the nearest degree. Even on a large circle like the earth's equator, a difference of one degree amounts to only about 69 miles. Furthermore, 360 can be divided evenly by many factors. This means that the measure of many geometrically significant angles is given by a whole number of degrees. For instance, a straight angle measures exactly 180° and a right angle measures exactly 90°, since these correspond to one half and one quarter of a circle, respectively. However, it must be noted that the choice of 360° is somewhat of an astronomical accident particular to our planet.

EXAMPLE 4.4. In navigation and surveying, directions are often described in terms of **bearings**, that is, as angles from one of the four cardinal directions: North, South, East, and West. For instance, consider the five arrows shown in Figure 4.3. These arrows divide a complete circle into five equal pieces, so they form five angles measuring $\frac{360}{5}^\circ = 72^\circ$ apiece.

To begin, we note that the first of our arrows points due East. The second arrow points in a northeasterly direction, making a counterclockwise angle of 72° with the first arrow, that is to say, with East. Our arrow also makes a clockwise angle of $90^\circ - 72^\circ = 18^\circ$ with the northerly direction. Now, it is customary to take the direction which produces the smaller of these two angles as our frame of reference for our bearing. In this case, our reference direction happens to be North. Therefore, our second arrow is said to have a bearing of 18° East of North.

The third arrow is directed towards the northwest, making a counterclockwise angle of $72^\circ - 18^\circ = 54^\circ$ from North and a clockwise angle of $90^\circ - 54^\circ = 36^\circ$ from West. Again, to obtain the smaller of these two angles, we select West as our reference direction. Hence, we say that this third arrow points with a bearing of 36° North of West.

The fourth arrow points towards the southwest, at an angle of $72^\circ - 36^\circ = 36^\circ$ counterclockwise from West and $90^\circ - 36^\circ = 54^\circ$ clockwise from South. Once again, we selecting the reference direction with the smaller angle; thus, this arrow is said to have a bearing of 36° South of West.

Finally, the fifth arrow points $72^\circ - 54^\circ = 18^\circ$ counterclockwise from South and $90^\circ - 18^\circ = 72^\circ$ clockwise from East. Therefore, we say that it points with a bearing of 18° East of South.

The shading in the figure indicates the angles used for each of these bearings.

---

[1] In the Babylonian calendar, a year consisted of 12 months, each with 30 days. An extra "leap month" was added every six years to synchronize with the seasons.

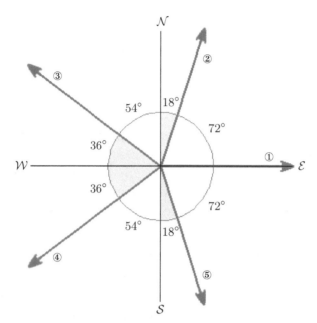

FIGURE 4.3. Describing directions in terms of bearings.

Such was the state of affairs until the beginning of the eighteenth century, when the British mathematician Roger Cotes (1682 – 1716) introduced a truly mathematical approach to angle measure. A collaborator of Sir Isaac Newton, Cotes was instrumental in the publication of the second edition of the *Principia*, Newton's masterpiece describing calculus and its application to the laws of motion. Cotes was generally regarded as one of the brightest minds of his generation, but his life was tragically cut short at the age of 33 by a violent fever. Hearing of his death, Isaac Newton is said to have remarked, "If he had lived we would have known something."

Cotes's idea was to take the radius of a circle, whatever length that might be, as the basic unit of measurement for any piece of that circle (and consequently for any angle). For example, on a small circle measuring one inch in radius, it is natural to measure the circumference in inches. On the other hand, if the radius of a circle measures one mile, then the circumference of that circle should also be measured in miles. In either case, the circumference will measure 2π (or approximately 6.283) of whatever units we used. The point is that the units we choose are not important in and of themselves, but only in how they relate to the radius of the circle in question. Even when the radius of a circle is not a standard unit of measure like an inch or a mile, we can still use it as the natural unit of measure for that particular circle. In this case, it is typical to refer to this length as one **radian**. Thus, a full rotation around a circle, regardless of its size, always corresponds to 2π radians.

Measuring angles in radians will, at first, feel strange and awkward. Angles which previously measured some whole number of degrees will, in radians, measure some fraction involving the irrational number π. For example, a straight angle measures

π radians, while a right angle measures $\frac{\pi}{2}$ radians, since these correspond to one half and one quarter of a full circle, respectively. Furthermore, radians are much larger than degrees. Indeed, as you can see in Figure 4.4, one radian is equivalent to approximately 57.296°. Consequently, on the equator of the earth, one radian of latitude is approximately 3 963 miles. This means that we need to measure our angles to the nearest hundredth of a radian in order to achieve the same level of precision as about half a degree.

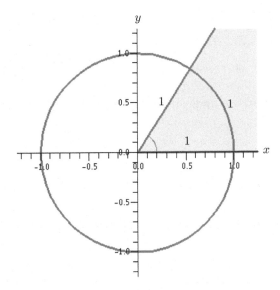

FIGURE 4.4. An angle measuring one radian.

EXAMPLE 4.5. Consider the two angles illustrated in Figure 4.1. We will denote the measure of these angles by using the Greek letters α (*alpha*) and β (*beta*), respectively. As we noted earlier, the first of these angles corresponds to $\frac{3}{8}$ of a full circle. Since a full circle corresponds to 360°, it follows that the degree measure for this angles is

$$\alpha = \tfrac{3}{8} \cdot 360° = 135°.$$

On the other hand, a full circle is equivalent to 2π radians, so the radian measure for this same angle is computed as

$$\alpha = \tfrac{3}{8} \cdot 2\pi = \tfrac{3}{4}\pi.$$

In contrast, the second angle in the figure measures $\frac{5}{8}$ of a *clockwise* circle, so its degree measure is given by

$$\beta = -\tfrac{5}{8} \cdot 360° = -225°.$$

By the same token, the radian measure for this angle is

$$\beta = -\tfrac{5}{8} \cdot 2\pi = -\tfrac{5}{4}\pi.$$

Note that we use negative angle measures to denote negative (in other words, clockwise) angles. It is also worth observing that we do not use any special symbols to denote radian measures.

In general, we can convert from the degree measure of an angle to its radian measure and back by multiplying by an appropriate conversion factor. In particular, since a the measure of a straight angle is given by either $180°$ or π radians, we have

$$\boxed{\frac{\text{Radian Measure}}{\pi} = \frac{\text{Degree Measure}}{180}.}$$

EXAMPLE 4.6. Let us consider the angle measurements that we made in Example 4.4. There we noted that five arrows in Figure 4.3 made five angles of $72°$. In radians, these angles amounts to:

$$72° = \tfrac{72}{180} \cdot \pi = \tfrac{2\pi}{5} \text{ radians.}$$

Note that, as before, this corresponds to one fifth of a full rotation of a circle (that is, one fifth of 2π radians).

In the following examples, it will be convenient to measure angles on the **unit circle**, that is, on the circle with a radius of one unit about the origin. Recall that this circle is given by the equation

$$x^2 + y^2 = 1.$$

In this circle, the radian measure is simply the length of the arc of the circle covered by the angle.

EXAMPLE 4.7. We can tile six **equilateral triangles** around the center of the unit circle, as illustrated in Figure 4.5. This means that the angle at each corner of these equilateral triangles measures one sixth of a full circle, that is to say, $60°$ or $\frac{\pi}{3}$ radians. However, we can say more than that: Since all equilateral triangles are **similar** to one another (meaning that corresponding angles are equal and corresponding sides are proportional), the angles in every equilateral triangle also measure $\frac{\pi}{3}$ radians.

Observe that the equilateral triangle shaded in the figure has one corner at the origin $(0,0)$ and another corner at the point $(1,0)$. The third corner, known as the **apex** of the triangle, is the same distance away from these two points, so it must have an x-coordinate of $x = \frac{1}{2}$. Furthermore, since the apex is on the unit circle, its coordinates must also satisfy the equation of that circle:

$$x^2 + y^2 = \left(\tfrac{1}{2}\right)^2 + y^2 = 1.$$

By solving this equation, we conclude that the apex has a y-coordinate of $y = \frac{\sqrt{3}}{2}$, as indicated in the figure.

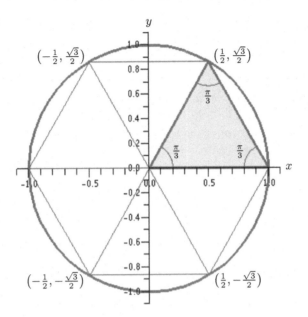

FIGURE 4.5. An equilateral triangle inside the unit circle.

EXAMPLE 4.8. The diagram in Figure 4.6 shows a different way to tile equilateral triangles around the center of the unit circle. In this case, the positive x-axis cuts one of the equilateral triangles down the middle, producing the smaller triangle shaded in the figure. At the origin, where one of the angles of the original equilateral triangle was cut in half, this new triangle has an angle measuring $30°$ or $\frac{\pi}{6}$ radians. At its apex, the triangle has an angle of

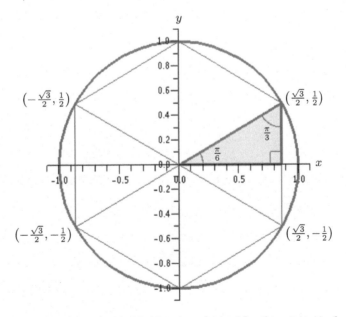

FIGURE 4.6. A 30-60-90 triangle inside the unit circle.

60° or $\frac{\pi}{3}$ radians, matching that of the original equilateral triangle. Finally to the right, where the vertical edge meets the x-axis, the triangle has an angle of 90° or $\frac{\pi}{2}$ radians. For obvious reasons, this type of triangle is often called a **30-60-90 triangle**.

Since the x-axis cuts the vertical edge of the original equilateral triangle in half, the apex for our 30-60-90 triangle must have a y-coordinate of $y = \frac{1}{2}$. Furthermore, since the apex is a point on the unit circle, its coordinates must again satisfy the equation of that circle:

$$x^2 + y^2 = x^2 + \left(\tfrac{1}{2}\right)^2 = 1.$$

After solving this equation, we conclude that the apex has an x-coordinate of $x = \frac{\sqrt{3}}{2}$, as indicated in Figure 4.6.

It should be noted that all 30-60-90 triangles are also similar to one another. This means that every 30-60-90 triangle has sides in the proportion of

$$\frac{1}{2} : \frac{\sqrt{3}}{2} : 1 \qquad \text{or} \qquad 1 : \sqrt{3} : 2,$$

just like the one in Figure 4.6. In particular, if we know that the shorter leg of a 30-60-90 triangle measures z units, then we automatically know that the longer leg measures $\sqrt{3}\,z$ units and the hypotenuse measures $2z$ units.

EXAMPLE 4.9. We can tile four squares around the center of the unit circle, as shown in Figure 4.7. In this diagram, one of the squares has a diagonal that comes out of the origin and cuts two of its right angles in half. Thus, each of the resulting triangles has two angles measuring 45° or $\frac{\pi}{4}$ radians, in

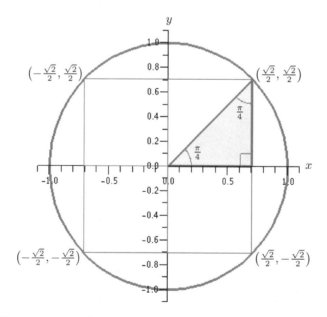

FIGURE 4.7. A 45-90-45 triangle inside the unit circle.

addition to the right angle that it shares with the square. Consequently, a triangle of this type is often called a *45-90-45 triangle*.

Note that the hypotenuse of the triangle shaded in Figure 4.7 has a slope of one. This means that the apex of this triangle has equal x- and y-coordinates. However, these equal coordinates must also satisfy the equation of the unit circle. Therefore, we can determine their value by solving the following system of equations:

$$\begin{cases} x = y, \\ x^2 + y^2 = 1. \end{cases}$$

After solving, we arrive at the conclusion that $x = y = \frac{\sqrt{2}}{2}$, as indicated in the figure.

Like our other families of triangles, all 45-90-45 triangles are also similar to one another, this time with sides in the proportion of

$$\frac{\sqrt{2}}{2} : \frac{\sqrt{2}}{2} : 1 \qquad \text{or} \qquad 1 : 1 : \sqrt{2}.$$

Therefore, if we know that the legs of a 45-90-45 triangle measure z units, then we automatically know that the hypotenuse measures $\sqrt{2}\, z$ units.

By combining the three apex points from Examples 4.7, 4.8, and 4.9, along with their reflections across the x- and y-axis, we obtain coordinates for sixteen distinct points on the unit circle, as shown in Figure 4.8. Each of these sixteen points describes the terminal side of some angle (in standard position) measuring between 0 and 2π radians, as indicated in the figure. In particular, we can obtain the points marked on the second, third, and fourth quadrants of the unit circle by rotating our three apex points by one quarter, one half, or three quarters of a turn, respectively. This means that the angles in the second, third, and fourth quadrants of the unit circle measure $\frac{\pi}{2}$, π, or $\frac{3\pi}{2}$ radians more than their respective angles in the first quadrant. You should commit these sixteen points, and their corresponding angles, to memory.

Observe that the points in Figure 4.8 also determine negative angles measuring between 0 and -2π radians. In order to find these negative angles, all we need to do is to rotate clockwise instead of counterclockwise around the unit circle. For instance, the point $\left(-\frac{\sqrt{2}}{2}, \frac{\sqrt{2}}{2}\right)$ corresponds to an angle of $\frac{3\pi}{4}$ (by turning counterclockwise) as well as to an angle of $-\frac{5\pi}{4}$ (by turning clockwise). Figure 4.1, back in page 323, shows what each of these angles looks like.

Of course, there is no reason to stop at 2π or -2π radians. We can go beyond these values by considering angles that rotate, either counterclockwise or clockwise, more than one full turn of the circle. For instance, the angle measuring $\frac{27\pi}{4}$ radians illustrated in Figure 4.9 consists of three and three eighths turns around the unit

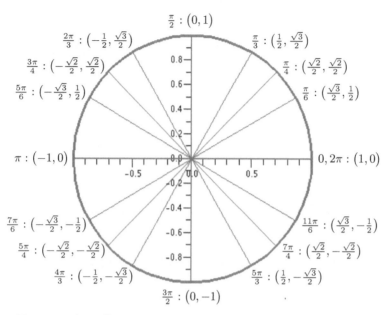

FIGURE 4.8. Sixteen important points on the unit circle.

circle:

$$\frac{27\pi}{4} = \underbrace{2\pi + 2\pi + 2\pi}_{\text{three full turns}} + \underbrace{\frac{3\pi}{4}}_{\frac{3}{8}\text{ turn}}.$$

This generalization of what we mean by an "angle" is a departure from our original definition in page 323, but it follows naturally from the picture of the unit circle.

EXAMPLE 4.10. The terminal side of the angle in Figure 4.9 intersects the unit circle at the point $\left(-\frac{\sqrt{2}}{2}, \frac{\sqrt{2}}{2}\right)$, making this angle coterminal with the $\frac{3\pi}{4}$ radian angle shown in Figure 4.1(a). In fact, we can describe all of the angles θ coterminal to $\frac{3\pi}{4}$ simply by adding some whole number of turns around the unit circle to this angle. In other words, we let

$$\theta = \underbrace{\frac{3\pi}{4}}_{\frac{3}{8}\text{ turn}} + \underbrace{2k\pi}_{k\text{ full turns}},$$

where k is an integer. For the case $k = 0$, this formula gives us our original angle of $\theta = \frac{3\pi}{4}$. For $k = -1$, our formula produces the coterminal angle in Figure 4.1(b):

$$\theta = \frac{3\pi}{4} - 2\pi = -\frac{5\pi}{4}.$$

Finally, when $k = 3$, we obtain the coterminal angle shown in Figure 4.9:

$$\theta = \frac{3\pi}{4} + 6\pi = \frac{27\pi}{4}.$$

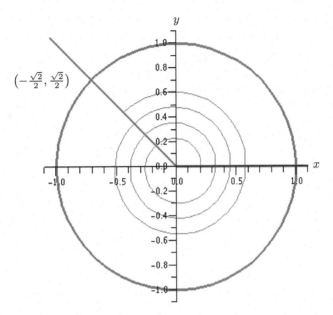

FIGURE 4.9. An angle measuring $\frac{27\pi}{4}$ radians.

Most importantly, by letting k be an arbitrary integer, θ can represent an infinite number of coterminal angles all at once.

Reading Comprehension Questions for Section 4.1

An angle in standard position consists of the region between two infinite rays that meet at the __(a)__. One of the rays, known as the __(b)__ side, points in the direction of the positive x-axis; the other ray is known as the __(c)__ side. A __(d)__ angle corresponds to a counterclockwise sweeping motion from the first to the second of these rays. In contrast, a __(e)__ angle corresponds to a clockwise sweeping motion. A right angle corresponds to __(f)__ of a full rotation. Thus, in standard position, this corresponds to placing the terminal side along the __(g)__ axis. In contrast, a straight angle corresponds to __(h)__ of a full rotation; in standard position, this corresponds to placing the terminal side along the __(i)__.

Angles can be measured using degrees, an ancient unit of measurement dating back to the __(j)__ calendar. There are __(k)__° in a full rotation, __(l)__° in a straight angle, and __(m)__° in a right angle. The choice of these numbers can be considered an __(n)__ particular to our planet. A better approach is to measure angles using radians. In this case, there are __(o)__ radians in a full rotation, __(p)__ radians in a straight angle, and __(q)__ radians in a right angle. We can convert degree measure to radian measure by multiplying times __(r)__ and dividing by __(s)__.

Six equilateral triangles may be placed inside the unit circle so they all meet at the origin. This means that the angle at every vertex of an equilateral triangle measures __(t)__ radians. If we arrange it so that one triangle sits on the first quadrant, with its base along the x-axis, then its apex will have coordinates __(u)__. Cutting these equilateral triangles in half creates twelve 30-60-90 triangles with acute angles measuring __(v)__ and __(w)__ radians. If we rotate one of these in the first quadrant so the longer leg lies along the x-axis, then its apex will have coordinates __(x)__. Finally, we can place eight 45-90-45 triangles in the unit circle so they all meet at the origin. These triangles have one right angle and two acute angles measuring __(y)__ radians. If we place one of these triangles in the first quadrant with one leg along the x-axis, then its apex will have coordinates __(z)__.

334

Exercises for Section 4.1

1. Convert each of the following angle measurements from degrees to radians.

    (a) $150°$ (b) $-315°$ (c) $144°$ (d) $-30\pi°$

2. Convert each of the following angle measurements from radians to degrees.

    (a) $\dfrac{5\pi}{2}$ (b) $-\dfrac{2\pi}{5}$ (c) $-\dfrac{7\pi}{12}$ (d) $\dfrac{5}{18}$

3. Find the quadrant containing the terminal side of the angle with the given measure.

    (a) $156°$ (b) $-24°$ (c) $262°$ (d) $-287°$

4. Find the quadrant containing the terminal side of the angle with the given measure.

    (a) $\dfrac{7\pi}{5}$ (b) $-\dfrac{7\pi}{4}$ (c) $\dfrac{18\pi}{7}$ (d) 5.67

5. Determine the coordinates for the point on the unit circle corresponding to the angle with the given measure.

    (a) $780°$ (b) $-270°$ (c) $405°$ (d) $-450°$

6. Determine the coordinates for the point on the unit circle corresponding to the angle with the given measure.

    (a) $-\dfrac{19\pi}{4}$ (b) $-\dfrac{5\pi}{3}$ (c) $\dfrac{7\pi}{2}$ (d) $-\dfrac{11\pi}{6}$

7. Determine the complementary angle of an angle with the given measure.

    (a) $\dfrac{\pi}{6}$ (b) $\dfrac{\pi}{5}$ (c) $\dfrac{2\pi}{9}$ (d) 1.23

8. Determine the supplementary angle of an angle with the given measure.

    (a) $\dfrac{\pi}{4}$ (b) $\dfrac{5\pi}{6}$ (c) $\dfrac{3\pi}{5}$ (d) 2.34

9. Find two coterminal angles, one positive and one negative, of an angle with the given measure.

    (a) $\dfrac{\pi}{12}$ (b) $-\dfrac{2\pi}{3}$ (c) $\dfrac{7\pi}{6}$ (d) $-\dfrac{11\pi}{6}$

In Exercises 10–15, find the missing lengths and angle measures in each 30-60-90 or a 45-90-45 triangle. (Note: The triangles are not drawn to scale.)

10.

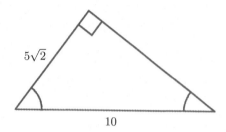

11.

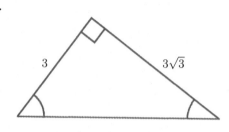

12.

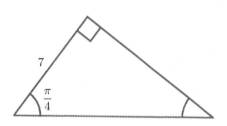

13.

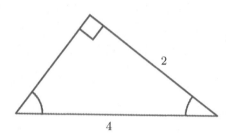

14.

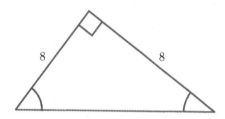

15.

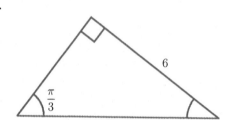

In Exercises 16–25, sketch a graph of the unit circle and the given line. Be sure to label the points of intersection.

16. $5x = 3$

17. $25y = -7$

18. $9y = -40x$

19. $13x = -5$

20. $17y = 8$

21. $20y = -21x$

22. $37x = 35$

23. $61y = 11$

24. $45x = -28y$

25. $13y = 84x$

In Exercises 26–29, describe the direction of the initial and terminal side of each angle in terms of bearings. Then find the degree and radian measure of the angle. You may assume that the angles in question have positive measure.

26.

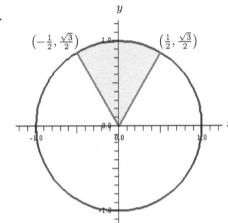

27.

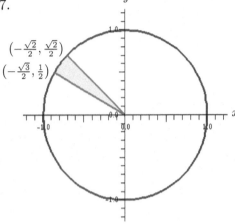

28.

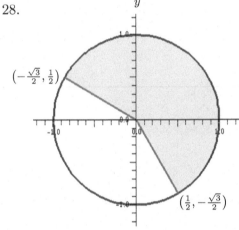

29.

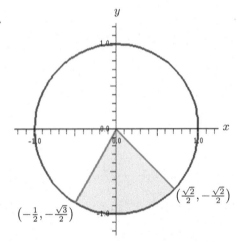

30. Draw an analog clock indicating each of the given times. In each case, describe the direction of the hour hand and the minute hand in terms of bearings. Then find the degree and radian measure of the angle whose initial and terminal sides point, respectively, along the hour and minute hands.

   (a) 3:00   (b) 1:00   (c) 10:00   (d) 3:30   (e) 9:45

4.2. Sine, Cosine, and Tangent

The relationship between the angles and the sides of a triangle, what we call **trigonometry**, dates back to the Greek astronomer and mathematician Hipparchus of Nicaea (c. 190 – 120 BC) and his table of chords. In time, these chords gave way to tables of "half-chords," and these eventually led to our modern trigonometric functions.

To start, let us consider an angle in standard position, and suppose that we denote its radian measure by the Greek letter θ (*theta*). Then, the point P where the terminal side of this angle crosses the unit circle determines our three trigonometric functions of interest, as shown in Figure 4.10. First of all, the y-coordinate of the point P is called the **sine** of the angle θ, and is abbreviated as $\sin(\theta)$. Next, the x-coordinate of the point P is called **cosine** of θ, which we denote as $\cos(\theta)$. Finally, the slope of the terminal side connecting the origin to the point P is known as the **tangent** of θ, or $\tan(\theta)$. In summary, we have:

The Functions of Trigonometry

$\sin(\theta) = y$-coordinate of intersection point P,

$\cos(\theta) = x$-coordinate of intersection point P,

$\tan(\theta) = $ slope of the line connecting the origin to P.

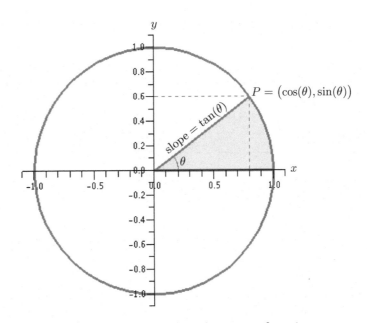

FIGURE 4.10. The sine, cosine, and tangent functions.

As you might expect, our three trigonometric functions are related to each other in various ways. For instance, the sine and cosine functions can be substituted into the equation for the unit circle, producing the useful formula

$$(4.1) \qquad \bigl(\cos(\theta)\bigr)^2 + \bigl(\sin(\theta)\bigr)^2 = x^2 + y^2 = 1.$$

Furthermore, since the tangent function is defined as a slope, we can write it as a difference quotient in terms of the sine and cosine functions:

$$(4.2) \qquad \tan(\theta) = \frac{\Delta y}{\Delta x} = \frac{\sin(\theta)}{\cos(\theta)}.$$

EXAMPLE 4.11. Since we already determined the coordinates for sixteen special points on the unit circle (see Figure 4.8), we know the values of the sine and cosine functions at several angles. We record these values, along with those for the tangent function, in Table 4.1. You should note that the tangent function is undefined for the angles $\theta = \frac{\pi}{2}$ and $\theta = \frac{3\pi}{2}$. This is due to the fact that, for these two angles, the terminal side in question is a vertical line with no slope. Additionally, if we tried to use formula (4.2) for these two angles, we would find that $\cos(\theta) = 0$ and thus be forced to divide by zero.

TABLE 4.1. A table of sines, cosines, and tangents.

θ	$\sin(\theta)$	$\cos(\theta)$	$\tan(\theta)$	θ	$\sin(\theta)$	$\cos(\theta)$	$\tan(\theta)$
0	0	1	0	π	0	-1	0
$\frac{\pi}{6}$	$\frac{1}{2}$	$\frac{\sqrt{3}}{2}$	$\frac{\sqrt{3}}{3}$	$\frac{7\pi}{6}$	$-\frac{1}{2}$	$-\frac{\sqrt{3}}{2}$	$\frac{\sqrt{3}}{3}$
$\frac{\pi}{4}$	$\frac{\sqrt{2}}{2}$	$\frac{\sqrt{2}}{2}$	1	$\frac{5\pi}{4}$	$-\frac{\sqrt{2}}{2}$	$-\frac{\sqrt{2}}{2}$	1
$\frac{\pi}{3}$	$\frac{\sqrt{3}}{2}$	$\frac{1}{2}$	$\sqrt{3}$	$\frac{4\pi}{3}$	$-\frac{\sqrt{3}}{2}$	$-\frac{1}{2}$	$\sqrt{3}$
$\frac{\pi}{2}$	1	0	undefined	$\frac{3\pi}{2}$	-1	0	undefined
$\frac{2\pi}{3}$	$\frac{\sqrt{3}}{2}$	$-\frac{1}{2}$	$-\sqrt{3}$	$\frac{5\pi}{3}$	$-\frac{\sqrt{3}}{2}$	$\frac{1}{2}$	$-\sqrt{3}$
$\frac{3\pi}{4}$	$\frac{\sqrt{2}}{2}$	$-\frac{\sqrt{2}}{2}$	-1	$\frac{7\pi}{4}$	$-\frac{\sqrt{2}}{2}$	$\frac{\sqrt{2}}{2}$	-1
$\frac{5\pi}{6}$	$\frac{1}{2}$	$-\frac{\sqrt{3}}{2}$	$-\frac{\sqrt{3}}{3}$	$\frac{11\pi}{6}$	$-\frac{1}{2}$	$\frac{\sqrt{3}}{2}$	$-\frac{\sqrt{3}}{3}$
π	0	-1	0	2π	0	1	0

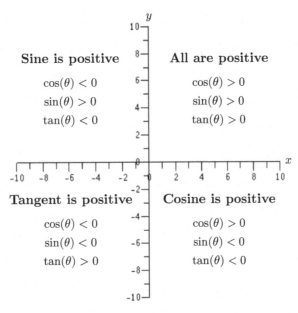

FIGURE 4.11. Signs of the trigonometric function in each quadrant.

Depending on the quadrant containing the terminal side of the angle θ, the three trigonometric functions can take on either positive or negative values. Figure 4.11 gives a visual summary of the four possibilities. One simple way to remember this is by reciting the following mnemonic phrase:

"All snow tastes cold."

Although this is quite a silly phrase (after all, cold is not something you can taste), the first letter of each word informs us of which function has positive values in each quadrant. Of course, "all" indicates that all three functions start out positive.

As we mentioned at the outset, the values of the three trigonometric functions give us information about the relationship between the sides and the angles of a triangle. We will explore this relationship in greater generality in Section 4.4. For now, we concentrate only on right triangles.

Theorem 4.1 (Right triangle trigonometry). Let θ be the measure of one of the acute angles in a right triangle. Denote the three sides of the triangle as "adjacent," "opposite," or "hypotenuse," based on their position in the triangle relative to the angle θ, as indicated in Figure 4.12(a). Then the values of the sine, cosine, and tangent functions for the angle θ are given as proportions of the lengths of the sides of the triangle as follows:

$$\cos(\theta) = \frac{\text{adjacent side}}{\text{hypotenuse}}, \quad \sin(\theta) = \frac{\text{opposite side}}{\text{hypotenuse}}, \quad \tan(\theta) = \frac{\text{opposite side}}{\text{adjacent side}}.$$

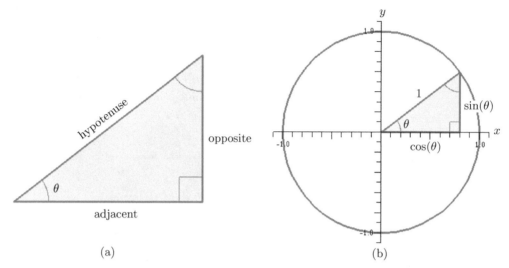

FIGURE 4.12. The trigonometric functions in a right triangle and the unit circle.

Proof. We can construct a new right triangle, similar to our original one but with a hypotenuse of one, by dividing the length each side by that of the hypotenuse. This will not alter the measure of any of the angles. This new triangle can be placed inside the unit circle as in Figure 4.12(b), so that the lengths of the two legs are equal to $\cos(\theta)$ and $\sin(\theta)$, respectively. The first two equations then follow from the fact that the sides of this new triangle were obtained by dividing the corresponding sides in the original triangle by the hypotenuse, while the final equation follows from formula (4.2).   □

The following mnemonic device gives us one way to remember the fractions presented in Theorem 4.1:

"Cows and horses snack on hay tossed over apples."

Again, this is a very silly sentence to say out loud, but by taking the initials of the words three at a time, we can easily remember which function corresponds to which fraction. For example, "cows and horses" corresponds to "*cosine* equals *adjacent* over *hypotenuse*," and so on.

EXAMPLE 4.12. Suppose that θ is an angle in the third quadrant of the unit circle that has $\cos(\theta) = -\frac{12}{13}$. Determine the values of $\sin(\theta)$ and $\tan(\theta)$.

Solution 1. (Unit circle approach) The angle θ corresponds to the point $\big(\cos(\theta), \sin(\theta)\big)$ on the unit circle. Thus, according to formula (4.1), we have

$$\big(\cos(\theta)\big)^2 + \big(\sin(\theta)\big)^2 = 1$$

$$\big(-\tfrac{12}{13}\big)^2 + \big(\sin(\theta)\big)^2 = 1$$

$$\tfrac{144}{169} + \big(\sin(\theta)\big)^2 = 1$$

$$\left(\sin(\theta)\right)^2 = 1 - \tfrac{144}{169} = \tfrac{25}{169}$$

$$\sin(\theta) = \pm\sqrt{\tfrac{25}{169}} = \pm\tfrac{5}{13}.$$

However, since our angle is in the third quadrant, both its sine and its cosine must be negative, so

$$\sin(\theta) = -\tfrac{5}{13}.$$

This, in turn, means that

$$\tan(\theta) = \frac{\sin(\theta)}{\cos(\theta)} = \frac{-\tfrac{5}{13}}{-\tfrac{12}{13}} = \tfrac{5}{12}.$$

Solution 2. (Right triangle approach) We begin by constructing a reference triangle using the information we have about our value of cosine, temporarily ignoring the negative sign. Since $\cos(\theta) = -\tfrac{12}{13}$, we shall construct a right triangle with an adjacent side of 12 and a hypotenuse of 13, as in Figure 4.13. We then determine the length of the opposite side, which we label as x in the figure, by recalling Pythagoras's Theorem (see page 81):

$$12^2 + x^2 = 13^2$$

$$144 + x^2 = 169$$

$$x^2 = 169 - 144 = 25$$

$$x = \sqrt{25} = 5.$$

Observe that we have selected the positive square root because x is a length.

Now, the acute angle $\tilde{\theta}$ in the figure is not the same as our angle θ. However, its values of sine, cosine, and tangent agree with those of our θ in everything but their sign. In particular, since θ is in the third quadrant, it has a negative sine and cosine, and a positive tangent. This means that

$$\sin(\theta) = -\sin(\tilde{\theta}) = -\tfrac{5}{13} \quad \text{and} \quad \tan(\theta) = \tan(\tilde{\theta}) = \tfrac{5}{12}.$$

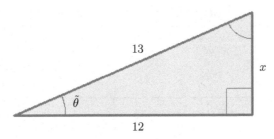

FIGURE 4.13. Using a right triangle to determine the values of the trigonometric functions.

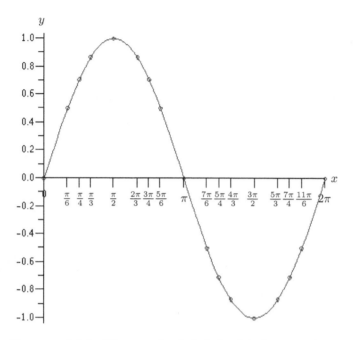

FIGURE 4.14. The graph of $\sin(x)$ with $0 \le x \le 2\pi$.

Suppose that we momentarily let the variable x take the place of the angle θ. Then, by plotting the values of the sine function given by Table 4.1, we obtain seventeen points outlining the waxing and waning of the ***sinusoidal waveform*** shown in Figure 4.14. Of course, we can evaluate $\sin(x)$ at inputs outside of the interval between 0 and 2π. In this case, we find that coterminal angles point to the same point on the unit circle, and therefore share the same values of sine (as well as cosine and tangent). This means that the graph of the sine function repeats indefinitely to the left and to the right, as in Figure 4.15. Observe that this graph has a y-intercept at $y = 0$ and x-intercepts at every integer multiple of π, at $x = k\pi$ where k is an arbitrary integer. Furthermore, it has a local maximum at $x = \frac{\pi}{2} + 2k\pi$ and a local minimum at $x = \frac{3\pi}{2} + 2k\pi$.

We can also plot the values of $\cos(x)$ from Table 4.1, obtaining a second sinusoidal waveform, illustrated in Figure 4.16. As before, coterminal angles have the same value of cosine, so this graph also repeats indefinitely to the left and to the right, as shown in

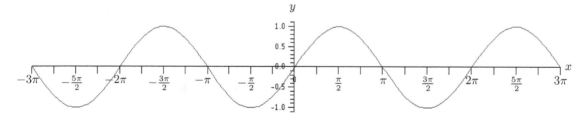

FIGURE 4.15. The graph of the sine function.

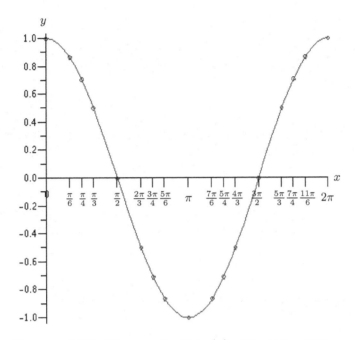

FIGURE 4.16. The graph of $\cos(x)$ with $0 \leq x \leq 2\pi$.

Figure 4.17. Observe that this graph has its y-intercept at $y = 1$ and its x-intercepts at $x = \frac{\pi}{2} + k\pi$ where k is an arbitrary integer. In addition, local maxima occur at all even multiples of π, when $x = 2k\pi$, while local minima occur at all odd multiples of π, when $x = (2k+1)\pi$.

At first sight, it seems that the sine and cosine functions define different waveforms, and from at least one point of view, they do. Whereas the graph in Figure 4.14 resembles a snake slithering on the desert sand, the wave in Figure 4.16 looks more like the head of a cow, with its horns sticking above the x-axis. (Conveniently, "cow" and "cos" only differ by one letter.) On the other hand, if we were to erase the coordinate axes in Figures 4.15 and 4.17, we would find that both waves are actually identical in shape. One way to see this is to note that the values in Table 4.1 for the cosine function are just five steps ahead of those for sine. Indeed, the cosine function is a horizontal translation of the sine function, moving the latter waveform $\frac{\pi}{2}$ units to the left.

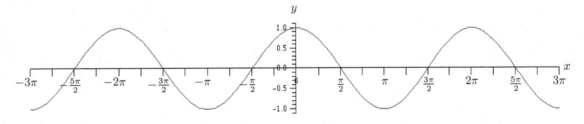

FIGURE 4.17. The graph of the cosine function.

Sinusoidal waveforms, like the graphs of sine and cosine, are just two examples in the larger class of **periodic functions** – functions whose graphs repeat the same pattern over and over again. Like other periodic functions, waveforms are typically described by two characteristic measurements of their graphs: their wavelength and their amplitude. The **wavelength** (sometimes also called the **period**) of a periodic function f is the smallest horizontal distance after which the graph of the function repeats itself. Often denoted by the Greek letter λ (*lambda*), wavelength can also be defined as the smallest positive number for which

$$f(x + \lambda) = f(x)$$

for all x in the domain of f. This gives a measure of how quickly the graph of f is oscillating, with longer wavelengths corresponding to slower oscillations. Perhaps the easiest way to visualize the wavelength of a sinusoidal wave is to look at the distance from one crest of the wave to the next. In the case of our model trigonometric functions, both sine and cosine have a wavelength of 2π. In contrast, the **amplitude** of a periodic function is the vertical span from the middle of the graph to its highest or lowest point. In other words, the amplitude of a waveform is half of the vertical distance from a crest to a trough. It measures how far the wave deviates from its average value. Observe that both the sine and the cosine functions have an amplitude of one.

Finally, Figure 4.18 shows the graph of $\tan(x)$. Thanks to formula (4.2),

$$\tan(x) = \frac{\sin(x)}{\cos(x)},$$

we can see that the tangent function shares its x-intercepts with sine, when $x = k\pi$ for arbitrary integers k. Furthermore, this formula reminds us that the tangent is

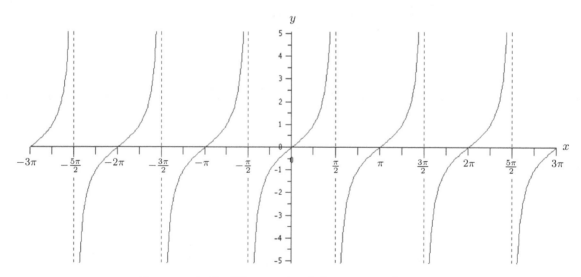

FIGURE 4.18. The graph of the tangent function.

undefined whenever the cosine is zero, namely at $x = \frac{\pi}{2} + k\pi$. In our graph, these input values correspond to vertical asymptotes, which we indicate using dotted lines. As you might expect, our graph goes through the same pattern after each asymptote. This means that it has a wavelength of π. On the other hand, note that the tangent function takes on arbitrarily large (positive or negative) values on either side of an asymptote. As a consequence, our graph has no maximum or minimum, and therefore its amplitude is undefined.

In addition to the sine, cosine, and tangent, there are three trigonometric functions worth a brief mention. These are the **cotangent**, **secant**, and **cosecant** functions, defined as the reciprocals of the three main trigonometric by the formulas

$$\cot(x) = \frac{1}{\tan(x)}, \qquad \sec(x) = \frac{1}{\cos(x)}, \qquad \csc(x) = \frac{1}{\sin(x)}.$$

The importance of these functions arise in calculus, so we shall not discuss these any further here, other than to point out that, like the tangent function, the graphs of these functions have infinitely many vertical asymptotes.

Reading Comprehension Questions for Section 4.2

The three trigonometric functions, $\sin(\theta)$, $\cos(\theta)$, and $\tan(\theta)$, are defined in terms of how an angle with measure θ intersects the unit circle. In particular, suppose that θ is the measure of an angle in standard position and that P is the point where the angle's __(a)__ intersects the unit circle. Then we define the sine of θ as the __(b)__ of the point P. Similarly, we define the cosine of θ as the __(c)__ of the point P. Additionally, the tangent of θ is defined as the __(d)__ of the line connecting P to the origin. This means that the sine and cosine functions are related to one another by the equation __(e)__, while the tangent can be expressed in terms of the other two functions by the equation __(f)__.

For angles in standard position, the signs of the trigonometric functions are determined by the quadrant containing the terminal side. In the first quadrant, all three functions are __(g)__. In the second quadrant, the __(h)__ is positive while the other two functions are negative. Similarly, in the third quadrant, only the __(i)__ is positive, while in the fourth quadrant, only the __(j)__ is positive. We can remember these facts by using the mnemonic phrase, "__(k)__."

On right triangles, the values of the trigonometric functions of the acute angles are determined by ratios of the __(l)__ of the triangle. For example, the cosine is given as the __(m)__ divided by the __(n)__, the sine is given as the __(o)__ divided by the __(p)__, and the tangent is given as the __(q)__ divided by the __(r)__. Again, we can remember these fractions by using the mnemonic phrase, "__(s)__."

The graphs of the sine and cosine functions form a long __(t)__ that repeatedly alternate between maximum values of __(u)__ and minimum values of __(v)__. Each graph takes __(w)__ radians to go from one maximum to the next. On the other hand, the graph of the tangent has vertical asymptotes occurring every __(x)__ radians, when the values of the function head off to positive and negative __(y)__. All three functions are said to be __(z)__ because their graphs repeat the same pattern indefinitely to the left and to the right.

Exercises for Section 4.2

In Exercises 1–4, match each function to the corresponding graph below.

(A)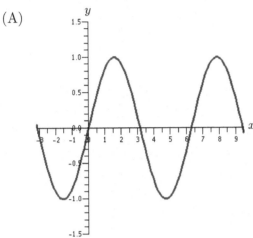

(B)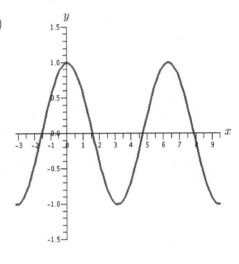

(C)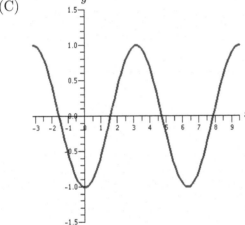

(D)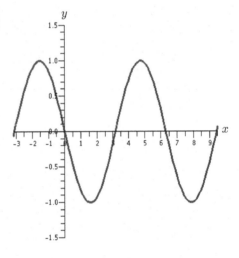

1. (a) $f(x) = -\sin(x)$ (b) $g(x) = -\cos(x)$ (c) $h(x) = \sin(-x)$

2. (a) $f(x) = \sin(x - \frac{\pi}{2})$ (b) $g(x) = \cos(x - \frac{\pi}{2})$ (c) $h(x) = \sin(x + \frac{\pi}{2})$

3. (a) $f(x) = \sin(x + \pi)$ (b) $g(x) = \cos(x + \pi)$ (c) $h(x) = -\cos(x + \pi)$

4. (a) $f(x) = \sin(\frac{\pi}{2} - x)$ (b) $g(x) = \cos(\frac{\pi}{2} - x)$ (c) $h(x) = -\sin(\pi - x)$

In Exercises 5–10, find the values of the missing trigonometric functions for the angle in the given quadrant.

5. $\sin(\theta) = \dfrac{15}{17}$ (Quadrant I)

6. $\sin(\theta) = -\dfrac{7}{25}$ (Quadrant IV)

7. $\cos(\theta) = -\dfrac{9}{41}$ (Quadrant II)

8. $\cos(\theta) = \dfrac{21}{29}$ (Quadrant IV)

9. $\tan(\theta) = -\dfrac{12}{35}$ (Quadrant II)

10. $\tan(\theta) = \dfrac{45}{28}$ (Quadrant III)

In Exercises 11–16, find two values of θ in the interval $[0, 2\pi]$ that satisfy each of the following conditions. Then describe each angle in terms of a bearing (in degrees) on a compass.

11. $\sin(\theta) = \dfrac{1}{2}$

12. $\sin(\theta) = -\dfrac{1}{\sqrt{2}}$

13. $\cos(\theta) = -\dfrac{\sqrt{3}}{2}$

14. $\cos(\theta) = \dfrac{\sqrt{2}}{2}$

15. $\tan(\theta) = -\sqrt{3}$

16. $\tan(\theta) = 1$

In Exercises 17–26, interpret each function as a linear transformation of the sine or cosine function. Use this information to determine its wavelength and amplitude, and sketch its graph.

17. $g(x) = 4\sin(x)$

18. $g(x) = 1 - 5\cos(x)$

19. $g(x) = 3\cos(2x)$

20. $g(x) = -\sin(5x)$

21. $g(x) = -6\sin\left(\frac{1}{2}x\right)$

22. $g(x) = -\frac{1}{3}\cos\left(\frac{2}{5}x\right)$

23. $g(x) = 2\sin(2\pi x)$

24. $g(x) = 3\cos\left(\frac{\pi}{2}x\right)$

25. $g(x) = 5\sin(\pi - x)$

26. $g(x) = 7\cos(x + 3)$

In Exercises 27–30, determine the wavelength and the amplitude of the sinusoidal wave shown in each graph. Then find a formula describing each waveform.

27.

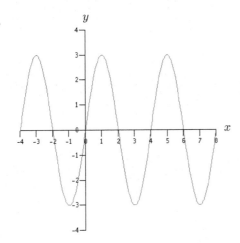

28.

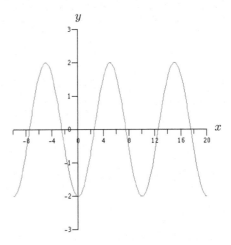

29.

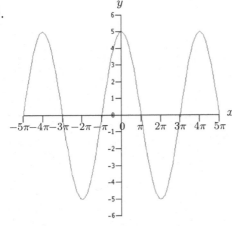

30.

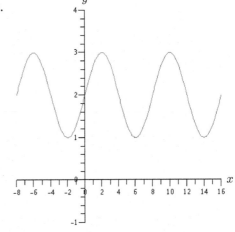

4.3. Identities and Inverses

Since the graphs of the sine and cosine function consist of essentially identical sinusoidal waveforms differing only on the position of their ebbs and flows, it should not be surprising that there is a variety of relationships between these two functions. These relationships are often expressed in terms of *identities*, or equations which hold true no matter which input values you substitute in.

Perhaps the simplest and most useful trigonometric identity is given by formula (4.1), which basically states that $\cos(\theta)$ and $\sin(\theta)$ represent the x- and y-coordinates of some point on the unit circle:

$$\big(\cos(\theta)\big)^2 + \big(\sin(\theta)\big)^2 = 1.$$

This equation, commonly called the **Pythagorean identity**, remains true regardless of what value we substitute in for θ. Often, for the sake of typographical convenience, the outside parentheses in this formula are dropped, and the little twos marking the squares are moved just to the right of "cos" and "sin," as in

$$\cos^2(\theta) + \sin^2(\theta) = 1.$$

This is, of course, only a notational shorthand. In particular, "cos" and "sin" are simply the names of two functions, so squaring these would be entirely nonsensical. However, it does make sense to square the numbers that we get *after* we evaluate each of these functions at the angle θ. This is precisely what our identity is suggesting that we do.

Notice that if we reflect the graph of the cosine function horizontally about the y-axis, we obtain a graph that matches the original graph of cosine point for point. In other words, the graph of the cosine function has **horizontal symmetry** about the y-axis. This is a consequence of the fact that, when we rotate clockwise around the unit circle, we see the exactly same x-coordinates as when we rotate counterclockwise. See Figure 4.19. We can express this simple fact by the formula

$$\cos(-\theta) = \cos(\theta).$$

In contrast, for the graph of the sine function, a horizontal reflection about the y-axis produces exactly the same result as a vertical reflection about the x-axis. In this case, we say that the graph of the sine function has **point symmetry** about the origin. Again, this follows from the fact that, when we rotate clockwise around the unit circle, we see opposite y-coordinates than when we rotate counterclockwise. Again, see Figure 4.19. We can express this fact with the formula

$$\sin(-\theta) = -\sin(\theta).$$

Both of these formulas hold true regardless of the value of θ we use, so they really are identities. They are often called the **negative angle identities** for cosine and sine.

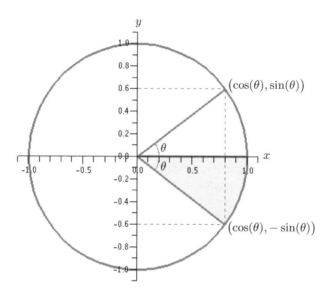

FIGURE 4.19. The negative angle identities on the unit circle.

Starting with the graph of either the sine or cosine function, consider performing a horizontal reflection about the y-axis followed by a horizontal translation to the right by $\frac{\pi}{2}$ radians. In the case of the sine function, this transformation produces the graph of the cosine function. This means that

$$\sin\left(\tfrac{\pi}{2} - \theta\right) = \sin\left(-\left(\theta - \tfrac{\pi}{2}\right)\right) = \cos(\theta).$$

In the case of the cosine function, we obtain the graph of the sine function, so that

$$\cos\left(\tfrac{\pi}{2} - \theta\right) = \cos\left(-\left(\theta - \tfrac{\pi}{2}\right)\right) = \sin(\theta).$$

Since $\frac{\pi}{2} - \theta$ represents the complementary angle to θ, the two equations above are called the **complementary angle identities** for sine and cosine. In particular, they show that the cosine of an angle is equal to the sine of the complement of the angle, and vice versa. See Figure 4.20.

Starting with the graph of either the sine or cosine function, consider performing a horizontal reflection about the y-axis followed by a horizontal translation to the right by π radians. In the case of the sine function, this transformation produces the original graph of the sine function. This means that

$$\sin(\pi - \theta) = \sin\left(-\left(\theta - \pi\right)\right) = \sin(\theta).$$

In the case of the cosine function, we obtain the graph of the cosine function reflected vertically, so that

$$\cos(\pi - \theta) = \cos\left(-\left(\theta - \pi\right)\right) = -\cos(\theta).$$

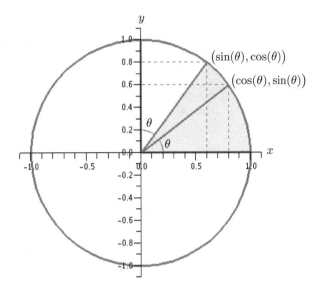

FIGURE 4.20. The complementary angle identities on the unit circle.

Since $\pi - \theta$ represents the supplementary angle to θ, the two equations above are called the ***supplementary angle identities*** for sine and cosine. See Figure 4.21.

The complementary and supplementary angle identities should dissuade us from the idea that there is some sort of distributive property for sines and cosines, by which adding or subtracting inside a sine or cosine produces the same result as adding or subtracting outside the sine or cosine. As the next example shows, this is patently not true!

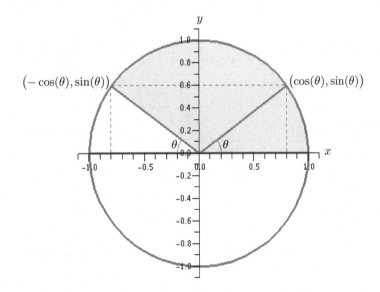

FIGURE 4.21. The supplementary angle identities on the unit circle.

Suppose that we know the values of the sine and cosine functions for two angles α and β. Consider the point $P = \big(\cos(\theta), \sin(\theta)\big)$ on the unit circle corresponding to the angle $\theta = \alpha + \beta$ in standard position, as illustrated in Figure 4.22 (a). Then, the distance from P to the point $A = (0, 1)$ on the y-axis is equal to

$$a = \sqrt{\big(\cos(\theta)\big)^2 + \big(1 - \sin(\theta)\big)^2}$$
$$= \sqrt{\cos^2(\theta) + 1 - 2\sin(\theta) + \sin^2(\theta)}$$
$$= \sqrt{2 - 2\sin(\theta)}\,,$$

while the distance from P to the point $B = (1, 0)$ on the x-axis is equal to

$$b = \sqrt{\big(1 - \cos(\theta)\big)^2 + \big(\sin(\theta)\big)^2}$$
$$= \sqrt{1 - 2\cos(\theta) + \cos^2(\theta) + \sin^2(\theta)}$$
$$= \sqrt{2 - 2\cos(\theta)}\,.$$

Now suppose that we rotate these points clockwise by an angle of β, as in Figure 4.22 (b). Although this rotation will change the position of our three points, observe that it will not affect the distances between them. In particular, our rotation moves P to the point P' corresponding to an angle of α, A to the point A' corresponding to an angle of $\frac{\pi}{2} - \beta$, and B to the point B' corresponding to an angle of $-\beta$. Hence, according to the complementary and negative angle identities above, we

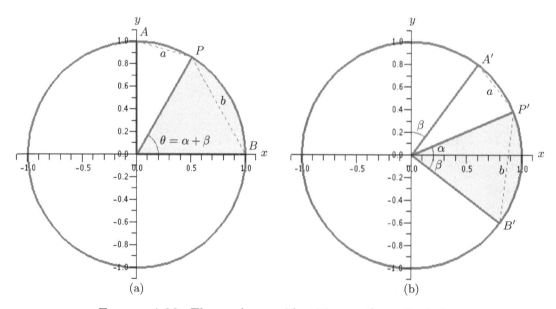

(a)   (b)

FIGURE 4.22. The angle sum identities on the unit circle.

have

$$P' = \big(\cos(\alpha), \sin(\alpha)\big),$$

$$A' = \big(\cos(\tfrac{\pi}{2} - \beta), \sin(\tfrac{\pi}{2} - \beta)\big) = \big(\sin(\beta), \cos(\beta)\big),$$

$$B' = \big(\cos(-\beta), \sin(-\beta)\big) = \big(\cos(\beta), -\sin(\beta)\big).$$

This means that the distance between P' and A' is equal to

$$a = \sqrt{\big(\cos(\alpha) - \sin(\beta)\big)^2 + \big(\sin(\alpha) - \cos(\beta)\big)^2}$$

$$= \sqrt{\cos^2(\alpha) - 2\cos(\alpha)\sin(\beta) + \sin^2(\beta) + \sin^2(\alpha) - 2\sin(\alpha)\cos(\beta) + \cos^2(\beta)}$$

$$= \sqrt{2 - 2\big(\cos(\alpha)\sin(\beta) + \sin(\alpha)\cos(\beta)\big)} \, ,$$

while the distance between P' and B' is

$$b = \sqrt{\big(\cos(\alpha) - \cos(\beta)\big)^2 + \big(\sin(\alpha) + \sin(\beta)\big)^2}$$

$$= \sqrt{\cos^2(\alpha) - 2\cos(\alpha)\cos(\beta) + \cos^2(\beta) + \sin^2(\alpha) + 2\sin(\alpha)\sin(\beta) + \sin^2(\beta)}$$

$$= \sqrt{2 - 2\big(\cos(\alpha)\cos(\beta) - \sin(\alpha)\sin(\beta)\big)} \, .$$

Since our rotation should not have altered these distances, these formulas must agree with the ones we computed earlier on, implying that

$$\sin(\alpha + \beta) = \sin(\alpha)\cos(\beta) + \cos(\alpha)\sin(\beta),$$

$$\cos(\alpha + \beta) = \cos(\alpha)\cos(\beta) - \sin(\alpha)\sin(\beta).$$

Since these formulas allow us to compute the sine and cosine of the sum of the angles α and β, they are known as the **angle sum identities**.

We can remember the angle sum identities by singing the following trigonometric cheer:

Sine – Cosine – Cosine – Sine,

Cosine – Cosine – Sign – Sine – Sine!

You should try repeating this to yourself a few times as you mentally prepare yourself for your homework. Practicing your "spirit fingers" at the same time can only help.

EXAMPLE 4.13. Determine the algebraic values of $\cos\big(\tfrac{5\pi}{12}\big)$ and $\sin\big(\tfrac{5\pi}{12}\big)$.

Solution. Since we can express the angle $\tfrac{5\pi}{12} = \tfrac{\pi}{6} + \tfrac{\pi}{4}$ as the sum of two smaller angles for which we know the exact algebraic values of the sine and cosine functions, we can use the angle sum identities by setting $\alpha = \frac{\pi}{6}$ and $\beta = \frac{\pi}{4}$. In this case, we first need to remember that

$$\cos\left(\tfrac{\pi}{6}\right) = \tfrac{\sqrt{3}}{2}, \qquad\qquad \cos\left(\tfrac{\pi}{4}\right) = \tfrac{\sqrt{2}}{2},$$

$$\sin\left(\tfrac{\pi}{6}\right) = \tfrac{1}{2}, \qquad\qquad \sin\left(\tfrac{\pi}{4}\right) = \tfrac{\sqrt{2}}{2}.$$

Thus, applying the identities to the angle sum $\alpha + \beta = \frac{2\pi}{3} + \frac{\pi}{4}$, we have

$$\sin\left(\tfrac{5\pi}{12}\right) = \sin\left(\tfrac{\pi}{6} + \tfrac{\pi}{4}\right) = \sin\left(\tfrac{\pi}{6}\right)\cos\left(\tfrac{\pi}{4}\right) + \cos\left(\tfrac{\pi}{6}\right)\sin\left(\tfrac{\pi}{4}\right)$$

$$= \tfrac{1}{2} \cdot \tfrac{\sqrt{2}}{2} + \tfrac{\sqrt{3}}{2} \cdot \tfrac{\sqrt{2}}{2} = \tfrac{\sqrt{2}+\sqrt{6}}{4},$$

$$\cos\left(\tfrac{5\pi}{12}\right) = \cos\left(\tfrac{\pi}{6} + \tfrac{\pi}{4}\right) = \cos\left(\tfrac{\pi}{6}\right)\cos\left(\tfrac{\pi}{4}\right) - \sin\left(\tfrac{\pi}{6}\right)\sin\left(\tfrac{\pi}{4}\right)$$

$$= \tfrac{\sqrt{3}}{2} \cdot \tfrac{\sqrt{2}}{2} - \tfrac{1}{2} \cdot \tfrac{\sqrt{2}}{2} = \tfrac{\sqrt{6}-\sqrt{2}}{4}.$$

Note that the results indicate a positive sine and cosine. This is precisely what we would expect from an acute angle in the first quadrant. Furthermore, just as a check on our arithmetic, we note that the two values satisfy the Pythagorean identity:

$$\cos^2\left(\tfrac{5\pi}{12}\right) + \sin^2\left(\tfrac{5\pi}{12}\right) = \left(\tfrac{\sqrt{2}+\sqrt{6}}{4}\right)^2 + \left(\tfrac{\sqrt{6}-\sqrt{2}}{4}\right)^2 = \tfrac{8+4\sqrt{3}}{16} + \tfrac{8-4\sqrt{3}}{16} = 1.$$

We can also combine the angle sum and the negative angle identities to produce the following **angle difference identities**:

$$\sin(\alpha - \beta) = \sin\big(\alpha + (-\beta)\big) = \sin(\alpha)\cos(\beta) - \cos(\alpha)\sin(\beta),$$

$$\cos(\alpha - \beta) = \cos\big(\alpha + (-\beta)\big) = \cos(\alpha)\cos(\beta) + \sin(\alpha)\sin(\beta).$$

Note that these look just like the angle sum identities, except that the plus and minus signs in the right hand sides have been swapped.

EXAMPLE 4.14. Determine the algebraic values of $\cos\left(\frac{\pi}{12}\right)$ and $\sin\left(\frac{\pi}{12}\right)$.

Solution. Since we can write $\frac{\pi}{12} = \frac{\pi}{3} - \frac{\pi}{4}$ as the difference of two angle, we can apply the angle difference identities by first setting $\alpha = \frac{\pi}{3}$ and $\beta = \frac{\pi}{4}$. As before, we begin by remembering that

$$\cos\left(\tfrac{\pi}{3}\right) = \tfrac{1}{2}, \qquad\qquad \cos\left(\tfrac{\pi}{4}\right) = \tfrac{\sqrt{2}}{2},$$

$$\sin\left(\tfrac{\pi}{3}\right) = \tfrac{\sqrt{3}}{2}, \qquad\qquad \sin\left(\tfrac{\pi}{4}\right) = \tfrac{\sqrt{2}}{2}.$$

Therefore, applying the identities to the angle difference $\alpha - \beta = \frac{\pi}{3} - \frac{\pi}{4}$, we have

$$\sin\left(\tfrac{\pi}{12}\right) = \sin\left(\tfrac{\pi}{3} - \tfrac{\pi}{4}\right) = \sin\left(\tfrac{\pi}{3}\right)\cos\left(\tfrac{\pi}{4}\right) - \cos\left(\tfrac{\pi}{3}\right)\sin\left(\tfrac{\pi}{4}\right)$$

$$= \tfrac{\sqrt{3}}{2} \cdot \tfrac{\sqrt{2}}{2} - \tfrac{1}{2} \cdot \tfrac{\sqrt{2}}{2} = \tfrac{\sqrt{6}-\sqrt{2}}{4},$$

$$\cos\left(\tfrac{\pi}{12}\right) = \cos\left(\tfrac{\pi}{3} - \tfrac{\pi}{4}\right) = \cos\left(\tfrac{\pi}{3}\right)\cos\left(\tfrac{\pi}{4}\right) + \sin\left(\tfrac{\pi}{3}\right)\sin\left(\tfrac{\pi}{4}\right)$$

$$= \tfrac{1}{2} \cdot \tfrac{\sqrt{2}}{2} + \tfrac{\sqrt{3}}{2} \cdot \tfrac{\sqrt{2}}{2} = \tfrac{\sqrt{2}+\sqrt{6}}{4}.$$

By comparing these values with those obtained in Example 4.13, we note that $\sin\left(\frac{5\pi}{12}\right) = \cos\left(\frac{\pi}{12}\right)$ and $\cos\left(\frac{5\pi}{12}\right) = \sin\left(\frac{\pi}{12}\right)$, as predicted by the complementary angle identities.

Occasionally, we know the output value of a trigonometric function and wish to find the angle that produced this value. The ***inverse trigonometric functions*** allow us to "cancel out" a sine, cosine, or tangent as follows:

$$
\begin{array}{lll}
\theta = \arcsin(x) & \Rightarrow & \sin(\theta) = x, \\[2mm]
\theta = \arccos(x) & \Rightarrow & \cos(\theta) = x, \\[2mm]
\theta = \arctan(x) & \Rightarrow & \tan(\theta) = x.
\end{array}
$$

In other words, the ***arcsine*** of x (denoted $\arcsin(x)$) is defined to be the angle whose sine is equal to x, the ***arccosine*** of x (denoted $\arccos(x)$) is defined to be the angle whose cosine is equal to x, and the ***arctangent*** of x (denoted $\arctan(x)$) is defined to be the angle whose tangent is equal to x. Of course, there are many angles that satisfy each of these conditions, so in order to make sure these three functions are well-defined, we will always choose angles in some restricted codomain, as follows:

$$\arcsin : [-1, 1] \to \left[-\tfrac{\pi}{2}, \tfrac{\pi}{2}\right],$$

$$\arccos : [-1, 1] \to [0, \pi],$$

$$\arctan : \mathbb{R} \to \left(-\tfrac{\pi}{2}, \tfrac{\pi}{2}\right).$$

Note that this means that $\arccos(x)$ always lives in the first or second quadrant of the unit circle, while $\arcsin(x)$ and $\arctan(x)$ always live in the first and fourth quadrants.

EXAMPLE 4.15. Evaluate the expression $\arccos\left(\frac{1}{2}\right)$.

Solution. The arccosine function asks us to find an angle that has a given cosine value, so we must find a value of θ that solves the equation

$$\cos(\theta) = \tfrac{1}{2}.$$

According to Table 4.1 (see page 340), this equation becomes true precisely when $\theta = \frac{\pi}{3}$, when $\theta = \frac{5\pi}{3}$, or when θ is an angle coterminal to one of these. In particular, note that these angles point to the first and fourth quadrants of the unit circle. Since the arccosine function only takes on values in the first and second quadrants, we can immediately discard the second of these angles and conclude that the angle that we are looking for must be

$$\arccos\left(\tfrac{1}{2}\right) = \tfrac{\pi}{3}.$$

Indeed, this is the only solution to the equation above that lives inside the arccosine's restricted codomain of $[0, \pi]$.

EXAMPLE 4.16. Evaluate the expression $\arctan\left(-\frac{\sqrt{3}}{3}\right)$.

Solution. The arctangent function asks us to find an angle with a given value of the tangent function, so we must solve the equation

$$\tan(\theta) = -\tfrac{\sqrt{3}}{3}.$$

Again, after consulting Table 4.1, we find that this equation holds when $\theta = \frac{5\pi}{6}$ or $\theta = \frac{11\pi}{6}$. Since the arctangent function only takes on values in the first and fourth quadrants, we can ignore the first of these angles, which points to the second quadrant. Unfortunately, although the second angle does point to the fourth quadrant, it does not fall in the restricted codomain for the arctangent, so it is also not the angle we need. Instead, we need to find an angle that is coterminal to $\frac{11\pi}{6}$ and lives in $\left(-\frac{\pi}{2}, \frac{\pi}{2}\right)$. We can do this by moving clockwise by one full rotation, getting us to $\theta = \frac{11\pi}{6} - 2\pi = -\frac{\pi}{6}$. Observe that this angle satisfies both of the conditions above, so

$$\arctan\left(-\tfrac{\sqrt{3}}{3}\right) = -\tfrac{\pi}{6}.$$

EXAMPLE 4.17. Consider the equation

$$25\sin(\theta) + 1 = 12\big(3 - \sin(\theta)\big).$$

We can find the exact solutions to this equation by first replacing the trigonometric expression $\sin(\theta)$ with the dummy variable y. This produces the linear equation

$$25y + 1 = 12(3 - y),$$

which we can solve by distributing the multiplication on the right hand side and then collecting all of the terms containing y:

$$25y + 1 = 36 - 12y$$

$$35y + 12y = 36 - 1$$

$$37y = 35.$$

$$y = \tfrac{35}{37}.$$

Evidently, we need to consider all angles θ with $\sin(\theta) = \frac{35}{37}$. The arcsine function provides us with one such angle, namely

$$\theta = \arcsin\left(\tfrac{35}{37}\right);$$

in this case, we can use a calculator to obtain an approximate value of $\theta \approx 1.240\,498\,972$ radians.[2] Observe that this angle is in the first quadrant; according to the supplementary angle identity, the angle

$$\theta = \pi - \arcsin\left(\tfrac{35}{37}\right)$$

must be another solution, this time in the second quadrant. Any additional solutions to our equation must be coterminal to one of these two angles. Therefore, we can express the most general solution for our equation as

$$\theta = \arcsin\left(\tfrac{35}{37}\right) + 2\pi k \qquad \text{or} \qquad \theta = \pi - \arcsin\left(\tfrac{35}{37}\right) + 2\pi k,$$

where where $k \in \mathbb{Z}$ is assumed to be an arbitrary integer.

EXAMPLE 4.18. Find all of the solutions of the equation

$$4\cos^2(\theta) + 11\cos(\theta) + 6 = 0.$$

Solution. We can solve this equation by first replacing $\cos(\theta)$ with the dummy variable x, producing the quadratic equation

$$4x^2 + 11x + 6 = 0.$$

This equation can be solved using the quadratic formula as follows:

$$x = \frac{-11 \pm \sqrt{121 - 96}}{8} = \frac{-11 \pm 5}{8}.$$

In other words, we either have $x = -2$ or $x = -\frac{3}{4}$. Therefore, we are looking for all angles θ which satisfy the conditions

$$\cos(\theta) = -2 \qquad \text{or} \qquad \cos(\theta) = -\tfrac{3}{4}.$$

Now, the first of these equations can be discarded outright, since the cosine function only gives values between -1 and 1, so that there is no angle for which cosine is equal to -2. On the other hand, the second equation has two solutions in the unit circle, one in the second quadrant and one in the third. The first of these is given by

$$\theta = \arccos\left(-\tfrac{3}{4}\right).$$

---

[2] On a standard scientific calculator, you can access each of the inverse trigonometric functions by pressing the buttons labeled `sin`⁻¹, `cos`⁻¹, and `tan`⁻¹. Before doing so, you should make sure that your calculator is set for "radian mode." Check your user manual for more details.

The solution in the third quadrant can be obtained from the negative angle identity. This gives us

$$\theta = -\arccos\left(-\tfrac{3}{4}\right).$$

Of course, any angle coterminal to either of these values will be yet another solution to our original equation. Therefore, can express all of these solutions at once by the expression

$$\theta = \pm\arccos\left(-\tfrac{3}{4}\right) + 2\pi k,$$

where $k \in \mathbb{Z}$ is assumed to be an arbitrary integer.

EXAMPLE 4.19. Find all of the solutions of the equation:

$$5\sin(\theta) - 3\cos(\theta) = 7\cos(\theta) + 2\sin(\theta).$$

Solution. As in the previous examples, we begin by introducing the dummy variables $x = \cos(\theta)$ and $y = \sin(\theta)$:

$$5\,y - 3\,x = 7\,x + 2\,y.$$

We can then separate these variables by moving the y's to the left hand side and the x's to the right hand side of the equation, as follows:

$$3\,y = 10\,x.$$

Solving for y then produces

$$y = \tfrac{10}{3}\,x.$$

Note that this is the equation of a line passing through the origin, so its slope corresponds to the tangent of our angle θ. Indeed, if we divide both sides by x and replace our trigonometric functions, we obtain

$$\frac{y}{x} = \frac{\sin(\theta)}{\cos(\theta)} = \frac{10}{3}.$$

Now, we can simplify this last equation by using formula (4.2):

$$\tan(\theta) = \tfrac{10}{3}.$$

As before, we note that there are infinitely many angles that satisfy this equation. The most notable of these is

$$\theta = \arctan\left(\tfrac{10}{3}\right) \approx 1.279\,339\,532,$$

which lives in the first quadrant. However, there is also a solution angle in the third quadrant. We can find it by rotating halfway around the unit circle; this takes us to

$$\theta = \arctan\left(\tfrac{10}{3}\right) + \pi \approx 4.420\,932\,186.$$

And again, any angle coterminal with these is also a solution. Therefore, we can express the general solution to our equation as

$$\theta = \arctan\left(\tfrac{10}{3}\right) + \pi k,$$

where $k \in \mathbb{Z}$ is assumed to be an arbitrary integer as above.

Reading Comprehension Questions for Section 4.3

Since the graphs of the sine and cosine functions form identical sinusoidal ___(a)___ (excepting for the ___(b)___ of the maxima and minima) there exist many relationships between these two functions. These relationships are expressed in terms of ___(c)___. The most important of these is the ___(d)___, given by the equation ___(e)___, which reminds us that the sine and cosine are defined in terms of the ___(f)___ of a point on the unit circle. Next come the ___(g)___, which remind us that the graph of the cosine is its own ___(h)___ reflection about the y-axis and that the sine is its own ___(i)___ reflection about the origin. These are expressed by the equations $\cos(-\theta) = $ ___(j)___ and $\sin(-\theta) = $ ___(k)___. The ___(l)___ tell us that the cosine of an acute angle equals the sine of the complement, and vice versa. In other words, $\cos\left(\frac{\pi}{2} - \theta\right) = $ ___(m)___ and $\sin\left(\frac{\pi}{2} - \theta\right) = $ ___(n)___. The ___(o)___ tell us that the sine of the supplement of an angle equals the sine of the original angle, while its cosine equals the opposite of the cosine of the original angle. That is, $\cos(\pi - \theta) = $ ___(p)___ and $\sin(\pi - \theta) = $ ___(q)___. The last four identities are special cases of the ___(r)___, which allow us to compute the sine and cosine of the sum of two arbitrary angles.

The inverse trigonometric functions allow us to ___(s)___ the sine, cosine, or tangent functions; this allows us to find the angle that these functions map to some given output value. For example, $\theta = \arcsin(x)$ is the angle having ___(t)___. Similarly, $\theta = \arccos(x)$ is the angle having ___(u)___, and $\theta = \arctan(x)$ is the angle having ___(v)___. Since there are many possible angles for any of these conditions, these functions select angles from specific quadrants. Thus, ___(w)___ always selects an angle in the first or second quadrant of the unit circle, while ___(x)___ and ___(y)___ always select an angle in the first and fourth quadrants. To select an angle in a different quadrant, we need to modify the output of the inverse functions in some way. For example, to find an angle θ in the third quadrant having $\tan(\theta) = x$ (where x is some positive number), we would need to compute $\theta = \arctan(x) + $ ___(z)___.

Exercises for Section 4.3

In Exercises 1–8, find the values of the sine, cosine, and tangent functions for the angle θ in each of the following right triangles. Then use a calculator to approximate the measure of θ to the nearest hundredth of a radian. (Note: The triangles are not drawn to scale.)

1.

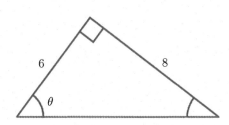

2.

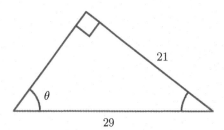

3.

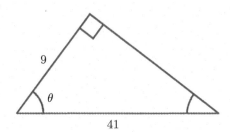

4.

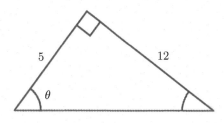

5.

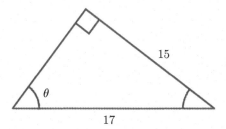

6.

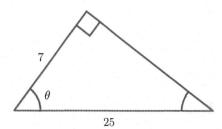

7.

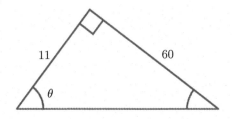

8.

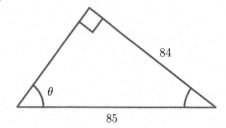

365

In Exercises 9–20, find algebraic expressions for the sine and cosine of each angle.

9. $\theta = \arcsin\left(-\frac{12}{37}\right)$

10. $\theta = \arccos\left(-\frac{28}{53}\right)$

11. $\theta = \arctan\left(\frac{84}{13}\right)$

12. $\theta = \arctan\left(-\frac{9}{40}\right)$

13. $\theta = \frac{11\pi}{12} = \frac{2\pi}{3} + \frac{\pi}{4}$

14. $\theta = \frac{17\pi}{12} = \frac{2\pi}{3} + \frac{3\pi}{4}$

15. $\theta = \frac{7\pi}{12} = \frac{5\pi}{6} - \frac{\pi}{4}$

16. $\theta = -\frac{13\pi}{12} = \frac{\pi}{4} - \frac{4\pi}{3}$

17. $\theta = \arcsin\left(\frac{24}{25}\right) + \frac{11\pi}{4}$

18. $\theta = \arccos\left(\frac{20}{29}\right) - \frac{20\pi}{3}$

19. $\theta = \arccos\left(\frac{8}{17}\right) + \arcsin\left(-\frac{13}{85}\right)$

20. $\theta = \arcsin\left(\frac{7}{25}\right) - \arccos\left(\frac{3}{5}\right)$

In Exercises 21–26, first find all of the values of $\sin(\theta)$ and $\cos(\theta)$ satisfying each equation. Then express the solution θ in its most general form.

21. $2\sin(\theta) = 3\big(1 - \sin(\theta)\big)$

22. $13\big(\cos(\theta) + 1\big) = 1$

23. $17\sin^2(\theta) + 9\sin(\theta) - 8 = 0$

24. $50\cos^2(\theta) = 61\cos(\theta) + 21$

25. $10\sin(\theta) - 11\cos(\theta) = 9\cos(\theta) - 10\sin(\theta)$

26. $17\cos(\theta) - 27\sin(\theta) = 26\cos(\theta) + 13\sin(\theta)$

27. Find the appropriate negative angle identity for the tangent function. In other words, express $\tan(-\theta)$ in terms of $\tan(\theta)$.

28. Find the appropriate complementary angle identity for the tangent function. In other words, express $\tan\left(\frac{\pi}{2} - \theta\right)$ in terms of $\tan(\theta)$.

29. Find the appropriate supplementary angle identity for the tangent function. In other words, express $\tan(\pi - \theta)$ in terms of $\tan(\theta)$.

30. Find the appropriate angle sum identity for the tangent function, as follows.

    (a) Express $\tan(\alpha + \beta)$ as a fraction involving $\sin(\alpha)$, $\cos(\alpha)$, $\sin(\beta)$, and $\cos(\beta)$.

    (b) Divide both the numerator and the denominator in your answer to part (a) by $\cos(\alpha)\cos(\beta)$. Then express your answer in terms of $\tan(\alpha)$ and $\tan(\beta)$.

4.4. Oblique Triangles

A triangle is said to be *oblique* if none of its angles is a right angle. Typically, we use the English letters a, b, and c to denote the lengths of the sides of an oblique triangle, and the Greek letters α (*alpha*), β (*beta*), and γ (*gamma*) to denote the measure of its angles. Our convention will be that α is the angle opposite of side a, that β is the angle opposite of side b, and that γ is the angle opposite of side c, as shown in Figure 4.23.

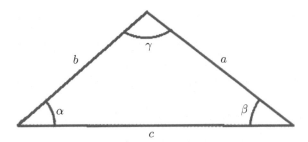

FIGURE 4.23. An oblique triangle.

If you were to consult a thesaurus, you would find that the word "oblique" means indirect, evasive, backhanded, roundabout, and surreptitious. As their name implies, oblique triangles are a mystery of sorts. This is certainly the case when we only know a few of its sides and angles, and have to solve for the rest. In particular, you will note that our usual right angle trigonometry from Theorem 4.1 would prove useless in such a situation. Luckily, this type of mystery does not require a little Belgian detective with an egg-shaped head and a magnificent waxed mustache. With only three clues on our side, we can put our own "little grey cells" to the task of solving the oblique triangle. To do so, we will call on the following three theorems:

Theorem 4.2 (The Law of Sines). The sine of each angle of a triangle is proportional to the length of the side opposite it:

$$\frac{\sin(\alpha)}{a} = \frac{\sin(\beta)}{b} = \frac{\sin(\gamma)}{c}.$$

Proof. Suppose that we construct an altitude of length x perpendicular to side c, as in Figure 4.24. This divides our oblique triangle into two right triangles. In the first of these, b is the hypotenuse and x is the leg opposite the angle α. In the second, a is the hypotenuse and x is the leg opposite the angle β. Therefore,

$$\sin(\alpha) = \frac{x}{b} \qquad \text{and} \qquad \sin(\beta) = \frac{x}{a}.$$

Thus, by dividing the first of these equations by a and the second by b, we find that

$$\frac{\sin(\alpha)}{a} = \frac{x}{a \cdot b} = \frac{\sin(\beta)}{b},$$

as desired. Repeating this process with a different altitude completes the proof. $\qquad \square$

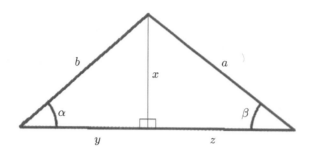

FIGURE 4.24. Proving the Laws of Sines and Cosines.

Theorem 4.3 (The Law of Cosines). The square of any side of a triangle is equal to the sum of the squares of the other two sides minus a correction factor involving the cosine of the angle opposite it:

$$a^2 = b^2 + c^2 - 2bc \cos(\alpha),$$

$$b^2 = a^2 + c^2 - 2ac \cos(\beta),$$

$$c^2 = a^2 + b^2 - 2ab \cos(\gamma).$$

Proof. As above, we construct an altitude perpendicular to side c, as shown in Figure 4.24. This divides our oblique triangle into two right triangles, and more critically, the side c in two pieces of length y and z, respectively. In the first triangle, b is the hypotenuse and y is the leg adjacent to the angle α, while, in the second triangle, a is the hypotenuse and z is the leg adjacent the angle β. Therefore,

$$\cos(\alpha) = \frac{y}{b} \qquad \text{and} \qquad \cos(\beta) = \frac{z}{a}.$$

If we solve these equations for y and z, and add the results together, we obtain

$$c = y + z = b \cos(\alpha) + a \cos(\beta).$$

Then, multiplying by c, gives

$$c^2 = bc \cos(\alpha) + ac \cos(\beta).$$

Repeating this process with the other sides of our triangle produces two similar equations:

$$a^2 = ab \cos(\gamma) + ac \cos(\beta),$$

$$b^2 = ab \cos(\gamma) + bc \cos(\alpha).$$

Finally, we take each of these equations minus the other two, producing

$$a^2 - b^2 - c^2 = 2bc \cos(\alpha),$$

$$b^2 - a^2 - c^2 = 2ac \cos(\beta),$$

$$c^2 - a^2 - b^2 = 2ab \cos(\gamma),$$

as desired.   □

Our last theorem dates back to Euclid of Alexandria (c. 325–265 BC), although it is likely that it is actually much older still. Euclid stands as one of the greatest mathematical minds of the ancient world thanks to the *Elements*, the voluminous text in which he collected much of the Greek mathematics of his time, arranging it all in a single logical framework. So influential was this one work that, over time, scholars chose to copy and recopy it over any earlier texts, leaving those earlier mathematical manuscripts to disappear into dust as the ravages of time disintegrated the papyrus on which they were written.

Theorem 4.4 (Euclid's theorem). The three angles in any triangle always add up to a straight angle:

$$\alpha + \beta + \gamma = \pi. \qquad \text{or} \qquad \alpha + \beta + \gamma = 180°.$$

Proof. Suppose that we construct a line parallel to side c passing through the vertex of angle γ, as in Figure 4.25. This line creates two new angles at this vertex, which together with γ, add up to a straight angle. Furthermore, the new angles are alternate interior angles with α and β, respectively, and therefore have measure equal to these angles. Therefore, the three angles of the triangle add up to a straight angle, as desired. $\square$

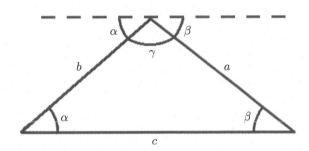

FIGURE 4.25. Proving Euclid's Theorem.

As it stands, Euclid's theorem gives us the measure of an angle only if we know the exact measure of the other two angles; otherwise, it can only provide us with an approximation. However, when combined with our complementary angle and angle sum identities, Euclid's theorem gives us the following formulas:

$$\sin(\gamma) = \sin\big(\pi - (\alpha + \beta)\big) = \sin(\alpha)\cos(\beta) + \cos(\alpha)\sin(\beta),$$

$$\cos(\gamma) = \cos\big(\pi - (\alpha + \beta)\big) = \sin(\alpha)\sin(\beta) - \cos(\alpha)\cos(\beta).$$

These are useful in expressing the third angle of a triangle when we know the values of the trigonometric functions at the other two angles.

Our strategy for solving each mystery will depend on our clues, that is, on which parts of the triangle we know, and which we do not. The following case studies go through all of the possible combinations.

Case 1 – Side-Side-Side (SSS)

Clues: The lengths of all three sides of the triangle.

Procedure: ① *Find the largest angle using the law of cosines.*

② *Find the other two angles using the law of sines.*

EXAMPLE 4.20. Consider the SSS oblique triangle shown in Figure 4.26. The sides of this triangle have length $a = 4$, $b = 5$, and $c = 6$.

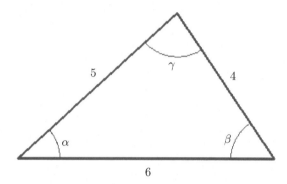

FIGURE 4.26. Solving an SSS oblique triangle.

① The largest angle will be the one opposite the largest side ($c = 6$). This is the only angle that could possibly be obtuse, so we apply the law of cosines to compute

$$6^2 = 4^2 + 5^2 - 2 \cdot 4 \cdot 5 \cdot \cos(\gamma).$$

This means that $\cos(\gamma) = \frac{1}{8}$, so $\gamma = \arccos\left(\frac{1}{8}\right) \approx 82.8°$. Before moving on, we compute $\sin(\gamma)$, which we will need for Step ②, by using the Pythagorean identity:

$$\sin(\gamma) = \sqrt{1 - \cos^2(\gamma)} = \sqrt{1 - \tfrac{1}{64}} = \frac{\sqrt{63}}{8} = \frac{3\sqrt{7}}{8}.$$

② Since the remaining two angles must be acute, we apply the law of sines as follows:

$$\frac{\sin(\alpha)}{4} = \frac{\sin(\beta)}{5} = \frac{\sin(\gamma)}{6} = \frac{\frac{3\sqrt{7}}{8}}{6} = \frac{\sqrt{7}}{16}.$$

This means that $\sin(\alpha) = \frac{\sqrt{7}}{4}$, so $\alpha = \arcsin\left(\frac{\sqrt{7}}{4}\right) \approx 41.4°$. Similarly, $\sin(\beta) = \frac{5\sqrt{7}}{16}$, so $\beta = \arcsin\left(\frac{5\sqrt{7}}{16}\right) \approx 55.8°$.

Case 2 – Side-Angle-Side (SAS)

Clues: The lengths of two sides of the triangle, as well as the measure of the angle between these two sides.

Procedure: ① *Find the third side using the law of cosines.*

② *Find the smallest angle using the law of sines.*

③ *Find the last angle using Euclid's theorem.*

EXAMPLE 4.21. Consider the SAS oblique triangle shown in Figure 4.27. In this case, we have $a = 3$, $b = 7$, and $\gamma = 60°$.

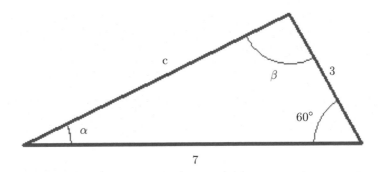

FIGURE 4.27. Solving an SAS oblique triangle.

① The third side is opposite $\gamma = 60°$, so the law of cosines tell us that

$$c^2 = 3^2 + 7^2 - 2 \cdot 3 \cdot 7 \cdot \cos(60°) = 9 + 49 - 42 \cdot \tfrac{1}{2} = 37.$$

This means that $c = \sqrt{37} \approx 6.083$.

② The smallest angle is opposite the smallest side ($a = 3$). This angle is necessarily acute, so by the law of sines,

$$\frac{\sin(\alpha)}{3} = \frac{\sin(60°)}{\sqrt{37}} = \frac{\frac{\sqrt{3}}{2}}{\sqrt{37}} = \frac{\sqrt{3}}{2\sqrt{37}}.$$

This means that $\sin(\alpha) = \frac{3\sqrt{3}}{2\sqrt{37}} = \frac{3\sqrt{111}}{74}$, so $\alpha = \arcsin\left(\frac{3\sqrt{111}}{74}\right) \approx 25.3°$. We can now compute $\cos(\alpha)$, which we will need for Step ③, by using the Pythagorean identity:

$$\cos(\alpha) = \sqrt{1 - \sin^2(\alpha)} = \sqrt{1 - \tfrac{27}{148}} = \tfrac{11}{2\sqrt{37}} = \tfrac{11\sqrt{37}}{74}.$$

③ We can find the exact value for the last angle by using the cosine formula arising from Euclid's theorem:

$$\cos(\beta) = \sin(\alpha)\,\sin(60°) - \cos(\alpha)\,\cos(60°)$$

$$= \frac{3\sqrt{3}}{2\sqrt{37}} \cdot \frac{\sqrt{3}}{2} - \frac{11}{2\sqrt{37}} \cdot \frac{1}{2}$$

$$= -\frac{1}{2\sqrt{37}} = -\frac{\sqrt{37}}{74}.$$

Therefore $\beta = \arccos\left(-\frac{\sqrt{37}}{74}\right) \approx 94.7°$.

Case 3 – Side-Angle-Angle (SAA)

Clues: The length of one side of the triangle, as well as the measures of any two of its angles.

Procedure: ① *Find the third angle using Euclid's theorem.*

② *Find the other two sides using the law of sines.*

EXAMPLE 4.22. Consider the SAA oblique triangle shown in Figure 4.28. This triangle has a side of length $a = 4$, as well as two angles measuring $\alpha = 45°$ and $\beta = 30°$.

① The third angle for this triangle can be easily computed as

$$\gamma = 180° - 45° - 30° = 105°.$$

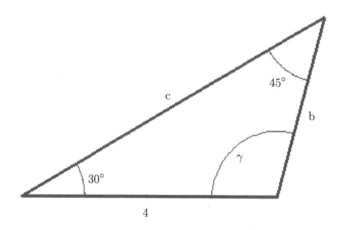

FIGURE 4.28. Solving an SAA oblique triangle.

We can then determine the exact value of $\sin(\gamma)$, which we will need in Step ②, using the sine formula for Euclid's theorem as follows:

$$\sin(\gamma) = \sin(45°)\cos(30°) + \cos(45°)\sin(30°)$$

$$= \frac{\sqrt{2}}{2} \cdot \frac{\sqrt{3}}{2} + \frac{\sqrt{2}}{2} \cdot \frac{1}{2}$$

$$= \frac{\sqrt{6}+\sqrt{2}}{4}.$$

② The law of sines now tells us that

$$\frac{\sin(45°)}{4} = \frac{\sin(30°)}{b} = \frac{\sin(105°)}{c}.$$

This means that

$$b = \frac{4\sin(30°)}{\sin(45°)} = \frac{4 \cdot \frac{1}{2}}{\frac{\sqrt{2}}{2}} = 2\sqrt{2} \approx 2.828$$

and

$$c = \frac{4\sin(105°)}{\sin(45°)} = \frac{4 \cdot \frac{\sqrt{6}+\sqrt{2}}{4}}{\frac{\sqrt{2}}{2}} = 2\sqrt{3} + 2 \approx 5.464.$$

Case 4 – Side-Side-Angle (SSA)

Clues: The length of two sides of the triangle, as well as the measure of an angle opposite to one of these sides.

Procedure: ① *Find the angle opposite the other known side using the law of sines.*

② *Find the third angle using Euclid's theorem.*

③ *Find the last side using either the law of sines or the law of cosines.*

Warning – Depending on the result of step ①, there can be three distinct outcomes for this case.

- The good: *The sine of the angle is determined to be less than or equal to one. Furthermore, we have reliable evidence that the angle is not obtuse. Outcome: one solution.*

- The bad: *The sine of the angle is determined to be greater than one. Outcome: no solution.*

- The ugly: *The sine of the angle is determined to be less than one. However, we have no reliable evidence that the angle must be acute. Outcome: two solutions.*

EXAMPLE 4.23. Consider the SSA oblique triangle shown in Figure 4.29. In this case, we have $a = 8$, $b = 7$, and $\alpha = 45°$.

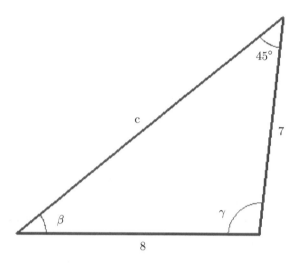

FIGURE 4.29. Solving an SSA oblique triangle (good version).

① According to the law of sines, we have

$$\frac{\sin(\beta)}{7} = \frac{\sin(45°)}{8} = \frac{\frac{\sqrt{2}}{2}}{8} = \frac{\sqrt{2}}{16}.$$

so that $\sin(\beta) = \frac{7\sqrt{2}}{16} \approx 0.619$. Now, β is not the largest angle in the triangle since it is opposite a side of length $b = 7$, which in turn is smaller than $a = 8$. This means that β must be an acute angle, and therefore

$$\beta = \arcsin\left(\frac{7\sqrt{2}}{16}\right) \approx 38.2°.$$

Before moving on, we can compute $\cos(\beta)$, which we will need for Step ②, by using the Pythagorean identity:

$$\cos(\beta) = \sqrt{1 - \sin^2(\beta)} = \sqrt{1 - \frac{98}{256}} = \frac{\sqrt{158}}{16}.$$

② We shall use the sine and cosine versions of Euclid's Theorem to find

$$\sin(\gamma) = \sin(45°)\cos(\beta) + \cos(45°)\sin(\beta)$$

$$= \frac{\sqrt{2}}{2} \cdot \frac{\sqrt{158}}{16} + \frac{\sqrt{2}}{2} \cdot \frac{7\sqrt{2}}{16}$$

$$= \frac{\sqrt{79}+7}{16} = \frac{7+\sqrt{79}}{16},$$

$$\cos(\gamma) = \sin(45°)\sin(\beta) - \cos(45°)\cos(\beta)$$

$$= \frac{\sqrt{2}}{2} \cdot \frac{7\sqrt{2}}{16} - \frac{\sqrt{2}}{2} \cdot \frac{\sqrt{158}}{16}$$

$$= \frac{7 - \sqrt{79}}{16}.$$

Note that the value of the cosine is negative, so γ must be obtuse. We can determine its measure by computing an arccosine as follows:

$$\gamma = \arccos\left(\frac{7 - \sqrt{79}}{16}\right) \approx 96.8°.$$

③ The law of cosines now says that

$$c^2 = 8^2 + 7^2 - 2 \cdot 8 \cdot 7 \cdot \frac{7 - \sqrt{79}}{16} = 64 + 49 - 7\left(7 - \sqrt{79}\right) = 64 + 7\sqrt{79},$$

which means that

$$c = \sqrt{64 + 7\sqrt{79}} \approx 11.235.$$

Alternatively, the law of sines says that

$$\frac{\sin(\gamma)}{c} = \frac{7 + \sqrt{79}}{16\,c} = \frac{\sqrt{2}}{16}.$$

Solving this equation gives a different (but equivalent) formula for c:

$$c = \frac{7 + \sqrt{79}}{\sqrt{2}} = \frac{7\sqrt{2} + \sqrt{158}}{2} \approx 11.235.$$

EXAMPLE 4.24. Consider the SSA oblique triangle shown in Figure 4.30, which has $a = 4$, $b = 7$, and $\alpha = 45°$.

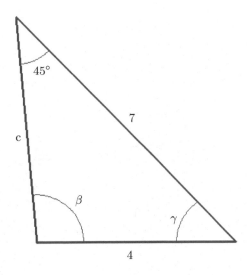

FIGURE 4.30. Solving an SSA oblique triangle (bad version).

① According to the law of sines, we have

$$\frac{\sin(\beta)}{7} = \frac{\sin(45°)}{4} = \frac{\frac{\sqrt{2}}{2}}{4} = \frac{\sqrt{2}}{8}.$$

so that

$$\sin(\beta) = \frac{7\sqrt{2}}{8} \approx 1.237.$$

Note that this value is larger than 1, which is impossible because the sine function can only take on values between -1 and 1. Since there is no angle β that can satisfy the law of sines, our oblique triangle has no solution.

EXAMPLE 4.25. Consider the SSA oblique triangle in Figure 4.31, which has sides of length $a = 6$, $b = 7$, and an angle measuring $\alpha = 45°$.

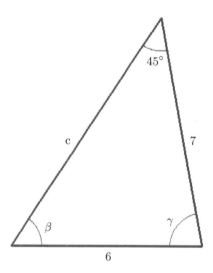

FIGURE 4.31. Solving an SSA oblique triangle (ugly version).

① In this case, the law of sines gives

$$\frac{\sin(\beta)}{7} = \frac{\sin(45°)}{6} = \frac{\frac{\sqrt{2}}{2}}{6} = \frac{\sqrt{2}}{12}.$$

so that $\sin(\beta) = \frac{7\sqrt{2}}{12} \approx 0.825$. Since this value is less than 1, we have two possibilities: The angle in question might be acute or it might be obtuse. In order to account for both of these possibilities, we first determine the value of $\cos(\beta)$ using the Pythagorean identity:

$$\cos(\beta) = \pm\sqrt{1 - \sin^2(\beta)} = \pm\sqrt{1 - \frac{98}{144}} = \pm\frac{\sqrt{46}}{12}.$$

This gives us two solutions to consider.

Acute Solution: $\beta = \arccos\left(\frac{\sqrt{46}}{12}\right) \approx 55.6°$.

② According to Euclid's theorem, we have

$$\sin(\gamma) = \sin(45°)\cos(\beta) + \cos(45°)\sin(\beta)$$
$$= \frac{\sqrt{2}}{2} \cdot \frac{\sqrt{46}}{12} + \frac{\sqrt{2}}{2} \cdot \frac{7\sqrt{2}}{12} = \frac{\sqrt{23}+7}{12} = \frac{7+\sqrt{23}}{12},$$

$$\cos(\gamma) = \sin(45°)\sin(\beta) - \cos(45°)\cos(\beta)$$
$$= \frac{\sqrt{2}}{2} \cdot \frac{7\sqrt{2}}{12} - \frac{\sqrt{2}}{2} \cdot \frac{\sqrt{46}}{12} = \frac{7-\sqrt{23}}{12}.$$

This means that

$$\gamma = \arcsin\left(\frac{7+\sqrt{23}}{12}\right) = \arccos\left(\frac{7-\sqrt{23}}{12}\right) \approx 79.4°.$$

③ Now, the law of cosines says that

$$c^2 = 6^2 + 7^2 - 2 \cdot 6 \cdot 7 \cdot \frac{7-\sqrt{23}}{12} = 36 + 49 - 7\left(7 - \sqrt{23}\right) = 36 + 7\sqrt{23}.$$

This means that

$$c = \sqrt{36 + 7\sqrt{23}} \approx 8.341.$$

Alternatively, the law of sines says that

$$\frac{\sin(\gamma)}{c} = \frac{7+\sqrt{23}}{12\,c} = \frac{\sqrt{2}}{12},$$

which gives the equivalent formulation

$$c = \frac{7+\sqrt{23}}{\sqrt{2}} = \frac{7\sqrt{2}+\sqrt{46}}{2} \approx 8.341.$$

Obtuse Solution: $\beta = \arccos\left(\frac{-\sqrt{46}}{12}\right) \approx 124.4°$.

② Again, by Euclid's theorem, we have

$$\sin(\gamma) = \sin(45°)\cos(\beta) + \cos(45°)\sin(\beta)$$
$$= \frac{\sqrt{2}}{2} \cdot \frac{-\sqrt{46}}{12} + \frac{\sqrt{2}}{2} \cdot \frac{7\sqrt{2}}{12} = \frac{-\sqrt{23}+7}{12} = \frac{7-\sqrt{23}}{12},$$

$$\cos(\gamma) = \sin(45°)\sin(\beta) - \cos(45°)\cos(\beta)$$
$$= \frac{\sqrt{2}}{2} \cdot \frac{7\sqrt{2}}{12} - \frac{\sqrt{2}}{2} \cdot \frac{-\sqrt{46}}{12} = \frac{7+\sqrt{23}}{12}.$$

This gives us

$$\gamma = \arcsin\left(\frac{7-\sqrt{23}}{12}\right) = \arccos\left(\frac{7+\sqrt{23}}{12}\right) \approx 10.6°.$$

③ The law of cosines now gives

$$c^2 = 6^2 + 7^2 - 2 \cdot 6 \cdot 7 \cdot \tfrac{7+\sqrt{23}}{12} = 36 + 49 - 7\big(7 + \sqrt{23}\big) = 36 - 7\sqrt{23},$$

so that

$$c = \sqrt{36 - 7\sqrt{23}} \approx 1.559.$$

Alternatively, the law of sines says that

$$\frac{\sin(\gamma)}{c} = \frac{7 - \sqrt{23}}{12\,c} = \frac{\sqrt{2}}{12},$$

giving the equivalent formulation

$$c = \tfrac{7 - \sqrt{23}}{\sqrt{2}} = \tfrac{7\sqrt{2} - \sqrt{46}}{2} \approx 1.559.$$

You will note that the key factor determining whether a given angle is found using the law of sines or the law of cosines is its size. In particular, you should recall that the codomain of the arcsine function includes only acute angles, while that of the arccosine function also includes obtuse angles. This means that if we know conclusively that an angle is acute, then it can be safely found using the law of sines, and consequently the arcsine function. On the other hand, if there is even a chance that an angle is obtuse, then its value should be found using the law of cosines and the arccosine function.

Reading Comprehension Questions for Section 4.4

A triangle is said to be ___(a)___ if none of its angles is a right angle. Solving this kind of triangle involves determining the lengths of all of the ___(b)___ and the measures of all of the ___(c)___, given some partial information. Even though they are designed to work explicitly with ___(d)___ triangles, the trigonometric functions allow us to also solve these triangles. The procedure to follow depends on the information known, but the tools are generally the same. These include ___(e)___, which says that the angles in any triangle always add up to ___(f)___. In addition, we have the ___(g)___, which says that the sine of each angle in a triangle is proportional to the ___(h)___. Finally, there is the ___(i)___, which is just Pythagoras's theorem minus a correction factor involving ___(j)___ times the lengths of two ___(k)___ times the ___(l)___ of the ___(m)___ between them.

For instance, consider a triangle with sides of length $a = 13$, $b = 14$, and $c = 15$. Label the angles opposite these sides as α, β, and γ, respectively. We first find the largest angle (which in this case is ___(n)___) using the law of ___(o)___. This gives us $15^2 = $ ___(p)___, which simplifies to $\cos(\gamma) = $ ___(q)___. Then, using a calculator in degree mode, we find that $\gamma \approx$ ___(r)___°. Next, we can find the other two angles using the law of ___(s)___. In particular, we first use the ___(t)___ identity to compute

$$\sin(\gamma) = \sqrt{\underline{\quad(u)\quad}} = \underline{\quad(v)\quad}.$$

Therefore,

$$\sin(\alpha) = \frac{a\sin(\gamma)}{c} = \underline{\quad(w)\quad}$$

and

$$\sin(\beta) = \frac{b\sin(\gamma)}{c} = \underline{\quad(x)\quad}.$$

Thus, using a calculator, we find that $\alpha \approx$ ___(y)___° and $\beta \approx$ ___(z)___°.

Exercises for Section 4.4

In Exercises 1–12, find the exact values of the missing lengths and angle measures in the following oblique triangles. (Note: The diagrams are not drawn to scale.)

1.

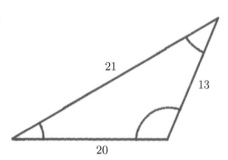

2.

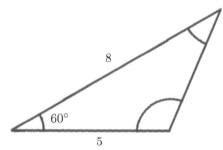

3.

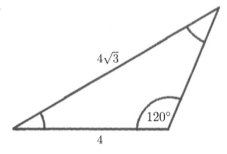

4.

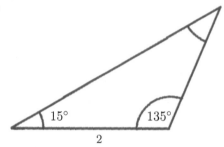

5.

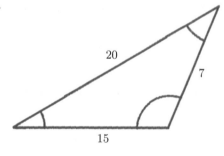

6.

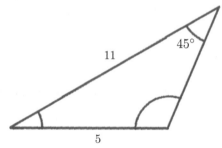

7.

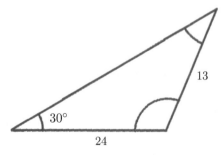

8.

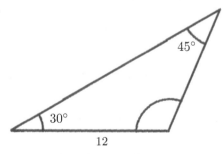

380

9.

10.

11.

12.

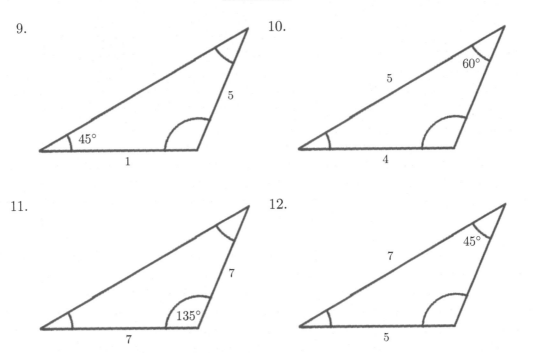

In Exercises 13–30, each problem describes one or more triangles. Find the answer to each problem by using a calculator to approximate the values of the angles in question. Round your final answer to the nearest tenth of a unit.

13. The sonar of a navy cruiser detects a nuclear submarine 4000 feet from the cruiser at an angle of 35° below the water level. How deep is the submarine submerged?

14. Acute Alice is admiring the architecture of an old New England church from a point 45 feet in front of the church. From where she is standing, the top of the steeple and the base of the steeple are, respectively, at an angle of 50° and 40° from the horizontal. How tall is the steeple?

15. Scalene Sallie is standing on the observation deck of a lighthouse 350 feet above sea level when she spots two ships directly offshore. The lines of sight to each of the ships make angles of 5° and 7.5° with the horizontal. How far apart are the ships?

16. Obtuse Ollie is flying on an airplane that is cruising at an altitude of 10 km when he spots two towns directly to the left of the plane. The angles of depression to the towns are 28° and 55° below the horizontal. How far apart are the towns?

17. Coast Guard Station Alpha is located 150 miles due south of Station Bravo. A ship at sea sends an S.O.S. call that is received by each station. The call to Station Alpha indicates that the ship is located at 35° North of West, while the call to Station Bravo indicates that the ship is located at 25° South of West. How far is the ship from each station?

18. Over winter break, Acute Alice is working at a ski resort. As she comes out of the ski lodge, she notes that the angle of elevation to the top of the ski lift is 15° from

the horizontal. Then she walks 1000 feet to the base of the ski lift and observes that the lift climbs at an angle of 25°. What is the length of the span of the ski lift?

19. Scalene Sallie finds that, on her map, Orlando is 178 millimeters due south of Niagara Falls. On the same map, Denver is 273 millimeters from Orlando and 235 millimeters from Niagara Falls. Find the bearings for Orlando and for Niagara Falls from Denver.

20. While playing golf, Obtuse Ollie hits a ball from the tee and it lands in the rough outside the fairway. A marker in the center of the fairway is 150 yards from the center of the green. While standing at the marker and facing the green, Ollie turns 110° and paces off 35 yards directly to his ball. How far is his ball from the center of the green?

21. Two fire towers are located 30 kilometers apart on a stretch of road running east to west. A forest fire is spotted from both towers with bearings of 15° East of North and 35° West of North, respectively. Find the shortest distance from the fire to the road between the towers.

22. Acute Alice is on vacation on a cruise ship from Puerto Rico to Barbados, a distance of 600 nautical miles. To avoid a tropical storm, the ship's captain sets out of Puerto Rico in an indirect path to Barbados, cruising for ten hours at a speed of 15 knots (nautical miles per hour). At that point in time, the path to Barbados becomes clear of storms, so the captain turns the ship 26° to starboard and heads directly to Barbados. If the ship continues at the same speed of 15 knots, how long will it be before it reaches Barbados?

23. Scalene Sallie is taking photographs of a 500-foot tall radio tower. The tower is secured by several guy wires attached to concrete blocks on the ground 100 feet from the base of the tower. On one side of the tower, where the ground is level, a guy wire connects to the point halfway up the tower; on the other side of the tower, where the ground slopes upward at an angle of 10°, a guy wire connects to the point of the tower. How long are the guy wires?

24. Obtuse Ollie is flying on an airplane from Boston to Los Angeles, a distance of 2600 miles, at a speed of 450 miles per hour. After takeoff, the pilot inadvertently took a course that was 10° in error. When the error is finally discovered, the aircraft is turned through an angle of 25° so it heads directly to Los Angeles. How much longer will it take Ollie to get to his destination?

25. A land surveyor wishes to find the distance between two alligator nests on opposite sides of a swamp in the Florida Everglades. She stands by one nest and records a bearing of 32° North of West to the other nest. Then she walks 50 meters South from the first nest and records a bearing of 22° West of North to the other nest. Find the distance between the alligator nests.

26. Acute Alice and Obtuse Ollie are standing at opposite ends of a 700-foot long bridge over a river. They each spot a rock at water level directly below the bridge

at angles of 70° and 65°, respectively, below the horizontal. How high is the bridge over the water?

27. While traveling on horseback across a flat prairie, Scalene Sallie noticed a tall butte directly in front of her. The butte's flat top makes angle of elevation of 2.5° above the horizontal. After riding 18 miles closer to the butte, Sallie notes that the angle of elevation to the top is now 10°. How tall is the butte?

28. A crew of astronauts travels on a shuttle from the International Space Station to an orbiting fuel station, a distance of 150 miles. After fueling, they turn through an angle of 50° and fly to a malfunctioning communications satellite, a distance of 100 miles. How far is it from the satellite back to the space station?

29. Obtuse Ollie is flying on an airplane heading due east when he sees the light from a lighthouse at 28° North of East. After the airplane has traveled 3 kilometers, the light is at 42° North of East. If the plane continues on the same heading, how close will it approach the lighthouse?

30. A television satellite traveling in a circular orbit 150 miles above the surface of the earth can broadcast its signal to any point below as far out as the horizon. Assuming that the radius of the earth is 4000 miles, what is the width of the satellite's broadcast range? (Hint: Model the surface of the earth as a circle, and the satellite's broadcast range as the arc on that circle determined by the two tangent lines emerging from the satellite.)

Review of Chapter 4

Vocabulary with which you should now be familiar:

- acute angle
- amplitude
- bearing
- complementary angle
- cosine function
- coterminal angle
- degree measure
- law of cosines
- law of sines
- negative angle
- oblique triangle
- obtuse angle

- periodic function
- positive angle
- radian measure
- reflex angle
- right angle
- sine function
- sinusoidal waveform
- standard position
- supplementary angle
- tangent function
- unit circle
- wavelength

Tasks you should now be prepared to perform:

- convert between the degree and radian measure of an angle.
- recognize 30-60-90 and 45-90-45 right triangles.
- sketch positive and negative angles in standard position.
- evaluate the sine, cosine, and tangent functions at $\theta = 0$, $\frac{\pi}{6}$, $\frac{\pi}{4}$, $\frac{\pi}{3}$, $\frac{\pi}{2}$, etc.
- use the Pythagorean, sign, and angle sum identities.
- sketch the graph of a sine, cosine, or tangent function.
- determine the equation of a sinusoidal waveform given its wavelength and amplitude.
- determine the sides and the angles of an oblique triangle, given sufficient information.

CHAPTER 5

The Complex Numbers

If you take any "ordinary" non-zero real number, be it positive or negative, and square it, you get a positive number. So $\sqrt{-1}$ (alias the number, if such a thing could be imagined to exist, whose square is -1) cannot be an "ordinary" quantity. The clear and sober judgment ... that such objects are "impossible" is echoed everywhere. "We do not perceive any quantity such as that its square is negative!"

Nevertheless, this $\sqrt{-1}$ did not go away. It showed itself as imperatively useful. Those who refused to deal with it did so at the price of limiting their powers as algebraists. By the beginning of the eighteenth century, square roots of negative quantities were routinely met with and jauntily handled, and their impossibility noted....

The story of the ripening act of coming to live with $\sqrt{-1}$, and eventually achieving a somewhat surprising but wholly satisfactory "imagining" of $\sqrt{-1}$, spans more than three centuries of mathematical activity.

B. Mazur

Imagining Numbers (particularly the square root of minus fifteen)
pages 35–36 (2003)

5.1. The Square Root of Negative One

The turn of the sixteenth century was a time of intellectual vitality in northern Italy. Geniuses the likes of Raphael (1483–1520), Michelangelo (1475–1564), and Leonardo da Vinci (1452–1519) dotted the landscape. It was also a time when mathematicians would vie for fortune, glory, and the always-illusive patronage of a rich sponsor in public problem-solving duels. The thought of such mathematical contests might seem strange to you or me, but at the time, university positions (even those in mathematics) were not particularly well-paid. At a public duel, an exceptional mathematician with the ability to solve problems that others could not stood a decent chance of making a tidy sum.

Antonio Maria Fior was not an exceptional mathematician. However, while studying at the University of Bologna, he had gained the trust of his professor, Scipione del Ferro (1465–1526), and at the master's deathbed, he learned from him the secret solution to the "depressed" cubic equation

$$x^3 + bx + c = 0.$$

What del Ferro had discovered, and what he revealed to Fior, was that the solution to this equation is given by the formula

(5.1) $$x = \sqrt[3]{-\frac{c}{2} + \sqrt{\left(\frac{c}{2}\right)^2 + \left(\frac{b}{3}\right)^3}} + \sqrt[3]{-\frac{c}{2} - \sqrt{\left(\frac{c}{2}\right)^2 + \left(\frac{b}{3}\right)^3}}.$$

You can think of this as the equivalent of the quadratic formula, but for a special type of cubic equation. According to this formula, for example, the solution to the equation

$$x^3 - 9x - 28 = 0,$$

for which $b = -9$ and $c = -28$, is given by the expression

$$\begin{aligned}
x &= \sqrt[3]{\frac{28}{2} + \sqrt{\left(-\frac{28}{2}\right)^2 + \left(-\frac{9}{3}\right)^3}} + \sqrt[3]{\frac{28}{2} - \sqrt{\left(-\frac{28}{2}\right)^2 + \left(-\frac{9}{3}\right)^3}} \\
&= \sqrt[3]{14 + \sqrt{14^2 - 3^3}} + \sqrt[3]{14 - \sqrt{14^2 - 3^3}} \\
&= \sqrt[3]{14 + \sqrt{196 - 27}} + \sqrt[3]{14 - \sqrt{196 - 27}} \\
&= \sqrt[3]{14 + \sqrt{169}} + \sqrt[3]{14 - \sqrt{169}} \\
&= \sqrt[3]{14 + 13} + \sqrt[3]{14 - 13} = \sqrt[3]{27} + \sqrt[3]{1} = 3 + 1 = 4.
\end{aligned}$$

You should take a minute to check that this is really a solution:

$$x = 4 \quad \Rightarrow \quad x^3 - 9x - 28 = 4^3 - 9 \cdot 4 - 28 = 64 - 36 - 28 = 0.$$

Armed with this secret knowledge, Fior foolishly challenged a superior mathematician named Niccolo Tartaglia (1500–1557) to a problem-solving contest. Originally a native of Brescia, Tartaglia now taught in Venice, where he had acquired somewhat of a reputation by taking part in this sort of mathematical duel. Each contestant was to pose thirty problems to his opponent, and then deliver his solutions to a notary on February 22, 1535. Unfortunately for poor Fior, after a late night of computations, Tartaglia was able to rediscover del Ferro's secret formula for himself. By the time the deadline arrived, he had solved all thirty of Fior's problems while Fior had not been able to solve a single one of Tartaglia's.

After this celebrated victory, Tartaglia was convinced (some would say "tricked") into sharing the secret of del Ferro's formula with a scoundrelly mathematician by the name of Girolamo Cardano (1501–1576). Tartaglia swore Cardano to secrecy, but this did not stop Cardano from publishing del Ferro's formula anyway. In fact, starting with del Ferro's formula, Cardano was able to derive a general method for solving any cubic equation (depressed or otherwise) and it was this general solution that he included in his 1545 masterpiece *Ars Magna*. Since he was dealing with a new, more general formula, Cardano felt that, morally speaking, he was in the clear to publish away. The embittered Tartaglia did not see things quite the same way, and spent the remainder of his life festering in self-pity and cursing Cardano's name.

Del Ferro's formula notwithstanding, there were still some cubic equations which posed insurmountable obstacles, even for Cardano. For instance, the equation

$$x^3 - 6x + 4 = 0$$

has the form of the depressed cubic above, this time with $b = -6$ and $c = 4$. In this case, however, del Ferro's formula gives the expression

$$x = \sqrt[3]{-\tfrac{4}{2} + \sqrt{\left(\tfrac{4}{2}\right)^2 + \left(-\tfrac{6}{3}\right)^3}} + \sqrt[3]{-\tfrac{4}{2} - \sqrt{\left(\tfrac{4}{2}\right)^2 + \left(-\tfrac{6}{3}\right)^3}}$$

$$= \sqrt[3]{-2 + \sqrt{2^2 - 2^3}} + \sqrt[3]{-2 - \sqrt{2^2 - 2^3}}$$

$$= \sqrt[3]{-2 + \sqrt{4 - 8}} + \sqrt[3]{-2 - \sqrt{4 - 8}}$$

$$= \sqrt[3]{-2 + \sqrt{-4}} + \sqrt[3]{-2 - \sqrt{-4}}.$$

If we were to proceed with this computation, we would now be required to produce the square root of -4 which, as we emphasized as far back as Chapter 1, is an impossibility. This is a basic tenet of the real numbers, where squares are never negative and negative numbers never have square roots. Cardano would have then concluded that, in this case, del Ferro's formula simply breaks down. "*Una tortura mentale,*" he would have lamented.

However, suppose that we could *extend* the set of real numbers by adding a *new* number i, living somewhere "outside" of the number line, whose square is equal to negative one:

$$\boxed{i^2 = -1.}$$

This is precisely what Rafael Bombelli (1526 – 1572) did, although initially with some amount of reservation and skepticism, some twenty-five years after Cardano. Since $i = \sqrt{-1}$ is not real – that is, it is not a *real number* – it was at first called "sophistic" and later "imaginary." Eventually, though, the resulting number system gained the acceptance of the mathematical community and became known as the set of **complex numbers**. We shall denote this set by the symbol $\mathbb{C}$.

Once you come to terms with accepting $i = \sqrt{-1}$ as an honest-to-goodness number (both your psychotherapist and your mathematics instructor can help you with this), you might ask yourself: Why not give other improbabilities a chance? For instance, how about adding square roots for other negative numbers like -4 or -17? As it turns out, all you need is i. In particular, you should notice that

$$(2 \cdot i)^2 = 2^2 \cdot i^2 = 4 \cdot (-1) = -4$$

and that

$$(\sqrt{17} \cdot i)^2 = \sqrt{17}^2 \cdot i^2 = 17 \cdot (-1) = -17.$$

Of course, these computations are based on our faith and hope that we should be allowed to perform the same arithmetic operations with i as with any other number, and that the familiar rules of arithmetic will still hold when we do so. As we shall see, this is nearly always the case.

To be precise, a complex number is defined as an expression of the form

$$\boxed{z = a + b\,i,}$$

where a and b are real numbers and i is the square root of negative one. This is called the **rectangular form** of the complex number z. The number a is called the **real part** of z and is denoted $a = \mathfrak{Re}\,z$. The number b is called the **imaginary part** of z and is denoted $b = \mathfrak{Im}\,z$. Notice that both $\mathfrak{Re}\,z$ and $\mathfrak{Im}\,z$ are real numbers.

Every real number is automatically a complex number; we simply take its imaginary part to be equal to zero. Thus,

$$5 = 5 + 0\,i \qquad \text{and} \qquad \sqrt{7} = \sqrt{7} + 0\,i$$

are both real *and* complex. On the other hand, if the real part of a complex number is zero, as is the case with

$$2\,i = 0 + 2\,i \qquad \text{and} \qquad \sqrt{17}\,i = 0 + \sqrt{17}\,i,$$

then we shall say that the complex number in question is **purely imaginary**.

Arithmetic in the complex numbers is defined in the only way that would be compatible with the familiar associative, commutative, and distributive properties. Thus, when we add two complex numbers, we simply add their real and imaginary parts separately, as follows:

$$(a + bi) + (c + di) = (a + c) + (b + d)i.$$

Subtraction works in a similar way:

$$(a + bi) - (c + di) = (a - c) + (b - d)i.$$

There is nothing fancy going on here. In each case, we are just grouping together the real and the imaginary parts of the two numbers in question. Multiplying two complex numbers is only a little bit more complicated:

$$(a + bi) \cdot (c + di) = ac + bci + adi + bdi^2 = ac + (bc + ad)i - bd.$$

Observe that this is just an application of the distributive property, closely followed by the fact that $i^2 = -1$. Collecting the real and imaginary parts together then gives:

$$(a + bi) \cdot (c + di) = (ac - bd) + (bc + ad)i.$$

Finally, when dividing two complex numbers, as in the fraction

$$\frac{a + bi}{c + di},$$

we shall first multiply both the numerator and the denominator by $c - di$. This new complex number is almost identical to the original denominator, except that the sign of the imaginary part was changed from positive to negative, or vice versa. It is called the **complex conjugate** of the denominator. Carrying through with this multiplication does not change the value our fraction, since it amounts to multiplying by one; nevertheless it does alter its appearance to a more manageable form:

$$\frac{a + bi}{c + di} = \frac{(a + bi) \cdot (c - di)}{(c + di) \cdot (c - di)} = \frac{ac + bci - adi - bdi^2}{c^2 + dci - cdi - d^2i^2} = \frac{(ac + bd) + (bc - ad)i}{c^2 + d^2}.$$

In particular, since $c^2 + d^2$ is real, all we need to do now is separate the real part from the imaginary part, as follows:

$$\frac{a + bi}{c + di} = \frac{ac + bd}{c^2 + d^2} + \frac{bc - ad}{c^2 + d^2}i.$$

With these definitions in place, the associative, commutative, and distributive properties are at our complex numerical beck and call. Of course, we ought not *memorize* these formulas, but rather *understand* how to reproduce them when the need arises.

EXAMPLE 5.1. Consider the complex numbers $z = -2 + 2i$ and $w = 3 + i$. According to the arithmetic operations defined above, we have:

$$z + w = (-2 + 2i) + (3 + i) = -2 + 3 + 2i + i = 1 + 3i,$$

$$z - w = (-2 + 2i) - (3 + i) = -2 - 3 + 2i - i = -5 + i,$$

$$z \cdot w = (-2 + 2i) \cdot (3 + i) = -6 + -2i + 6i + 2i^2 = -8 + 4i,$$

$$\frac{z}{w} = \frac{-2 + 2i}{3 + i} \cdot \frac{3 - i}{3 - i} = \frac{-6 + 2i + 6i - 2i^2}{9 + 3i - 3i - i^2} = \frac{-4 + 8i}{10} = -\frac{2}{5} + \frac{4}{5}i.$$

EXAMPLE 5.2. Remember that, by definition, $i^2 = -1$. This means that

$$i^3 = (i \cdot i) \cdot (i) = (-1) \cdot (i) = -i,$$

$$i^4 = (i \cdot i) \cdot (i \cdot i) = (-1) \cdot (-1) = 1,$$

$$i^5 = (i \cdot i \cdot i \cdot i) \cdot (i) = (1) \cdot (i) = i,$$

$$i^6 = (i \cdot i \cdot i \cdot i) \cdot (i \cdot i) = (1) \cdot (-1) = -1,$$

$$i^7 = (i \cdot i \cdot i \cdot i) \cdot (i \cdot i \cdot i) = (1) \cdot (-i) = -i,$$

$$i^8 = (i \cdot i \cdot i \cdot i) \cdot (i \cdot i \cdot i \cdot i) = (1) \cdot (1) = 1,$$

$$i^9 = (i \cdot i \cdot i \cdot i) \cdot (i \cdot i \cdot i \cdot i) \cdot (i) = (1) \cdot (1) \cdot (i) = i,$$

and so on. Notice that by continuing in this fashion, we can simplify any power of i by simply "peeling off" as many factors of $i^4 = 1$ as we can, until we get down to 1, i, i^2, or i^3. Of course, this amounts to just finding the remainder when the exponent is divided by 4. For instance, consider raising i to the historically significant 1492nd, 1621st, and 1775th powers. Dividing each of these powers by 4 produces remainders of 0, 1, and 3, respectively:

$$1492 \div 4 = 373 \qquad \Rightarrow \qquad 1492 = 4 \cdot 373 + 0,$$

$$1621 \div 4 = 405.25 \qquad \Rightarrow \qquad 1621 = 4 \cdot 405 + 1,$$

$$1775 \div 4 = 443.75 \qquad \Rightarrow \qquad 1775 = 4 \cdot 443 + 3.$$

Therefore, we can simplify each power of i as follows:

$$i^{1492} = i^{(4 \cdot 373 + 0)} = \left(i^4\right)^{373} \cdot i^0 = (1)^{373} \cdot i^0 = i^0 = 1,$$

$$i^{1621} = i^{(4 \cdot 405 + 1)} = \left(i^4\right)^{405} \cdot i^1 = (1)^{405} \cdot i^1 = i^1 = i,$$

$$i^{1963} = i^{(4 \cdot 490 + 3)} = \left(i^4\right)^{490} \cdot i^3 = (1)^{490} \cdot i^3 = i^3 = -i.$$

EXAMPLE 5.3. Since arithmetic in the complex numbers obeys the usual properties of arithmetic, we can proceed with any computation as if our imaginary unit i were simply an unknown like x or y, and only later worry about the fact that $i^2 = -1$. In particular, this means that we are allowed to use all of our notable formulas from Theorem 1.1 in page 25. For instance, adapting the perfect square formulas (1.3) and (1.4) to complex numbers, we have:

$$\left(\tfrac{\sqrt{2}}{2} + \tfrac{\sqrt{2}}{2}\,i\right)^2 = \left(\tfrac{\sqrt{2}}{2}\right)^2 + 2\left(\tfrac{\sqrt{2}}{2}\right)\left(\tfrac{\sqrt{2}}{2}\,i\right) + \left(\tfrac{\sqrt{2}}{2}\,i\right)^2$$
$$= \tfrac{1}{2} + i + \tfrac{1}{2}\,i^2$$
$$= \tfrac{1}{2} + i - \tfrac{1}{2} = i,$$

$$\left(-\tfrac{\sqrt{2}}{2} + \tfrac{\sqrt{2}}{2}\,i\right)^2 = \left(-\tfrac{\sqrt{2}}{2}\right)^2 + 2\left(-\tfrac{\sqrt{2}}{2}\right)\left(\tfrac{\sqrt{2}}{2}\,i\right) + \left(\tfrac{\sqrt{2}}{2}\,i\right)^2$$
$$= \tfrac{1}{2} - i + \tfrac{1}{2}\,i^2$$
$$= \tfrac{1}{2} - i - \tfrac{1}{2} = -i,$$

$$\left(-\tfrac{\sqrt{2}}{2} - \tfrac{\sqrt{2}}{2}\,i\right)^2 = \left(-\tfrac{\sqrt{2}}{2}\right)^2 + 2\left(-\tfrac{\sqrt{2}}{2}\right)\left(-\tfrac{\sqrt{2}}{2}\,i\right) + \left(-\tfrac{\sqrt{2}}{2}\,i\right)^2$$
$$= \tfrac{1}{2} + i + \tfrac{1}{2}\,i^2$$
$$= \tfrac{1}{2} + i - \tfrac{1}{2} = i,$$

$$\left(\tfrac{\sqrt{2}}{2} - \tfrac{\sqrt{2}}{2}\,i\right)^2 = \left(\tfrac{\sqrt{2}}{2}\right)^2 + 2\left(\tfrac{\sqrt{2}}{2}\right)\left(-\tfrac{\sqrt{2}}{2}\,i\right) + \left(-\tfrac{\sqrt{2}}{2}\,i\right)^2$$
$$= \tfrac{1}{2} - i + \tfrac{1}{2}\,i^2$$
$$= \tfrac{1}{2} - i - \tfrac{1}{2} = -i.$$

These computations show that i has two square roots:

$$\tfrac{\sqrt{2}}{2} + \tfrac{\sqrt{2}}{2}\,i \qquad \text{and} \qquad -\tfrac{\sqrt{2}}{2} - \tfrac{\sqrt{2}}{2}\,i.$$

By the same token, $-i$ also has two square roots:

$$\tfrac{\sqrt{2}}{2} - \tfrac{\sqrt{2}}{2}\,i \qquad \text{and} \qquad -\tfrac{\sqrt{2}}{2} + \tfrac{\sqrt{2}}{2}\,i.$$

It should not come as a surprise that the square roots come in pairs, or that in each case they are negatives of one another.

EXAMPLE 5.4. As with real numbers, we compute powers of any complex number simply by repeated multiplication. Thus,

$$(1+i)^3 = (1+i) \cdot (1+i) \cdot (1+i)$$

$$= (1+i) \cdot (1 + 2i + i^2)$$

$$= (1+i) \cdot 2i$$

$$= 2i + 2i^2 = 2i - 2,$$

$$(1-i)^3 = (1-i) \cdot (1-i) \cdot (1-i)$$

$$= (1-i) \cdot (1 - 2i + i^2)$$

$$= (1-i) \cdot (-2i)$$

$$= -2i + 2i^2 = -2i - 2.$$

Notice that this means that $1+i$ and $1-i$ are cube roots of $-2+2i$ and $-2-2i$, respectively.

EXAMPLE 5.5. According to Example 5.2, $-i$ is a cube root of i, since

$$(-i)^3 = (i^3)^3 = i^9 = i.$$

However, this is not the only cube root of i. To see this, consider the following computations:

$$\left(\tfrac{\sqrt{3}}{2} + \tfrac{1}{2}i\right)^3 = \left(\tfrac{\sqrt{3}}{2} + \tfrac{1}{2}i\right) \cdot \left(\tfrac{\sqrt{3}}{2} + \tfrac{1}{2}i\right) \cdot \left(\tfrac{\sqrt{3}}{2} + \tfrac{1}{2}i\right)$$

$$= \left(\tfrac{\sqrt{3}}{2} + \tfrac{1}{2}i\right) \cdot \left(\tfrac{3}{4} + \tfrac{\sqrt{3}}{2}i + \tfrac{1}{4}i^2\right)$$

$$= \left(\tfrac{\sqrt{3}}{2} + \tfrac{1}{2}i\right) \cdot \left(\tfrac{1}{2} + \tfrac{\sqrt{3}}{2}i\right)$$

$$= \tfrac{\sqrt{3}}{4} + \left(\tfrac{3}{4} + \tfrac{1}{4}\right)i + \tfrac{\sqrt{3}}{4}i^2 = i,$$

$$\left(-\tfrac{\sqrt{3}}{2} + \tfrac{1}{2}i\right)^3 = \left(-\tfrac{\sqrt{3}}{2} + \tfrac{1}{2}i\right) \cdot \left(-\tfrac{\sqrt{3}}{2} + \tfrac{1}{2}i\right) \cdot \left(-\tfrac{\sqrt{3}}{2} + \tfrac{1}{2}i\right)$$

$$= \left(-\tfrac{\sqrt{3}}{2} + \tfrac{1}{2}i\right) \cdot \left(\tfrac{3}{4} - \tfrac{\sqrt{3}}{2}i + \tfrac{1}{4}i^2\right)$$

$$= \left(-\tfrac{\sqrt{3}}{2} + \tfrac{1}{2}i\right) \cdot \left(\tfrac{1}{2} - \tfrac{\sqrt{3}}{2}i\right)$$

$$= -\tfrac{\sqrt{3}}{4} + \left(\tfrac{3}{4} + \tfrac{1}{4}\right)i - \tfrac{\sqrt{3}}{4}i^2 = i.$$

These calculations show that i has *three* different cube roots. As we shall soon see, this behavior is typical of all non-zero complex numbers!

EXAMPLE 5.6. Consider the following equation:

$$5z - i = (4 - i)z + 3.$$

This is a simple linear equation, just like the ones we studied back in Section 1.2, except that here we will allow both the coefficients and the unknown to be complex numbers. This distinction is brought home by the fact that we are now using the letter z, instead of the familiar x, to denote our unknown. Aside from that, however, there is really nothing new going on here.

Suppose that we wish to solve this equation for the unknown z. Since it appears on both sides of the equation, we will begin by first moving all of the unknowns to one side of the equation and all of the constants to the other:

$$5z - (4 - i)z = 3 + i$$

After collecting like terms, this simplifies to

$$\big(5 - (4 - i)\big)z = 3 + i,$$

or better yet, to

$$(1 + i)z = 3 + i.$$

Our one and only solution is then found by dividing both sides of the equation by $1 + i$ as follows:

$$z = \frac{3 + i}{1 + i} = \frac{3 + i}{1 + i} \cdot \frac{1 - i}{1 - i} = \frac{3 - 2i - i^2}{1 - i^2} = \frac{4 - 2i}{2} = 2 - i.$$

EXAMPLE 5.7. Suppose that we wish to solve the equation

$$z^2 + 5 = 4z,$$

again, assuming that z can be any complex number. Then we can proceed in the usual way, first setting one side equal to zero,

$$z^2 - 4z + 5 = 0,$$

and then recalling the quadratic formula:

$$z = \frac{4 \pm \sqrt{4^2 - 4 \cdot 1 \cdot 5}}{2} = \frac{4 \pm \sqrt{16 - 20}}{2} = \frac{4 \pm \sqrt{-4}}{2}.$$

Observe that our discriminant turned out to be negative. If were restricted to only thinking about real numbers, that would be the end of the road. There would be no solution. We would not pass "Go." We would not collect $200. However, since we are thinking of z as a complex number, we can continue without much difficulty. In particular, our equation has two solutions:

$$z = \frac{4 \pm \sqrt{-4}}{2} = \frac{4 \pm 2i}{2} = 2 \pm i.$$

EXAMPLE 5.8. Find the complex solutions to the equation

$$z^2 - 9\,i\,z - 20 = 0.$$

Solution. This is a quadratic equation with complex coefficients, so we shall once again use the quadratic equation, this time with $a = 1$, $b = -9\,i$, and $c = -20$:

$$z = \frac{9\,i \pm \sqrt{(-9\,i)^2 + 4 \cdot 1 \cdot 20}}{2} = \frac{9\,i \pm \sqrt{-81 + 80}}{2} = \frac{9\,i \pm \sqrt{-1}}{2} = \frac{9\,i \pm i}{2}$$

Evidently, our two solutions are $z = \frac{1}{2}(9\,i + i) = 5\,i$ and $z = \frac{1}{2}(9\,i - i) = 4\,i$, as you can verify by substituting back into our equation.

EXAMPLE 5.9. Now that we have gone through some of the rules of arithmetic that hold for complex numbers, we should point out one that does not hold. As we saw in Example 1.39 on page 60, the square root of the product of two positive real numbers is equal to the product of the square roots of the two numbers:

$$\sqrt{a \cdot b} = \sqrt{a} \cdot \sqrt{b}.$$

This is *not* the case when we are dealing with complex numbers. To see why not, consider the following fallacious "proof" that negative one is equal to positive one:

$$-1 = \sqrt{-1} \cdot \sqrt{-1} = \sqrt{(-1) \cdot (-1)} = \sqrt{1} = 1.$$

In order to understand what went wrong with this computation, we need to recall what we meant by the symbol $\sqrt{x}$ in the first place. As we noted in Section 1.4, every positive real number x has a positive square root as well as a negative square root. We defined $\sqrt{x}$ to be the positive one of these roots. Now that we are dealing with complex numbers, we will find that, once again, every non-zero complex number has two distinct square roots. For instance, as we saw in Example 5.3, both

$$\frac{\sqrt{2}}{2} - \frac{\sqrt{2}}{2}\,i \qquad \text{and} \qquad -\frac{\sqrt{2}}{2} + \frac{\sqrt{2}}{2}\,i$$

are square roots of $-i$. As expected, these are opposites of one another. The problem is that neither of these is positive and neither of these is negative, so there does not appear to be a reasonable way to choose which one of these should be declared *the* square root $\sqrt{-i}$. In this case, both roots seem to share an equal claim to this symbol!

Indeed, one could go as far as to claim that the square roots of a positive real number are like a pair of shoes, which we can easily distinguish as either left or right (or positive and negative). On the other hand, or should we say foot, the square roots of a complex number are like a pair of socks, in which case left and right is an arbitrary distinction.

Coming back to the alleged proof above, let us reconsider the meaning of $\sqrt{-1} \cdot \sqrt{-1}$. On the one hand, we would certainly be correct in saying that

$$\sqrt{-1} \cdot \sqrt{-1} = i \cdot i = -1.$$

Here, of course, we are letting the symbol $\sqrt{-1}$ stand for the number i. However, we could just as easily take $\sqrt{-1}$ to mean $-i$, in which case we would have

$$\sqrt{-1} \cdot \sqrt{-1} = (-i) \cdot (-i) = -1.$$

Again, no problem. However, suppose that we let the first instance of $\sqrt{-1}$ stand for $-i$, while at the same time, we let the second instance of $\sqrt{-1}$ stand for i. We would then have

$$\sqrt{-1} \cdot \sqrt{-1} = -i \cdot i = 1.$$

This is precisely what the second half of our so-called proof says. The problem is that we changed the meaning of $\sqrt{-1}$ halfway through the equation. The moral to be learned from all this is that, at least for the time being, complex roots are not to be trusted. Be careful in your dealings with them!

Mathematics students often feel some amount of apprehension when they first encounter complex numbers, and justifiably so! Computations like the one we just saw should remind us to proceed with caution when we toss i into our calculations. Furthermore, the idea that we can work with an "imaginary" square root of minus one goes against all of our previous training. Even if you can accept the fact that i is some sort of symbolic object which you can manipulate by following some well-prescribed set of rules, that still does not answer the question of how an abstract object can be of any use in solving concrete, real-world problems.

As it turns out, complex numbers *have* proven themselves extremely useful in providing real solutions to real problems over the years. For instance, let us once again consider Cardano's troublesome depressed cubic:

$$x^3 - 6x + 4 = 0.$$

As we noted earlier, del Ferro's formula produces the strange solution

$$x = \sqrt[3]{-2 + \sqrt{-4}} + \sqrt[3]{-2 - \sqrt{-4}}.$$

Because he was only familiar with the real numbers, this is as far as Cardano could go. However, after introducing complex numbers, Bombelli could rewrite this solution as

$$x = \sqrt[3]{-2 + 2i} + \sqrt[3]{-2 - 2i}.$$

Now, in Example 5.4, we found that $(1+i)^3 = -2+2i$ and that $(1-i)^3 = -2-2i$. Therefore, using $1+i$ and $1-i$ as the desired cube roots, we arrive at the solution

$$x = (1+i) + (1-i) = 2.$$

And, indeed, despite its unusual genesis, $x = 2$ is a real solution to Cardano's cubic:

$$x = 2 \quad \Rightarrow \quad x^3 - 6x + 4 = 2^3 - 6 \cdot 2 + 4 = 8 - 12 + 4 = 0.$$

However, that is not the end of the story. As we asserted in Example 5.5, every non-zero complex number has *three* distinct cube roots. In particular,

$$\left(1 + i\right)^3 = -2 + 2\,i, \qquad\qquad \left(1 - i\right)^3 = -2 - 2\,i,$$

$$\left(\tfrac{-1-\sqrt{3}}{2} + \tfrac{-1+\sqrt{3}}{2}\,i\right)^3 = -2 + 2\,i, \qquad \left(\tfrac{-1-\sqrt{3}}{2} + \tfrac{1-\sqrt{3}}{2}\,i\right)^3 = -2 - 2\,i,$$

$$\left(\tfrac{-1+\sqrt{3}}{2} + \tfrac{-1-\sqrt{3}}{2}\,i\right)^3 = -2 + 2\,i, \qquad \left(\tfrac{-1+\sqrt{3}}{2} + \tfrac{1+\sqrt{3}}{2}\,i\right)^3 = -2 - 2\,i,$$

as you can verify for yourself. The solution $x = 2$ came from substituting the first pair of cube roots in this list into del Ferro's formula. If we use the other two pairs of cube roots, we can find two more solutions to our cubic equation:

$$x = \left(\tfrac{-1-\sqrt{3}}{2} + \tfrac{-1+\sqrt{3}}{2}\,i\right) + \left(\tfrac{-1-\sqrt{3}}{2} + \tfrac{1-\sqrt{3}}{2}\,i\right) = -1 - \sqrt{3} = -2.732\,050\,807\ldots$$

and

$$x = \left(\tfrac{-1+\sqrt{3}}{2} + \tfrac{-1-\sqrt{3}}{2}\,i\right) + \left(\tfrac{-1+\sqrt{3}}{2} + \tfrac{1+\sqrt{3}}{2}\,i\right) = -1 + \sqrt{3} = 0.732\,050\,807\ldots.$$

As was the case with $x = 2$, these are perfectly acceptable *real number* solutions to Cardano's cubic equation. The only thing unusual about them is that they were conjured up out of the shadows by means of the mysterious alchemy of the complex numbers.

Reading Comprehension Questions for Section 5.1

A complex number is an expression of the form $z = a + bi$, where i is the ___(a)___.
Since the square of any real number is ___(b)___ zero, i is not a real number. Historically, i was said to be ___(c)___ or ___(d)___, but this does not mean that it is a
product of someone's imagination. Instead, i is a valid symbolic object that allows
us to answer concrete, real-world problems like solving depressed ___(e)___ equations.

The expression $z = a + bi$ is known as the ___(f)___ form of the complex number z.
In this case, a and b are real numbers; the first is known as the ___(g)___ of z, while the
second is known as the ___(h)___ of z. We sometimes use the notations ___(i)___ and
___(j)___ to refer to these numbers. Every real number is a complex number whose
___(k)___ is equal to zero. In contrast, any complex number that has a real part equal
to zero is said to be ___(l)___.

Arithmetic in the complex numbers is defined to be compatible with the familiar
___(m)___, ___(n)___, and ___(o)___ properties of the real numbers. This means that,
in order to add or subtract two complex numbers, we simply add or subtract their
corresponding ___(p)___ and ___(q)___ parts. On the other hand, multiplying and
dividing complex numbers is a little more complicated. If $z = a + bi$ and $w = c + di$, then their product is $z \cdot w = $ ___(r)___ $+ $ ___(s)___ i, while their quotient is
$z/w = $ ___(t)___ $+$ ___(u)___ i. The latter is found by first multiplying z and w times the
complex number ___(v)___, which is known as the ___(w)___ of w.

One interesting property of the complex numbers is that $i^4 = $ ___(x)___. This
means that the powers of i cycle through the four values 1, i, -1, and $-i$ over
and over again. Thus, to determine the value of i^{1849}, all we need to do is divide
the exponent by four. This gives a remainder of ___(y)___, which then tells us that
$i^{1849} = $ ___(z)___. Unfortunately, this convenient shortcut only works for powers of i!

Exercises for Section 5.1

In Exercises 1–10, write each complex number in the rectangular form $a + bi$.

1. $(2 - 3i) + (6 + 8i)$

2. $(3 - 2i) - (4 - 4i)$

3. $(2 + 4i) \cdot (3 + 2i)$

4. $(1 - 3i) \cdot (1 + 3i)$

5. $\dfrac{10}{3 + 4i}$

6. $\dfrac{13i}{12 + 5i}$

7. $\dfrac{24 + 7i}{4 - 3i}$

8. $\dfrac{7 + 3i}{1 - i}$

9. $i^{1066} + i^{1776} + i^{1863}$

10. $(\sqrt{3} + i)^6$

In Exercises 11–25, find all of the complex solutions for each equation. Express your answers in the rectangular form $a + bi$.

11. $z + 2 - 3i = 0$

12. $z - 7 + i = 0$

13. $(2 + 2i)z = 0$

14. $(\sqrt{3} - i)z = 4$

15. $(5 + 12i)z = 169i$

16. $4z - 1 - i = 0$

17. $-5z + 7 + i = 0$

18. $-iz - 2 = 0$

19. $3iz + 6i = 0$

20. $(-1 - i)z + (5 - 4i) = 0$

21. $z^2 - 4z + 13 = 0$

22. $z^2 + 2z + 5 = 0$

23. $2z^2 - 4z + 1 = 0$

24. $9z^2 + 12z + 5 = 0$

25. $13z^2 + 6z + 1 = 0$

26. $8z^2 - 4z + 1 = 0$

27. Obtuse Ollie is trying to find all the solutions to the depressed cubic equation
$$z^3 - 9z - 28 = 0,$$
by first factoring the left hand side as follows:
$$z^3 - 9z - 28 = (z - 4)(z^2 + Az + B).$$

   (a) Determine the values of the constants A and B.

   (b) Use Ollie's factorization to find all complex solutions for the equation above.

   (c) How many of these complex solutions are real?

28. Acute Alice is trying to verify that the complex number

$$z = \frac{-1-\sqrt{3}}{2} + \frac{-1+\sqrt{3}}{2}\, i$$

is a cube root of $-2 + 2i$. She begins by using the results of Example 4.14 (see page 358) to rewrite z in terms of the sine and cosine of $\frac{\pi}{12}$ as follows:

$$z = -\sqrt{2}\cos\left(\tfrac{\pi}{12}\right) + \sqrt{2}\sin\left(\tfrac{\pi}{12}\right) i.$$

(a) Verify that Alice is correct in her assertion.

(b) Express z^2 in the rectangular form $a + bi$ in terms of the sine and cosine of $\frac{\pi}{12}$. Then use the angle sum identities to rewrite this expression in terms of the sine and cosine of $\frac{\pi}{6}$.

(c) Use the angle sum identities a second time to express z^3 in terms of the sine and cosine of $\frac{\pi}{4}$. Then verify that this gives $-2 + 2i$.

29. Scalene Sallie is trying to find the square root of $7 + 24i$ by using the Babylonian algorithm. She starts with an initial guess of $y_1 = 1$ and proceeds to complete the first row of the following table:

n	y_n	$\dfrac{7+24i}{y_n}$	$\dfrac{1}{2}\left(y_n + \dfrac{7+24i}{y_n}\right)$
1	1	$7 + 24i$	$4 + 12i$
2	$4 + 12i$		
3			
4			
5			

(a) Complete the table above. You may use a calculator or computer to round the real and imaginary parts of each number in the table to the nearest hundredth.

(b) What complex number do Sallie's approximations appear to be approaching?

(c) Verify that your answer to (b) really is a square root of $7 + 24i$.

30. (a) Verify that the product of the conjugates of two complex numbers is equal to the conjugate of the product of the two numbers. In other words, show that the following complex numbers are conjugates of each other:

$$(a - bi)\cdot(c - di) \qquad \text{and} \qquad (a + bi)\cdot(c + di).$$

(b) Verify that the quotient of the conjugates of two complex numbers is equal to the conjugate of the quotient of the two numbers. In other words, show that the following complex numbers are conjugates of each other:

$$\frac{a - bi}{c - di} \qquad \text{and} \qquad \frac{a + bi}{c + di}.$$

5.2. The Complex Plane

The greatest difficulty that seventeenth and eighteenth century mathematicians faced when working with complex numbers was that, at the time, there was no good way of visualizing the number i. Whereas the real numbers became truly "real" when viewed as points on the number line via the ruler postulate (see page 39), an equivalent geometric interpretation of the complex numbers was required before they could also be accepted as "real" entities. Finally, in 1806, a Parisian bookseller and amateur mathematician named Jean Robert Argand (1768–1822) came up with just the right idea. And there was much rejoicing. (Yay!)

What Argand, along with several others, realized at the turn of the nineteenth century was that multiplication by -1 performs a $180°$ rotation of the number line about zero, as in Figure 5.1.

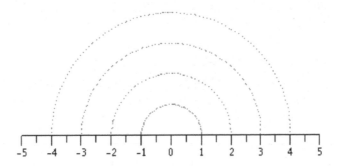

FIGURE 5.1. Multiplication by -1 as a rotation by $180°$.

Since i is a square root of -1, it stands to reason that multiplying by i should accomplish half of this rotation. In other words, multiplication by i should correspond to a $90°$ rotation. Of course, performing a $90°$ rotation does not make sense in the number line, but it does in a plane, as shown in Figure 5.2.

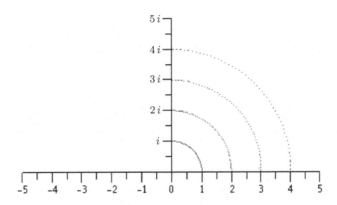

FIGURE 5.2. Multiplication by i as a rotation by $90°$.

403

Argand proposed that the usual real number line be identified with the x-axis in the Cartesian plane. Furthermore, since a 90° rotation about the origin takes the x-axis to the y-axis, the y-axis should represent the set of purely imaginary numbers, each of which is the product of a real number times i. In particular, Argand let the point $(1, 0)$ on the x-axis correspond to the number 1. A 90° counterclockwise rotation about the origin will take this point to $(0, 1)$, which Argand identified with the number i. With these two points as his frame of reference, Argand could then view any complex number $a + b\,i$ as the point (a, b) on the Cartesian plane:

$$a + b\,i \quad \leftrightarrow \quad (a, b)$$

The beauty of Argand's idea shines through in the way that arithmetic notions in the complex numbers appear as simple geometric notions in the Cartesian plane. For example, complex conjugation, in which the imaginary part of a complex number $a + b\,i$ changes sign to form $a - b\,i$, simply corresponds to a vertical reflection across the x-axis. Nevertheless, this new geometric representation of the complex numbers was not without its detractors, and it soon caused a minor controversy in the pages of the mathematical journals of the day. Some mathematicians like François Joseph Servois (1768–1847) argued vigorously against it, warning that the complex numbers could only be safely handled by using pure algebra. In the end, however, Argand and his supporters won the day, and the set $\mathbb{C}$ of complex numbers, now interpreted geometrically as a plane, became known as the ***complex plane***. Adopting this point of view, instead of referring to the x- and y-axes, we shall now talk about the ***real*** and ***imaginary axes***, respectively.

EXAMPLE 5.10. In the complex plane, the number $z = 4 + 3\,i$ corresponds to the point $P = (4, 3)$, while $z \cdot i = (4 + 3\,i) \cdot i = -3 + 4\,i$ corresponds to the point $Q = (-3, 4)$:

$$z = 4 + 3\,i \quad \leftrightarrow \quad P = (4, 3)$$

$$z \cdot i = -3 + 4\,i \quad \leftrightarrow \quad Q = (-3, 4)$$

Now, according to the distance formula, both of these points are 5 units away from the origin:

$$d_{OP} = \sqrt{(4 - 0)^2 + (3 - 0)^2} = \sqrt{16 + 9} = \sqrt{25} = 5,$$

$$d_{OQ} = \sqrt{(-3 - 0)^2 + (4 - 0)^2} = \sqrt{9 + 16} = \sqrt{25} = 5.$$

Furthermore, the distance between P and Q is

$$d_{PQ} = \sqrt{(-3 - 4)^2 + (4 - 3)^2} = \sqrt{49 + 1} = \sqrt{50} = 5\sqrt{2}.$$

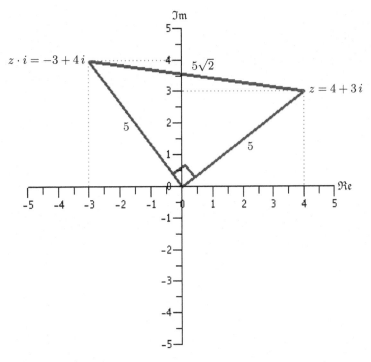

FIGURE 5.3. Multiplication by i is a rotation by $90°$.

This means that P and Q, together with the origin, form a 45-90-45 right triangle, as indicated in Figure 5.3. Of course, this is precisely what we would expect should happen if multiplying by i were indeed to rotate the complex plane by an angle of $90°$ about the origin.

As we spend more and more time exploring the complex plane, we will let the distinction between complex numbers and their corresponding points on the Cartesian plane fade into the background. We shall casually refer to the *points* in the complex plane as real or purely imaginary or complex *numbers*, and let the words *origin* and *zero* become completely interchangeable. For instance, as we look back to the example above, we might say that the complex numbers $3 + 4i$ and $-4 + 3i$ are a distance of $5\sqrt{2}$ units apart, even though this statement is technically only true for the points that represent these complex numbers.

Pushing our linguistic limits even further, we will define the ***absolute value*** of a complex number to be the distance between that complex number and the origin. A simple application of the distance formula then gives the absolute value of a complex number as the square root of the sum of its real and imaginary parts squared:

$$\boxed{\left| a + b\,i \right| = \sqrt{a^2 + b^2}.}$$

In the special case of a real number, for which the imaginary part $b = 0$ vanishes, this expression becomes

$$\left|a + 0\,i\right| = \sqrt{a^2 + 0^2} = \sqrt{a^2} = |a|,$$

which, thanks to the curious formula from Example 1.47 on page 65, agrees with our familiar notion of the absolute value of a real number.

EXAMPLE 5.11. Consider the complex numbers $z = -2 + 2\,i$ and $w = 3 + i$. We compute the absolute value of each of these numbers by squaring their real and imaginary parts separately, adding these together, and then taking the square root of the sum:

$$|z| = |-2 + 2\,i| = \sqrt{(-2)^2 + 2^2} = \sqrt{4 + 4} = \sqrt{8} = 2\sqrt{2},$$
$$|w| = |3 + i| = \sqrt{3^2 + 1^2} = \sqrt{9 + 1} = \sqrt{10}.$$

As you might suspect, $\mathbb{C}$ suffers from a slight case of multiple-personality disorder. On the one hand, it is a set of numbers which can be added and multiplied together. On the other hand, it is a copy of the Cartesian plane. Our goal now is to understand how these two different personalities interact with one another. We shall achieve this goal by observing the way in which various linear functions $f : \mathbb{C} \to \mathbb{C}$ affect the complex plane.

EXAMPLE 5.12. Consider the linear function

$$f(z) = z + (3 + i),$$

in which the complex number $3 + i$ is added to the input z, which again is an arbitrary complex number. By evaluating f at several key input values, we arrive at the following five output values, which we have arranged suggestively in the shape of a plus sign:

$$f(i) = 3 + 2\,i$$
$$f(-1) = 2 + i \qquad f(0) = 3 + i \qquad f(1) = 4 + i$$
$$f(-i) = 3$$

These five values, which we plot in Figure 5.4 (a), will serve as a sort of "mathematical crosshairs" that will help us gauge how the function f is affecting the complex plane. As you will observe, the output values in the horizontal piece of the crosshairs (those corresponding to input values of 1, 0, and -1) all have the same imaginary part, so they fall on a single horizontal line in the complex plane. In fact, this function maps the entire real axis to this horizontal line, since the image of any real number will turn out to be a complex number with an imaginary part equal to 1. On the other hand, the output values in the vertical part of our crosshairs (those corresponding to inputs of i, 0, and $-i$) all have the same real part of 3, and therefore fall on a single vertical line. Again, the same is true for any purely imaginary

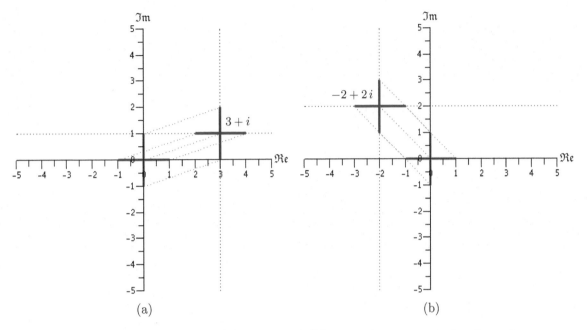

FIGURE 5.4. Effects of adding (a) $3 + i$ and (b) $-2 + 2i$, respectively. In each case, the addition causes a translation of the complex plane.

number, so f maps the entire imaginary axis to this vertical line. Evidently, our function translated our crosshairs (and with it, the entire complex plane) three units to the right and one unit up.

EXAMPLE 5.13. Consider the linear function

$$f(z) = z + (-2 + 2i),$$

which adds the complex number $-2 + 2i$ to its complex input z. As before, we evaluate f at a few choice input values, obtaining the following crosshairs of output values:

$$f(i) = -2 + 3i$$

$$f(-1) = -3 + 2i \qquad f(0) = -2 + 2i \qquad f(1) = -1 + 2i$$

$$f(-i) = -2 + i$$

Observe that f maps any real input to an output value with an imaginary part equal to 2, like those in the horizontal piece of the crosshairs above. Similarly, purely imaginary inputs are mapped to output values with a real part of -2, such as those in the vertical piece of the crosshairs. Therefore, the images of the real and imaginary axes form a horizontal and a vertical line, respectively, as shown in Figure 5.4 (b). In particular, our crosshairs allow us to see how the function translated the complex plane two units to the left and two units up.

As the last two examples suggest, adding a complex number corresponds to a **translation** of the complex plane. This is perfectly consistent with our original definition of addition from Section 5.1: When we add two complex numbers, we add their real and imaginary parts separately. Thus, when adding $a + b\,i$ to an arbitrary complex number, we will increase its real part (in other words, its x-coordinate) by a, while we increase its imaginary part (its y-coordinate) by b. It is precisely these increments that cause the observed translation (a units to the right and b units up) of the complex plane.

EXAMPLE 5.14. Consider the linear function

$$f(z) = (-2 + 2\,i) \cdot z,$$

which multiplies its complex input z times the complex number $-2 + 2\,i$. Evaluating f at several key points yields the following crosshairs values:

$$f(i) = -2 - 2\,i$$

$$f(-1) = 2 - 2\,i \qquad f(0) = 0 \qquad f(1) = -2 + 2\,i$$

$$f(-i) = 2 + 2\,i$$

We plot these values in Figure 5.5 (a), observing that, although f still maps the real and imaginary axes to straight lines, these lines are no longer horizontal or vertical. In fact, f maps our original crosshairs of input values about the origin to a much larger, tilted crosshairs of output values. Whereas one of the arms of the original crosshairs, say the one between 0 and 1, was one unit long, the corresponding arm of the tilted crosshairs goes between 0 and $-2 + 2\,i$, and therefore measures

$$\left| -2 + 2\,i \right| = 2\sqrt{2}.$$

Indeed, f has rotated the entire complex plane counterclockwise by an angle of $\frac{3\pi}{4}$ radians (or 135°), all while dilating it radially (that is to say, in all directions) away from the origin by a factor of $2\sqrt{2}$.

EXAMPLE 5.15. Consider the linear function

$$f(z) = (3 + i) \cdot z,$$

which multiplies its complex input z times the complex number $3 + i$. As before, a few computations reveal the following output data, arranged as before in the shape of a crosshairs:

$$f(i) = -1 + 3\,i$$

$$f(-1) = -3 - i \qquad f(0) = 0 \qquad f(1) = 3 + i$$

$$f(-i) = 1 - 3\,i$$

We plot these values in Figure 5.5 (b), observing that f is again rotating and dilating the crosshairs, and with them, the entire complex plane. This time,

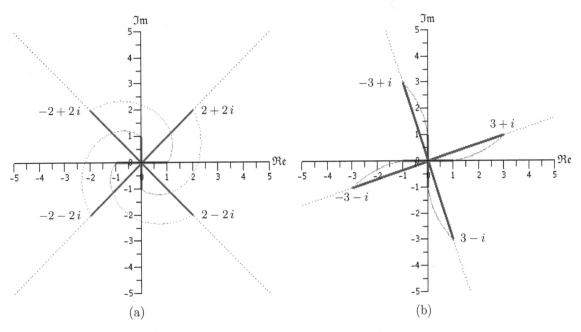

FIGURE 5.5. Effects of multiplying by (a) $-2 + 2i$ and (b) $3 + i$, respectively. In each case, the multiplication causes the complex plane to rotate and to dilate radially away from the origin.

the arm of the crosshairs connecting 0 and 1 is mapped to the hypotenuse of a right triangle with a base of 3 and a height of 1. (You can see this triangle if you draw a vertical line connecting the point $3 + i$ to the x-axis.) Therefore, the dilation factor in this case is

$$|3 + i| = \sqrt{10},$$

while the angle of rotation is given by

$$\arctan\left(\tfrac{1}{3}\right) \approx 0.562 \text{ radians},$$

or about $32.175°$.

As we see in the last two examples, multiplication by a complex number causes a **_radial dilation_** away from (or perhaps towards) the origin. The dilation factor in question is given by the absolute value of the number by which we multiply. In particular, a straight-forward algebraic manipulation shows that the absolute value of a product is equal to the product of the respective absolute values:

$$\big|(a + bi) \cdot (c + di)\big| = \big|a + bi\big| \cdot \big|c + di\big|.$$

Therefore, multiplication by $a + bi$ maps each point on the complex plane to a location $|a + bi|$ times farther away from the origin than it originally was. If this dilation factor is greater than one, then the complex plane will expand away from the origin; if it is less than one, then the plane will contract towards the origin. In either case, the origin is the only point on the plane that remains fixed in place.

Multiplication by a complex number also causes a **_rotation_** of the complex plane. The angle of rotation can be found from the position of the complex number by using a little trigonometry. However, it is somewhat more complicated to express in general, if only because it depends on whether the real part of the number in question is positive, negative, or zero. In particular, if $a > 0$, then the complex number $a + bi$ lives on either the first or fourth quadrants. In this case, multiplication by $a + bi$ rotates the complex plane by an angle of $\theta = \arctan\left(\frac{b}{a}\right)$. On the other hand, if $a < 0$, then the point $a + bi$ lives on either the second or third quadrants; this makes the angle of rotation equal to $\theta = \arctan\left(\frac{b}{a}\right) + \pi$. Finally, if $a = 0$, then $a + bi$ is purely imaginary and the angle of rotation is $\theta = \pm\frac{\pi}{2}$, depending on whether b is positive or negative. Therefore, we can express the angle of rotation by the piecewise function

$$\theta = \begin{cases} \arctan\left(\frac{b}{a}\right) & \text{if } a > 0, \\ \arctan\left(\frac{b}{a}\right) + \pi & \text{if } a < 0, \\ \frac{\pi}{2} & \text{if } a = 0 \text{ and } b > 0, \\ -\frac{\pi}{2} & \text{if } a = 0 \text{ and } b < 0. \end{cases}$$

EXAMPLE 5.16. We can consider the linear function

$$f(z) = (-3 - 4i) \cdot z + (1 + 2i)$$

as a composition of two simpler functions: one which multiplies the input z by the "slope" of $-3 - 4i$, followed by one which adds the "y-intercept" of $1 + 2i$ to this product. To begin with, multiplication by $-3 - 4i$ causes a radial dilation by a factor of

$$\left|-3 - 4i\right| = \sqrt{(-3)^2 + (-4)^2} = \sqrt{9 + 16} = \sqrt{25} = 5$$

as well as a rotation by an angle of

$$\theta = \arctan\left(\frac{4}{3}\right) + \pi \approx 4.069$$

or about $233.1°$. (This follows from the fact that the real part of slope in question is negative.) Then, adding $1 + 2i$ translates the plane one unit to the right and two units up. We can see the effect of these transformations when we evaluate f at our usual inputs and produce the following set of output values:

$$f(i) = 5 - i$$

$$f(-1) = 4 + 6i \qquad f(0) = 1 + 2i \qquad f(1) = -2 - 2i$$

$$f(-i) = -3 + 5i$$

We plot these values in Figure 5.6. Note that, as expected, f dilates, rotates, and translates our mathematical crosshairs as predicted above.

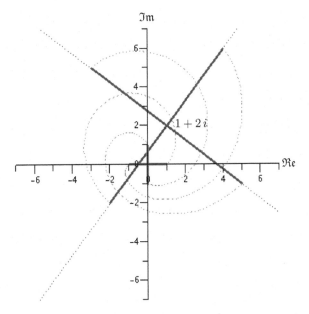

FIGURE 5.6. The function $f(z) = (-3 - 4i) \cdot z + (1 + 2i)$ rotates the complex plane clockwise by an angle of $\arctan\left(\frac{4}{3}\right) + \pi$, dilates it by a factor of 5, and translates it one unit to the right and two units up.

We shall now put our newly acquired understanding of complex multiplication to work as we determine the exact algebraic value of cosine of $\frac{\pi}{5}$ radians or 36°. You will note that we cannot use any of our trigonometric identities to write this value as a combination of the other algebraic values of sine or cosine that we know. To begin, we let $z = \cos\left(\frac{2\pi}{5}\right) + i \sin\left(\frac{2\pi}{5}\right)$ and consider the sum

$$S = 1 + z + z^2 + z^3 + z^4.$$

Notice that $|z| = 1$, so multiplication by z corresponds to a rotation by $\frac{2\pi}{5}$ radians, or one fifth of a full circle, with no dilation. Therefore, each of the terms in the sum above is the vertex of a regular pentagon inscribed in the unit circle, as shown in Figure 5.7. In particular, we have

$$z = \cos\left(\tfrac{2\pi}{5}\right) + i \sin\left(\tfrac{2\pi}{5}\right),$$

$$z^2 = \cos\left(\tfrac{4\pi}{5}\right) + i \sin\left(\tfrac{4\pi}{5}\right),$$

$$z^3 = \cos\left(\tfrac{6\pi}{5}\right) + i \sin\left(\tfrac{6\pi}{5}\right),$$

$$z^4 = \cos\left(\tfrac{8\pi}{5}\right) + i \sin\left(\tfrac{8\pi}{5}\right),$$

$$z^5 = \cos\left(2\pi\right) + i \sin\left(2\pi\right) = 1.$$

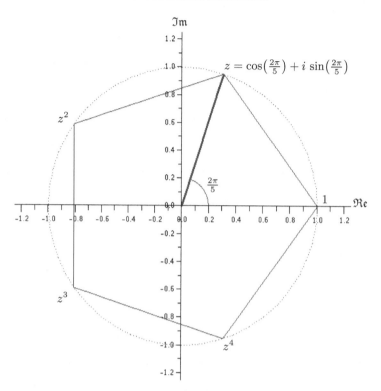

FIGURE 5.7. The complex numbers 1, z, z^2, z^3, and z^4 form the vertices of a regular pentagon on the complex plane.

Hence, multiplying by z will leave our sum unchanged:

$$z \cdot S = z \cdot (1 + z + z^2 + z^3 + z^4) = z + z^2 + z^3 + z^4 + z^5 = z + z^2 + z^3 + z^4 + 1 = S.$$

However, zero is the only number that does not move to a new location when the complex plane is rotated by $\frac{2\pi}{5}$. We must, therefore, have

$$S = 1 + z + z^2 + z^3 + z^4 = 0,$$

or, equivalently,

$$z + z^2 + z^3 + z^4 = -1.$$

Now suppose that we let $A = z^2 + z^3$ and $B = z + z^4$. Both of these are real numbers since each is a sum of a pair of complex conjugates whose imaginary parts cancel out. In fact, it is easy to see in Figure 5.7 that A is negative and B is positive:

$$A = z^2 + z^3 = \cos\left(\tfrac{4\pi}{5}\right) + \cos\left(\tfrac{6\pi}{5}\right) = -2 \cdot \cos\left(\tfrac{\pi}{5}\right)$$

and

$$B = z + z^4 = \cos\left(\tfrac{2\pi}{5}\right) + \cos\left(\tfrac{8\pi}{5}\right) = 2 \cdot \cos\left(\tfrac{2\pi}{5}\right).$$

Furthermore, notice that

$$A + B = (z^2 + z^3) + (z + z^4) = z + z^2 + z^3 + z^4 = -1$$

and that

$$A \cdot B = (z^2 + z^3) \cdot (z + z^4) = z^3 + z^6 + z^4 + z^7 = z + z^2 + z^3 + z^4 = -1.$$

(Note that for this last computation, we used the fact that $z^6 = z^5 \cdot z = 1 \cdot z = z$ and that $z^7 = z^5 \cdot z^2 = 1 \cdot z^2 = z^2$.) This means that the numbers A and B give us a new way to factor the quadratic equation from Example 1.23 in page 31:

$$x^2 - x - 1 = x^2 + (A + B)\, x + AB = (x + A)(x + B) = 0.$$

According to this factorization, this equation has solutions of

$$x = -A = 2\cos\left(\tfrac{\pi}{5}\right) \qquad \text{and} \qquad x = -B = -2\cos\left(\tfrac{2\pi}{5}\right).$$

On the other hand, by using the quadratic formula, we found in page 203 that these solutions are actually equal to

$$x = \varphi = \tfrac{1+\sqrt{5}}{2} \qquad \text{and} \qquad x = -\tfrac{1}{\varphi} = \tfrac{1-\sqrt{5}}{2}.$$

By comparing these two sets of solutions, and in particular which solution is positive and which solution is negative, we arrive at the inevitable conclusion that

$$\cos\left(\tfrac{\pi}{5}\right) = -\tfrac{A}{2} = \tfrac{1+\sqrt{5}}{4} = \tfrac{\varphi}{2}.$$

In other words, the cosine of $\frac{\pi}{5}$ is half of our old friend, the golden ratio!

Reading Comprehension Questions for Section 5.2

The first geometrical interpretation of the complex numbers came at the beginning of the nineteenth century with ___(a)___. His idea was that, since multiplying times ___(b)___ corresponds to a 180° rotation of the real line, then multiplying times ___(c)___ should correspond to a rotation by ___(d)___°. On the Cartesian plane, such a rotation would take the x-axis to the ___(e)___. Thus, the x-axis is identified with the set of ___(f)___ numbers, the y-axis is identified with the set of ___(g)___ numbers, and more generally, the point (a, b) in the Cartesian plane is identified with the complex number ___(h)___. With this geometric interpretation, the set of complex numbers became known as the ___(i)___.

We can extend the absolute value function to the domain of all complex numbers, defining $|z|$ as the ___(j)___ between z and the ___(k)___. In particular, for $z = a + bi$, this means that $|z| = |a + bi| = $ ___(l)___.

By examining the behavior of linear functions on the complex plane, we find that the various arithmetic operations can cause three distinct effects: First of all, adding a complex number causes a ___(m)___ of the complex plane. In particular, the real part of the complex number being added controls the ___(n)___ (horizontal or vertical) motion, while its imaginary part controls the ___(o)___ (horizontal or vertical) motion. Thus adding $3 - 4i$ moves the complex plane horizontally ___(p)___ units to the ___(q)___ (left or right) and vertically ___(r)___ units ___(s)___ (up or down). On the other hand, multiplying times a complex number causes the complex plane to ___(t)___ radially away from the origin by a factor equal to the ___(u)___ of the complex number being multiplied. In addition, it causes the complex plane to ___(v)___ around the origin by an angle given by the ___(w)___ function. For example, multiplying times $3 - 4i$ ___(x)___ (expands or contracts) the complex plane by a factor of ___(y)___ and rotates it by an angle of ___(z)___.

Exercises for Section 5.2

In Exercises 1–9, plot each complex number in the complex plane and indicate its absolute value. Draw the line segment connecting zero to the number and find the angle from the positive real axis to this line segment.

1. $-1 + i$

2. $-3i$

3. $5 - 12i$

4. $7 - i$

5. $4 - 3i$

6. $9\sqrt{3} + 9i$

7. $-2 - 3i$

8. $1 - 3i$

9. $-21 + 20i$

In Exercises 10–15, plot the complex solutions of each equation in the complex plane.

10. $z^2 + 8 = 4z$

11. $3z^2 + 5 = 4z$

12. $2z^2 + 4z = 1$

13. $13z^2 + 6z + 1 = 0$

14. $9z^2 - 6z + 1 = 0$

15. $8z^2 + 1 = 4z$

In Exercises 16–25, sketch the image of the real and imaginary lines under the action of each linear function. Then describe what each function is doing to the complex plane in terms of dilations, rotations, and translations.

16. $f(z) = z + 2 - 3i$

17. $f(z) = z - 7 + i$

18. $f(z) = (2 + 2i)z$

19. $f(z) = (\sqrt{3} - i)z$

20. $f(z) = (5 + 12i)z$

21. $f(z) = 4z - 1 - i$

22. $f(z) = -5z + 7 + i$

23. $f(z) = -iz - 2$

24. $f(z) = 3iz + 6i$

25. $f(z) = (-1 - i)z + (5 - 4i)$

26. Suppose that z is a complex number with $|z| = 5$. Suppose further that that the ray on the complex plane starting at the origin and passing through z makes an angle of $-\frac{\pi}{6}$ with the positive real axis. Write z in the rectangular form $a + bi$.

27. Suppose that z is a complex number with $|z| = 2$ such that $\mathfrak{Re}\, z = 3 \cdot \mathfrak{Im}\, z$. Write z in the rectangular form $a + bi$.

28. Obtuse Ollie is trying to understand why the complex number

$$w = \frac{\sqrt{2}}{2} + \frac{\sqrt{2}}{2}i$$

is a square root of i. Acute Alice suggests that he consider the linear function that multiplies its input times w. Assuming that w really is a square root of i, what should this function do to the complex plane? Verify your conjecture.

29. Scalene Sallie is trying to understand why the complex number

$$w = \frac{\sqrt{3}}{2} + \frac{1}{2}\,i$$

is a cube root of i. Acute Alice suggests that she consider the linear function that multiplies its input times w. Assuming that w really is a cube root of i, what should this function do to the complex plane? Verify your conjecture.

30. Expand both sides of the equation below in order to show that the absolute value of a product of two complex numbers is always equal to the product of the absolute values of the individual numbers:

$$\bigl|(a + b\,i) \cdot (c + d\,i)\bigr| = \bigl|a + b\,i\bigr| \cdot \bigl|c + d\,i\bigr|.$$

5.3. Euler's Formula

In the last section we used linear functions to explore the geometric nature of the complex plane. As we saw, addition and subtraction have the effect of translating the entire complex plane up and down and side to side, while multiplication causes the complex plane to dilate radially and to rotate about the origin. Indeed, Argand's very idea of the complex plane originated with the thought that since multiplying by -1 performs a 180° rotation, then multiplying by i should perform a 90° rotation.

In order to further investigate the rotation associated with each complex number, we now shall consider a new function cis: $\mathbb{R} \to \mathbb{C}$ defined by the formula

$$\operatorname{cis}(\theta) = \cos(\theta) + i \cdot \sin(\theta).$$

The name "c-i-s" is a bit of tongue-in-cheek mathematical shorthand meant to remind you of its definition as the *cosine* plus i times *sine* of an angle (measured in radians, of course). You should observe that, regardless of the value of the input θ, the absolute value of cis (θ) is always one:

$$\left|\operatorname{cis}(\theta)\right| = \sqrt{\cos^2(\theta) + \sin^2(\theta)} = 1.$$

Furthermore, any complex number w whose absolute value equals one can be written in the form $w = \operatorname{cis}(\theta)$ by simply letting θ be the measure of the angle between the

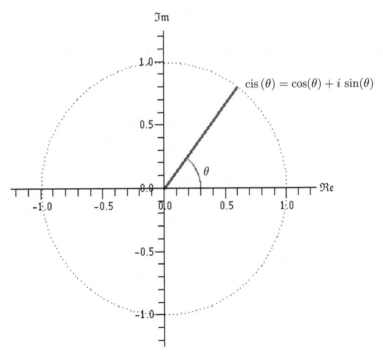

FIGURE 5.8. The image set of the function cis (θ).

positive real axis and the ray pointing from the origin to z, as in Figure 5.8. This means that this function's image set is equal to the unit circle in the complex plane. In fact, one way to describe this function is to say that it "winds" the real line around the unit circle.

Now, let us take an arbitrary non-zero complex number $z = a + b\,i$, and set

$$r = |a + b\,i| = \sqrt{a^2 + b^2}\,.$$

Then z will be located on the circle of radius r around the origin, as in Figure 5.9. We can think of this circle as the dilation of the unit circle by a factor of r. This means that z can be decomposed as the product of the positive number r times some complex number on the unit circle which, as we noted earlier, can always be written in the form $\mathrm{cis}\,(\theta)$:

$$\boxed{z = r\left(\cos(\theta) + i\sin(\theta)\right) = r\,\mathrm{cis}\,(\theta).}$$

This decomposition is called the **polar form** of the complex number z. In this case, the number r is called the **magnitude** of the complex number, while the angle θ is called its **argument**.

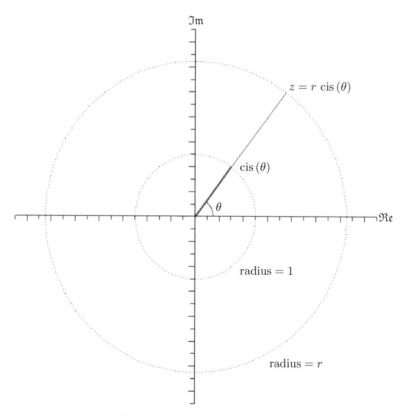

FIGURE 5.9. The polar form of a complex number.

EXAMPLE 5.17. Consider the complex number $z = -2 + 2i$, which, as we saw in Example 5.11, has a magnitude of $r = |-2 + 2i| = 2\sqrt{2}$. In order to find the argument for z, we first divide z by r and obtain the point on the unit circle closest to z:

$$\frac{z}{r} = \frac{-2 + 2i}{2\sqrt{2}} = -\frac{2}{2\sqrt{2}} + \frac{2}{2\sqrt{2}} i = -\frac{\sqrt{2}}{2} + \frac{\sqrt{2}}{2} i.$$

Since this is a point on the unit circle, it can be written as $z/r = \operatorname{cis}(\theta)$ for an appropriate angle θ with

$$\cos(\theta) = -\frac{\sqrt{2}}{2} \qquad \text{and} \qquad \sin(\theta) = \frac{\sqrt{2}}{2}.$$

Now, we recognize that the argument $\theta = \frac{3\pi}{4}$ satisfies both of these requirements, so we can write z in polar form as

$$z = -2 + 2i = 2\sqrt{2}\left(-\frac{\sqrt{2}}{2} + \frac{\sqrt{2}}{2} i\right) = 2\sqrt{2} \operatorname{cis}\left(\frac{3\pi}{4}\right).$$

Figure 5.10 illustrates this polar form graphically. Of course, since sine and cosine are periodic functions whose values repeat every 2π radians, there are infinitely many other choices of θ that satisfy the requirements above. Consequently, there are infinitely many distinct polar forms for the same complex number z. All of these polar forms, however, differ only by an integer multiple of 2π in their argument. Therefore, every polar form of the number z can be written as

$$z = -2 + 2i = 2\sqrt{2} \operatorname{cis}\left(\frac{3\pi}{4} + 2\pi k\right)$$

for an appropriate choice of the integer k. The polar form above happens to correspond to the choice of $k = 0$.

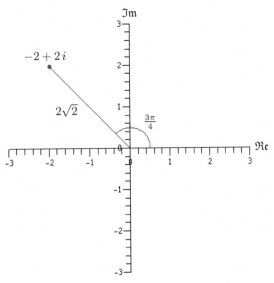

FIGURE 5.10. The polar form of the complex number $z = -2 + 2i$.

EXAMPLE 5.18. According to Example 5.11, the complex number $w = 3 + i$ has a magnitude of $r = |3 + i| = \sqrt{10}$. In order to write w in polar form, we begin by dividing w by r as follows:

$$\frac{w}{r} = \frac{3 + i}{\sqrt{10}} = \frac{3}{\sqrt{10}} + \frac{1}{\sqrt{10}}\, i = \frac{3\sqrt{10}}{10} + \frac{\sqrt{10}}{10}\, i.$$

The result is a complex number on the unit circle and can therefore be written in the form $w/r = \operatorname{cis}(\theta)$ for an appropriate choice of θ. In particular, we will need to find an angle θ with

$$\cos(\theta) = \frac{3\sqrt{10}}{10} \qquad \text{and} \qquad \sin(\theta) = \frac{\sqrt{10}}{10}.$$

Again, there are several possible choices for θ. One possibility is

$$\theta = \arccos\!\left(\tfrac{3\sqrt{10}}{10}\right) = \arcsin\!\left(\tfrac{\sqrt{10}}{10}\right) = \arctan\!\left(\tfrac{1}{3}\right) \approx 0.562.$$

With this choice of argument, we can write w in polar form as follows:

$$w = 3 + i = \sqrt{10}\,\operatorname{cis}\!\left(\arctan\!\left(\tfrac{1}{3}\right)\right).$$

Figure 5.11 gives a graphical representation of this polar form. However, we can choose any other angle that is coterminal to $\arctan\!\left(\tfrac{1}{3}\right)$ as our argument. Hence, the most general polar form for w becomes

$$w = 3 + i = \sqrt{10}\,\operatorname{cis}\!\left(\arctan\!\left(\tfrac{1}{3}\right) + 2\pi k\right),$$

where k is an arbitrary integer.

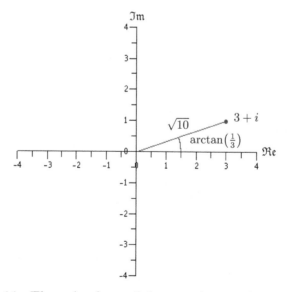

FIGURE 5.11. The polar form of the complex number $w = 3 + i$.

Observe that the arguments we computed in the last two examples were equal to the angles of rotation in Examples 5.14 and 5.15. To see why this is the case, consider the product of two arbitrary complex numbers expressed in polar form:

$$\big(r\,\text{cis}\,(\theta)\big) \cdot \big(s\,\text{cis}\,(\psi)\big)$$

$$= (r \cdot s) \cdot \big(\cos(\theta) + i\,\sin(\theta)\big) \cdot \big(\cos(\psi) + i\,\sin(\psi)\big)$$

$$= (r \cdot s) \cdot \big(\big(\cos(\theta)\cos(\psi) - \sin(\theta)\sin(\psi)\big) + i\,\big(\sin(\theta)\cos(\psi) + \cos(\theta)\sin(\psi)\big)\big)$$

$$= (r \cdot s) \cdot \big(\cos(\theta + \psi) + i\,\sin(\theta + \psi)\big)$$

$$= (r \cdot s) \cdot \text{cis}\,(\theta + \psi).$$

Here, the first equality is simply a rearrangement of our factors. The second follows from the rule for complex multiplication. Next, the third line comes from the angle sum identities from page 357. Finally, the last equation simply rearranges our product back to polar form. Take particular note of the fact that the magnitude of the final product is equal to the product of the original two magnitudes (that is, of r and s), while its argument is the sum of the original arguments (that is, of θ and ψ):

Complex Multiplication

When multiplying complex numbers in polar form together:

    ① magnitudes multiply,

    ② arguments add.

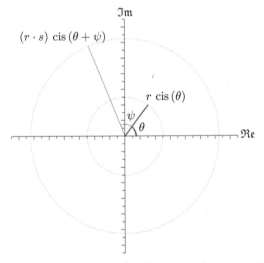

FIGURE 5.12. Multiplying times $s\,\text{cis}\,(\psi)$ dilates and rotates the complex plane.

This characterization gives us a complete picture of the type of transformation experienced by the complex plane when we multiply times a complex number. That magnitudes multiply is just a fancy way of stating our initial observation that multiplication dilates the complex plane radially away from the origin. Furthermore, the fact that arguments add explains why the complex plane also undergoes a rotation. In particular, as we can see in Figure 5.12, the magnitude and argument of a complex number give, respectively, the dilation factor and the angle of rotation at work when we multiply by that number.

EXAMPLE 5.19. Since multiplying times i corresponds to a quarter turn of the complex plane with no dilation, i must have a magnitude of $r = 1$ and an argument of $\theta = \frac{\pi}{2} + 2\pi k$, where k can be any integer. Therefore, it must take the polar form

$$i = \operatorname{cis}\left(\tfrac{\pi}{2} + 2\pi k\right),$$

Indeed, we can verify this assertion by noting that

$$\mathfrak{Re}\, i = \cos\left(\tfrac{\pi}{2} + 2\pi k\right) = 0 \qquad \text{and} \qquad \mathfrak{Im}\, i = \sin\left(\tfrac{\pi}{2} + 2\pi k\right) = 1.$$

EXAMPLE 5.20. As we saw in Example 5.16, multiplying by $-3 - 4i$ dilates the complex plane radially by a factor of $r = 5$, all while rotating it by an angle of $\theta = \arctan\left(\frac{4}{3}\right) + \pi$. We can therefore express this complex number in its most general polar form as

$$-3 - 4i = 5\operatorname{cis}\left(\arctan\left(\tfrac{4}{3}\right) + (2k+1)\pi\right).$$

As before, the value of k in this formula can be any integer whatsoever. Now, realizing that $\arctan\left(\frac{4}{3}\right)$ is located in the first quadrant of the unit circle, and that $(2k+1)\pi$ is always an odd multiple of π, we find that our choice of argument, regardless of the value of k, places this complex number in the third quadrant of the complex plane. In particular, we have

$$\cos\left(\arctan\left(\tfrac{4}{3}\right) + (2k+1)\pi\right) = -\cos\left(\arctan\left(\tfrac{4}{3}\right)\right) = -\tfrac{3}{5},$$

$$\sin\left(\arctan\left(\tfrac{4}{3}\right) + (2k+1)\pi\right) = -\sin\left(\arctan\left(\tfrac{4}{3}\right)\right) = -\tfrac{4}{5}.$$

As expected, this means that

$$5\operatorname{cis}\left(\arctan\left(\tfrac{4}{3}\right) + (2k+1)\pi\right) = 5\left(-\tfrac{3}{5} - \tfrac{4}{5}i\right) = -3 - 4i.$$

There is a second lesson to be learned from the computation in page 421. By considering only the parts of this result involving the cis function, we find that a product outside of this function can be moved into a sum inside as follows:

$$\operatorname{cis}(x) \cdot \operatorname{cis}(y) = \operatorname{cis}(x + y).$$

This behavior is reminiscent of that of an exponential function, in which case we had:

$$b^x \cdot b^y = b^{x+y}.$$

In other words, the cis function obeys the defining property (3.1) for exponential functions. It should, therefore, not be surprising that the cis function shares many other properties with the exponential functions. For instance, suppose that x and y are positive integers; then $(\operatorname{cis}(x))^y$ is equal to y copies of $\operatorname{cis}(x)$ multiplied together. By repeatedly applying the property above, we can see that this product is equal to the value that the cis function assigns to the sum of y copies of x added together:

$$\big(\operatorname{cis}(x)\big)^y = \underbrace{\operatorname{cis}(x) \cdots\cdots \operatorname{cis}(x)}_{y \text{ copies of } \operatorname{cis}(x)} = \operatorname{cis}\underbrace{(x + x + \cdots + x + x)}_{y \text{ copies of } x} = \operatorname{cis}(y \cdot x).$$

You should compare this formula to Exponential Rule ③ in page 248. With a bit of care, we can show that all of the exponential rules also hold for the cis function, even for non-integer inputs. In fact, by considering first negative inputs, then rational inputs, and finally using limits to handle real number inputs, we can show that $\operatorname{cis}(x)$ not only *behaves* like an exponential function; it *is* an exponential function:

$$\operatorname{cis}(x) = \operatorname{cis}(x \cdot 1) = \big(\operatorname{cis}(1)\big)^x.$$

You might feel somewhat dismayed by how to interpret the last statement since, after all, the base of this "exponential" appears to be a strange complex number whose real and imaginary parts are both irrational:

$$\operatorname{cis}(1) = \cos(1) + i\sin(1) = (0.540\,302\,305\ldots) + i \cdot (0.841\,470\,984\ldots).$$

To better appreciate how the cis function can be treated as an exponential, let us recall from Chapter 3 that every exponential function can be rewritten in two different forms:

$$f(x) = b^x \qquad \text{or} \qquad f(x) = e^{kx}.$$

In the second of these, the constant $k = \ln(b)$ was the growth rate of the exponential, which we defined as the instantaneous rate of change of $f(x)$ at the moment that its graph crosses the y-axis, that is, when $x = 0$. Back in Section 3.2, we computed this growth rate as the limit of a sequence of difference quotients of the form

$$\frac{\Delta f}{\Delta x} = \frac{f(h) - f(-h)}{h - (-h)} = \frac{b^h - b^{-h}}{2h}$$

where we let the number h take on values closer and closer to zero. Since the function $\operatorname{cis}(x)$ also behaves like an exponential, we shall assume that the same computation may be made in this situation, and therefore write

$$\operatorname{cis}(x) = \big(\operatorname{cis}(1)\big)^x = e^{kx}$$

where k is the "natural logarithm" (whatever that means) of the complex number $\operatorname{cis}(1)$. In particular, we shall interpret k as the growth rate of $\operatorname{cis}(x)$, and determine

TABLE 5.1. The average rate of change of the exponential function $\operatorname{cis}(x)$ over a sequence of smaller and smaller intervals about $x = 0$.

interval	average rate of change
$[-1, 1]$	$\dfrac{\Delta \operatorname{cis}}{\Delta x} = \dfrac{\operatorname{cis}(1) - \operatorname{cis}(-1)}{2} \approx 0.841\,470\,984\,808\,i$
$[-0.1, 0.1]$	$\dfrac{\Delta \operatorname{cis}}{\Delta x} = \dfrac{\operatorname{cis}(0.1) - \operatorname{cis}(-0.1)}{0.2} \approx 0.998\,334\,166\,468\,i$
$[-0.01, 0.01]$	$\dfrac{\Delta \operatorname{cis}}{\Delta x} = \dfrac{\operatorname{cis}(0.01) - \operatorname{cis}(-0.01)}{0.02} \approx 0.999\,983\,333\,416\,i$
$[-0.001, 0.001]$	$\dfrac{\Delta \operatorname{cis}}{\Delta x} = \dfrac{\operatorname{cis}(0.001) - \operatorname{cis}(-0.001)}{0.002} \approx 0.999\,999\,833\,333\,i$
$[-0.000\,1, 0.000\,1]$	$\dfrac{\Delta \operatorname{cis}}{\Delta x} = \dfrac{\operatorname{cis}(0.000\,1) - \operatorname{cis}(-0.000\,1)}{0.000\,2} \approx 0.999\,999\,999\,983\,i$

its value by computing the difference quotient

$$\frac{\Delta \operatorname{cis}}{\Delta x} = \frac{\operatorname{cis}(h) - \operatorname{cis}(-h)}{h - (-h)} = \frac{\cos(h) - \cos(-h)}{2h} + \frac{\sin(h) - \sin(-h)}{2h} i$$

for a progression of smaller and smaller values of h. As you will observe from Table 5.1, each of these difference quotients is a purely imaginary number, each one a little bit closer to $k = i$. This computation shows that the growth rate of the cis function is equal to i, and therefore that

$$\boxed{e^{ix} = \cos(x) + i\sin(x).}$$

This last result is known as **Euler's formula** since it was first discovered using analytic methods by Leonhard Euler (whom we met briefly back in page 267) more than a half-century before Argand even proposed his geometric model for the complex plane. As our next examples show, this formula allows us to avoid the repetitive arithmetic involved in computing high powers of a complex number, much like the our observation from Example 5.2 did for the special case of powers of i. It can also help us "extract" the roots of complex numbers by using trigonometry.

EXAMPLE 5.21. Recall that the complex number $z = -2 + 2i$ takes the polar form of

$$z = -2 + 2i = 2\sqrt{2}\left(\cos\left(\tfrac{3\pi}{4}\right) + i\sin\left(\tfrac{3\pi}{4}\right)\right).$$

Using Euler's formula, we can now rewrite this in a more elegant fashion as a complex exponential as follows:

$$z = -2 + 2i = 2^{3/2}\, e^{3\pi i/4}.$$

With this formulation in hand, can easily compute powers of z. For instance,

$$
\begin{aligned}
\left(-2 + 2i\right)^5 &= \left(2^{3/2}\, e^{3\pi i/4}\right)^5 \\
&= 2^{15/2}\, e^{15\pi i/4} \\
&= 128\sqrt{2}\, \operatorname{cis}\left(\tfrac{15\pi}{4}\right) \\
&= 128\sqrt{2}\left(\cos\left(\tfrac{15\pi}{4}\right) + i\sin\left(\tfrac{15\pi}{4}\right)\right) \\
&= 128\sqrt{2}\left(\tfrac{\sqrt{2}}{2} - \tfrac{\sqrt{2}}{2}i\right) \\
&= 128 - 128i.
\end{aligned}
$$

Similarly, we have

$$
\begin{aligned}
\left(-2 + 2i\right)^{-5} &= \left(2^{3/2}\, e^{3\pi i/4}\right)^{-5} \\
&= 2^{-15/2}\, e^{-15\pi i/4} \\
&= \tfrac{\sqrt{2}}{256}\, \operatorname{cis}\left(-\tfrac{15\pi}{4}\right) \\
&= \tfrac{\sqrt{2}}{256}\left(\cos\left(-\tfrac{15\pi}{4}\right) + i\sin\left(-\tfrac{15\pi}{4}\right)\right) \\
&= \tfrac{\sqrt{2}}{256}\left(\tfrac{\sqrt{2}}{2} + \tfrac{\sqrt{2}}{2}i\right) \\
&= \tfrac{1}{256} + \tfrac{1}{256}i.
\end{aligned}
$$

Note that, in each of the computations above, we start by distributing the power (either 5 or -5) to both the magnitude and complex exponential. We can then rewrite the result, first in polar form by using Euler's formula, and then in rectangular form by evaluating the sine and cosine functions at the appropriate argument. As expected, when we multiply these two numbers together, using the distributive property, we obtain a result of one:

$$
\begin{aligned}
\left(-2 + 2i\right)^5 \cdot \left(-2 + 2i\right)^{-5} &= \left(128 - 128i\right)\cdot\left(\tfrac{1}{256} + \tfrac{1}{256}i\right) \\
&= \tfrac{1}{2} + \tfrac{1}{2}i - \tfrac{1}{2}i + \tfrac{1}{2} \\
&= 1 + 0i.
\end{aligned}
$$

EXAMPLE 5.22. Since we can write $i = \cos\left(\frac{\pi}{2}\right) + i\,\sin\left(\frac{\pi}{2}\right) = e^{\pi i/2}$, we can determine its square root as

$$\left(e^{\pi i/2}\right)^{1/2} = e^{\pi i/4} = \cos\left(\tfrac{\pi}{4}\right) + i\,\sin\left(\tfrac{\pi}{4}\right) = \tfrac{\sqrt{2}}{2} + \tfrac{\sqrt{2}}{2}\,i.$$

On the other hand, we also have $i = \cos\left(\frac{5\pi}{2}\right) + i\,\sin\left(\frac{5\pi}{2}\right) = e^{5\pi/2\,i}$, so

$$\left(e^{5\pi i/2}\right)^{1/2} = e^{5\pi i/4} = \cos\left(\tfrac{5\pi}{4}\right) + i\,\sin\left(\tfrac{5\pi}{4}\right) = -\tfrac{\sqrt{2}}{2} - \tfrac{\sqrt{2}}{2}\,i$$

is another square root of i. This result should hardly come as a surprise, since we had already discovered these two square roots, albeit indirectly, in Example 5.3. However, by writing $i = e^{\pi i/2} = e^{5\pi i/2} = e^{9\pi i/2}$, we can now see why i has three cube roots:

$$\left(e^{\pi i/2}\right)^{1/3} = e^{\pi i/6} = \cos\left(\tfrac{\pi}{6}\right) + i\,\sin\left(\tfrac{\pi}{6}\right) = \tfrac{\sqrt{3}}{2} + \tfrac{1}{2}\,i,$$

$$\left(e^{5\pi i/2}\right)^{1/3} = e^{5\pi i/6} = \cos\left(\tfrac{5\pi}{6}\right) + i\,\sin\left(\tfrac{5\pi}{6}\right) = -\tfrac{\sqrt{3}}{2} + \tfrac{1}{2}\,i,$$

$$\left(e^{9\pi i/2}\right)^{1/3} = e^{3\pi i/2} = \cos\left(\tfrac{3\pi}{2}\right) + i\,\sin\left(\tfrac{3\pi}{2}\right) = -i.$$

This fact is confirmed by our earlier computations in Example 5.5.

The last example illustrates why every non-zero complex number has p distinct complex p^{th} roots. The main fact to remember is that we can add an integer multiple of 2π to any complex number's argument without changing the number. This means that, as long as k is an integer, we have

$$r\,e^{i\,(\theta + 2\pi k)} = r\,e^{i\,\theta}.$$

Therefore, every complex number of the form

$$\left(r\,e^{i\,(\theta + 2\pi k)}\right)^{1/p} = \sqrt[p]{r}\;e^{i\,(\theta + 2\pi k)/p}$$

will be a pth root of $r\,e^{i\,\theta}$ regardless of the value of the integer k. Since each choice of k between 0 and $p-1$ will produce a different p^{th} root, this means that there are at least p distinct p^{th} roots of $r\,e^{i\,\theta}$. In particular, to extract the pth roots of a complex number, we must consider p consecutive coterminal arguments and divide each one of them by p. Of course, we will also need to take the pth root of the magnitude. For instance, starting with an argument of θ, we might have:

$$\sqrt[p]{r}\;e^{i\,\theta/p} \quad \sqrt[p]{r}\;e^{i\,(\theta + 2\pi)/p} \quad \sqrt[p]{r}\;e^{i\,(\theta + 4\pi)/p} \quad \ldots \quad \sqrt[p]{r}\;e^{i\,(\theta + 2(p-1)\pi)/p}.$$

On the other hand, every value of k outside of this range will repeat one of these p roots. For instance, setting $k = p$ produces the same root as setting $k = 0$:

$$\sqrt[p]{r}\;e^{i\,(\theta + 2\pi p)/p} = \sqrt[p]{r}\;e^{i\,(\theta/p + 2\pi)} = \sqrt[p]{r}\;e^{i\,(\theta/p)} = \sqrt[p]{r}\;e^{i\,\theta/p}.$$

EXAMPLE 5.23. At the end of Section 5.1 (see page 398), we saw how del Ferro's formula gave the expression

$$x = \sqrt[3]{-2 + 2\,i} + \sqrt[3]{-2 - 2\,i}$$

as the solution to the cubic equation

$$x^3 - 6x + 4 = 0.$$

We can use Euler's formula to extract these cube roots. In particular, we first note that both $-2 + 2\,i$ and $-2 - 2\,i$ have a magnitude of

$$|-2 + 2\,i| = |-2 - 2\,i| = 2\sqrt{2}.$$

Hence, we can write each of these numbers in polar form in three distinct ways, using three consecutive coterminal arguments, as follows:

$$-2 + 2\,i = 2\sqrt{2}\left(-\tfrac{\sqrt{2}}{2} + \tfrac{\sqrt{2}}{2}\,i\right) = \begin{cases} 2^{3/2}\,e^{3\pi/4\,i}, \\[2mm] 2^{3/2}\,e^{(3\pi/4 + 2\pi)i} = 2^{3/2}\,e^{11\pi/4\,i}, \\[2mm] 2^{3/2}\,e^{(3\pi/4 + 4\pi)i} = 2^{3/2}\,e^{19\pi/4\,i}, \end{cases}$$

$$-2 - 2\,i = 2\sqrt{2}\left(-\tfrac{\sqrt{2}}{2} - \tfrac{\sqrt{2}}{2}\,i\right) = \begin{cases} 2^{3/2}\,e^{5\pi/4\,i}, \\[2mm] 2^{3/2}\,e^{(5\pi/4 + 2\pi)i} = 2^{3/2}\,e^{13\pi/4\,i}, \\[2mm] 2^{3/2}\,e^{(5\pi/4 + 4\pi)i} = 2^{3/2}\,e^{21\pi/4\,i}. \end{cases}$$

Each of these polar forms gives us a different cube root:

$$\sqrt[3]{-2 + 2\,i} = \begin{cases} \left(2^{3/2}\,e^{3\pi/4\,i}\right)^{1/3} = 2^{1/2}\,e^{\pi/4\,i} = 1 + i, \\[2mm] \left(2^{3/2}\,e^{11\pi/4\,i}\right)^{1/3} = 2^{1/2}\,e^{11\pi/12\,i} = \tfrac{-1-\sqrt{3}}{2} + \tfrac{-1+\sqrt{3}}{2}\,i, \\[2mm] \left(2^{3/2}\,e^{19\pi/4\,i}\right)^{1/3} = 2^{1/2}\,e^{19\pi/12\,i} = \tfrac{-1+\sqrt{3}}{2} + \tfrac{-1-\sqrt{3}}{2}\,i, \end{cases}$$

$$\sqrt[3]{-2 - 2\,i} = \begin{cases} \left(2^{3/2}\,e^{5\pi/4\,i}\right)^{1/3} = 2^{1/2}\,e^{5\pi/12\,i} = \tfrac{-1+\sqrt{3}}{2} + \tfrac{1+\sqrt{3}}{2}\,i, \\[2mm] \left(2^{3/2}\,e^{13\pi/4\,i}\right)^{1/3} = 2^{1/2}\,e^{13\pi/12\,i} = \tfrac{-1-\sqrt{3}}{2} + \tfrac{1-\sqrt{3}}{2}\,i, \\[2mm] \left(2^{3/2}\,e^{21\pi/4\,i}\right)^{1/3} = 2^{1/2}\,e^{7\pi/4\,i} = 1 - i. \end{cases}$$

Notice that these cube roots form three pairs of complex conjugates. In other words, for each cube root of $-2 + 2\,i$, we can find a corresponding cube root of $-2 - 2\,i$ with an equal, but opposite, imaginary part. These imaginary parts cancel out when the conjugate pairs are added together in del Ferro's formula, producing the three real solutions to our depressed cubic equation:

$$x = \left(1 + i\right) + \left(1 - i\right) = 2,$$

$$x = \left(\tfrac{-1-\sqrt{3}}{2} + \tfrac{-1+\sqrt{3}}{2}\, i\right) + \left(\tfrac{-1-\sqrt{3}}{2} + \tfrac{1-\sqrt{3}}{2}\, i\right) = -1 - \sqrt{3},$$

$$x = \left(\tfrac{-1+\sqrt{3}}{2} + \tfrac{-1-\sqrt{3}}{2}\, i\right) + \left(\tfrac{-1+\sqrt{3}}{2} + \tfrac{1+\sqrt{3}}{2}\, i\right) = -1 + \sqrt{3}.$$

Euler was, without a doubt, the preeminent mathematician of the eighteenth century, and some might argue of all time. He is said to have produced more mathematical papers and explored more areas of mathematics than anyone else in history. He was known to work on difficult problems while his children and grandchildren played on his lap. Even on the very day that he died, Euler spent his morning running through some calculations concerning the orbit of the planet Uranus. Of particular significance to us is Euler's 1748 masterpiece *Introductio in Analysin Infinitorum*, in which he not only derived the famous formula discussed above, but also introduced our modern notation for e, π, i, and $f(x)$. It was here that, for the first time, Euler put the concept of function on the center stage of mathematics. Therefore, it seems only fitting that Euler also marks the end of our brief mathematical tour.

Reading Comprehension Questions for Section 5.3

The function cis : $\mathbb{R} \to \mathbb{C}$, defined by the formula $\operatorname{cis}(\theta) = \underline{\quad(a)\quad} + i \underline{\quad(b)\quad}$, winds the real line around the unit circle. This function allows us to express any complex number in the form $z = r \operatorname{cis}(\theta)$. This is known as the $\underline{\quad(c)\quad}$ form of the complex number. The number r is sometimes called the $\underline{\quad(d)\quad}$ of the complex number; it is determined by evaluating the $\underline{\quad(e)\quad}$ of z. On the other hand, the angle θ is sometimes called the $\underline{\quad(f)\quad}$ of the complex number. It can be computed by dividing the real and imaginary parts of z by r; the first of these ratios gives the $\underline{\quad(g)\quad}$ of θ while the second gives its $\underline{\quad(h)\quad}$.

When we multiply two complex numbers, their $\underline{\quad(i)\quad}$ are added while their $\underline{\quad(j)\quad}$ are multiplied. This result follows from the definition of complex multiplication and the $\underline{\quad(k)\quad}$ identities for sine and cosine. In particular, we find that the cis function maps a sum into a $\underline{\quad(l)\quad}$, that is, $\operatorname{cis}(x + y) = \underline{\quad(m)\quad}$. In other words, the cis function obeys the same defining property as an $\underline{\quad(n)\quad}$ function. Indeed, we can show that the cis function can be written as $\operatorname{cis}(x) = (\underline{\quad(o)\quad})^x$. We can compute the $\underline{\quad(p)\quad}$ of this exponential function by considering a sequence of difference quotients of the form

$$\frac{\Delta \operatorname{cis}}{\Delta x} = \frac{\operatorname{cis}(h) - \operatorname{cis}(-h)}{h - (-h)} = \underline{\quad(q)\quad} + \underline{\quad(r)\quad} i,$$

where h becomes smaller and smaller. The results of these computations get closer and closer to $\underline{\quad(s)\quad}$. Therefore, we can use the growth rate formulation of an exponential to express the polar form of a complex number as

$$z = r \operatorname{cis}(\theta) = \underline{\quad(t)\quad}.$$

This result is known as $\underline{\quad(u)\quad}$.

As an application of this formula, we can "extract" n different n^{th} roots of a non-zero complex number $z = r \operatorname{cis}(\theta)$. First, we take the $\underline{\quad(v)\quad}$ of the magnitude, and use this as our new magnitude. Then, we consider n consecutive, coterminal arguments and divide each of them by $\underline{\quad(w)\quad}$. This gives us

$$\sqrt[n]{r} \operatorname{cis}(\underline{\quad(x)\quad}), \ \sqrt[n]{r} \operatorname{cis}(\underline{\quad(y)\quad}), \ \ldots, \ \sqrt[n]{r} \operatorname{cis}(\underline{\quad(z)\quad}),$$

all of which are valid n^{th} roots of z.

Exercises for Section 5.3

In Exercises 1–9, find the polar form for each complex number. Then plot the number in the complex plane, labeling both its magnitude and argument. Express the argument in both radians and degrees.

1. $1 + i$

2. $1 - i$

3. $1 - \sqrt{3}\,i$

4. $\sqrt{3} - i$

5. $-5\,i$

6. $9\sqrt{3} + 9\,i$

7. $3 - 4\,i$

8. $2 - 3\,i$

9. $\sqrt{5} - i$

In Exercises 10–21, write each complex number in rectangular form $a + b\,i$. In each case, you should start by using Euler's formula to write each number as a complex exponential of the form $r\,e^{i\theta}$.

10. $\left(4\left(\cos\left(\frac{2\pi}{9}\right) + i\,\sin\left(\frac{2\pi}{9}\right)\right)\right)^3$

11. $\left(3\left(\cos\left(\frac{4\pi}{9}\right) + i\,\sin\left(\frac{4\pi}{9}\right)\right)\right)^3$

12. $\left(2\left(\cos\left(\frac{\pi}{10}\right) + i\,\sin\left(\frac{\pi}{10}\right)\right)\right)^5$

13. $\left(\sqrt{2}\left(\cos\left(\frac{5\pi}{16}\right) + i\,\sin\left(\frac{5\pi}{16}\right)\right)\right)^4$

14. $\left(\sqrt{5}\left(\cos\left(\frac{3\pi}{16}\right) + i\,\sin\left(\frac{3\pi}{16}\right)\right)\right)^4$

15. $\left(\sqrt{3}\left(\cos\left(\frac{5\pi}{18}\right) + i\,\sin\left(\frac{5\pi}{18}\right)\right)\right)^6$

16. $\left(\frac{1}{2}\left(\cos\left(\frac{2\pi}{5}\right) + i\,\sin\left(\frac{2\pi}{5}\right)\right)\right)^5$

17. $\left(\frac{2}{3}\left(\cos\left(\frac{\pi}{15}\right) + i\,\sin\left(\frac{\pi}{15}\right)\right)\right)^5$

18. $(1 - i)^5$

19. $(\sqrt{3} - i)^6$

20. $(\sqrt{2} - \sqrt{2}\,i)^6$

21. $(\sqrt{5} + \sqrt{15}\,i)^6$

In Exercises 22–30, find all of the complex roots in polar form. Express each answer using both the cis function and as a complex exponential of the form $r\,e^{i\theta}$.

22. $\sqrt[3]{-8}$

23. $\sqrt[3]{1 + i}$

24. $\sqrt[3]{-8 - 8\,i}$

25. $\sqrt[4]{4 - 4\sqrt{3}\,i}$

26. $\sqrt[4]{-16\,i}$

27. $\sqrt[4]{\sqrt{3} - i}$

28. $\sqrt[5]{i}$

29. $\sqrt[5]{-i}$

30. $\sqrt[6]{64}$

5.4. Epilogue

The renown cellist Yo-Yo Ma once said that the job of the artist is to go to the brink of the imagination and report back. This is precisely what Euler's formula does for us, and the good news is that there is much yet to be explored. Euler gives us a bridge between the geometry of rotations and the arithmetic of exponentials. It quite literally breaks boundaries and allows us to define functions on ever larger domains than initially seemed possible.

For instance, consider the sign identities for the cosine and sine functions:

$$\cos(-x) = \cos(x) \qquad \text{and} \qquad \sin(-x) = -\sin(x).$$

In Euler's hands, they become

$$e^{-xi} = \cos(-x) + i\,\sin(-x) = \cos(x) - i\,\sin(x).$$

Adding or subtracting this equation to the standard version of Euler's formula allows us to think about our old-fashioned trigonometric functions in terms of exponentials in the complex plane:

$$\cos(z) = \frac{e^{iz} + e^{-iz}}{2} \qquad \text{and} \qquad \sin(z) = \frac{e^{iz} - e^{-iz}}{2i}.$$

The beauty of these formulas is that they are no longer bound to domain of the real numbers: The formulas on the right hand sides of these equations are well-defined regardless of whether z is real or complex. Take a moment to let this sink in! These formulas can be used to define $\cos(z)$ and $\sin(z)$ for any complex number $z \in \mathbb{C}$ whatsoever. For example, we now have

$$\cos(i) = \frac{e^{i^2} + e^{-i^2}}{2} = \frac{e^{-1} + e^1}{2} \approx 1.543\,080\,634\,815$$

and

$$\sin(i) = \frac{e^{i^2} - e^{-i^2}}{2i} = \frac{e^{-1} - e^1}{2i} \approx 1.175\,201\,193\,644\,i.$$

Trigonometry is not the only arena where Euler's formula makes domains more malleable. As you will recall, we originally restricted the natural logarithm function to the domain $(0, \infty)$. With Euler's formula, this is no longer necessary. In particular, since we can express any non-zero complex number in polar form as

$$z = r\,(\cos(\theta) + i\sin(\theta)) = r\,e^{\theta i},$$

then it seems reasonable to define its natural logarithm as

$$\ln(z) = \ln(r\,e^{\theta i}) = \ln(r) + \theta\,i.$$

The only restriction now is that z be non-zero. There is still the small matter of making our function well-defined (remember that a single complex number can take many different polar forms, each with an argument that differs by an integer multiple of 2π) but this is easily dealt with by making sure that we always choose arguments in the interval $[0, 2\pi)$. With this definition in place, we have

$$\ln(i) = \ln\!\left(e^{\pi/2\,i}\right) = \tfrac{\pi}{2}\, i \approx 1.570\,796\,326\,795\, i.$$

Logarithms and exponentials, sines and cosines, roots and powers, all dance together to the beat of Euler's drum!

Throughout this book, we have tried to illustrate both the power and beauty of mathematics. However, can mathematics *really* be beautiful? For the sake of the nonbeliever, we shall close with one final observation: Since $\cos(\pi) = -1$ and $\sin(\pi) = 0$, Euler's formula produces one of the most remarkable and, yes, beautiful equations in all of mathematics:

$$\boxed{e^{\pi i} = -1.}$$

After deriving this equation in one of his classes at Harvard University, Prof. Benjamin Peirce (1809 – 1880) is reported to have exclaimed:

> Gentlemen, that is surely true, it is absolutely paradoxical; we cannot understand it, and we don't know what it means. But we have proved it, and therefore we know it must be the truth.[1]

Indeed, this is mysterious! That these fundamental constants of mathematics – the irrationals π and e, the imaginary i, and the sinister minus one, the mathematical prince of darkness himself – should all come together at once, interwoven in such a simple little formula, is both amazing and beautiful. And yet, when we picture minus one sitting at the leftmost point of the unit circle in the complex plane, perhaps things do not seem so paradoxical, after all. . . .

❈ ❈ ❈ ❈ ❈

> I used to think math was no fun,
> 'Cause I couldn't see how it was done.
> Now Euler's my hero,
> For I now see why zero
> Equals $e^{\pi i} + 1$.

P. J. Nahim
Dr. Euler's Fabulous Formula
page 12 (2006)

---

[1] E. Kasner and J. Newman, *Mathematics and the Imagination* (1940).

Reading Comprehension Questions for Section 5.4

One of the consequences of Euler's formula is that the domain of functions like ___(a)___, ___(b)___, and ___(c)___ can be extended to include ___(d)___ numbers. In the case of the trigonometric functions like sine and cosine, the domain can be extended to all complex numbers by the formulas

$$\sin(z) = \frac{\underline{(e)} - \underline{(f)}}{\underline{(g)}} \quad \text{and} \quad \cos(z) = \frac{\underline{(h)} + \underline{(i)}}{\underline{(j)}}.$$

For instance, these formulas give us $\sin(i) \approx$ ___(k)___ and $\cos(i) \approx$ ___(l)___. In the case of the natural logarithm, we first need to express the complex input in polar form as $z =$ ___(m)___, and then we can write

$$\ln(z) = \underline{\quad(n)\quad} + \underline{\quad(o)\quad} i \, .$$

For example, $\ln(i) \approx$ ___(p)___. With this formula, we can extend the domain of the natural logarithm to all complex numbers except ___(q)___. However, to make sure our function is well-defined, we must always pick arguments in the interval ___(r)___.

Another consequence of Euler's formula is an amazing identity that combines the four mathematical constants ___(s)___ (marking the first extension over and above the "natural numbers" $\mathbb{N}$), ___(t)___ (usually associated with the geometry of circles), ___(u)___ (associated with exponential growth and decay), and ___(v)___ (the imaginary unit in complex numbers). In equation form, our identity is:

$$\underline{\quad(w)\quad} = \underline{\quad(x)\quad}.$$

After proving this beautiful formula in class, one professor famously noted that despite the fact that it is absolutely ___(y)___, we know it must be the ___(z)___.

Review of Chapter 5

Vocabulary with which you should now be familiar:

- absolute value
- argument
- complex conjugate
- complex number
- complex plane
- dilation of complex plane
- Euler's formula
- i
- imaginary axis

- imaginary part
- magnitude
- polar form
- purely imaginary number
- real axis
- real part
- rotation of complex plane
- rectangular form
- translation of complex plane

Tasks you should now be prepared to perform:

- Write complex numbers in both rectangular and polar form.
- Add, subtract, multiply, and divide complex numbers.
- Extract all n^{th} roots of a complex number.
- Find the complex zeroes of any linear or quadratic polynomial.
- Describe a linear function of complex numbers in terms of rotations, dilations, and translations of the complex plane.

Brief Answers to the Exercises

Section 1.1

1. The months not containing an r happen to be warm summer months (May through August). Perhaps oysters pick up more toxins from warm water than from cooler water, making them more dangerous during these months.

2. (a) Yes   (b) No   (c) No   (d) Yes

3. (a) Yes   (b) No   (c) Yes   (d) No

4. After 30 minutes of sitting outside, the temperature of Acute Alice's hot cocoa is 10°C.

5. Obtuse Ollie would have to pay $6000 for a 5 year old car.

6. Scalene Sallie's hometown had a population of 12 000 people in 1985.

7. (a) 3
   (b) Four (1, 2, 6, 10)
   (c) $n = 60$

8. (a) $n = 18$ or 23 or 27 or 32 or 34 or ...
   (b) Greater (since $j(5) = 1$)
   (c) 8 (since $88 = $ LXXXVIII)

9. (a) *Bubble diagram*
   (b) Domain $M = \{1, 2, 3, \ldots, 8\}$
   (c) Codomain $M = \{0, 1, 2, 3, \ldots\}$
   (d) Image $M = \{0, 1, 2, 13, 27, 60, 63\}$

10. (a) $n = 5$
    (b) $n = 1$ and $n = 2$
    (c) $n = 8$

11. No: $f(4)$ is ambiguous.

12. Yes.

13. No: $f(3)$ is ambiguous.

14. No: $f(1)$ is not specified.

15. Yes.

16. No: $f(1)$ is ambiguous; $f(2)$, $f(3)$, and $f(4)$ are not specified.

17. No: $f(1)$ and $f(2)$ are ambiguous; $f(3)$ and $f(4)$ are not specified.

18. Yes.

19. Yes.

20. No: $f(2)$ and $f(4)$ are ambiguous.

21. (a) fib : $1, 1, 2, 3, 5, 8, 13, 21, 34, 55$

(b) $n = 3, 6, 9$ are all multiples of three.

(c) Since the first two values of fib are odd, the third must be even by the recursive formula:
$$odd + odd = even.$$
Similarly, the next two values must be odd, since
$$odd + even = odd$$
and
$$even + odd = odd.$$
This makes the pattern of values repeat indefinitely as
$$odd, odd, even, odd, odd, even, \ldots$$
with the even values occurring at every multiple of three.

22. (a) $f : 1, 3, 5, 7, 9, 11, 13, 15, 17, 19$
    (b) The values are all odd numbers, so f can be described by the formula $f(n) = 2n - 1$.
    (c) The two functions will agree at every positive integer. However, they are different functions because they have different domains and codomains.

23. (a) $g : 1, 4, 9, 16, 25, 36, 49, 64, 81, 100$
    (b) The values are all perfect squares, so g can be described by the formula $g(n) = n^2$.
    (c) The two functions will agree at every positive integer. However, they are different functions because they have different domains and codomains.

24. (a) $H : 3, 82.5, 130, 145.5, 129.0, 80.5, 0, 0, 0, 0$
    (b) The clown is at his peak at $t \approx 3$ seconds.
    (c) When $t = 6$ seconds, the clown hits the ground. After that point in time, he stays on the ground, so that $H(t) = 0$ feet for all $t \geq 6$.

25. (a) The flat fee is $24.99.
    (b) The flat fee covers a maximum of 400 peak-time minutes.
    (c) Each additional minute costs $0.05.

26. $D(x) = \begin{cases} 28 & \text{if } x = \text{February,} \\ 30 & \text{if } x = \text{April, June, September,} \\ & \quad \text{or November,} \\ 31 & \text{otherwise.} \end{cases}$

27. In the bubble diagram for the absolute value function, there is exactly one line coming out of each real number in the domain. There are two lines coming into each positive number x

in the codomain (one from x and one from $-x$). There is only one line coming into zero (from zero). There are no lines coming into any negative number in the codomain.

28. (a) There are eight such functions. For six of these, the image set equals the codomain. For the remaining two, the image set contains only one element.

    (b) There are nine such functions. For three of these, the image set contains only one element. For the remaining six, the image set contains two elements. Thus, the image set is never equal to the codomain.

29. $A = 5$

30. $B = 9$ and $C = 3$

Section 1.2

1. $\dfrac{1}{100}$

2. (a) 1, 1, 1

    (b) 9, 0, 0

    (c) 0, 1, 2

3. (a) $\frac{3}{2} = 1.5$

    (b) $\frac{5}{3} = 1.666\,666\ldots$

    (c) $\frac{8}{5} = 1.6$

    (d) $\frac{13}{8} = 1.625$

    (e) Four more iterations of the pattern gives

$$\frac{89}{55} = 1.618\,181\ldots$$

which agrees with the first four digits of

$$\varphi = 1.618\,033\ldots.$$

4. (a) $3 + (2 \cdot (10 - 1)) = 21$

    (b) $(3 + (2 \cdot 10)) - 1 = 22$

    (c) $(3 + 2) \cdot (10 - 1) = 45$

    (d) $((3 + 2) \cdot 10) - 1 = 49$

5. (a) $(3 \cdot (8 - 4)) \div 2 = 6$

    (b) $((3 \cdot 8) - 4) \div 2 = 10$

    (c) $3 \cdot (8 - (4 \div 2)) = 18$

    (d) $(3 \cdot 8) - (4 \div 2) = 22$

6. $3^2 = 4 + 5$

7. Ollie cannot cancel the 3's:

$$\frac{5x^2 + 3}{x + 3} \neq \frac{5x^2}{x}$$

8. Sallie did not multiply correctly:

$$(4x + 1)(x + 3) = 4x^2 + 13x + 3 \neq 4x^2 + 3$$

9. (a) $1\,x^3 + 0\,x^2 + 0\,x - 8$

    (b) $1\,x^3 - 6\,x^2 + 12\,x - 8$

    (c) $1\,x^3 + 0\,x^2 + 0\,x + 8$

    (d) $1\,x^3 + 6\,x^2 + 12\,x + 8$

10. (a) $-15\,x^3 - 14\,x^2 - 47\,x + 22$

    (b) $-15\,x^3 - 14\,x^2 + 83\,x - 30$

    (c) $-15\,x^3 + 66\,x^2 + 51\,x - 30$

    (d) $-15\,x^3 + 26\,x^2 + 67\,x - 30$

11. $x = 3$

12. $x = 7$

13. $x = -\frac{4}{3}$

14. $x = \frac{7}{5}$

15. $x = \frac{4}{\pi - 2}$

16. $x = 5$ or $x = -5$

17. $x = -4$

18. $x = 2$

19. $x = 4$ or $x = 3$

20. $x = -2$ or $x = -5$

21. $x = 2$ or $x = -3$

22. $x = \frac{2}{5}$ or $x = -1$

23. $x = \frac{1}{2}$ or $x = -3$

24. $x = -\frac{1}{2}$ or $x = -\frac{1}{3}$

25. $x = \frac{3}{2}$ or $x = \frac{2}{5}$

26. $x = 4$ or $x = \frac{1}{7}$

27. $x = 2$ or $x = 0$ or $x = -\frac{1}{5}$

28. $x = 7$ or $x = \frac{1}{2}$ or $x = 0$

29. Only one integer (-1) has that property.

30. $x = -2$ or $x = 0$ or $x = 1$

Section 1.3

1. $\{x : x > -7\} = (-7, \infty)$

2. $\{x : x \leq 5\} = (-\infty, 5]$

3. $\{x : x \geq 0\} = [0, \infty)$

4. $\{x : x < 7\} = (-\infty, 7)$

5. $\{x : x > 10\} = (10, \infty)$

6. $\{x : x \leq -1\} = (-\infty, -1]$

7. $\{x : 3 \leq x \leq 6\} = [3, 6]$

8. $\{x : \frac{2}{3} < x \leq 3\} = (\frac{2}{3}, 3]$

9. $\{x : x < -1 \text{ or } x > 8\} = (-\infty, -1) \cup (8, \infty)$

10. $\{x : x \leq 1 \text{ or } 2 \leq x \leq 3\} = (-\infty, 1] \cup [2, 3]$

11. $\{x : -2 < x < 1 \text{ or } x > 1\} = (-2, 1) \cup (1, \infty)$

12. $\{x : x < -1 \text{ or } 0 < x < 3\} =$
    $(-\infty, -1) \cup (0, 3)$

13. $\{x : -\frac{2}{3} \leq x \leq \frac{3}{2}\} = [-\frac{2}{3}, \frac{3}{2}]$

14. $\{x : x \leq -2 \text{ or } x = 0 \text{ or } x \geq 2\} =$
    $(-\infty, -2] \cup \{0\} \cup [2, \infty)$

15. $\{x : 0 \leq x < 3\} = [0, 3)$

16. $\{x : -\frac{11}{2} < x < \frac{17}{2}\} = (-\frac{11}{2}, \frac{17}{2})$

17. $\{x : x < -1 \text{ or } x > 3\} = (-\infty, -1) \cup (3, \infty)$

18. $\{x : -1 < x < 1 \text{ or } x = 3\} = (-1, 1) \cup \{3\}$

19. $\{x : x \leq -1 \text{ or } 0 < x \leq 1\} =$
    $(-\infty, -1] \cup (0, 1]$

20. $\{x : x < 0 \text{ or } 0 < x \leq 1 \text{ or } x \geq 2\} =$
    $(-\infty, 0) \cup (0, 1] \cup [2, \infty)$

21. $\{x : -5 < x < 2\} = (-5, 2)$

22. $\{x : -2 < x < 0 \text{ or } x > 3\} = (-2, 0) \cup (3, \infty)$

23. $\{x : -6 < x \leq 3\} = (-6, 3]$

24. $\{x : -26 \leq x < -2 \text{ or } x > 6\} =$
    $[-26, -2) \cup (6, \infty)$

25. (a) $(-3, 3]$

    (b) $[-2, 4)$

    (c) $(3, 6)$

    (d) $(1, 7]$

* 26. $\dfrac{(x+2)(x-1)}{(x+1)(x-2)} \leq 0$

* 27. $(x-5)(x+5)^2 \geq 0$

28. $(-\infty, -2] \cup \{0\} \cup [\frac{2}{3}, \infty)$

29. (a) $\mathbb{Q}$ (b) $\mathbb{R}$ (c) $\varnothing$

30. (a) Yes. Alice just needs to divide the original inequality by q.

    (b) Yes. Sallie just needs to divide the last inequality by p.

    (c) No. Since p and q are negative, Ollie will need to change the direction of the inequalities each time he divides. Thus, he should have
    $$\frac{p}{q} > 1$$

---

* Other answers are possible for these exercises.

after switching directions once, and
$$\frac{1}{q} < \frac{1}{p}$$
after switching directions a second time. This means that the second inequality is correct, but the first one is not.

Section 1.4

1. (a) $(-\infty, 0) \cup (12, 18)$

   (b) Domain $V = [0, 12]$

2. (a) $W(x)$ is undefined when $x = 0$ and when $x = 406$. These values correspond to the center of the earth and the center of the moon.

   (b) Domain $W = [6.4, 404.3]$

3. (a) $V(x) = x(24 - 2x)^2$

   (b) Alice's suggestion will produce a larger box, since $V(3) = 972$ cubic inches while $V(6) = 864$ cubic inches.

   (c) Cut a 4-inch square from each corner, making a box measuring $V(4) = 1024$ cubic inches.

4. $2.645751\ldots$ (computed in 5 steps)

5. $1.709975\ldots$ (computed in 5 steps)

6. (a) $1.414213\ldots$

   (b) $1.553773\ldots$

   (c) $1.598053\ldots$

   (d) $1.611847\ldots$

   (e) $\phi = 1.618033\ldots$

7. (a) $2.828427\ldots$

   (b) $3.061467\ldots$

   (c) $3.121445\ldots$

   (d) $3.136548\ldots$

   (e) $\pi = 3.141592\ldots$

8. (a) III   (b) IV   (c) II   (d) I

9. $x = 11$

10. $x = 2$

11. $x = 7$ ($x = 1$ is spurious)

12. $x = 2$ ($x = 5$ is spurious)

13. $x = 0$ or $x = -3$

14. $x = 14$ or $x = -10$

15. $x = \frac{5}{3}$ or $x = -\frac{1}{3}$

16. $x = -1 \pm \sqrt{5}$

17. $(-\infty, -4) \cup (-4, \infty)$

18. $(-\infty, -\frac{3}{2}) \cup (-\frac{3}{2}, 3) \cup (3, \infty)$

19. $(-\infty, -1) \cup (-1, -\frac{2}{3}) \cup (-\frac{2}{3}, \infty)$

20. $(-\infty, 1) \cup (1, \frac{3}{2}) \cup (\frac{3}{2}, \infty)$

21. $[2, \infty)$

22. $(-\infty, -6]$

23. $(-\infty, 3] \cup [4, \infty)$

24. $(8, \infty)$

25. $[-3, 3)$

26. $(-\infty, -7) \cup (-7, -2] \cup [2, \infty)$

* 27. $f(x) = \dfrac{1}{x-1}$

* 28. $f(x) = \sqrt{7-x}$

* 29. $f(x) = \sqrt{(x+1)(x-5)}$

* 30. $f(x) = \sqrt{\dfrac{1}{(x+2)(x-4)}}$

Section 1.5

1. (a) II   (b) III   (c) III

   (d) I   (e) IV   (f) II

2. (a) $(1, 4)$ (b) $(-3, -4)$ (c) $(-3, 4)$

   (d) $(4, 1)$ (e) $(0, 1)$ (f) $(-3, 0)$

3. (a) Yes   (b) No   (c) No

   (d) Yes   (e) No   (f) Yes

4. (a) No   (b) No   (c) Yes

   (d) Yes   (e) Yes   (f) No

5. x-intercept: -2; y-intercept: $\frac{3}{2}$

6. (a) The triangle has a perimeter of $12\sqrt{2}$.

   (b) Sallie's triangle is a scalene triangle.

   (c) Sallie's triangle is a right triangle.

7. (a) The triangle would have two sides of length $\sqrt{2}$ and one of length 2.

   (b) $1^2 + y^2 = 2^2$.

   (c) The third vertex should be placed at either $(0, \sqrt{3})$ or $(0, -\sqrt{3})$.

8. $A = (-5, 6)$, $B = (7, 1)$,   length $= 13$

9. $C = (3, 6)$, $D = (-6, -6)$,   length $= 15$

10. $E = (-4, 7)$, $F = (4, -8)$,   length $= 17$

11. $G = (-4, -2)$, $H = (4, 6)$,   length $= 8\sqrt{2}$

12. x-intercept: 2; y-intercept: 5

13. x-intercepts: ± 2; y-intercept: 4

14. x-intercepts: $-7, -1$; y-intercepts: ± 1

15. x-intercepts: $-1, 5$; y-intercepts: $-5, -2$

16. $x = 7$

17. $y = 3$

18. $(x-4)^2 + (y+2)^2 = 5^2$

19. $(x-5)^2 + (y-12)^2 = 13^2$

20. $(x-4)^2 + (y-\frac{15}{2})^2 = (\frac{17}{2})^2$

21. circle with $r = 7$,   center $= (0, 0)$
x-intercepts: ± 7; y-intercepts: ± 7.

22. vertical line
x-intercept: 5; y-intercept: none.

23. horizontal line
x-intercept: none; y-intercept: 5.

24. circle with $r = 5$,   center $= (-3, 0)$
x-intercepts: $-8, 2$; y-intercepts: ± 4.

25. circle with $r = 4$,   center $= (-5, 0)$
x-intercepts: $-9, -1$; y-intercepts: none.

26. circle with $r = 5$,   center $= (0, -3)$
x-intercepts: ± 4; y-intercepts: $-8, 2$.

27. vertical line
x-intercept: 7; y-intercept: none.

28. circle with $r = 2$,   center $= (2, 0)$
x-intercepts: $0, 4$; y-intercept: 0.

29. horizontal line
x-intercept: none; y-intercept: $\frac{3}{2}$.

30. circle with $r = 3$,   center $= (1, 2)$
x-intercepts: $1 \pm \sqrt{5}$; y-intercepts: $2 \pm \sqrt{8}$.

Section 1.6

1. While standing on the far side of the moon, where $x = 407.7$, the cat will feel gravity pulling towards Earth. Therefore $W(407.7)$ should be positive, contrary to what the graph indicates. The problem is that $x = 407.7$ is outside of the domain of W.

2. *Graph.* The temperature of the cocoa will continue to decrease, but never dip below $-30°$C. The y-intercept is the initial tempera-

* Other answers are possible for these exercises.

ture of the cocoa. The x-intercept is the time when it reaches $0°C$ and freezes; an accurate graph will cross the axis tangentially as the cocoa changes from liquid to solid.

3. *Graph.* The graph is decreasing because the car will eventually lose its value with time. The y-intercept is the cost of a new car. The x-intercept is the time when the car is completely worthless.

4. *Graph.* There is a local maximum at around 1970 and a local minimum at around 1980. In addition, there is a second maximum, higher than the first one, which stretches from 1995 to the present.

5. $H : 3, 82.5, 130, 145.5, 129.0, 80.5, 0, 0, 0, 0$

   Graph. The first part is a parabolic arc, increasing from $(0, 3)$ to a local maximum at around $(3, 145.5)$ and then decreasing to an x-intercept at $(6, 0)$. This is followed by a horizontal line segment along the x-axis.

6. $C : 24.99, 24.99, 24.99, 24.99, 24.99, 29.99,$
   $34.99, 39.99, 44.99, 49.99$

   Graph. The first part is a horizontal line segment connecting $(0, 24.99)$ to $(400, 24.99)$; the second is a diagonal line segment from $(400, 24.99)$ to $(900, 49.99)$.

7. $f : -6.1, -4.5, 4.2, 3.9, 0, 2, 0.5, 1, 6.8$

8. $g : 2.5, -4.5, 6.5, -8.5, 9, -8.5, 6.5, -4.5, 2.5$

9. (a) Image $f = \left[-7.2, 8.5\right]$.
   (b) x-ints: $x = -10, -5, 0, 5, 0$; y-ints: $y = 0$.
   (c) $x \in \left(-5, 0\right) \cup \left(0, 5\right) \cup \left(5, 10\right]$.
   (d) $x \in \left(-10, -5\right)$.
   (e) There are 3 values of x for which $f(x) = 5$: $x \approx -3.7, -2.5,$ and 7.4.

10. (a) Image $g = \left[-8.5, 9\right]$.
    (b) Local maxima at $x = -8, -4, 0, 4, 8$.
    (c) $x \in \left(-10, -8\right) \cup \left(-6, -4\right) \cup \left(-2, 0\right) \cup \left(2, 4\right) \cup \left(6, 8\right)$.
    (d) $x \in \left(-8, -6\right) \cup \left(-4, -2\right) \cup \left(0, 2\right) \cup \left(4, 6\right) \cup \left(8, 10\right)$.
    (e) There are 5 values of x for which $g(x) = x$: $x \approx -2.7, -1.1, 0.9, 3.3,$ and 4.7.

11. *Graph*:
    x-intercepts: $-3, \frac{7}{2}$ (both transversal),
    no asymptotes,
    left and right ends go towards $+\infty$.

12. *Graph*:
    x-intercepts: $-9, 2, \frac{8}{3}$ (all transversal),
    no asymptotes,

left ends goes towards $-\infty$,
right ends goes towards $+\infty$.

13. *Graph*:
    x-intercepts: $\frac{1}{2}$ (transversal), 5 (turning);
    no asymptotes,
    left ends goes towards $+\infty$,
    right ends goes towards $-\infty$.

14. *Graph*:
    x-intercepts: $-4, -3, -2, -1$ (all transversal),
    no asymptotes,
    left and right ends go towards $+\infty$.

15. *Graph*:
    x-intercepts: -4 (tangential), $\frac{1}{6}$ (transversal),
    no asymptotes,
    left and right ends go towards $+\infty$.

16. *Graph*:
    x-intercepts: -6 (transversal), $\frac{7}{4}$ (turning),
    no asymptotes,
    left ends goes towards $-\infty$,
    right ends goes towards $+\infty$.

17. *Graph*:
    x-intercepts: $-3, -\frac{1}{2}$ (both transversal),
    no asymptotes,
    left and right ends go towards $+\infty$.

18. *Graph*:
    x-intercept: 4 (tangential),
    no asymptotes,
    left and right ends go towards $+\infty$.

19. *Graph*:
    x-intercept: 5 (transversal),
    vertical asymptotes: $x = -8, x = \frac{2}{3}$,
    horizontal asymptote: $y = 0$.

20. *Graph*:
    x-intercepts: $-4, -6$ (both transversal),
    vertical asymptote: $x = 4$,
    no horizontal asymptotes,
    left ends goes towards $-\infty$,
    right ends goes towards $+\infty$.

21. *Graph*:
    x-intercept: $\frac{5}{2}$ (transversal),
    vertical asymptote: $x = 6$,
    horizontal asymptote: $y = 0$.

22. *Graph*:
    x-intercept: $-\frac{1}{4}$ (transversal),
    vertical asymptote: $x = -7$,
    horizontal asymptote: $y = 4$.

23. *Graph*:
    x-intercept: -4 (tangential),
    vertical asymptotes: $x = 4, x = \frac{9}{2}$,
    horizontal asymptote: $y = \frac{1}{2}$.

24. *Graph*:
    x-intercept: $-\frac{3}{7}$ (turning),
    vertical asymptotes: $x = -1, x = 9$,
    horizontal asymptote: $y = 0$.

25. Yes.

26. No.

27. No.

28. Yes.

29. No.

30. Yes.

Section 2.1

1. (a) 540   (b) 36   (c) -252 (d) -324

2. Both are equal to 0.

3. Average rate of change $= -\frac{12.9}{397.9} \approx 0.032\,420$. The function is not linear because its graph is not a line.

4. *Graph.*

5. The function is not linear since the average rate of change varies from -1 in the interval $[1, 100]$ to -0.001 in the interval $[100, 1000]$.

6. $f(x) = 3x - 13$

7. $g(x) = 6 - x$

8. $h(x) = 3$

9. $j(x) = -\frac{1}{3}x + 2$

10. slope: 2 y-intercept: 3

11. slope: $-\frac{1}{2}$ y-intercept: 3

12. slope: $\frac{2}{5}$ y-intercept: 2

13. slope: $-\frac{2}{7}$ y-intercept: $\frac{13}{7}$

14. slope: $-\frac{1}{5}$ y-intercept: $\frac{3}{5}$

15. slope: 9 y-intercept: 1

16. x-intercept:-2 y-intercept:2

17. x-intercept:10 y-intercept:10

18. x-intercept:$\frac{32}{5}$ y-intercept:8

19. x-intercept:$\frac{5}{2}$ y-intercept:5

20. x-intercept:$\frac{5}{2}$ y-intercept:-10

21. x-intercept:5 y-intercept:$\frac{5}{4}$

22. $f(x) = -\frac{3}{2}x + 3$

23. $f(x) = \frac{1}{2}x + 2$

24. $f(x) = 3x - 6$

25. $f(x) = -x - 5$

26. (a) slope: 0; y-intercept: $(0, 24.99)$; *Graph*.

    (b) slope: 0.05; y-intercept: $(0, 4.99)$; *Graph*.

    (c) *Graph*. Yes, it forms a connected graph because the two pieces meet at the point $(400, 24.99)$.

27. (a) $C(x) = 19 - 1.5x$

    (b) $\frac{34}{3} \approx 11.333$ years.

28. (a) $T(x) = 1.6x + 64$

    (b) 3 hours and 45 minutes.

29. (a) $d(x) = 1450 - 250x$

    (b) $s(x) = \frac{1600}{3}x + \frac{100}{3}$

30. (a) If supply is greater than demand, the store will have too much cat food left over in its shelves.

    (b) If demand is greater than supply, the store will run out of cat food before the next shipment.

    (c) The equilibrium price is $\frac{85}{47} \approx \$1.81$.

Section 2.2

1. Yes. $f(x) = 3x - 2$

2. No. $f_*(x) \approx -2.1x + 17.5$

3. No. $f_*(x) \approx 1.8x + 0.6$

4. Yes. $f(x) = 2x + 1$

5. No. $f_*(x) \approx -2.5x + 9.9$

6. Yes. $f(x) = 4x - 11$

7. Yes. $f(x) = 10 - 2x$

8. No. $f_*(x) \approx 3.5x - 3.5$

9. No. $f_*(x) \approx -1.7x + 8.9$

10. Yes. $f(x) = 29 - 4x$

11. (a) *Scatter Plot.*
    Positive correlation.

    (b) Slope $= 0.285\,714\ldots$.
    Six points above. Six points below.

    (c) Slope $= 0.307\,142\ldots$.
    Eight points above. Seven points below.

12. (a) *Scatter Plot.*
    Positive correlation.

    (b) Slope $= 0.071\,428\ldots$.
    Eleven points above. Two points below.

    (c) Slope $= 0.078\,571\ldots$.
    Seven points above. Eight points below.

13. (a) *Scatter Plot.*

(b) Slope = 4.125.
No points above. Seven points below.

(c) Slope = 3.65.
Four points above. Five points below.

14. (a) *Scatter Plot.*

(b) Slope = 88.
No points above. Ten points below.

(c) Slope = 88.
Six points above. Six points below.

15. $f_*(x) \approx 5.457\,x - 37.459$.
Positive correlation.

16. $f_*(x) \approx 6.551\,x + 100.698$.
Positive correlation.

17. $f_*(x) \approx 26.948\,x + 48.514$.
Positive correlation.

18. $f_*(x) \approx 24.567\,x + 112.323$.
Positive correlation.

19. (a) Mercury: 440.6, Venus: 1 125.5,
Earth: 1 829.8, Mars: 3 440.5,
Jupiter: 21 725.6, Saturn: 54 274.6,
Uranus: 153 953.7, Neptune: 301 376.3

(b) $f_*(x) \approx 0.198\,452\,x + 3.947$.

* 20. The errors range from -0.36% (for Jupiter) to 3.8% (for Mercury). These errors are fairly small, indicating a strong correlation in the data. In particular, $b_* \approx 3.947$ is also small, so the length of a year is (almost) proportional to the square root of the cube of the distance to the sun, confirming Kepler's third law.

21. The predicted duration of a year in Pluto is approximately 89 255 days.

22. The error is about 1 333 days or 1.5%. This error is comparable to those computed for the other planets, so the IAU must have had other reasons for downgrading Pluto.

23. (a) $f_*(x) \approx -2.817\,x + 80.2$.

(b) Negative correlation.

* (c) No. In poorer countries, higher birth rates might contribute to widespread famines and therefore to shorter life spans. However, in the richer countries of Europe, it seems unlikely that higher birth rates should be the direct cause of shorter life spans.

24. (a) $f_*(x) \approx 1.007\,x + 12.0$.

(b) Positive correlation.

* (c) Yes. A higher gross domestic product indicates a more affluent population that is

more likely to own computers and make use of the internet.

25. The predicted life expectancy in the U.S. is about 76.2 years, corresponding to an error of approximately 1.8 years or 2.3%.

26. The predicted internet usage in the U.S. is about 56.327%, corresponding to an overall error of 14.656% and a relative error of 20.6%.

* 27. (a) Correlation. More information is required in order to determine causation.

(b) Correlation but not causation. Presumably, the cause should precede the effect, not lag behind it.

(c) Neither correlation nor causation. This anomaly indicates that other factors are also responsible for warming and cooling trends.

(d) Perhaps correlation, but perhaps neither. Two data points is probably not enough to determine either correlation or causation.

28. $m_* = \dfrac{x_1 y_1 - x_2 y_1 - x_1 y_2 + x_2 y_2}{x_1{}^2 - 2\,x_1 x_2 + x_2{}^2}$

$= \dfrac{(x_1 - x_2)(y_1 - y_2)}{(x_1 - x_2)^2} = \dfrac{y_1 - y_2}{x_1 - x_2}.$

This shows that the line that best fits two points will be precisely the line determined by those two points.

29. In each case we would be dividing by

$$Sn - X^2 = (3\,x_1{}^2) \cdot 3 - (3\,x_1)^2 = 0$$

This shows that the line that best fits three points with the same x-coordinate will be a vertical line.

30. (a) $S\,m_* + X\,b_*$

$= \dfrac{SPn - SXY + XSY - PX^2}{Sn - X^2} = P.$

(b) $X\,m_* + n\,b_*$

$= \dfrac{XPn - X^2Y + nSY - nPX}{Sn - X^2} = Y.$

Section 2.3

1. model function: $f(x) = x^2$;
horizontal translation ($\leftarrow 2$),
vertical translation ($\downarrow 4$);
$g(x) = (x+2)^2 - 4$.

2. model function: $f(x) = x^3$;
horizontal translation ($\leftarrow 2$),

---

* Other answers are possible for these exercises.

vertical translation ($\uparrow 1$);
$g(x) = (x+2)^3 + 1$.

3. model function: $f(x) = |x|$;
vertical dilation ($\times \frac{5}{2}$),
vertical translation ($\downarrow 5$);
$g(x) = \frac{5}{2}|x| - 5$.

4. model function: $f(x) = x^3$;
horizontal reflection,
horizontal dilation ($\times 3$),
vertical translation ($\uparrow 1$);
$g(x) = \left(-\frac{1}{3}x\right)^3 + 1$.

5. model function: $f(x) = \frac{1}{x}$;
vertical reflection,
vertical translation ($\uparrow 2$);
$g(x) = -\frac{1}{x} + 2$.

6. model function: $f(x) = x^2$;
vertical reflection,
vertical dilation ($\times 2$),
vertical translation ($\uparrow 2$);
$g(x) = -2x^2 + 2$.

7. *Graph*:
model function: $f(x) = x^2$;
horizontal translation ($\rightarrow 2$).

8. *Graph*:
model function: $f(x) = |x|$;
vertical translation ($\downarrow 7$).

9. *Graph*:
model function: $f(x) = \frac{1}{x}$;
vertical reflection,
vertical dilation ($\times 2$).

10. *Graph*:
model function: $f(x) = \sqrt{x}$;
horizontal dilation ($\times \frac{1}{3}$).

11. *Graph*:
model function: $f(x) = |x|$;
horizontal translation ($\leftarrow 5$).

12. *Graph*:
model function: $f(x) = \frac{1}{x}$;
vertical reflection,
horizontal translation ($\rightarrow 4$).

13. *Graph*:
model function: $f(x) = x^2$;
vertical dilation ($\times 3$),
horizontal translation ($\leftarrow 1$).

14. *Graph*:
model function: $f(x) = |x|$;
horizontal dilation ($\times \frac{1}{2}$),
vertical translation ($\uparrow 1$).

15. *Graph*:
model function: $f(x) = \sqrt{x}$;
vertical dilation ($\times 5$),
vertical translation ($\downarrow 2$).

16. *Graph*:
model function: $f(x) = \frac{1}{x}$;
horizontal dilation ($\times \frac{1}{3}$),
vertical translation ($\uparrow 1$).

17. *Graph*:
model function: $f(x) = x^3$;
horizontal reflection,
horizontal dilation ($\times \frac{1}{2}$),
horizontal translation ($\rightarrow 3$).

18. *Graph*:
model function: $f(x) = \frac{1}{x}$;
horizontal dilation ($\times \frac{1}{3}$),
horizontal translation ($\rightarrow 1$),
vertical translation ($\uparrow 1$).

19. *Graph 1*:
x-intercepts at $x = -5, 1$,
no asymptotes,
left and right ends go towards $+\infty$;

Graph 2:
model function: $f(x) = x^2$,
horizontal translation ($\leftarrow 2$),
vertical translation ($\downarrow 9$).

20. *Graph 1*:
x-intercept at $x = 3$,
vertical asymptote at $x = 4$,
horizontal asymptote at $y = 1$;

Graph 2:
model function: $f(x) = \frac{1}{x}$,
horizontal translation ($\rightarrow 4$),
vertical translation ($\uparrow 1$).

21. *Graph 1*:
x-intercepts at $x = 1, 9$,
no asymptotes;
left and right ends go towards $-\infty$;

Graph 2:
model function: $f(x) = x^2$,
vertical reflection,
horizontal translation ($\rightarrow 5$),
vertical translation ($\uparrow 16$).

22. *Graph 1*:
x-intercept at $x = \frac{7}{3}$,
vertical asymptote at $x = 2$,
horizontal asymptote at $y = 3$;

Graph 2:
model function: $f(x) = \frac{1}{x}$,
vertical reflection,

horizontal translation ($\to 2$),
vertical translation ($\uparrow 3$).

23. *Graph 1:*
    x-intercepts at $x = -4, -2,$
    no asymptotes;
    left and right ends go towards $+\infty$;

    Graph 2:
    model function: $f(x) = x^2,$
    vertical dilation ($\times 2$),
    horizontal translation ($\leftarrow 3$),
    vertical translation ($\downarrow 2$).

24. *Graph 1:*
    x-intercept at $x = 3,$
    vertical asymptote at $x = 4,$
    horizontal asymptote at $y = 2$;

    Graph 2:
    model function: $f(x) = \frac{1}{x},$
    vertical dilation ($\times 2$),
    horizontal translation ($\to 4$),
    vertical translation ($\uparrow 2$).

25. $f(x) = |x|$ and $f(x) = x^2$ are even.

26. $f(x) = x$, $f(x) = x^3$, and $f(x) = \frac{1}{x}$ are odd.

27. (a) even   (b) odd

    (c) even   (d) even

    (e) odd   (f) odd

28. (a) odd   (b) neither

    (c) neither   (d) even

29. $A = 1$, $B = -\frac{1}{2}$, $C = 0$

30.

	integers	functions
even + even	even	even
odd + odd	even	odd
even + odd	odd	neither
even × even	even	even
odd × odd	odd	even
even × odd	even	odd

Section 2.4

1. No; change to $f(3) = \frac{22}{3}$.

2. Yes; $f(x) = -x^2 + 6x + 3$.

3. No; must change at least three values.

4. Yes; $f(x) = x^2 + 2x - 10$.

5. Yes; $f(x) = -\frac{1}{2}x^2 - \frac{1}{2}x + 11$.

6. No; change to $f(2) = -5$.

7. $x = 2$ or $x = 5$

8. $x = 2 \pm \sqrt{3}$

9. No solution

10. $x = -4 \pm \sqrt{7}$

11. $x = -\frac{1}{2}$ or $x = -2$

12. No solution

13. $x = \dfrac{-1 \pm \sqrt{3}}{2}$

14. $x = 2 \pm \sqrt{2}$

15. $x = \dfrac{3 \pm \sqrt{29}}{10}$

16. No solution

17. *Graph:* Concave down parabola;
    vertex: $(0, 25)$;
    x-intercepts: $(-5, 0), (5, 0)$;
    y-intercept: $(0, 25)$.

18. *Graph:* Concave up parabola;
    vertex: $(\frac{1}{4}, 0)$;
    x-intercept: $(\frac{1}{4}, 0)$;
    y-intercept: $(0, 1)$.

19. *Graph:* Concave up parabola;
    vertex: $(-3, -8)$;
    x-intercepts: $(-5, 0), (-1, 0)$;
    y-intercept: $(0, 10)$.

20. *Graph:* Concave down parabola;
    vertex: $\left(-\frac{1}{3}, -\frac{2}{3}\right)$;
    no x-intercepts;
    y-intercept: $(0, -1)$.

21. *Graph:* Concave up parabola;
    vertex: $\left(-\frac{3}{4}, -\frac{25}{8}\right)$;
    x-intercepts: $(-2, 0), (\frac{1}{2}, 0)$;
    y-intercept: $(0, -2)$.

22. *Graph:* Concave down parabola;
    vertex: $\left(\frac{2}{3}, \frac{10}{3}\right)$;
    x-intercepts: $\left(\frac{2-\sqrt{10}}{3}, 0\right), \left(\frac{2+\sqrt{10}}{3}, 0\right)$;
    y-intercept: $(0, 2)$.

23. *Graph:* Concave up parabola;
    vertex: $\left(-\frac{\sqrt{2}}{2}, \frac{1}{2}\right)$;

no x-intercepts;

y-intercept: $(0, 1)$.

24. *Graph*: Concave up parabola;

vertex: $\left(\frac{\sqrt{2}}{2}, -\frac{3}{2}\right)$;

x-intercepts: $\left(\frac{\sqrt{2}-\sqrt{6}}{2}, 0\right), \left(\frac{\sqrt{2}+\sqrt{6}}{2}, 0\right)$;

y-intercept: $(0, -1)$.

25. The clown is at his maximum height when $t = \frac{191}{64} = 2.984\,375$ seconds. This is just shy of our answer to Exercise 24 in Section 1.1.

26. (a) The best formula is (ii).

(b) $h = 3$, $k = -8$.

(c) $d = 5$.

(d) $b = 6$.

(e) $a = 2$.

(f) $c = 10$.

27. $A = \pm 1$

28. $B \in \left(-\infty, -\sqrt{32}\right) \cup \left(\sqrt{32}, \infty\right)$

29. (a) $(y - d)^2 - (y - k)^2$

$$= \big((y - d) - (y - k)\big)\big((y - d) + (y - k)\big)$$
$$= (k - d)(2y - k - d)$$
$$= (k - d)\big(2y - (k + d)\big).$$

(b) $(k - d)\big(2y - (k + d)\big)$

$$= \left(\frac{1}{2a}\right)\left(2y - 2c + \frac{b^2}{2a}\right)$$
$$= \frac{y - c}{a} + \frac{b^2}{4a^2} = \frac{y - c}{a} + h^2.$$

(c) $\dfrac{y - c}{a} + h^2$

$$= \frac{(ax^2 + bx + c) - c}{a} + h^2$$
$$= x^2 + \frac{b}{a}x + h^2 = x^2 + 2hx + h^2.$$

(d) The left hand side of the equation gives the square of the distance from the point $\big(x, f(x)\big)$ to the focus; the right hand side gives the square of the distance from the same point to the directrix. Therefore, the two distances are equal.

30. (a) $m_* = \dfrac{2(P - b_* X)}{2S} = \dfrac{P - b_* X}{S}$.

(b) $b_* = \dfrac{2(Y - m_* X)}{2n} = \dfrac{Y - m_* X}{n}$.

(c) Multiply the first equation by S and solve for P; then multiply the second equation by n and solve for Y.

Section 2.5

1. $x = 1 \quad y = 2$

2. $x = 2 \quad y = -1$

3. $x = 5 \quad y = 3$

4. $x = 3 \quad y = 5$ or $x = 7 \quad y = 13$

5. (a) Alice pays \$6.40 and Sallie pays \$9.60.

(b) Ollie pays Alice \$2.40 and Sallie \$3.60.

6. At the top of Mount McKinley, the boiling point of water would be about $78.47°$C; at the top of Mount Everest, it would be about $69.26°$C.

7. Alice paid \$106 for her tripod.

8. A total of 36 seniors went on Sallie's trip. Each one will pay \$13.40 for their ticket.

9. Ollie should charge \$1900 per lawnmower.

10. Starting at age 36, a man can court a woman eleven years younger than he is.

11. (a) Alice will have to walk for 9 minutes.

(b) Alice will have to walk for 19.5 minutes.

12. The foundation can acquire 12.5 square miles of forest.

13. Ollie earns \$7.50 per hour.

14. The trains will meet at 5:52 pm.

15. Alice invested \$700 in one stock and \$300 in the other.

16. Sallie travelled a total of 8 miles.

17. Ollie made deliveries on 26 nights, and was on call the other 14 nights.

18. The largest window is a rectangle $\frac{15}{4+\pi} \approx 2.1$ feet tall by $\frac{30}{4+\pi} \approx 4.2$ feet wide, crowned by a semicircle of radius $\frac{15}{4+\pi} \approx 2.1$ feet.

19. Alice can finish painting her room in 9 hours, while her roommate can finish in 18 hours.

20. There was a total of 19 tables.

21. Planting 75 trees per acre will produce the maximum yield of $11\,250$ boxes per acre.

22. The passenger train will pass the freight train at 12:45 pm.

23. (a) Alice should let 9 kilograms of water evaporate away.

(b) Alice should add 1 kilogram of salt.

24. Sallie can travel 15 kilometers each way.

25. Ollie should start with a 24 cm by 24 cm square of sheet metal.

26. The tank can be emptied in 2 hours 6 minutes.

27. Alice triangle will enclose 30 square feet of area.

28. Ollie has 12 quarters, 4 dimes, 6 nickels, and 22 pennies.

29. Sallie was rowing at 2 miles per hour.

30. (a) They will run past each other every 3.75 minutes if they run in opposite directions.

    (b) They will run past each every 15 minutes if they run in the same direction.

Section 3.1

1. No; f is quadratic.

2. Yes; $f(x) = 0.25 \, 4^x$.

3. Yes; $f(x) = \frac{2}{3}\left(\frac{3}{2}\right)^x$.

4. No; f is linear.

5. Yes; $f(x) = 100 \, 0.1^x$.

6. No; f is quadratic.

7. (a) $8^{5/3} = 32$

   (b) $32^{2/5} = 4$

   (c) $49^{3/2} = 343$

   (d) $81^{3/4} = 27$

8. (a) $0.707\,106\,781\ldots$

   (b) $0.375\,214\,227\ldots$

   (c) $0.594\,426\,997\ldots$

   (d) $0.438\,651\,165\ldots$

   (e) $b^* = 0.5$

9. (a) *Table.*

   (b) They are the values of Fibonacci's function fib, and therefore model a population of rabbits.

10. model function: $f(x) = 4^x$;
    vertical dilation ($\times 3$);
    horizontal asymptote: $y = 0$.

11. model function: $f(x) = 2^x$;
    vertical translation ($\uparrow 5$);
    horizontal asymptote: $y = 5$.

12. model function: $f(x) = 7^x$;
    horizontal reflection,
    horizontal dilation ($\times 2$);
    horizontal asymptote: $y = 0$.

13. model function: $f(x) = 2^x$;
    horizontal translation ($\rightarrow 4$),

vertical translation ($\uparrow 1$);
horizontal asymptote: $y = 1$.

14. model function: $f(x) = 2^x$;
    vertical reflection,
    horizontal reflection,
    vertical translation ($\uparrow 7$);
    horizontal asymptote: $y = 7$.

15. model function: $f(x) = 5^x$;
    horizontal reflection,
    horizontal translation ($\rightarrow 2$),
    vertical translation ($\downarrow 3$);
    horizontal asymptote: $y = -3$.

16. $x = 3$

17. $x = 4$

18. $x = -4$ or $x = -3$

19. $x = -1$ or $x = \frac{1}{3}$

20. No solution

21. $x = 1$ or $x = -7^3 = -343$

22. $f(x) = \frac{3\sqrt{5}}{5}\left(\sqrt{5}\right)^x$.

23. $A = 1$ and $B = 3$. (Note that $A = 6$ and $B = -2$ is not acceptable because Domain f should be all of $\mathbb{R}$.)

24. $p(10) \approx 73.742\%$, and $p(25) \approx 46.697\%$.

25. $C(3) = 12\,123.27$, and $C(9) \approx 6\,442.80$.

26. In 5 days, half of the residents will have heard the rumor. In 10 days, 75% will have heard it.

27. (a) \$4.04

    (b) \$4.060\,401

    (c) \$4.074\,154\ldots

    (d) Short-term investors will get some of their interest in less time, so they do not have to commit their assets to a single investment. Long-term investors will get more interest in the long run because their interest builds up new interest quicker. Banks will appear to be more attractive to both kinds of investors and thus be more competitive.

28. $p = 1.584\,962\ldots$

29. (a) Yes; if x is a positive integer then $y = 0^x$ would be a product of several zeroes multiplied together, so $y = 0$.

    (b) No; for instance, 0^{-1} should be the reciprocal of zero $\left(\frac{1}{0}\right)$ and this is undefined since it would mean dividing by zero.

    (c) Maybe; as long as x is a positive rational number, $y = 0^x$ is a root of zero and hence $y = 0$. However, it is not defined for negative values of x since that would mean

447

dividing by zero.

(d) Maybe; as long as x is a positive irrational number, $y = 0^x$ would be computed as the limit of a sequence of positive rational powers of zero (all zero), and thus $y = 0$. However, it is not defined for negative values of x, since that would mean dividing by zero.

30. (a) Yes; if x is an even integer, then $y = (-1)^x$ is either a product of an even number of copies of minus one multiplied together, or the reciprocal of such a product. In either case, $y = 1$.

(b) Yes; if x is an odd integer, then $y = (-1)^x$ is either a product of an odd number of copies of minus one multiplied together, or the reciprocal of such a product. In either case, $y = -1$.

(c) Maybe; $y = (-1)^x$ is well-defined as long as x is a rational number with an odd denominator. In that case, the value of y depends on whether the numerator of x is even or odd:
$$(-1)^{\text{even/odd}} = 1$$
and
$$(-1)^{\text{odd/odd}} = -1.$$
It is not defined for rational numbers with even denominators since that would mean taking the square root of a negative number.

(d) No; every irrational number can be approximated by two sequences of fractions, one with odd numerators and denominators and the other with even numerators and odd denominators. Using the first sequence, we arrive at the limit
$$(-1)^{\text{odd/odd}} = -1,$$
but using the second, we would arrive at the limit
$$(-1)^{\text{even/odd}} = 1.$$
Since $(-1)^x$ cannot take on both of these values at once, it must remain undefined.

Section 3.2

1. $2.302\,585\,092\ldots \approx \ln 10$

2. $2.197\,224\,576\ldots \approx \ln 9$

3. $0.693\,147\,180\ldots \approx \ln 2$

4. $n!: 1, 2, 6, 24, 120, 720, 5\,040, 40\,320, 362\,880, 3\,628\,800$

5. (a) $10^2 < 2^{10} < 10! < 10^{10}$

   (b) 10^2 has 3 digits;

2^{10} has 4 digits;
10! has 7 digits;
10^{10} has 11 digits.

(c) 10^2 ends with 2 zeroes;
2^{10} ends with no zeroes;
10! ends with 2 zeroes;
10^{10} ends with 10 zeroes.

6. (a) 2.5

   (b) $2.666\,666\,666\ldots$

   (c) $2.708\,333\,333\ldots$

   (d) $2.716\,666\,666\ldots$

   (e) 4 more steps

7. (a) 2.8

   (b) 2.7

   (c) $2.721\,649\,484\ldots$

   (d) $2.717\,770\,034\ldots$

   (e) 3 more steps

8. (a) $2.593\,742\,460\ldots$

   (b) $2.691\,588\,029\ldots$

   (c) $2.704\,813\,829\ldots$

   (d) $2.715\,568\,520\ldots$

   (e) At least $n = 4\,822$

9. model function: $f(x) = e^x$;
   horizontal reflection;
   horizontal asymptote: $y = 0$.

10. model function: $f(x) = e^x$;
    vertical reflection;
    horizontal asymptote: $y = 0$.

11. model function: $f(x) = e^x$;
    horizontal translation ($\leftarrow 1$);
    horizontal asymptote: $y = 0$.

12. model function: $f(x) = e^x$;
    vertical translation ($\downarrow 1$);
    horizontal asymptote: $y = -1$.

13. model function: $f(x) = e^x$;
    horizontal reflection,
    vertical translation ($\uparrow 5$);
    horizontal asymptote: $y = 5$.

14. model function: $f(x) = e^x$;
    vertical dilation ($\times 3$),
    translation ($\uparrow 9$);
    horizontal asymptote: $y = 9$.

15. $x = -5$

16. $x = 3$

17. $x = \pm 5$

18. $x = 3$

19. $x = -8$ or $x = -1$

20. $x = 1$ or $x = 2$

21. $x = -6$ or $x = 2$

22. $x = 8$ or $x = 64$

23. $x = 1 \pm \frac{\sqrt{3}}{3}$

24. $x = \frac{1}{2}$

25. $x = 2$ or $x = 3$

26. $x = 0$

27. $x = e$

28. $x = 1$ or $x = e$

29. (a) $m = \ln(b)$ and $\Delta x = 1$, so $\Delta y = \ln(b)$.

   (b) $\Delta y = \ln(b)$ and $\Delta x = \frac{1}{k}$, so $m = k \ln(b)$.

   (c) $m = 1.585 \cdot \ln(2) \approx 1.098\,638\,281 \approx \ln(3)$

30. (a) $m = \ln(b)$ and $\Delta x = 1$, so $\Delta y = \ln(b)$.

   (b) $\Delta y = k \ln(b)$ and $\Delta x = 1$, so $m = k \ln(b)$.

   (c) The graphs of g and h exhibit exponential growth and cross the y-axis with the same slope. However, the graphs have different y-intercepts, one at $(0, 1)$ and the other at $(0, 1.585)$. The graphs cross each other at $x \approx 1.136$, so g heads to infinity and asymptotes to zero faster than h.

Section 3.3

1. (a) $\log_a 5 = 3$

   (b) $\log_b \pi = 4$

   (c) $\ln x = 15$

   (d) $\log_{10} 4y = \sqrt{2}$

2. (a) $a^6 = 3$

   (b) $b^2 = 4$

   (c) $3^x = 2$

   (d) $10^4 = y$

3. 3

4. -2

5. $\frac{3}{2}$

6. $\frac{2}{3}$

7. 8

8. -4

9. 71

10. 7

11. 5

12. 12

13. $x = 9$

14. $x = \sqrt{17} \approx 4.123\,105\,626$

15. $x = \frac{11}{3} \approx 3.666\,666\,666$

16. $x = \frac{7}{2} = 3.5$

17. $x = -2$ or $x = \frac{5}{2}$

18. $x = -8$ or $x = 3$

19. $x = -1 - \sqrt{1 + e} \approx -2.928\,284\,686$

   or $x = -1 + \sqrt{1 + e} \approx 0.928\,284\,686$

20. $x = \frac{\ln(5) - 4}{3} \approx -0.796\,854\,029$

21. $x = \frac{\log_2(7) + 2}{5} \approx 0.961\,470\,984$

22. $x = 3$ or $x = 4$

23. No solution: $\log_2(-4)$ is undefined

24. No solution: $\sqrt{4 \log_3(7) - 8}$ is undefined

25. $(3, \infty)$

26. $(-\infty, -1) \cup (1\infty)$

27. $(-\infty, 1) \cup (1\infty)$

28. $(0, 1) \cup (2\infty)$

29. $(-\infty, -1) \cup (0\infty)$

30. $\left(-\infty, \frac{7}{2}\right)$

Section 3.4

1. 1

2. 2

3. 1

4. 1

5. 2

6. 2

7. $\frac{5}{4}$

8. $\frac{6}{7}$

9. 4

10. 15

11. (a) $\log_5\left(u^3 v^4\right)$

   (b) $\log_3\left(\dfrac{u^2}{v}\right)$

   (c) $\log_4\left(\dfrac{x - 1}{x + 1}\right)$

   (d) $\ln\left(\dfrac{x + 1}{x + 2}\right)$

12. (a) $\ln(2) + \ln(3)$

    (b) $\ln(3) - \ln(2)$

    (c) $\ln(2) + 3\ln(3)$

    (d) $\frac{1}{5}\big(\ln(2) + \ln(3)\big)$

13. (a) $\dfrac{3\ln(2) + \ln(3)}{\ln(3)}$

    (b) $\dfrac{\ln(2) + 2\ln(3)}{\ln(2)}$

    (c) $\dfrac{2\ln(2) - 2\ln(3)}{\ln(2) + \ln(3)}$

    (d) $\dfrac{4\ln(2) + \ln(3)}{\ln(2) - \ln(3)}$

14. $\dfrac{\ln(128)}{\ln(2)} = \log_2(128) = 7$

15. $x = \frac{1}{3}\ln(10) \approx 0.767\,528$

16. $x = \frac{1}{2}\big(\ln(13) - 5\big) \approx -1.217\,525$

17. $x = 6$

18. $x = 16$

19. $x = 8$

20. $x = 5$

21. $x = 3$

22. $x = 4$

23. $x = -1 + \sqrt{1 + e^4} \approx 6.454\,416$

24. $x = \dfrac{1}{e^2 - 1} \approx 0.156\,517$

25. No solution

26. $x = \log_2(5) \approx 2.321\,928$

27. $x = 0$ or $x = \log_3(2) \approx 0.630\,930$

28. $x = \ln\!\big(\frac{3}{4}\big) \approx -0.287\,682$

    or $x = \ln\!\big(\frac{4}{3}\big) \approx 0.287\,682$

29. $x = \dfrac{3\ln(7) + 4\ln(2)}{5\ln(2) - \ln(7)} \approx 5.665\,333$

30. $x = \dfrac{5\ln(4) + 7\ln(3)}{3\ln(4) + 12\ln(3)} \approx 0.843\,131$

Section 3.5

1. (a) 500 insects

    (b) $e^{0.02} - 1 \approx 0.020\,201$ or about 2.02%

    (c) 0.02 or 2% per day

    (d) $\frac{\ln 2}{0.02} \approx 34.66$ days

2. (a) 250 cells

    (b) 0.4 or 40%

    (c) $\ln 1.4 = 0.336\ldots$ or about 33.6% per hour

    (d) $\frac{\ln 2}{\ln 1.4} \approx 2.06$ hours

3. (a) \$700

    (b) 0.05 or 5%

    (c) $(1.05^{1/12} - 1)\cdot 12 \approx 0.048\,889$
        or about 4.889%

    (d) $\ln 1.05 \approx 0.048\,790$ or about 4.879%

4. (a) \$625

    (b) $12\cdot 0.005 = 0.06$ or 6%

    (c) $1.005^{12} - 1 \approx 0.061\,678$ or about 6.168%

    (d) $\ln 1.005^{12} \approx 0.059\,850$ or about 5.985%

5. (a) \$435

    (b) 0.03 or 3%

    (c) $e^{0.03} - 1 \approx 0.030\,455$ or about 3.046%

    (d) $(e^{0.03/12} - 1)\cdot 12 \approx 0.030\,038$
        or about 3.004%

6. (a) 37.5 grams

    (b) 0.131\,527 or about 13.15%

    (c) $1 - e^{-0.131\,527} \approx 0.123\,244$
        or about 12.32%

    (d) $\dfrac{\ln 2}{0.131\,527} \approx 5.27$ years

7. (a) 3.5 grams

    (b) $\dfrac{\ln 2}{1\,601} \approx 0.000\,432\,946$
        or about 0.043\,295%

    (c) $1 - 2^{-1/1\,601} \approx 0.000\,432\,853$
        or about 0.043\,285%

    (d) 1601 years

8. (a) 74 micrograms per milliliter

    (b) 0.175 or about 17.5%

    (c) $\dfrac{\ln 2}{0.175} \approx 3.96$ hours

    (d) $\dfrac{\ln 740}{0.175} \approx 37.75$ hours

9. (a) 7°C

    (b) $\dfrac{\ln(93/15)}{0.19} \approx 9.6$ minutes

    (c) $T(60) = 100 - 93\cdot e^{-11.4}$
        $\approx 99.998\,958\,819°\text{C}$,

        $T(120) = 100 - 93\cdot e^{-22.8}$
        $\approx 99.999\,999\,988°\text{C}$

        $T(600) = 100 - 93\cdot e^{-114}$
        $\approx 100°\text{C}$

10. $127 \cdot 3^{5/4} \approx 501$ cells

11. Since $e^{0.34} \approx 1.405$, an investment that pays 34% interest compounded continuously is better than one that pays 40% interest compounded yearly.

12. $3 \dfrac{\ln(4/19)}{\ln(23/38)} \approx 9.3$ minutes

13. $5730 \dfrac{\ln 0.63}{\ln 0.5} \approx 3819.5$ years

14. $3 \dfrac{\ln 10}{\ln 1.8} \approx 11.75$ days

15. $2 \dfrac{\ln(5/23)}{\ln(35/46)} \approx 11.17$ years

16. $93°$C

17. $\dfrac{\ln 2}{0.09} \approx 7.7$ years

18. $12 \dfrac{\ln 3}{\ln 2} \approx 19.02$ hours

19. $6.006 \dfrac{\ln 1000}{\ln 2} \approx 59.85$ hours

20. Since $3500 \cdot e^{-0.16 \cdot 0.25} \cdot e^{0.11 \cdot 0.75} \approx 3651.96$, after one year Sallie's investment grew by $151.96, or about 4.34%.

21. $-10°$F

22. $38 + 34 \left(\dfrac{22}{34}\right)^{7/2} \approx 45.4°$ F

23. $2200 \left(\dfrac{29}{11}\right)^4 \approx 106\,278$ people

24. Since $2500 \left(1 + \dfrac{0.08}{365}\right)^{365} \approx 2708.19$, interest in Ollie's CD is compounded daily.

25. $8 \dfrac{\ln 10}{\ln 2} \approx 26.6$ days.

26. (a) $-5730 \dfrac{\ln .92}{\ln 2} \approx 689$ years

    (b) $2^{-200/573} \approx .785$ or about 78.5%

27. (a) $\dfrac{1}{50} \ln \dfrac{3\,959}{755} \approx 0.033\,141$ or about 3.314%

    (b) $528\,500 \left(\dfrac{3\,959}{755}\right)^2 \approx 14\,531\,890$ people

    (c) The actual value is greater than the predicted value.

    (d) Two possibilities include the development of air conditioning and the arrival of retiring baby-boomers.

28. (a) $P(t) = 3\,043 \left(\dfrac{3\,712}{3\,043}\right)^{(t-1960)/10}$

    (b) $P(1980) \approx 4528$, $P(1990) \approx 5524$,

    $P(2000) \approx 6738$, and $P(2010) \approx 8219$

    (c) The actual values are less than the predicted values.

29. $150 \dfrac{\ln 2}{\ln(13/9)} \approx 282.7$ years

30. (a) $2^{-10/3} \approx 0.099\,213$ or about 9.92%

    (b) $100 \dfrac{\ln 0.5}{\ln 0.9} \approx 657.9$ years

Section 4.1

1. (a) $\dfrac{5\pi}{6}$ (b) $-\dfrac{7\pi}{4}$

   (c) $\dfrac{4\pi}{5}$ (d) $-\dfrac{\pi^2}{6}$

2. (a) $450°$ (b) $-72°$

   (c) $-105°$ (d) $\dfrac{50°}{\pi} \approx 15.9°$

3. (a) II   (b) IV

   (c) III   (d) I

4. (a) III   (b) I

   (c) II   (d) IV

5. (a) $\left(\frac{1}{2}, \frac{\sqrt{3}}{2}\right)$ (b) $(0, 1)$

   (c) $\left(\frac{\sqrt{2}}{2}, \frac{\sqrt{2}}{2}\right)$ (d) $(0, -1)$

6. (a) $\left(-\frac{\sqrt{2}}{2}, -\frac{\sqrt{2}}{2}\right)$ (b) $\left(\frac{1}{2}, \frac{\sqrt{3}}{2}\right)$

   (c) $(0, -1)$ (d) $\left(\frac{\sqrt{3}}{2}, \frac{1}{2}\right)$

7. (a) $\dfrac{\pi}{3}$ (b) $\dfrac{3\pi}{10}$

   (c) $\dfrac{5\pi}{18}$ (d) $\dfrac{\pi - 2.46}{2}$

8. (a) $\dfrac{3\pi}{4}$ (b) $\dfrac{\pi}{6}$

   (c) $\dfrac{2\pi}{5}$ (d) $\pi - 2.34$

9. (a) $\dfrac{25\pi}{12}, \dfrac{-23\pi}{12}$ (b) $\dfrac{4\pi}{3}, -\dfrac{8\pi}{3}$

   (c) $\dfrac{19\pi}{6}, -\dfrac{5\pi}{6}$ (d) $\dfrac{\pi}{6}, -\dfrac{23\pi}{6}$

10. 45-90-45 triangle:
    $a = 5\sqrt{2}; \quad \alpha = \dfrac{\pi}{4}, \quad \beta = \dfrac{\pi}{4}$

11. 30-60-90 triangle:
    $c = 6; \quad \alpha = \dfrac{\pi}{3}, \quad \beta = \dfrac{\pi}{6}$

12. 45-90-45 triangle:
    $a = 7, \quad c = 7\sqrt{2}; \quad \beta = \dfrac{\pi}{4}$

13. 30-60-90 triangle:
    $b = 2\sqrt{3}; \quad \alpha = \dfrac{\pi}{6}, \quad \beta = \dfrac{\pi}{3}$

14. 45-90-45 triangle:

$c = 8\sqrt{2}; \quad \alpha = \dfrac{\pi}{4}, \quad \beta = \dfrac{\pi}{4}$

15. 30-60-90 triangle:

$b = 2\sqrt{3}, \quad c = 4\sqrt{3}; \quad \beta = \dfrac{\pi}{6}$

16. Intersections at $\left(\dfrac{3}{5}, \dfrac{4}{5}\right), \left(\dfrac{3}{5}, -\dfrac{4}{5}\right)$

17. Intersections at $\left(\dfrac{24}{25}, -\dfrac{7}{25}\right), \left(-\dfrac{24}{25}, -\dfrac{7}{25}\right)$

18. Intersections at $\left(\dfrac{9}{41}, -\dfrac{40}{41}\right), \left(-\dfrac{9}{41}, \dfrac{40}{41}\right)$

19. Intersections at $\left(-\dfrac{5}{13}, \dfrac{12}{13}\right), \left(-\dfrac{5}{13}, -\dfrac{12}{13}\right)$

20. Intersections at $\left(\dfrac{15}{17}, \dfrac{8}{17}\right), \left(-\dfrac{15}{17}, \dfrac{8}{17}\right)$

21. Intersections at $\left(\dfrac{20}{29}, -\dfrac{21}{29}\right), \left(-\dfrac{20}{29}, \dfrac{21}{29}\right)$

22. Intersections at $\left(\dfrac{35}{37}, \dfrac{12}{37}\right), \left(\dfrac{35}{37}, -\dfrac{12}{37}\right)$

23. Intersections at $\left(\dfrac{60}{61}, \dfrac{11}{61}\right), \left(-\dfrac{60}{61}, \dfrac{11}{61}\right)$

24. Intersections at $\left(\dfrac{28}{53}, -\dfrac{45}{53}\right), \left(-\dfrac{28}{53}, \dfrac{45}{53}\right)$

25. Intersections at $\left(\dfrac{13}{85}, \dfrac{84}{85}\right), \left(-\dfrac{13}{85}, -\dfrac{84}{85}\right)$

26. Initial side: bearing 30° east of north

Terminal side: bearing 30° west of north

Angle measure: $60° = \dfrac{\pi}{3}$

27. Initial side: bearing 45° north of west

Terminal side: bearing 30° north of west

Angle measure: $15° = \dfrac{\pi}{12}$

28. Initial side: bearing 30° east of south

Terminal side: bearing 30° north of west

Angle measure: $210° = \dfrac{7\pi}{6}$

29. Initial side: bearing 30° west of south

Terminal side: bearing 45° south of east

Angle measure: $75° = \dfrac{5\pi}{12}$

30. (a) Hour hand: bearing due east

Minute hand: bearing due north

(b) Angle measure: $90° = \dfrac{\pi}{2}$

(c) Hour hand: bearing 30° east of north

Minute hand: bearing due north

Angle measure: $30° = \dfrac{\pi}{6}$

(d) Hour hand: bearing 30° north of west

Minute hand: bearing due north

Angle measure: $-60° = -\dfrac{\pi}{3}$

or $300° = \dfrac{5\pi}{3}$

(e) At 3:30, the hour hand is halfway between 3 and 4 o'clock, so:

Hour hand: bearing 15° south of east

Minute hand: bearing due south

Angle measure: $-75° = -\dfrac{5\pi}{12}$

or $285° = \dfrac{19\pi}{12}$

(f) At 9:45, the hour hand is three-fourths of the way between 9 and 10 o'clock, so:

Hour hand: bearing 22.5° north of west

Minute hand: bearing due west

Angle measure: $22.5° = \dfrac{\pi}{8}$

Section 4.2

1. (a) D   (b) C   (c) D

2. (a) C   (b) A   (c) B

3. (a) D   (b) C   (c) B

4. (a) B   (b) A   (c) D

5. $\cos\theta = \dfrac{8}{17}, \quad \sin\theta = \dfrac{15}{17}, \quad \tan\theta = \dfrac{15}{8}$

6. $\cos\theta = \dfrac{24}{25}, \quad \sin\theta = -\dfrac{7}{25}, \quad \tan\theta = -\dfrac{7}{24}$

7. $\cos\theta = -\dfrac{9}{41}, \quad \sin\theta = \dfrac{40}{41}, \quad \tan\theta = -\dfrac{40}{9}$

8. $\cos\theta = \dfrac{21}{29}, \quad \sin\theta = -\dfrac{20}{29}, \quad \tan\theta = -\dfrac{20}{21}$

9. $\cos\theta = -\dfrac{35}{37}, \quad \sin\theta = \dfrac{12}{37}, \quad \tan\theta = -\dfrac{12}{35}$

10. $\cos\theta = -\dfrac{28}{53}$, $\sin\theta = -\dfrac{45}{53}$, $\tan\theta = \dfrac{45}{28}$

11. $\theta = \dfrac{\pi}{6}$ (bearing 30° north of east) or

$\theta = \dfrac{5\pi}{6}$ (bearing 30° north of west)

12. $\theta = \dfrac{5\pi}{4}$ (bearing 45° south of west) or

$\theta = \dfrac{7\pi}{4}$ (bearing 45° south of east)

13. $\theta = \dfrac{5\pi}{6}$ (bearing 30° north of west) or

$\theta = \dfrac{7\pi}{6}$ (bearing 30° south of west)

14. $\theta = \dfrac{\pi}{4}$ (bearing 45° north of east) or

$\theta = \dfrac{7\pi}{4}$ (bearing 45° south of east)

15. $\theta = \dfrac{2\pi}{3}$ (bearing 30° west of north) or

$\theta = \dfrac{5\pi}{3}$ (bearing 30° east of south)

16. $\theta = \dfrac{\pi}{4}$ (bearing 45° north of east) or

$\theta = \dfrac{5\pi}{4}$ (bearing 45° south of west)

17. Graph. $A = 4$, $\lambda = 2\pi$

18. Graph. $A = 5$, $\lambda = 2\pi$

19. Graph. $A = 3$, $\lambda = \pi$

20. Graph. $A = 1$, $\lambda = \frac{2\pi}{5}$

21. Graph. $A = 6$, $\lambda = 4\pi$

22. Graph. $A = \frac{1}{3}$, $\lambda = 5\pi$

23. Graph. $A = 2$, $\lambda = 1$

24. Graph. $A = 3$, $\lambda = 4$

25. Graph. $A = 5$, $\lambda = 2\pi$

26. Graph. $A = 7$, $\lambda = 2\pi$

27. $A = 3$ $\lambda = 4$, $f(x) = 3\sin\left(\frac{\pi}{2}x\right)$,

28. $A = 2$ $\lambda = 10$, $f(x) = -2\cos\left(\frac{\pi}{5}x\right)$,

29. $A = 5$ $\lambda = 4\pi$, $f(x) = 5\cos\left(\frac{1}{2}x\right)$,

30. $A = 1$ $\lambda = 8$, $f(x) = \sin\left(\frac{\pi}{4}x\right) + 2$,

Section 4.3

1. $\cos\theta = \dfrac{3}{5}$, $\sin\theta = \dfrac{4}{5}$, $\tan\theta = \dfrac{4}{3}$,

$\theta \approx 0.93 \approx 53.1°$

2. $\cos\theta = \dfrac{20}{29}$, $\sin\theta = \dfrac{21}{29}$, $\tan\theta = \dfrac{21}{20}$,

$\theta \approx 0.81 \approx 46.4°$

3. $\cos\theta = \dfrac{9}{41}$, $\sin\theta = \dfrac{40}{41}$, $\tan\theta = \dfrac{40}{9}$,

$\theta \approx 1.35 \approx 77.3°$

4. $\cos\theta = \dfrac{5}{13}$, $\sin\theta = \dfrac{12}{13}$, $\tan\theta = \dfrac{12}{5}$,

$\theta \approx 1.18 \approx 67.4°$

5. $\cos\theta = \dfrac{8}{17}$, $\sin\theta = \dfrac{15}{17}$, $\tan\theta = \dfrac{15}{8}$,

$\theta \approx 1.08 \approx 61.9°$

6. $\cos\theta = \dfrac{7}{25}$, $\sin\theta = \dfrac{24}{25}$, $\tan\theta = \dfrac{24}{7}$,

$\theta \approx 1.29 \approx 73.7°$

7. $\cos\theta = \dfrac{11}{61}$, $\sin\theta = \dfrac{60}{61}$, $\tan\theta = \dfrac{60}{11}$,

$\theta \approx 1.39 \approx 79.6°$

8. $\cos\theta = \dfrac{13}{85}$, $\sin\theta = \dfrac{84}{85}$, $\tan\theta = \dfrac{84}{13}$,

$\theta \approx 1.42 \approx 81.2°$

9. $\cos\theta = \dfrac{35}{37}$, $\sin\theta = -\dfrac{12}{37}$

10. $\cos\theta = -\dfrac{28}{53}$, $\sin\theta = \dfrac{45}{53}$

11. $\cos\theta = \dfrac{13}{85}$, $\sin\theta = \dfrac{84}{85}$

12. $\cos\theta = \dfrac{40}{41}$, $\sin\theta = -\dfrac{9}{41}$

13. $\cos\theta = -\dfrac{\sqrt{6}+\sqrt{2}}{4}$, $\sin\theta = \dfrac{\sqrt{6}-\sqrt{2}}{4}$

14. $\cos\theta = \dfrac{\sqrt{2}-\sqrt{6}}{4}$, $\sin\theta = -\dfrac{\sqrt{2}+\sqrt{6}}{4}$

15. $\cos\theta = \dfrac{\sqrt{2}-\sqrt{6}}{4}$, $\sin\theta = \dfrac{\sqrt{2}+\sqrt{6}}{4}$

16. $\cos\theta = -\dfrac{\sqrt{6}+\sqrt{2}}{4}$, $\sin\theta = \dfrac{\sqrt{6}-\sqrt{2}}{4}$

17. $\cos\theta = -\dfrac{31\sqrt{2}}{50}$, $\sin\theta = -\dfrac{17\sqrt{2}}{50}$

18. $\cos\theta = \dfrac{-20+21\sqrt{3}}{58}$, $\sin\theta = \dfrac{-21-20\sqrt{3}}{58}$

19. $\cos\theta = \dfrac{3}{5}$, $\sin\theta = \dfrac{4}{5}$

20. $\cos\theta = \dfrac{4}{5}$, $\sin\theta = -\dfrac{3}{5}$

21. $\sin(\theta) = \frac{3}{5}$, $\cos(\theta) = \frac{4}{5}$:
$$\theta = \arcsin\left(\tfrac{3}{5}\right) + 2\pi k$$
$\sin(\theta) = \frac{3}{5}$, $\cos(\theta) = -\frac{4}{5}$:
$$\theta = \pi - \arcsin\left(\tfrac{3}{5}\right) + 2\pi k$$

22. $\sin(\theta) = \frac{5}{13}$, $\cos(\theta) = -\frac{12}{13}$:
$$\theta = \arccos\left(-\tfrac{12}{13}\right) + 2\pi k$$
$\sin(\theta) = -\frac{5}{13}$, $\cos(\theta) = -\frac{12}{13}$:
$$\theta = -\arccos\left(-\tfrac{12}{13}\right) + 2\pi k$$

23. $\sin(\theta) = -1$, $\cos(\theta) = 0$:
$$\theta = \tfrac{3\pi}{2} + 2\pi k$$
$\sin(\theta) = \frac{8}{17}$, $\cos(\theta) = \frac{15}{17}$:
$$\theta = \arcsin\left(\tfrac{8}{17}\right) + 2\pi k$$
$\sin(\theta) = \frac{8}{17}$, $\cos(\theta) = -\frac{15}{17}$:
$$\theta = \pi - \arcsin\left(\tfrac{8}{17}\right) + 2\pi k$$

24. $\sin(\theta) = \frac{24}{25}$, $\cos(\theta) = -\frac{7}{25}$:
$$\theta = \arccos\left(-\tfrac{7}{25}\right) + 2\pi k$$
$\sin(\theta) = -\frac{24}{25}$, $\cos(\theta) = -\frac{7}{25}$:
$$\theta = -\arccos\left(-\tfrac{7}{25}\right) + 2\pi k$$

25. $\sin(\theta) = \frac{\sqrt{2}}{2}$, $\cos(\theta) = \frac{\sqrt{2}}{2}$:
$$\theta = \tfrac{\pi}{4} + 2\pi k$$
$\sin(\theta) = -\frac{\sqrt{2}}{2}$, $\cos(\theta) = -\frac{\sqrt{2}}{2}$:
$$\theta = \tfrac{5\pi}{4} + 2\pi k$$

26. $\sin(\theta) = \frac{9}{41}$, $\cos(\theta) = -\frac{40}{41}$
$$\theta = \arccos\left(-\tfrac{40}{41}\right) + 2\pi k$$
$\sin(\theta) = -\frac{9}{41}$, $\cos(\theta) = \frac{40}{41}$
$$\theta = \arcsin\left(-\tfrac{9}{41}\right) + 2\pi k$$

27. $\tan(-\theta) = -\tan(\theta)$

28. $\tan\left(\frac{\pi}{2} - \theta\right) = \dfrac{1}{\tan(\theta)}$

29. $\tan(\pi - \theta) = -\tan(\theta)$

30. (a) $\tan(\alpha+\beta) = \dfrac{\sin(\alpha)\cos(\beta) + \cos(\alpha)\sin(\beta)}{\cos(\alpha)\cos(\beta) - \sin(\alpha)\sin(\beta)}$

(b) $\tan(\alpha + \beta) = \dfrac{\tan(\alpha) + \tan(\beta)}{1 - \tan(\alpha)\tan(\beta)}$

Section 4.4

1. $\gamma = \arccos\left(\frac{16}{65}\right) \approx 75.7°$
$\alpha = \arcsin\left(\frac{3}{5}\right) \approx 36.9°$
$\beta = \arcsin\left(\frac{12}{13}\right) \approx 67.4°$

2. $c = 7$
$\alpha = \arcsin\left(\frac{5\sqrt{3}}{14}\right) \approx 38.2°$
$\beta = \arccos\left(\frac{1}{7}\right) \approx 81.8°$

3. $\alpha = \beta = 30°$
$b = 4$

4. $\alpha = 30°$
$b = 2\sqrt{2}$
$c = 4\sin 15° = \sqrt{6} - \sqrt{2}$

5. $\gamma = \arccos\left(-\frac{3}{5}\right) \approx 126.9°$
$\beta = \arcsin\left(\frac{3}{5}\right) \approx 36.9°$
$\alpha = \arcsin\left(\frac{7}{25}\right) \approx 16.3°$

6. No solution

7. Acute solution:
$\beta = \arccos\left(\frac{5}{13}\right) \approx 67.4°$
$\gamma = \arccos\left(\frac{12-5\sqrt{3}}{26}\right)$
$\quad = \arcsin\left(\frac{5+12\sqrt{3}}{26}\right) \approx 82.6°$
$c = \sqrt{457 + 120\sqrt{3}} = 5 + 12\sqrt{3}$

Obtuse solution:
$\beta = \arccos\left(-\frac{5}{13}\right) \approx 112.6°$
$\gamma = \arcsin\left(\frac{12\sqrt{3}-5}{26}\right) \approx 37.4°$
$c = \sqrt{457 - 120\sqrt{3}} = 12\sqrt{3} - 5$

8. $\gamma = 105°$
$a = 6\sqrt{2}$
$c = 12\sqrt{2}\sin 105° = 6(\sqrt{3} + 1)$

9. $\alpha = \arcsin\left(\frac{\sqrt{2}}{10}\right) \approx 8.1°$
$\gamma = \arccos\left(-\frac{3}{5}\right) \approx 126.9°$
$c = 4\sqrt{2}$

10. No solution

11. $c = 7\sqrt{2 + \sqrt{2}}$

$\alpha = \beta = \arcsin\left(\frac{\sqrt{2-\sqrt{2}}}{2}\right) = 22.5°$

12. Acute solution:

$\beta = \arccos\left(\frac{\sqrt{2}}{10}\right) \approx 81.9°$

$\gamma = \arccos\left(\frac{3}{5}\right) = \arcsin\left(\frac{4}{5}\right) \approx 53.1°$

$c = 4\sqrt{2}$

Obtuse solution:

$\beta = \arccos\left(-\frac{\sqrt{2}}{10}\right) \approx 98.1°$

$\gamma = \arcsin\left(\frac{3}{5}\right) \approx 36.9°$

$c = 3\sqrt{2}$

13. $4000 \sin 35° \approx 2294.3$ feet

14. $45\left(\tan 50° - \tan 40°\right) \approx 15.9$ feet

15. $350\left(\tan 85° - \tan 82.5°\right) \approx 1342.0$ feet

16. $10\left(\tan 62° - \tan 35°\right) \approx 11.8$ km

17. $100\sqrt{3} \sin 65° \approx 157.0$ miles from Alpha

$100\sqrt{3} \sin 55° \approx 141.9$ miles from Bravo

18. $\dfrac{1000 \sin 15°}{\sin 10°} \approx 1490.5$ feet

19. Orlando is $\arcsin\left(\frac{607}{1157}\right) \approx 0.552 \approx 31.6°$ south of east from Denver

Niagara Falls is $\arcsin\left(\frac{619}{4183}\right) \approx 0.149 \approx 8.5°$ north of east from Denver

20. $5\sqrt{949 - 420\cos 110°} \approx 165.3$ yards

21. $\dfrac{30 \sin 55° \sin 75°}{\sin 50°} \approx 31.0$ kilometers

22. $10\left(\cos 154° + \sqrt{15 + \cos^2 154°}\right) \approx 30.8$ hours

23. 1st wire: $50\sqrt{29} \approx 269.3$ feet

2nd wire: $100\sqrt{26 - 10\cos 80°} \approx 492.6$ feet

24. $\dfrac{52}{9}\left(\dfrac{\sin 15° + \sin 10°}{\sin 155°} - 1\right) \approx 0.135$ hrs

or 8.1 minutes.

25. $\dfrac{50 \sin 22°}{\sin 36°} \approx 31.9$ meters

26. $700\sqrt{2} \sin 65° \sin 70° \approx 843.1$ feet

27. $\dfrac{18 \sin 2.5° \sin 10°}{\sin 7.5°} \approx 1.0$ miles

28. $50\sqrt{13 - 12\cos 130°} \approx 227.6$ miles

29. $\dfrac{3 \sin 28° \sin 42°}{\sin 14°} \approx 3.9$ kilometers

30. $8000 \arccos\left(\frac{80}{83}\right) \approx 2157.5$ miles

Section 5.1

1. $8 + 5i$

2. $-1 + 2i$

3. $-2 + 16i$

4. $10 + 0i$

5. $\frac{6}{5} - \frac{8}{5}i$

6. $\frac{5}{13} + \frac{12}{13}i$

7. $3 + 4i$

8. $2 + 5i$

9. $0 - 1i$

10. $-64 + 0i$

11. $-2 + 3i$

12. $7 - i$

13. $0 + 0i$

14. $\sqrt{3} + i$

15. $12 + 5i$

16. $\frac{1}{4} + \frac{1}{4}i$

17. $\frac{7}{5} + \frac{1}{5}i$

18. $0 + 2i$

19. $-2 + 0i$

20. $\frac{1}{2} - \frac{9}{2}i$

21. $2 \pm 3i$

22. $-1 \pm 2i$

23. $1 \pm \frac{\sqrt{2}}{2}$

24. $\frac{2}{3} \pm \frac{1}{3}i$

25. $-\frac{3}{13} \pm \frac{2}{13}i$

26. $\frac{1}{4} \pm \frac{1}{4}i$

27. (a) $A = 4, \quad B = 7$

(b) $z = 4, z = -2 \pm \sqrt{3}\,i$

(c) Only one of these solutions ($z = 4$) is real.

28. (b) $z^2 = 2\left(\cos\left(\frac{\pi}{6}\right) - i\sin\left(\frac{\pi}{6}\right)\right)$

(c) $z^3 = 2\sqrt{2}\left(-\cos\left(\frac{\pi}{4}\right) + i\sin\left(\frac{\pi}{4}\right)\right) = -2 + 2i$

29. (a) The third column of the table reads:

$2.99 + 6.04i$

$3.32 + 3.34i$

$3.99 + 2.94i$

$4.00 + 3.00i$

(b) $4 + 3i$

(c) $(4 + 3i)^2 = 16 + 24i + 9i^2 = 7 + 24i$

30. *Verify values are conjugates.*

Section 5.2

1. $|-1 + i| = \sqrt{2}$

2. $|-3i| = 3$

3. $|5 - 12i| = 13$

4. $|7 - i| = 5\sqrt{2}$

5. $|4 - 3i| = 5$

6. $|9\sqrt{3} + 9i| = 18$

7. $|-2 - 3i| = \sqrt{13}$

8. $|1 - 3i| = \sqrt{10}$

9. $|-21 + 20i| = 29$

10. $2 \pm 2i$

11. $\frac{2}{3} \pm \frac{\sqrt{11}}{3}i$

12. $-1 \pm \frac{\sqrt{6}}{2}$

13. $-\frac{3}{13} \pm \frac{2}{13}i$

14. $\frac{1}{3} + 0i$

15. $\frac{1}{4} \pm \frac{1}{4}i$

16. right 2, down 3

17. left 7, up 1

18. dilation by $2\sqrt{2}$, rotation by $\frac{\pi}{4}$

19. dilation by 2, rotation by $-\frac{\pi}{6}$

20. dilation by 13, rotation by $\arctan\frac{12}{5}$

21. dilation by 4, left 1, down 1

22. dilation by 5, rotation by π, right 7, up 1

23. rotation by $-\frac{\pi}{2}$, left 2

24. dilation by 3, rotation by $\frac{\pi}{2}$, up 6

25. dilation by $\sqrt{2}$, rotation by $\frac{5\pi}{4}$, right 5, down 4

26. $\frac{5\sqrt{3}}{2} - \frac{5}{2}i$

27. $\frac{3\sqrt{10}}{5} + \frac{\sqrt{10}}{5}i$ or $-\frac{3\sqrt{10}}{5} - \frac{\sqrt{10}}{5}i$

28. rotation by $\frac{\pi}{4}$

29. rotation by $\frac{\pi}{6}$

30. *Verify values are equal.*

Section 5.3

1. $\sqrt{2}\operatorname{cis}\left(\frac{\pi}{4}\right) = \sqrt{2}\operatorname{cis}\left(45°\right)$

2. $\sqrt{2}\operatorname{cis}\left(-\frac{\pi}{4}\right) = \sqrt{2}\operatorname{cis}\left(-45°\right)$

3. $2\operatorname{cis}\left(-\frac{\pi}{3}\right) = 2\operatorname{cis}\left(-60°\right)$

4. $2\operatorname{cis}\left(-\frac{\pi}{6}\right) = 2\operatorname{cis}\left(-30°\right)$

5. $5\operatorname{cis}\left(-\frac{\pi}{2}\right) = 5\operatorname{cis}\left(-90°\right)$

6. $18\operatorname{cis}\left(\frac{\pi}{6}\right) = 18\operatorname{cis}\left(30°\right)$

7. $5\operatorname{cis}\left(-\arccos\left(\frac{3}{5}\right)\right) = 5\operatorname{cis}\left(-\arcsin\left(\frac{4}{5}\right)\right)$

8. $\sqrt{13}\operatorname{cis}\left(-\arccos\left(\frac{2}{\sqrt{13}}\right)\right) = \sqrt{13}\operatorname{cis}\left(-\arcsin\left(\frac{3}{\sqrt{13}}\right)\right)$

9. $\sqrt{6}\operatorname{cis}\left(-\arccos\left(\frac{\sqrt{5}}{\sqrt{6}}\right)\right) = \sqrt{6}\operatorname{cis}\left(-\arcsin\left(\frac{1}{\sqrt{6}}\right)\right)$

10. $64\operatorname{cis}\left(\frac{2\pi}{3}\right) = -32 + 32\sqrt{3}i$

11. $27\operatorname{cis}\left(\frac{4\pi}{3}\right) = -\frac{27}{2} + \frac{27\sqrt{3}}{2}i$

12. $32\operatorname{cis}\left(\frac{\pi}{2}\right) = 0 + 32i$

13. $4\operatorname{cis}\left(\frac{5\pi}{4}\right) = -2\sqrt{2} - 2\sqrt{2}i$

14. $25\operatorname{cis}\left(\frac{3\pi}{4}\right) = -\frac{25\sqrt{2}}{2} + \frac{25\sqrt{2}}{2}i$

15. $27\operatorname{cis}\left(\frac{5\pi}{3}\right) = \frac{27}{2} - \frac{27\sqrt{3}}{2}i$

16. $\frac{1}{32}\operatorname{cis}\left(2\pi\right) = \frac{1}{32} + 0i$

17. $\frac{32}{243}\operatorname{cis}\left(\frac{\pi}{3}\right) = \frac{16}{243} + \frac{16\sqrt{3}}{243}i$

18. $4\sqrt{2}\operatorname{cis}\left(-\frac{5\pi}{4}\right) = -4 + 4i$

19. $64\operatorname{cis}\left(-\pi\right) = -64 + 0i$

20. $64\operatorname{cis}\left(-\frac{3\pi}{2}\right) = 0 + 64i$

21. $8000\operatorname{cis}\left(2\pi\right) = 8000 + 0i$

22. $2\operatorname{cis}\left(\frac{\pi}{3}\right) = 2e^{\pi/3\,i}$
    $2\operatorname{cis}\left(\pi\right) = 2e^{\pi\,i}$
    $2\operatorname{cis}\left(\frac{5\pi}{3}\right) = 2e^{5\pi/3\,i}$

23. $\sqrt[6]{2}\operatorname{cis}\left(\frac{\pi}{12}\right) = \sqrt[6]{2}\,e^{\pi/12\,i}$
    $\sqrt[6]{2}\operatorname{cis}\left(\frac{3\pi}{4}\right) = \sqrt[6]{2}\,e^{3\pi/4\,i}$
    $\sqrt[6]{2}\operatorname{cis}\left(\frac{17\pi}{12}\right) = \sqrt[6]{2}\,e^{17\pi/12\,i}$

24. $2\sqrt[6]{2}\operatorname{cis}\left(\frac{5\pi}{12}\right) = 2\sqrt[6]{2}\,e^{5\pi/12\,i}$
    $2\sqrt[6]{2}\operatorname{cis}\left(\frac{13\pi}{12}\right) = 2\sqrt[6]{2}\,e^{13\pi/12\,i}$
    $2\sqrt[6]{2}\operatorname{cis}\left(\frac{7\pi}{4}\right) = 2\sqrt[6]{2}\,e^{7\pi/4\,i}$

25. $\sqrt[4]{8}\operatorname{cis}\left(\frac{5\pi}{12}\right) = \sqrt[4]{8}\,e^{5\pi/12\,i}$
    $\sqrt[4]{8}\operatorname{cis}\left(\frac{11\pi}{12}\right) = \sqrt[4]{8}\,e^{11\pi/12\,i}$
    $\sqrt[4]{8}\operatorname{cis}\left(\frac{17\pi}{12}\right) = \sqrt[4]{8}\,e^{17\pi/12\,i}$
    $\sqrt[4]{8}\operatorname{cis}\left(\frac{23\pi}{12}\right) = \sqrt[4]{8}\,e^{23\pi/12\,i}$

26. $2\operatorname{cis}\left(\frac{3\pi}{8}\right) = 2e^{3\pi/8\,i}$
    $2\operatorname{cis}\left(\frac{7\pi}{8}\right) = 2e^{7\pi/8\,i}$
    $2\operatorname{cis}\left(\frac{11\pi}{8}\right) = 2e^{11\pi/8\,i}$
    $2\operatorname{cis}\left(\frac{15\pi}{8}\right) = 2e^{15\pi/8\,i}$

27. $\sqrt[4]{2}\operatorname{cis}\left(\frac{11\pi}{24}\right) = \sqrt[4]{2}\,e^{11\pi/24\,i}$

$\sqrt[4]{2}\operatorname{cis}\left(\frac{23\pi}{24}\right) = \sqrt[4]{2}\,e^{23\pi/24\,i}$

$\sqrt[4]{2}\operatorname{cis}\left(\frac{35\pi}{24}\right) = \sqrt[4]{2}\,e^{35\pi/24\,i}$

$\sqrt[4]{2}\operatorname{cis}\left(\frac{47\pi}{24}\right) = \sqrt[4]{2}\,e^{47\pi/24\,i}$

28. $\operatorname{cis}\left(\frac{\pi}{10}\right) = e^{\pi/10\,i}$

$\operatorname{cis}\left(\frac{\pi}{2}\right) = e^{\pi/2\,i}$

$\operatorname{cis}\left(\frac{9\pi}{10}\right) = e^{9\pi/10\,i}$

$\operatorname{cis}\left(\frac{13\pi}{10}\right) = e^{13\pi/10\,i}$

$\operatorname{cis}\left(\frac{17\pi}{10}\right) = e^{17\pi/10\,i}$

29. $\operatorname{cis}\left(\frac{3\pi}{10}\right) = e^{3\pi/10\,i}$

$\operatorname{cis}\left(\frac{7\pi}{10}\right) = e^{7\pi/10\,i}$

$\operatorname{cis}\left(\frac{11\pi}{10}\right) = e^{11\pi/10\,i}$

$\operatorname{cis}\left(\frac{3\pi}{2}\right) = e^{3\pi/2\,i}$

$\operatorname{cis}\left(\frac{19\pi}{10}\right) = e^{19\pi/10\,i}$

30. $2\operatorname{cis}\left(0\right) = 2\,e^{0\,i}$

$2\operatorname{cis}\left(\frac{\pi}{3}\right) = 2\,e^{\pi/3\,i}$

$2\operatorname{cis}\left(\frac{2\pi}{3}\right) = 2\,e^{2\pi/3\,i}$

$2\operatorname{cis}\left(\pi\right) = 2\,e^{\pi\,i}$

$2\operatorname{cis}\left(\frac{4\pi}{3}\right) = 2\,e^{4\pi/3\,i}$

$2\operatorname{cis}\left(\frac{5\pi}{3}\right) = 2\,e^{5\pi/3\,i}$

Index

of complex plane, **410**
ruler postulate, 39, 403
run, 130
Russell, Bertrand, 11
  paradox, 11

scatter plot, **146**
secant function, **347**
sequence
  arithmetic, 143
  geometric, 241
  quadratic, 191
Servois, François Joseph, 404
set-builder notation, 19
similar triangles, 328, 330, 331, 342
sine function, **339**
sines, law of, 367
sinusoidal waveform, **344**
sledgehammer method, 28–32
slope, **128**
  and personality, 131–132
  of a line, 136
slope-intercept formula, **129**
solidus, 22
solution
  of equation, **23**
  of inequality, **40**
  of system, 210
  spurious, 62, 298
solving
  equations, 23
  inequalities, 40
  systems, 210
sophistic numbers, 391
speed, 125, 221
spurious solution, 62, 298
square root, 56
  of minus one, 391
  of negative numbers, 56, 67, 390–391
  of two, 21, 57–58
square root function
  graph, 99–100
square root method, 64–65
stable digits, 58, 247, 262
standard position, **323**
start-up cost, 127
story problems, 215
straight angle, 324
strong correlation, 152
substituting, 24

substitution method, 211–215
sum
  angle identity, 357
  of two squares, 32
supplementary angle, **324**
  identities, 355
supply function, 209
symmetry
  bilateral, 163
  horizontal, 353
  point, 353
syntax, 155
system of equations, **210**

tangent function, **339**
tangential intercept, **101**
Tartaglia, Niccolo, 390
terminal side, 323
terminal velocity, 137
theorem
  Euclid, 369
  factoring, 25
  law of cosines, 368
  law of sines, 367
  least squares regression, 148
  Pythagoras, 81
  right triangle trigonometry, 341
  vertical line test, 111, 136
30-60-90 triangle, 329–330
time, 221
transcendental numbers, 268
translation
  horizontal, 174
  of complex plane, **408**
  vertical, 174
transversal intercept, **101**
triangle
  equilateral, 328
  oblique, 367
  right, 81–82, 341
    30-60-90, 329–330
    45-90-45, 330–331
  similar, 328, 330, 331, 342
trigonometry, 339
  of right triangles, 341
turning intercept, **101**

uninhibited growth, **305**
union, 44
unit circle, **328**